This is the substantially revised and updated second edition of Terence Mills' best-selling graduate textbook *The Econometric Modelling of Financial Time Series*. The book provides detailed coverage of the variety of models that are currently being used in the empirical analysis of financial markets. Covering bond, equity and foreign exchange markets, it is aimed at scholars and practitioners wishing to acquire an understanding of the latest research techniques and findings, and also graduate students wishing to research into financial markets.

This second edition includes a great deal of new material that has been developed in the last six years, and also provides a more in-depth treatment of two crucial, and related, areas: the theory of integrated processes and cointegration. Completely new material discusses the distributional properties of asset returns and recent and novel techniques of analysing and interpreting vector autoregressions that contain integrated and possibly cointegrated variables.

Terence Mills is Professor of Economics at Loughborough University. He obtained his Ph.D. at the University of Warwick, lectured at the University of Leeds, and has held professorial appointments at City University Business School and the University of Hull. He has over 100 publications, including articles in the *American Economic Review, Journal of Econometrics* and *Journal of Applied Econometrics*.

Data appendix available on http://www.lboro.ac.uk/departments/ec/cup/.

The Econometric Modelling of Financial Time Series

Second edition

Terence C. Mills

Professor of Economics,
Loughborough University

CAMBRIDGE
UNIVERSITY PRESS

PUBLISHED BY THE PRESS SYNDICATE OF THE UNIVERSITY OF CAMBRIDGE
The Pitt Building, Trumpington Street, Cambridge, United Kingdom

CAMBRIDGE UNIVERSITY PRESS
The Edinburgh Building, Cambridge CB2 2RU, UK
40 West 20th Street, New York, NY 10011–4211, USA
10 Stamford Road, Oakleigh, VIC 3166, Australia
Ruiz de Alarcón 13, 28014 Madrid, Spain
Dock House, The Waterfront, Cape Town 8001, South Africa

http://www.cambridge.org

First published 1993
Reprinted 1994, 1996, 1997
Second edition 1999
Reprinted 2000 (twice)

Printed in the United Kingdom at the University Press, Cambridge

Typeset in Times 10/12 [KW]

British Library Cataloguing in Publication Data
Mills, Terence C.
The econometric modelling of financial time series / Terence C.
Mills. – 2nd edn
p. cm.
Includes bibliographical references (p.).
ISBN 0-521-62413-4. – ISBN 0-521-62492-4 (pbk.)
1. Finance–Econometric models. 2. Time-series analysis.
3. Stochastic processes. I. Title
HG174.M55 1999
332′.01′5195–dc21 98-53587 CIP

First edition
ISBN 0 521 41046 7 hardback
ISBN 0 521 42257 4 paperback

Second edition
ISBN 0 521 62413 4 hardback
ISBN 0 521 62492 4 paperback

Contents

Preface to the second edition

In the six years since I completed the manuscript for the first edition of *The Econometric Modelling of Financial Time Series*, there have been many advances in time series econometrics, some of which have been in direct response to features found in the data coming from financial markets, while others have found ready application in financial fields. Incorporating these developments, and omitting some techniques that have since fallen out of favour, has led to a second edition rather different to the first. Although the basic structure of the book remains the same, it is worth pointing out these changes in some detail.

Chapters 1 and 2 remain essentially the same, although examples have been updated. It is in chapter 3 that the first major changes appear. Like it or not, the analysis of unit roots has come to dominate much of time series econometrics during the 1990s. Although much of the recent published research on unit roots has been highly technical without being particularly illuminating, I felt that a more formal analysis of unit root testing and inference than appeared in the first edition was warranted. To this end, there is now a more detailed treatment of the asymptotic distributions of the various test statistics and an emphasis on Monte Carlo simulation to obtain estimates of these distributions and hence critical values. Newer developments incorporating breaking and evolving trends and stochastic unit roots are also discussed. This chapter also includes a rather more detailed treatment of fractionally integrated processes.

Evidence of non-linearity in financial time series has accumulated over the years, although the initial enthusiasm at the start of the decade for chaotic dynamics has rather dissipated. Stochastic variance models and the many extensions of the ARCH process have become very popular, the latter leading to an impressive array of acronyms! Both of these classes of models are analysed in greater detail than before in chapter 4. Artificial neural networks also have their devotees, and these are also now briefly discussed in this chapter. Non-linearity goes hand-in-hand with non-normality, and the completely new chapter 5 looks at various methods of modelling return distributions and transformations of returns, introducing a wealth of techniques that have only recently made their appearance in the literature.

Much of the material of chapter 6 (previously chapter 5) remains as before, although new sections on GMM and robust estimation and testing parameter stability are included and alternative methods of computing variance decompositions are introduced. As developments in the analysis of unit roots in univariate time series led to many changes in chapter 3, so analogous developments in the analysis of unit roots and cointegration in a multivariate framework has led to a complete rewriting of the chapter, now chapter 7, on regression techniques for integrated financial time series. A more formal approach is taken here as well, with Monte Carlo simulation again being used to bring out the differences in the various asymptotic distributions of estimators that result from alternative setups. The VECM framework is now used to analyse cointegration in non-stationary VARs, and a detailed treatment of causality testing, alternative estimation methods, and impulse response asymptotics is also provided. The final chapter, chapter 8, introduces further topics in the analysis of integrated financial time series, such as common trends and cycles and estimating permanent and transitory components, and looks at some non-linear generalisations of cointegration and error correction mechanisms. It also includes material on present value models and excess volatility, but only within the VAR framework: the discussion of the 'first generation' of excess volatility tests has been omitted from this edition as they no longer appear to be used.

Many new examples have been developed using several new data sets. I would like to thank Chris Brooks and Scott Spears for generously supplying their exchange rate and stock market data, respectively, and Raphael Markellos for providing the neural network example. My thanks also go to the kind reviewers of the first edition and to the many people who have contacted me since the book appeared: their encouraging comments convinced me that a second edition was worthwhile embarking upon. Since the appearance of the first edition I have once more changed universities. Loughborough has provided me with a very congenial atmosphere in which to research and even to be able to teach some of the material contained in the book! The production team at Cambridge University Press continue to do a fine job, and Patrick McCartan, and now Ashwin Rattan, can always be relied upon for encouragement and some entertaining gossip! Finally, but of course they should be at the head of any list of acknowledgements, my thanks and love go to my family, Thea and Alexa, and to my mother, Rose.

1 Introduction

The aim of this book is to provide the researcher in financial markets with the techniques necessary to undertake the empirical analysis of financial time series. To accomplish this aim we introduce and develop both univariate modelling techniques and multivariate methods, including those regression techniques for time series that seem to be particularly relevant to the finance area.

Why do we concentrate exclusively on time series techniques when, for example, cross-sectional modelling plays an important role in empirical investigations of the Capital Asset Pricing Model (CAPM): see, as an early and influential example, Fama and MacBeth (1973)? Our answer is that, apart from the usual considerations of personal expertise and interest, plus manuscript length considerations, it is because time series analysis, in both its theoretical and empirical aspects, has been for many years an integral part of the study of financial markets, with empirical research beginning with the papers by Working (1934), Cowles (1933, 1944) and Cowles and Jones (1937).

Working focused attention on a previously noted characteristic of commodity and stock prices: namely, that they resemble cumulations of purely random changes. Cowles investigated the ability of market analysts and financial services to predict future price changes, finding that there was little evidence that they could. Cowles and Jones reported evidence of positive correlation between successive price changes but, as Cowles (1960) was later to remark, this was probably due to their taking monthly averages of daily or weekly prices before computing changes: a 'spurious correlation' phenomenon analysed by Working (1960).

The predictability of price changes has since become a major theme of financial research but, surprisingly, little more was published until Kendall's (1953) study, in which he found that the weekly changes in a wide variety of financial prices could not be predicted from either past changes in the series or from past changes in other price series. This seems to have been the first explicit reporting of this oft-quoted property of financial prices, although further impetus to research on price predictability was only provided by the publication of the papers by Roberts (1959) and Osborne (1959). The former presents a largely heuristic argument for why successive price changes should be independent, while the latter develops the proposition that it is not absolute price changes but the logarithmic price changes which are independent of each other: with the auxiliary assumption that the changes themselves are normally distributed, this implies that prices are generated as Brownian motion.

The stimulation provided by these papers was such that numerous articles appeared over the next few years investigating the hypothesis that price changes (or logarithmic price changes) are independent, a hypothesis that came to be termed the random walk model, in recognition of the similarity of the evolution of a price series to the random stagger of a drunk. Indeed, the term 'random walk' is believed to have first been used in an exchange of correspondence appearing in *Nature* in 1905 (see Pearson and Rayleigh, 1905), which was concerned about the optimal search strategy for finding a drunk who had been left in the middle of a field. The solution is to start exactly where the drunk had been placed, as that point is an unbiased estimate of the drunk's future position since he will presumably stagger along in an unpredictable and random fashion.

The most natural way to state formally the random walk model is as

$$P_t = P_{t-1} + a_t \tag{1.1}$$

where P_t is the price observed at the beginning of time t and a_t is an error term which has zero mean and whose values are independent of each other. The price change, $\Delta P_t = P_t - P_{t-1}$, is thus simply a_t and hence is independent of past price changes. Note that, by successive backward substitution in (1.1), we can write the current price as the cumulation of all past errors, i.e.

$$P_t = \sum\nolimits_{i=1}^{t} a_i$$

so that the random walk model implies that prices are indeed generated by Working's 'cumulation of purely random changes'. Osborne's model of Brownian motion implies that equation (1.1) holds for the logarithms of P_t and, further, that a_t is drawn from a zero mean normal distribution having constant variance.

Most of the early papers in this area are contained in the collection of Cootner (1964), while Granger and Morgenstern (1970) provide a detailed development and empirical examination of the random walk model and various of its refinements. Amazingly, much of this work had been anticipated by the French mathematician Louis Bachelier (1900, English translation in Cootner, 1964) in a remarkable Ph.D. thesis in which he developed an elaborate mathematical theory of speculative prices, which he then tested on the pricing of French government bonds, finding that such prices were consistent with the random walk model. What made the thesis even more remarkable was that it also developed many of the mathematical properties of Brownian motion which had been thought to have first been derived some years later in the physical sciences, particularly by Einstein! Yet, as Mandelbrot (1989) remarks, Bachelier had great difficulty in even getting himself a university appointment, let alone getting his theories disseminated throughout the academic community!

It should be emphasised that the random walk model is only a hypothesis about how financial prices move. One way in which it can be tested is by examining the autocorrelation properties of price changes: see, for example, Fama (1965). A more general perspective is to view (1.1) as a particular model within the class of autoregressive-integrated-moving average (ARIMA) models popularised by Box and Jenkins (1976). Chapter 2 thus develops the theory of such models within the general context of (univariate) linear stochastic processes.

We should avoid giving the impression that the only financial time series of interest are stock prices. There are financial markets other than those for stocks, most notably for bonds and foreign currency, but there also exist the various futures, commodity and derivative markets, all of which provide interesting and important series to analyse. For certain of these, it is by no means implausible that models other than the random walk may be appropriate or, indeed, models from a class other than the ARIMA. Chapter 3 discusses various topics in the general analysis of linear stochastic models, most notably that of determining the order of integration of a series and, associated with this, the appropriate way of modelling trends and structural breaks. It also considers methods of decomposing an observed series into two or more unobserved components and of determining the extent of the 'memory' of a series, by which is meant the behaviour of the series at low frequencies or, equivalently, in the very long run. A variety of examples taken from the financial literature are provided throughout the chapter.

During the 1960s much research was also carried out on the theoretical foundations of financial markets, leading to the development of the theory of efficient capital markets. As LeRoy (1989) discusses, this led to some serious questions being raised about the random walk hypothesis as a *theoretical* model of financial markets, the resolution of which required situating the hypothesis within a framework of economic equilibrium. Unfortunately, the assumption in (1.1) that price changes are independent was found to be too restrictive to be generated within a reasonably broad class of optimising models. A model that is appropriate, however, can be derived for stock prices in the following way (similar models can be derived for other sorts of financial prices, although the justification is sometimes different: see LeRoy, 1982). The return on a stock from t to $t+1$ is defined as the sum of the dividend yield and the capital gain, i.e., as

$$r_{t+1} = \frac{P_{t+1} + D_t - P_t}{P_t} \tag{1.2}$$

where D_t is the dividend paid during period t. Let us suppose that the expected return is constant, $E_t(r_{t+1}) = r$, where $E_t(\ )$ is the expectation conditional on information available at t: r_t is then said to be a *fair game*. Taking expectations at t of both sides of (1.2) and rearranging yields

$$P_t = (1+r)^{-1} E_t(P_{t+1} + D_t) \tag{1.3}$$

which says that the stock price at the beginning of period t equals the sum of the expected future price and dividend, discounted back at the rate r. Now assume that there is a mutual fund that holds the stock in question and that it reinvests dividends in future share purchases. Suppose that it holds h_t shares at the beginning of period t, so that the value of the fund is $x_t = h_t P_t$. The assumption that the fund ploughs back its dividend income implies that h_{t+1} satisfies

$$h_{t+1} P_{t+1} = h_t (P_{t+1} + D_t)$$

Thus

$$\begin{aligned} E_t(x_{t+1}) &= E_t(h_{t+1} P_{t+1}) = h_t E_t(P_{t+1} + D_t) \\ &= (1+r) h_t P_t = (1+r) x_t \end{aligned}$$

i.e., that x_t is a *martingale* (if, as is common, $r > 0$ we have that $E_t(x_{t+1}) \geq x_t$, so that x_t is a *submartingale*: LeRoy (1989, pp. 1593–4), however, offers an example in which r could be negative, in which case x_t

will be a *supermartingale*). LeRoy (1989) emphasises that price itself, without dividends added in, is not generally a martingale, since from (1.3) we have

$$r = E_t(D_t)/P_t + E_t(P_{t+1})/P_t - 1$$

so that only if the expected dividend–price ratio (or dividend yield) is constant, say $E_t(D_t)/P_t = d$, can we write P_t as the submartingale (assuming $r > d$)

$$E_t(P_{t+1}) = (1 + r - d)P_t$$

The assumption that a stochastic process, y_t say, follows a random walk is more restrictive than the requirement that y_t follows a martingale. The martingale rules out any dependence of the conditional expectation of Δy_{t+1} on the information available at t, whereas the random walk rules out not only this but also dependence involving the higher conditional moments of Δy_{t+1}. The importance of this distinction is thus evident: financial series are known to go through protracted quiet periods and also protracted periods of turbulence. This type of behaviour could be modelled by a process in which successive conditional variances of Δy_{t+1} (but *not* successive levels) are positively autocorrelated. Such a specification would be consistent with a martingale, but not with the more restrictive random walk.

Martingale processes are discussed in chapter 4, and lead naturally on to non-linear stochastic processes that are capable of modelling higher conditional moments, such as the autoregressive conditionally heteroskedastic (ARCH) model introduced by Engle (1982), stochastic variance models, and the bilinear process analysed by Granger and Andersen (1978). Also discussed in this chapter are a variety of other non-linear models, including Markov switching processes, smooth transitions and chaotic models, and the various tests of non-linearity that have been developed. The chapter also includes a discussion of the computer intensive technique of artificial neural network modelling. The various techniques are illustrated using exchange rates and stock price series.

The focus of chapter 5 is on the unconditional distributions of asset returns. The most noticeable feature of such distributions is their leptokurtic property: they have fat tails and high peakedness compared to a normal distribution. Although ARCH processes can model such features, much attention in the finance literature since Mandelbrot's (1963a, 1963b) path-breaking papers has concentrated on the possibility that returns are generated by a stable process, which has the property of having an infinite variance. Recent developments in statistical analysis have allowed a much deeper investigation of the tail shapes of empirical distributions, and methods of estimating tail shape indices are introduced and applied to a variety of returns series. The chapter then looks at the implications of fat-tailed distributions for testing the covariance stationarity assumption of time series analysis, data analytic methods of modelling skewness and kurtosis, and the impact of analysing transformations of returns, rather than the returns themselves.

The remaining three chapters focus on multivariate techniques of time series analysis, including regression methods. Chapter 6 concentrates on analysing the relationships between a set of *stationary* or, more precisely, *non-integrated*, financial time series and considers such topics as general dynamic regression, robust estimation, generalised methods of moments estimation, multivariate regression, vector autoregressions, Granger-causality, variance decompositions and impulse response analysis. These topics are illustrated with a variety of examples drawn from the finance literature: using forward exchange rates as optimal predictors of future spot rates, modelling the volatility of stock returns and the risk premium in the foreign exchange market, testing the CAPM, and investigating the interaction of the equity and gilt markets in the UK.

Chapter 7 concentrates on the modelling of *integrated* financial time series, beginning with a discussion of the spurious regression problem, introducing cointegrated processes and demonstrating how to test for cointegration, and then moving on to consider how such processes can be estimated. Vector error correction models are analysed in detail, along with associated issues in causality testing and impulse response analysis. The techniques introduced in this chapter are illustrated with extended examples analysing the market model and the interactions of the UK financial markets.

Finally, chapter 8 considers further issues in multivariate time series analysis, such as alternative approaches to testing for the presence of a long-run relationship, the analysis of both common cycles and trends, methods of computing permanent and transitory decompositions in a multivariate framework, and extensions to deal with infinite variance errors and structural breaks. Modelling issues explicit to finance are also discussed. Samuelson (1965, 1973) and Mandelbrot (1966) analysed the implications of equation (1.3), that the stock price at the beginning of time t equals the discounted sum of next period's expected future price and dividend, to show that this stock price equals the expected discounted, or present, value of *all* future dividends, i.e., that

$$P_t = \sum_{i=0}^{\infty} (1+r)^{-(i+1)} E_t(D_{t+i}) \tag{1.4}$$

which is obtained by recursively solving (1.3) forwards and assuming that $(1+r)^{-n}E_t(P_{t+n})$ converges to zero as $n \to \infty$. Present value models of the type (1.4) are analysed extensively in chapter 8, with the theme of whether stock markets are excessively volatile, perhaps containing speculative bubbles, being used extensively throughout the discussion and in a succession of examples, although the testing of the expectations hypothesis of the term structure of interest rates is also used as an example of the general present value framework.

Having emphasised earlier in this chapter that the book is exclusively about modelling financial time series, we should state at this juncture what the book is not about. It is certainly not a text on financial market theory, and any such theory is only discussed when it is necessary as a motivation for a particular technique or example. There are numerous texts on the theory of finance and the reader is referred to these for the requisite financial theory: two notable texts that contain both theory and empirical techniques are Campbell, Lo and MacKinlay (1997) and Cuthbertson (1996). Neither is it a textbook on econometrics. We assume that the reader already has a working knowledge of probability, statistics and econometric theory. Nevertheless, it is also non-rigorous, being at a level roughly similar to my *Time Series Techniques for Economists* (1990), in which references to the formal treatment of the theory of time series are provided.

When the data used in the examples throughout the book have already been published, references are given. Previous unpublished data are defined in the data appendix, which contains details on how they may be accessed. All standard regression computations were carried out using *EVIEWS 2.0* (EViews, 1995) or *MICROFIT* 4.0 (Pesaran and Pesaran, 1997). *PcFiml* 9.0 (Doornik and Hendry, 1997), *STAMP* 5.0 (Koopman *et al.*, 1995), *SHAZAM* (Shazam, 1993) and *COINT 2.0a* (Ouliaris and Phillips, 1995) were also used for particular examples and 'non-standard' computations were made using algorithms written by the author in *GAUSS 3.1*.

2 Univariate linear stochastic models: basic concepts

Chapter 1 has emphasised the standard representation of a financial time series as that of a (univariate) linear stochastic process, specifically as being a member of the class of ARIMA models popularised by Box and Jenkins (1976). This chapter provides the basic theory of such models within the general framework of the analysis of linear stochastic processes. As already stated in chapter 1, our treatment is purposely non-rigourous. For detailed theoretical treatments, but which do not, however, focus on the analysis of financial series, see, for example, Brockwell and Davis (1991), Hamilton (1994) or Fuller (1996).

2.1 Stochastic processes, ergodicity and stationarity

2.1.1 Stochastic processes, realisations and ergodicity

When we wish to analyse a financial time series using formal statistical methods, it is useful to regard the observed series, $(x_1, x_2, \ldots, x_T)$, as a particular *realisation* of a stochastic process. This realisation is often denoted $\{x_t\}_1^T$ while, in general, the stochastic process itself will be the family of random variables $\{X_t\}_{-\infty}^{\infty}$ defined on an appropriate probability space. For our purposes it will usually be sufficient to restrict the index set $\mathrm{T} = (-\infty, \infty)$ of the parent stochastic process to be the same as that of the realisation, i.e., $\mathrm{T} = (1, T)$, and also to use x_t to denote both the stochastic process and the realisation when there is no possibility of confusion.

With these conventions, the stochastic process can be described by a T-dimensional probability distribution, so that the relationship between a realisation and a stochastic process is analogous to that between the sample and the population in classical statistics. Specifying the complete form of the probability distribution will generally be too ambitious a task and we usually content ourselves with concentrating attention on the first and second moments: the T means

$$E(x_1), E(x_2), \ldots, E(x_T)$$

T variances

$$V(x_1), V(x_2), \ldots, V(x_T)$$

and $T(T-1)/2$ covariances

$$Cov(x_i, x_j), \quad i < j$$

If we could assume joint normality of the distribution, this set of expectations would then completely characterise the properties of the stochastic process. As we shall see, however, such an assumption is unlikely to be appropriate for many financial series. If normality cannot be assumed, but the process is taken to be *linear*, in the sense that the current value of the process is generated by a linear combination of previous values of the process itself and current and past values of any other related processes, then again this set of expectations would capture its major properties. In either case, however, it will be impossible to infer all the values of the first and second moments from just one realisation of the process, since there are only T observations but $T + T(T+1)/2$ unknown parameters. Hence further simplifying assumptions must be made to reduce the number of unknown parameters to more manageable proportions.

We should emphasise that the procedure of using a single realisation to infer the unknown parameters of a joint probability distribution is only valid if the process is *ergodic*, which roughly means that the sample moments for finite stretches of the realisation approach their population counterparts as the length of the realisation becomes infinite. For more on ergodicity see, for example, Granger and Newbold (1986, chapter 1) or Hamilton (1994, chapter 3.2), and since it is impossible to test for ergodicity using just (part of) a single realisation, it will be assumed from now on that all time series have this property.

2.1.2 Stationarity

One important simplifying assumption is that of *stationarity*, which requires the process to be in a particular state of 'statistical equilibrium' (Box and Jenkins, 1976, p. 26). A stochastic process is said to be *strictly stationary* if its properties are unaffected by a change of time origin. In other words, the joint probability distribution at *any* set of times $t_1, t_2, \ldots, t_m$ must be the same as the joint probability distribution at times $t_1 + k, t_2 + k, \ldots, t_m + k$, where k is an arbitrary shift in time. For $m = 1$, this implies that the marginal probability distributions do not depend on time, which in turn implies that, so long as $E|x_t|^2 < \infty$, both the mean and variance of x_t must be constant, i.e.

$$E(x_1) = E(x_2) = \cdots = E(x_T) = E(x_t) = \mu$$

and

$$V(x_1) = V(x_2) = \cdots = V(x_T) = V(x_t) = \sigma_x^2$$

If $m = 2$, strict stationarity implies that all bivariate distributions do not depend on t: thus all covariances are functions only of the time-shift (or lag) k, i.e., for all k

$$\begin{aligned} Cov(x_1, x_{1+k}) &= Cov(x_2, x_{2+k}) = \cdots = Cov(x_{T-k}, x_T) \\ &= Cov(x_t, x_{t-k}) \end{aligned}$$

Hence we may define the *autocovariances* and *autocorrelations* as

$$\gamma_k = Cov(x_t, x_{t-k}) = E[(x_t - \mu)(x_{t-k} - \mu)]$$

and

$$\rho_k = \frac{Cov(x_t, x_{t-k})}{[V(x_t) \cdot V(x_{t-k})]^{1/2}} = \frac{\gamma_k}{\gamma_0}$$

respectively, both of which depend only on the lag k. Since these conditions apply just to the first- and second-order moments of the process, this is known as *second-order* or *weak stationarity* (and sometimes *covariance stationarity* or *stationarity in the wide sense*). While strict stationarity (with finite second moments) thus implies weak stationarity, the converse does not hold, for it is possible for a process to be weakly stationary but *not* strictly stationary: this would be the case if higher moments, such as $E(x_t^3)$, were functions of time. If, however, joint normality could be assumed, so that the distribution was entirely characterised by the first two moments, weak stationarity does indeed imply strict stationarity. More complicated relationships between these concepts of stationarity hold for some types of non-linear processes, as is discussed in chapter 4.

The autocorrelations considered as a function of k are referred to as the *autocorrelation function* (ACF). Note that since

$$\gamma_k = Cov(x_t, x_{t-k}) = Cov(x_{t-k}, x_t) = Cov(x_t, x_{t+k}) = \gamma_k$$

it follows that $\rho_k = \rho_{-k}$ and so only the positive half of the ACF is usually given. The ACF plays a major role in modelling dependencies among observations since it characterises, along with the process mean $\mu = E(x_t)$ and variance $\sigma_x^2 = \gamma_0 = V(x_t)$, the stationary stochastic process describing the evolution of x_t. It therefore indicates, by measuring the extent to which one value of the process is correlated with previous values, the length and strength of the 'memory' of the process.

2.2 Stochastic difference equations

A fundamental theorem in time series analysis, known as *Wold's decomposition* (Wold, 1938: see Hamilton, 1994, chapter 4.8), states that every weakly stationary, purely non-deterministic, stochastic process $(x_t - \mu)$ can be written as a linear combination (or linear *filter*) of a sequence of uncorrelated random variables. By purely non-deterministic we mean that any linearly deterministic components have been subtracted from $(x_t - \mu)$. Such a component is one that can be perfectly predicted from past values of itself and examples commonly found are a (constant) mean, as is implied by writing the process as $(x_t - \mu)$, periodic sequences, and polynomial or exponential sequences in t. A formal discussion of this theorem, well beyond the scope of this book, may be found in, for example, Brockwell and Davis (1991, chapter 5.7), but Wold's decomposition underlies all the theoretical models of time series that are subsequently to be introduced.

This linear filter representation is given by

$$x_t - \mu = a_t + \psi_1 a_{t-1} + \psi_2 a_{t-2} + \ldots = \sum_{j=0}^{\infty} \psi_j a_{t-j}, \quad \psi_0 = 1 \qquad (2.1)$$

The $\{a_t : t = 0, \pm 1, \pm 2, \cdots\}$ are a sequence of uncorrelated random variables, often known as *innovations*, drawn from a fixed distribution with

$$E(a_t) = 0, \quad V(a_t) = E(a_t^2) = \sigma^2 < \infty$$

and

$$Cov(a_t, a_{t-k}) = E(a_t a_{t-k}) = 0, \text{ for all } k \neq 0$$

We will refer to such a sequence as a *white-noise* process, often denoting it as $a_t \sim WN(0, \sigma^2)$. The coefficients (possibly infinite in number) in the linear filter are known as *ψ-weights*.

We can easily show that the model (2.1) leads to autocorrelation in x_t. From this equation it follows that

$$\begin{aligned}
E(x_t) &= \mu \\
\gamma_0 = V(x_t) &= E(x_t - \mu)^2 \\
&= E(a_t + \psi_1 a_{t-1} + \psi_2 a_{t-2} + \ldots)^2 \\
&= E(a_t^2) + \psi_1^2 E(a_{t-1}^2) + \psi_2^2 E(a_{t-2}^2) + \ldots \\
&= \sigma^2 + \psi_1^2\sigma^2 + \psi_2^2\sigma^2 + \ldots \\
&= \sigma^2 \sum\nolimits_{j=0}^{\infty} \psi_j^2
\end{aligned}$$

by using the result that $E(a_{t-i}a_{t-j}) = 0$ for $i \neq j$. Now

$$\begin{aligned}
\gamma_k &= E(x_t - \mu)(x_{t-k} - \mu) \\
&= E(a_t + \psi_1 a_{t-1} + \cdots + \psi_k a_{t-k} + \cdots)(a_{t-k} + \psi_1 a_{t-k-1} + \cdots) \\
&= \sigma^2(1 \cdot \psi_k + \psi_1\psi_{k+1} + \psi_2\psi_{k+2} + \cdots) \\
&= \sigma^2 \sum\nolimits_{j=0}^{\infty} \psi_j \psi_{j+k}
\end{aligned}$$

and this implies

$$\rho_k = \frac{\sum_{j=0}^{\infty} \psi_j \psi_{j+k}}{\sum_{j=0}^{\infty} \psi_j^2}$$

If the number of ψ-weights in (2.1) is infinite, we have to assume that the weights are absolutely summable, i.e., that $\sum_{j=0}^{\infty}|\psi_j| < \infty$, in which case the linear filter representation is said to *converge*. This condition can be shown to be equivalent to assuming that x_t is stationary, and guarantees that all moments exist and are independent of time, in particular that the variance of x_t, γ_0, is finite.

2.3 ARMA processes

2.3.1 Autoregressive processes

Although equation (2.1) may appear complicated, many realistic models result from particular choices of the ψ-weights. Taking $\mu = 0$ without loss of generality, choosing $\psi_j = \phi^j$ allows (2.1) to be written

$$\begin{aligned} x_t &= a_t + \phi a_{t-1} + \phi^2 a_{t-2} + \ldots \\ &= a_t + \phi(a_{t-1} + \phi a_{t-2} + \ldots) \\ &= \phi x_{t-1} + a_t \end{aligned}$$

or

$$x_t - \phi x_{t-1} = a_t \tag{2.2}$$

This is known as a *first-order autoregressive* process, often given the acronym AR(1). The *backshift* (or *lag*) *operator* B is now introduced for notational convenience. This shifts time one step back, so that

$$Bx_t \equiv x_{t-1}$$

and, in general

$$B^m x_t = x_{t-m}$$

noting that $B^m \mu \equiv \mu$. The lag operator allows (possibly infinite) distributed lags to be written in a very concise way. For example, by using this notation the AR(1) model can be written as

$$(1 - \phi B)x_t = a_t$$

so that

$$\begin{aligned} x_t &= (1 - \phi B)^{-1} a_t = (1 + \phi B + \phi^2 B^2 + \ldots)a_t \\ &= a_t + \phi a_{t-1} + \phi^2 a_{t-2} + \ldots \end{aligned} \tag{2.3}$$

This linear filter representation will converge as long as $|\phi| < 1$, which is therefore the stationarity condition.

We can now deduce the ACF of an AR(1) process. Multiplying both sides of (2.2) by x_{t-k}, $k > 0$, and taking expectations yields

$$\gamma_k - \phi\gamma_{k-1} = E(a_t x_{t-k}) \tag{2.4}$$

From (2.3), $a_t x_{t-k} = \sum_{i=0}^{\infty} \phi^i a_t a_{t-k-i}$. As a_t is white noise, any term in $a_t a_{t-k-i}$ has zero expectation if $k+i>0$. Thus (2.4) simplifies to

$$\gamma_k = \phi\gamma_{k-1}, \text{ for all } k>0$$

and, consequently, $\gamma_k = \phi^k\gamma_0$. An AR(1) process therefore has an ACF given by $\rho_k = \phi^k$. Thus, if $\phi>0$, the ACF decays exponentially to zero, while if $\phi<0$, the ACF decays in an oscillatory pattern, both decays being slow if ϕ is close to the non-stationary boundaries of $+1$ and -1.

The ACFs for two AR(1) processes with (a) $\phi=0.5$, and (b) $\phi=-0.5$, are shown in figure 2.1, along with generated data from the processes with a_t assumed to be normally and independently distributed with $\sigma^2 = 25$, denoted $a_t \sim NID(0{,}25)$, and with starting value $x_0=0$. With $\phi>0$, adjacent values are positively correlated and the generated series has a tendency to exhibit 'low-frequency' trends. With $\phi<0$, however, adjacent values have a negative correlation and the generated series displays violent, rapid oscillations.

2.3.2 Moving average processes

Now consider the model obtained by choosing $\psi_1 = -\theta$ and $\psi_j = 0, j\geq 2$, in (2.1)

$$x_t = a_t - \theta a_{t-1}$$

or

$$x_t = (1-\theta B)a_t \tag{2.5}$$

This is known as the *first-order moving average* [MA(1)] process and it follows immediately that

$$\gamma_0 = \sigma^2(1+\theta^2), \ \gamma_1 = -\sigma^2\theta, \ \gamma_k = 0 \text{ for } k>1$$

and hence its ACF is described by

$$\rho_1 = \frac{-\theta}{1+\theta^2}, \ \rho_k = 0, \ \text{for } k>1$$

Thus, although observations one period apart are correlated, observations more than one period apart are not, so that the 'memory' of the process is just one period: this 'jump' to zero autocorrelation at $k=2$

may be contrasted with the smooth, exponential decay of the ACF of an AR(1) process.

The expression for ρ_1 can be written as the quadratic equation $\theta^2\rho_1 + \theta + \rho_1 = 0$. Since θ must be real, it follows that $-\frac{1}{2} < \rho_1 < \frac{1}{2}$. However, both θ and $1/\theta$ will satisfy this equation and thus two MA(1) processes can always be found that correspond to the same ACF. Since any moving average model consists of a finite number of ψ-weights, all MA models are stationary. In order to obtain a converging autoregressive representation, however, the restriction $|\theta| < 1$ must be imposed. This restriction is known as the *invertibility* condition and implies that the process can be written in terms of an infinite autoregressive representation

$$x_t = \pi_1 x_{t-1} + \pi_2 x_{t-2} + \ldots + a_t$$

where the π-*weights* converge, i.e. $\sum_{j=0}^{\infty}|\pi_j| < \infty$. In fact, the MA(1) model can be written as

$$(1 - \theta B)^{-1} x_t = a_t$$

and expanding $(1 - \theta B)^{-1}$ yields

$$(1 + \theta B + \theta^2 B^2 + \ldots) x_t = a_t$$

The weights $\pi_j = -\theta^j$ will converge if $|\theta| < 1$, i.e., if the model is invertible. This implies the reasonable assumption that the effect of past observations decreases with age.

Figure 2.2 represents plots of generated data from two MA(1) processes with (a) $\theta = 0.8$ and (b) $\theta = -0.8$, in each case with $a_t \sim NID(0, 25)$. On comparison of these plots with those of the AR(1) processes in figure 2.1, it is seen that realisations from the two types of processes are often quite similar, suggesting that it may, on occasions, be difficult to distinguish between the two.

2.3.3 General AR and MA processes

Extensions to the AR(1) and MA(1) models are immediate. The general autoregressive model of order p [AR(p)] can be written as

$$x_t - \phi_1 x_{t-1} - \phi_2 x_{t-2} - \ldots - \phi_p x_{t-p} = a_t$$

or

$$(1 - \phi_1 B - \phi_2 B^2 - \ldots - \phi_p B^p) x_t = \phi(B) x_t = a_t$$

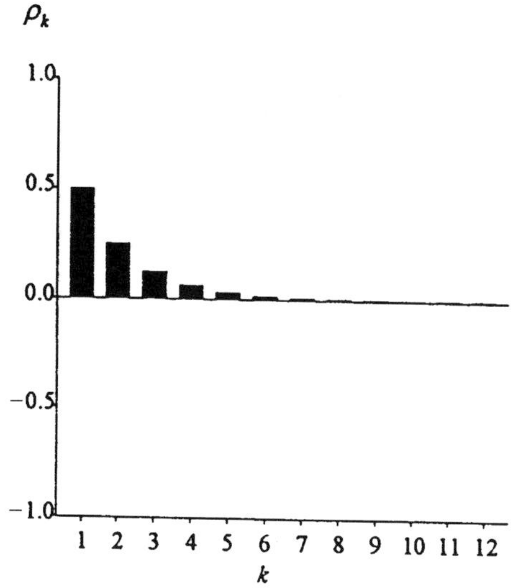

(a) $\phi = 0.5$

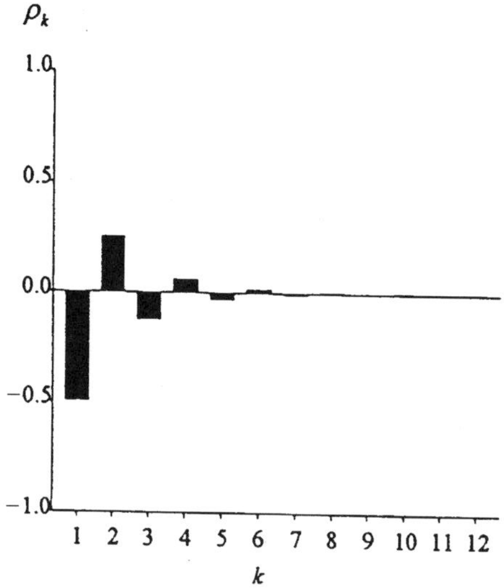

(b) $\phi = -0.5$

The linear filter representation $x_t = \psi(B)a_t$ can be obtained by equating coefficients in $\phi(B)\psi(B) = 1$ (see Mills, 1990, chapter 5, for examples of how to do this). The stationarity conditions required for convergence of the ψ-weights are that the roots of the characteristic equation

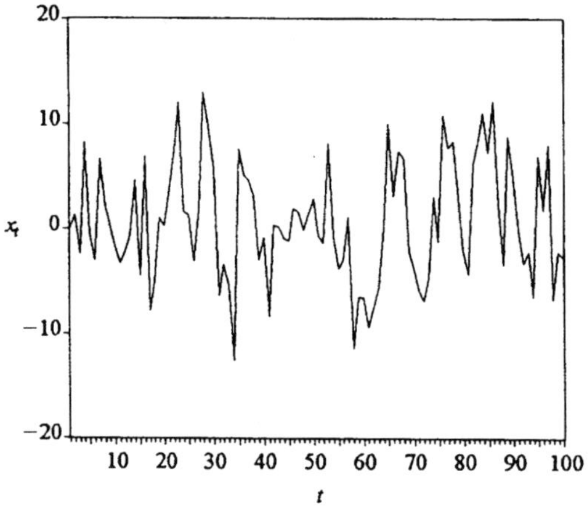

(c) $\phi = 0.5,\ x_0 = 0$

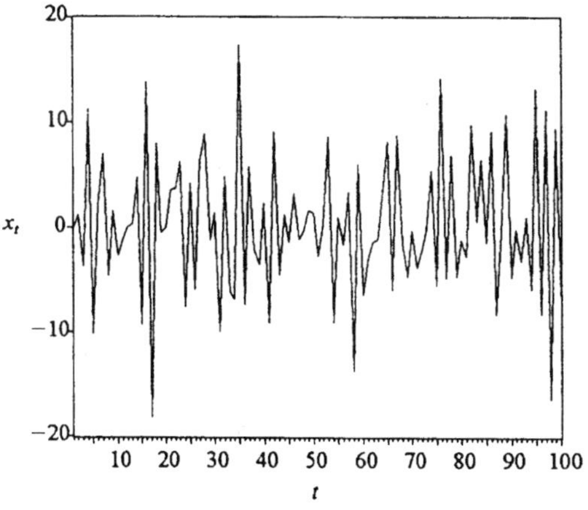

(d) $\phi = -0.5,\ x_0 = 0$

Figure 2.1 ACFs and simulations of AR(1) processes

$$\phi(B) = (1 - g_1 B)(1 - g_2 B) \ldots (1 - g_p B) = 0$$

are such that $|g_i| < 1$ for $i = 1, 2, \ldots, p$, an equivalent phrase being that the roots g_i^{-1} all lie outside the unit circle. The behaviour of the ACF is determined by the difference equation.

$$\phi(B)\rho_k = 0, \ k > 0 \tag{2.6}$$

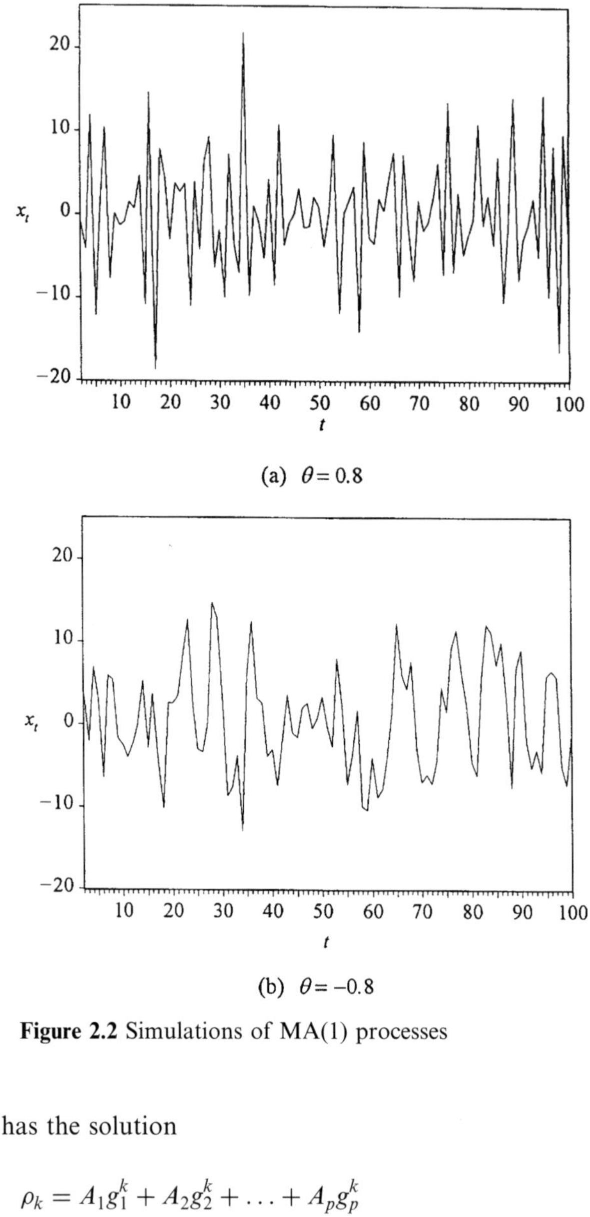

Figure 2.2 Simulations of MA(1) processes

which has the solution

$$\rho_k = A_1 g_1^k + A_2 g_2^k + \ldots + A_p g_p^k$$

Since $|g_i| < 1$, the ACF is thus described by a mixture of damped exponentials (for real roots) and damped sine waves (for complex roots). As an example, consider the AR(2) process

$$(1-\phi_1 B-\phi_2 B^2)x_t = a_t$$

with characteristic equation

$$\phi(B) = (1-g_1B)(1-g_2B) = 0$$

The roots g_1 and g_2 are given by

$$g_1, g_2 = \left(\phi_1 \pm (\phi_1^2+4\phi_2)^{1/2}\right)/2$$

and can both be real, or they can be a pair of complex numbers. For stationarity, it is required that the roots be such that $|g_1| < 1$ and $|g_2| < 1$, and it can be shown that these conditions imply the following set of restrictions on ϕ_1 and ϕ_2

$$\phi_1+\phi_2 < 1, \quad -\phi_1+\phi_2 < 1, \quad -1 < \phi_2 < 1$$

The roots will be complex if $\phi_1^2+4\phi_2 < 0$, although a necessary condition for complex roots is simply that $\phi_2 < 0$.

The behaviour of the ACF of an AR(2) process for four combinations of (ϕ_1, ϕ_2) is shown in figure 2.3. If g_1 and g_2 are real (cases (a) and (c)), the ACF is a mixture of two damped exponentials. Depending on their sign, the autocorrelations can also damp out in an oscillatory manner. If the roots are complex (cases (b) and (d)), the ACF follows a damped sine wave. Figure 2.4 shows plots of generated time series from these four AR(2) processes, in each case with $a_t \sim NID(0{,}25)$. Depending on the signs of the real roots, the series may be either smooth or jagged, while complex roots tend to induce 'pseudo-periodic' behaviour.

Since all AR processes have ACFs that 'damp out', it is sometimes difficult to distinguish between processes of different orders. To aid with such discrimination, we may use the *partial autocorrelation function* (PACF). In general, the correlation between two random variables is often due to both variables being correlated with a third. In the present context, a large portion of the correlation between x_t and x_{t-k} may be due to the correlation this pair have with the intervening lags $x_{t-1}, x_{t-2}, \ldots, x_{t-k+1}$. To adjust for this correlation, the *partial autocorrelations* may be calculated.

The kth partial autocorrelation is the coefficient ϕ_{kk} in the AR(k) process

$$x_t = \phi_{k1}x_{t-1} + \cdots + \phi_{kk}x_{t-k} + a_t \tag{2.7}$$

and measures the additional correlation between x_t and x_{t-k} after adjustments have been made for the intervening lags.

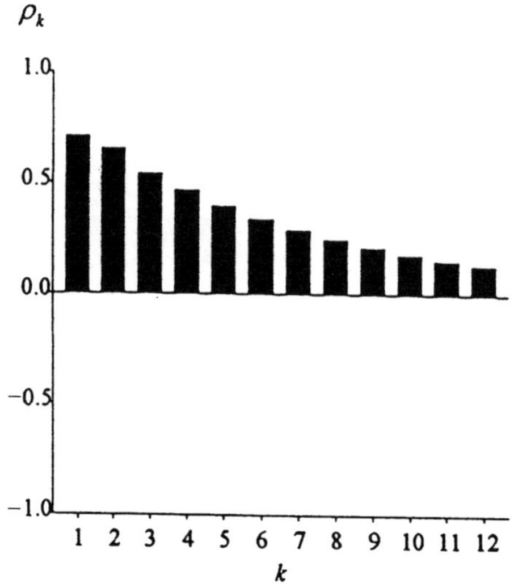

(a) $\phi_1 = -0.5,\ \phi_2 = 0.3$

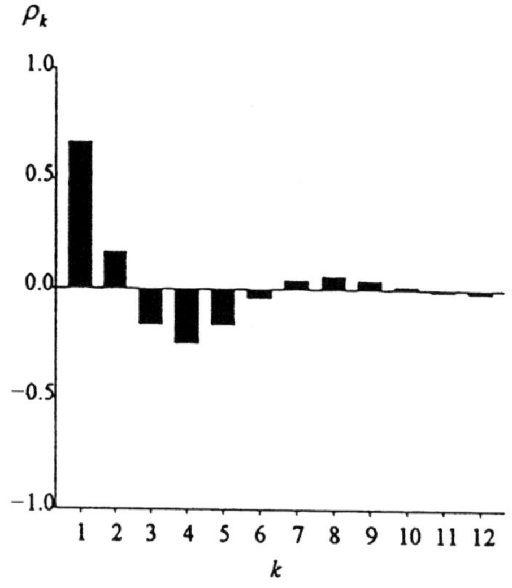

(b) $\phi_1 = 1,\ \phi_2 = -0.5$

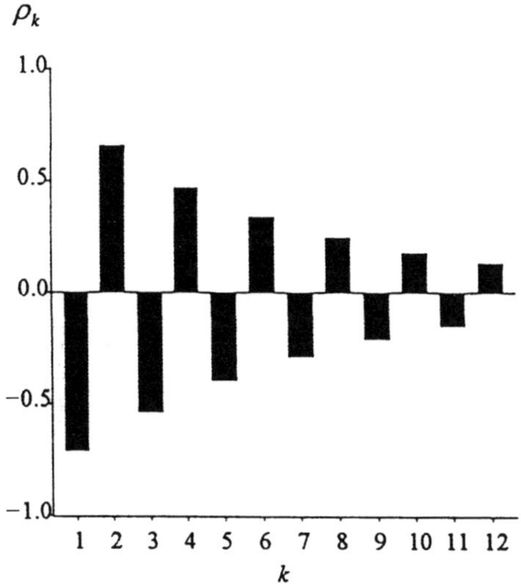

(c) $\phi_1 = -0.5,\ \phi_2 = 0.3$

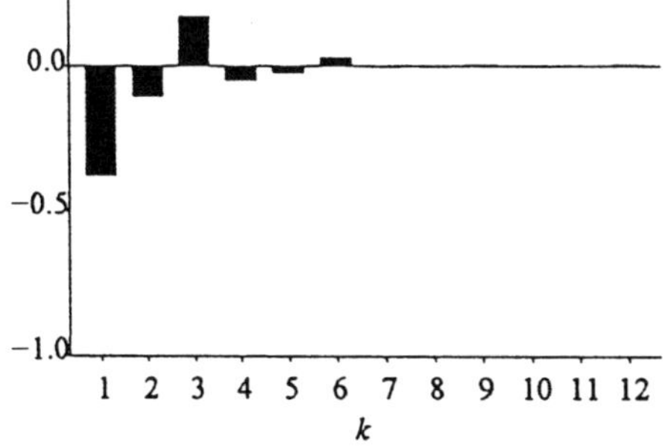

(d) $\phi_1 = -0.5,\ \phi_2 = -0.3$

Figure 2.3 ACFs of various AR(2) processes

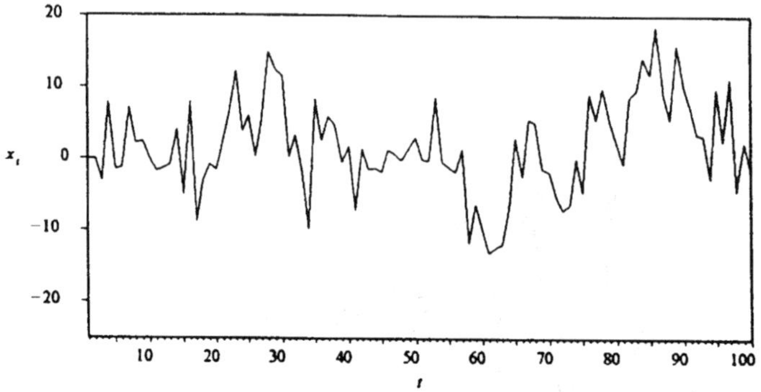

(a) $\phi_1 = 0.5$, $\phi_2 = 0.3$, $x_0 = x_1 = 0$

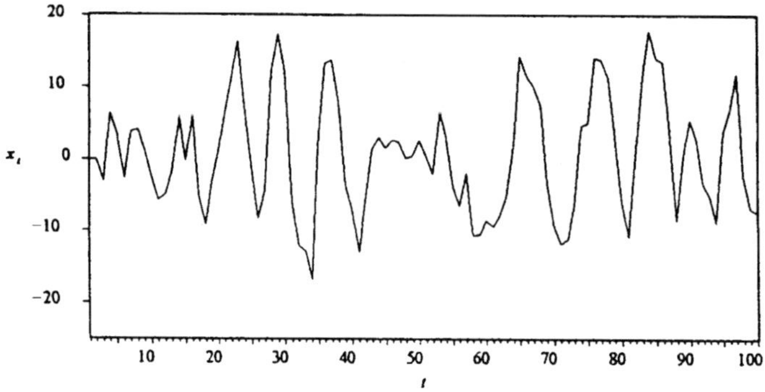

(b) $\phi_1 = 1$, $\phi_2 = -0.5$, $x_0 = x_1 = 0$

In general, ϕ_{kk} can be obtained from the *Yule–Walker* equations that correspond to (2.7). These are given by the set of equations (2.6) with $p = k$ and $\phi_i = \phi_{ii}$, and solving for the last coefficient ϕ_{kk} using Cramer's Rule leads to

$$\phi_{kk} = \frac{\begin{vmatrix} 1 & \rho_1 & \cdots & \rho_{k-2} & \rho_1 \\ \rho_1 & 1 & \cdots & \rho_{k-3} & \rho_2 \\ \cdot & \cdot & \cdots & \cdot & \cdot \\ \cdot & \cdot & \cdots & \cdot & \cdot \\ \rho_{k-1} & \rho_{k-2} & \cdots & \rho_1 & \rho_k \end{vmatrix}}{\begin{vmatrix} 1 & \rho_1 & \cdots & \rho_{k-2} & \rho_{k-1} \\ \rho_1 & 1 & \cdots & \rho_{k-3} & \rho_{k-2} \\ \cdot & \cdot & \cdots & \cdot & \cdot \\ \cdot & \cdot & \cdots & \cdot & \cdot \\ \rho_{k-1} & \rho_{k-2} & \cdots & \rho_1 & 1 \end{vmatrix}}$$

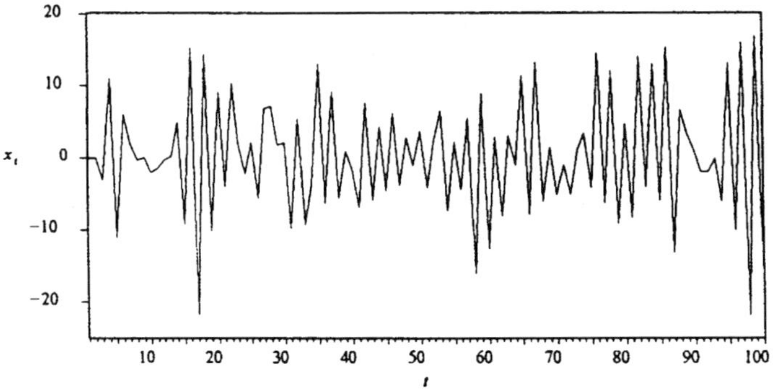

(c) $\phi_1 = -0.5$, $\phi_2 = 0.3$, $x_0 = x_1 = 0$

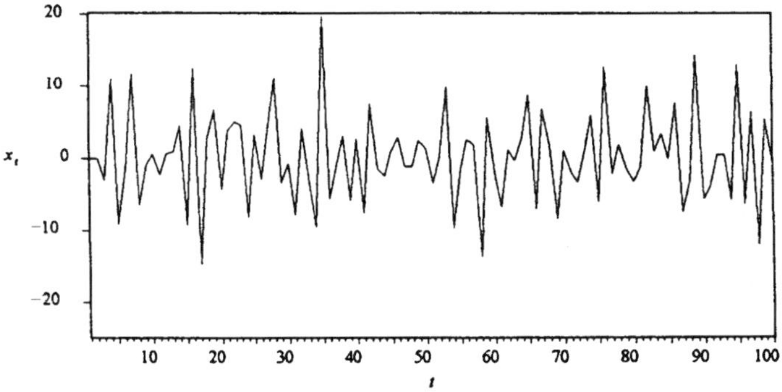

(d) $\phi_1 = -0.5$, $\phi_2 = -0.3$, $x_0 = x_1 = 0$

Figure 2.4 Simulations of various AR(2) processes

It follows from the definition of ϕ_{kk} that the PACFs of AR processes are of a particular form

$$\mathrm{AR}(1): \phi_{11} = \rho_1 = \phi, \qquad \phi_{kk} = 0 \text{ for } k > 1.$$

$$\mathrm{AR}(2): \phi_{11} = \rho_1, \phi_{22} = \frac{\rho_2 - \rho_1^2}{1 - \rho_1^2}, \qquad \phi_{kk} = 0 \text{ for } k > 2.$$

$$\mathrm{AR}(3): \phi_{11} \neq 0, \phi_{22} \neq 0, \cdots, \phi_{pp} \neq 0, \quad \phi_{kk} = 0 \text{ for } k > p.$$

Thus the partial autocorrelations for lags larger than the order of the process are zero. Hence an AR(p) process is described by:

(i) an ACF that is infinite in extent and is a combination of damped exponentials and damped sine waves, and
(ii) a PACF that is zero for lags larger than p.

The general moving average of order q [MA(q)] can be written as

$$x_t = a_t - \theta_1 a_{t-1} - \ldots - \theta_q a_{t-q}$$

or

$$x_t = (1 - \theta_1 B - \ldots - \theta_q B^q)a_t = \theta(B)a_t$$

The ACF can be shown to be

$$\rho_k = \frac{-\theta_k + \theta_1\theta_{k+1} + \ldots + \theta_{q-k}\theta_q}{1 + \theta_1^2 + \ldots + \theta_q^2}, \quad k = 1, 2, \ldots, q,$$

$$\rho_k = 0, \ k > q$$

The ACF of an MA(q) process therefore cuts off after lag q: the memory of the process extends q periods, observations more than q periods apart being uncorrelated.

The weights in the AR(∞) representation $\pi(B)x_t = a_t$ are given by $\pi(B) = \theta^{-1}(B)$ and can be obtained by equating coefficients of B^j in $\pi(B)\theta(B) = 1$. For invertibility, the roots of

$$(1 - \theta_1 B - \ldots - \theta_q B^q) = (1 - h_1 B) \cdots (1 - h_q B) = 0$$

must satisfy $|h_i| < 1$ for $i = 1, 2, \ldots, q$.

Figure 2.5 presents generated series from two MA(2) processes, again using $a_t \sim NID(0,25)$. The series tend to be fairly jagged, similar to AR(2) processes with real roots of opposite signs, and, of course, such MA processes are unable to capture periodic-type behaviour.

The PACF of an MA(q) process can be shown to be infinite in extent (i.e., it tails off). Explicit expressions for the PACFs of MA processes are complicated but, in general, are dominated by combinations of exponential decays (for the real roots in $\theta(B)$) and/or damped sine waves (for the complex roots). Their patterns are thus very similar to the ACFs of AR processes. Indeed, an important duality between AR and MA processes exists: while the ACF of an AR(p) process is infinite in extent, the PACF cuts off after lag p. The ACF of an MA(q) process,

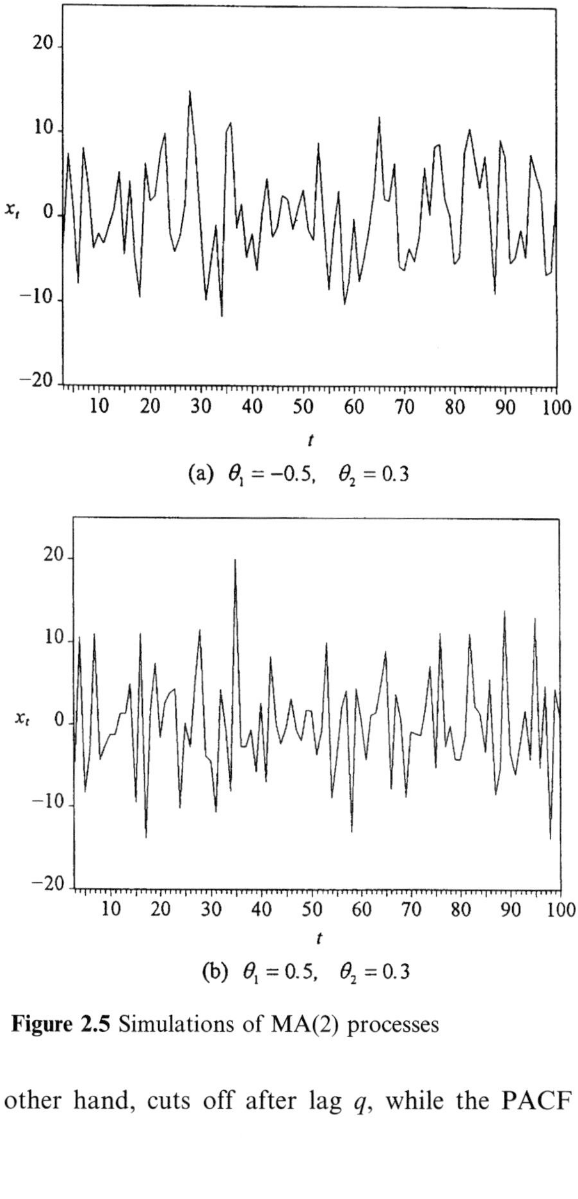

Figure 2.5 Simulations of MA(2) processes

on the other hand, cuts off after lag q, while the PACF is infinite in extent.

2.3.4 Autoregressive-moving average models

We may also consider combinations of autoregressive and moving average models. For example, consider the natural combination of the AR(1) and MA(1) models, known as the *first-order autoregressive-moving average*, or ARMA(1,1), model

$$x_t - \phi x_{t-1} = a_t - \theta a_{t-1}$$

or (2.8)

$$(1 - \phi B)x_t = (1 - \theta B)a_t$$

The ψ-weights in the MA(∞) representation are given by

$$\psi(B) = \frac{(1 - \theta B)}{(1 - \phi B)}$$

i.e.

$$x_t = \psi(B)a_t = \left(\sum_{i=0}^{\infty} \phi^i B^i\right)(1 - \theta B)a_t = a_t + (\phi - \theta)\sum_{i=1}^{\infty} \phi^{i-1} a_{t-i} \tag{2.9}$$

Likewise, the π-weights in the MA(∞) representation are given by

$$\pi(B) = \frac{(1 - \phi B)}{(1 - \theta B)}$$

i.e.

$$\pi(B)x_t = \left(\sum_{i=0}^{\infty} \theta^i B^i\right)(1 - \phi B)x_t = a_t$$

or

$$x_t = (\phi - \theta)\sum_{i=1}^{\infty} \theta^{i-1} x_{t-i} + a_t$$

The ARMA(1,1) model thus leads to both moving average and autoregressive representations having an infinite number of weights. The ψ-weights converge for $|\phi| < 1$ (the stationarity condition) and the π-weights converge for $|\theta| < 1$ (the invertibility condition). The stationarity condition for the ARMA(1,1) model is thus the same as that of an MA(1) model.

From equation (2.9) it is clear that any product $x_{t-k}a_{t-j}$ has zero expectation if $k > j$. Thus multiplying both sides of (2.8) by x_{t-k} and taking expectations yields

$$\gamma_k = \phi\gamma_{k-1}, \text{ for } k > 1$$

whilst for $k = 0$ and $k = 1$ we obtain, respectively

$$\gamma_0 = \phi\gamma_1 = \sigma^2 - \theta(\phi - \theta)\sigma^2$$

and

$$\gamma_1 - \phi\gamma_0 = -\theta\sigma^2$$

Eliminating σ^2 from these two equations allows the ACF of the ARMA(1,1) process to be given by

$$\rho_1 = \frac{(1 - \phi\theta)(\phi - \theta)}{1 + \theta^2 - 2\phi\theta}$$

and

$$\rho_k = \phi\rho_{k-1}, \text{ for } k > 1$$

The ACF of an ARMA(1,1) process is therefore similar to that of an AR(1) process, in that the autocorrelations decay exponentially at a rate ϕ. Unlike the AR(1), however, this decay starts from ρ_1 rather than from $\rho_0 = 1$. Moreover, $\rho_1 \neq \phi$ and, since for typical financial series both ϕ and θ will be positive with $\phi > \theta$, ρ_1 can be much less than ϕ if $\phi - \theta$ is small.

More general ARMA processes are obtained by combining AR(p) and MA(q) processes

$$x_t - \phi_1 x_{t-1} - \ldots - \phi_p x_{t-p} = a_t - \theta_1 a_{t-1} - \ldots - \theta_q a_{t-q}$$

or

$$(1 - \phi_1 B - \ldots - \phi_p B^p)x_t = (1 - \theta_1 B - \ldots - \theta_q B^q)a_t \tag{2.10}$$

i.e.

$$\phi(B)x_t = \theta(B)a_t$$

The resultant ARMA(p, q) process has the stationarity and invertibility conditions associated with the constituent AR(p) and MA(q) processes respectively. Its ACF will eventually follow the same pattern as that of an AR(p) process after $q-p$ initial values $\rho_1, \ldots, \rho_{q-p}$, while its PACF eventually (for $k > p-q$) behaves like that of an MA(q) process.

Throughout this development, we have assumed that the mean of the process, μ, is zero. Non-zero means are easily accommodated by replacing x_t with $x_t - \mu$ in (2.10), so that in the general case of an ARMA(p, q) process, we have

$$\phi(B)(x_t - \mu) = \theta(B)a_t$$

Noting that $\phi(B)\mu = (1 - \phi_1 - \ldots - \phi_p)\mu = \phi(1)\mu$, the model can equivalently be written as

$$\phi(B)x_t = \theta_0 + \theta(B)a_t$$

where $\theta_0 = \phi(1)\mu$ is a constant or intercept.

2.4 Linear stochastic processes

In this development of ARMA models, we have assumed that the innovations $\{a_t\}$ are uncorrelated and drawn from a fixed distribution with finite variance, and hence the sequence has been termed white noise, i.e., $a_t \sim WN(0, \sigma^2)$. If these innovations are also *independent*, then the sequence is termed *strict* white noise, denoted $a_t \sim SWN(0, \sigma^2)$, and a stationary process $\{x_t\}$ generated as a linear filter of strict white noise is said to be a linear process. It is possible, however, for a linear filter of a white noise process to result in a non-linear stationary process. The distinctions between white and strict white noise and between linear and non-linear stationary processes are extremely important when modelling financial time series and, as was alluded to in section 2.1.2, will be discussed in more detail in chapter 4.

2.5 ARMA model building

2.5.1 Sample autocorrelation and partial autocorrelation functions

An essential first step in fitting ARMA models to observed time series is to obtain estimates of the generally unknown parameters, μ, σ_x^2 and the ρ_k. With our stationarity and (implicit) ergodicity assumptions, μ and σ_x^2

can be estimated by the sample mean and sample variance, respectively, of the realisation $\{x_t\}_1^T$

$$\bar{x} = T^{-1} \sum_{t=1}^{T} x_t$$

$$s^2 = T^{-1} \sum_{t=1}^{T} (x_t - \bar{x})^2$$

An estimate of ρ_k is then given by the lag k *sample autocorrelation*

$$r_k = \frac{\sum\limits_{t=k+1}^{T} (x_t - \bar{x})(x_{t-k} - \bar{x})}{Ts^2}, \quad k = 1, 2, \ldots$$

the set of r_ks defining the *sample autocorrelation function* (SACF).

For independent observations drawn from a fixed distribution with finite variance ($\rho_k = 0$, for all $k \neq 0$), the variance of r_k is approximately given by T^{-1} (see, for example, Box and Jenkins, 1976, chapter 2). If, as well, T is large, $\sqrt{T} r_k$ will be approximately standard normal, i.e., $\sqrt{T} r_k \overset{a}{\sim} N(0, 1)$, so that an absolute value of r_k in excess of $2T^{-1/2}$ may be regarded as 'significantly' different from zero. More generally, if $\rho_k = 0$ for $k > q$, the variance of r_k, for $k > q$, is

$$V(r_k) = T^{-1}\left(1 + 2\rho_1^2 + \ldots + 2\rho_q^2\right)$$

Thus, by successively increasing the value of q and replacing the ρ_ks by their sample estimates, the variances of the sequence $r_1, r_2, \ldots, r_k$ can be estimated as $T^{-1}, T^{-1}(1 + 2r_1^2), \ldots, T^{-1}(1 + 2r_1^2 + \ldots + 2r_{k-1}^2)$ and, of course, these will be larger, for $k > 1$, than those calculated using the simple formula T^{-1}.

The *sample partial autocorrelation function* (SPACF) is usually calculated by fitting autoregressive models of increasing order: the estimate of the last coefficient in each model is the sample partial autocorrelation, $\hat{\phi}_{kk}$. If the data follow an AR(p) process, then for lags greater than p the variance of $\hat{\phi}_{kk}$ is approximately T^{-1}, so that $\sqrt{T}\hat{\phi}_{kk} \overset{a}{\sim} N(0, 1)$.

2.5.2 Model-building procedures

Given the r_k and $\hat{\phi}_{kk}$, with their respective standard errors, the approach to ARMA model building proposed by Box and Jenkins (1976) is essentially to match the behaviour of the SACF and SPACF of a particular time series with that of various theoretical ACFs and PACFs, picking the best match (or set of matches), estimating the unknown model parameters (the ϕ_is, θ_is and σ^2), and checking the residuals from the fitted models for any possible misspecifications.

Another popular method is to select a set of models based on prior considerations of maximum possible settings of p and q, estimate each possible model and select that model which minimises a chosen selection criterion based on goodness of fit considerations. Details of these model building procedures, and their various modifications, may be found in many texts, e.g., Mills (1990, chapter 8), and hence will not be discussed in detail: rather, they will be illustrated by way of a sequence of examples.

Example 2.1 Are the returns on the S&P 500 a fair game?

An important and often analysed financial series is the real return on the annual Standard & Poor (S&P) 500 stock index for the US. Annual observations from 1872 to 1995 are plotted in figure 2.6 and its SACF up to $k = 12$ is given in table 2.1. It is seen that the series appears to be stationary around a constant mean, estimated to be 3.08 per cent. This is confirmed by the SACF and a comparison of each of the r_k with their corresponding standard errors, computed using equation

Table 2.1. *SACF of real S&P 500 returns and accompanying statistics*

k	r_k	$s.e.(r_k)$	$Q(k)$
1	0.043	0.093	0.24 [0.62]
2	−0.169	0.093	3.89 [0.14]
3	0.108	0.093	5.40 [0.14]
4	−0.057	0.094	5.83 [0.21]
5	−0.117	0.094	7.61 [0.18]
6	0.030	0.094	7.73 [0.26]
7	0.096	0.094	8.96 [0.25]
8	−0.076	0.096	9.74 [0.28]
9	−0.000	0.097	9.74 [0.37]
10	0.086	0.097	10.76 [0.38]
11	−0.038	0.099	10.96 [0.45]
12	−0.148	0.099	14.00 [0.30]

Note: Figures in [..] give $P(\chi^2_k > Q(k))$.

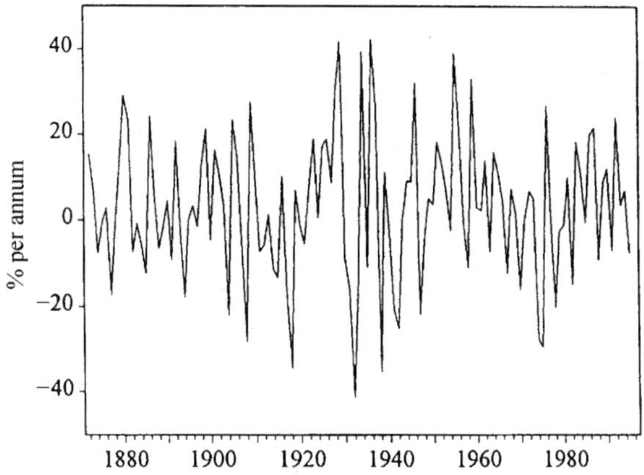

Figure 2.6 Real S&P 500 returns (annual 1872–1995)

(2.10), shows that none are individually significantly different from zero, thus suggesting that the series is, in fact, white noise.

We can construct a 'portmanteau' statistic based on the complete set of r_ks. On the hypothesis that $x_t \sim WN(\mu, \sigma^2)$, Box and Pierce (1970) show that the statistic

$$Q^*(k) = T \sum_{i=1}^{k} r_i^2$$

is asymptotically distributed as χ^2 with k degrees of freedom, i.e., $Q^*(k) \overset{a}{\sim} \chi_k^2$. Unfortunately, simulations have shown that, even for quite large samples, the true significance levels of $Q^*(k)$ could be much smaller than those given by this asymptotic theory, so that the probability of incorrectly rejecting the null hypothesis will be smaller than any chosen significance level. Ljung and Box (1978) argue that a better approximation is obtained when the modified statistic

$$Q(k) = T(T+2) \sum_{i=1}^{k} (T-i)^{-1} r_i^2 \overset{a}{\sim} \chi_k^2$$

is used. $Q(k)$ statistics, with accompanying marginal significance levels of rejecting the null, are also reported in table 2.1 for $k = 1, \ldots, 12$, and they confirm that there is no evidence against the null hypothesis that returns are white noise. Real returns on the S&P 500 would therefore appear to be consistent with the fair game model in which the expected return is constant, being 3.08 per cent per annum.

Example 2.2 Modelling the UK interest rate spread

As we shall see in chapter 8, the 'spread', the difference between long and short interest rates, is an important variable in testing the expectations hypothesis of the term structure of interest rates. Figure 2.7 shows the spread between 20 year UK gilts and 91 day Treasury bills using monthly observations for the period 1952 to 1995 ($T = 526$), while table 2.2 reports the SACF and SPACF up to $k = 12$, with accompanying standard errors. (The spread may be derived from the interest rate series $R20$ and RS given in the data appendix.)

The spread is seen to be considerably smoother than one would expect if it was a realisation from a white-noise process, and this is confirmed by the SACF, all of whose values are positive and significant (the accompanying portmanteau statistic is $Q(12) = 3701!$). The SPACF has both $\hat{\phi}_{11}$ and $\hat{\phi}_{22}$ significant, thus identifying an AR(2) process. Fitting such a model to the series by ordinary least squares (OLS) regression yields

$$\underset{}{x_t =} \underset{(0.023)}{0.045} + \underset{(0.043)}{1.182}\, x_{t-1} - \underset{(0.043)}{0.219}\, x_{t-2} + \hat{a}_t, \quad \hat{\sigma} = 0.448$$

Figures in parentheses are standard errors and the intercept implies a fitted mean of $\hat{\mu} = \hat{\theta}_0/(1 - \hat{\phi}_1 - \hat{\phi}_2) = 1.204$, with standard error 0.529. Since $\hat{\phi}_1 + \hat{\phi}_2 = 0.963$, $-\hat{\phi}_1 + \hat{\phi}_2 = -1.402$ and $\hat{\phi}_2 = -0.219$, the stationarity conditions associated with an AR(2) process are satisfied but,

Table 2.2. *SACF and SPACF of the UK spread*

k	r_k	$s.e.(r_k)$	$\hat{\phi}_{kk}$	$s.e.(\hat{\phi}_{kk})$
1	0.969	0.044	0.969	0.044
2	0.927	0.075	−0.217	0.044
3	0.884	0.094	0.011	0.044
4	0.844	0.109	0.028	0.044
5	0.803	0.121	−0.057	0.044
6	0.761	0.131	−0.041	0.044
7	0.719	0.139	−0.007	0.044
8	0.678	0.146	−0.004	0.044
9	0.643	0.152	0.057	0.044
10	0.613	0.157	0.037	0.044
11	0.586	0.162	0.008	0.044
12	0.560	0.166	−0.020	0.044

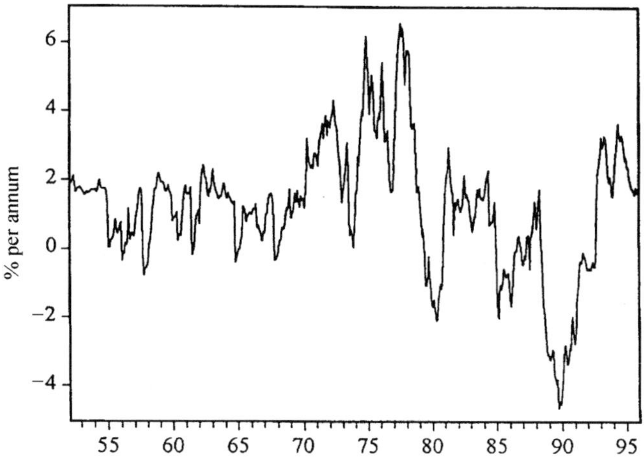

Figure 2.7 UK interest rate spread (monthly 1952.03–1995.12)

although $\hat{\phi}_2$ is negative, $\hat{\phi}_1^2 + 4\hat{\phi}_2 = 0.522$, so that the roots are real, being $\hat{g}_1 = 0.95$ and $\hat{g}_2 = 0.23$. The closeness of $\hat{g}_1$ to unity will be discussed further later in the chapter.

Having fitted an AR(2) process, it is now necessary to check whether such a model is adequate. As a 'diagnostic check', we may examine the properties of the residuals $\hat{a}_t$. Since these are estimates of a_t, they should mimic its behaviour, i.e., they should behave as white noise. The portmanteau statistics Q^* and Q can be used for this purpose, although the degrees of freedom attached to them must be amended: if an ARMA(p, q) process is fitted, they are reduced to $k - p - q$. With $k = 12$, our residuals yield the value $Q(12) = 6.62$, which is now asymptotically distributed as χ^2_{10} and hence gives no evidence of model inadequacy.

An alternative approach to assessing model adequacy is to overfit. For example, we might consider fitting an AR(3) process or, perhaps, an ARMA(2,1) to the series. These yield the following pair of models (methods of estimating MA processes are discussed in, for example, Hamilton, 1994, chapter 5. We use here maximum likelihood (ML))

$$\underset{}{x_t =} \underset{(0.023)}{0.044} + \underset{(0.044)}{1.185}\, x_{t-1} - \underset{(0.067)}{0.235}\, x_{t-2} + \underset{(0.044)}{0.013}\, x_{t-3} + \hat{a}_t,$$

$$\hat{\sigma} = 0.449$$

$$x_t = \underset{(0.025)}{0.046} + \underset{(0.196)}{1.137}\, x_{t-1} - \underset{(0.191)}{0.175}\, x_{t-2} + \hat{a}_t + \underset{(0.199)}{0.048}\, \hat{a}_{t-1},$$

$$\hat{\sigma} = 0.449$$

In both models, the additional parameter is insignificant, thus confirming the adequacy of our original choice of an AR(2) process.

Other methods of testing model adequacy are available. In particular, we may construct formal tests based on the Lagrange Multiplier (LM) principle: see Godfrey (1979), with Mills (1990, chapter 8.8) providing textbook discussion.

Example 2.3 Modelling returns on the FTA All Share index

The broadest-based stock index in the UK is the *Financial Times-Actuaries (FTA) All Share*. Table 2.3 reports the SACF and SPACF (up to $k = 12$) of its nominal return calculated using equation (1.2) from monthly observations from 1965 to 1995 ($T = 371$). The portmanteau statistic is $Q(12) = 26.4$, with a marginal significance level of 0.009, and both r_k and $\hat{\phi}_{kk}$ at lags $k = 1$ and 3 are greater than two standard errors. This suggests that the series is best modelled by some ARMA process of reasonably low order, although a number of models could be consistent with the behaviour shown by the SACF and SPACF.

In such circumstances, there are a variety of selection criteria that may be used to choose an appropriate model, of which perhaps the most popular is Akaike's (1974) Information Criteria, defined as

$$AIC(p, q) = \log \hat{\sigma}^2 + 2(p+q)T^{-1}$$

although a criterion that has better theoretical properties is Schwarz's (1978)

Table 2.3. *SACF and SPACF of* FTA All Share *nominal returns*

k	r_k	$s.e.(r_k)$	$\hat{\phi}_{kk}$	$s.e.(\hat{\phi}_{kk})$
1	0.153	0.052	0.153	0.052
2	−0.068	0.053	−0.094	0.052
3	0.109	0.053	0.139	0.052
4	0.093	0.054	0.046	0.052
5	−0.066	0.054	−0.072	0.052
6	−0.017	0.054	−0.006	0.052
7	0.056	0.054	0.030	0.052
8	−0.022	0.054	−0.030	0.052
9	0.101	0.055	0.138	0.052
10	0.044	0.055	−0.017	0.052
11	−0.025	0.055	−0.014	0.052
12	0.019	0.055	0.017	0.052

$$BIC(p, q) = \log \hat{\sigma}^2 + (p + q)T^{-1} \log T$$

A number of other criteria have been proposed, but all are structured in terms of the estimated error variance $\hat{\sigma}^2$ plus a penalty adjustment involving the number of estimated parameters, and it is in the extent of this penalty that the criteria differ. For more discussion about these, and other, selection criteria, see Judge *et al.* (1985, chapter 7.5).

The criteria are used in the following way. Upper bounds, say $p_{\max}$ and $q_{\max}$, are set for the orders of $\phi(B)$ and $\theta(B)$, and with $\bar{p} = \{0, 1, \ldots, p_{\max}\}$ and $\bar{q} = \{0, 1, \ldots, q_{\max}\}$, orders p_1 and q_1 are selected such that, for example

$$AIC(p_1, q_1) = \min AIC(p, q), \quad p \in \bar{p}, q \in \bar{q}$$

with parallel strategies obviously being employed in conjunction with *BIC* or any other criterion. One possible difficulty with the application of this strategy is that no specific guidelines on how to determine $\bar{p}$ and $\bar{q}$ seem to be available, although they are tacitly assumed to be sufficiently large for the range of models to contain the 'true' model, which we may denote as having orders (p_0, q_0) and which, of course, will not necessarily be the same as (p_1, q_1), the orders chosen by the criterion under consideration.

Given these alternative criteria, are there reasons for preferring one to another? If the true orders (p_0, q_0) are contained in the set $(p, q), p \in \bar{p}, q \in \bar{q}$, then for all criteria, $p_1 \geq p_0$ and $q_1 \geq q_0$, almost surely, as $T \to \infty$. However, *BIC* is *strongly consistent* in that it determines the true model asymptotically, whereas for *AIC* an overparameterised model will emerge no matter how long the available realisation. Of course, such properties are not necessarily guaranteed in finite samples, as we find below.

Given the behaviour of the SACF and SPACF of our returns series, we set $\bar{p} = \bar{q} = 3$ and table 2.4 shows the resulting *AIC* and *BIC* values. *AIC* selects the orders (2,2), i.e., an ARMA(2,2) process, while *BIC* selects the orders (0,1), so that an MA(1) process is chosen. The two estimated models are

$$\begin{aligned} x_t = \underset{(0.10)}{1.57} - \underset{(0.059)}{1.054}\, x_{t-1} - \underset{(0.056)}{0.822}\, x_{t-2} + \hat{a}_t + \underset{(0.049)}{1.204}\, \hat{a}_{t-1} \\ + \underset{(0.044)}{0.895}\, \hat{a}_{t-2}, \quad \hat{\sigma} = 5.89 \end{aligned}$$

$$x_t = \underset{(0.04)}{0.55} + \hat{a}_t + \underset{(0.051)}{0.195}\, \hat{a}_{t-1}, \quad \hat{\sigma} = 5.98$$

Table 2.4. *Model selection criteria for nominal returns*

	q / p	0	1	2	3
	0	−5.605	−5.629	−5.632	−5.633
AIC	1	−5.621	−5.631	−5.626	−5.629
	2	−5.622	−5.624	−5.649	−5.647
	3	−5.634	−5.629	−5.629	−5.646
	0	−5.594	−5.608	−5.601	−5.590
BIC	1	−5.600	−5.599	−5.584	−5.576
	2	−5.591	−5.582	−5.596	−5.583
	3	−5.591	−5.576	−5.565	−5.571

Although these models appear quite different, they are, in fact, similar in two respects. The estimate of the mean return implied by the ARMA(2,2) model is 0.55, the same as that obtained directly from the MA(1) model, while the sum of the weights of the respective AR(∞) representations are 0.93 and 0.84 respectively. The short-run dynamics are rather different, however. For the ARMA(2,2) model the initial weights are $\pi_1 = -0.150$, $\pi_2 = 0.108$, $\pi_3 = 0.005$, $\pi_4 = -0.102$; while for the MA(1) they are $\pi_1 = -0.195$, $\pi_2 = 0.038$, $\pi_3 = -0.007$, $\pi_4 = 0.001$.

There is, however, one fundamental difference between the two models: the MA(1) does not produce an acceptable fit to the returns series, for it has a $Q(12)$ value of 20.9, with a marginal significance level of 0.035. The ARMA(2,2) model, on the other hand, has a $Q(12)$ value of only 8.42.

Thus, although theoretically the *BIC* has advantages over the *AIC*, it would seem that the latter selects the model that is preferable on more general grounds. However, we should observe that, for both criteria, there are other models that yield criterion values very close to that of the model selected. Using this idea of being 'close to', Poskitt and Tremayne (1987) introduce the concept of a *model portfolio*. Models are compared to the selected (p_1, q_1) process by way of the statistic, using *AIC* for illustration

$$\Re = \exp\left[-\frac{1}{2}T\{AIC(p_1, q_1) - AIC(p, q)\}\right]$$

Although $\Re$ has no physical meaning, its value may be used to 'grade the decisiveness of the evidence' against a particular model. Poskitt and

Tremayne (1987) suggest that a value of $\mathfrak{R}$ less than $\sqrt{10}$ may be thought of as being a close competitor to (p_1, q_1), with the set of closely competing models being taken as the model portfolio.

Using this concept, with $\sqrt{10}$ taken as an approximate upper bound, *no* models are found to be close to (0,1) for the *BIC*. For the *AIC*, however, a model portfolio containing (2,2), (2,3) and (3,3) is obtained.

All these models have similar fits and, although it is difficult to compare them using the estimated AR and MA polynomials, their 'closeness' can be seen by looking at the roots of the characteristic equations associated with the $\phi(B)$ and $\theta(B)$ polynomials. The (2,2) model has complex AR roots $-0.53 \pm 0.74i$ and MA roots of $-0.60 \pm 0.73i$. The (3,3) model has AR roots of 0.82 and $-0.58 \pm 0.75i$ and MA roots 0.76 and $-0.64 \pm 0.75i$: the real roots are close to each other and hence 'cancel out' to leave the (2,2) model. The (0,1) model has a real MA root of -0.20, while the (2,3) model has a real MA root of -0.30 and complex AR roots of $-0.49 \pm 0.77i$ and MA roots of $-0.54 \pm 0.81i$. 'Cancelling out' these complex roots yields the (0,1) model.

We should also note the similarity of the complex AR and MA roots in the higher-order models. This could lead to problems of parameter redundancy, with roots again approximately cancelling out. From this perspective, the (2,2) model selected by the *AIC* may be thought of as providing a trade-off between the parsimonious, but inadequate, (0,1) model selected by *BIC* and the other, more profligately parameterised, models contained in the *AIC* portfolio.

2.6 Non-stationary processes and ARIMA models

The class of ARMA models developed in the previous sections of this chapter relies on the assumption that the underlying process is weakly stationary, thus implying that the mean, variance and autocovariances of the process are invariant under time translations. As we have seen, this restricts the mean and variance to be constant and requires the autocovariances to depend only on the time lag. Many financial time series, however, are certainly not stationary and, in particular, have a tendency to exhibit time-changing means and/or variances.

2.6.1 Non-stationarity in variance

We begin by assuming that a time series can be decomposed into a *non-stochastic* mean level and a random error component

$$x_t = \mu_t + \varepsilon_t \tag{2.11}$$

and we suppose that the variance of the errors, ε_t, is functionally related to the mean level μ_t by

$$V(x_t) = V(\varepsilon_t) = h^2(\mu_t)\sigma^2$$

where $h(\cdot)$ is some known function. Our objective is to find a transformation of the data, $g(x_t)$, that will stabilise the variance, i.e., the variance of the transformed variable $g(x_t)$ should be constant. Expanding $g(x_t)$ as a first-order Taylor series around μ_t yields

$$g(x_t) \cong g(\mu_t) + (x_t - \mu_t)g'(\mu_t)$$

where $g'(\mu_t)$ is the first derivative of $g(x_t)$ evaluated at μ_t. The variance of $g(x_t)$ can then be approximated as

$$\begin{aligned} V[g(x_t)] &\cong V[g(\mu_t) + (x_t - \mu_t)g'(\mu_t)] \\ &= [g'(\mu_t)]^2 V(x_t) \\ &= [g'(\mu_t)]^2 h^2(\mu_t)\sigma^2 \end{aligned}$$

Thus, in order to stabilise the variance, we have to choose the transformation $g(\cdot)$ such that

$$g'(\mu_t) = \frac{1}{h(\mu_t)}$$

For example, if the standard deviation of x_t is proportional to its level, $h(\mu_t) = \mu_t$ and the variance-stabilising transformation $g(\mu_t)$ has then to satisfy $g'(\mu_t) = \mu_t^{-1}$. This implies that $g(\mu_t) = \log(\mu_t)$ and thus (natural) logarithms of x_t should be used to stabilise the variance. If the variance of x_t is proportional to its level, $h(\mu_t) = \mu_t^{1/2}$ so that $g'(\mu_t) = \mu_t^{-1/2}$. Thus, since $g(\mu_t) = 2\mu_t^{1/2}$, the square root transformation $x_t^{1/2}$ will stabilise the variance. These two examples are special cases of the Box and Cox (1964) class of power transformations

$$g(x_t) = \frac{x_t^{\lambda} - 1}{\lambda}$$

where we note that $\lim_{\lambda \to 0}\left[\left(x_t^\lambda - 1\right)/\lambda\right] = \log(x_t)$. While the use of logarithms is a popular transformation for financial time series, a constant variance is rarely completely induced by this transformation alone. Chapter 4 considers various models in which time varying variances are explicitly modelled.

2.6.2 *Non-stationarity in mean*

A non-constant mean level in equation (2.11) can be modelled in a variety of ways. One possibility is that the mean evolves as a polynomial of order d in time. This will arise if x_t can be decomposed into a trend component, given by the polynomial, and a stochastic, stationary, but possibly autocorrelated, zero mean error component. This is always possible given Cramer's (1961) extension of Wold's decomposition theorem to non-stationary processes. Thus we may have

$$x_t = \mu_t + \varepsilon_t = \sum_{j=0}^{d} \beta_j t^j + \psi(B)a_t \tag{2.12}$$

Since

$$E(\varepsilon_t) = \psi(B)E(a_t) = 0$$

we have

$$E(x_t) = E(\mu_t) = \sum_{j=0}^{d} \beta_j t^j$$

and, as the β_j coefficients remain constant through time, such a trend in the mean is said to be *deterministic*. Trends of this type can be removed by a simple transformation. Consider the linear trend obtained by setting $d = 1$, where, for simplicity, the error component is assumed to be a white-noise sequence

$$x_t = \beta_0 + \beta_1 t + a_t \tag{2.13}$$

Lagging (2.13) one period and subtracting this from (2.13) yields

$$x_t - x_{t-1} = \beta_1 + a_t - a_{t-1} \tag{2.14}$$

The result is a difference equation following an ARMA(1,1) process in which, since $\phi = \theta = 1$, both autoregressive and moving average roots are unity and the model is neither stationary nor invertible. If we consider the *first differences* of x_t, w_t say, then

$$w_t = x_t - x_{t-1} = (1 - B)x_t = \Delta x_t$$

where $\Delta = 1 - B$ is known as the *first difference operator*. Equation (2.14) can then be written as

$$w_t = \Delta x_t = \beta_1 + \Delta a_t$$

and w_t is thus generated by a stationary (since $E(w_t) = \beta_1$ is a constant), but not invertible, MA(1) process.

In general, if the trend polynomial is of order d, and ε_t is characterised by the ARMA process $\phi(B)\varepsilon_t = \theta(B)a_t$, then

$$\Delta^d x_t = (1 - B)^d x_t$$

obtained by differencing x_t d times, will follow the process

$$\Delta^d x_t = \theta_0 + \frac{\Delta^d \theta(B)}{\phi(B)} a_t$$

where $\theta_0 = d!\beta_d$. Thus the MA part of the process generating $\Delta^d x_t$ will contain the factor Δ^d and will therefore have d roots of unity. Note also that the variance of x_t will be the same as the variance of ε_t, which will be constant for all t. Figure 2.8 shows plots of generated data for both linear and quadratic trend models. Because the variance of the error component, here assumed to be white noise and distributed as $NID(0,9)$, is constant and independent of the level, the variability of the two series are bounded about their expected values, and the trend components are clearly observed in the plots.

An alternative way of generating a non-stationary mean level is to consider ARMA models whose autoregressive parameters do not satisfy stationarity conditions. For example, consider the AR(1) process

$$x_t = \phi x_{t-1} + a_t \tag{2.15}$$

where $\phi > 1$. If the process is assumed to have started at time $t = 0$, the difference equation (2.15) has the solution

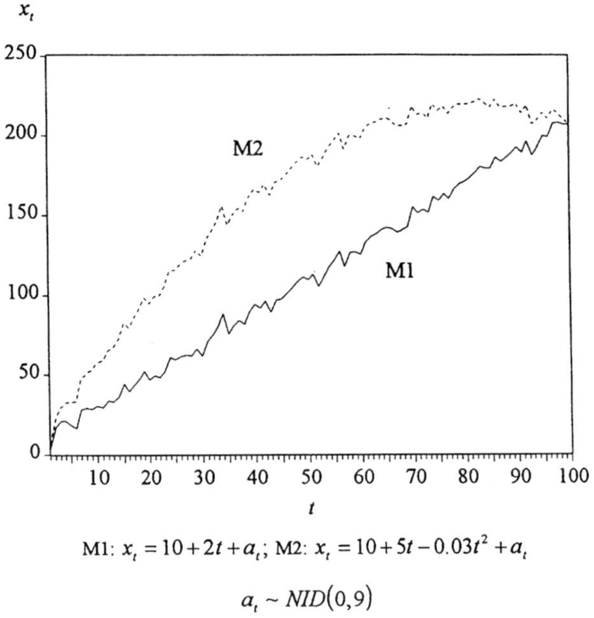

Figure 2.8 Linear and quadratic trends

$$x_t = x_0\phi^t + \sum_{i=0}^{t} \phi^i a_{t-i} \tag{2.16}$$

The 'complementary function' $x_0\phi^t$ can be regarded as the *conditional expectation* of x_t at time $t = 0$ (Box and Jenkins, 1976, chapter 4), and is an increasing function of t. The conditional expectation of x_t at times $t = 1, 2, \ldots, t-2, t-1$ depends on the random shocks $a_0, a_1, \ldots, a_{t-3}$, a_{t-2} and hence, since this conditional expectation may be regarded as the trend of x_t, the trend changes *stochastically*.

The variance of x_t is given by

$$V(x_t) = \sigma^2 \frac{\phi^{2(t+1)} - 1}{\phi^2 - 1}$$

which is an increasing function of time and becomes infinite as $t \to \infty$. In general, x_t will have a trend in both mean and variance, and such processes are said to be *explosive*. A plot of generated data from the process (2.15) with $\phi = 1.05$ and $a_t \sim NID(0, 9)$, and having starting value $x_0 = 10$, is shown in figure 2.9. We see that, after a short 'induction

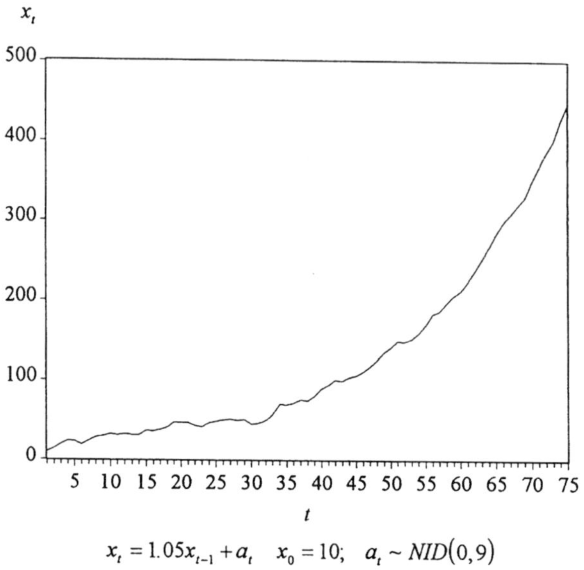

Figure 2.9 Explosive AR(1) model

period', the series follows essentially an exponential curve with the generating a_ts playing almost no further part. The same behaviour would be observed if additional autoregressive and moving average terms were added to the model, as long as the stationarity conditions are violated.

As we can see from (2.16), the solution of (2.15) is explosive if $\phi > 1$ but stationary if $\phi < 1$. The case $\phi = 1$ provides a process that is neatly balanced between the two. If x_t is generated by the model

$$x_t = x_{t-1} + a_t \tag{2.17}$$

then x_t is said to follow a *random walk*. If we allow a constant, θ_0, to be included, so that

$$x_t = x_{t-1} + \theta_0 + a_t \tag{2.18}$$

then x_t will follow a *random walk with drift*. If the process starts at $t = 0$, then

$$x_t = x_0 + t\theta_0 + \sum_{i=0}^{t} a_{t-i}$$

so that

$$\mu_t = E(x_t) = x_0 + t\theta_0$$
$$\gamma_{0,t} = V(x_t) = t\sigma^2$$

and

$$\gamma_{k,t} = Cov(x_t, x_{t-k}) = (t-k)\sigma^2, \quad k \geq 0$$

Thus the correlation between x_t and x_{t-k} is given by

$$\rho_{k,t} = \frac{t-k}{\sqrt{t(t-k)}} = \sqrt{\frac{t-k}{t}}$$

If t is large compared to k, all $\rho_{k,t}$ will be approximately unity. The sequence of x_t values will therefore be very smooth, but will also be non-stationary since both its mean and variance will increase with t. Figure 2.10 shows generated plots of the random walks (2.17) and (2.18) with $x_0 = 10$ and $a_t \sim NID(0, 9)$. In part (a) of the figure the drift parameter, θ_0, is set to zero, while in part (b) we have set $\theta_0 = 2$. The two plots differ considerably, but neither show any affinity whatsoever with the initial value x_0: indeed, the expected length of time for a random walk to pass again through an arbitrary value is infinite.

The random walk is an example of a class of non-stationary processes known as *integrated processes*. Equation (2.18) can be written as

$$\Delta x_t = \theta_0 + a_t$$

and so first differencing x_t leads to a stationary model, in this case the white noise process a_t. Generally, a series may need first differencing d times to attain stationarity, and the series so obtained may itself be autocorrelated.

If this autocorrelation is modelled by an ARMA(p, q) process, then the model for the original series is of the form

$$\phi(B)\Delta^d x_t = \theta_0 + \theta(B)a_t \tag{2.19}$$

which is said to be an *autoregressive-integrated-moving average* process of orders p, d and q, or ARIMA(p, d, q), and x_t is said to be integrated of order d, denoted $I(d)$.

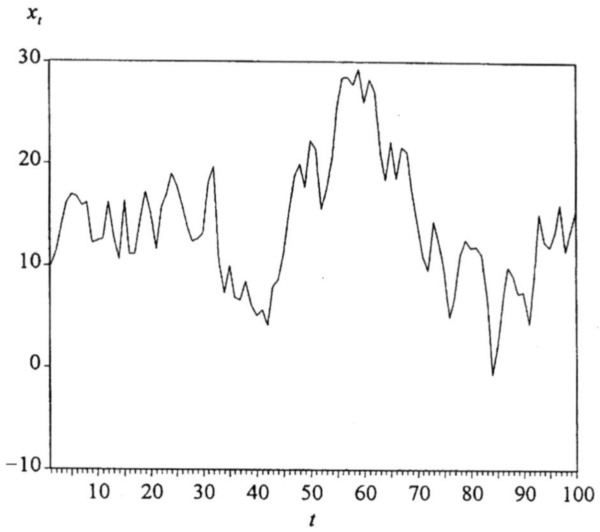

(a) $x_t = x_{t-1} + a_t \quad x_0 = 10; \quad a_t \sim NID(0,9)$

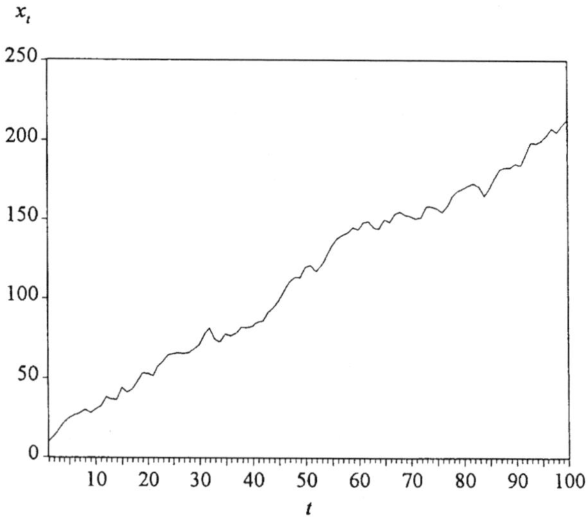

(b) $x_t = x_{t-1} + 2 + a_t \quad x_0 = 10; \quad a_t \sim NID(0,9)$

Figure 2.10 Random walks

It will usually be the case that the order of integration, d, or, equivalently, the degree of differencing, will be 0, 1, or, very occasionally, 2. Again it will be the case that the autocorrelations of an ARIMA process will be near one for all non-large k. For example, consider the (stationary) ARMA(1,1) process

$$x_t - \phi x_{t-1} = a_t - \theta a_{t-1}$$

whose ACF has been shown to be

$$\rho_1 = \frac{(1-\phi\theta)(\phi-\theta)}{1+\theta^2-2\phi\theta}, \quad \rho_k = \phi\rho_{k-1}, \text{ for } k > 1$$

As $\phi \to 1$, the ARIMA(0,1,1) process

$$\Delta x_t = a_t - \theta a_{t-1}$$

results, and all the ρ_k tend to unity.

A number of points concerning the ARIMA class of models are of importance. Consider again (2.19), with $\theta_0 = 0$ for simplicity

$$\phi(B)\Delta^d x_t = \theta(B)a_t \tag{2.20}$$

This process can equivalently be defined by the two equations

$$\phi(B)w_t = \theta(B)a_t \tag{2.21}$$

and

$$w_t = \Delta^d x_t \tag{2.22}$$

so that, as we have noted above, the model corresponds to assuming that $\Delta^d x_t$ can be represented by a stationary and invertible ARMA process. Alternatively, for $d \geq 1$, (2.22) can be inverted to give

$$x_t = S^d w_t \tag{2.23}$$

where S is the infinite summation, or *integral*, operator defined by

$$S = \left(1 + B + B^2 + \ldots\right) = (1-B)^{-1} = \Delta^{-1}$$

Equation (2.23) implies that the process (2.20) can be obtained by summing, or 'integrating', the stationary process d times: hence the term integrated process.

Box and Jenkins (1976, chapter 4) refer to this type of non-stationary behaviour as *homogenous non-stationarity*, and it is important to discuss why this form of non-stationarity is felt to be useful in describing the behaviour of many financial time series. Consider again the first-order autoregressive process (2.2). A basic characteristic of the AR(1) model is that, for both $|\phi| < 1$ and $|\phi| > 1$, the local behaviour of a series generated from the model is heavily dependent upon the level of x_t. For many financial series, local behaviour appears to be roughly independent of level, and this is what we mean by homogenous non-stationarity.

If we want to use ARMA models for which the behaviour of the process is indeed independent of its level, then the autoregressive operator $\phi(B)$ must be chosen so that

$$\phi(B)(x_t + c) = \phi(B)x_t$$

where c is any constant. Thus

$$\phi(B)c = 0$$

implying that $\phi(1) = 0$, so that $\phi(B)$ must be able to be factorised as

$$\phi(B) = \phi_1(B)(1 - B) = \phi_1(B)\Delta$$

in which case the class of processes that need to be considered will be of the form

$$\phi_1(B)w_t = \theta(B)a_t$$

where $w_t = \Delta x_t$. Since the requirement of homogenous non-stationarity precludes w_t increasing explosively, either $\phi_1(B)$ is a stationary operator, or $\phi_1(B) = \phi_2(B)(1 - B)$, so that $\phi_2(B)w_t^* = \theta(B)a_t$, where $w_t^* = \Delta^2 x_t$. Since this argument can be used recursively, it follows that for time series that are homogenously non-stationary, the autoregressive operator must be of the form $\phi(B)\Delta^d$, where $\phi(B)$ is a stationary autoregressive operator. Figure 2.11 plots generated data from the model $\Delta^2 x_t = a_t$, where $a_t \sim NID(0, 9)$ and $x_0 = x_1 = 10$, and such a series is seen to display random movements in both level and slope.

We see from figures 2.10(a) and 2.11 that ARIMA models without the constant θ_0 in (2.19) are capable of representing series that have *stochastic*

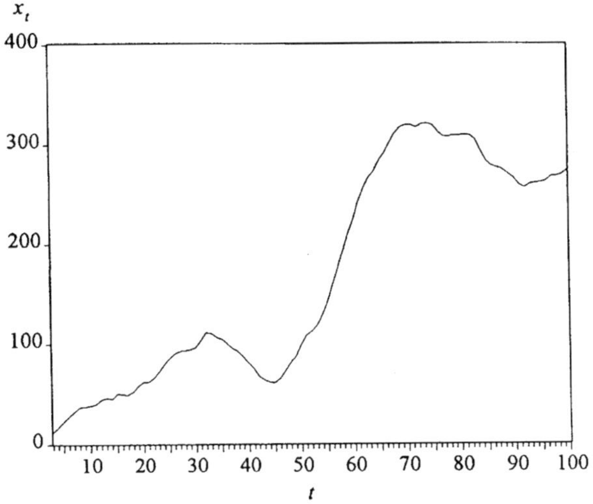

$(1-B)^2 x_t = a_t \quad x_0 = x_1 = 10; \quad a_t \sim NID(0,9)$

Figure 2.11 'Second difference' model

trends, which typically will consist of random changes in both the level and slope of the series. As seen from figure 2.10(b) and equation (2.18), however, the inclusion of a non-zero drift parameter introduces a deterministic trend into the generated series, since $\mu_t = E(x_t) = \beta_0 + \theta_0 t$ if we set $\beta_0 = x_0$. In general, if a constant is included in the model for dth differences, then a deterministic polynomial trend of degree d is automatically allowed for. Equivalently, if θ_0 is allowed to be non-zero, then

$$E(w_t) = E\left(\Delta^d x_t\right) = \mu_w = \theta_0 / (1 - \phi_1 - \phi_2 - \ldots - \phi_p)$$

is non-zero, so that an alternative way of expressing (2.19) is as

$$\phi(B)\tilde{w}_t = \theta(B)a_t$$

where $\tilde{w}_t = w_t - \mu_w$. Figure 2.12 plots generated data for $\Delta^2 x_t = 2 + a_t$, where again $a_t \sim NID(0, 9)$ and $x_0 = x_1 = 10$. The inclusion of the deterministic quadratic trend has a dramatic effect on the evolution of the series, with the non-stationary 'noise' being completely swamped after a few periods.

Model (2.19) therefore allows both stochastic and deterministic trends to be modelled. When $\theta_0 = 0$, a stochastic trend is incorporated, while if

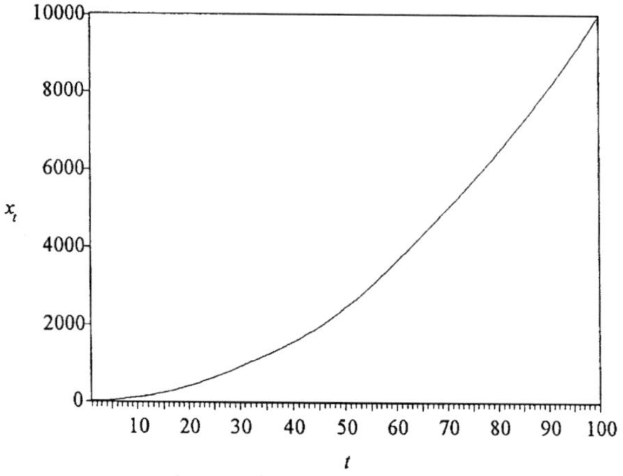

Figure 2.12 'Second difference with drift' model

$\theta_0 \neq 0$, the model may be interpreted as representing a deterministic trend (a polynomial in time of order d) buried in non-stationary noise, which will typically be autocorrelated. The models presented earlier in this section could be described as deterministic trends buried in *stationary* noise, since they can be written as

$$\phi(B)\Delta^d x_t = \phi(1)\beta_d d! + \Delta^d \theta(B) a_t$$

the stationary nature of the noise in the level of x_t being manifested in d roots of the moving average operator being unity. Further discussion of the relationships between stochastic and deterministic trends is contained in chapter 3.

2.7 ARIMA modelling

Once the order of differencing d has been established then, since $w_t = \Delta^d x_t$ is by definition stationary, the ARMA techniques discussed in section 2.5.2 may be applied to the suitably differenced series. Establishing the correct order of differencing is by no means straightforward, however, and is discussed in detail in chapter 3. We content ourselves here with a sequence of examples illustrating the modelling of ARIMA processes when d has already been chosen: the suitability of these choices are examined through examples in the subsequent chapter.

Example 2.4 Modelling the UK spread as an integrated process

In example 2.2 we modelled the spread of UK interest rates as a stationary, indeed AR(2), process. Here we consider modelling the spread assuming that it is an $I(1)$ process, i.e., we examine the behaviour of the SACF and SPACF of $w_t = \Delta x_t$. Table 2.5 provides these estimates up to $k = 12$ and suggests that, as both cut-off at $k = 1$, either an AR(1) or an MA(1) process is identified. Estimation of the former obtains

$$w_t = \underset{(0.0198)}{-0.0002} + \underset{(0.043)}{0.201}\, w_{t-1} + \hat{a}_t\,, \qquad \hat{\sigma} = 0.453$$

The residuals are effectively white noise, as they yield a portmanteau statistic of $Q(12) = 9.03$, and the mean of w_t is seen to be insignificantly different from zero. The spread can thus be modelled as an ARIMA(1,1,0) process without drift. In fact, fitting an ARIMA(0,1,1) process obtained almost identical estimates, with θ estimated to be 0.200 and $\hat{\sigma} = 0.452$.

Example 2.5 Modelling the dollar/sterling exchange rate

Figure 2.13 plots daily observations of both the level and first differences of the dollar/sterling exchange rate from January 1974 to December 1994, a total of 5,192 observations. The levels exhibit the wandering movement of a driftless random walk: the SACF has $r_1 = 0.999$, $r_{10} = 0.989$, $r_{20} = 0.977$, $r_{50} = 0.933$ and $r_{100} = 0.850$ and thus

Table 2.5. *SACF and SPACF of the first difference of the UK spread*

k	r_k	$s.e.(r_k)$	$\hat{\phi}_{kk}$	$s.e.(\hat{\phi}_{kk})$
1	0.201	0.044	0.201	0.044
2	0.006	0.045	−0.036	0.044
3	−0.053	0.045	−0.048	0.044
4	0.014	0.045	0.036	0.044
5	0.028	0.045	0.018	0.044
6	−0.006	0.045	−0.019	0.044
7	−0.028	0.045	−0.021	0.044
8	−0.088	0.046	−0.079	0.044
9	−0.087	0.046	−0.059	0.044
10	−0.049	0.046	−0.025	0.044
11	−0.006	0.046	0.000	0.044
12	0.017	0.046	0.015	0.044

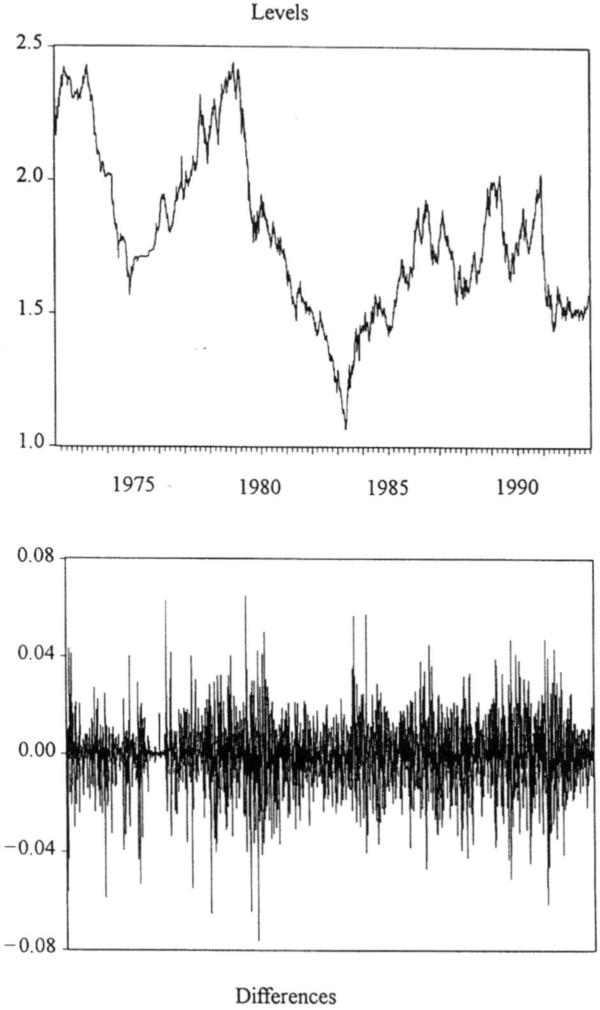

Figure 2.13 Dollar/sterling exchange rate (daily 1974–1994)

displays the slow, almost linear, decline typical of an $I(1)$ process (this is discussed further in chapter 3). The differences are stationary about zero and appear to show no discernable pattern. They are very close to being a white-noise process, the only significant sample autocorrelation being $r_1 = 0.071$. On fitting either an AR(1) or MA(1) process, although the parameter estimates were significant, the R^2 statistic associated with each model was less than 0.005, which, of course, is approximately equal to r_1^2.

Example 2.6 Modelling the *FTA All Share* index

Figure 2.14 plots monthly observations from January 1965 to December 1995 of the *FTA All Share* index and, as expected, shows the series to exhibit a prominent upward, but not linear, trend, with pronounced and persistent fluctuations about it, which increase in variability as the level of the series increases. This behaviour thus suggests a logarithmic transformation to be appropriate. The so transformed observations are also shown in figure 2.14: taking logarithms does indeed both linearise the trend and stabilise the variance.

Eliminating the trend by taking first differences yields the SACF and SPACF shown in table 2.6. Although the r_ks show no discernible pattern, the $\hat{\phi}_{kk}$s suggest an AR(3) process, whose adequacy is confirmed through overfitting and residual diagnostic tests. The fitted model is

$$\begin{aligned}\Delta x_t = {} & \underset{(0.0032)}{0.0069} + \underset{(0.052)}{0.152}\,\Delta x_{t-1} - \underset{(0.052)}{0.140}\,\Delta x_{t-2} \\ & + \underset{(0.052)}{0.114}\,\Delta x_{t-3} + \hat{a}_t, \quad \hat{\sigma} = 0.0603\end{aligned}$$

Table 2.6. *SACF and SPACF of the first difference of the* FTA All Share index

k	r_k	$s.e.(r_k)$	$\hat{\phi}_{kk}$	$s.e.(\hat{\phi}_{kk})$
1	0.122	0.052	0.122	0.052
2	−0.108	0.053	−0.125	0.052
3	0.080	0.055	0.114	0.052
4	0.061	0.056	0.021	0.052
5	−0.101	0.056	−0.094	0.052
6	−0.044	0.057	−0.014	0.052
7	0.033	0.057	0.010	0.052
8	−0.047	0.058	−0.048	0.052
9	0.083	0.058	0.123	0.052
10	0.025	0.059	−0.029	0.052
11	−0.044	0.059	−0.022	0.052
12	0.044	0.059	0.008	0.052

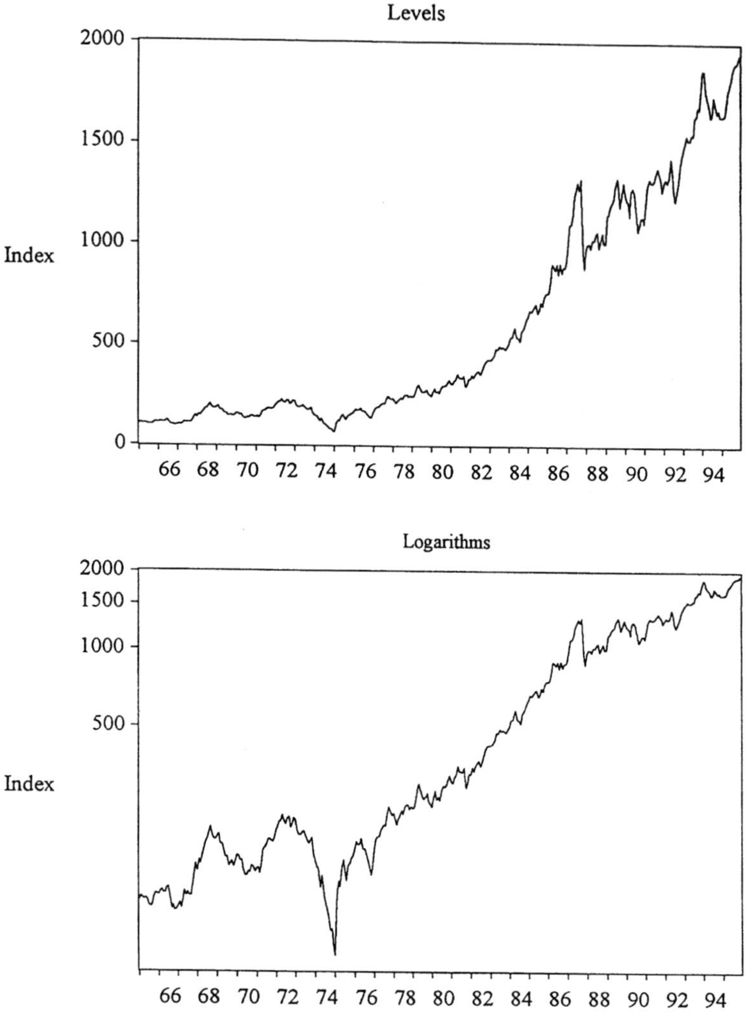

Figure 2.14 *FTA All Share* index (monthly 1965–95)

The implied estimate of μ is 0.0079 which, since Δx_t can be interpreted as the monthly growth of the index, implies an annual mean growth rate of approximately 9.5 per cent. Here x_t is defined as $\log(P_t)$, where P_t is the level of the index. Thus $\Delta x_t = \log(P_t/P_{t-1})$, which can be compared with the nominal return on the index analysed in example 2.3

$$\begin{aligned} r_t &= \frac{P_t + D_t - P_{t-1}}{P_{t-1}} \approx \log\left(\frac{P_t + D_t}{P_{t-1}}\right) \\ &= \log\left(\frac{P_t}{P_{t-1}}\right) + \log\left(1 + \frac{D_t}{P_t}\right) \approx \Delta x_t + \frac{D_t}{P_t} \end{aligned}$$

i.e., the nominal return is equal to the growth of the index plus the dividend yield. The dividend yield appears to be best modelled as an ARMA(1,3) process. Granger and Morris (1976) prove that if two independent series y_1 and y_2 are ARMA(p_i, q_i), $i = 1, 2$, processes then their sum is an ARMA(p, q) process, where

$$p \leq p_1 + p_2 \quad \text{and} \quad q \leq \max(p_1 + q_2, q_1 + p_2)$$

The assumption of independence can be weakened to allow for contemporaneous correlation between the innovations of y_1 and y_2, which is the case for Δx and D/P, so that r_t should be generated by an ARMA process with orders $p \leq 4$ and $q \leq 6$, which is consistent with what was found in example 2.3.

2.8 Forecasting using ARIMA models

Given a realisation $\{x_t\}_{1-d}^{T}$ from a general ARIMA(p, d, q) process

$$\phi(B)\Delta^d x_t = \theta_0 + \theta(B)a_t$$

it is often the case that we wish to forecast a future value x_{T+h}. If we let

$$\alpha(B) = \phi(B)\Delta^d = \left(1 - \alpha_1 B - \alpha_2 B^2 - \ldots - \alpha_{p+d}B^{p+d}\right)$$

then a *minimum mean square error* (MMSE) forecast, denoted $f_{T,h}$, made at time T, is given by the conditional expectation

$$\begin{aligned} f_{T,h} =& E(\alpha_1 x_{T+h-1} + \alpha_2 x_{T+h-2} + \ldots + \alpha_{p+d} x_{T+h-p-d} + \theta_0 \\ & + a_{T+h} - \theta_1 a_{T+h-1} - \ldots - \theta_q a_{T+h-q} | x_T, x_{T-1}, \ldots) \end{aligned}$$

Now

$$E(x_{T+j} | x_T, x_{T-1}, \ldots) = \begin{cases} x_{T+j}, & j \leq 0 \\ f_{T,j}, & j > 0 \end{cases}$$

and

$$E\left(a_{T+j}|x_T, x_{T-1}, \ldots\right) = \begin{cases} a_{T+j}, & j \leq 0 \\ 0, & j > 0 \end{cases}$$

so that, to evaluate $f_{T,h}$, all we need to do is: (i) replace past expectations ($j \leq 0$) by known values, x_{T+j} and a_{T+j}, and (ii) replace future expectations ($j > 0$) by forecast values, $f_{T,j}$ and 0.

Three examples will illustrate the procedure. Consider first the AR(2) model $\left(1 - \phi_1 B - \phi_2 B^2\right)x_t = \theta_0 + a_t$, so that $\alpha(B) = \left(1 - \phi_1 B - \phi_2 B^2\right)$. Here

$$x_{T+h} = \phi_1 x_{T+h-1} + \phi_2 x_{T+h-2} + \theta_0 + a_{T+h}$$

and hence, for $h = 1$, we have

$$f_{T,1} = \phi_1 x_T + \phi_2 x_{T-1} + \theta_0$$

for $h = 2$

$$f_{T,2} = \phi_1 f_{T,1} + \phi_2 x_T + \theta_0$$

and for $h > 2$

$$f_{T,h} = \phi_1 f_{T,h-1} + \phi_2 f_{T,h-2} + \theta_0$$

An alternative expression for $f_{T,h}$ can be obtained by noting that

$$f_{T,h} = (\phi_1 + \phi_2) f_{T,h-1} - \phi_2\left(f_{T,h-1} - f_{T,h-2}\right) + \theta_0$$

from which, by repeated substitution, we obtain

$$\begin{aligned} f_{T,h} =& (\phi_1 + \phi_2)^h x_T - \phi_2 \sum_{j=0}^{h-1} (\phi_1 + \phi_2)^j \left(f_{T,h-1-j} - f_{T,h-2-j}\right) \\ & + \theta_0 \sum_{j=0}^{h-1} (\phi_1 + \phi_2)^j \end{aligned}$$

where, by convention, we take $f_{T,0} = x_T$ and $f_{T,-1} = x_{T-1}$. Thus, for stationary processes ($\phi_1 + \phi_2 < 1$, $|\phi_2| < 1$), as $h \to \infty$

$$f_{T,h} = \frac{\theta_0}{1 - \phi_1 - \phi_2} = E(x_t) = \mu$$

so that for large lead times the best forecast of a future observation is eventually the mean of the process.

Next consider the ARIMA(0,1,1) model $\Delta x_t = (1 - \theta B)a_t$. Here $\alpha(B) = (1 - B)$ and so

$$x_{T+h} = x_{T+h-1} + a_{T+h} - \theta a_{T+h-1}$$

For $h = 1$, we have

$$f_{T,1} = x_T - \theta a_T$$

for $h = 2$

$$f_{T,2} = f_{T,1} = x_T - \theta a_T$$

and, in general

$$f_{T,h} = f_{T,h-1}, \quad h > 1$$

Thus, for all lead times, the forecasts from origin T will follow a straight line parallel to the time axis passing through $f_{T,1}$. Note that, since

$$f_{T,h} = x_T - \theta a_T$$

and

$$a_T = (1 - B)(1 - \theta B)^{-1} x_T$$

the h-step ahead forecast can be written as

$$\begin{aligned} f_{T,h} &= (1 - \theta)(1 - \theta B)^{-1} x_T \\ &= (1 - \theta)\left(x_T + \theta x_{T-1} + \theta^2 x_{T-2} + \ldots\right) \end{aligned}$$

i.e., the forecast for all future values of x is an exponentially weighted moving average of current and past values.

Finally, consider the ARIMA(0,2,2) model $\Delta^2 x_t = \left(1 - \theta_1 B - \theta_2 B^2\right) a_t$, with $\alpha(B) = (1 - B)^2 = \left(1 - 2B + B^2\right)$

$$x_{T+h} = 2x_{T+h-1} - x_{T+h-2} + a_{T+h} - \theta_1 a_{T+h-1} - \theta_2 a_{T+h-2}$$

For $h = 1$, we have

$$f_{T,1} = 2x_T - x_{T-1} - \theta_1 a_T - \theta_2 a_{T-1}$$

for $h = 2$

$$f_{T,2} = 2f_{T,1} - x_T - \theta_2 a_T$$

for $h = 3$

$$f_{T,3} = 2f_{T,2} - f_{T,1}$$

and thus, for $h \geq 3$

$$f_{T,h} = 2f_{T,h-1} - f_{T,h-2}$$

Hence, for all lead times, the forecasts from origin T will follow a straight line passing through the forecasts $f_{T,1}$ and $f_{T,2}$.

The h-step ahead forecast error for origin T is

$$e_{T,h} = x_{T+h} - f_{T,h} = a_{T+h} + \psi_1 a_{T+h-1} + \ldots + \psi_{h-1} a_{T+1}$$

where $\psi_1, \ldots, \psi_{h-1}$ are the first $h-1$ ψ-weights in $\psi(B) = \alpha^{-1}(B)\theta(B)$. The variance of this forecast error is then

$$V(e_{T,h}) = \sigma^2(1 + \psi_1^2 + \psi_2^2 + \ldots + \psi_{h-1}^2) \tag{2.24}$$

The forecast error is therefore a linear combination of the unobservable future shocks entering the system after time T and, in particular, the one-step ahead forecast error is

$$e_{T,1} = x_{T,1} - f_{T,1} = a_{T+1}$$

Thus, for a MMSE forecast, the one-step ahead forecast errors must be uncorrelated. However, h-step ahead forecasts made at different origins will not be uncorrelated, and neither will be forecasts for different lead times made at the same origin (see, for example, Box and Jenkins, 1976, appendix A5.1).

For the AR(2) example given above, we have $\psi_1 = \phi_1$, $\psi_2 = \phi_1^2 + \phi_2$ and, for $j > 2$, $\psi_j = \phi_1 \psi_{j-1} + \phi_2 \psi_{j-2}$. Since we are assuming stationarity, these ψ-weights converge absolutely. As absolute convergence $(\sum_{j=1}^{h} |\psi_j| < \infty)$ implies $\sum_{j=1}^{h} \psi_j^2 < \infty$, known as square-summability (Hamilton, 1994, chapter 3), $V(e_{T,h})$ converges to a finite value, which is the variance of the process about the ultimate forecast μ.

For the ARIMA(0,1,1) model, $\psi_j = 1 - \theta, j = 1, 2, \ldots$. Thus we have

$$V(e_{T,h}) = \sigma^2\left(1 + (h-1)(1-\theta)^2\right)$$

which increases with h. Similarly, the ARIMA(0,2,2) model has ψ-weights given by $\psi_j = 1 + \theta_2 + j(1 - \theta_1 - \theta_2), j = 1, 2, \ldots$ and an h-step ahead forecast error variance of

$$V(e_{T,h}) = \sigma^2\left(1 + (h-1)(1+\theta_2)^2 + \tfrac{1}{6}h(h-1)(2h-1)(1-\theta_1-\theta_2)^2 + h(h-1)(1+\theta_2)(1-\theta_1-\theta_2)\right)$$

which again increases with h.

The examples in this section thus show how the degree of differencing, or order of integration, determines not only how successive forecasts are related to each other, but also the behaviour of the associated error variances.

Example 2.7 ARIMA forecasting of financial time series

Here we examine the properties of ARIMA forecasts for some of the series analysed in the examples of this chapter.

Example 2.2 fitted an AR(2) model to the UK interest rate spread, yielding parameter estimates $\hat{\phi}_1 = 1.182, \hat{\phi}_2 = -0.219, \quad \hat{\theta}_0 = 0.045$ and $\hat{\sigma} = 0.448$. With the last two observations being $x_{T-1} = 1.63$ and $x_T = 1.72$, forecasts are obtained as

$$\begin{aligned} f_{T,1} &= 1.182x_T - 0.219x_{T-1} &= 1.676 \\ f_{T,2} &= 1.182f_{T,1} - 0.219x_T &= 1.604 \\ f_{T,3} &= 1.182f_{T,2} - 0.219f_{T,1} &= 1.529 \end{aligned}$$

and so on. As h increases, the forecasts eventually tend to 1.216, the sample mean of the spread. The ψ-weights are given by

$$\begin{aligned} \psi_1 &= \phi_1 = 1.182 \\ \psi_2 &= \phi_1^2 + \phi_2 = 1.178 \\ \psi_3 &= \phi_1^3 + 2\phi_1\phi_2 = 1.134 \\ \psi_4 &= \phi_1^4 + 3\phi_1^2\phi_2 + \phi_2^2 = 1.082 \end{aligned}$$

and, hence

$$\psi_h = 1.182\psi_{h-1} - 0.219\psi_{h-2}$$

The forecast error variances are

$$\begin{aligned}
V(e_{T,1}) &= 0.448^2 = 0.201 \\
V(e_{T,2}) &= 0.448^2(1 + 1.182^2) = 0.482 \\
V(e_{T,3}) &= 0.448^2(1 + 1.182^2 + 1.178^2) = 0.761 \\
V(e_{T,4}) &= 0.448^2(1 + 1.182^2 + 1.178^2 + 1.134^2) = 1.019
\end{aligned}$$

the forecast error variances converging to the sample variance of the spread, 3.53.

If, however, we use the ARIMA(0,1,1) process of example 2.4 to model the spread, with $\hat{\theta} = 0.2$ and $\hat{\sigma} = 0.452$, then our forecasts are (using the final residual $\hat{a}_T = 0.136$)

$$f_{T,1} = 1.72 - 0.2(0.136) = 1.693$$

and, for $h > 1$

$$f_{T,h} = f_{T,1} = 1.693$$

so that there is no tendency for the forecasts to converge to the sample mean or, indeed, to any other value. Furthermore, the forecast error variances are given by

$$V(e_{T,h}) = 0.452^2(1 + 0.64(h - 1)) = 0.204 + 0.131(h - 1)$$

which, of course, increase with h, rather than tending to a constant. This example thus illustrates within the forecasting context the radically different properties of ARMA models which have, on the one hand, a unit autoregressive root and, on the other, a root that is large but less than unity.

The dollar/sterling exchange rate was found, in example 2.5, effectively to be a driftless random walk, which thus implies that, given an end-of-sample exchange rate of 1.557, all future forecasts of the rate are that particular value, although the precision of the forecasts, given by the accompanying forecast error variance, diminishes as the forecasting horizon increases: with σ estimated to be 0.011, we have $V(e_{T,h}) = 0.00012h$.

In example 2.6 we modelled the logarithms of the *FTA All Share* index as an ARIMA(3,1,0) process. Since

$$\phi(B) = 1 - 0.152B + 0.140B^2 - 0.114B^3$$

we have

$$\alpha(B) = 1 - 1.152B + 0.292B^2 - 0.254B^3 + 0.114B^4$$

so that forecasts can be computed recursively by

$$\begin{aligned}
f_{T,1} &= 1.152x_T - 0.292x_{T-1} + 0.254x_{T-2} - 0.114x_{T-3} + 0.0069,\\
f_{T,2} &= 1.152f_{T,1} - 0.292x_T + 0.254x_{T-1} - 0.114x_{T-2} + 0.0069,\\
f_{T,3} &= 1.152f_{T,2} - 0.292f_{T,1} + 0.254x_T - 0.114x_{T-1} + 0.0069,\\
f_{T,4} &= 1.152f_{T,3} - 0.292f_{T,2} + 0.254f_{T,1} - 0.114x_T + 0.0069
\end{aligned}$$

and, for $h \geq 5$

$$\begin{aligned}
f_{T,h} = {} & 1.152f_{T,h-1} - 0.292f_{T,h-2} + 0.254f_{T,h-3} - 0.114f_{T,h-4}\\
& + 0.0069
\end{aligned}$$

By computing the coefficients in the polynomial $\psi(B) = \alpha^{-1}(B)$ as

$$\psi(B) = 1 + 1.152B + 1.107B^2 + 1.193B^3 + 1.230B^4 + \ldots \quad (2.25)$$

and using the estimate $\hat{\sigma} = 0.0603$, forecast error variances can then be computed using the formula (2.24): since the series is $I(1)$, these variances increase with h.

Additional interpretation of the nature of these forecasts is provided by the *eventual forecast function*, which is obtained by solving the difference equation implicit in the ARIMA(3,1,0) representation of x_t at time $T+h$ (see, for example, Mills, 1990, chapter 7.3, for a general development and McKenzie, 1988, for further discussion)

$$\begin{aligned}
& x_{T+h} - 1.152x_{T+h-1} + 0.292x_{T+h-2} - 0.254x_{T+h-3} + 0.114x_{T+h-4}\\
& = 0.0069 + a_{T+h}
\end{aligned}$$

At origin T, this difference equation has the solution

$$x_{T+h} = \sum_{i=1}^{4} b_i^{(T)} f_i(h) + 0.0069 \sum_{j=T+1}^{T+h} \psi_{T+h-j}$$

where the ψs are as in (2.25) and the functions $f_1(h), \ldots, f_4(h)$ depend upon the roots of the polynomial $\alpha(B)$, which are unity, a real root of 0.43, and a pair of complex roots, $-0.14 \pm 0.49i$. Hence the solution can be written as

$$x_{T+h} = b_0 + b_1^{(T)} + b_2^{(T)}(0.43)^h + b_3^{(T)}(-0.14 + 0.49i)^h \\ + b_4^{(T)}(-0.14 - 0.49i)^h$$

where

$$b_0 = 0.0069 \sum_{j=T+1}^{T+h} \psi_{T+h-j}$$

For a given origin T, the coefficients $b_j^{(T)}, j = 1, \ldots, 4$ are constants applying to all lead times h, but they change from one origin to the next, adapting themselves to the observed values of x_t. They can be obtained by solving a set of recursive equations containing the $f_i(h)s$, ψ_h and a_T.

Since the ψ_hs increase with h, b_0 imparts a deterministic drift into x_{T+h}, so that $b_0 + b_1^{(T)}$ gives the forecasted 'trend' of the series. Around this trend are a geometrically declining component, provided by the real, but stationary, root, and a damped sine wave provided by the pair of complex roots, its damping factor, frequency and phase being functions of the process parameters (Box and Jenkins, 1976, pages 58–63). These complex roots provide a damped cyclical AR(2) component with parameters $\phi_1^* = -0.28$, $\phi_2^* = -0.26$, a damping factor of 0.51 and an average period of approximately 5 months.

3 Univariate linear stochastic models: further topics

The previous chapter has demonstrated that the order of integration, *d*, is a crucial determinant of the properties that a time series exhibits. This chapter begins with an exposition of the techniques available for determining the order of integration of a time series, emphasising the importance of the chosen alternative hypothesis to the null of a unit root: in particular, whether the alternative is that of a constant mean, a linear trend, or a segmented trend. The importance of these models to finance is demonstrated through a sequence of examples.

We then move, in section 2, to examining methods of decomposing an observed time series into two or more unobserved components, emphasising the signal extraction approach to estimating these components. This approach is particularly suited to estimating, under assumptions of market efficiency, expected, or *ex ante*, values using only observed, or *ex post*, observations, and is illustrated by showing how expected real interest rates can be extracted from observed rates.

The final sections of the chapter focus attention on long-term properties of financial time series. A number of models of stock market behaviour yield the prediction that stock returns, far from being unpredictable, should exhibit negative autocorrelation over long time horizons, i.e., that they should be *mean reverting*. Section 3 thus develops techniques for measuring and testing for such mean reversion, or *persistence* as it is often referred to. Section 4 introduces an alternative method of modelling long-term memory in a time series, through the use of a *fractional* value of *d*. Fractionally integrated extensions of ARIMA models are developed and methods of testing for fractional integration and estimating such models are introduced. Both methods of modelling long-run behaviour are illustrated through examples using stock returns.

3.1 Determining the order of integration of a time series

3.1.1 Distinguishing between different values of d.

As stated above, the order of integration, d, is a crucial determinant of the properties that a time series exhibits. If we restrict ourselves to the most common values of zero and one for d, so that x_t is either $I(0)$ or $I(1)$, then it is useful to bring together the properties of such processes.

If x_t is $I(0)$, which we will denote $x_t \sim I(0)$ even though such a notation has been used previously to denote the distributional characteristics of a series, then, assuming for convenience that it has zero mean:

(i) the variance of x_t is finite and does not depend on t,
(ii) the innovation a_t has only a temporary effect on the value of x_t,
(iii) the expected length of times between crossings of $x = 0$ is finite, i.e., x_t fluctuates around its mean of zero,
(iv) the autocorrelations, ρ_k, decrease steadily in magnitude for large enough k, so that their sum is finite.

If $x_t \sim I(1)$ with $x_0 = 0$ then:

(i) the variance of x_t goes to infinity as t goes to infinity,
(ii) an innovation a_t has a permanent effect on the value of x_t because x_t is the sum of all previous innovations: see, e.g., equation (2.16),
(iii) the expected time between crossings of $x = 0$ is infinite,
(iv) the autocorrelations $\rho_k \to 1$ for all k as t goes to infinity.

The fact that a time series is non-stationary is often self-evident from a plot of the series. Determining the actual form of non-stationarity, however, is not so easy from just a visual inspection, and an examination of the SACFs for various differences may be required.

To see why this may be so, recall that a stationary AR(p) process requires that all roots g_i in

$$\phi(B) = (1 - g_1 B)(1 - g_2 B) \ldots \left(1 - g_p B\right)$$

are such that $|g_i| < 1$. Now suppose that one of them, say g_1, approaches 1, i.e., $g_1 = 1 - \delta$, where δ is a small positive number. The autocorrelations

$$\rho_k = A_1 g_1^k + A_2 g_2^k + \ \ldots \ + A_p g_p^k \cong A_1 g_1^k$$

will then be dominated by $A_1 g_1^k$, since all other terms will go to zero more rapidly. Furthermore, as g_1 is close to 1, the exponential decay $A_1 g_1^k$ will be slow and almost linear, since

$$A_1 g_1^k = A_1(1 - \delta)^k = A_1\left(1 - \delta k + \delta^2 k^2 - \ \ldots\right) \cong A_1(1 - \delta k)$$

Hence, failure of the SACF to die down quickly is therefore an indication of non-stationarity, its behaviour tending to be that of a slow, linear decline. If the original series x_t is found to be non-stationary, the first difference Δx_t is then analysed. If Δx_t is still non-stationary, the next difference $\Delta^2 x_t$ is analysed, the procedure being repeated until a stationary difference is found, although it is seldom the case in practice that d exceeds 2.

Sole reliance on the SACF can sometimes lead to problems of *overdifferencing*. Although further differences of a stationary series will themselves be stationary, overdifferencing can lead to serious difficulties. Consider the stationary MA(1) process $x_t = (1 - \theta B)a_t$. The first difference of this is

$$\begin{aligned}\Delta x_t &= (1 - B)(1 - \theta B)a_t \\ &= \left(1 - (1 + \theta)B + \theta B^2\right)a_t \\ &= \left(1 - \theta_1 B - \theta_2 B^2\right)a_t\end{aligned}$$

We now have a more complicated model containing two parameters rather than one and, moreover, one of the roots of the $\theta(B)$ polynomial is unity since $\theta_1 + \theta_2 = 1$. The model is therefore not invertible, so that the AR(∞) representation does not exist and attempts to estimate this model will almost surely run into difficulties.

Note also that the variance of x_t is given by

$$V(x) = \gamma_0(x) = \left(1 + \theta^2\right)\sigma^2$$

whereas the variance of $w_t = \Delta x_t$ is given by

$$\begin{aligned}V(w) = \gamma_0(w) &= \left(1 + (1 + \theta)^2 + \theta^2\right)\sigma^2 \\ &= 2\left(1 + \theta + \theta^2\right)\sigma^2\end{aligned}$$

Hence

$$V(w) - V(x) = (1 + \theta)^2\sigma^2 > 0$$

thus showing that the variance of the overdifferenced process will be larger than that of the original MA(1) process. The behaviour of the sample variances associated with different values of d can provide a useful means of deciding the appropriate level of differencing: the sample variances will decrease until a stationary sequence has been found, but will tend to increase on overdifferencing. However, this will not always be the case, and a comparison of sample variances for successive differences of a series is best employed as a useful auxiliary method for determining the appropriate value of d.

3.1.2 Testing for a unit root: an introduction

Given the importance of choosing the correct order of differencing, it is clear that we require a formal testing procedure to determine d. To introduce the issues involved in developing such a procedure, we begin by considering the simplest case, that of the zero mean AR(1) process with normal innovations

$$x_t = \phi x_{t-1} + a_t, \qquad t = 1, 2, \ldots, T \tag{3.1}$$

where $a_t \sim NID(0, \sigma^2)$ and $x_0 = 0$. The OLS estimate of ϕ is given by

$$\hat{\phi}_T = \frac{\sum_{t=1}^{T} x_{t-1}x_t}{\sum_{t=1}^{T} x_{t-1}^2}$$

and, from the algebra of OLS, we have

$$\left(\hat{\phi}_T - \phi\right) = \frac{\sum_{t=1}^{T} x_{t-1}a_t}{\sum_{t=1}^{T} x_{t-1}^2}$$

Assuming that the true value of ϕ is less than 1 in absolute value, then, from Hamilton (1994, page 216)

$$\sqrt{T}\left(\hat{\phi}_T - \phi\right) \overset{a}{\sim} N\left(0, \sigma^2 E\left(x_{t-1}^2\right)^{-1}\right)$$

Since

$$E\left(x_{t-1}^2\right) = E\left(\sum_{i=0}^{\infty} \phi^i a_{t-i}\right)^2 = \sigma^2 \sum_{i=0}^{\infty} \phi^{2i} = \sigma^2/\left(1 - \phi^2\right)$$

it follows that

$$\sqrt{T}\left(\hat{\phi}_T - \phi\right) \overset{a}{\sim} N\left(0, \left(1 - \phi^2\right)\right)$$

from which hypothesis tests concerning ϕ may be constructed. However, when $\phi = 1$ there is an immediate problem with this result, for it seems to imply that $\sqrt{T}\left(\hat{\phi}_T - \phi\right)$ has a zero variance, which is not very helpful for hypothesis testing! To obtain a non-degenerate asymptotic distribution for $\hat{\phi}_T$ when $\phi = 1$ we need to scale $\left(\hat{\phi}_T - 1\right)$ by T rather than $\sqrt{T}$. To see why this is so, we need to investigate the distributional properties of the two sums making up the ratio

$$\left(\hat{\phi}_T - 1\right) = \frac{\sum_{t=1}^{T} x_{t-1}a_t}{\sum_{t=1}^{T} x_{t-1}^2}$$

When $\phi = 1$, (3.1) is the random walk

$$x_t = \sum_{s=1}^{t} a_s$$

from which it follows that $x_t \sim N\left(0, \sigma^2 t\right)$. Note also that

$$x_t^2 = (x_{t-1} + a_t)^2 = x_{t-1}^2 + 2x_{t-1}a_t + a_t^2$$

implying that

$$x_{t-1}a_t = (1/2)\left(x_t^2 - x_{t-1}^2 - a_t^2\right)$$

Thus, the numerator of the ratio can be written as

$$\sum_{t=1}^{T} x_{t-1}a_t = (1/2)\left(x_T^2 - x_0^2\right) - (1/2)\sum_{t=1}^{T} a_t^2$$

Recalling that $x_0 = 0$, we then have

$$\left(\frac{1}{\sigma^2 T}\right)\sum_{t=1}^{T} x_{t-1}a_t = \left(\frac{1}{2}\right)\left(\frac{x_T}{\sigma\sqrt{T}}\right)^2 - \left(\frac{1}{2\sigma^2}\right)\left(\frac{1}{T}\right)\sum_{t=1}^{T} a_t^2$$

$x_T/\left(\sigma\sqrt{T}\right)$ is $N(0,1)$, so its square is χ_1^2, and $T^{-1}\sum_{t=1}^{T} a_t^2$ converges in probability to σ^2. Thus

$$T^{-1}\sum_{t=1}^{T} x_{t-1}a_t \overset{a}{\sim} (1/2)\sigma^2(X - 1)$$

where $X \sim \chi_1^2$.

Since $E\left(x_t^2\right) = \sigma^2 t$, it follows that the expectation of the denominator of the ratio is

$$E\left[\sum_{t=1}^{T} x_{t-1}^2\right] = \sigma^2 \sum_{t=1}^{T} (t-1) = \sigma^2 (T-1)T/2$$

which has to be scaled by T^{-2} in order to converge to a finite value

$$E\left[T^{-2}\sum_{t=1}^{T} x_{t-1}^2\right] = (\sigma^2/2)(1 - 1/T) \to \sigma^2/2 \text{ as } T \to \infty$$

Hence

$$T\left(\hat{\phi}_T - 1\right) = \frac{T^{-1}\sum_{t=1}^{T} x_{t-1}a_t}{T^{-2}\sum_{t=1}^{T} x_{t-1}^2} \tag{3.2}$$

has an asymptotic distribution that is a ratio of a (scaled) χ_1^2 variable to a non-standard distribution. But what is this distribution? To answer this question, let us consider the limiting distribution of the standardised variable $x_t/\sigma\sqrt{T}$. For this, it is convenient to map the increasing interval from 0 to T into the fixed interval [0,1] so that results will be invariant to the actual value of T. We thus define the random *step function* $R_T(r)$ as follows. Denote $[rT]$ as the integer part of rT, where $r \in [0, 1]$, and define

$$R_T(r) = x_{[rT]}(r)\Big/\sigma\sqrt{T} = x_{t-1}\Big/\sigma\sqrt{T}$$

In effect, the interval [0,1] is divided into $T+1$ parts at $r = 0,\ 1/T,\ 2/T,\ \ldots,\ 1$ and $R_T(r)$ is constant at values of r but with jumps at successive integers. As $T \to \infty$, $R_T(r)$ becomes increasingly 'dense' on [0,1]. In the limit, $R_T(r)$ *weakly converges* to *standard Brownian motion* (or the Weiner process), $W(r)$, denoted

$$R_T(r) \Rightarrow W(r) \sim N(0, r)$$

Hamilton (1994, chapter 17) and Banerjee *et al.* (1993) provide detailed treatments of this result, known as *Donsker's theorem* but often referred to as the *Functional Central Limit Theorem*. Three implications of the theorem are

$$W(1) \sim N(0, 1)$$

$$\sigma \cdot W(r) \sim N\left(0, \sigma^2 r\right)$$

$$[W(r)]^2/r \sim \chi_1^2$$

A further implication is that, if $f(\cdot)$ is a continuous functional on [0, 1], then through the *continuous mapping theorem*,

$$f(R_T(r)) \Rightarrow f(W(r))$$

We are now in a position to derive the asymptotic distribution of the denominator of (3.2) (see Phillips, 1987a, theorem 3.1)

$$\begin{aligned} T^{-2}\sum_{t=1}^{T} x_{t-1}^2 &= (\sigma^2 T^{-1})\sum_{t=1}^{T}\left(\frac{x_{t-1}}{\sigma\sqrt{T}}\right)^2 \\ &= \sigma^2 \sum_{t=1}^{T} T^{-1}\left(R_T\left(\frac{t-1}{T}\right)\right)^2 \\ &= \sigma^2 \sum_{t=1}^{T} \int_{(i-1)/T}^{i/T} [R_T(r)]^2 \mathrm{d}r = \sigma^2 \int_0^1 [R_T(r)]^2 \mathrm{d}r \\ &\Rightarrow \sigma^2 \int_0^1 [W(r)]^2 \mathrm{d}r \end{aligned}$$

Note also that, because $[W(1)]^2$ is distributed as χ_1^2, the numerator of (3.2) can be written as

$$T^{-1}\sum_{t=1}^{T} x_{t-1}a_t \Rightarrow (1/2)\sigma^2\left([W(1)]^2-1\right)$$

Hence

$$T\left(\hat{\phi}_T - 1\right) \Rightarrow \frac{(1/2)\left([W(1)]^2-1\right)}{\int_0^1 [W(r)]^2 \mathrm{d}r} \tag{3.3}$$

The denominator of (3.3) must be positive. Since $[W(1)]^2$ is χ_1^2 and the probability that a χ_1^2 variable is less than unity is 0.68, the probability that $T\left(\hat{\phi}_T - 1\right)$ is negative approaches 0.68 as T becomes large. Thus, in two-thirds of samples generated by a random walk, the estimate $\hat{\phi}_T$ will be less than unity. Furthermore, when $[W(1)]^2$ is large so will be the denominator of (3.3), implying that the limiting distribution of $T\left(\hat{\phi}_T - 1\right)$ will be skewed to the left, with negative values twice as likely as positive values. Note that, from Phillips (1987a)

$$(1/2)\left([W(1)]^2-1\right) = \int_0^1 W(r)\mathrm{d}W(r)$$

so an equivalent expression is

$$T\left(\hat{\phi}_T - 1\right) \Rightarrow \frac{\int_0^1 W(r)\mathrm{d}W(r)}{\int_0^1 [W(r)]^2 \mathrm{d}r}$$

A conventional way of testing the null hypothesis $\phi = 1$ is to construct the t-statistic

$$t_\phi = \frac{\left(\hat{\phi}_T - 1\right)}{\hat{\sigma}_{\hat{\phi}_T}} = \frac{\left(\hat{\phi}_T - 1\right)}{\left(s_T^2 \Big/ \sum_{t=1}^T x_{t-1}^2\right)^{1/2}} \tag{3.4}$$

where

$$\hat{\sigma}_{\hat{\phi}_T} = \left(s_T^2 \Big/ \sum_{t=1}^T x_{t-1}^2\right)^{1/2}$$

is the usual OLS standard error for $\hat{\phi}_T$ and s_T^2 is the OLS estimate of σ^2

$$s_T^2 = \sum_{t=1}^T \left(x_t - \hat{\phi}_T x_{t-1}\right)^2 \Big/ (T-1)$$

The distribution of t_ϕ does not have a limiting normal distribution when $\phi = 1$. To find the appropriate limiting distribution, rewrite (3.4) as

$$\tau = (T/s_T)\left(\hat{\phi}_T - 1\right)\left(T^{-2}\sum_{t=1}^T x_{t-1}^2\right)^{1/2}$$

where, following Fuller (1996), we denote the statistic as τ to distinguish it from the conventional t-statistic. Substituting from (3.2) yields

$$\tau = \frac{T^{-1}\sum_{t=1}^T x_{t-1}a_t}{s_T\left(T^{-2}\sum_{t=1}^T x_{t-1}^2\right)^{1/2}}$$

Since s_T^2 is a consistent estimator of σ^2, it then follows from our previous results that

$$\tau \Rightarrow \frac{(1/2)\sigma^2([W(1)]^2-1)}{\sigma\left(\sigma^2\int_0^1[W(r)]^2\mathrm{d}r\right)^{1/2}} = \frac{(1/2)([W(1)]^2-1)}{\left(\int_0^1[W(r)]^2\mathrm{d}r\right)^{1/2}} = \frac{\int_0^1 W(r)\mathrm{d}W(r)}{\left(\int_0^1[W(r)]^2\mathrm{d}r\right)^{1/2}} \tag{3.5}$$

An alternative test of the null hypothesis results from the fact that $\hat{\phi}_T$ is a *superconsistent* estimate of $\phi = 1$. Dividing (3.2) by $\sqrt{T}$ yields

$$\sqrt{T}\left(\hat{\phi}_T - 1\right) = \frac{T^{-3/2}\sum_{t=1}^T x_{t-1}a_t}{T^{-2}\sum_{t=1}^T x_{t-1}^2}$$

The numerator converges to $(1/2)T^{-1/2}\sigma^2(X-1)$. Since X, being χ_1^2, has a variance of 2, the variance of this numerator is of order T^{-1}, so that the numerator converges in probability to zero. Hence

$$\sqrt{T}\left(\hat{\phi}_T - 1\right) \xrightarrow{p} 0$$

where $\xrightarrow{p}$ denotes convergence in probability (for a formal definition, see Hamilton, 1994, chapter 7.1). This result allows $T(\hat{\phi}_T - 1)$, which has the limiting distribution given by (3.3), to be used on its own as a test statistic without needing to calculate its standard error. These tests, particularly τ, are known as *Dickey–Fuller* (*DF*) tests, after the original analyses in Fuller (1976) and Dickey and Fuller (1979).

To make hypothesis testing operational, the limiting distributions (3.3) and (3.5) have to be tabulated, and critical values computed. This is typically done by Monte Carlo simulation (see Hendry, 1995, chapter 3.6, for a discussion of Monte Carlo techniques). To tabulate the limiting distribution (3.3), for example, a_t might be simulated by drawing T pseudo-random $N(0, 1)$ variates and calculating

$$\frac{T\sum_{t=1}^T\left(\sum_{s=0}^{t-1}a_s\right)a_t}{\sum_{t=1}^T\left(\sum_{s=0}^{t-1}a_s\right)^2}$$

Repeating this calculation n times and compiling the results into an empirical probability distribution will yield a close approximation to the limiting distribution. Simulated limiting distributions of $T(\hat{\phi}_T - 1)$ and τ are shown in figures 3.1 and 3.2, using $\sigma^2 = 1$, $T = 1000$ and

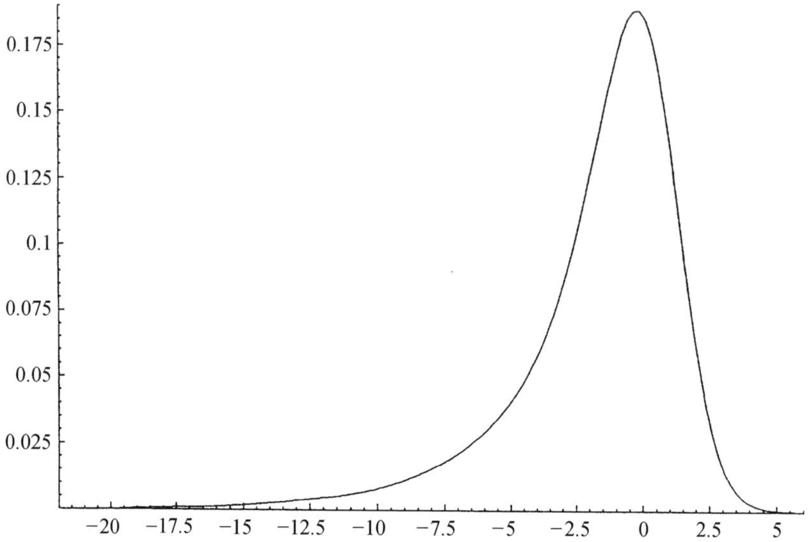

Figure 3.1 Simulated limiting distribution of $T(\hat{\phi}_T - 1)$

$n = 25{,}000$. These distributions are computed as smoothed functions of the histogram constructed from the simulated series using a normal kernel: Silverman (1986) provides an excellent reference to this technique, which is provided as part of the *GIVEWIN* package (Doornik and

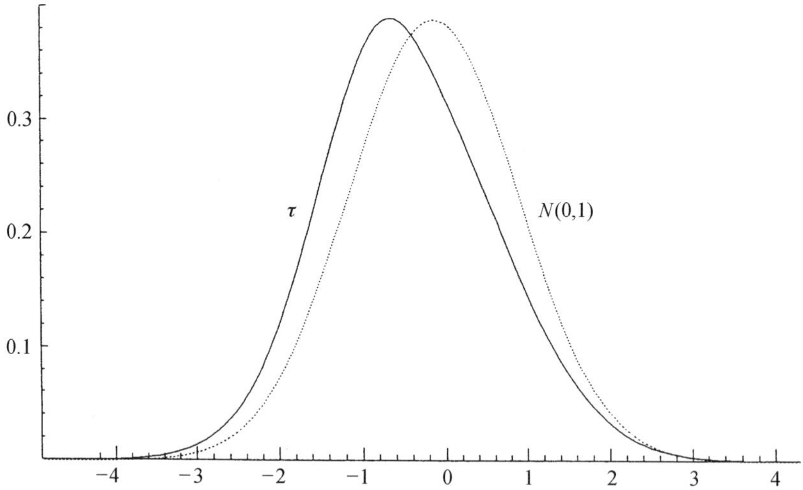

Figure 3.2 Simulated limiting distribution of τ

Hendry, 1996, chapter 7.4). The parameter that controls the amount of smoothing that is carried out was chosen to show the limiting distributions to be as smooth as possible whilst retaining their distinctive shapes relative to the standard normal.

Figure 3.1 shows clearly the skewed limiting distribution of $T(\hat{\phi}_T - 1)$. Critical values are available from many sources (see, for example, Hamilton, 1994, table B.5 case 1, and Banerjee *et al.*, 1993, table 4.1a, as well as the original source: Fuller, 1976, p. 371). For example, for T as large as it is in these simulations, the 5 per cent, 2.5 per cent and 1 per cent critical values are −8.1, −10.5 and −13.8 respectively.

Figure 3.2 shows that the limiting distribution of τ is approximately standard normal but shifted to the left by roughly 0.3: the large T 5 per cent, 2.5 per cent and 1 per cent critical values for τ are −1.95, −2.23 and −2.58, rather than the $N(0,1)$ critical values of −1.65, −1.96 and −2.33.

More extensive critical values than those given in standard tables are available in most econometric packages. These are obtained using the *response surfaces* computed by MacKinnon (1991). For example, 1 per cent critical values of τ for a given sample size T can be calculated from

$$\tau_{.01}(T) = -2.5658 - 1.960T^{-1} - 10.04T^{-2}$$

and response surfaces for 5 per cent and 10 per cent critical values are reported in MacKinnon (1991, table 1) and repeated in Banerjee *et al.* (1993, table 7.2). Much more extensive simulations carried out in MacKinnon (1996) also allow p-values (i.e., marginal significance levels) to be calculated for a wide range of sample sizes.

3.1.3 Extensions to the Dickey–Fuller test

The case discussed in the previous section has the merit of being simple, but is not particularly realistic, for it implies that the alternative to a driftless random walk is a stationary AR(1) process about a *zero* mean. A more sensible alternative would be for the AR(1) process to fluctuate about a non-zero mean, i.e., that we have the model

$$x_t = \theta_0 + \phi x_{t-1} + a_t, \qquad t = 1, 2, \ldots, T \tag{3.6}$$

in which the unit root null is parameterised as $\theta_0 = 0, \phi = 1$. The presence of an intercept in (3.6) alters the distribution of the test statistics: rather than (3.3) and (3.5), we have (see, for example, Hamilton, 1994, chapter 17.4)

$$T\left(\hat{\phi}_T - 1\right) \Rightarrow \frac{(1/2)\left([W(1)]^2 - 1\right) - W(1) \cdot \int_0^1 W(r)\mathrm{d}r}{\int_0^1 [W(r)]^2 \mathrm{d}r - \left(\int_0^1 W(r)\mathrm{d}r\right)^2}$$

and

$$\tau_\mu \Rightarrow \frac{(1/2)\left([W(1)]^2 - 1\right) - W(1) \cdot \int_0^1 W(r)\mathrm{d}r}{\left\{\int_0^1 [W(r)]^2 \mathrm{d}r - \left(\int_0^1 W(r)\mathrm{d}r\right)^2\right\}^{1/2}}$$

This statistic is denoted τ_μ to emphasise that a non-zero mean is allowed for in the regression (3.6). Figure 3.3 presents the simulated distribution of τ_μ, using the same settings of σ^2, T and n as before, and again with a standard normal superimposed for comparison. With the non-zero mean, the distribution under the unit root null deviates further from a standard normal than when the mean is zero (compare figure 3.2). The large T 5 per cent, 2.5 per cent and 1 per cent critical values are now -2.86, -3.12 and -3.43 and again critical values for other sample sizes can be obtained from response surfaces, e.g.

$$\tau_{\mu,.01}(T) = -3.4335 - 5.999T^{-1} - 29.25T^{-2}$$

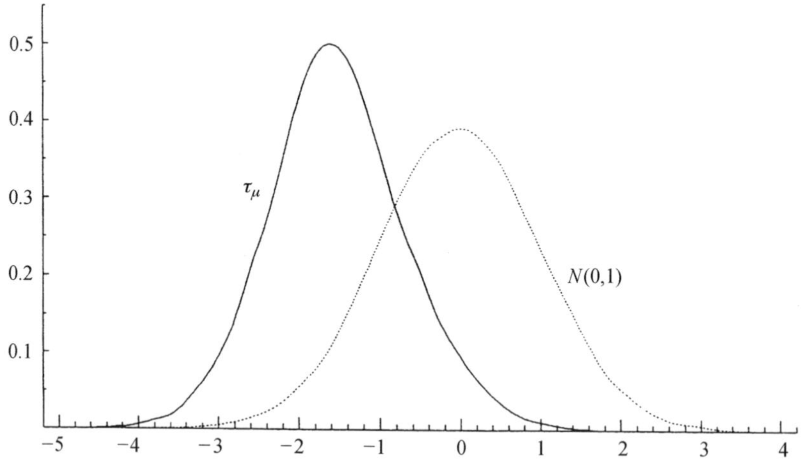

Figure 3.3 Simulated limiting distribution of τ_μ

These statistics actually concentrate on testing the null hypothesis $\phi = 1$, *conditional upon* the maintained assumption that $\theta_0 = 0$. It might seem more natural to test the joint hypothesis $\theta_0 = 0, \phi = 1$, which can be done by constructing, for example, a conventional Wald test. Under this null the model is the driftless random walk, so that $\sum_{t=1}^{T} \Delta x_t^2$ can be regarded as the *restricted residual sum of squares*, which should be compared to the *unrestricted residual sum of squares*

$$\sum_{t=1}^{T} \hat{a}_t^2 = \sum_{t=1}^{T} \left(x_t - \hat{\theta}_0 - \hat{\phi}_T x_{t-1}\right)^2$$

by constructing the statistic

$$\Phi = \frac{\left(\sum_{t=1}^{T} \Delta x_t^2 - \sum_{t=1}^{T} \hat{a}_t^2\right) \Big/ 2}{\sum_{t=1}^{T} \hat{a}_t^2 \Big/ (T-2)}$$

However, rather than being distributed as $F(2, T-2)$, the limiting distribution of Φ is tabulated in Dickey and Fuller (1981) (again, also in Hamilton, 1994, table B.7 case 2, and Banerjee *et al.*, 1993, table 4.5(a)). For example, for large T, 5 per cent and 1 per cent critical values of Φ are 4.59 and 6.43, rather than 2.99 and 4.60.

All the simulated distributions have been computed using normal innovations. If the innovations are not normal but have finite variance, the distributions are valid as long as T is large, which will typically be the case with financial applications. The infinite variance case is considered briefly in chapter 5. A more important generalisation is to allow the innovations to be serially correlated. Suppose that x_t is generated by the AR(p) process

$$\left(1 - \phi_1 B - \phi_2 B^2 - \ \ldots \ - \phi_p B^p\right) x_t = \theta_0 + a_t$$

or

$$x_t = \theta_0 + \sum_{i=1}^{p} \phi_i x_{t-i} + a_t \tag{3.7}$$

A more convenient representation is obtained by defining

$$\phi = \sum_{i=1}^{p} \phi_i$$
$$\delta_i = -\sum_{j=i+1}^{p-1} \phi_j\,, \quad i = 1, 2, \ldots, p-1$$

so that (3.7) can be written, with $k = p - 1$

$$x_t = \theta_0 + \phi x_{t-1} + \sum\nolimits_{i=1}^{k} \delta_i \Delta x_{t-i} + a_t \tag{3.8}$$

The null of one unit root is thus $\phi = \sum_{i=1}^{p} \phi_i = 1$. OLS provides consistent estimates of (3.7) and a test of $\phi = 1$ can be constructed as

$$\tau_\mu = \frac{\hat{\phi}_T - 1}{se\left(\hat{\phi}_T\right)}$$

where $se(\hat{\phi}_T)$ is the OLS standard error attached to the estimate $\hat{\phi}_T$. This statistic is also denoted τ_μ because it has the *same* limiting distribution as the statistic obtained from the AR(1) model (3.6), although it is often referred to as the *augmented Dickey–Fuller* (ADF) test (Dickey and Fuller, 1979: see Hamilton, 1994, chapter 17.7, for a detailed derivation). Similarly, $T(\hat{\phi}_T - 1)$ and the Wald Φ test have identical distributions to those obtained in the AR(1) case.

The above analysis has implicitly assumed that the AR order p is known, so that we are certain that x_t is generated by a pth-order autoregression. If the generating process is an ARMA(p, q), then Said and Dickey (1985) show that the τ_μ statistic obtained from estimating the model

$$x_t = \theta_0 + \phi x_{t-1} + \sum\nolimits_{i=1}^{k} \delta_i \Delta x_{t-i} + a_t - \sum\nolimits_{j=1}^{q} \theta_j a_{t-j}$$

has the same limiting distribution as that calculated from (3.8). The problem here, of course, is that p and q are assumed known, and this is unlikely to be the case in practice. When p and q are unknown, Said and Dickey (1984) show that, under the null hypothesis of a unit root, the test statistic obtained from (3.8) can still be used if k, the number of lags of Δx_t introduced as regressors, increases with the sample size at a controlled rate of $T^{1/3}$. With typical financial data, which do not contain pronounced seasonal variation, the results of Schwert (1987) and Diebold and Nerlove (1990) suggest that setting k at $\left[T^{0.25}\right]$ should work well in practice, where $[\cdot]$ again denotes the operation of taking the integer part of the argument. This adjustment is necessary because, as the sample size increases, the effects of the correlation structure of the residuals on the shape of the distribution of τ_μ become more precise. However, any choice of k will involve questions of test size and power and of trade-offs between the two and we shall return to this issue in section 3.1.7.

3.1.4 Non-parametric tests for a unit root

An alternative approach to dealing with autocorrelation in a_t, and which also allows for heterogeneity of variance, has been proposed by Phillips (1987a, 1987b; see also Phillips and Perron, 1988). Rather than including extra lags of Δx_t to ensure that the errors in (3.8) are white noise, the idea here is to modify the statistics after estimation of the simple model, (3.6) say, in order to take into account the effects of autocorrelated errors and to enable the same limiting distributions, and hence critical values, to apply. Thus consider again the model

$$x_t = \theta_0 + \phi x_{t-1} + a_t, \qquad t = 1, 2, \ldots, T \tag{3.9}$$

but where we now place the following set of conditions on the stochastic process $\{a_t\}_1^\infty$

$E(a_t) = 0$ for all t; (3.10*a*)
$\sup_t E(|a_t|^\beta) < \infty$ for some $\beta > 2$; (3.10*b*)
$\sigma_S^2 = \lim_{T\to\infty} E(T^{-1} S_T^2)$ exists and is positive, where $S_T = \sum_{t=1}^T a_t$ (3.10*c*)

Condition (*b*) is sufficient to ensure the existence of the variance and at least one higher-order moment of a_t. Normality entails that all moments of finite order exist and, as we shall see in later chapters, the existence of fourth moments is often required when dealing with financial time series. However, $E(|a_t|^\beta)$ is not assumed to be constant, so that heterogeneity is allowed. Condition (*c*) is needed to ensure non-degenerate limiting distributions, while (*a*) is the conventional one of assuring that all unconditional means are constant, namely zero. A fourth condition is necessary, which requires that

a_t is *strong mixing*, with mixing numbers α_m that satisfy $\sum_{m=1}^\infty \alpha_m^{1-2/\beta} < \infty$ (3.10*d*)

Strong mixing is related to ergodicity, which was briefly introduced in chapter 2, and implies ergodicity if a_t is stationary, which it need not be. The mixing numbers α_m measure the strength and extent of temporal dependence within the sequence a_t and condition (*d*) ensures that dependence declines as the length of memory, represented by m, increases. Strong mixing allows a considerable degree of serial dependence in a_t, but there is a trade-off between the extent of such dependence and the presence of heterogeneity (i.e., the probability of outliers), as is seen by the fact that the same coefficient β is present in both conditions (*b*) and (*d*). The overall set of conditions (3.10), which are described in detail in

Phillips (1987a), may be characterised by the statement that a_t is *weakly dependent*.

If a_t is stationary in (3.9), then

$$\sigma_S^2 = E(a_1^2) + 2\sum_{j=2}^{\infty} E(a_1 a_j)$$

For example, if a_t is the MA(1) process $a_t = \varepsilon_t - \theta\varepsilon_{t-1}$, where $E(\varepsilon_t^2) = \sigma_\varepsilon^2$, then

$$\sigma_S^2 = \sigma_\varepsilon^2(1+\theta^2) - 2\sigma_\varepsilon^2\theta = \sigma_\varepsilon^2(1-\theta)^2$$

Only if a_t is white noise will σ_S^2 equal σ^2, the variance of a_t. In the MA(1) case $\sigma^2 = \sigma_\varepsilon^2(1+\theta^2)$; in general it can be defined as

$$\sigma^2 = \lim_{T\to\infty} T^{-1}\sum_{t=1}^{T} E(a_t^2)$$

It is this inequality that necessitates the 'non-parametric' corrections to the DF statistics proposed by Phillips. For example, rather than $T(\hat{\phi}_T - 1)$, an asymptotically valid test is

$$Z(\phi) = T\left(\hat{\phi}_T - 1\right) - (1/2)(\hat{\sigma}_{S\ell}^2 - \hat{\sigma}^2)\left[T^{-2}\sum_{t=2}^{T}(x_{t-1} - \bar{x}_{-1})^2\right]^{-1}$$

Here $\bar{x}_{-1} = (T-1)^{-1}\sum_{t=1}^{T-1} x_t$, while $\hat{\sigma}_{S\ell}^2$ and $\hat{\sigma}^2$ are consistent estimates of the variances σ_S^2 and σ^2, respectively. The latter is simply given by

$$\hat{\sigma}^2 = T^{-1}\sum_{t=1}^{T}\hat{a}_t^2$$

where the $\hat{a}_t$ are the residuals from estimating (3.9). The former is typically calculated as

$$\hat{\sigma}_{S\ell}^2 = T^{-1}\sum_{t=1}^{T}\hat{a}_t^2 + 2T^{-1}\sum_{j=1}^{\ell}\omega_j(\ell)\sum_{t=j+1}^{T}\hat{a}_t\hat{a}_{t-j} \qquad (3.11)$$

The use of the triangular set of lag weights $\omega_j(\ell) = 1 - j/(\ell+1)$ ensures that this estimate is positive (Newey and West, 1987). Alternatively, τ_μ can be adjusted to become

$$Z(\tau_\mu) = \tau_\mu(\hat{\sigma}^2/\hat{\sigma}_{S\ell}^2) - (1/2)(\hat{\sigma}_{S\ell}^2 - \hat{\sigma}^2)T\left[\hat{\sigma}_{S\ell}^2\sum_{t=2}^{T}(x_{t-1} - \bar{x}_{-1})^2\right]^{-1/2}$$

Under the unit root null, these statistics have the same limiting distributions as $T(\hat{\phi}_T - 1)$ and τ_μ, respectively, and hence the same sets of critical values may be used. When x_t has a zero mean, the adjusted statistics are the same as $Z(\phi)$ and $Z(\tau_\mu)$ but with $\bar{x}_{-1}$ removed; these have the same limiting distributions as the zero-mean DF statistics.

For these non-parametric statistics to become operational, the lag truncation parameter ℓ has to be set. Phillips (1987a) shows that ℓ has to increase with T, but at a rate slower than $T^{0.25}$. This does not, however, tell us how to set ℓ in practice, and no simple rule has emerged from the Monte Carlo investigations of Phillips and Perron (1988), Schwert (1987) and Kim and Schmidt (1990). We will use the $[T^{0.25}]$ rule in the examples that follow.

As we have seen in chapter 1, the presence of a unit root is often a theoretical implication of models which postulate the rational use of information available to economic agents, and thus unit roots occur in many theoretical financial models. For example, variables such as futures contracts and stock prices (Samuelson, 1965, 1973), dividends and earnings (Kleidon, 1986a), spot and exchange rates (Meese and Singleton, 1982), and interest rates (Campbell and Shiller, 1987), should all contain unit roots under rational expectations. Unit root tests are thus extremely important in the analysis of financial time series.

Example 3.1 Unit root tests on financial time series

Examples 2.2 and 2.4 examined two models for the UK interest rate spread, a stationary AR(2) process and an $I(1)$ process without drift; while example 2.7 compared and contrasted the two models. We are now in a position to discriminate between the two through an application of a unit root test. The fitted AR(2) model

$$\underset{}{x_t} = \underset{(0.023)}{0.045} + \underset{(0.043)}{1.182}\, x_{t-1} - \underset{(0.043)}{0.219}\, x_{t-2} + a_t$$

can equivalently be written as

$$x_t = \underset{(0.023)}{0.045} + \underset{(0.011)}{0.963}\, x_{t-1} - \underset{(0.043)}{0.219}\, \Delta x_{t-1} + a_t$$

so that, with $T = 526$, $T(\hat{\phi}_T - 1) = 526(0.963 - 1) = -19.5$, which is significant at the 2.5 per cent level. Alternatively, $\tau_\mu = (0.963 - 1)/0.011 = -3.52$, which is significant at the 1 per cent level, this critical value being -3.445, as obtained from the MacKinnon response surface.

Note that the τ_μ statistic can be obtained directly as the t-ratio on x_{t-1} from rewriting the model again as

$$\underset{}{\Delta x_t =} \underset{(0.023)}{0.045} - \underset{(0.011)}{0.037}\, x_{t-1} - \underset{(0.043)}{0.219}\, \Delta x_{t-1} + a_t$$

The non-parametric τ_μ statistic, computed with $\ell = 5$, is $Z(\tau_\mu) = -3.49$, and thus confirms the rejection of a unit root at the 1 per cent significance level, while the joint test of $\theta_0 = 0, \phi = 1$ yields a statistic of $\Phi = 6.19$, which is significant at the 2.5 per cent level. We can thus conclude that the appropriate model for the spread is a stationary AR(2) process. We should also note that the estimate of the innovation standard deviation σ under the unit root null is 0.452, higher than its estimate under the AR(2) model (0.448), both of which are reported in example 2.7. This is in accordance with our earlier discussion of overdifferencing.

A similar approach to testing for a unit root in the dollar/sterling exchange rate, the presence of which was assumed in example 2.5, leads to the estimated equation

$$\Delta x_t = \underset{(0.0009)}{0.0015} - \underset{(0.00052)}{0.00093}\, x_{t-1} + \underset{(0.014)}{0.071}\, \Delta x_{t-1}$$

Here, with $T = 5192$, we have $T(\hat{\phi}_T - 1) = -4.83$, $\tau_\mu = -1.79$, $\Phi = 1.93$, and, for $\ell = 9$, $Z(\tau_\mu) = -1.90$. All are clearly insignificant, thus confirming that the appropriate model is indeed a random walk.

Figure 3.4 plots the dividend yield (D/P) of the UK *All Share* index for the period January 1965 to December 1995. Recall that in example 2.6 we stated that it appeared to be generated by an ARMA(1,3) process. Although the series does not contain a trend, its wandering pattern could be a consequence of it being generated by an $I(1)$ process and hence a unit root test may be performed. Since we are by no means certain that the ARMA orders are correct, it would seem appropriate to compute an ADF test with the lag augmentation order k chosen using the $[T^{0.25}]$ rule. Since $T = 372$, this sets $k = 4$, from which we obtain $\tau_\mu = -3.46$, which is significant at the 1 per cent level. The non-parametric version confirms this, for with $\ell = 5$, $Z(\tau_\mu) = -3.26$, which is significant at the 2.5 per cent level. The joint test statistic is $\Phi = 6.00$, also significant at the 2.5 per cent level.

Although ϕ is estimated to be 0.940, its standard error, 0.017, is sufficiently small enough for us to reject the null of a unit root in favour of the alternative that the dividend yield is stationary, a finding that will be shown in chapter 8 to be consistent with the implications of one of the

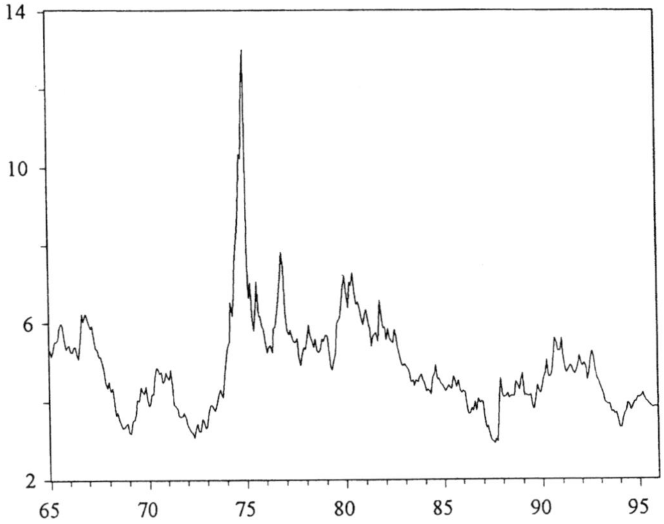

Figure 3.4 *FTA All Share* dividend yield (monthly 1965–95)

most fundamental models in finance, that of the present value relationship linking real stock prices and dividends.

3.1.5 Trend stationarity versus difference stationarity

In the unit root testing strategy outlined above, the implicit null hypothesis is that the series is generated as a driftless random walk with, possibly, a serially correlated error. In the terminology of Nelson and Plosser (1982), x_t is said to be *difference stationary* (DS)

$$\Delta x_t = \varepsilon_t \tag{3.12}$$

where $\varepsilon_t = \theta(B)a_t$, while the alternative is that x_t is *stationary* in levels. While the null of a driftless random walk is appropriate for many financial time series such as interest rates and exchange rates, other series often do contain a drift, so that the relevant null becomes

$$\Delta x_t = \theta + \varepsilon_t \tag{3.13}$$

In this case, a plausible alternative is that x_t is generated by a linear trend buried in stationary noise (see chapter 2.6), i.e., it is *trend stationary* (TS)

$$x_t = \beta_0 + \beta_1 t + \varepsilon_t \tag{3.14}$$

Perron (1988, theorem 1) shows that neither the τ_μ statistic obtained from (3.8) nor its non-parametric counterpart $Z(\tau_\mu)$ are capable of distinguishing a stationary process around a linear trend (model (3.14)) from a process with a unit root and drift (model (3.13)). Indeed, rejection of a null hypothesis of a unit root is unlikely if the series is stationary around a linear trend and becomes impossible as the sample size increases.

A test of (3.13) against (3.14) is, however, straightforward to carry out by using an extension of the testing methodology discussed above. If the parametric testing procedure is used, then (3.8) is extended by the inclusion of the time trend t as an additional regressor

$$x_t = \beta_0 + \beta_1 t + \phi x_{t-1} + \sum\nolimits_{i=1}^{k} \delta_i \Delta x_{t-i} + a_t \tag{3.15}$$

and the statistic

$$\tau_\tau = \frac{\hat{\phi}_T - 1}{se\left(\hat{\phi}_T\right)}$$

is constructed. This 't-statistic' is denoted τ_τ to distinguish it from τ_μ because it has a different limiting distribution, this time given by

$$\tau_\tau = \frac{(1/2)\left([W(1)]^2 - 1\right) - W(1)\int_0^1 W(r)\mathrm{d}r + A}{\left\{\int_0^1 [W(r)]^2 \mathrm{d}r - \left(\int_0^1 W(r)\mathrm{d}r\right)^2 + B\right\}^{1/2}}$$

where

$$\begin{aligned} A = 12&\left[\int_0^1 rW(r)\mathrm{d}r - (1/2)\int_0^1 W(r)\mathrm{d}r\right] \\ &\times \left[\int_0^1 W(r)\mathrm{d}r - (1/2)W(1)\right] \end{aligned}$$

and

$$B = 12\left[\int_0^1 W(r)\mathrm{d}r \int_0^1 rW(r)\mathrm{d}r - \left(\int_0^1 rW(r)\mathrm{d}r\right)^2\right] - 3\left(\int_0^1 W(r)\mathrm{d}r\right)^2$$

It is perhaps more informative to observe the simulated limiting distribution shown in figure 3.5, once again computed with $\sigma^2 = 1$, T=1000 and $n = 25{,}000$ and here with drift $\theta = 1$. The large T 5 per cent, 2.5 per cent and 1 per cent critical values are now −3.41, −3.66 and −3.96 and again critical values for other sample sizes can be obtained from the MacKinnon (1991) response surfaces, e.g.

$$\tau_{\tau,.01}(T) = -3.9638 - 8.353T^{-1} - 47.44T^{-2}$$

If the non-parametric approach is employed, then a time trend may be added to (3.9) and the analogous adjusted t-ratio can again be compared to the τ_τ distribution. The adjustment in this case is

$$Z(\tau_\tau) = \tau_\tau\left(\hat{\sigma}^2/\hat{\sigma}^2_{S\ell}\right) - (1/2)\left(\hat{\sigma}^2_{S\ell} - \hat{\sigma}^2\right)T^3\left[4\hat{\sigma}_{S\ell}(3D_x)^{1/2}\right]^{-1}$$

where

$$D_x = \left(T^2(T^2-1)/12\right)\sum x_{t-1}^2 - T\left(\sum tx_{t-1}\right)^2 + T(T+1)\sum tx_{t-1}\sum x_{t-1} - \left(T(T+1)(2T+1)/6\right)\left(\sum x_{t-1}\right)^2$$

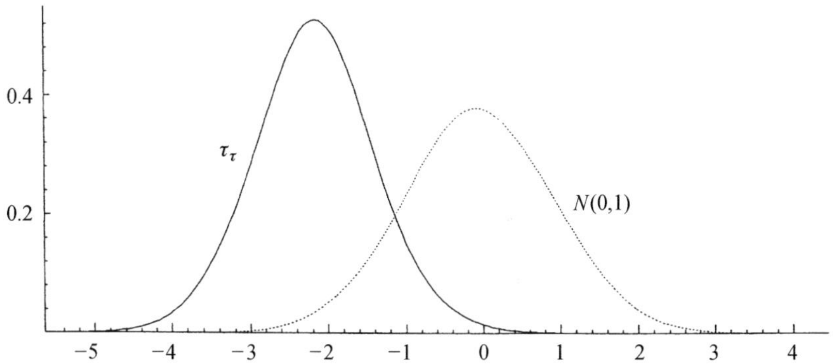

Figure 3.5 Simulated limiting distribution of τ_τ

is the determinant of the regressor moment matrix of the time trend augmented regression (3.9).

Strictly, the unit root null requires not only that $\phi = 1$ in (3.15) but also that $\beta_1 = 0$, because if $\beta_1 \neq 0$, x_t will contain a *quadratic* trend. This is easily seen if we set $p = 1$ for simplicity, for then (3.15) can also be written as

$$x_t = \beta_0 \sum_{j=1}^{t} \phi^{t-j} + \beta_1 \sum_{j=1}^{t} j\phi^{t-j} + \sum_{j=1}^{t} a_j \phi^{t-j}$$

Under the null $\phi = 1$, this becomes

$$x_t = \beta_0 t + \beta_1 \sum_{j=1}^{t} j + \sum_{j=1}^{t} a_j = \beta_0 t + \beta_1 t(t+1)/2 + S_t$$

A quadratic trend might be thought unlikely, because if, for example, x_t is in logarithms, a non-zero β_1 under the null would imply an ever-increasing (or decreasing) rate of change Δx_t. Nevertheless, a parametric joint test of $\phi = 1$ and $\beta_1 = 0$ is given by the conventional Wald test comparing the residual sum of squares from the regression of (3.15) with the residual sum of squares from the 'restricted' regression of Δx_t on an intercept and k lags of Δx_t. Rather than having an F-distribution, the statistic has a non-standard distribution whose critical values are given, for example, in Hamilton (1994, table B.7 case 4) or Banerjee *et al.* (1993, table 4.5(c)). A non-parametric version of this test is given in Perron (1988).

It is always possible, of course, that β_1 could be non-zero. If this was the case, the quadratic trend in x_t would dominate the $I(1)$ component S_t so that the variance of x_t, when appropriately normalised, converges to a constant: from Dolado *et al.* (1990), $T^{-5}\sum x_t^2 \Rightarrow \beta_1^2/20$. As Banerjee *et al.* (1993, chapter 6.2.1) show, this implies that τ_τ, for example, is asymptotically normal rather than converging to a non-standard distribution. Similarly, if $\beta_1 = 0$ but $\beta_0 \neq 0$ in (3.15), $T^{-3}\sum x_t^2 \Rightarrow \beta_0^2/3$ and τ_μ is asymptotically normal.

To circumvent such complications, Dolado *et al.* (1990) propose the following strategy for testing for unit roots in the presence of possible trends. Equation (3.15) is first estimated and τ_τ used to test the null hypothesis that $\phi = 1$. If the null is rejected, there is no need to go further and the testing procedure stops. If the null is not rejected, we test for the significance of β_1 under the null, i.e., we estimate

$$\Delta x_t = \beta_0 + \beta_1 t + \sum_{i=1}^{k} \delta_i \Delta x_{t-i} + a_t$$

and test whether β_1 is zero or not using conventional testing procedures. If β_1 is significant, we compare τ_τ with the standard normal and make our inference on the null accordingly. If, on the other hand, β_1 is not significant, we estimate (3.15) without the trend ($\beta_1 = 0$)

$$x_t = \beta_0 + \phi x_{t-1} + \sum\nolimits_{i=1}^{k} \delta_i \Delta x_{t-i} + a_t$$

and test the unit root null of $\phi = 1$ using τ_μ. If the null is rejected, the testing procedure is again terminated. If it is not rejected, we test for the significance of the constant β_0 under the null using the regression

$$\Delta x_t = \beta_0 + \sum\nolimits_{i=1}^{k} \delta_i \Delta x_{t-i} + a_t$$

If β_0 is insignificant, we conclude that x_t contains a unit root, while if $\beta_0 \neq 0$, we compare τ_μ with the standard normal, again making our inference accordingly.

This procedure is, of course, based on the *asymptotic* normality of τ_τ and τ_μ in the presence of a trend or drift in the relevant unit root null. An interesting question is what happens in small samples? Both Hylleberg and Mizon (1989) and Schmidt (1990) present evidence that, when the drift parameter β_0 is small compared to σ^2, the small sample distribution of τ_μ is very much closer to the Dickey–Fuller distribution than to the standard normal. Schmidt (1990) and Banerjee *et al.* (1993) present tabulations of the τ_μ distribution for various values of the 'standardised drift' β_0/σ: it is only when this ratio exceeds 0.5 that the critical values are closer to the normal than to the Dickey–Fuller distribution. We should therefore be careful when applying the asymptotic normality result in the testing strategy outlined above.

3.1.6 Other approaches to testing for unit roots

Various other approaches to testing for unit roots have been proposed. Hall's (1989) instrumental variable method for the case when x_t contains a moving average component (see also Pantula and Hall, 1991, for an ARMA extension), Bhargava's (1986) most powerful invariant tests when $k = 0$ in (3.15), and Phillips and Ouliaris' (1988) technique of using the 'long-run variance' of Δx_t are all surveyed in Stock (1994), while Park (1990) provides a survey of the 'variable addition' class of unit root tests. Likelihood ratio tests for a unit root in an ARMA model have been proposed by Yap and Reinsel (1995), while Perron and Ng (1996) provide modifications to the Phillips–Perron non-parametric tests.

A related development is the set of confidence intervals for the largest autoregressive root provided by Stock (1991). Stock assumes that the true value of ϕ can be modelled as $\phi = 1 + c/T$, where c is a fixed constant, and then uses 'local-to-unity' asymptotic distribution theory to construct asymptotic confidence intervals for ϕ based on computed τ_μ and τ_τ statistics. Since the distributions of these statistics are non-normal and the dependence on c is not a simple location shift, such confidence intervals cannot be constructed using a simple rule such as '± 2 standard errors'. The intervals are highly non-linear, exhibiting a sharp 'bend' for c just above zero (see Stock, 1991, figures 1 and 2): for positive values of the test statistics the intervals are tight, for large negative values they are wide.

Stock provides tables from which confidence intervals for ϕ can be calculated given a value of τ_μ or τ_τ and the sample size T. As an illustration of such a calculation, recall that the τ_μ statistic for the UK interest rate spread was reported in example 3.1 to be -3.52. From part A of table A.1 in Stock (1991), such a value corresponds to a 95 per cent confidence interval for c of $(-34.48, -2.02)$. Since the statistic was computed from a sample size of $T = 526$, this corresponds to an interval for ϕ of $(1 - 34.48/526,\ 1 - 2.02/526)$, i.e., $0.934 \leq \phi \leq 0.996$. Since $\hat{\phi} = 0.963$, this shows the complicated nature of the relationship between $\hat{\phi}$ and the confidence interval constructed by 'inverting' the τ statistic: the point estimate is not, and generally will not be, at the centre of the interval. Nevertheless, unity is excluded from the interval, thus confirming our choice of a stationary process for modelling this series.

Local-to-unity asymptotic approximation theory has also been used to develop extensions to DF tests. Elliott, Rothenberg and Stock (1996: see also Stock, 1994), using the concepts of an 'asymptotic power envelope' and 'local detrending', propose the DF-GLS test. This is computed in two steps. If we let $z_t = (1, t)$, then the first step involves obtaining estimates of $\beta = (\beta_0, \beta_1)$ by regressing $x_t^* = \left[x_1, x_2 - \bar{\phi}x_1, \ldots, x_T - \bar{\phi}x_{T-1}\right]'$ on $z_t^* = \left[z_1, z_2 - \bar{\phi}z_1, \ldots, z_T - \bar{\phi}z_{T-1}\right]'$, where $\bar{\phi} = 1 + \bar{c}/T$. Denoting the resulting estimator $\bar{\beta}$, detrended $\bar{x}_t = x_t - z_t\bar{\beta}'$ is then computed. For the second step, the regression (3.15) is then run using $\bar{x}_t$ but without an intercept or time trend. Elliott *et al.* suggest choosing $\bar{c} = -13.5$ and provide critical values for the t-statistic on $\bar{x}_{t-1}$. If no trend is to be included then $\bar{c} = -7.5$ and the t-statistic has the τ distribution.

Throughout this development of unit root testing procedures, the null hypothesis has been that of a unit root, with a stationary hypothesis (either trend or level stationarity) as the alternative. How might we go about testing the null of stationarity against a unit root alternative? This has been considered by Kwiatkowski *et al.* (1992) and Leybourne and McCabe (1994, 1996) and, in a related fashion, by Tanaka (1990) and

Saikkonen and Luukkonen (1993). Consider again the ARIMA(0,1,1) process

$$\Delta x_t = \theta_0 + a_t - \theta a_{t-1} \tag{3.16}$$

As was pointed out in chapter 2, a TS process is obtained if $\theta = 1$, so that this restriction parameterises the trend stationary null, with the unit root alternative being that $\theta < 1$. Equivalently, the null of $\theta = 1$ may be regarded as a case of *overdifferencing*. The statistic that has been proposed to test this null when the a_t are strict white noise and normal is

$$\eta_\tau = T^{-2} \sum\nolimits_{t=1}^{T} \hat{S}_t^2 \Big/ \hat{\sigma}_e^2$$

Here

$$\hat{S}_t = \sum\nolimits_{i=1}^{t} e_i, \qquad e_t = x_t - \hat{\beta}_0 - \hat{\beta}_1 t$$

and

$$\hat{\sigma}_e^2 = T^{-1} \sum\nolimits_{t=1}^{T} e_t^2$$

Kwiatkowski *et al.* (1992) show that the limiting distribution of η_τ is

$$\eta_\tau \Rightarrow \int_0^1 [V_2(r)]^2 \mathrm{d}r$$

where $V_2(r)$ is a demeaned and detrended Brownian motion process, also known as a second-level Brownian bridge, given by

$$V_2(r) = W(r) - \left(3r^2 - 2r\right) W(1) + \left(6r^2 - 6r\right) \int_0^1 W(s)\mathrm{d}s$$

On the null of $\theta = 1$, $\eta_\tau = 0$, while under the alternative, $\eta_\tau > 0$ (Kwiatkowski *et al.*, 1992, show that the test is consistent: a test is consistent if the probability of rejecting a false null goes to one as $T \to \infty$). Upper tail critical values of η_τ are reported in table 1 of Kwiatkowski *et al.*: the 5 per cent critical value is 0.146, while the 1 per cent value is 0.216.

If there is no trend in x_t under the null then the residuals are defined as $e_t = x_t - \bar{x}$. The level stationarity test statistic is then denoted as η_μ, whose limiting distribution is

$$\eta_\mu \Rightarrow \int_0^1 [V(r)]^2 \mathrm{d}r$$

Here $V(r) = W(r) - rW(1)$ is a demeaned Brownian motion process, a Brownian bridge. Upper tail critical values of η_μ are also reported in table 1 of Kwiatkowski *et al.*: 5 per cent and 1 per cent critical values are 0.463 and 0.739 respectively.

Of course, restricting a_t to be strict white noise will typically be inappropriate, but extensions are readily available if we assume the weak dependence conditions (3.10) and replace $\hat{\sigma}_e^2$ by an estimator of the form of (3.11)

$$\hat{\sigma}_{e\ell}^2 = T^{-1}\sum\nolimits_{t=1}^{T} \hat{e}_t^2 + 2T^{-1}\sum\nolimits_{j=1}^{\ell} \omega_j(\ell) \sum\nolimits_{t=j+1}^{T} \hat{e}_t \hat{e}_{t-j}$$

These statistics, which we denote $\eta_\mu(\ell)$ and $\eta_\tau(\ell)$, have the same limiting distributions as η_μ and η_τ. Leybourne and McCabe's (1994, 1996) variant of this test corrects for any serial correlation by considering an ARIMA(p,1,1) process rather than (3.16).

Example 3.2 Are UK equity prices trend or difference stationary?

In example 2.6 we modelled the logarithms of the UK *FTA All Share* index as an ARIMA(3,1,0) process on noting that it had a pronounced tendency to drift upwards, albeit with some major 'wanderings' about trend. We may thus investigate whether this DS representation is appropriate or whether a TS model would be preferable. Let us first test the null hypothesis that the series contains a unit root against the alternative that it is generated as stationary deviations about a linear trend.

Following the testing strategy outlined in section 3.1.5 requires estimating the following regressions (with absolute t-ratios now shown in parentheses):

$$\text{(i)}\ \Delta x_t = \underset{(2.59)}{0.128} + \underset{(2.56)}{0.00026t} - \underset{(2.53)}{0.0287x_{t-1}} + \sum_{i=1}^{3} \hat{\delta}_i \Delta x_{t-i} + \hat{a}_t$$

$$\text{(ii)}\ \Delta x_t = \underset{(0.67)}{0.0043} + \underset{(0.48)}{0.00001t} + \sum_{i=1}^{3} \hat{\delta}_i \Delta x_{t-i} + \hat{a}_t$$

$$\text{(iii)}\ \Delta x_t = \underset{(0.61)}{0.0121} - \underset{(0.27)}{0.00087x_{t-1}} + \sum_{i=1}^{3} \hat{\delta}_i \Delta x_{t-i} + \hat{a}_t$$

$$\text{(iv)}\ \Delta x_t = \underset{(2.15)}{0.0069} + \sum_{i=1}^{3} \hat{\delta}_i \Delta x_{t-i} + \hat{a}_t$$

From regression (i) a τ_τ test cannot reject the DS null, but β_1 is found to be insignificant under this null from regression (ii). This necessitates estimating regression (iii), from which a τ_μ test still cannot reject the null. Estimating equation (iv) shows that β_0 is non-zero under the null, so that τ_μ strictly should be tested against a standard normal. Since $\tau_\mu = -0.27$, however, this does not alter our conclusion that a unit root in x_t cannot be rejected. Note that the implied estimate of ϕ from regression (i) is 0.971 and, with $T = 368$, the associated confidence interval, calculated using Part B of Table A.1 of Stock (1991), is $0.946 \leq \phi \leq 1.011$. The DF-GLS test statistic is -2.04, again insignificant.

If we assume the null of trend stationarity, we find $\eta_\tau(5) = 0.861$, which is a clear rejection and thus confirms that equity prices do follow an $I(1)$ process with drift, so that the model estimated in example 2.6 is indeed the appropriate one.

3.1.7 Size and power considerations

This discussion of unit root testing would not be complete without some remarks about size and power and a related theme, that of the observational equivalence of TS and DS processes. Unlike many hypothesis testing situations, the power of tests of the unit root hypothesis against stationary alternatives depends less on the number of observations per se and more on the *span* of the data. For a given number of observations, the power is largest when the span is longest. Conversely, for a given span, additional observations obtained using data sampled more frequently lead only to a marginal increase in power, the increase becoming negligible as the sampling interval is decreased: see Shiller and Perron (1985), Perron (1991) and Pierse and Snell (1995). Hence a data set containing fewer annual observations over a long time period will lead to unit root tests having higher power than those computed from a data set containing more observations over a shorter time period. This is of some consequence when analysing financial time series, which often have a large number of observations obtained by sampling at very fine intervals over a fairly short time span. In such circumstances, the unit root null may be very difficult to reject even if false, particularly when the alternative is a root that is close to, but less than, unity. Monte Carlo evidence supporting this line of argument is provided by DeJong *et al.* (1992a, 1992b). One caveat to these conclusions is worth mentioning, however. Choi and Chung (1995) find that when there is a drift under the unit root null, Dickey–Fuller type tests that use higher sampling frequencies can provide higher finite sample power.

These are general power considerations. How do the alternative tests compare in power and empirical size? On the basis of various simulation results, in particular the detailed study contained in Stock's (1994) survey, it appears that the ADF tests tend to have empirical sizes closer to nominal size than the non-parametric alternatives, but that the GLS variants of Elliott *et al.* (1996) dominate the conventional ADF tests (the empirical size is the observed frequency of a test rejecting the true unit root null in a particular simulation experiment using the critical value given by a chosen significance level – the nominal size). The non-parametric tests generally have higher power (the ability to reject a false unit root null) for MA models such as (3.16) which have a negative coefficient, but the ADF family of tests perform better for MA models with θ positive and also for AR models. An important finding is that the choice of lag length or truncation parameter can strongly influence test performance. Use of the BIC to choose lag length is recommended.

The model (3.16) can also be used to illustrate the important concept of *observational equivalence*. Assuming $\theta_0 = 0$ for simplicity, the model can be written as

$$x_t = a_t + (1 - \theta)S_{t-1}$$

For large t, x_t will be dominated by the unit root component $(1 - \theta)S_{t-1}$. However, if θ is close to 1, then in a finite sample x_t will behave essentially like the white-noise process a_t. In such circumstances, unit root tests will almost always reject the unit root null, even though it is true! As Cochrane (1991) points out, in general any TS process can be approximated arbitrarily well by a unit root process, and vice versa, in the sense that the ACFs of the two processes will be arbitrarily close.

While attempting to discriminate between the two classes of processes in such circumstances might well be regarded as impossible, distinguishing between the two can yield important advantages. Campbell and Perron (1991) argue that near-stationary integrated processes (θ close to 1) seem to be better forecast using stationary models ($\theta = 1$), while near-integrated stationary models, e.g.

$$x_t = \phi x_{t-1} + a_t - \theta a_{t-1}$$

with ϕ close to, but less than, 1, are better forecast using integrated models. It may also be better to use integrated asymptotic theory to approximate finite sample distributions for near-integrated stationary models, and stationary asymptotic theory for near-stationary integrated models.

We should emphasise that all these testing procedures rely on classical methods of statistical inference. An alternative Bayesian methodology has also developed from the work of Sims (1988), Sims and Uhlig (1991), DeJong and Whiteman (1991a, 1991b) and Koop (1992). Special issues of the *Journal of Applied Econometrics*, (1991, volume 6, number 4), *Econometric Theory* (1994, volume 10, number 4/5) and the *Journal of Econometrics* (1995, volume 69, number 1) are devoted to Bayesian developments in unit root testing, but it seems fair to say that, perhaps because of both the technical and computational complexity of the Bayesian methodology, the classical approach remains the most convenient for the applied practitioner to adopt.

3.1.8 Testing for more than one unit root

The above development of unit root tests has been predicated on the assumption that x_t contains *at most* one unit root, i.e., that it is at most $I(1)$. If the null hypothesis of a unit root is not rejected, then it may be necessary to test whether the series contains a second unit root, i.e., whether it is $I(2)$ and thus needs differencing twice to induce stationarity. Unfortunately, the 'standard' testing procedure on non-rejection of a unit root in the levels x_t, that of testing whether the differences Δx_t contain a unit root, is not justified theoretically, as Dickey–Fuller type tests are based on the assumption of at most one unit root. If the true number of unit roots is greater than one, the empirical size of such tests is greater than the nominal size, so that the probability of finding any, let alone all, unit roots is reduced.

Dickey and Pantula (1987) propose a sequence of tests that does have a theoretical justification when we assume that x_t may contain more than one unit root. For example, suppose we assume that x_t contains a maximum of two unit roots. To test the null hypothesis of two unit roots against the alternative of one, we compare the t-ratio on β_2 from the regression

$$\Delta^2 x_t = \beta_0 + \beta_2 \Delta x_{t-1} + a_t$$

with the τ_μ critical values. If the null is rejected, we may then test the hypothesis of exactly one unit root against the alternative of none by comparing with τ_μ the t-ratio on β_1 from

$$\Delta^2 x_t = \beta_0 + \beta_1 x_{t-1} + \beta_2 \Delta x_{t-1} + a_t$$

Example 3.3 Do UK interest rates contain two unit roots?

Figure 3.6 shows plots of the UK short and long interest rates from which the spread, analysed in example 3.1, was calculated. To test for the presence of at most two unit roots we first estimate, under the null hypothesis of exactly two unit roots, the regressions

$$\Delta^2 RS_t = \underset{(0.023)}{-\ 0.007} - \underset{(0.042)}{0.714}\ \Delta RS_{t-1}$$

and

$$\Delta^2 R20_t = \underset{(0.014)}{0.005} - \underset{(0.042)}{0.702}\ \Delta R20_{t-1}$$

where RS_t and $R20_t$ are the short and long rates, respectively, and standard errors are shown in parentheses. The τ_μ statistics are computed to be -17.05 and -16.83, thus conclusively rejecting the hypothesis of two unit roots in both series. On estimating the regressions

$$\Delta^2 RS_t = \underset{(0.053)}{-\ 0.137} - \underset{(0.006)}{0.017}\ RS_{t-1} - \underset{(0.042)}{0.708}\ \Delta RS_{t-1}$$

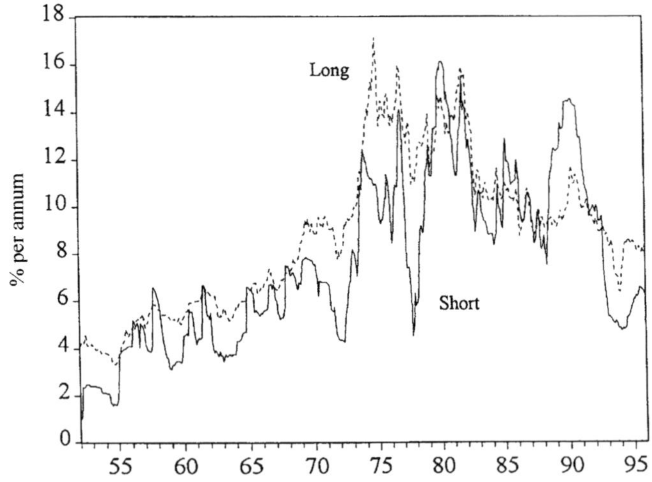

Figure 3.6 UK interest rates (monthly 1952–95)

$$\Delta^2 R20_t = \underset{(0.040)}{0.077} - \underset{(0.004)}{0.008}\, R20_{t-1} - \underset{(0.042)}{0.699}\, \Delta R20_{t-1}$$

however, we find that the τ_μ statistics from the estimates of β_1 are -2.69 and -1.90, thus providing no evidence against the hypothesis that both series contain a single unit root.

3.1.9 Segmented trends, structural breaks and smooth transitions

The difference stationary null hypothesis that has so far been considered is that the observed series $\{x_t\}_0^T$ is a realisation from a process characterised by the presence of a unit root and possibly a non-zero drift. Perron (1989) generalised the approach so as to allow for a one-time change in the structure occurring at a time T_B $(1 < T_B < T)$. He considered three different models under the null hypothesis: one that permits an exogenous change in the level of the series (a 'crash', for example), one that permits an exogenous change in the rate of growth, and one that allows both changes. The hypotheses can be parameterised as follows:

Null hypotheses:

Model (A): $x_t = \mu + x_{t-1} + bDTB_t + e_t,$
Model (B): $x_t = \mu_1 + x_{t-1} + (\mu_2 - \mu_1)DU_t + e_t,$
Model (C): $x_t = \mu_1 + x_{t-1} + \varsigma DTB_t + (\mu_2 - \mu_1)DU_t + e_t,$

where

$$DTB_t = 1 \quad \text{if } t = T_B + 1, \quad 0 \text{ otherwise;}$$
$$DU_t = 1 \quad \text{if } t > T_B, \quad 0 \text{ otherwise;}$$

and where e_t is an error process having the properties (3.10). Perron considers the following alternative hypotheses:

Alternative hypotheses:

Model (A): $x_t = \mu_1 + \beta t + (\mu_2 - \mu_1)DU_t + e_t,$
Model (B): $x_t = \mu + \beta_1 t + (\beta_2 - \beta_1)DT_t^* + e_t,$
Model (C): $x_t = \mu_1 + \beta_1 t + (\mu_2 - \mu_1)DU_t + (\beta_2 - \beta_1)DT_t^* + e_t,$

where $DT_t^* = t - T_B$ if $t > T_B$ and 0 otherwise. T_B is the time of the break, i.e., the period at which the change in the parameters of the trend function occurs.

Model (A) characterises the 'crash' in the null hypothesis by a dummy variable which takes the value one at the time of the break. Under the alternative of a trend stationary system, Model (A) allows for a one-time change in the intercept of the trend function, the magnitude of this change being $\mu_2 - \mu_1$. Model (B), the 'changing growth' model, specifies under the null that the drift parameter changes from μ_1 to μ_2 at time T_B, while under the alternative, a change in the slope of the trend function (of magnitude $\beta_2 - \beta_1$), without any sudden change in the level, is allowed (a segmented trend). Model (C) allows both effects to take place simultaneously, i.e., a sudden change in the level followed by a different growth path.

Perron (1989) showed that standard tests of the unit root hypothesis are not consistent against 'trend stationary' alternatives where the trend function contains a shift in the slope (see also Rappoport and Reichlin, 1989, Reichlin, 1989, and Montañés and Reyes, 1998). Although such tests are consistent against a shift in the intercept of the trend function (if the change is fixed as T increases), their power is likely to be substantially reduced due to the fact that the limiting value of the estimate of the largest autoregressive root is inflated above its true value. (Leybourne, Mills and Newbold, 1998, investigate a converse phenomenon: standard tests can spuriously reject the unit root null if the break occurs early in the series.)

Perron (1989) thus extends the unit root testing strategy to ensure a consistent testing procedure against shifting trend functions. Rather than use the observed series x_t to construct test statistics, we follow Perron and use the 'detrended' series $\tilde{x}_t^i$, whose form depends on which model is being considered. Thus we let $\tilde{x}_t^i$, $i = A,B,C$, be the residuals from a regression of x_t on:

(1) $i = A$: a constant, a time trend, and DU_t;
(2) $i = B$: a constant, a time trend, and DT_t^*;
(3) $i = C$: a constant, a time trend, DU_t, and DT_t^*.

Test statistics can then be constructed in the usual way, but the standard DF percentiles are now inappropriate. Perron (1989) provides the appropriate tables, which now depend not on T but on the time of the break relative to the sample size, i.e., on the ratio T_B/T. In general, these percentiles are larger (in absolute value) than their DF counterparts, with the largest value occurring when the break is in mid-sample ($T_B/T = 0.5$).

One drawback of these models is that they imply that the change in the trend function occurs instantaneously. Perron (1989) generalises the models by assuming that x_t responds to a shock in the trend function in the same way as it reacts to any other shock. Concentrating attention on the most general case, that of a sudden change in level followed by a different growth path (Model C), the procedure is to estimate the regression

$$x_t = \mu + \theta DU_t + \beta t + \gamma DT_t^* + \varsigma DTB_t + \phi x_{t-1} + \sum\nolimits_{i=1}^{k} \delta_i \Delta x_{t-i} + e_t \tag{3.17}$$

Under the null hypothesis of a unit root, $\phi = 1$ and $\theta = \beta = \gamma = 0$, whereas under the alternative of a 'segmented trend stationary' process, $\phi < 1$ and $\theta, \beta, \gamma \neq 0$. The case where there is no trend in the model is considered in Perron (1990).

A major problem with testing for unit roots in the suspected presence of a structural break is that, as Christiano (1992) and Zivot and Andrews (1992) demonstrate, the choice of timing of the break (or set of breaks) is unlikely to be selected exogenously. In practice, a break point will be decided upon by a combination of visual examination of data plots, consultation with colleagues, and formal testing techniques, with the chosen break point then being tested for formal significance. Christiano shows that whether or not the computed significance level takes into account pre-test examination of the data can make a drastic difference: the true significance levels are usually very much higher than the nominal ones that assume that the break point was chosen exogenously.

Zivot and Andrews (1992) consider the null hypothesis to be simply that x_t is $I(1)$ without an exogenous structural break (i.e., that in the null models $b = 0$ and $\mu_1 = \mu_2$), and view the selection of the break point as the outcome of an estimation procedure designed to fit x_t to a certain TS representation: they assume that the alternative hypothesis stipulates that x_t can be represented by a TS process with a single break in trend occurring at an unknown point in time. Their approach is to choose the break point κ which minimises the DF unit root test statistic computed from the regression

$$x_t = \mu + \theta DU_t(\kappa) + \beta t + \gamma DT_t^*(\kappa) + \phi x_{t-1} + \sum\nolimits_{i=1}^{k} \delta_i \Delta x_{t-i} + e_t \tag{3.18}$$

where $DU_t(\kappa) = 1$ and $DT_t^*(\kappa) = t - \kappa$ if $t > \kappa$, and 0 otherwise, the regression being estimated with the break point ranging from κ_0 to $T - \kappa_0$, so that the set of statistics $\tau_\tau^*(\kappa)$ are obtained. Note that, under the null that x_t is $I(1)$ with no structural break, the dummy DTB_t is no longer needed as $\varsigma = 0$.

When the selection of κ is treated as the outcome of an estimation procedure, Perron's critical values can no longer be used: they are too small in absolute value and hence biased towards rejecting the unit root null. Zivot and Andrews (1992) and Banerjee *et al.* (1992) provide critical values for the limiting distributions of these *sequential* 'minimum DF' statistics, $\tau_\tau^{\min *} = \min_\kappa \tau_\tau^*(\kappa)$. The difference between the critical values is substantial: for κ fixed at 0.5, the 5 per cent critical value is -4.24, whereas the corresponding value for κ estimated is -5.08.

Banerjee *et al.* (1992) also investigate the behaviour of *recursive* and *rolling* DF tests. Recursive DF statistics are obtained by estimating (3.18), with $\theta = \gamma = 0$, using the expanding subsamples $t = 1, \ldots, \kappa$, for $\kappa = \kappa_0, \ldots, T$. This leads to the set of statistics $\hat{\tau}_\tau(\kappa)$, noting that $\hat{\tau}_\tau(T) = \tau_\tau$, the full sample DF statistic. Rolling DF statistics can be computed from subsamples that are a constant fraction κ_0 of the full sample, but which 'roll' through the sample: the subsamples are thus $t = \kappa - \kappa_0 + 1, \ldots, \kappa$, yielding the set of statistics $\tilde{\tau}_\tau(\kappa)$.

Banerjee *et al.* provide asymptotic critical values and examine the size and power of various functions of these sets of unit root statistics. Their simulations suggest that the most useful statistics for examining the possibility of shifting roots and shifting trends are the maximal and minimal statistics $\hat{\tau}_\tau^{\max} = \max_\kappa \hat{\tau}_\tau(\kappa)$ and $\hat{\tau}_\tau^{\min} = \min_\kappa \hat{\tau}_\tau(\kappa)$, with similar definitions for $\tilde{\tau}_\tau^{\max}$ and $\tilde{\tau}_\tau^{\min}$.

More recent work has concentrated on extending these techniques to situations of multiple structural breaks (Bai, 1997, Bai and Perron, 1998) and of general, and possibly non-stationary, serial correlation in the errors (Perron, 1997, Vogelsang, 1997).

Rather than including lags of Δx_t, as in (3.17), to relax the instantaneous impact of the break, an alternative is to allow the trend to change gradually and smoothly between the two regimes. One possibility is to use a *logistic smooth transition regression* (LSTR) model. Leybourne, Newbold and Vougas (1998) propose the following three LSTR models to replace the segmented trend alternative hypotheses introduced above:

Model A: $x_t = \mu_1 + \mu_2 S_t(\gamma, m) + e_t$,
Model B: $x_t = \mu_1 + \beta_1 t + \mu_2 S_t(\gamma, m) + e_t$,
Model C: $x_t = \mu_1 + \beta_1 t + \mu_2 S_t(\gamma, m) + \beta_2 t S_t(\gamma, m) + e_t$,

where $S_t(\gamma, m)$ is the logistic smooth transition function

$$S_t(\gamma, m) = (1 + \exp(-\gamma(t - mT)))^{-1}$$

which controls the transition between regimes. The parameter m determines the timing of the transition midpoint since, for $\gamma > 0$, $S_{-\infty}(\gamma, m) = 0$, $S_{+\infty}(\gamma, m) = 1$ and $S_{mT}(\gamma, m) = 0.5$. The speed of transition is determined by the parameter γ. If γ is small then $S_t(\gamma, m)$ takes a long period of time to traverse the interval (0,1) and, in the limiting case when $\gamma = 0$,

$S_t(\gamma, m) = 0.5$ for all t. For large values of γ, $S_t(\gamma, m)$ traverses the interval (0,1) very rapidly, and as γ approaches $+\infty$ it changes from 0 to 1 instantaneously at time mT. Thus, in model A, x_t is stationary around a mean which changes from an initial value of μ_1 to a final value of $\mu_1 + \mu_2$. Model B is similar, with the intercept changing from μ_1 to $\mu_1 + \mu_2$, but allows for a fixed slope. In model C, in addition to the change in intercept from μ_1 to $\mu_1 + \mu_2$, the slope also changes, with the same speed of transition, from β_1 to $\beta_1 + \beta_2$. If we allow $\gamma < 0$ then the initial and final model states are reversed but the interpretation of the parameters remains the same.

The smooth transition $S_t(\gamma, m)$ does impose certain restrictions, in that the transition path is monotonic and symmetric around the midpoint. More flexible specifications, which allow for non-monotonic and non-symmetric transition paths, could be obtained by including a higher-order time polynomial in the exponential term of $S_t(\gamma, m)$. The constraints that the transitions in intercept and slope occur only once, simultaneously and at the same speed, could also be relaxed, although at some cost to interpretation and ease of estimation.

Leybourne *et al.* investigate the question of distinguishing between LSTR models and models containing unit roots, analogous to the analysis developed above with segmented trends. Their proposal is simple. Estimate the models by non-linear least squares (NLS), (i.e., detrend x_t), obtain the residuals, and compute an ADF test using these residuals. Once again, standard DF percentiles are invalid and Leybourne *et al.* provide the necessary critical values, which depend upon which LSTR model is fitted. If the null hypothesis is an $I(1)$ process without drift, then all three models are possible alternatives, while if the null is an $I(1)$ with drift, only models B and C can be realistic alternatives.

Example 3.4 Unit roots and structural breaks in US stock prices

Figure 3.7 plots the logarithms of the nominal annual (January average) S&P stock index for the period 1871 to 1997. A conventional unit root test obtained the value of $\tau_\tau = -1.15$ which, since $\tau_{\tau,.10} = -3.15$, thus provides no evidence to reject the null hypothesis that stock prices are DS in favour of the alternative that they are TS. Following Perron (1989), however, we first consider the possibility of both a change in level and, thereafter, an increased trend rate of growth of the series in the wake of the Great Crash of 1929. We thus set the break point T_B at 1929 and estimate the regression

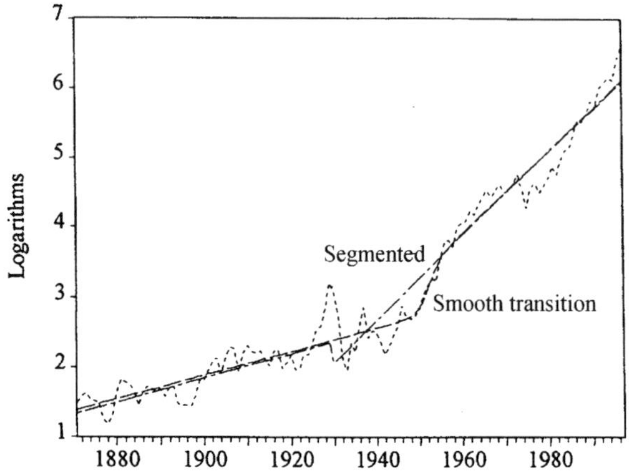

Figure 3.7 Nominal S&P 500 index (1871–1997)

$$\begin{aligned} x_t = {} & \underset{(0.089)}{0.334} + \underset{(0.0017)}{0.0066}\, t - \underset{(0.065)}{0.235}\, DU_t + \underset{(0.003)}{0.012}\, DT_t^* \\ & + \underset{(0.181)}{0.184}\, DTB_t + \underset{(0.058)}{0.731}\, x_{t-1} + \underset{(0.088)}{0.128}\, \Delta x_{t-1} \end{aligned}$$

The t-ratio for testing $\phi = 1$ yields a value of -4.65 and, since T_B/T is approximately 0.5, this is significant at the 5 per cent level. Moreover, since θ, β and γ are all significant and ς is insignificantly different from zero, all findings are consistent with x_t being generated by a segmented trend process. Indeed, the following model can be obtained

$$\begin{aligned} x_t &= \underset{(0.206)}{1.335} + \underset{(0.0053)}{0.0175}\, t + \underset{(0.0074)}{0.0430}\, DT_t^* - \underset{(0.156)}{0.346}\, DU_t + u_t \\ u_t &= \underset{(0.091)}{0.945}\, u_{t-1} - \underset{(0.092)}{0.177}\, u_{t-2} + e_t\,, \quad \hat{\sigma}_e = 0.1678 \end{aligned}$$

The trend function from this model is superimposed on the stock price series in figure 3.7: prices grew at a trend rate of growth of 1.75 per cent per annum up to 1929 and 6.05 per cent thereafter, the Crash provoking a decrease of almost 25 per cent in the trend level of the series. The roots of the error process are 0.69 and 0.26, which give no evidence of any non-stationarity.

However, we may not wish to impose the break point onto the series and might prefer to estimate it using the procedure proposed by Zivot and Andrews (1992). This led to the break point being estimated at 1931, with an associated test statistic of −4.89, which is significant at the 10 per cent level. Rolling DF tests also produced a significant $\hat{\tau}_\tau^{\min}$ test statistic, which occurred at 1929.

The significance of the estimate of θ, which produces the crash, implies that the trend function is not continuous at the break point, thus ruling out a piecewise linear trend with a break at 1929. Nevertheless, it is worth investigating the possibility that the trend function could be modelled as a smooth transition. Since it seems sensible to allow for a transition in both intercept and trend, LSTR model C was estimated by NLS, yielding

$$\begin{aligned} x_t = \; & \underset{(0.054)}{1.389} + \underset{(0.0012)}{0.0171}\, t - \underset{(0.352)}{2.714}\, S_t(0.738, 0.637) \\ & + \underset{(0.0034)}{0.0418}\, tS_t(0.738, 0.637) + u_t \end{aligned}$$

This model can be interpreted as implying that the intercept decreased from 1.389 to −1.325, while trend growth increased from 1.71 per cent per annum to 5.89 per cent. The midpoint of the smooth transition is estimated to be 1951, and as $\hat{\gamma} = 0.738$, the speed of the transition is fairly quick. As can be seen from the smooth transition trend also shown in figure 3.7, the transition takes about six years to complete. A unit root test computed using the residuals from this model yielded a value of −5.27. From table 1 of Leybourne *et al.*, this is certainly significant at the 5 per cent level, and the residuals are well fitted by the AR(2) process

$$u_t = \underset{(0.089)}{0.883}\, u_{t-1} - \underset{(0.090)}{0.194}\, u_{t-2} + e_t\,, \quad \hat{\sigma}_e = 0.1596$$

which has roots of 0.48 and 0.40 and a standard error somewhat smaller than that obtained from the segmented trend model. Whichever model is preferred, the finding that stock prices can be modelled as the sum of a deterministic trend and a stationary innovation is, as Perron (1989, p. 1384) remarks, ‘particularly striking given the vast amount of theoretical and empirical studies supporting the random walk hypothesis in this situation’.

3.1.10 Stochastic unit root processes

Granger and Swanson (1997), McCabe and Tremayne (1995) and Leybourne, McCabe and Tremayne (1996) investigate an extension of the $I(1)$ model to the case where the process has a *stochastic* unit root. A simple example is the *random coefficient* AR(1) process

$$x_t = \phi_t x_{t-1} + a_t \tag{3.19}$$

$$\phi_t = 1 + \delta_t$$

where a_t and δ_t are independent zero mean strict white-noise processes with variances σ_a^2 and σ_δ^2. If $\sigma_\delta^2 = 0$ then, clearly, $\phi_t = 1$ for all t, whereas if $\sigma_\delta^2 > 0$, ϕ_t has a mean of unity and x_t hence has a stochastic unit root (STUR). Why should such models be of interest here? Suppose x_t is the price of a financial asset, which then has a time t expected return of

$$E(r_t) = \frac{E(x_t) - x_{t-1}}{x_{t-1}}$$

if any dividend payments are ignored for simplicity. Rearranging yields

$$E(x_t) = (1 + E(r_t))x_{t-1}$$

Setting $a_t = x_t - E(x_t)$ and defining $\delta_t = E(r_t)$ thus yields the STUR(1) model (3.19). The assumption that a_t is white noise, i.e., returns are white noise, thus implies that the price *levels* have a stochastic unit root.

The STUR model can be extended in various ways, apart from considering higher-order processes with possible trends. Granger and Swanson (1997) consider (3.19) but with

$$\phi_t = \exp(\alpha_t)$$

where α_t is a zero mean stationary stochastic process. Since we can write

$$\phi_t = (x_t/x_{t-1})(1 - a_t/x_t)$$

we have

$$\alpha_t = \Delta \log(x_t) + \log(1 - a_t/x_t) \approx \Delta \log(x_t) - a_t/x_t$$

again showing that, while $\log(x_t)$ has an exact unit root, x_t has a stochastic unit root. Leybourne, McCabe and Mills (1996) allow δ_t to be an AR(1) process which may itself contain a unit root, so that the transition between stationary ($\phi_t < 1$) and explosive ($\phi_t > 1$) regimes does not necessarily occur randomly but is allowed to evolve in a more gradual fashion.

Granger and Swanson (1997) show that standard DF tests usually have little power to distinguish a STUR model from a standard unit root process, but Leybourne, McCabe and Tremayne (1996) and Leybourne, McCabe and Mills (1996) provide alternative tests that perform much better.

These papers also discuss ML estimation and forecasting of STUR models and provide some evidence in favour of such models over standard unit root models for both the levels and logarithms of a variety of stock market indices and interest rates. For example, Leybourne, McCabe and Mills find that the following STUR model fits the daily levels of the London Stock Exchange *FTSE 350* index over the period 1 January 1986 to 28 November 1994

$$\begin{aligned}\Delta x_t &= \beta + \phi_1 \Delta x_{t-1} + \phi_4 \Delta x_{t-4} \\ &\quad + \delta_t(x_{t-1} - \beta(t-1) - \phi_1 x_{t-2} - \phi_4 x_{t-5}) + a_t \\ \delta_t &= \delta_{t-1} + \eta_t\end{aligned}$$

Here the level of the index, x_t, follows a (restricted) STUR(4) process with drift in which the stochastic unit root is itself a random walk. The root $\phi_t = 1 + \delta_t$ fluctuates in a narrow band around 0.96, and hence is stationary. This model is found to produce a 7 per cent reduction in error variance over the competing ARIMA(4,1,0) model and some evidence of a better forecasting performance.

3.2 Decomposing time series: unobserved component models and signal extraction

3.2.1 Unobserved component models

If a time series is difference stationary, then it can be decomposed into a stochastic non-stationary, or trend, component and a stationary, or noise, component, i.e.

$$x_t = z_t + u_t \tag{3.20}$$

Such a decomposition can be performed in various ways. For instance, Muth's (1960) classic example assumes that the trend component z_t is a random walk

$$z_t = \mu + z_{t-1} + v_t$$

while u_t is white noise and independent of v_t, i.e., $u_t \sim WN(0, \sigma_u^2)$ and $v_t \sim WN(0, \sigma_v^2)$, with $E(u_t v_{t-i}) = 0$ for all i. It thus follows that Δx_t is a stationary process

$$\Delta x_t = \mu + v_t + u_t - u_{t-1} \tag{3.21}$$

and has an ACF that cuts off at lag one with coefficient

$$\rho_1 = -\frac{\sigma_u^2}{\sigma_u^2 + 2\sigma_v^2} \tag{3.22}$$

It is clear that $-0.5 \leq \rho_1 \leq 0$, the exact value depending on the relative sizes of the two variances, and that Δx_t is an MA(1) process

$$\Delta x_t = \mu + e_t - \theta e_{t-1} \tag{3.23}$$

where $e_t \sim WN(0, \sigma_e^2)$. On defining $\kappa = \sigma_v^2 / \sigma_u^2$ to be the *signal-to-noise* variance ratio, the relationship between the parameters of (3.21) and (3.23) can be shown to be

$$\theta = \left\{(\kappa + 2) - \left(\kappa^2 + 4\kappa\right)^{1/2}\right\} \Big/ 2, \qquad \kappa = (1-\theta)^2/\theta,$$

$$\kappa \geq 0, \ |\theta| < 1$$

and

$$\sigma_u^2 = \theta\sigma_e^2$$

Thus $\kappa = 0$ corresponds to $\theta = 1$, so that the unit roots in (3.23) 'cancel out' and the overdifferenced x_t is stationary, while $\kappa = \infty$ corresponds to $\theta = 0$, in which case x_t is a pure random walk. A test of the stationarity null of $\theta = 1$ has been set out in section 3.1.6. It can therefore also be regarded as a test of the null $\sigma_v^2 = 0$, for if this is the case then z_t is a deterministic linear trend.

Models of the form (3.20) are known as *unobserved component* (UC) models, a more general formulation for the components being

$$\Delta z_t = \mu + \gamma(B) v_t$$

and (3.24)

$$u_t = \lambda(B) a_t$$

where v_t and a_t are independent white-noise sequences with finite variances σ_v^2 and σ_a^2 and where $\gamma(B)$ and $\lambda(B)$ are stationary polynomials having no common roots. It can be shown that x_t will then have the form

$$\Delta x_t = \mu + \theta(B)e_t \tag{3.25}$$

where $\theta(B)$ and σ_e^2 can be obtained from

$$\sigma_e^2 \frac{\theta(B)\theta(B^{-1})}{(1-B)(1-B^{-1})} = \sigma_v^2 \frac{\gamma(B)\gamma(B^{-1})}{(1-B)(1-B^{-1})} + \sigma_a^2 \lambda(B)\lambda(B^{-1}) \tag{3.26}$$

From this we see that it is not necessarily the case that the parameters of the components can be identified from knowledge of the parameters of (3.25) alone: indeed, in general the components will not be identified. However, if z_t is restricted to be a random walk ($\gamma(B) = 1$), the parameters of the UC model will be identified. This is clearly the case for Muth's model since σ_u^2 can be estimated by the lag one autocovariance of Δx_t (the numerator of (3.22)) and σ_v^2 can be estimated from the variance of Δx_t (the denominator of (3.22)) and the estimated value of σ_u^2.

This example illustrates, however, that even though the variances are identified, such a decomposition may not always be feasible, for it is unable to account for positive first-order autocorrelation in Δx_t. To do so requires relaxing either the assumption that z_t is a random walk, so that the trend component contains both permanent and transitory movements, or the assumption that v_t and a_t are independent. If either of these assumptions is relaxed, the parameters of the Muth model will not be identified.

As a second example, consider Poterba and Summers (1988) model for measuring mean reversion in stock prices. Rather than assume the noise component to be purely random, they allow it to follow an AR(1) process

$$u_t = \lambda u_{t-1} + a_t$$

so that

$$\Delta x_t = \mu + v_t + (1 - \lambda B)^{-1}(1 - B)a_t$$

or

$$\Delta x_t^* = (1 - \lambda)\mu + (1 - \lambda B)v_t + (1 - B)a_t$$

where $x_t^* = (1 - \lambda B)x_t$. Δx_t thus follows the ARMA(1,1) process

$$(1 - \lambda B)\Delta x_t = \theta_0 + (1 - \theta_1 B)e_t$$

where $e_t \sim WN(0, \sigma_e^2)$ and $\theta_0 = \mu(1 - \lambda)$. The formula (3.26) can be used to obtain

$$\theta_1 = \left\{2 + (1+\lambda)^2\kappa - (1-\lambda)\left((1+\lambda)^2\kappa^2 + 4\kappa\right)^{1/2}\right\} \Big/ 2(1 + \lambda\kappa)$$
$$\sigma_e^2 = \left(\lambda\sigma_v^2 + \sigma_a^2\right)/\theta_1$$

which, of course, reduce to the Muth formulae when $\lambda = 0$.

The assumption that the trend component, z_t, follows a random walk is not as restrictive as it may first seem. Consider the Wold decomposition for Δx_t

$$\Delta x_t = \mu + \psi(B)e_t = \mu + \sum\nolimits_{j=0}^{\infty} \psi_j e_{t-j} \tag{3.27}$$

Beveridge and Nelson (1981) show that x_t can be decomposed as (3.20) with

$$\Delta z_t = \mu + \left(\sum_{j=0}^{\infty} \psi_j\right) e_t$$

and

$$-u_t = \left(\sum_{j=1}^{\infty} \psi_j\right) e_t + \left(\sum_{j=2}^{\infty} \psi_j\right) e_{t-1} + \left(\sum_{j=3}^{\infty} \psi_j\right) e_{t-2} + \ldots$$

Since e_t is white noise, the trend component is therefore a random walk with rate of drift equal to μ and an innovation equal to $(\sum_{j=0}^{\infty} \psi_j)e_t$, which is thus proportional to that of the original series. The noise component is clearly stationary, but since it is driven by the same innovation as the trend component, z_t and u_t must be *perfectly correlated*, in direct contrast to the Muth decomposition that assumes that they are independent. For example, the Beveridge–Nelson decomposition of the IMA(1,1) process (3.23) is

$$\Delta z_t = \mu + (1 - \theta)e_t$$
$$u_t = \theta e_t$$

In a more general context, it is possible for an x_t with Wold decomposition (3.27) to be written as (3.20) with z_t being a random walk and u_t being stationary and where the innovations of the two components are correlated to an arbitrary degree. However, only the Beveridge–Nelson decomposition is *guaranteed* to exist.

3.2.2 Signal extraction

Given a UC model of the form (3.20) and models for z_t and u_t, it is often useful to provide estimates of these two unobserved components: this is known as *signal extraction.* A MMSE estimate of z_t is an estimate $\hat{z}_t$ which minimises $E\left(\zeta_t^2\right)$, where ζ_t is the estimation error $z_t - \hat{z}_t$. From, for example, Pierce (1979), given the *infinite sample* $\{x_t\}_{-\infty}^{\infty}$, such an estimator is

$$\hat{z}_t = \nu_z(B)x_t = \sum\nolimits_{j=-\infty}^{\infty} \nu_{zj}x_{t-j}$$

where the filter $\nu_z(B)$ is defined as

$$\nu_z(B) = \frac{\sigma_v^2\gamma(B)\gamma\left(B^{-1}\right)}{\sigma_e^2\theta(B)\theta\left(B^{-1}\right)}$$

in which case the noise component can be estimated as

$$\hat{u}_t = x_t - \hat{z}_t = (1 - \nu_z(B))x_t = \nu_u(B)x_t$$

For example, for the Muth model of a random walk overlaid with stationary noise

$$\nu_z(B) = \frac{\sigma_v^2}{\sigma_e^2}(1 - \theta B)^{-1}\left(1 - \theta B^{-1}\right)^{-1} = \frac{\sigma_v^2}{\sigma_e^2}\frac{1}{\left(1 - \theta^2\right)}\sum\nolimits_{j=-\infty}^{\infty} \theta^{|j|}B^j$$

so that, using $\sigma_v^2 = (1 - \theta)^2\sigma_e^2$, obtained using (3.25), we have

$$\hat{z}_t = \frac{(1 - \theta)^2}{1 - \theta^2}\sum_{j=-\infty}^{\infty} \theta^{|j|}x_{t-j}$$

Thus, for values of θ close to unity, $\hat{z}_t$ will be given by a very long moving average of future and past values of x. If θ is close to zero, however, $\hat{z}_t$ will be almost equal to the most recently observed value of x. From (3.22) it is clear that large values of θ correspond to small values of the signal-to-noise ratio $\kappa = \sigma_v^2/\sigma_u^2$: when the noise component dominates, a long moving average of x values provides the best estimate of trend, while if the noise component is only small the trend is given by the current position of x.

The estimation error, $\zeta_t = z_t - \hat{z}_t$, can be written as

$$\zeta_t = \nu_z(B)z_t - \nu_u(B)u_t$$

and Pierce (1979) shows that ζ_t will be stationary if z_t and u_t are generated by processes of the form (3.23). In fact, ζ_t will follow the process

$$\zeta_t = \theta_\zeta(B)\xi_t$$

where

$$\theta_\zeta(B) = \frac{\gamma(B)\lambda(B)}{\theta(B)} \qquad \sigma_\xi^2 = \frac{\sigma_a^2\sigma_v^2}{\sigma_e^2}$$

and $\xi_t \sim WN(0, \sigma_\xi^2)$.

For the Muth model we thus have that ζ_t follows the AR(1) process

$$(1 - \theta B)\zeta_t = \xi_t$$

and the MSE of the optimal signal extraction procedure is

$$E(\zeta_t^2) = \frac{\sigma_a^2\sigma_v^2}{\sigma_e^2(1 - \theta^2)}$$

As noted earlier, if we are given only $\{x_t\}$ and its model, i.e., (3.25), then models for z_t and u_t are in general unidentified. If x_t follows the IMA(1,1) process

$$(1 - B)x_t = (1 - \theta B)e_t \tag{3.28}$$

then the most general signal-plus-*white*-noise UC model has z_t given by

$$(1 - B)z_t = (1 - \Theta B)v_t \tag{3.29}$$

and for any Θ value in the interval $-1 \leq \Theta \leq \theta$ there exists values of σ_a^2 and σ_v^2 such that $z_t + u_t$ yields (3.28). It can be shown that setting $\Theta = -1$ minimises the variance of both z_t and u_t and is known as the *canonical decomposition* of x_t. Choosing this value implies that $\gamma(B) = 1 + B$ and we thus have

$$\hat{z}_t = \frac{\sigma_v^2(1+B)(1+B^{-1})}{\sigma_e^2(1-\theta B)(1-\theta B^{-1})}$$

and

$$(1-\theta B)\zeta_t = (1+B)\xi_t$$

In this development we have assumed that in estimating z_t the future as well as the past of $\{x_t\}$ is available. In many situations it is necessary to estimate z_t given only data on x_t up to $s = t - m$, for finite m. This includes the problems of signal extraction based either on current data ($m = 0$) or on recent data ($m < 0$), and the problem of forecasting the signal ($m > 0$). We thus need to extend the analysis to consider signal extraction given only the *semi-infinite* sample $\{x_s, s \leq t - m\}$. Pierce (1979) shows that, in this case, an estimate of z_t is given by

$$\hat{z}_t^{(m)} = \nu_z^{(m)}(B)x_t$$

where

$$\nu_z^{(m)}(B) = \frac{(1-B)}{\sigma_e^2\theta(B)}\left[\frac{\sigma_v^2\gamma(B)\gamma(B^{-1})}{(1-B)\theta(B^{-1})}\right]_m$$

in which we use the notation

$$[h(B)]_m = \sum\nolimits_{j=m}^{\infty} h_j B^j$$

Thus for the Muth model we have

$$\nu_z^{(m)}(B) = \frac{\sigma_v^2(1-B)}{\sigma_e^2(1-\theta B)}\left[\frac{(1-B)^{-1}}{(1-\theta B^{-1})}\right]_m$$

and Pierce (1979) shows that this becomes, for $m \geq 0$

$$\nu_z^{(m)}(B) = \frac{\sigma_v^2 B^m}{\sigma_e^2(1-\theta)}\sum_{j=0}^{\infty}(\theta B)^j = (1-\theta)B^m\sum_{j=0}^{\infty}(\theta B)^j$$

while for $m < 0$

$$\nu_z^{(m)}(B) = \theta^{-m}(1-\theta)B^m \sum_{j=0}^{\infty} (\theta B)^j + \frac{1}{(1-\theta B)} \sum_{j=0}^{-m-1} \theta^j B^{-j}$$

Thus, when either estimating z_t for the current time period ($m = 0$) or forecasting z_t ($m > 0$), we apply an exponentially weighted moving average to the observed series, beginning with the most recent data available, but not otherwise depending on the value of m. For $m < 0$, when we are estimating z_t based on some, but not all, of the relevant future observations of x_t, the filter comprises two parts: the same filter as in the $m \geq 0$ case applied to the furthest forward observation but with a declining weight (θ^{-m}) placed upon it, and a second term capturing the additional influence of the observed future observations.

UC models can also be analysed within a *state space* framework, in which the Kalman filter plays a key role in providing both optimal forecasts and a method of estimating the unknown model parameters. In this framework, models such as the random walk plus white noise are known as *structural models*, and a thorough discussion of the methodological and technical ideas underlying such formulations is contained in Harvey (1989) and Harvey and Shephard (1992), while Koopman *et al.* (1995) provide computer software.

Example 3.5 Estimating expected real rates of interest

An important example of the unobserved random walk buried in white noise is provided by the analysis of expected real rates of interest under the assumption of rational expectations or, equivalently, financial market efficiency: see, for example, Fama (1975), Nelson and Schwert (1977), and Mills and Stephenson (1985). In this model, the unobservable expected real rate, z_t, is assumed to follow a driftless random walk, i.e., equation (3.29) with $\Theta = 0$, and it differs from the observed real rate, x_t, by the amount of unexpected inflation, u_t, which, under the assumption of market efficiency, will be a white-noise process. The observed real rate will thus follow the ARIMA(0,1,1) process shown in (3.28).

Such a model fitted to the real UK Treasury bill rate over the period 1952Q1 to 1995Q3 yielded

$$\Delta x_t = (1 - 0.694B)e_t, \quad \hat{\sigma}_e^2 = 7.62\,, \quad Q(12) = 9.1$$

From the relationships linking σ_v^2 and σ_u^2 to θ and σ_e^2, it follows that the unobserved variances may be estimated as

$$\hat{\sigma}_v^2 = (1 - 0.694)^2 \hat{\sigma}_e^2 = 0.71$$
$$\hat{\sigma}_u^2 = 0.694 \hat{\sigma}_e^2 = 5.29$$

yielding a signal-to-noise variance ratio of $\kappa = \hat{\sigma}_v^2 / \hat{\sigma}_u^2 = 0.134$, so that variations in the expected real rate are small compared to variations in unexpected inflation. Expected real rates based on information up to and including time t, i.e., $m = 0$, can then be estimated using the exponentially weighted moving average

$$\hat{z}_t = \nu_z^{(0)}(B) x_t$$

where

$$\nu_z^{(0)}(B) = (1 - \theta) \sum_{j=0}^{\infty} (\theta B)^j = 0.306 \sum_{j=0}^{\infty} (0.694 B)^j$$

Unexpected inflation can then be obtained as $\hat{u}_t = x_t - \hat{z}_t$. Figure 3.8 provides plots of x_t, $\hat{z}_t$ and $\hat{u}_t$, showing that the expected real rate is considerably smoother than the observed real rate, as was suggested by the small signal-to-noise ratio. In the early part of the 1950s expected real rates were generally negative, but from 1956 to 1970 they were consistently positive. From the middle of 1970 and for the subsequent decade the expected real rate was always negative, reaching a minimum in 1975Q1 after inflation peaked in the previous quarter as a consequence of the OPEC price rise, and a local minimum in 1979Q2, this being a result of the VAT increase in the budget of that year. From mid 1980 the series is again positive and remains so until the end of the sample period. Fluctuations in unexpected inflation are fairly homogenous except for the period from 1974 to 1982.

3.3 Measures of persistence and trend reversion

3.3.1 Alternative measures of persistence

Let us suppose that x_t contains a unit root, so that it has the representation

$$\Delta x_t = \mu + \psi(B) a_t = \mu + \sum_{j=0}^{\infty} \psi_j a_{t-j} \tag{3.30}$$

From (3.30), the impact of a shock in period t, a_t, on the change in x in period $t+k$, Δx_{t+k}, is ψ_k. The impact of the shock on the *level* of x in period $t+k$, x_{t+k}, is therefore $1 + \psi_1 + \ldots + \psi_k$. The ultimate impact of

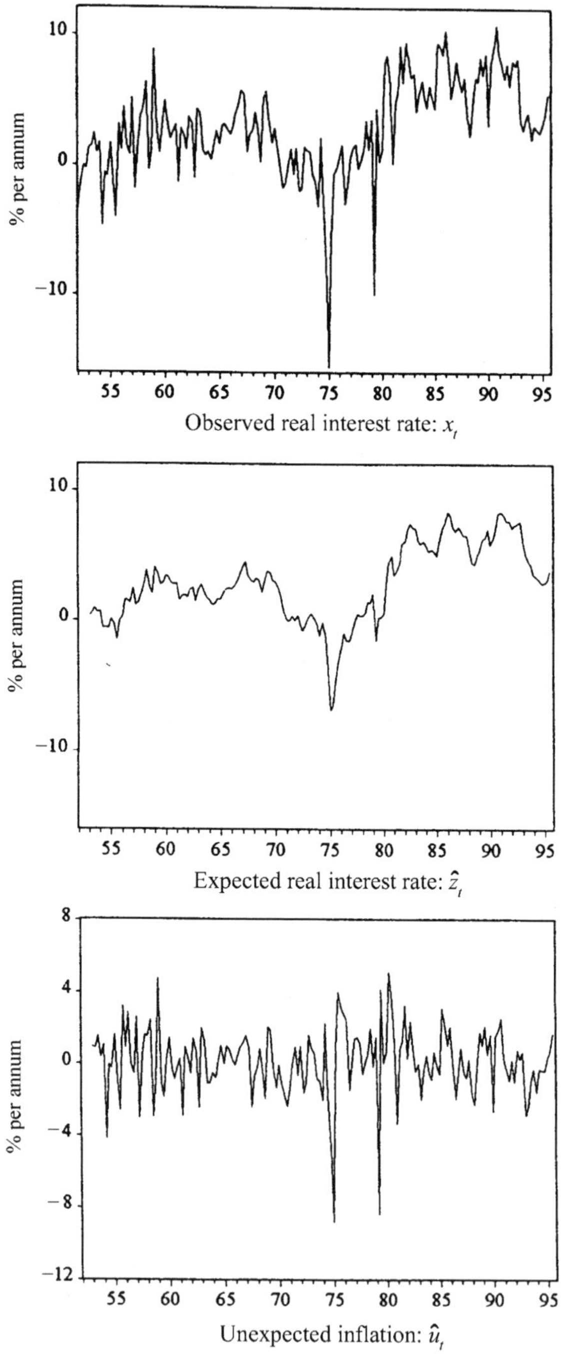

Figure 3.8 Interest rate decomposition

the shock on the level of x is the infinite sum of these moving average coefficients, defined as

$$A(1) = 1 + \psi_1 + \psi_2 + \ldots = \sum_{j=0}^{\infty} \psi_j$$

The value of $A(1)$ can then be taken as a measure of how persistent shocks to x are. For example, $A(1) = 0$ for any trend stationary series, since $A(B)$ must contain a factor $(1 - B)$, whereas $A(1) = 1$ for a random walk, since $\psi_j = 0$ for $j > 0$. Other positive values of $A(1)$ are, of course, possible for more general DS processes, depending upon the size and signs of the ψ_j.

Difficulties arise in estimating $A(1)$ because it is an infinite sum, thus requiring the estimation of an infinite number of coefficients. Various measures have thus been proposed in the literature to circumvent this problem, two of the most popular being the *impulse response* measure proposed by Campbell and Mankiw (1987) and the *variance ratio* of Cochrane (1988).

Campbell and Mankiw offer a measure of $A(1)$ based on approximating $A(B)$ by a ratio of finite-order polynomials. This is possible because, since it is assumed that Δx_t is a linear stationary process, it follows that it has an ARMA(p, q) representation

$$\phi(B)\Delta x_t = \theta_0 + \theta(B)a_t$$

Equation (3.30) is then interpreted as the moving average representation, or *impulse response function*, of Δx_t

$$\Delta x_t = \phi(1)^{-1}\theta_0 + \phi(B)^{-1}\theta(B)a_t$$

From the equality $A(B) = \phi(B)^{-1}\theta(B)$, the measure $A(1)$ can then be calculated directly as $A(1) = \theta(1)/\phi(1)$.

Cochrane (1988), on the other hand, proposes a non-parametric measure of persistence known as the *variance ratio*, defined as $V_k = \sigma_k^2/\sigma_1^2$, where

$$\sigma_k^2 = k^{-1}V(x_t - x_{t-k}) = k^{-1}V(\Delta_k x_t)$$

$\Delta_k = 1 - B^k$ being the kth differencing operator. This measure is based on the following argument. If x_t is a pure random walk with drift, $\Delta x_t = \theta + a_t$, then the variance of its kth differences will grow linearly with k: using the fact that $\Delta_k = \Delta(1 + B + \ldots + B^{k-1})$

$$\begin{aligned} V(\Delta_k x_t) &= V\big((x_t - x_{t-1}) + (x_{t-1} - x_{t-2}) + \ldots + (x_{t-k+1} - x_{t-k})\big) \\ &= \textstyle\sum_{j=1}^{k} V\big(x_{t-j+1} - x_{t-j}\big) = \textstyle\sum_{j=1}^{k} V\big(a_{t-j+1}\big) = k\sigma^2 \end{aligned}$$

If, on the other hand, x_t is trend stationary, the variance of its kth-differences approaches a constant, this being twice the unconditional variance of the series: if $x_t = \beta_0 + \beta_1 t + a_t$, $V(\Delta_k x_t) = V(a_t) + V(a_{t-k}) = 2\sigma^2$.

Cochrane thus suggests plotting a sample estimate of σ_k^2 as a function of k. If x_t is a random walk, the plot should be constant at σ^2, whereas if x_t is trend stationary the plot should decline towards zero. If fluctuations in x_t are partly permanent and partly temporary, so that the series can be modelled as a combination of random walk and stationary components, the plot of σ_k^2 versus k should settle down to the variance of the innovation to the random walk component.

In providing a sample estimate of σ_k^2, Cochrane corrects for two possible sources of small sample bias. First, the sample mean of Δx_t is used to estimate the drift term μ at all k, rather than a different trend term at each k being estimated from the mean of the k-differences. Second, a degrees of freedom correction $T/(T-k-1)$ is included, for, without this, σ_k^2 will decline towards zero as $k \to T$ because a variance cannot be taken with one observation. These corrections produce an estimator of σ_k^2 that is unbiased when applied to a pure random walk with drift. The actual formula used to compute the estimator from the sample $\{x_t\}_0^T$ is (Cochrane, 1988, equation (A3), page 917)

$$\hat{\sigma}_k^2 = \frac{T}{k(T-k)(T-k+1)} \sum_{t=k}^{T} \left(x_t - x_{t-k} - \frac{k}{T}(x_T - x_0) \right)^2 \tag{3.31}$$

From Cochrane (1988), the asymptotic standard error of $\hat{\sigma}_k^2$ is $(4k/3T)^{0.5}\hat{\sigma}_k^2$. The variance ratio can then be estimated as $\hat{V}_k = \hat{\sigma}_k^2 / \hat{\sigma}_1^2$. Cochrane shows that V_k can also be written as

$$V_k = 1 + 2\sum_{j=1}^{k-1} \frac{k-j}{k} \rho_j$$

so that the *limiting variance ratio*, V, can be defined as

$$V \equiv \lim_{k\to\infty} V_k = 1 + 2\textstyle\sum_{j=1}^{\infty} \rho_j$$

Furthermore, since it can also be shown that

$$\lim_{k\to\infty} \sigma_k^2 = \frac{\left(\sum \psi_j\right)^2}{\sum \psi_j^2}\sigma_1^2 = \left(\sum \psi_j\right)^2\sigma^2 = |A(1)|^2\sigma^2$$

V can also be written as

$$V = \left(\sigma^2/\sigma_1^2\right)|A(1)|^2$$

which provides the link between the two persistence measures. By defining $R^2 = 1 - \left(\sigma^2/\sigma_1^2\right)$, the fraction of the variance that is predictable from knowledge of the past history of Δx_t, we have

$$A(1) = \sqrt{\frac{V}{1 - R^2}}$$

so that $A(1) \geq \sqrt{V}$: the more predictable is Δx_t, the greater the difference between the two measures.

3.3.2 Testing for trend reversion

Whether a random walk is present in a financial time series has been shown to be a question of some importance. The various unit root tests discussed in section 3.1 are, of course, one approach to testing whether a series contains a random walk component. As we have seen, however, such tests can have difficulties in detecting some important departures from a random walk, and the associated distributions of the test statistics tend to have awkward dependencies on nuisance parameters.

When the null hypothesis under examination is that the series is generated by a random walk with strict white-noise normal increments, a test based on the variance ratio may be preferred. Consider again the observed series $\{x_t\}_0^T$ and suppose that x_t is generated by the random walk

$$x_t = \theta + x_{t-1} + a_t$$

where $a_t \sim NID(0, \sigma^2)$. For this model, the variance ratio, V, is unity. Lo and MacKinlay (1988, 1989) consider the test statistic

$$M(k) = \hat{\sigma}_k^2 \Big/ \hat{\sigma}_1^2 - 1 = \hat{V}_k - 1$$

and show that

$$z_1(k) = M(k) \cdot \left(\frac{2(2k-1)(k-1)}{3Tk} \right)^{-\frac{1}{2}} \overset{a}{\sim} N(0, 1)$$

They also derive a version of the variance ratio test that is robust to serial correlation and heteroskedasticity. If a_t takes the conditions (3.10), the test statistic becomes

$$z_2(k) = M(k) \cdot \Omega^{-\frac{1}{2}}(k)$$

where

$$\Omega(k) = \sum_{j=1}^{k-1} \left(\frac{2(k-j)}{k} \right)^2 \delta_j$$

$$\delta_j = \frac{\sum_{t=j+1}^{T} \alpha_{0t}\alpha_{jt}}{\left(\sum_{t=1}^{T} \alpha_{0t}\right)^2}, \quad \alpha_{jt} = \left(x_{t-j} - x_{t-j-1} - \frac{1}{T}(x_T - x_0) \right)^2$$

The δ_j are heteroskedastic-consistent estimators of the asymptotic variances of the estimated autocorrelations of Δx_t.

Lo and MacKinlay (1989) find that this large-sample normal approximation works well when k is small and T is large. They emphasise, however, that it can become unsatisfactory for large k because the empirical distribution of $M(k)$ is highly skewed in these circumstances. Although the empirical sizes of the test statistic are close to their nominal values, almost all of the rejections occur in the upper tail of the distribution. It is thus clear that the normal approximation to the distribution of $M(k)$ is likely to be of only limited practical use. As a consequence, the empirical distributions of the test statistics need to be evaluated by simulation.

In any case, the asymptotic normality of $M(k)$ relies on fixing k and allowing T to increase, so that $k/T \to 0$. Richardson and Stock (1989), however, consider a different perspective in which k is allowed to tend asymptotically to a non-zero fraction (δ) of T, i.e., $k/T \to \delta$. Under this asymptotic theory, $M(k)$ has a limiting distribution that is not normal, but has a representation in terms of functionals of Brownian motion, $W(r)$, which under the null does not depend on any unknown parameters

$$M(k) \Rightarrow \frac{1}{\delta}\int_{\delta}^{1} [Y(r)]^2 \mathrm{d}r$$

where

$$Y(r) = W(r) - W(r - \delta) - \delta W(1)$$

Richardson and Stock argue that the $k/T \rightarrow \delta$ theory provides a much better approximation to the finite sample distribution of $M(k)$ than does the fixed k theory. Moreover, this limiting distribution is valid even under non-normality and certain forms of heteroskedasticity. Lo and MacKinlay (1989) find that the power of the variance ratio test is comparable in power to τ_τ when x_t is trend stationary.

Example 3.6 Persistence and mean reversion in UK stock prices

In example 2.6 we fitted an ARIMA(3,1,0) process to the logarithms of the *FTA All Share* index, with $\phi(B) = (1 - 0.152B + 0.140B^2 - 0.114B^3)$. Thus $A(1) = 1/0.874 = 1.144$, which provides some evidence in favour of *mean aversion*, whereby a series will continue to diverge from its previously forecasted value following a shock. Cochrane (1988) has criticised the use of fitted ARIMA models for constructing the long-run measure $A(1)$ because they are designed to capture *short-run* dynamics (recall their development for short-term forecasting by Box and Jenkins, 1976), rather than the *long-run* correlations that are of interest here. More general ARIMA processes were unable to provide reliable estimates of $A(1)$ here because of the presence of approximate common factors in the AR and MA polynomials (recall the discussion in example 2.3).

Table 3.1 presents $M(k)$ statistics for a sequence of k values associated with 'long-differences' of prices of between one and eight years. Also provided are the p-values using the normal approximation and simulated upper tail percentiles using the Richardson and Stock (1989) $k/T \rightarrow \delta$ asymptotic theory. Using either distribution, there is evidence to reject the random walk null at low levels of significance for values of $k > 48$ (i.e., more than four years): the marginal significance levels are a little smaller for the $k/T \rightarrow \delta$ distributions. We thus conclude that there is mean aversion in UK stock prices, with returns being positively correlated at long horizons.

Table 3.1. *Variance ratio test statistics for UK stock prices (monthly data 1965–95)*

k	M	$p_1(M)$	95%	97.5%	99%
12	0.39	0.024	0.34	0.43	0.54
24	0.42	0.071	0.47	0.59	0.75
36	0.44	0.107	0.52	0.69	0.88
48	0.45	0.136	0.58	0.80	1.07
60	0.68	0.069	0.67	0.90	1.17
72	0.92	0.034	0.69	0.95	1.29
84	1.01	0.032	0.68	0.97	1.33
96	1.16	0.023	0.70	1.05	1.45

Note: $p_1(\cdot)$ denotes the probability under the null hypothesis of observing a larger variance ratio than that observed using the asymptotic $N(0, 1)$ distribution. 95%, 97.5%, 99% are percentiles of the empirical distributions of $M(k)$ computed under the $k/T \rightarrow \delta$ asymptotic theory using $NID(0, 1)$ returns with 5000 replications for each k.

3.4 Fractional integration and long memory processes

3.4.1 ARFIMA models

Much of the analysis of financial time series considers the case when the order of differencing, d, is either 0 or 1. If the latter, x_t is $I(1)$ and its ACF declines linearly. If the former, x_t is $I(0)$ and its ACF will exhibit an exponential decay: observations separated by a long time span may, therefore, be assumed to be independent, or at least nearly so. As we have seen, $I(1)$ behaviour of the levels of financial time series is an implication of many models of efficient markets, and the previous sections of this chapter have discussed the analysis of such behaviour in considerable detail. However, many empirically observed time series, although appearing to satisfy the assumption of stationarity (perhaps after some differencing transformation), seem to exhibit a dependence between distant observations that, although small, is by no means negligible.

Such series are particularly found in hydrology, where the 'persistence' of river flows is known as the Hurst effect (see, for example, Mandlebrot and Wallis, 1969, and Hosking, 1984), but many economic time series also exhibit similar characteristics of extremely long persistence. This may be characterised as a tendency for large values to be followed by large values of the same sign in such a way that the series seem to go through a succession of 'cycles', including long cycles whose length is comparable to the total sample size.

This viewpoint has been persuasively argued by Mandelbrot (1969, 1972) in extending his work on non-Gaussian (marginal) distributions in economics, particularly financial prices (see Mandelbrot, 1963b: this is discussed in chapter 5), to an exploration of the structure of serial dependence in economic time series. While Mandelbrot considered processes that were of the form of discrete time 'fractional Brownian motion', attention has more recently focused on an extension of the ARIMA class to model long-term persistence.

We have so far considered only integer values of d. If d is non-integer, x_t is said to be *fractionally integrated*, and models for such values of d are referred to as ARFIMA (AR Fractionally IMA). This notion of fractional integration seems to have been proposed independently by Hosking (1981) and Granger and Joyeux (1980), while Beran (1992), Baillie (1996) and Robinson (1994) provide detailed surveys of such models. To make the concept operational, we may use the binomial series expansion for any real $d > -1$

$$\begin{aligned}\Delta^d = (1-B)^d &= \sum_{k=0}^{\infty} \begin{bmatrix} d \\ k \end{bmatrix} (-B)^k \\ &= 1 - dB + \frac{d(d-1)}{2!}B^2 - \frac{d(d-1)(d-2)}{3!}B^3 + \ldots\end{aligned} \tag{3.32}$$

How does the ARFIMA model incorporate 'long memory' behaviour? Let us first consider the ARFIMA(0,d,0) process

$$(1-B)^d x_t = a_t$$

This process is often referred to as *fractional white noise* and is the discrete time analog of fractional Brownian motion, just as the random walk is the discrete time analog of Brownian motion. For $d = 0$, x_t is simply white noise and its ACF declines immediately to zero, whereas for $d = 1$, x_t is a random walk and hence has an ACF that remains (approximately) at unity. For non-integer values of d, it can be shown that the ACF of x_t declines *hyperbolically* to zero. To be precise, the autocorrelations are given by $\rho_k = \Gamma k^{2d-1}$, where Γ is the ratio of two gamma functions, so that the autocorrelations exhibit a hyperbolic decay, the speed of which depends upon d. The process is weakly stationary for $d < 0.5$ and invertible for $d > -0.5$. For $d \geq 0.5$, the variance of x_t is infinite, and so the process is non-stationary, but Robinson (1994) refers to it as being 'less non-stationary' than a unit root process, so smoothly bridging the gulf between $I(0)$ and $I(1)$ processes. The autocorrelation properties of fractional white noise are conveniently set out as table 2 of Baillie (1996). As with the ACF, both the π- and ψ-weights exhibit slow hyperbolic decay for large k.

These same properties are displayed by the more general ARFIMA(p, d, q) process

$$\phi(B)(1-B)^d x_t = \theta(B)a_t$$

although parametric expressions for the π- and ψ-weights are particularly complicated: again see Baillie (1996). The impulse response function is defined from

$$\Delta x_t = (1-B)^{1-d}\phi(B)^{-1}\theta(B)a_t = A(B)a_t$$

From Baillie (1996), $(1-B)^{1-d} = 0$ for $d < 1$, so that any ARFIMA process is trend reverting since $A(1) = 0$.

The intuition behind the concept of long memory and the limitation of the integer-d restriction emerge more clearly in the frequency domain. The series x_t will display long memory if its spectral density, $f_x(\omega)$, increases without limit as the frequency ω tends to zero

$$\lim_{\omega \to 0} f_x(\omega) = \infty$$

If x_t is ARFIMA then $f_x(\omega)$ behaves like ω^{-2d} as $\omega \to 0$, so that d parameterises its low-frequency behaviour. When $d = 1$, $f_x(\omega)$ thus behaves like ω^{-2} as $\omega \to 0$, whereas when the integer-d restriction is relaxed a much richer range of spectral behaviour near the origin becomes possible. Indeed, the 'typical spectral shape' of economic time series (Granger, 1966), which exhibits monotonically declining power as frequency increases (except at seasonals), is well captured by an $I(d)$ process with $0 < d < 1$. Moreover, although the levels of many series have spectra that appear to be infinite at the origin, and so might seem to warrant first differencing, after such differencing they often have no power at the origin. This suggests that first differencing takes out 'too much' and that using a fractional d is thus a more appropriate form of 'detrending'. This difficulty is compounded by the finding that unit root tests have even lower power than usual against fractional alternatives, so that $d = 1$ will often be chosen rather than a correct d that is less than unity: see Sowell (1990), Diebold and Rudebusch (1991) and Hassler and Wolters (1994).

3.4.2 Testing for fractional differencing

A 'classic' approach to detecting the presence of long-term memory in a time series, or long-range dependence as it is also known, is to use the 'range over standard deviation' or 'rescaled range' statistic, originally developed by Hurst (1951) when studying river discharges and proposed in the economic context by Mandelbrot (1972). This 'R/S' statistic is the range of partial sums of deviations of a time series from its mean, rescaled by its standard deviation, i.e.

$$R_0 = \hat{\sigma}_0^{-1}\left[\underset{1\leq i\leq T}{\text{Max}}\sum_{t=1}^{i}(x_t - \bar{x}) - \underset{1\leq i\leq T}{\text{Min}}\sum_{t=1}^{i}(x_t - \bar{x})\right] \tag{3.33}$$

where

$$\hat{\sigma}_0^2 = T^{-1}\sum_{t=1}^{T}(x_t - \bar{x})^2$$

The first term in brackets is the maximum (over T) of the partial sums of the first i deviations of x_t from the sample mean. Since the sum of all T deviations of the x_ts from their mean is zero, this maximum is always non-negative. The second term is the minimum of the same sequence of partial sums, and hence is always non-positive. The difference between the two quantities, called the 'range' for obvious reasons, is therefore always non-negative: hence $R_0 \geq 0$.

Although it has long been established that the R/S statistic has the ability to detect long-range dependence, it is sensitive to short-range dependence, so that any incompatibility between the data and the predicted behaviour of the R/S statistic under the null hypothesis of no long-run dependence need not come from long-term memory, but may be merely a symptom of short-term autocorrelation.

Lo (1991) therefore considers a modified R/S statistic in which short-run dependence is incorporated into its denominator, which becomes (the square root of) a consistent estimator of the variance of the partial sum in (3.33)

$$R_q = \hat{\sigma}_q^{-1}\left[\underset{1\leq i\leq T}{\text{Max}}\sum_{t=1}^{i}(x_t - \bar{x}) - \underset{1\leq i\leq T}{\text{Min}}\sum_{t=1}^{i}(x_t - \bar{x})\right]$$

where $\hat{\sigma}_q^2$ is of the form (3.11) and may be written as

$$\hat{\sigma}_q^2 = \hat{\sigma}_0^2\left(1 + \frac{2}{T}\sum\nolimits_{j=1}^{q} w_{qj} r_j\right), \quad w_{qj} = 1 - \frac{j}{q+1}, \quad q < T$$

the $r_j, j = 1, \ldots, q$, being the sample autocorrelations of x_t as defined in chapter 2.5.1. Lo provides the assumptions and technical details to allow the asymptotic distribution of R_q to be obtained. $T^{-1/2}R_q$ converges in distribution to a well-defined random variable (the range of a Brownian bridge on the unit interval), whose distribution and density functions are plotted and significance levels reported in Lo (1991, figure I and table II respectively). The statistics are consistent against a class of long-range dependent alternatives that include all ARFIMA(p, d, q) models with $-0.5 \leq d \leq 0.5$. However, the appropriate choice of q (i.e., how to distinguish between short- and long-range dependencies) remains an unresolved issue (see, for example, Pagan, 1996) and there is evidence that, if the distribution of x_t is 'fat-tailed', a phenomenon that is discussed in detail in chapter 5, then the sampling distribution of R_q is shifted to the left relative to the asymptotic distribution. This would imply that rejection rates on the left tail (rejections in favour of $d < 0$: anti-persistence) are above the nominal sizes given by the asymptotic distribution, whereas rejection rates on the right tail (rejections in favour of $d > 0$: persistent long memory) are below the nominal size (see Hiemstra and Jones, 1997). Lo thus argues that the R/S approach may perhaps be best regarded as a kind of portmanteau test that may complement, and come prior to, a more comprehensive analysis of long-range dependence.

An obvious approach to testing for fractional differencing is to construct tests against the null of either $d = 1$ or $d = 0$. The ADF and non-parametric tests of $d = 1$ discussed in section 3.1 are consistent against fractional d alternatives (see Diebold and Rudebusch, 1991, and Hassler and Wolters, 1994), although the power of the tests grows more slowly as d diverges from unity than with the divergence of the AR parameter ϕ from unity. Similarly, Lee and Schmidt (1996) show that the η statistics of Kwiatkowski *et al.* (1992) for testing the null of $d = 0$ are consistent against fractional d alternatives in the range $-0.5 < d < 0.5$, and their power compares favourably to Lo's modified R/S statistic.

Alternatively, we may be able to construct tests based on the residuals from fitting an ARIMA$(p, 0, q)$ model to x_t. Suppose the fitted model is $\hat{\phi}(B)x_t = \hat{\theta}(B)\hat{a}_t$. Agiakloglou and Newbold (1994) derive an LM test of $d = 0$ as the t-ratio on δ in the regression

$$\hat{a}_t = \sum\nolimits_{i=1}^{p} \beta_i W_{t-i} + \sum\nolimits_{j=1}^{q} \gamma_j Z_{t-j} + \delta K_t(m) + u_t$$

where

$$\hat{\theta}(B)W_t = x_t\,, \quad \hat{\theta}(B)Z_t = \hat{a}_t$$

and

$$K_t(m) = \sum\nolimits_{j=1}^{m} j^{-1}\hat{a}_{t-j}$$

Agiakloglou and Newbold also derive a test based on the residual autocorrelations, $\hat{r}_1, \hat{r}_2, \ldots, \hat{r}_m$, but this requires a rather greater computational effort. They find that, although both tests have empirical size close to nominal size, low power is a particular problem when p and q are positive rather than zero and when a non-zero mean of x_t has to be estimated.

Mean estimation for long memory processes is a general problem, as the sample mean is a poor estimate of the true mean in these models (see Samarov and Taqqu, 1988). Indeed, Newbold and Agiakloglou (1993) also find that the SACF of fractional white noise (when $d > 0$) is a severely biased estimator of the true ACF, so that it will be very difficult to detect long memory behaviour from the SACFs of moderate length series.

3.4.3 *Estimation of ARFIMA models*

The fractional differencing parameter d can be estimated by a variety of methods. An early and popular approach is that proposed by Geweke and Porter-Hudak (GPH, 1983). The spectral density of x_t is given by

$$f_x(\omega) = |1 - \exp(-i\omega)|^{-2d} f_w(\omega) = \left(4\sin^2(\omega/2)\right)^{-d} f_w(\omega)$$

where $f_w(\omega)$ is the spectral density of $w_t = (1 - B)^d x_t$. It then follows that

$$\log(f_x(\omega)) = \log(f_w(\omega)) - d\log\left(4\sin^2(\omega/2)\right)$$

and, given the sample $\{x_t\}_1^T$, this leads GPH to propose estimating d as (minus) the slope estimator of the regression of the periodogram $I_T(\omega_j)$ on a constant and $\log\left(4\sin^2(\omega_j/2)\right)$, at frequencies $\omega_j = 2\pi j/T$, $j = 1, \ldots, K$, where typically $K = \left[T^{1/2}\right]$ (other choices for K are discussed in Baillie, 1996).

Although the GPH estimator is consistent, asymptotically normal, and potentially robust to non-normality, so that inference on d can be carried out in the usual fashion, it is severely affected by autocorrelation in w_t, i.e., when x_t is an ARFIMA process rather than fractional white noise. Agiakloglou, Newbold and Wohar (1992) show that it is both biased and inefficient in these circumstances. In particular, when there are large positive AR or MA roots the estimator of d is seriously biased upwards, so that the null of $d = 0$ would be rejected far too often.

In fact, as Baillie (1996) notes, semi-parametric estimators of d, of which the GPH estimator is but an example, are notably poor in terms of bias and MSE. Attention has therefore focused on joint ML estimation of all the parameters in the ARFIMA(p, d, q) model, as developed by Sowell (1992a, 1992b) and surveyed by Baillie (1996).

Example 3.7 Long memory and fractional differencing in exchange rates and stock returns

In example 3.1 we confirmed that the dollar/sterling exchange rate contains a unit root, while in example 3.2 we confirmed that this was also the case for the *FTA All Share* index. We now consider whether the differences of the two series, the returns, are really stationary or whether they exhibit long memory.

We first compute the modified R/S statistic, $T^{-1/2}R_q$, for the exchange rate differences. Lo (1991) recommends choosing q as $\left[T^{0.25}\right] = 9$, as with the non-parametric unit root statistic. Using this setting we obtain $T^{-1/2}$ $R_9 = 1.692$ and, since a 95 per cent confidence interval for this statistic is, from Lo (1991, table II), (0.809, 1.862), we cannot reject the hypothesis that exchange rate returns are short memory. This finding is confirmed by both LM tests and the GPH estimate of d. Using the residuals from an ARIMA(1,1,0) model (see example 2.5), t-ratios for δ were 1.03, 1.23, 1.30 and 1.21 for m set equal to 25, 50, 75 and 100 respectively. The GPH estimate computed using $K = \left[T^{1/2}\right] = 22$ was $\hat{d} = -0.07$ with standard error 0.08.

For the *FTA All Share* returns, we obtain $T^{-1/2}R_4 = 2.090$, which is significant. This finding of long memory is confirmed by the GPH estimate of $\hat{d} = 0.39$ with standard error 0.19, computed using $K = 19$. However, the LM t-ratios were never remotely significant for a wide range of m values. This is, in fact, consistent with the simulation results of Agiakloglou and Newbold (1994), who find that the power of this test to reject $d = 0$ is very weak when the sample mean (the drift in the index here) has to be estimated. The empirical evidence is thus consistent with the *FTA All Share* index being an $I(1.4)$, rather than an $I(1)$, process.

As a final example, we investigate the daily returns for the S&P 500 index from January 1928 to August 1991, a total of $T = 17{,}054$ observations, a series that was originally analysed in Ding, Granger and Engle

(1993). The GPH estimate for the returns was $\hat{d} = 0.11$, with a standard error of 0.06, so that there is little evidence that the series is long memory. However, for the *squared returns* series we obtain $\hat{d} = 0.56$, while for the *absolute returns* we obtain $\hat{d} = 0.73$. Thus, simple non-linear transformations of returns do appear to be long memory, and this is also found to be the case for a wide variety of other financial series: see the results in Ding and Granger (1996), Granger and Ding (1996) and Mills (1996a, 1997a). These type of models are analysed in greater detail in the next chapter.

4 Univariate non-linear stochastic models

As we have seen in previous chapters, financial time series often appear to be well approximated by random walks. The relationship between random walks and the theory of efficient capital markets was briefly discussed in chapter 1, where it was argued that the random walk assumption that asset price changes are independent is usually too restrictive to be consistent with a reasonably broad class of optimising models: what is in fact required is that a variable related to the asset price is a martingale.

Martingales and random walks are discussed formally in section 1, with tests of the random walk hypothesis being the subject of section 2. The relaxation of the assumption that changes in a time series must be independent and identically distributed allows the possibility of examining non-linear stochastic processes and the remainder of the chapter thus introduces various non-linear models that are now used regularly in the analysis of financial time series. Stochastic variance models are discussed in section 3, ARCH processes in section 4, and bilinear and other non-linear models in section 5, including artificial neural networks and chaotic models. Finally, section 6 looks at some tests for non-linearity.

4.1 Martingales, random walks and non-linearity

A *martingale* is a stochastic process that is a mathematical model of a 'fair game'. The term martingale, which also denotes part of a horse's harness or a ships rigging, refers in addition to a gambling system in which every losing bet is doubled, a usage that may be felt to be rather apposite when considering the behaviour of financial data!

A martingale may be formally defined as a stochastic process $\{x_t\}$ having the following properties:

(a) $E(|x_t|) < \infty$ for each t;

(b) $E(x_t|\Im_s) = x_s$, whenever $s \leq t$, where $\Im_s$ is the σ-algebra comprising events determined by observations over the interval [0, t], so that $\Im_s \subseteq \Im_t$ when $s \leq t$. This is known as the 'martingale property'.

While the 'history' $\{\Im_t\}_0^t$ can, in general, include observations on any number of variables, it is often restricted to be just the past history of $\{x_t\}_0^t$ itself, i.e., $\Im_t = \sigma(x_s; s \leq t)$. Written as

$$E(x_t - x_s|\Im_s) = 0, \quad s \leq t \tag{4.1}$$

the martingale property implies that the MMSE forecast of a future increment of a martingale is zero. This property can be generalised to situations, quite common in finance, where

$$E(x_t - x_s|\Im_s) \geq 0, \quad s \leq t$$

in which case we have a *submartingale*, and to the case where the above inequality is reversed, giving us a *supermartingale*.

The martingale given by (4.1) can be written equivalently as

$$x_t = x_{t-1} + a_t$$

where a_t is the martingale increment or *martingale difference*. When written in this form, the sequence $\{x_t\}_0^t$ looks superficially identical to the random walk, a model that was first introduced formally in chapter 2. There a_t was defined to be a stationary and uncorrelated sequence drawn from a fixed distribution, i.e., to be white noise. As was discussed in chapter 2.4, however, alternative definitions are possible: a_t could be defined to be strict white noise, so that it is both a stationary and independent sequence, rather than just being uncorrelated. Moreover, it is possible for a_t to be uncorrelated but not necessarily stationary. While the white-noise assumptions rule this out, such behaviour is allowed for in martingale differences: this implies that there could be dependence between higher conditional moments, most notably conditional variances.

The possibility of this form of dependence in financial time series, which often go through protracted quiet periods interspersed with bursts of turbulence, leads naturally to the consideration of *non-linear* stochastic processes capable of modelling such volatility. Non-linearity can, however, be introduced in many other ways, some of which may violate the martingale model. As an illustration, suppose that x_t is generated by the process $\Delta x_t = \eta_t$, with η_t being defined as

$$\eta_t = a_t + \beta a_{t-1} a_{t-2}$$

where a_t is strict white noise. It follows immediately that η_t has zero mean, constant variance, and ACF given by

$$E(\eta_t \eta_{t-k}) = E(a_t a_{t-k} + \beta a_{t-1} a_{t-2} a_{t-k} + \beta a_t a_{t-k-1} a_{t-k-2} + \beta^2 a_{t-1} a_{t-2} a_{t-k-1} a_{t-k-2})$$

For all $k \neq 0$, each of the terms in the ACF has zero expectation, so that, as far as its second-order properties are concerned, η_t behaves just like an independent process. However, the MMSE forecast of a future observation, η_{t+1}, is not zero (the unconditional expectation), but is the conditional expectation

$$\hat{\eta}_{t+1} = E(\eta_{t+1} | \eta_t, \eta_{t-1}, \ldots) = \beta a_t a_{t-1}$$

It then follows that x_t is not a martingale, because

$$E(x_{t+1} - x_t | \eta_t, \eta_{t-1}, \ldots) = \hat{\eta}_{t+1} \neq 0$$

and the non-linear structure of the η_t process could be used to improve the forecasts of x_t over the simple 'no-change' forecast associated with the martingale model.

4.2 Testing the random walk hypothesis

Notwithstanding the above discussion, the random walk model has played a major role in the empirical analysis of financial time series: see, for example, the seminal research of Fama (1965) and Granger and Morgenstern (1970). In chapter 3 we examined various tests of an observed time series being a random walk. In the main these were developed by assuming that there was a specific alternative to the random walk null: for example, the stationary AR(1) process used for expository purposes in chapter 3.1.2 but also advanced by Shiller (1981a) as a model of stock market fads, and the Poterba and Summers (1988) UC model in which this AR(1) process is added to a pure random walk. There have also been numerous other tests developed against a variety of different alternatives, some of which we now discuss.

4.2.1 *Autocorrelation tests*

Using the results stated in chapter 2.5.1, if $w_t = \Delta x_t$ is strict white noise then the asymptotic distribution of the sample autocorrelations (standardised by $\sqrt{T}$) calculated from the realisation $\{w_t\}_1^T$ will be $N(0, 1)$, so that the random walk null would be rejected at the 5 per cent significance level if, for example, $\sqrt{T}|r_1| > 1.96$.

If a set of sample autocorrelations are considered, say $r_1, \ldots, r_K$, then some will probably be significant even if the null is true: on average one out of twenty will be significant at the 5 per cent level. As noted in example 2.1, the portmanteau statistics $Q^*(K)$ and $Q(K)$ may be used in these circumstances. On the random walk null, both statistics are distributed as χ^2_K, so that the null would be rejected for sufficiently high values. Note that these tests do not require a specific alternative hypothesis: they may thus be regarded as 'diagnostic' tests with, hopefully, some power against the null for a wide range of alternatives.

The tests do, however, require that the innovations to the random walk be strict white noise. As other assumptions are possible, other types of test might be appropriate. Taylor (1986, chapter 6.4) discusses both the non-parametric runs test and certain spectral tests, which may be considered when the alternative to random walk behaviour is a cyclical model.

4.2.2 *Calendar effects*

As remarked above, autocorrelation tests are generally diagnostic checks aimed at detecting general departures from white noise and do not consider autocorrelations associated with specific timing patterns, i.e., patterns associated with 'calendar effects'. There has been a great deal of research carried out in recent years on detecting such effects. To date, researchers have found evidence of a January effect, in which stock returns in this month are exceptionally large when compared to the returns observed for other months; a weekend effect, in which Monday mean returns are negative rather than positive as for all other weekdays; a holiday effect, showing a much larger mean return for the day before holidays; a turn-of-the-month effect, in which the four-day return around the turn of a month is *greater* than the average total monthly return; an intramonth effect, in which the return over the first half of a month is significantly larger than the return over the second half; and a variety of intraday effects.

Early reviews of these 'anomalies' are Thaler (1987a, 1987b), while Mills and Coutts (1995) provide a more recent survey and additional evidence. A wide range of statistical techniques have been employed to detect such anomalies and discussion of them here would take us too far afield from our development of formal time series models. Taylor (1986, pp. 41–4) discusses some of the techniques and the interested reader is recommended to examine both this and further papers cited in the above references.

4.2.3 Consequences of non-linearities for random walk tests

As has been emphasised, the test statistics introduced above rely on the assumption that the random walk innovation is strict white noise. What happens if this innovation is just white noise, so that the sequence is merely uncorrelated rather than independent? Consider the following example, taken from Taylor (1986, p. 117). Suppose that $\{w_t\}_1^T$ is constructed from the strict white-noise process $\{a_t\}_1^T$ by

$$w_t = \begin{cases} \sigma_1 a_t, & \text{for } 1 \leq t \leq m, \\ \sigma_2 a_t, & \text{for } m+1 \leq t \leq T \end{cases}$$

Ignoring the sample mean $\bar{w}$, the autocorrelations are given by

$$r_k = \frac{\sum_{t=1}^{T-k} w_t w_{t+k}}{\sum_{t=1}^{T} w_t^2}$$

Keeping σ_1 fixed at a positive number and letting $\sigma_2 \to 0$, we have

$$r_k \to \frac{\sum_{t=1}^{m-k} a_t a_{t+k}}{\sum_{t=1}^{m} a_t^2}$$

which are the autocorrelations of the sequence $\{a_t\}_1^m$. These have variances of approximately m^{-1}, so that $T \cdot V(r_i) \to T/m$, which can be arbitrarily high, and certainly bigger than the value of unity that occurs when w_t is strict white noise rather than just uncorrelated, as it is here by construction.

4.3 Stochastic volatility

A simple way in which non-linearity can be introduced into a time series is to allow the variance (or conditional variance) of the process to change either at certain discrete points in time or continuously. Although a stationary process must have a constant variance, certain conditional variances can change. For a non-linear stationary process x_t, the variance, $V(x_t)$, is a constant for all t, but the conditional variance $V(x_t|x_{t-1}, x_{t-2}, \ldots)$ depends on the observations and thus can change from period to period.

4.3.1 Stochastic volatility models

Suppose that the sequence $\{x_t\}_1^t$ is generated by the *product process*

$$x_t = \mu + \sigma_t U_t \tag{4.2}$$

where U_t is a standardised process, so that $E(U_t) = 0$ and $V(U_t) = 1$ for all t, and σ_t is a sequence of positive random variables usually such that $V(x_t|\sigma_t) = \sigma_t^2$: σ_t is thus the conditional standard deviation of x_t.

Typically $U_t = (x_t - \mu)/\sigma_t$ is assumed to be normal and independent of σ_t: we will further assume that it is strict white noise. Equation (4.2) can then be shown to be obtained as the discrete time approximation to the stochastic differential equation

$$\frac{dP}{P} = d(\log(P)) = \mu dt + \sigma dW$$

where $x_t = \Delta \log(P_t)$ and $W(t)$ is standard Brownian motion. This is the usual *diffusion process* used to price financial assets in theoretical models of finance (see, for example, Wilmott, Howison and DeWynne, 1995, chapter 2).

The above assumptions together imply that x_t has mean μ, variance

$$E(x_t - \mu)^2 = E(\sigma_t^2 U_t^2) = E(\sigma_t^2)E(U_t^2) = E(\sigma_t^2)$$

and autocovariances

$$E(x_t - \mu)(x_{t-k} - \mu) = E(\sigma_t \sigma_{t-k} U_t U_{t-k}) = E(\sigma_t \sigma_{t-k} U_t)E(U_{t-k}) = 0$$

i.e., it is white noise. However, note that both the squared and absolute deviations, $S_t = (x_t - \mu)^2$ and $M_t = |x_t - \mu|$, can be autocorrelated. For example

$$\begin{aligned}Cov(S_t, S_{t-k}) &= E(S_t - E(S_t))(S_{t-k} - E(S_t)) = E(S_t S_{t-k}) - (E(S_t))^2 \\ &= E(\sigma_t^2 \sigma_{t-k}^2) E(U_t^2 U_{t-k}^2) - (E(\sigma_t^2))^2 \\ &= E(\sigma_t^2 \sigma_{t-k}^2) - (E(\sigma_t^2))^2\end{aligned}$$

in which case we have

$$\rho_{k,S} = \frac{E(\sigma_t^2 \sigma_{t-k}^2) - (E(\sigma_t^2))^2}{E(\sigma_t^4) - (E(\sigma_t^2))^2}$$

where $\rho_{k,S}$ is the kth autocorrelation of S_t.

What models are plausible for the conditional standard deviation σ_t? Since it is a sequence of positive random variables, a normal distribution is inappropriate, but as it is likely that σ_t will be skewed to the right, a log-normal distribution would seem to be a plausible choice. Let us define

$$h_t = \log(\sigma_t^2) = \gamma_0 + \gamma_1 h_{t-1} + \eta_t \tag{4.3}$$

where $\eta_t \sim NID(0, \sigma_\eta^2)$ and is independent of U_t. A common interpretation of h_t is that it represents the random and uneven flow of new information into financial markets: see Clark (1973) and Tauchen and Pitts (1983). We then have

$$x_t = \mu + U_t \exp(h_t/2)$$

Since U_t is always stationary, x_t will be (weakly) stationary if and only if h_t is, which will be the case if $|\gamma_1| < 1$. Assuming this, then using the properties of the log-normal distribution shows that all even moments of x_t and S_t will exist, being given by

$$\begin{aligned}E(x_t - \mu)^r &= E(S_t)^{r/2} = E(U_t^r) E\left(\exp\left(\frac{r}{2} h_t\right)\right) \\ &= \left(r!/\left(2^{r/2}(r/2!)\right)\right) \exp\left(\frac{r}{2}\mu_h + \left(\frac{r}{2}\right)\left(\frac{\sigma_h^2}{2}\right)\right)\end{aligned}$$

where $\mu_h = E(h_t) = \gamma_0/(1 - \gamma_1)$ and $\sigma_h^2 = V(h_t) = \sigma_\eta^2/(1 - \gamma_1^2)$. All odd moments are zero. The moment measure of kurtosis is then given by

$$\frac{E(S_t^2)}{(E(S_t))^2} = \frac{E(x_t - \mu)^4}{\left(E(x_t - \mu)^2\right)^2} = 3\exp(\sigma_h^2) > 3$$

so that the process has fatter tails than a normal distribution. The autocorrelation function of S_t follows from the fact that

$$\begin{aligned} E(S_t S_{t-k}) &= E\left(\sigma_t^2 \sigma_{t-k}^2\right) = E(\exp(h_t)\exp(h_{t-k})) = E(\exp(h_t + h_{t-k})) \\ &= \exp\left(\left(\mu_h + \sigma_h^2\right) + \left(\mu_h + \gamma_1^k \sigma_h^2\right)\right) = \exp\left(2\mu_h + \sigma_h^2\left(1 + \gamma_1^k\right)\right) \end{aligned}$$

Hence

$$\begin{aligned} Cov(S_t, S_{t-k}) &= \exp\left(2\mu_h + \sigma_h^2\left(1 + \gamma_1^k\right)\right) - \exp\left(2\mu_h + \sigma_h^2\right) \\ &= \exp\left(2\mu_h + \sigma_h^2\right)\left(\exp\left(\sigma_h^2 \gamma_1^k\right) - 1\right) \end{aligned}$$

and

$$\rho_{k,S} = \frac{\left(\exp\left(\sigma_h^2 \gamma_1^k\right) - 1\right)}{3\left(\exp\left(\sigma_h^2\right) - 1\right)}$$

Taking logarithms of (4.2) yields

$$\log(S_t) = h_t + \log\left(U_t^2\right) = \mu_h + \frac{\eta_t}{(1 - \gamma_1 B)} + \log\left(U_t^2\right)$$

which shows that $\log(S_t) \sim$ ARMA(1, 1), but with non-normal innovations: if U_t is normal then $\log\left(U_t^2\right)$ has mean -1.27 and variance 4.93 and a very long left-hand tail, caused by taking logarithms of very small numbers. The autocorrelation function of $\log(S_t)$ is

$$\rho_{k,\log(S)} = \frac{\gamma_1^k}{\left(1 + 4.93/\sigma_h^2\right)}$$

Note that it is possible that some values of S_t may be zero, in which case their logarithms cannot be taken. One way of overcoming this difficulty is to employ the transformation used by Koopman *et al.* (1995)

$$\log(S_t) \cong \log\left(S_t + cs_S^2\right) - cs_S^2 / \left(S_t + cs_S^2\right)$$

where s_S^2 is the sample variance of S_t and c is a small number, set by Koopman *et al.* to be 0.02.

4.3.2 Estimation of stochastic volatility models

The main difficulty with using stochastic volatility (SV) models is that they are rather difficult to estimate. A survey of estimation techniques is provided by Shephard (1996): for example, ML-based estimation can only be carried out by a computer-intensive technique such as that described in Jacquier, Polson and Rossi (1994). A convenient estimation method is, however, quasi-maximum likelihood (QML), as outlined in Koopman *et al.* (1995, chapter 7.5) and available in their STAMP 5.0 software package. This technique, which uses the Kalman filter, also provides an estimate of the volatility σ_t^2.

Example 4.1 A stochastic volatility model for the dollar/sterling exchange rate
In this example we fit the SV model

$$x_t = U_t \exp(h_t/2)$$

$$h_t = \log(\sigma_t^2) = \gamma_0 + \gamma_1 h_{t-1} + \eta_t$$

to the daily series of dollar/sterling first differences initially examined in example 2.5, where it was found to be close to zero mean white noise. To use the QML technique of Koopman *et al.* (1995), the model is rewritten as

$$x_t = \sigma U_t \exp(h_t/2)$$

$$h_t = \gamma_1 h_{t-1} + \eta_t$$

where $\sigma = \exp(\gamma_0/2)$, or as

$$\log(x_t^2) = \kappa + h_t + u_t$$

$$h_t = \gamma_1 h_{t-1} + \eta_t$$

where

$$u_t = \log(U_t^2) - E(\log(U_t^2))$$

and

$$\kappa = \log(\sigma^2) + E(\log(U_t^2))$$

QML estimation using STAMP 5.0 yields the following estimates: $\hat{\sigma}_\eta = 0.125$, $\hat{\sigma} = 1.685$, $\hat{\gamma}_0 = 1.044$ and $\hat{\gamma}_1 = 0.989$, and a plot of the exchange rate volatility, given by the 'smoothed' estimates (of the square root) of $\exp(h_t/2)$, are shown in figure 4.1. The conditional variance equation is close to a random walk and the time-varying nature of the volatility can clearly be seen.

4.4 ARCH processes

4.4.1 Development of generalised ARCH processes

In the previous section the process determining the conditional standard deviations of x_t was assumed not to be a function of x_t. For example, for the AR(1) log-normal model of equation (4.3), σ_t was dependent upon the information set $\{\eta_t, \sigma_{t-1}, \sigma_{t-2}, \ldots\}$. We now consider the case when the conditional standard deviations are a function of past values of x_t, i.e.

$$\sigma_t = \Im(x_{t-1}, x_{t-2}, \ldots)$$

A simple example is

$$\sigma_t = \Im(x_{t-1}) = \left(\alpha_0 + \alpha_1(x_{t-1} - \mu)^2\right)^{1/2} \qquad (4.4)$$

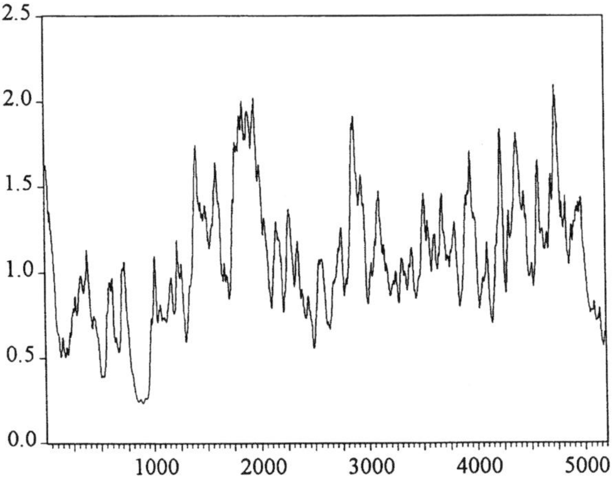

Figure 4.1 Dollar/sterling exchange rate 'volatility'

where α_0 and α_1 are both positive. With $U_t \sim NID(0, 1)$ and independent of σ_t, $x_t = \mu + U_t\sigma_t$ is then white noise and conditionally normal, i.e.

$$x_t|x_{t-1}, x_{t-2}, \ldots \sim NID(\mu, \sigma_t^2)$$

so that

$$V(x_t|x_{t-1}) = \alpha_0 + \alpha_1(x_{t-1} - \mu)^2$$

If $\alpha_1 < 1$ the unconditional variance is $V(x_t) = \alpha_0/(1 - \alpha_1)$ and x_t is weakly stationary. The fourth moment of x_t is finite if $3\alpha_1^2 < 1$ and, if so, the kurtosis is given by $3(1 - \alpha_1^2)/(1 - 3\alpha_1^2)$. This exceeds 3, so that the unconditional distribution of x_t is fatter tailed than the normal. If this moment condition is not satisfied, then the variance of x_t^2 will not be finite and hence x_t^2 will not be weakly stationary.

This model was first introduced by Engle (1982) and is known as the *first-order autoregressive conditional heteroskedastic* [ARCH(1)] process. ARCH processes have proved to be an extremely popular class of non-linear models for financial time series, as can be seen from the various surveys of the literature that have been published: Engle and Bollerslev (1986), Bollerslev, Chou and Kroner (1992), Bera and Higgins (1993), Bollerslev, Engle and Nelson (1994) and Palm (1996) is by no means an exhaustive list.

A more convenient notation is to define $\varepsilon_t = x_t - \mu = U_t\sigma_t$, so that the ARCH(1) model can be written as

$$\varepsilon_t|x_{t-1}, x_{t-2}, \ldots \sim NID(0, \sigma_t^2)$$

$$\sigma_t^2 = \alpha_0 + \alpha_1\varepsilon_{t-1}^2$$

Defining $\nu_t = \varepsilon_t^2 - \sigma_t^2$, the model can also be written as

$$\varepsilon_t^2 = \alpha_0 + \alpha_1\varepsilon_{t-1}^2 + \nu_t$$

Since $E(\nu_t|x_{t-1}, x_{t-2}, \ldots) = 0$, the model corresponds directly to an AR(1) model for the squared innovations ε_t^2. However, as $\nu_t = \sigma_t^2(U_t^2 - 1)$, the errors are obviously heteroskedastic.

The ARCH(1) model can be interpreted in various ways. For example, suppose the parameters in the ARCH equation are defined as $\alpha_0 = V(u_t)$ and $\alpha_1 = V(\phi_t)$, where u_t and ϕ_t are independent. Thus

$$V(\varepsilon_t) = V(u_t) + V(\phi_t)\varepsilon_{t-1}^2$$

which is consistent with ε_t being generated by a *random coefficient* AR(1) process

$$\begin{aligned}\varepsilon_t &= \phi_t\varepsilon_{t-1} + u_t \\ &= \phi_t\sigma_{t-1}U_{t-1} + u_t\end{aligned}$$

where $E(\phi_t) = \phi$ and u_t has mean zero (see Bera and Higgins, 1993, for more on this interpretation).

A natural extension is the ARCH(q) process, where (4.4) is replaced by

$$\Im(x_{t-1}, x_{t-2}, \ldots, x_{t-q}) = \left(\alpha_0 + \sum\nolimits_{i=1}^{q} \alpha_i(x_{t-i} - \mu)^2\right)^{1/2}$$

where $\alpha_0 > 0$ and $\alpha_i \geq 0,\ 1 \leq i \leq q$. The process will be weakly stationary if all the roots of the characteristic equation associated with the ARCH parameters, $\alpha(B)$, lie outside the unit circle, i.e., if $\sum_{i=1}^{q} \alpha_i < 1$, in which case the unconditional variance is $V(x_t) = \alpha_0 / \left(1 - \sum_{i=1}^{q} \alpha_i\right)$. In terms of ε_t and σ_t^2, the conditional variance function is

$$\sigma_t^2 = \alpha_0 + \sum\nolimits_{i=1}^{q} \alpha_i \varepsilon_{t-i}^2$$

or, equivalently

$$\varepsilon_t^2 = \alpha_0 + \alpha(B)\varepsilon_{t-1}^2 + \nu_t$$

Detailed discussion of the ARCH(q) model, setting out further technical conditions that need not concern us here, may be found in, for example, Engle (1982), Milhøj (1985) and Weiss (1986a).

A practical difficulty with ARCH models is that, with q large, unconstrained estimation (to be discussed later) will often lead to the violation of the non-negativity constraints on the α_is that are needed to ensure that the conditional variance σ_t^2 is always positive. In many early applications of the model a rather arbitrary declining lag structure was thus imposed on the α_is to ensure that these constraints were met. To obtain more flexibility, a further extension, to the *generalised* ARCH (GARCH) process, was proposed (Bollerslev, 1986, 1988): the GARCH(p,q) process has the conditional variance function

$$\sigma_t^2 = \alpha_0 + \sum_{i=1}^{q} \alpha_i \varepsilon_{t-i}^2 + \sum_{i=1}^{p} \beta_i \sigma_{t-i}^2$$

$$= \alpha_0 + \alpha(B)\varepsilon_t^2 + \beta(B)\sigma_t^2$$

where $p > 0$ and $\beta_i \geq 0,\ 1 \leq i \leq p$. For the conditional variance of the GARCH(p,q) model to be well defined, all the coefficients in the corresponding ARCH(∞) model $\sigma_t^2 = \theta_0 + \theta(B)\varepsilon_t^2$ must be positive. Provided that $\alpha(B)$ and $\beta(B)$ have no common roots and that the roots of $\beta(B)$ lie outside the unit circle, this positivity constraint is satisfied if and only if all the coefficients in $\theta(B) = \alpha(B)/(1 - \beta(B))$ are non-negative. Necessary and sufficient conditions for this are given in Nelson and Cao (1992). For the GARCH(1,1) process

$$\sigma_t^2 = \alpha_0 + \alpha_1 \varepsilon_{t-1}^2 + \beta_1 \sigma_{t-1}^2$$

a model that has proved extremely popular for modelling financial time series, these conditions require that all three parameters are non-negative.

The equivalent form of the GARCH(p,q) process is

$$\varepsilon_t^2 = \alpha_0 + (\alpha(B) + \beta(B))\varepsilon_{t-1}^2 + \nu_t - \beta(B)\nu_{t-1} \tag{4.5}$$

so that $\varepsilon_t^2 \sim$ ARMA(m,p), where $m = \max(p, q)$. This process will be weakly stationary if and only if the roots of $\alpha(B) + \beta(B)$ lie outside the unit circle, i.e., if $\alpha(1) + \beta(1) < 1$. This also ensures that ε_t is weakly stationary, but it is only a sufficient, rather than a necessary, condition for strict stationarity. Because ARCH processes are thick tailed, the conditions for weak stationarity are often more stringent than those for strict stationarity. For example, Nelson (1990a) shows that ε_t and σ_t^2 will be strictly stationary in the GARCH(1,1) model if and only if

$$E\left(\log\left(\beta_1 + \alpha_1 U_t^2\right)\right) < 0$$

and this will be satisfied if, for example, $U_t \sim N(0, 1), \alpha_1 = 3$ and $\beta_1 = 0$, although the conditions for weak stationarity are clearly violated. Stationarity conditions for the general GARCH(p,q) process are derived in Bougerol and Picard (1992).

These complications with stationarity conditions carry over to the concept of 'volatility persistence' in GARCH models. If $\alpha(1) + \beta(1) = 1$ in (4.5) then $\alpha(B) + \beta(B)$ contains a unit root and we say that the model is integrated GARCH, or IGARCH(p,q) (see Engle and Bollerslev, 1986). It is often the case that $\alpha(1) + \beta(1)$ is very close to unity for financial time series and, if this condition holds, a shock to the conditional variance is persistent in the sense that it remains important for all future forecasts. As Bollerslev *et al.* (1994) argue, however, the concept of persistence in GARCH models is ambiguous. One reasonable definition is to say that shocks fail to persist when σ_t^2 is stationary, so that the conditional expectation $E(\sigma_{t+s}^2|\varepsilon_t, \varepsilon_{t-1}, \ldots)$ converges, as $s \to \infty$, to the unconditional variance $\alpha_0/(1-\alpha(1)-\beta(1))$. An alternative definition concentrates on forecast moments and says that shocks fail to persist if and only if $E(\sigma_{t+s}^{2\eta}|\varepsilon_t, \varepsilon_{t-1}, \ldots)$, for some $\eta > 0$, converges to a finite limit independent of $\varepsilon_t, \varepsilon_{t-1}, \ldots$.

Unfortunately, whether or not shocks persist can depend on which definition is adopted. For example, consider the GARCH(1,1) model

$$\sigma_{t+1}^2 = \alpha_0 + \alpha_1\varepsilon_t^2 + \beta_1\sigma_t^2 = \alpha_0 + \alpha_1\sigma_t^2(U_t^2 + \beta_1)$$

from which we have that

$$E(\sigma_{t+s}^2|\varepsilon_t, \varepsilon_{t-1}, \ldots) = \alpha_0\left(\sum\nolimits_{k=0}^{s-1}(\alpha_1+\beta_1)^k\right) + \sigma_t^2(\alpha_1+\beta_1)^s$$

It is easy to see that the conditional expectation converges to the unconditional variance $\alpha_0/(1-\alpha_1-\beta_1)$ if and only if $\alpha_1+\beta_1 < 1$, whereas in the IGARCH model with $\alpha_1+\beta_1 = 1$ the conditional expectation will tend to infinity as s increases, i.e.

$$E(\sigma_{t+s}^2|\varepsilon_t, \varepsilon_{t-1}, \ldots) = s\alpha_0 + \sigma_t^2$$

Yet IGARCH models are strictly stationary and, in this case, $E(\sigma_{t+s}^{2\eta}|\varepsilon_t, \varepsilon_{t-1}, \ldots)$ converges to a finite limit whenever $0 < \eta < 1$ (see Nelson, 1990a). The implication of this is that any apparent persistence of shocks may be a consequence of thick-tailed distributions rather than of inherent non-stationarity.

Persistence may also be characterised by the impulse response coefficients. The GARCH(1,1) process can be written, with $\phi_1 = \alpha_1 + \beta_1$, as

$$(1-\phi_1 B)\varepsilon_t^2 = \alpha_0 + (1-\beta_1 B)\nu_t$$

or as

$$\Delta\varepsilon_t^2 = (1-B)(1-\phi_1 B)^{-1}(1-\beta_1 B)\nu_t = \theta(B)\nu_t$$

The impulse response coefficients are found from the coefficients in the $\theta(B)$ lag polynomial

$$\theta_0 = 1, \quad \theta_1 = \phi_1 - \beta_1 - 1, \quad \theta_j = (\phi_1 - \beta_1)(\phi_1 - 1)\phi_1^{j-2}, \; j \geq 2$$

The cumulative impulse response $\theta(1)$ is zero because $\theta(B)$ contains a unit root or, equivalently, because $\sum_j \theta_j = (\phi_1 - \beta_1)\phi_1^{j-1}$, which exponentially tends to zero in the limit as long as $\phi_1 = \alpha_1 + \beta_1 < 1$. However, when $\phi_1 = \alpha_1 + \beta_1 = 1$, so that we have an IGARCH(1,1) process

$$\Delta\varepsilon_t^2 = \alpha_0 + (1 - \beta_1 B)\nu_t$$

$\sum_j \theta_j = 1 - \beta_1 = \theta(1) \neq 0$, and hence shocks persist indefinitely.

4.4.2 Modifications of GARCH processes

Although we have assumed that the distribution of ε_t was conditionally normal, this is not essential. Bollerslev (1987), for example, considers the case when the distribution is standardised t with unknown degrees of freedom υ that may be estimated from the data: for $\upsilon > 4$ such a distribution is leptokurtic and hence has thicker tails than the normal. Other distributions that have been considered include the normal-Poisson mixture distribution (Jorion, 1988), the power exponential distribution (Baillie and Bollerslev, 1989), the normal–lognormal mixture (Hsieh, 1989a), and the generalised exponential distribution (Nelson, 1991). There has also been developed recently estimation procedures which either estimate semi-parametrically the density of ε_t (Engle and Gonzalez-Rivera, 1991) or adaptively estimate the parameters of ARCH models in the presence of non-normal ε_t (Linton, 1993).

Further modifications result from allowing the relationship between σ_t^2 and ε_t to be more flexible than the quadratic mapping that has so far been assumed. To simplify the exposition, we shall concentrate on variants of the GARCH(1,1) process

$$\sigma_t^2 = \alpha_0 + \alpha_1\varepsilon_{t-1}^2 + \beta_1\sigma_{t-1}^2 = \alpha_0 + \alpha_1\sigma_{t-1}^2 U_{t-1}^2 + \beta_1\sigma_{t-1}^2 \tag{4.6}$$

An early alternative was to model conditional standard deviations rather than variances (Taylor, 1986, Schwert, 1989)

$$\sigma_t = \alpha_0 + \alpha_1|\varepsilon_{t-1}| + \beta_1\sigma_{t-1} = \alpha_0 + \alpha_1\sigma_{t-1}|U_{t-1}| + \beta_1\sigma_{t-1} \tag{4.7}$$

This makes the conditional variance the square of a weighted average of absolute shocks, rather than the weighted average of squared shocks. Consequently, large shocks have a smaller effect on the conditional variance than in the standard GARCH model.

A non-symmetric response to shocks is made explicit in Nelson's (1991) *exponential* GARCH (EGARCH) model

$$\log(\sigma_t^2) = \alpha_0 + \alpha_1 f(\varepsilon_{t-1}/\sigma_{t-1}) + \beta_1 \log(\sigma_{t-1}^2) \tag{4.8}$$

where

$$f(\varepsilon_{t-1}/\sigma_{t-1}) = \theta_1 \varepsilon_{t-1}/\sigma_{t-1} + (|\varepsilon_{t-1}/\sigma_{t-1}| - E|\varepsilon_{t-1}/\sigma_{t-1}|)$$

The 'news impact curve', $f(\cdot)$, relates revisions in conditional volatility, here given by $\log(\sigma_t^2)$, to 'news', ε_{t-1}. It embodies a non-symmetric response since $\partial f/\partial\varepsilon_{t-1} = \theta_1 + 1$ when $\varepsilon_{t-1} > 0$ and $\partial f/\partial\varepsilon_{t-1} = \theta_1 - 1$ when $\varepsilon_{t-1} < 0$. (Note that volatility will be at a minimum when there is no news, $\varepsilon_{t-1} = 0$). This asymmetry is potentially useful as it allows volatility to respond more rapidly to falls in a market than to corresponding rises, which is an important stylized fact for many financial assets and is known as the 'leverage' effect. It is easy to show that $f(\varepsilon_{t-1})$ is strict white noise with zero mean and constant variance, so that $\log(\sigma_t^2)$ is an ARMA(1,1) process and will be stationary if $\beta_1 < 1$.

A model which nests (4.6), (4.7) and (4.8) is the non-linear ARCH (NARCH) model (Higgins and Bera, 1992), a general form of which is

$$\sigma_t^\gamma = \alpha_0 + \alpha_1 f^\gamma(\varepsilon_{t-1}) + \beta_1 \sigma_{t-1}^\gamma$$

while an alternative is the threshold ARCH process

$$\sigma_t^\gamma = \alpha_0 + \alpha_1 g^{(\gamma)}(\varepsilon_{t-1}) + \beta_1 \sigma_{t-1}^\gamma$$

where

$$g^{(\gamma)}(\varepsilon_{t-1}) = \theta I(\varepsilon_{t-1} > 0) \cdot |\varepsilon_{t-1}|^\gamma + \theta I(\varepsilon_{t-1} \leq 0) \cdot |\varepsilon_{t-1}|^\gamma$$

$I(\cdot)$ being the indicator function. If $\gamma = 1$, we have the threshold ARCH (TARCH) model of Zakoian (1994), while for $\gamma = 2$ we have the GJR model of Glosten, Jagannathan and Runkle (1993), which allows a quadratic response of volatility to news but with different coefficients for good and bad news, although it maintains the assertion that the minimum volatility will result when there is no news.

Ding, Granger and Engle (1993) and Hentschel (1995) define very general classes of models which nest all the above ARCH models; the details of how to do so may be found in the two papers. Hentschel's model, for example, can be written using the Box and Cox (1964) transformation as

$$\frac{\sigma_t^\lambda - 1}{\lambda} = \alpha_0 + \alpha_1 \sigma_{t-1}^\lambda f^\gamma(U_{t-1}) + \beta_1 \frac{\sigma_{t-1}^\lambda - 1}{\lambda} \tag{4.9}$$

where

$$f(U_t) = |U_t - b| - c(U_t - b)$$

Several variants cannot be nested within (4.9). Engle's (1990) asymmetric ARCH (AARCH) and Sentana's (1995) quadratic ARCH (QARCH) are two such models. These can be written in the simple case being considered here as

$$\sigma_t^2 = \alpha_0 + \alpha_1 \varepsilon_{t-1}^2 + \delta \varepsilon_{t-1} + \beta_1 \sigma_{t-1}^2$$

where a negative value of δ means that good news increases volatility less than bad news. It is the presence of a quadratic form in ε_{t-1} that precludes them from being included as special cases of (4.9).

An alternative way of formalising the GARCH(1,1) model (4.6) is to define $\alpha_0 = \varpi(1 - \alpha_1 - \beta_1)$, where ϖ is the unconditional variance, or long-run volatility, to which the process reverts to

$$\sigma_t^2 = \varpi + \alpha_1\left(\varepsilon_{t-1}^2 - \varpi\right) + \beta_1\left(\sigma_{t-1}^2 - \varpi\right)$$

EVIEWS extends this formalisation to allow reversion to a varying level defined by q_t

$$\sigma_t^2 = q_t + \alpha_1\left(\varepsilon_{t-1}^2 - q_{t-1}\right) + \beta_1\left(\sigma_{t-1}^2 - q_{t-1}\right)$$

$$q_t = \varpi + \xi(q_{t-1} - \varpi) + \zeta\left(\varepsilon_{t-1}^2 - \sigma_{t-1}^2\right)$$

Here q_t is long-run volatility, which converges to ϖ through powers of ξ, while $\sigma_t^2 - q_t$ is the transitory component, converging to zero via powers of $\alpha_1 + \beta_1$.

This *component* GARCH model can also be combined with the TARCH model to allow asymmetries in both the permanent and transitory parts: this *asymmetric component* GARCH model automatically introduces the asymmetry into the transitory equation.

Two additional classes of models have also been proposed, the structural ARCH (STARCH) model of Harvey, Ruiz and Sentana (1992) and the switching ARCH (SWARCH) model proposed by both Cai (1994) and Hamilton and Susmel (1994). Both require estimation by the Kalman filter: the former decomposes ε_{t-1} into various unobserved components, each of which have ARCH forms, the latter postulates several different ARCH models between which the process switches via a Markov chain.

The stochastic variance and GARCH classes of models have some obvious similarities and a comparison between them is provided in Taylor (1994).

4.4.3 Long memory volatility processes: the FIGARCH model

An apparent stylized fact of return series is that the absolute values or powers, particularly squares, of returns tend to have very slowly decaying autocorrelations. For example, Ding, Granger and Engle (1993) find that the first negative autocorrelation of the squared returns of the daily S&P 500 index over the period 1928 to 1991, analysed in example 3.7, occurs at lag 2598, and a similar finding has been provided by Mills (1996a) for the daily returns of the London FT30 for the period 1935 to 1994. Additional evidence of this feature for other types of financial series is contained in, for example, Taylor (1986) and Dacarogna *et al.* (1993).

In response to these findings, Baillie, Bollerslev and Mikkelson (1996) consider the *Fractionally Integrated* GARCH (FIGARCH) process. The FIGARCH(1,d,1) process is most transparently defined as an extension of (4.5)

$$\Delta^d \varepsilon_t^2 = \alpha_0 + (\alpha_1 + \beta_1)\Delta^d \varepsilon_{t-1}^2 + \nu_t - \beta_1 \nu_{t-1} \tag{4.10}$$

Equivalently, but perhaps less transparently, it can be written as

$$\sigma_t^2 = \alpha_0 + \left(1 - \Delta^d\right)\varepsilon_t^2 - \left(\beta_1 - (\alpha_1 + \beta_1)\Delta^d\right)\varepsilon_{t-1}^2 + \beta_1 \sigma_{t-1}^2 \tag{4.11}$$

(4.10) can be expressed as

$$\Delta \varepsilon_t^2 = \alpha_0^* + \Delta^{1-d}(1 - (\alpha_1 + \beta_1)B)^{-1}(1 - \beta_1 B)\nu_t = \alpha_0^* + \theta(B)\nu_t$$

and (4.11) as

$$\begin{aligned}\sigma_t^2 &= \alpha_0 \Big/ (1-\beta_1) + \left(1 - (1-(\alpha_1+\beta_1)B)(1-\beta_1 B)^{-1}\Delta^d\right)\varepsilon_t^2 \\ &= \alpha_0^{**} + \pi(B)\varepsilon_t^2\end{aligned}$$

Baillie *et al.* (1996) show that the FIGARCH(p,d,q) class of processes is strictly but not weakly stationary for $0 \leq d \leq 1$. FIGARCH processes with $0 < d < 1$ have $\theta(1) = 0$, so that shocks to the conditional variance ultimately die out. Unlike the $d = 0$ case, however, $\sum_j \theta_j$ decays eventually at an hyperbolic, rather than an exponential, rate, so that the fractional differencing parameter provides important information about the pattern and speed with which shocks to volatility are propagated. For $d > 1$, $\theta(1)$ is undefined and the conditional variance is explosive. The conditions that ensure a positive conditional variance for the FIGARCH($1,d,1$) process are $\alpha_0 > 0$, $\alpha_1 + d \geq 0$ and $1 - 2(\alpha_1 + \beta_1) \geq d \geq 0$.

Baillie *et al.* (1996) argue that the presence of FIGARCH processes may explain the common finding of IGARCH type behaviour in high-frequency financial data. It is commonly argued (Nelson, 1990b, Nelson and Foster, 1994) that GARCH(1,1) models provide consistent discrete time approximations to continuous time diffusion processes and, as the sampling interval goes to zero, the sum of the two GARCH parameters tends to one, indicating IGARCH behaviour. However, IGARCH implies that shocks to the conditional variance persist indefinitely and this is difficult to reconcile with the persistence observed after large shocks, such as the Crash of October 1987, and also with the perceived behaviour of agents who do not appear to frequently and radically alter the composition of their portfolios, as would be implied by IGARCH. Temporal aggregation issues also cast doubt on the reasonableness of IGARCH models. Drost and Nijman (1993) show that an IGARCH generating process at high frequencies should carry over to low frequencies of observation, but this seems at odds with most reported empirical findings.

Given these anomalies, Baillie *et al.* (1996) suggest that the widespread observation of IGARCH behaviour may be an artifact of a long memory FIGARCH data generating process and provide a simulation experiment that provides considerable support for this line of argument. It would thus seem that FIGARCH models should be seriously considered when modelling volatility.

4.4.4 Estimation of ARMA models with ARCH errors

The analysis so far has proceeded on the assumption that $\varepsilon_t = x_t - \mu$ is serially uncorrelated. A natural extension is to allow x_t to follow an ARMA(P,Q) process, so that the combined ARMA-ARCH model becomes

$$\Phi(B)(x_t - \mu) = \Theta(B)\varepsilon_t \tag{4.12}$$

$$\sigma_t^2 = E\left(\varepsilon_t^2 | \varepsilon_{t-1}, \varepsilon_{t-2}, \ldots\right) = \alpha_0 + \sum\nolimits_{i=1}^{q} \alpha_i \varepsilon_{t-i}^2 + \sum\nolimits_{i=1}^{p} \beta_i \sigma_{t-i}^2 \tag{4.13}$$

This latter equation can be written as

$$\sigma_t^2 = z_t' \omega = z_{1t}' \omega_1 + z_{2t}' \omega_2$$

where

$$z_t' = \left(z_{1t}' : z_{2t}'\right) = \left(1, \varepsilon_{t-1}^2, \ldots, \varepsilon_{t-q}^2 : \sigma_{t-1}^2, \ldots, \sigma_{t-p}^2\right)$$

and

$$\omega' = \left(\omega_1' : \omega_2'\right) = \left(\alpha_0, \alpha_1, \ldots, \alpha_q : \beta_1, \ldots, \beta_p\right)$$

Using this notation, ML estimates of the model can be obtained in the following way. Define Ω as the vector of parameters in the model given by equations (4.12) and (4.13) and partition it as $\Omega = \left(\omega' : \psi'\right)$, $\psi' = \left(\Phi_1, \ldots, \Phi_P, \Theta_1, \ldots, \Theta_Q, \mu\right)$ being a vector containing the parameters in the ARMA equation. We may also define $\Omega_0 = \left(\omega_0' : \psi_0'\right)$ as the true parameter vector.

The log likelihood function for a sample of T observations is, apart from some constants

$$L_T(\Omega) = T^{-1} \sum\nolimits_{t=1}^{T} l_t(\Omega)$$

where

$$l_t(\Omega) = \log\left\{f\left(\varepsilon_t / \sigma_t : \varsigma\right)\right\} - 0.5 \log \sigma_t^2$$

is the log likelihood for the tth observation and $f\left(\varepsilon_t / \sigma_t : \varsigma\right)$ denotes the conditional density function for the standardised innovations ε_t / σ_t, which has mean zero, variance one, and nuisance parameters ς. Precise details of ML estimation may be found in, for example, Engle (1982), Weiss (1986a, 1986b) and Bollerslev (1988). The Berndt, Hall, Hall and Hausman (BHHH, 1974) algorithm is a convenient method of computation. If $\hat{\Omega}^{(i)}$ denotes the parameter estimates after the ith iteration, then $\hat{\Omega}^{(i+1)}$ is calculated by the algorithm as

$$\hat{\Omega}^{(i+1)} = \hat{\Omega}^{(i)} + \lambda_i \left(\sum_{t=1}^{T} \frac{\partial l_t}{\partial \Omega} \frac{\partial l_t}{\partial \Omega'} \right)^{-1} \sum_{t=1}^{T} \frac{\partial l_t}{\partial \Omega}$$

where $\partial l_t / \partial \Omega$ is evaluated at $\hat{\Omega}^{(i)}$ and λ_i is a variable step length chosen to maximise the likelihood function in the given direction. Because the information matrix, $\eta = -E(\partial^2 l_t / \partial \Omega \partial \Omega')$, is block diagonal, ω can be estimated without loss of asymptotic efficiency based on a consistent estimate of ψ, and vice versa, so that the iterations for $\omega^{(i)}$ and $\psi^{(i)}$ can be carried out separately.

The ML estimate $\hat{\Omega}$ is strongly consistent for Ω_0 and asymptotically normal with mean Ω_0 and covariance matrix η^{-1}, consistently estimated by $T^{-1}(\sum_{t=1}^{T} (\partial l_t / \partial \Omega)(\partial l_t / \partial \Omega'))^{-1}$, which may be obtained from the last BHHH iteration.

Of course, the actual implementation of the ML procedure requires an explicit assumption about the conditional density $f(\varepsilon_t / \sigma_t : \varsigma)$. The most commonly employed distribution is the normal

$$f(\varepsilon_t / \sigma_t : \varsigma) = (2\pi)^{-1/2} \exp(-0.5(\varepsilon_t^2 / \sigma_t^2))$$

From the discussion in section 4.4.1, the ARCH model with conditionally normal errors results in a leptokurtic unconditional distribution. However, the degree of leptokurtosis so induced often does not capture all of the fat tails present in financial data: this is discussed in detail in chapter 5. Consequently, various alternatives were discussed in section 4.4.2. Perhaps the two most popular, Bollerslev's (1987) standardised t-distribution and Nelson's (1991) generalised exponential distribution (GED), are special cases of the *generalised* t-distribution (see McDonald and Newey, 1988), which has the density function

$$f(\varepsilon_t / \sigma_t : \varsigma, \xi) = \frac{\xi}{2\sigma_t b \cdot B(1/\xi, \varsigma) \cdot \left[1 + |\varepsilon_t|^{\xi} \left(\varsigma b^{\xi} \sigma_t^{\xi} \right) \right]^{\varsigma + 1/\xi}}$$

where $B(1/\varsigma, \xi) = \Gamma(1/\xi)\Gamma(\varsigma)\Gamma(1/\xi + \varsigma)$ denotes the beta function, $\Gamma(\cdot)$ denotes the gamma function, $b \equiv \left(\Gamma(\varsigma)\Gamma(1/\xi)/\Gamma(3/\xi)\Gamma(\varsigma - 2/\xi)\right)^{1/2}$ is a scale factor that makes $V(\varepsilon_t/\sigma_t) = 1$ and $\varsigma\xi > 2$, $\varsigma > 0$ and $\xi > 0$. The standardised t is obtained when $\xi = 2$, in which case the degrees of freedom are given by 2ς. As is well known, the t-distribution is symmetric around zero and converges to the normal distribution as $\varsigma \to \infty$, but for $2 < \varsigma < \infty$ the conditional kurtosis equals $3(\varsigma - 1)/(\varsigma - 2)$, which exceeds the normal value of three. The GED is obtained as $\varsigma \to \infty$ and for $\xi > 2$ (<2) has fatter (thinner) tails than the normal. For a detailed discussion of the issues involved in estimation and inference in GARCH models, see Bollerslev *et al.* (1994).

What are the consequences of ignoring possible non-normality and continuing to use the normal density for $f(\varepsilon_t/\sigma_t : \varsigma)$? This is known as *quasi*-ML (QML) estimation and produces an estimate $\tilde{\Omega}$ that is consistent and asymptotically normal but with standard errors that are inconsistent. However, these can be corrected by using robust standard errors (Bollerslev and Wooldridge, 1992). For symmetric departures from conditional normality, the QML estimator $\tilde{\Omega}$ is generally close to the exact ML estimator $\hat{\Omega}$, but for non-symmetric conditional distributions both the asymptotic and the finite sample loss in efficiency may be quite large, and semi-parametric estimation might be preferred.

4.4.5 Testing for the presence of ARCH errors

Let us suppose that an ARMA model for x_t has been estimated, from which the residuals e_t have been obtained. The presence of ARCH can lead to serious model misspecification if it is ignored: as with all forms of heteroskedasticity, analysis assuming its absence will result in inappropriate parameter standard errors, and these will typically be too small. For example, Weiss (1984) shows that ignoring ARCH will lead to the identification of ARMA models that are overparameterised.

Methods for testing whether ARCH is present are therefore essential, particularly as estimation incorporating it requires the complicated iterative techniques discussed above. Equation (4.5) has shown that if ε_t is GARCH(p,q) then ε_t^2 is ARMA(m,p), where $m = \max(p, q)$, and Bollerslev (1986) shows that standard ARMA theory follows through in this case. This implies that the squared residuals e_t^2 can then be used to identify m and p, and therefore q, in a fashion similar to the way the usual residuals are used in conventional ARMA modelling. McLeod and Li (1983), for example, show that the sample autocorrelations of e_t^2 have asymptotic variance T^{-1} and that portmanteau statistics calculated from them are asymptotically χ^2 if the ε_t^2 are independent.

Formal tests are also available. Engle (1982) shows that a test of the null hypothesis that ε_t has a constant conditional variance against the alternative that the conditional variance is given by an ARCH(q) process, i.e., a test of $\alpha_1 = \ldots = \alpha_q = 0$ in (4.13) conditional upon $\beta_1 = \ldots = \beta_p = 0$ may be based on the Lagrange Multiplier principle. The test procedure is to run a regression of e_t^2 on $e_{t-1}^2, \ldots, e_{t-q}^2$ and to test the statistic $T \cdot R^2$ as a χ_q^2 variate, where R^2 is the squared multiple correlation coefficient of the regression. An asymptotically equivalent form of the test, which may have better small sample properties, is to compute the standard F-test from the regression. The intuition behind this test is clear. If the data are indeed homoskedastic, then the variance cannot be predicted and variations in e_t^2 will be purely random. If ARCH effects are present, however, such variations will be predicted by lagged values of the squared residuals. Of course, if the residuals themselves contain some remaining autocorrelation or, perhaps, some other form of non-linearity, then it is quite likely that this test for ARCH will reject, since these errors may induce autocorrelation in the squared residuals: we cannot simply assume that ARCH effects are necessarily present when the ARCH test rejects.

Strictly, since the parameters of an ARCH model must be positive, a test of ARCH should be formulated as a one-sided test, which should presumably be more powerful than the above $T \cdot R^2$ test. Engle, Hendry and Trumble (1985) thus suggested a one-sided test for ARCH(1) by using the square root of the LM test with an appropriate sign, but this approach cannot be extended to test higher-order ARCH(q) alternatives. In this situation, either the test proposed by Lee and King (1993), and extended by Hong (1997), or that of Demos and Sentana (1998) may be employed. These tests are necessarily more complicated to derive and compute and we refer the reader to the above references for details.

When the alternative is a GARCH(p, q) process, some complications arise. In fact, a general test of $p > 0$, $q > 0$ against a white-noise null is not feasible, nor is a test of GARCH $(p + r_1, q + r_2)$ errors, where $r_1 > 0$ and $r_2 > 0$, when the null is GARCH(p,q). Furthermore, under this null, the LM test for GARCH(p,r) and ARCH($p + r$) alternatives coincide. What can be tested is the null of an ARCH(p) process against a GARCH(p,q) alternative, i.e., a test of $\omega_2 = 0$ using the notation of the previous section: Bollerslev (1988) provides details.

4.4.6 ARCH and theories of asset pricing

The importance of ARCH processes in modelling financial time series is seen most clearly in models of asset pricing which involve agents maximising expected utility over uncertain future events. To illustrate this, consider the following example, taken from Engle and Bollerslev (1986). Suppose a representative agent must allocate his wealth, W_t, between shares of a risky asset q_t at a price p_t and those of a risk-free asset x_t, whose price is set equal to 1. The shares of the risky asset will be worth y_{t+1} each at the end of the period (if there are no dividends, then $y_{t+1} = p_{t+1}$). The risk-free asset will be worth $r_t x_t$, where r_t denotes one plus the risk-free rate of interest. If the agent has a mean-variance utility function in end-of-period wealth, $W_{t+1} = q_t y_{t+1} + r_t x_t$, then the allocation problem for the agent is to maximise this utility function with respect to holdings of the risky asset, q_t, i.e., to maximise

$$2E_t(q_t y_{t+1} + r_t x_t) - \gamma_t V_t(q_t y_{t+1})$$

subject to the start of period wealth constraint

$$W_t = x_t + p_t q_t$$

This has the solution

$$p_t = r_t^{-1} E_t(y_{t+1}) - \gamma_t q_t r_t^{-1} V_t(y_{t+1}) \tag{4.14}$$

If the outstanding stock of the risky asset is fixed at q, and γ_t and r_t are taken as constants (γ and r respectively), then (4.14) describes the asset pricing model.

If the risky asset is interpreted as a forward contract for delivery in s periods time, the price that a pure speculator would be willing to pay is

$$p_t = r^{-s}\left(E_t(y_{t+s}) - \delta V_t(y_{t+s})\right) \tag{4.15}$$

where r^{-s} gives the present discounted value at the risk-free rate r and $\delta = \gamma q$. A simple redating of the model shows that the price of the forward contract at time $t+1$, for $s \geq 2$ periods remaining to maturity, can be expressed as

$$p_{t+1} = r^{1-s}\left(E_{t+1}(y_{t+s}) - \delta V_{t+1}(y_{t+s})\right)$$

Taking expectations at time t, multiplying by r^{-1}, and subtracting from (4.15) gives

$$p_t = r^{-1} E_t(p_{t+1}) - \delta r^{-s}\left(V_t(y_{t+s}) - E_t\left(V_{t+1}(y_{t+s})\right)\right) \tag{4.16}$$

Now, suppose y_t can be represented by an infinite moving average process where the innovations are uncorrelated but have time-varying conditional variance σ_t^2

$$y_t = \varepsilon_t + \sum_{i=1}^{\infty} \theta_i \varepsilon_{t-i} = \theta(B)\varepsilon_t \tag{4.17}$$

$$V_t(y_{t+1}) = V_t(\varepsilon_{t+1}) = \sigma_{t+1}^2$$

Thus

$$V_t(y_{t+s}) = E_t\left(\sum_{i=1}^{s} \theta_{s-i}\varepsilon_{t+i}\right)^2 = \sum_{i=1}^{s} \theta_{s-i}^2 E_t(\sigma_{t+i}^2)$$

Consequently

$$V_t(y_{t+s}) - E_t(V_{t+1}(y_{t+s})) = \theta_{s-1}^2 \sigma_{t+1}^2$$

and (4.16) becomes

$$p_t = r^{-1}E_t(p_{t+1}) - \delta r^{-s}\theta_{s-1}^2\sigma_{t+1}^2$$

which is the familiar formula for a one-period holding yield with the explicit calculation of the effect of the changing variance of y_{t+s} for a risk averse agent.

In this simple model the only source of uncertainty derives from the future spot price to which the contract relates. In many other situations, however, there is a flow of uncertain distributions which accrue to the owner of the asset: for example, the price of a share is determined by the present discounted value of the expected dividend stream. The precise form in which the variability of future payoffs enters the asset pricing formulation will depend, amongst other things, on the utility function of the agents and the intertemporal substitutability of the payouts. A simple formulation might be

$$p_t = \sum_{s=1}^{\infty} r^{-s}\left(E_t(y_{t+s}) - \delta V_t(y_{t+s})\right)$$

where $\{y_t\}_{t+1}^{\infty}$ is the future income stream generated by the asset. If y_t again follows the process (4.17), this pricing equation can be converted to the holding yield expression

$$p_t = r^{-1}\left(E_t(p_{t+1}) + E_t(y_{t+1}) - \delta\lambda\sigma_{t+1}^2\right)$$

where λ depends upon $\theta(B)$ and r.

It is thus clear that, if $\delta \neq 0$, the conditional variance of y_t in the future will affect the price of the asset today. If such variances can be forecast as in a GARCH process, then the current information on y_t and the current conditional variance will have an effect on the current price. The size of the effect, however, will depend upon the persistence of the variance, i.e., on how important current information is in predicting future variances.

A closed-form solution to the simple asset pricing formula (4.15) depends upon the process assumed to generate the 'forcing variable' y_t. Suppose y_t is a random walk with innovations that follow an IGARCH(1,1) process. Then $E_t(y_{t+s}) = y_t$ and

$$V_t(y_{t+s}) = E_t\left(\sum\nolimits_{i=1}^{s} \varepsilon_{t+i}^2\right) = E_t\left(\sum\nolimits_{i=1}^{s} \sigma_{t+i}^2\right) = s\sigma_{t+1}^2$$

so that

$$p_t = r^{-s}\left(y_t - \delta s\sigma_{t+1}^2\right)$$

For a future contract where no money changes hands until the terminal date $t+s$, the risk-free rate of return is zero so that $r = 1$, i.e., the solution simplifies to

$$p_t = y_t - \delta s\sigma_{t+1}^2$$

If $\delta \neq 0$ there will be a time-varying risk premium in the future contract. For contracts far in the future, new information will have a substantial effect on asset prices as it changes agents' perceptions of the variance of the final payoff as well as all the intermediate variances. This persistence gives time-varying risk premia even for contracts many periods into the future and thus implies sizeable effects on asset prices.

Alternatively, suppose that the random walk innovations to y_t are serially independent with constant variance σ^2. In this case $V_t(y_{t+s}) = s\sigma^2$ and the solution to (4.15) is

$$p_t = y_t - \delta s\sigma^2$$

so that, although the variance of the spot price enters the pricing equation, it does not give rise to a time-varying risk premium since new information casts no light on future uncertainty.

Finally, consider an intermediate case where the innovations are GARCH(1,1) such that $\alpha_1 + \beta_1 < 1$. The unconditional variance will be $\sigma^2 = \alpha_0/(1 - \alpha_1 - \beta_1)$ and it is easy to show that

$$E_t(\sigma_{t+s}^2 - \sigma^2) = (\alpha_1 + \beta_1)^{s-1}(\sigma_{t+1}^2 - \sigma^2)$$

and

$$V_t(y_{t+s}) = \sum_{i=1}^{s}(\sigma^2 + E_t(\sigma_{t+i}^2 - \sigma^2)) = s\sigma^2 + (\sigma_{t+1}^2 - \sigma^2)\left(\frac{1 - (\alpha_1 + \beta_1)^s}{1 - \alpha_1 - \beta_1}\right)$$

Substituting into (4.15), the solution of the future contract is

$$p_t = y_t - \delta s\sigma^2 + \delta(\sigma_{t+1}^2 - \sigma^2)\left(\frac{1 - (\alpha_1 + \beta_1)^s}{1 - \alpha_1 - \beta_1}\right)$$

Current information, embodied in the term $\sigma_{t+1}^2 - \sigma^2$, continues to be an important part of the time-varying risk premium even for large s but, in contrast to the solution for the IGARCH(1,1) model, where $\alpha_1 + \beta_1 = 1$, its importance decreases with the length of the contract.

These examples thus establish that a solution to an asset pricing equation depends in a crucial way on the distribution of the forcing variable, y_t, in particular on its conditional variance, which is naturally modelled as an ARCH process.

We should also note that, analogous to stochastic variance models being discrete approximations to continuous time option valuation models that use diffusion processes, ARCH models can also approximate a wide range of stochastic differential equations. This was first shown by Nelson (1990b) and further developments are contained in, for example, Nelson and Foster (1994), Drost and Nijman (1993), and Drost and Werker (1996). Further analysis of the predictive aspects of ARMA-ARCH models is developed in Baillie and Bollerslev (1992). The survey by Bollerslev, Chou and Kroner (1992) focuses on the application of ARCH models to stock return and interest rate data, emphasising the use of ARCH to model volatility persistence, and to foreign exchange rate data, where the characterisation of exchange rate movements have important implications for many issues in international finance.

Example 4.2 GARCH models for the dollar/sterling exchange rate

Table 4.1 presents the results of fitting various AR(1)–GARCH(p,q) models to the first differences of the dollar/sterling exchange rate, x_t. The choice of an AR(1) model for the conditional mean equation is based on our findings from examples 2.5 and 3.1. Assuming homoskedasticity, i.e., GARCH(0,0), produces the estimates in the first column of table 4.1. The ARCH(12) statistic, the LM test for 12th-order ARCH, shows that there is strong evidence of conditional heteroskedasticity and, as eight of the twelve lag coefficients in the autoregression of the squared residuals are significant, a GARCH formulation is suggested. Not surprisingly, the residuals are highly non-normal, being fat tailed and asymmetric.

Table 4.1. *Dollar/sterling exchange rate: QML estimates,* $x_t \sim$ AR(1) – ARCH(p, q)

	GARCH(0,0)	GARCH(1,1)	GARCH(2,1)	GARCH(1,2)
$\tilde{\Phi}_1$	0.0710 (5.13)	0.0777 (5.34)	0.0754 (4.19)	0.0700 (3.88)
$\tilde{\alpha}_0$	–	7.32 (2.13)	5.44 (1.63)	9.20 (1.87)
$\tilde{\alpha}_1$	–	0.0981 (5.95)	0.1365 (3.49)	0.1480 (5.01)
$\tilde{\alpha}_2$	–	–	−0.0476 (1.03)	–
$\tilde{\beta}_1$	–	0.9075 (63.6)	0.9161 (53.4)	0.4378 (2.76)
$\tilde{\beta}_2$	–	–	–	0.4233 (3.00)
$\Sigma(\tilde{\alpha}_i + \tilde{\beta}_i)$	–	1.0056	1.0050	1.0091
ARCH(12)	240.3 [0.00]	16.8 [0.16]	12.6 [0.40]	11.7 [0.47]
Skewness	−0.23	−0.07	−0.02	−0.04
Kurtosis	6.48	7.75	8.02	7.68
Normality	2666	4885	5461	4739
Log-L	15935.23	16390.38	16394.63	16394.88
L_1	0.000454	0.000444	0.000444	0.000446
L_2	29325.67	26406.22	26385.32	26376.15

Notes: Figures in ( ) are robust t-statistics; figures in [ ] are prob-values. Under the null of strict white-noise normally distributed standardised residuals, *skewness* should be $N(0, 0.083)$ and *kurtosis* should be $N(3, 0.333)$. *Normality* is the Jarque-Bera (1980) statistic testing for normality and is distributed as χ^2_2 under the above null (see chapter 6 for details). *Log-L* is the log likelihood. L_1 and L_2 are loss functions described in the text. Estimation was performed in *EVIEWS* using the BHHH algorithm. Estimates of α_0 are scaled by 10^{-7}.

A GARCH(1,1) conditional variance is fitted in the second column. As the standardised residuals are now symmetric, although fat tailed, these QML estimates should have reasonable properties. Nevertheless, the t-ratios are computed using the Bollerslev and Wooldridge (1992) robust standard errors. Both GARCH parameters are significant, and the LM test for any neglected ARCH is insignificant. Note that the GARCH parameters sum to just over unity, suggesting an IGARCH formulation. The third and fourth columns investigate neglected ARCH via overfitting. The alternative models are compared in three ways, by their log likelihoods and by two loss criteria suggested by Pagan and Schwert (1990a) and Bollerslev *et al.* (1994), respectively

$$L_1 = \sum_{t=1}^{T} \left(\varepsilon_t^2 - \sigma_t^2\right)^2$$

and

$$L_2 = \sum_{t=1}^{T} \left(\log\left(\varepsilon_t^2 / \sigma_t^2\right)\right)^2$$

These show that, on balance, a GARCH(1,2) specification produces a marginally better fit. The conditional standard deviations from this model are shown in figure 4.2. A comparison with the volatility series from the SV model fitted in example 4.1, shown in figure 4.1, reveals a close similarity. This is not surprising, since an SV model with an approx-

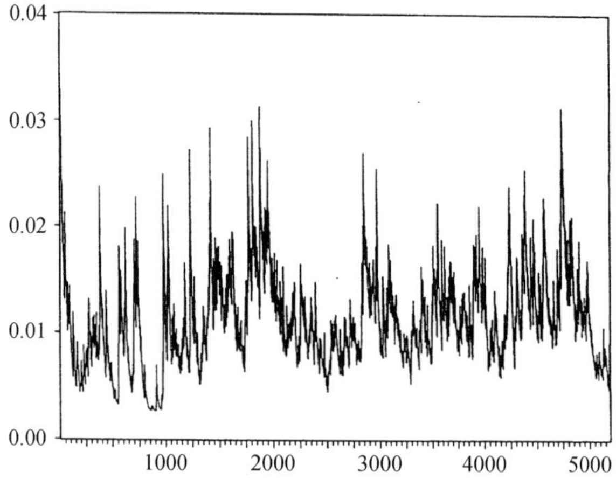

Figure 4.2 Conditional standard deviations from GARCH(1,2) model

imate random walk conditional variance equation will fit similarly to an IGARCH(1,1) model, which we effectively have here.

A variety of non-linear GARCH variants were also entertained. Noting that the EGARCH model (4.8) can be written as

$$\log(\sigma_t^2) = \alpha + \alpha_1 |\varepsilon_{t-1}/\sigma_{t-1}| + \gamma\varepsilon_{t-1}/\sigma_{t-1} + \beta_1 \log(\sigma_{t-1}^2)$$

where $\alpha = \alpha_0 - \alpha_1\sqrt{2/\pi}$ and $\gamma = \alpha_1\theta_1$, BHHH estimation in *EVIEWS* obtained, with Bollerslev and Wooldridge robust t-statistics

$$x_t = \underset{(3.36)}{0.0579}\, x_{t-1} + \varepsilon_t$$

$$\log(\sigma_t^2) = -\underset{(6.08)}{14.76} + \underset{(2.12)}{0.104} |\varepsilon_{t-1}/\sigma_{t-1}| - \underset{(0.47)}{0.016}\, \varepsilon_{t-1}/\sigma_{t-1} - \underset{(2.31)}{0.624} \log(\sigma_{t-1}^2)$$

$\tilde{\gamma}$ is insignificantly different from zero, so there does not appear to be any asymmetric news effect. Moreover, the LM test for neglected conditional heteroskedasticity is ARCH(12) = 208.6 and *LogL* = 15971.70, so that this model is inferior to the GARCH specifications. Both TARCH and component GARCH models produced similarly inferior fits, but the combined model did prove to be marginally superior

$$x_t = \underset{(4.21)}{0.0712}\, x_{t-1} + \varepsilon_t$$

$$q_t = \underset{(1.23)}{0.00021} + \underset{(292)}{0.996}(q_{t-1} - 0.00021) + \underset{(4.68)}{0.074}\, (\varepsilon_{t-1}^2 - \sigma_{t-1}^2)$$

$$\sigma_t^2 - q_t = \underset{(0.71)}{0.031}\, (\varepsilon_{t-1}^2 - q_{t-1}) + \underset{(2.36)}{0.127}\, I(\varepsilon_{t-1} < 0) \cdot (\varepsilon_{t-1}^2 - q_{t-1})$$
$$+ \underset{(0.98)}{0.243}\, (\sigma_{t-1}^2 - q_{t-1})$$

The long-run component q_t converges to its long-run level of 0.00021 very slowly (with powers of 0.996), while the transitory component is only influenced significantly by previous 'bad news', so that there is some evidence of a leverage effect. For this model ARCH(12) = 10.2 and *LogL* = 16401.87.

Example 4.3 GARCH models for S&P 500 daily returns

In this example we again analyse the daily returns (logarithmic first differences) of the S&P 500 index from January 1928 to August 1991, first looked at in example 3.7. Ding, Granger and Engle (1993) initially fitted an MA(1)–GARCH(1,1) model to the returns, x_t. We find that the MA(1)–GARCH(1,2) model provides a slightly better fit

$$x_t = \underset{(6.38)}{0.00045} + \varepsilon_t + \underset{(16.8)}{0.146}\, \varepsilon_{t-1}$$

$$\sigma_t^2 = \underset{(7.04)}{1.49 \times 10^{-6}} + \underset{(10.0)}{0.152}\, \varepsilon_{t-1}^2 + \underset{(3.72)}{0.397}\, \sigma_{t-1}^2 + \underset{(4.58)}{0.445}\, \sigma_{t-2}^2$$

$$LogL = 56825;\ \mathrm{ARCH}(12) = 12.4$$

The GARCH parameters sum to 0.994, indicating IGARCH behaviour. The model can, nevertheless, be improved upon. The TARCH extension is

$$x_t = \underset{(3.34)}{0.00023} + \varepsilon_t + \underset{(17.6)}{0.149}\, \varepsilon_{t-1}$$

$$\sigma_t^2 = \underset{(7.25)}{1.58 \times 10^{-6}} + \underset{(5.55)}{0.063}\, \varepsilon_{t-1}^2 + \underset{(7.04)}{0.150}\, I(\varepsilon_{t-1} < 0) \cdot \varepsilon_{t-1}^2$$

$$+ \underset{(4.15)}{0.383}\, \sigma_{t-1}^2 + \underset{(5.57)}{0.470}\, \sigma_{t-2}^2$$

with $LogL = 56935$, while the EGARCH variant is

$$x_t = \underset{(2.54)}{0.00017} + \varepsilon_t + \underset{(16.3)}{0.139}\, \varepsilon_{t-1}$$

$$\sigma_t^2 = -\underset{(9.77)}{0.330} + \underset{(10.6)}{0.230} \left| \varepsilon_{t-1}/\sigma_{t-1} \right| - \underset{(5.72)}{0.096}\, \varepsilon_{t-1}/\sigma_{t-1}$$

$$+ \underset{(3.96)}{0.403}\, \sigma_{t-1}^2 + \underset{(5.76)}{0.580}\, \sigma_{t-2}^2$$

with $LogL = 56961$. Both models provide a significant leverage effect, with 'bad news', $\varepsilon_{t-1} < 0$, increasing volatility more than 'good news', and they also show more volatility persistence than the conventional GARCH model.

Ding *et al.* (1993) provide yet a further model, extending the TARCH model to the *asymmetric Power* ARCH (APARCH), estimated as

$$x_t = 0.00021 + \varepsilon_t + 0.145\,\varepsilon_{t-1}$$

$$\sigma_t^{1.43} = 0.000014 + 0.083\left(|\varepsilon_{t-1}| - 0.373\varepsilon_{t-1}\right)^{1.43} + 0.920\sigma_t^{1.43}$$

t-ratios are not provided as Ding *et al.* do not report robust statistics, but the model has $LogL = 56974$, which is a significant improvement on the previous models. Note that rather than σ_t being raised to either the power 1 (the conditional standard deviation model; see (4.7)), or the power 2 (the traditional conditional variance model), the estimated power coefficient is 1.43, which Ding *et al.* find is significantly different from either. Nevertheless, the leverage effect remains significant.

4.5 Other non-linear univariate models

4.5.1 Bilinear processes

An important class of non-linear model is the *bilinear*, which takes the general form

$$\phi(B)(x_t - \mu) = \theta(B)\varepsilon_t + \sum_{i=1}^{R}\sum_{j=1}^{S} \gamma_{ij} x_{t-i}\varepsilon_{t-j} \tag{4.18}$$

where $\varepsilon_t \sim SWN(0, \sigma_\varepsilon^2)$. The second term on the right-hand side of (4.18) is a bilinear form in ε_{t-j} and x_{t-i}, and this accounts for the non-linear character of the model: if all the γ_{ij} are zero, (4.18) reduces to the familiar ARMA model.

Little analysis has been carried out on this general bilinear form, but Granger and Andersen (1978) have analysed the properties of several simple bilinear forms, characterised as

$$x_t = \varepsilon_t + \gamma_{ij} x_{t-i}\varepsilon_{t-j}$$

If $i > j$ the model is called superdiagonal, if $i = j$ it is diagonal, and if $i < j$ it is subdiagonal. If we define $\lambda = \gamma_{ij}\sigma$, then for superdiagonal models, x_t has zero mean and variance $\sigma^2/(1 - \lambda^2)$, so that $|\lambda| < 1$ is a necessary condition for stability. Conventional identification techniques using the

SACF of x_t would identify this series as white noise, but Granger and Andersen show that, in theory at least, the SACF of the squares of x_t would identify x_t^2 as an ARMA(i, j) process, so that we could distinguish between white noise and this bilinear model by analysing x_t^2.

Diagonal models will also be stationary if $|\lambda| < 1$. If $i = j = 1$, x_t will be identified as MA(1), with $0 < \rho_1 < 0.1547$ (corresponding to $\lambda = \pm 0.605$), while x_t^2 will be identified as ARMA(1,1). However, if x_t actually was MA(1), then x_t^2 will also be MA(1), so that this result allows the bilinear model to be distinguished from the linear model. In general, the levels of a diagonal model will be identified as MA(i).

Subdiagonal models are essentially similar to superdiagonal models in that they appear to be white noise but generally have x_t^2 following an ARMA(i, j) process. Detailed analysis of the properties of bilinear models can be found in Granger and Andersen (1978), Subba Rao (1981), Subba Rao and Gabr (1984), and Guégan (1987). Most of the results are of considerable theoretical interest but are of little relevance in practice: for example, most of the conditions for stationarity and invertibility are too complicated to be used as constraints on the parameters in actual models.

4.5.2 A comparison of ARCH and bilinearity

Weiss (1986b) provides a detailed comparison of the ARMA–ARCH model, given by equations (4.12) and (4.13), and the bilinear model (4.18). At first sight, the models appear quite different: whereas the addition of the ARCH equation to the pure ARMA process (4.12) introduces non-linearity by affecting the conditional variance, the addition of the bilinear terms contained in (4.18) changes the *conditional mean* of x_t. Weiss argues that, despite these different influences, the two processes can have similar properties and, for example, the bilinear process may be mistaken for an ARMA model with ARCH errors.

Why might this be? Suppose the true model for x_t is (4.18) but the ARMA model

$$\tilde{\phi}(B)(x_t - \tilde{\mu}) = \tilde{\theta}(B)\tilde{\varepsilon}_t$$

is fitted. The residual $\tilde{\varepsilon}_t$ is given by

$$\tilde{\varepsilon}_t = \vartheta_1(B)\varepsilon_t + \vartheta_2(B)\sum_{i=1}^{R}\sum_{j=1}^{S}\gamma_{ij}x_{t-i}\varepsilon_{t-j}$$

where $\vartheta_1(B) = \phi^{-1}(B)\tilde{\theta}^{-1}(B)\tilde{\phi}(B)\theta(B)$ and $\vartheta_2(B) = \tilde{\phi}^{-1}(B)\tilde{\theta}^{-1}(B)\phi(B)$. On squaring this expression and taking conditional expectations, it is clear that $E(\tilde{\varepsilon}_t^2|x_{t-1}, x_{t-2}, \ldots)$ is not constant but will be a function of lagged ε_t^2, and hence may be thought to have ARCH. For example, suppose the true model is

$$x_t = \varepsilon_t + \gamma_{21} x_{t-1} \varepsilon_{t-1} \tag{4.19}$$

As $E(x_t) = 0$ and $E(x_t x_{t+i}) = 0, i > 0$, the use of traditional modelling techniques may identify the trivial ARMA model $x_t = \tilde{\varepsilon}_t$, where

$$\tilde{\varepsilon}_t = \varepsilon_t + \gamma_{21} \varepsilon_{t-1} \tilde{\varepsilon}_{t-1}$$

Squaring this and taking expectations gives

$$E(\tilde{\varepsilon}_t^2|x_{t-1}, x_{t-2}, \ldots) = \sigma_\varepsilon^2 + \gamma_{21}^2 \sigma_\varepsilon^2 \tilde{\varepsilon}_{t-1}^2$$

Now, the LM statistic for testing whether $\tilde{\varepsilon}_t$ is ARCH(1) is $T \cdot R^2$ from the regression of $\tilde{\varepsilon}_t^2$ on a constant and $\tilde{\varepsilon}_{t-1}^2$: given the above expectation, such a statistic may well be large even if the correct model is really the bilinear process (4.19).

The correct LM statistic for testing $x_t = \tilde{\varepsilon}_t$ against the bilinear alternative (4.19) is, in fact, $T \cdot R^2$ from the regression of $\tilde{\varepsilon}_t$ on a constant, $\tilde{\varepsilon}_{t-1}$ and $\tilde{\varepsilon}_{t-1}^2$. In general, if $\phi(B)$ and $\theta(B)$ in (4.18) are of orders P and Q respectively, then the LM statistic for testing (4.18) against the simple linear ARMA specification (4.12) is $T \cdot R^2$ from the regression of $\tilde{\varepsilon}_t$ on a constant, $x_{t-1}, \ldots, x_{t-P}, \tilde{\varepsilon}_{t-1}, \ldots, \tilde{\varepsilon}_{t-Q}$, and $x_{t-i}\tilde{\varepsilon}_{t-j}$, $i = 1, \ldots, R$, $j = 1, \ldots, S$; the statistic being distributed as χ_{RS}^2. Weiss shows, however, that such a test will not have the correct size if, in fact, ARCH is present as well: nor, indeed, will the LM test for ARCH if bilinearity is present.

Weiss (1986b) shows that LS and ML estimates of the bilinear model (4.18) coincide. However, although estimation of a bilinear model is straightforward, identification of that model can pose difficulties, particularly when, as we have seen, both bilinearity and ARCH are present and one can be confused with the other.

Weiss thus considers the combined bilinear model with ARCH errors, i.e., the bilinear process (4.18) with the ARCH specification (4.13). The identification of this model is based on the relative difficulties introduced by the different specification errors. First, ignoring bilinearity can lead to residuals appearing to have ARCH even though they may not be autocorrelated. On the other hand, misspecifying the ARCH will affect the variance of a process but not the specification of the mean equation. Given the greater complexity of bilinear models and the difficulties faced in their specification, this suggests that it is easier to mistake bilinearity for ARCH than vice versa. Weiss thus suggests that the bilinear model should be specified before ARCH is considered explicitly.

The suggested procedure is to use the SACFs of x_t^2, $\tilde{\varepsilon}_t$ and $\tilde{\varepsilon}_t^2$ and associated LM tests to specify the bilinear process after a pure ARMA model has been identified and fitted by conventional techniques. The SACFs, which do not allow for ARCH, will suggest possible bilinear specifications or extra bilinear terms, and the formal tests, which do allow for ARCH, can then be used to determine which specifications are appropriate. However, because we wish to test for bilinearity in the possible presence of ARCH, the LM test, although not requiring the actual form of ARCH, nevertheless does not have a $T \cdot R^2$ representation: the exact form, derived in Weiss (1986b), is

$$\left(\sum \tilde{\varepsilon}_t \frac{\partial \varepsilon_t}{\partial \Lambda}\right)' \left(\sum \tilde{\varepsilon}_t^2 \frac{\partial \varepsilon_t}{\partial \Lambda} \frac{\partial \varepsilon_t}{\partial \Lambda'}\right) \left(\sum \tilde{\varepsilon}_t \frac{\partial \varepsilon_t}{\partial \Lambda}\right)$$

where Λ contains both the ARMA and bilinear parameters.

Once the bilinearity has been determined, the ARCH equation can be specified using the ACF of the squared residuals obtained from the estimation of the bilinear model. Estimation of the combined model then follows, and overfitting and LM tests for extra ARCH or bilinear parameters can be undertaken.

Since the LM test for bilinearity in the presence of ARCH does not have the usual $T \cdot R^2$ form, and because the subsequent ARCH test requires first estimating a bilinear model, this procedure is rather burdensome if we just want a simple test for non-linearity which is sensitive to both ARCH and bilinear alternatives. Higgins and Bera (1988) thus propose an easily computed simultaneous test for a joint ARCH and bilinear alternative. This is an LM test whose construction exploits the result that the individual LM tests for ARCH and bilinearity are additive: the joint test statistic is thus the sum of the individual test statistics. Moreover, because the two forms of non-linearity are considered simultaneously, the LM test for bilinearity again has the standard $T \cdot R^2$ representation, being the test outlined above. Hence the combined test statistic will be distributed as χ^2_{RS+p}.

Maravall (1983) considers an alternative form of bilinearity in which x_t is given by the ARMA process

$$\phi(B)(x_t - \mu) = \theta(B)a_t$$

but where the *uncorrelated* sequence $\{a_t\}$ is bilinear in a_t and the strict white-noise sequence $\{\varepsilon_t\}$:

$$a_t = \varepsilon_t + \sum_{i=1}^{R}\sum_{j=1}^{S}\gamma_{ij}a_{t-i}\varepsilon_{t-j}$$

This may be interpreted as a bilinear model 'forecasting white noise'.

How useful are bilinear models in modelling financial time series? De Gooijer (1989) presents evidence to suggest that such processes can provide useful models for certain daily stock return series, although the residual variance of the bilinear models were usually only marginally smaller than those obtained from alternative linear models.

Example 4.4 Is the dollar/sterling exchange rate bilinear?

Given the above discussion, is it possible that the GARCH model fitted to the dollar/sterling exchange rate in example 4.2 is a misspecification and the true process generating the series is of bilinear form? An obvious way to proceed is to consider the SACFs and PACFs of the differences and squared differences. Recall that in example 2.5 it was found that the only significant sample autocorrelation for x_t was the first, which is consistent with an MA(1) process, although an AR(1) provided a slightly better fit. For x_t^2, the first twelve sample autocorrelations are significant, as are the first seven partial autocorrelations, which suggests that an ARMA(1,1) process could be appropriate. This pair of findings is consistent with a diagonal bilinear model with $R = S = 1$. The LM test for such bilinearity obtained from regressing the MA(1) residuals, $\tilde{\varepsilon}_t$, on $\tilde{\varepsilon}_{t-1}$ and $x_{t-1}\tilde{\varepsilon}_{t-1}$ produced a $T \cdot R^2$ of just 0.26, distributed as χ_1^2, thus indicating no evidence in favour of bilinearity. Of course, this statistic is only strictly valid in the absence of ARCH, which we know exists (see table 4.1). Construction of the ARCH adjusted statistic produced a value of only 0.48, however, confirming the absence of bilinearity.

Example 4.5 Modelling IBM stock prices as a combined bilinear and ARCH process

The daily closing price for IBM common stock for the 169 trading days starting 17 May 1961, presented as part of series B in Box and Jenkins (1976) and plotted as figure 4.3, has been investigated by various researchers (see, in particular, Weiss, 1986b). Conventional (linear)

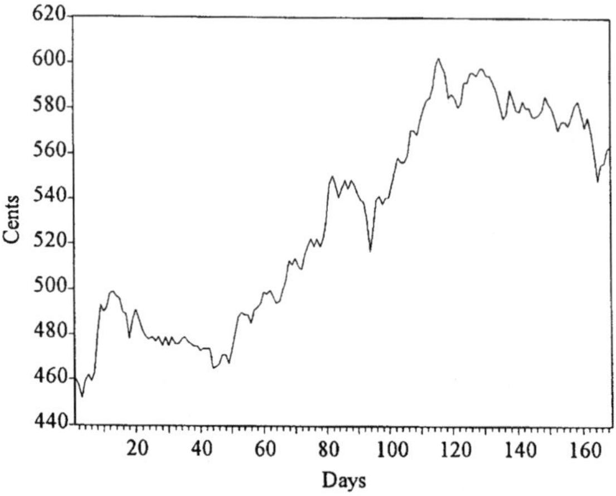

Figure 4.3 IBM common stock price (daily from 17 May 1961)

identification procedures suggest that the differences of the series, denoted x_t, follow an MA(1) process, LS estimation of which yields

$$x_t = \tilde{\varepsilon}_t - 0.26\tilde{\varepsilon}_{t-1}, \quad \sigma^2_{\tilde{\varepsilon}} = 24.8, \quad r_{1,\tilde{\varepsilon}} = -0.02, \quad r_{1,\tilde{\varepsilon}^2} = 0.18$$

An LM test for ARCH(1) errors, ignoring the possibility of bilinearity, yields a $T \cdot R^2$ statistic of 15.1, which is clearly significant (note that this confirms the evidence of non-linearity provided by the lag one autocorrelation of $\tilde{\varepsilon}^2_t$). Tests for first-order diagonal bilinearity yield values of 7.9 and 8.1, the latter being corrected for first-order ARCH. Incorporating an ARCH(1) error specification yields, on ML estimation

$$x_t = \varepsilon_t - 0.24\varepsilon_{t-1}, \quad \sigma^2_{\varepsilon} = 24.8, \quad r_{\varepsilon} = 0.01, \quad r_{1,\varepsilon^2} = 0.02$$

$$\sigma^2 = \underset{(2.6)}{17.9} + \underset{(0.12)}{0.28}\ \varepsilon^2_{t-1}$$

and then including bilinear terms produces either

$$x_t = \varepsilon_t - \underset{(0.08)}{0.24}\ \varepsilon_{t-1} + \underset{(0.010)}{0.023}\ x_{t-1}\varepsilon_{t-1}, \qquad \sigma^2_{\varepsilon} = 23.7$$

$$\sigma^2 = \underset{(2.6)}{18.3} + \underset{(0.11)}{0.23}\ \varepsilon^2_{t-1}$$

or

$$x_t = a_t - \underset{(0.08)}{0.23}\, a_{t-1}, \qquad \sigma_a^2 = 23.7$$

$$a_t = \varepsilon_t + \underset{(0.010)}{0.023}\, a_{t-1}\varepsilon_{t-1}$$

$$\sigma^2 = \underset{(2.6)}{18.3} + \underset{(0.11)}{0.23}\, \varepsilon_{t-1}^2$$

The bilinear terms are significant and their introduction decreases the estimate of the ARCH parameter somewhat. Note that the mean equation for the second model can be written as

$$x_t = \varepsilon_t - 0.23\varepsilon_{t-1} + 0.023x_{t-1}\varepsilon_{t-1} - 0.005(a_{t-2}\varepsilon_{t-1} - a_{t-2}\varepsilon_{t-2})$$

so that it is no surprise that the fit of the two models are virtually identical. The same specification is also arrived at if a bilinear process is first fitted after tests for bilinearity on the original MA(1) model are performed.

4.5.3 State dependent and related models

Using the concept of 'Volterra expansions', Priestley (1980, 1988) shows that a general relationship between x_t and ε_t can be represented as

$$x_t = f(x_{t-1}, \ldots, x_{t-p}, \varepsilon_{t-1}, \ldots, \varepsilon_{t-q}) \tag{4.20}$$

If $f(\,)$ is assumed analytic, the right-hand side of (4.20) can be expanded in a Taylor's series expansion about an arbitrary but fixed time point, allowing the relationship to be written as the State Dependent Model (SDM) of order (p, q)

$$x_t - \sum_{i=1}^{p} \phi_i(\mathbf{x}_{t-1})x_{t-i} = \mu(\mathbf{x}_{t-1}) + \sum_{i=1}^{q} \theta_i(\mathbf{x}_{t-1})\varepsilon_{t-i} \tag{4.21}$$

where $\mathbf{x}_t$ denotes the state vector

$$\mathbf{x}_t = (x_t, \ldots, x_{t-p+1}, \varepsilon_t, \ldots, \varepsilon_{t-q+1})$$

Priestley (1980, p. 54) remarks that this model has the interpretation of a locally linear ARMA model in which the evolution of the process at time $t-1$ is governed by a set of AR coefficients, $\{\phi_i(\cdot)\}$, a set of MA coefficients, $\{\theta_i(\cdot)\}$, and a local 'mean', $\mu(\cdot)$, all of which depend on the 'state' of the process at time $t-1$.

If $\mu(\cdot)$, $\{\phi_i(\cdot)\}$ and $\{\theta_i(\cdot)\}$ are all taken as constants, i.e., as independent of $\mathbf{x}_{t-1}$, (4.21) reduces to the usual ARMA(p, q) model. Moreover, if only $\mu(\cdot)$ and $\{\phi_i(\cdot)\}$ are taken as constants but we set

$$\theta_i(\mathbf{x}_{t-1}) = \theta_i + \sum\nolimits_{j=1}^{p} \gamma_{ij} x_{t-j}, \qquad i = 1, ..., q$$

then the SDM reduces to the bilinear model (4.18), with $R = p$ and $S = q$.

The SDM class of non-linear models can also be shown to include the *threshold AR* model (Tong and Lim, 1980), the *exponential AR* model (Haggan and Ozaki, 1981), and various other non-linear specifications that have been developed over recent years: for example, a *non-linear AR(1)* model could be

$$x_t = \phi_1 x_{t-1} + \exp\left(-\gamma x_{t-1}^2\right)\phi_2 x_{t-1} + \varepsilon_t$$

Haggan, Heravi and Priestley (1984) provide an extensive study of the application of SDMs to a wide variety of non-linear time series, although they use no financial, or even economic, data.

Various other non-linear models related to the SDM class have been proposed over the years, although relatively few have had much impact in the financial area. Wecker's (1981) *asymmetric ARMA* model, in which x_t responds in a different fashion to an innovation depending on whether the innovation is positive or negative, looked to have potential but does not seem to have become popular, while a related model, Rocke's (1982) 'limited response' model, seems to be unknown in the finance literature.

4.5.4 Regime switching models: Markov chains and STARs

An alternative way of introducing asymmetry is to consider 'regime switching' models. We consider here two of the most popular of these, the two-state Markov model and the smooth transition autoregression. Hamilton (1989, 1990), Engle and Hamilton (1990) and Lam (1990) propose variants of a switching-regime Markov model, which can be regarded as a non-linear extension of an ARMA process that can accommodate complicated dynamics, such as asymmetry and conditional heteroskedasticity. The setup is that of the UC model developed in chapter 3.2, i.e.

$$x_t = z_t + u_t \tag{4.22}$$

where again z_t is a non-stationary random walk component, but where its drift now evolves according to a two-state Markov process

$$z_t = \mu(S_t) + z_{t-1} = \alpha_0 + \alpha_1 S_t + z_{t-1} \tag{4.23}$$

where

$$\begin{aligned}
P(S_t = 1|S_{t-1} = 1) &= p \\
P(S_t = 0|S_{t-1} = 1) &= 1 - p \\
P(S_t = 1|S_{t-1} = 0) &= 1 - q \\
P(S_t = 0|S_{t-1} = 0) &= q
\end{aligned}$$

The component u_t is assumed to follow an AR(r) process

$$\phi(B)u_t = \varepsilon_t \tag{4.24}$$

where the innovation sequence $\{\varepsilon_t\}$ is strict white noise, but the case when $\phi(B)$ contains a unit root is allowed so that, unlike the conventional UC specification, u_t can be non-stationary. In fact, a special case of the conventional UC model results when $p = 1 - q$: the random walk component then has an innovation restricted to being a two-point random variable, taking the values 0 and 1 with probabilities q and $1 - q$ respectively, rather than a zero mean random variable drawn from a continuous distribution such as the normal.

The stochastic process for S_t is strictly stationary, having the AR(1) representation

$$S_t = (1 - q) + \lambda S_{t-1} + V_t$$

where $\lambda = p + q - 1$ and where the innovation V_t has the conditional probability distribution

$$\begin{aligned}
P(V_t = (1 - p)|S_{t-1} = 1) &= p, \\
P(V_t = -p|S_{t-1} = 1) &= 1 - p, \\
P(V_t = -(1 - q)|S_{t-1} = 0) &= q, \\
P(V_t = q|S_{t-1} = 0) &= 1 - q
\end{aligned}$$

This innovation is uncorrelated with lagged values of S_t for

$$E(V_t|S_{t-j}=1)=E(V_t|S_{t-j}=0)=0 \text{ for } j\geq 1$$

but it is not independent of such lagged values, since, for example

$$E(V_t^2|S_{t-1}=1)=p(1-p),$$

$$E(V_t^2|S_{t-1}=0)=q(1-q).$$

The variance of the Markov process can be shown to be

$$\alpha_1^2\frac{(1-p)(1-q)}{(2-p-q)^2}$$

As this variance approaches zero, i.e., as p and q approach unity, so the random walk component (4.23) approaches a deterministic trend. If $\phi(B)$ contains no unit roots, x_t will thus approach a TS process, whereas if $\phi(B)$ does contain a unit root, x_t approaches a DS process.

Given $\{x_t\}_0^T$, ML estimates of the model are obtained by first expressing (4.22) as

$$u_t=u_{t-1}-x_t-x_{t-1}-\alpha_0-\alpha_1 S_t$$

and solving backwards in time to yield

$$u_t=x_t-x_0-\alpha_0 t-\alpha_1\sum\nolimits_{i=1}^{t}S_i+u_0 \tag{4.25}$$

Using (4.24) and (4.25), the innovations ε_t can be expressed as

$$\varepsilon_t=\phi(B)(x_t-x_0-\alpha_0 t)+\phi(1)u_0-\alpha_1\phi(1)\sum_{i=1}^{t}S_i+\alpha_1\sum_{j=1}^{r}\left(\sum_{k=j}^{r}\phi_k\right)S_{t-j+1}$$

Assuming that the innovations are normal, this expression can be utilised to calculate the log likelihood function on noting that this can be decomposed as the sum of the conditional (on past observations) log likelihoods. These conditional log likelihoods depend on unobserved current and past realisations of the Markov states. A recursive relationship can be shown to hold between the conditional distribution of the states and the conditional likelihood of the observations and this can be exploited to obtain an algorithm for evaluating the log likelihood function. Inferences about the unobserved components and states are then obtained as byproducts of this evaluation: details of the algorithm may be found in Hamilton (1989) and Lam (1990).

Example 4.6 Are there long swings in the dollar/sterling exchange rate?

In this example, inspired by Engel and Hamilton (1990), we fit a two-state Markov process to quarterly observations on the dollar/sterling exchange rate from 1972I to 1996IV and, in the spirit of Engel and Hamilton, ask whether the series is characterised by 'long swings', i.e., as a sequence of stochastic segmented trends.

This exchange rate is close to being a driftless random walk, so that the differences are approximately white noise, but not strict white noise, as they are conditionally heteroskedastic. We thus fitted the two-state Markov model, with $\phi(B) = (1 - B)$, to the series using Hamilton's (1990) EM algorithm (see also Engle and Hamilton, 1990). The differences are thus given by

$$\Delta x_t = \alpha_0 + \alpha_1 S_t + \varepsilon_t$$

which can equivalently be interpreted as a model in which Δx_t is assumed to be drawn from a $N(\mu_0, \sigma_0^2)$ distribution when $S_t = 0$ and a $N(\mu_1, \sigma_1^2)$ distribution when $S_t = 1$, where $\mu_0 = \alpha_0$ and $\mu_1 = \alpha_0 + \alpha_1$.

This simple model allows a wide variety of exchange rate behaviour. For example, asymmetry in the persistence of the two regimes can be characterised by μ_0 being large and positive and p being small, so that upward moves are short and sharp, and μ_1 being negative and small and q being large, so that downward moves are drawn out and gradual. If the change in the exchange rate is completely independent of the previous state, then we have a random walk with $p = 1 - q$. The long swings hypothesis can be represented by μ_0 and μ_1 being opposite in sign and p and q both being large.

The following ML estimates were obtained, with standard errors shown in parentheses

$$\hat{\mu}_0 = 2.605\ (0.964), \qquad \hat{\mu}_1 = -3.277\ (1.582),$$
$$\hat{p} = 0.857\ (0.084), \qquad \hat{q} = 0.866\ (0.097),$$
$$\hat{\sigma}_0^2 = 13.56\ (3.34), \qquad \hat{\sigma}_1^2 = 20.82\ (4.79).$$

The ML estimates associate regime 0 with a 2.61 per cent quarterly rise in sterling and regime 1 with a fall of 3.28 per cent. Figure 4.4 shows the levels of the exchange rate and a plot of the 'smoothed' probability that the process was in regime 0 at each date in the sample. These smoothed probabilities are estimates of the probability that $S_t = 0$ conditional upon the full sample of observations and the ML estimates of the parameters (see Engel and Hamilton, 1990, for further discussion). The dates at which the exchange rate was in an 'upswing', i.e., periods for which these smoothed probabilities are greater than 0.5, are shown as shaded areas.

These estimates show that movements in the exchange rate are indeed characterised by long swings, since the point estimates of p and q are both greater than 0.85 and those of μ_0 and μ_1, as we have seen, are opposite in sign. Hence, once the exchange rate is in a particular regime, it is likely to stay there, although there is an indication that such swings are shorter in the 1990s. The expected length of stay in regime 0 is given by $(1-p)^{-1}=$

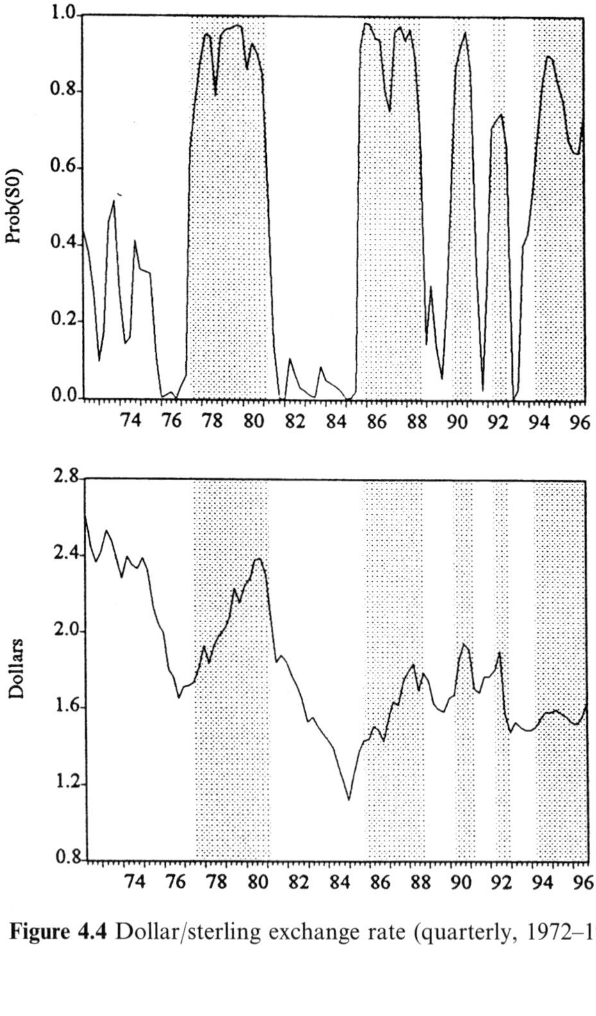

Figure 4.4 Dollar/sterling exchange rate (quarterly, 1972–1996)

7.0 quarters, while that for regime 1 is $(1-q)^{-1} = 7.5$ quarters. Two hypothesis tests are of interest. The first is the random walk (strictly, the martingale) hypothesis that $p = 1 - q$, for which a Wald test, distributed asymptotically as χ_1^2, yields the statistic 26.9, which clearly rejects the null. The second is the hypothesis that the mean appreciation and depreciation rates are the same, i.e., $\mu_0 = -\mu_1$. This produces a Wald statistic of only 0.09 and so clearly cannot be rejected.

The Markov approach assumes that the process can shift randomly and abruptly from one regime to the other. An alternative is to consider a process in which the transition from one regime to the other occurs only once and in a smooth fashion. We have already encountered a model of this type in chapter 3.1.9, the logistic smooth transition (LSTR) trend model, and this idea is easily extended to *smooth transition* AR models, termed STAR models by Teräsvirta (1994). The LSTAR(p) model is defined as

$$x_t = \pi_{10} + \sum\nolimits_{i=1}^{p} \pi_{1i} x_{t-i} + \left(\pi_{20} + \sum\nolimits_{i=1}^{p} \pi_{2i} x_{t-i}\right) \cdot S_{t,d}(\gamma, c) + u_t$$

where $S_{t,d}(\gamma, c) = (1 + \exp(-\gamma(x_{t-d} - c)))^{-1}$ is the smooth transition. An alternative model replaces $S_{t,d}(\gamma, c)$ with $S^*_{t,d}(\gamma^*, c^*) = (1 - \exp(-\gamma^*(x_{t-d} - c^*)^2))$, which is known as the *exponential* STAR (ESTAR) model. Either model can be estimated by NLS for a given value of the delay parameter d, although as Teräsvirta (1994) discusses, obtaining convergence and accurately estimating the 'smoothing' parameter γ or γ^* is not always easy.

Example 4.7 An LSTAR model for UK gilt yields

In this example we fit a smooth transition model to the 20 year UK gilt series, *R*20, used to derive the spread analysed in examples 2.2, 2.4 and 3.1. As *R*20 is $I(1)$, we analyse the differences of the series, $\Delta R20$, whose plot is shown in figure 4.5. The plot shows a pattern of changing variability, so that there is certainly the potential for successfully fitting a non-linear model. Within the class of linear ARMA models, an AR(2) provides an adequate fit

$$\Delta R20_t = \underset{(0.043)}{0.340}\ \Delta R20_{t-1} - \underset{(0.043)}{0.137}\ \Delta R20_{t-2} + e_t$$

$$\hat{\sigma} = 0.315; \quad Q(12) = 9.2; \quad Q^2(12) = 225$$

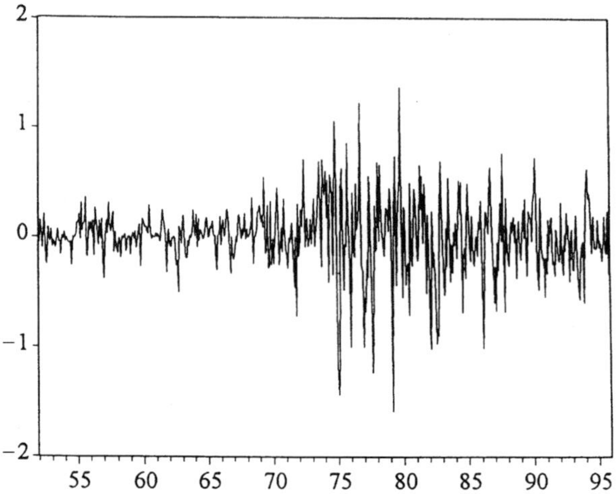

Figure 4.5 20-year gilt yield differences (monthly 1952–1995)

However, the Q^2 statistic, which is a portmanteau statistic using the *squared* residuals (see section 4.4.5), reveals considerable evidence of non-linearity. We thus initially fitted an LSTAR(2) model (with the delay set at $d = 1$), but this did not eliminate the non-linearity and we thus extended the model to a combined LSTAR(2)–GARCH(1,1) process, for which estimation yielded

$$\Delta R20_t = \underset{(0.205)}{0.753}\ \Delta R20_{t-1} - \underset{(0.299)}{0.633}\ \Delta R20_{t-2} + \left(- \underset{(0.211)}{0.511}\ \Delta R20_{t-1} + \underset{(0.301)}{0.585}\ \Delta R20_{t-2} \right) \cdot S_{t,1}\left(\underset{(1868)}{357}, \underset{(0.026)}{-0.834} \right) + \varepsilon_t$$

$$\sigma_t^2 = \underset{(0.00015)}{0.00030} + \underset{(0.015)}{0.061}\ \varepsilon_{t-1}^2 + \underset{(0.013)}{0.938}\ \sigma_{t-1}^2$$

For this model we have $\hat{\sigma} = 0.312$ and $Q^2(12) = 5.6$, so that the GARCH error process successfuly removes the non-linearity but, nevertheless, the smooth transition component enters significantly (the smoothness parameter γ is very imprecisely estimated but, as Teräsvirta (1994) discusses, this is not unusual for such models). The transition is, however, abrupt at a value for $\Delta R20$ of -0.834, with $S_{t,1}(\cdot)$ switching from 0 to 1 at this point. When $S = 0$, which we might refer to as the 'lower' regime, the mean process for $\Delta R20$ is an AR(2) with complex roots $0.38 \pm 0.70i$, having a modulus of 0.80 and a period of 5.8 months. When $S = 1$, the 'upper' regime, the AR(2) process has roots $0.12 \pm 0.18i$ with modulus 0.22 and period of 6.4 months. By way of contrast, the linear AR(2) model has roots $0.17 \pm 0.33i$ with modulus 0.37 and period 5.7 months. Thus, while the periods of the cycles are roughly similar, the lower regime has a cycle with a much greater amplitude than the upper regime. As usual, the GARCH process for the errors is almost integrated, the sum of the coefficients being 0.999.

4.5.5 Neural networks

A currently popular technique of non-linear model building is that of *artificial neural networks* (ANNs), which are data processing systems based loosely on the topology of the brain. They are artificial intelligence techniques that suggest that intelligence can emerge through the interaction of a large number of processing elements connected together, each performing a simple task.

These numerous, simple and highly interconnected elements, called *neurons*, are crude analogs of human brain cells and are organised in at least two layers: the *input* and *output* layers. The input layer has as many neurons as the number of the input variables that we use. The output layer has as many neurons as the variables we wish to forecast. Between the input and output layers there usually exist one or more *hidden layers*. The number of hidden layers and the number of neurons in each are defined manually. They are called hidden layers because they do not communicate with the external environment either by taking in the external input or sending out the system output. They are considered to be 'feature detectors', since they are designed to identify special attributes of the data.

Each hidden and output layer neuron receives messages (numbers) from several other neurons (except for the input layer neurons, which receive messages from only one source, the input variable we provide). Incoming messages do not all have the same significance and effect: these depend on the strength of the association between each of the transmitter neurons and the receiver neuron. This strength of association is expressed by a number, called the *weight of connection* between the two neurons.

Each neuron computes the sum of its inputs and applies to it a simple non-linear mathematical formula, called the *transfer function*. If the result exceeds a certain value (the neuron threshold or activation level) then a single output message (number) is produced, which is multiplied by a weight if it is to be used as an input for other neurons. In this way, there is a separate, adjustable weight for each connection between neurons. The development of a neural network does not require a specific computer program or algorithm, but rather requires the specification of a *network topology* or *architecture* by defining:

The number of input and output neurons
The number of hidden layers
The number of neurons in each hidden layer

After defining the network architecture, the problem is to find the optimal values of the interconnection weights that best describe the relationship between the input and output variables. This is done by a process known as *training* (or learning), which starts with an initial set of random weights and then repeatedly adjusts them so as to minimise the difference between the output produced and the output desired. This difference is measured by a simple formula called the *cost function*.

Training is done on the basis of presented examples of paired input/output patterns from the so-called training set. The most popular and successful method of training is *back-propagation*, where the error at the output layer propagates backwards to the hidden layer(s), until it reaches the input layer. During training, back-propagation adjusts the network weights on the basis of the cost function until a minimum is reached. This optimisation problem is solved using a mathematical technique called *gradient descent*, which searches for the solution where the error is smallest (i.e., steepest descent). The cost function that is most commonly used is the mean squared difference between the output desired and the output produced by the model.

The neural network model described above refers to a widely used paradigm known as the *multi-layer perceptron* (MLP). Although it is only one of many existing ANN types, the MLP has been found to be the most successful and reliable approach to a wide class of problems, including those found in finance. In most cases MLPs are trained using the back-propagation method. In brief, they can be described by the following key characteristics:

Their neurons are organised in *at least three layers*: an input layer, an output layer, and one or more hidden layers.

They are *fully connected*, since all neurons are fully connected between adjacent layers.

They are *feedforward* networks, since all connections point in one direction, from the input towards the output layer. Thus a neuron output cannot go to any neuron in its own layer or to a lower one.

They are *supervised* neural networks, since the user provides examples of both inputs and outputs.

Supervised neural networks 'learn' from examples and experience. If the network is trained too much on the same set of information it becomes 'narrow-minded' and unable to recognise similar patterns. When this situation, called *overtraining* (or overfitting), occurs then a network performs worse instead of better after a certain point during training. This is because extensive training may result in the network memorising rather than learning the training patterns, including all their peculiarities and the noise that surrounds them. An overtrained network has poor *generalisation* abilities, i.e., the ability to recognise examples not seen during training. Memorising exactly the examples of the training set makes the generalisation properties of the network worse since it should only learn the general, abstract structure of the examples.

A common procedure when training a neural network is to divide the data into a *training set*, a *cross-validation set*, and a *test set*. The training set is used to estimate the neural network weights. As the network is learning the training set its performance is also monitored on the cross-validation set. Finally, the test set is used to observe how the trained neural network actually performs on unknown data. The reason for using a test set is that any neural network performs better on cases it has seen in its training process. Thus it is not enough to measure the performance of the model on just the data used for its training: an exogenous set must be used for an 'honest' test of neural network performance.

The performance of the network on the training and test sets can be assessed by simple mathematical formulae, called *error functions*, which measure the difference between the observed and actual examples. Several error functions exist, for example the Root Mean Square Error, the Digital Error and the Absolute Error. The difference between the cost function and the error functions must be noted: the cost function is minimised automatically through back-propagation, whereas the values of the error functions are only monitored during training for performance evaluation purposes.

In terms of the models presented in this chapter, an ANN can be expressed as

$$x_t = \theta_0 + \sum\nolimits_{i=1}^{k} \beta_i \phi(\gamma' \mathbf{x}_{t-1}) + u_t$$

where $\phi(\ )$ is a 'squashing' function, such as the logistic or a cumulative distribution function. For detailed discussion of ANNs in an econometric context, see White (1989) and Kuan and White (1994), while Qi (1996) presents a survey of financial applications of ANNs.

4.5.6 Non-linear dynamics and chaos

The processes introduced so far in this chapter all have in common the aim of modelling *stochastic* non-linearities in financial time series. This would seem a natural approach to take by those used to dealing with stochastic time series processes, but recently a literature has developed that considers the question of whether such series could have been generated, at least in part, by non-linear *deterministic* laws of motion.

This literature has been prompted by findings in the natural sciences of completely deterministic processes that generate behaviour which looks random under statistical tests: processes that are termed 'deterministic' or 'white chaos'. An example of such a process is one that is generated by a deterministic difference equation

$$x_t = f(x_{t-1}, \ldots, x_{t-p})$$

such that x_t does not tend to a constant or a (limit) cycle and has estimated covariances that are very small or zero. A simple example is provided by Brock (1986), where a formal development of deterministic chaos models is provided. Consider the difference equation

$$x_t = f(x_{t-1}), \quad x_0 \in [0, 1]$$

where

$$f(x) = \begin{cases} x/\alpha, & x \in [0, \alpha] \\ (1-x)/(1-\alpha), & x \in [\alpha, 1], \quad 0 < \alpha < 1 \end{cases}$$

Most realisations (or trajectories) of this difference equation generate the same SACFs as an AR(1) process for x_t with parameter $\phi = (2\alpha - 1)$. Hence, for $\alpha = ½$, the realisation will be indistinguishable from white noise, although it has been generated by a purely deterministic non-linear process. For further discussion of this particular function, called a *tent map* because the graph of x_t against x_{t-1} (known as the *phase diagram*) is shaped like a 'tent', see Hsieh (1991), who also considers other relevant examples of chaotic systems, such as the *logistic map*

$$x_t = 4x_{t-1}(1 - x_{t-1}) = 4x_{t-1} - 4x_{t-1}^2, \qquad 0 < x_0 < 1$$

This also has the same autocorrelation properties as white noise, although x_t^2 has an SACF consistent with an MA(1) process.

Are such models useful in finance? Brock (1988) considers some models of equilibrium asset pricing that might lead to chaos and complex dynamics: the idea that there should be no arbitrage profits in financial equilibrium is linked with the theory of economic growth to show how dynamics in the 'dividend' process are transmitted through the equilibrating mechanism to equilibrium asset prices. These dynamics can be linear, non-linear or chaotic depending on the constraints imposed on the models. Apart from this, there has been few attempts to build theoretical financial models from chaotic foundations. There has also been little empirical evidence of chaotic dynamics uncovered in financial time series, although much evidence of other types of stochastic non-linearities. This has been obtained from a variety of tests for non-linearity, to which we now turn.

4.6 Testing for non-linearity

As the previous sections have demonstrated, there has been a wide variety of non-linear models proposed for modelling financial time series. We have, in particular, compared and contrasted the ARCH and bilinear models, and in so doing have discussed LM tests for each. Nevertheless, given the range of alternative non-linear models, it is not surprising that a number of other tests for non-linearity have also been proposed, but since the form of the departure from linearity is often difficult to specify a priori, many tests are 'diagnostic' in nature, i.e., a clear alternative to the null hypothesis of linearity is not specified, and this, of course, leads to difficulties in discriminating between the possible causes of 'non-linear misspecification'.

Ramsey (1969), Keenan (1985) and Tsay (1986) provide a regression type test that appears to have good power against the non-linear moving average (see Robinson, 1977) and bilinear alternatives, but possibly has low power against ARCH models. In developing this test, we assume that an AR(p) process has been fitted to the observed series x_t and the residuals, e_t, and the fitted values, $\hat{x}_t = x_t - e_t$, calculated. Ramsey's original *Regression Error Specification Test* (RESET) is constructed from the auxiliary regression

$$e_t = \sum_{i=1}^{p} \varphi_i x_{t-i} + \sum_{j=2}^{h} \delta_j \hat{x}_t^j + v_t$$

and is the F-test of the hypothesis $H_0 : \delta_j = 0,\ j = 2, \ldots, h$. If $h = 2$ this is equivalent to Keenan's test, while Tsay augments the auxiliary regression with second-order terms

$$e_t = \sum_{i=1}^{p} \varphi_i x_{t-i} + \sum_{i=1}^{p} \sum_{j=i}^{p} \delta_{ij} x_{t-i} x_{t-j} + v_t$$

in which the linearity hypothesis is $H_0 : \delta_{ij} = 0,\ \forall i, j$. These tests have LM interpretations and Tsay's test has power against a greater variety of non-linear models than the RESET. A further extension is provided by Teräsvirta, Lin and Granger (1993), in which the auxiliary regression becomes

$$e_t = \sum_{i=1}^{p} \varphi_i x_{t-i} + \sum_{i=1}^{p} \sum_{j=i}^{p} \delta_{ij} x_{t-i} x_{t-j}$$

$$+ \sum_{i=1}^{p} \sum_{j=i}^{p} \sum_{k=j}^{p} \delta_{ijk} x_{t-i} x_{t-j} x_{t-k} + v_t$$

with the linearity hypothesis now being $H_0 : \delta_{ij} = 0,\ \delta_{ijk} = 0,\ \forall i, j, k$. This is related to the 'neural network' test proposed by Lee, White and Granger (1993) and appears to have better power.

A further test that has created considerable interest is the BDS statistic, based on the concept of the *correlation integral*: see, for example, Brock (1986), Brock, Hsieh and LeBaron (1991), Brock and Dechert (1991) and Dechert (1996). For an observed series $\{x_t\}_1^T$, the correlation integral $C_N(\ell, T)$ is defined as

$$C_N(\ell, T) = \frac{2}{T_N(T_N - 1)} \sum_{t<s} I_t\left(x_t^N, x_s^N\right)$$

where

$$x_t^N = \left(x_t, x_{t+1}, \ldots, x_{t+N-1}\right)$$

and

$$x_s^N = \left(x_s, x_{s+1}, \ldots, x_{s+N-1}\right)$$

are called 'N-histories', $I_t(x_t^N, x_s^N)$ is an indicator function that equals one if $\|x_t^N - x_s^N\| < \ell$ and zero otherwise, $\|\cdot\|$ being the sup-norm, and $T_N = T - N + 1$.

The correlation integral is an estimate of the probability that any two N-histories, x_t^N and x_s^N, are within ℓ of each other. If the x_ts are strict white noise, then

$$C_N(\ell, T) \to C_1(\ell, T)^N, \text{ as } T \to \infty$$

and

$$w_N(\ell, T) = \sqrt{T}\left(C_N(\ell, T) - C_1(\ell, T)^N\right) \Big/ \sigma_N(\ell, T)$$

has a standard normal limiting distribution, where the expression for the variance $\sigma_N^2(\ell, T)$ may be found in, for example, Hsieh (1989b, p. 343). Thus the BDS statistic $w_N(\ell, T)$ tests the null hypothesis that a series is strict white noise: it is a diagnostic test since a rejection of this null is consistent with some type of dependence in the data, which could result from a linear stochastic system, a non-linear stochastic system, or a non-linear deterministic system. Additional diagnostic tests are therefore needed to determine the source of the rejection, but simulation experiments do suggest that the BDS test has power against simple linear deterministic systems as well as non-linear stochastic processes.

Tests are also available for specific non-linear alternatives. Tests against ARCH and bilinear alternatives have already been discussed in sections 4.4 and 4.5 and there is also a fully developed testing procedure against STAR models. From Teräsvirta (1994), an LM-type test statistic for the null of linearity against an LSTAR alternative can be constructed from the auxiliary regression

$$e_t = \sum_{i=1}^{p} \varphi_i x_{t-i} + \sum_{j=1}^{p} \delta_{1j} x_{t-j} x_{t-d}$$

$$+ \sum_{j=1}^{p} \delta_{2j} x_{t-j} x_{t-d}^2 + \sum_{j=1}^{p} \delta_{3j} x_{t-j} x_{t-d}^3 + v_t$$

with the linearity hypothesis being $H_0 : \delta_{ij} = 0, \ \forall i, j$. To test against an ESTAR alternative the same auxiliary regression is estimated, but without the fourth-order terms, i.e., we set $\delta_{3j} = 0$ a priori. This relationship between the two tests leads naturally to a method for discriminating between the two types of STAR models (see Teräsvirta, 1994, for details, and example 4.8 below). Of course, these tests assume that the delay parameter d is known. Typically its value will be unknown and Teräsvirta suggests that it should be chosen on the basis of a sequence of LM tests for alternative values of d: we choose the value that minimises the p-value of the individual tests in the sequence. The auxiliary regression can also be estimated with x_t rather than e_t as the regressand and this may be preferred as it provides a direct comparison with the AR(p) model under the null of linearity.

Further tests are discussed, within a general econometric context, in Granger and Teräsvirta (1993, chapter 6) and in the survey by Teräsvirta, Tjostheim and Granger (1994). It should be emphasised, however, that all these tests are designed to distinguish between linear and non-linear *stochastic* dynamics. They are not, as yet, capable of distinguishing non-linear stochastic dynamics from deterministic chaotic dynamics, although the rejection of linearity may, of course, motivate the investigation of chaotic models. A test that is claimed to be able to detect chaos in noisy data is the Lyaponuv exponent estimator of Nychka *et al.* (1992), which has been subject to rigorous scrutiny in Barnett *et al.* (1996, 1997).

Example 4.8 Non-linearity tests and an ANN model for UK gilt yields

The residuals from the linear AR(2) model fitted to $\Delta R20$ in example 4.7 were used to construct various tests of non-linearity. The LM test for twelfth-order ARCH produced the statistic $\chi^2_{12} = 89.6$, which is obviously significant, and LM tests for bilinearity with $R = S = 1$ and $R = S = 2$, respectively, obtained $\chi^2_1 = 4.10$ and $\chi^2_4 = 9.52$, both significant at the 5 per cent level. The RESET test with $h = 2$ (i.e., Keenan's test) has a p-value of 0.031, Tsay's test a p-value of 0.17, and Teräsvirta *et al.*'s test a p-value of 0.011. Thus, all bar Tsay's test indicate substantial non-linear dependence in the data: the non-rejection of linearity by this test occurring because the additional regressors over the RESET test, $x_{t-1}x_{t-2}$ and x^2_{t-2}, are individually insignificant.

Following, for example, Hsieh (1989b), the BDS tests were computed for a selection of ℓ and N values and are shown in table 4.2. For $N > 2$, all statistics are highly significant, thus again indicating substantial non-linear dependence in the residuals.

Why was an LSTAR(2) model with delay parameter set at $d = 1$ fitted to $\Delta R20$ in example 4.7? Auxiliary regressions for $d = 1$ and 2 suggested that the former setting was appropriate: after deletion of insignificant regressors the auxiliary regression was

Table 4.2 *BDS statistics for 20 year gilts*

$\ell = 0.5$		$\ell = 1$		$\ell = 1.5$	
N	w_N	N	w_N	N	w_N
2	0.78	2	0.80	2	0.61
3	10.14	3	9.64	3	8.38
4	13.56	4	12.05	4	9.67
5	17.93	5	14.07	5	10.38

Note: ℓ is set in terms of the standard deviation of the residuals from the AR(2) fit, i.e., $\ell = 1$ is one standard deviation.

$$\begin{aligned} x_t = {} & \underset{(0.060)}{0.268}\, x_{t-1} - \underset{(0.051)}{0.083}\, x_{t-2} + \underset{(0.068)}{0.180}\, x_{t-1}^3 \\ & - \underset{(0.141)}{0.383}\, x_{t-1}^2 x_{t-2} - \underset{(0.087)}{0.224}\, x_{t-1}^3 x_{t-2} \end{aligned}$$

To choose between an LSTAR and an ESTAR model, Teräsvirta (1994) suggests the following procedure: (i) test whether all 'fourth-order' terms are insignificant; (ii) conditional on all fourth-order terms being zero, test the joint significance of all third-order terms; and (iii) conditional on all third- and fourth-order terms being zero, test the significance of the second-order terms. If the test in (ii) produces the smallest p-value, select an ESTAR model; if not, choose an LSTAR model. The p-values are found to be (i) 0.011, (ii) 0.100 and (iii) effectively zero as no second-order terms appear. Thus we chose to fit an LSTAR model.

Methods of testing the adequacy of fitted STAR models are discussed in Eitrhem and Teräsvirta (1996). To check whether such a model is adequate, we can use the approach discussed above for linear models, e.g., to test against general 'neglected' non-linearity, second- and third-order terms of the form $x_{t-i}x_{t-j}$ and $x_{t-i}x_{t-j}x_{t-k}$ may be added to the LSTAR model and tested for significance. Doing so for the fitted LSTAR(2) model leads to a statistic that is significant at less than the 0.01 level. However, Eitrhem and Teräsvirta remark that this does not give us much of a clue as to what model we should fit next: given the nature of the residuals from the LSTAR(2) model, we decided to fit GARCH(1,1) errors, leading to the model discussed in example 4.7.

Given the evidence of non-linearity, we also investigated the performance of ANNs. The *logarithmic* changes, $\Delta r20$, were used in this

Table 4.3 *Within-sample and forecasting performance of three models for* $\Delta r20$

	RMSE In-sample: 1952–1990	*RMSE* Outside-sample: 1991–1995
AR(2)	0.0311	0.0289
LSTAR(2)	0.0309	0.0294
ANN(2:5)	0.0294	0.0298

exercise, as this series is used in a sequence of examples in subsequent chapters. An AR(2), an LSTAR(2) with $d = 1$, and an ANN, a MLP with two inputs, $\Delta r20_{t-1}$ and $\Delta r20_{t-2}$, and five hidden neurons organised in one layer, denoted ANN(2:5), were estimated over the sample January 1952 to December 1990. The MLP was estimated using 1500 training cycles and cross-validisation. Table 4.3 presents the within-sample root mean squared errors (RMSEs) for the three models, where we see that both non-linear models have smaller RMSEs than the AR(2) process, the ANN quite considerably so. The three models were also used to forecast the remaining five years of data, these outside-sample RMSEs also being shown in table 4.3. Now we see that goodness of fit is reversed: the linear AR(2) model has the smallest RMSE and the ANN the largest, leading to the suspicion that perhaps the ANN had been overtrained.

5 Modelling return distributions

Empirical research on returns distributions has been ongoing since the early 1960s: see, for example, the surveys in Kon (1984), Badrinath and Chatterjee (1988) and Mittnik and Rachev (1993a). These have almost universally found that such distributions are characterised by the 'stylised facts' of fat tails and high peakedness – excess kurtosis – and are often skewed. However, there have been several recent developments in statistics and econometrics that have led to considerable advances in the analysis of such distributions. To set the scene for subsequent analysis, section 1 presents initial descriptive analysis of the distributional properties of three typical return series, before section 2 reviews two of the most important theoretical models for examining return distributions, the stable process and, much more briefly since it was analysed in great detail in the previous chapter, the ARCH process. Section 3 generalises the discussion to consider tail shapes of distributions and methods of estimating indices of these shapes, while section 4 reviews existing empirical research and offers new evidence from our own returns series. Section 5 considers the implications of fat-tailed distributions for testing the conventional maintained assumption of time series models of returns, that of weak, or covariance, stationarity. Section 6 switches attention to modelling the central part of returns distributions and section 7 reviews data analytic methods of modelling skewness and kurtosis. The distributional properties of absolute returns are the focus of section 8, and a summary and some further extensions are provided in section 9.

5.1 Descriptive analysis of three returns series

The techniques to be discussed in this chapter will be illustrated using three return series: (i) the daily returns of the London FT30 for a sixty year period from 1935 to 1994, which has previously been analysed in terms of its long memory properties and the profitability of technical trading rules in Mills (1996a, 1997b); (ii) the daily returns of the S&P500, and (iii) the daily dollar/sterling exchange rate, the latter two having been used in earlier examples. Unlike other chapters, however, because the use of these series is integral to the development of the techniques, separate, numbered, examples will not be presented: rather, the techniques will be illustrated within the main body of the text itself.

Descriptive distributional statistics are thus presented in table 5.1 and graphical representations of these distributions are shown in figure 5.1. The empirical densities shown are computed as a smoothed function of the histogram using a normal kernel (see Silverman, 1986, chapter 3: the computations were performed in *GIVEWIN* (Doornik and Hendry, 1996)). Superimposed on the empirical density is a normal distribution having the same variance as that estimated from the sample.

The empirical cumulative distributions are plotted against the cumulative reference normal distributions in the form of normal probability or *Q–Q* plots (see Mills, 1990, chapter 3). From this information it is clear that all returns distributions diverge substantially from the normal in the manner expected – they have fatter tails, are more highly peaked, and are skewed.

5.2 Two models for returns distributions

The 'fat-tailed and highly peaked' stylised fact about financial return series was first emphasised by Mandelbrot (1963a, 1963b), who proposed using the stable (also known as the stable Paretian, Pareto-Lévy, or Lévy flight) class of distributions, which includes the normal as a special case, to model the fat-tailed nature of stock returns. Since then, many, but certainly by no means all, researchers have found that the stable distribution provides a good fit to a wide variety of returns series: see, for example, the references provided by Ghose and Kroner (1995). Alternative lines of modelling take the empirical returns distribution to be a mixture

Table 5.1. *Descriptive statistics on returns distributions*

	T	mean	median	std.dev	max	min	range	skew	kurt
FT30	15003	0.022	0.000	1.004	10.78	−12.40	23.1	−0.14	14.53
S&P500	17054	0.020	0.047	1.154	15.37	−22.80	33.1	−0.49	25.04
Dollar	5192	−0.008	0.000	0.647	4.67	−3.87	13.2	−0.70	6.51

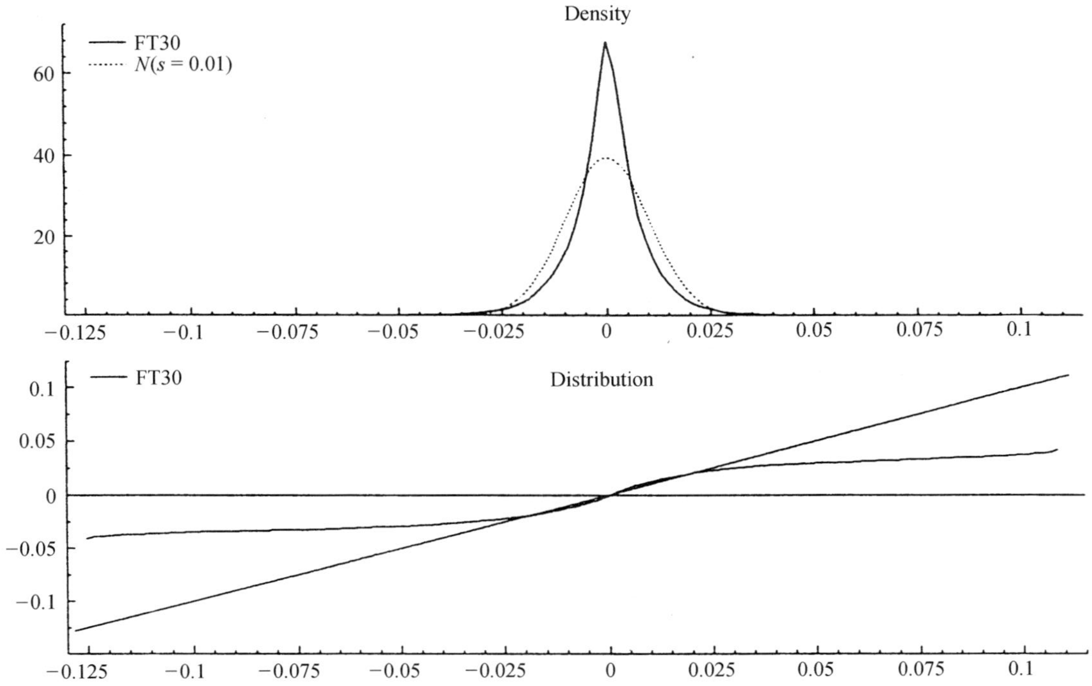

(a) FT30

Figure 5.1 Distributional properties of three returns series

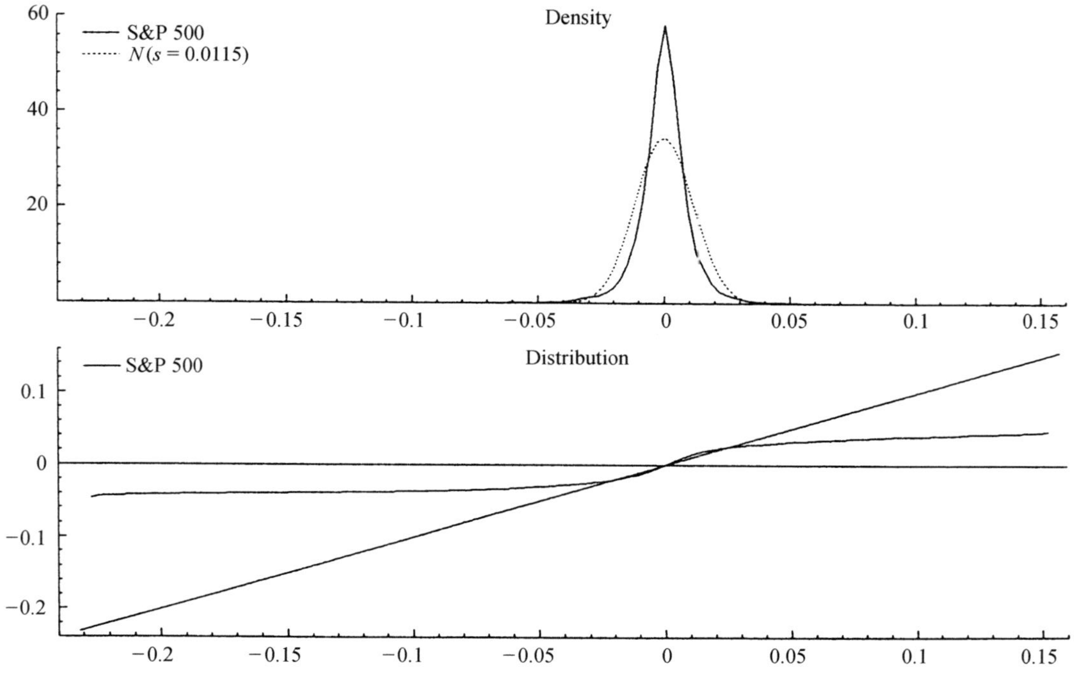

(b) S&P 500

Figure 5.1 (*cont.*)

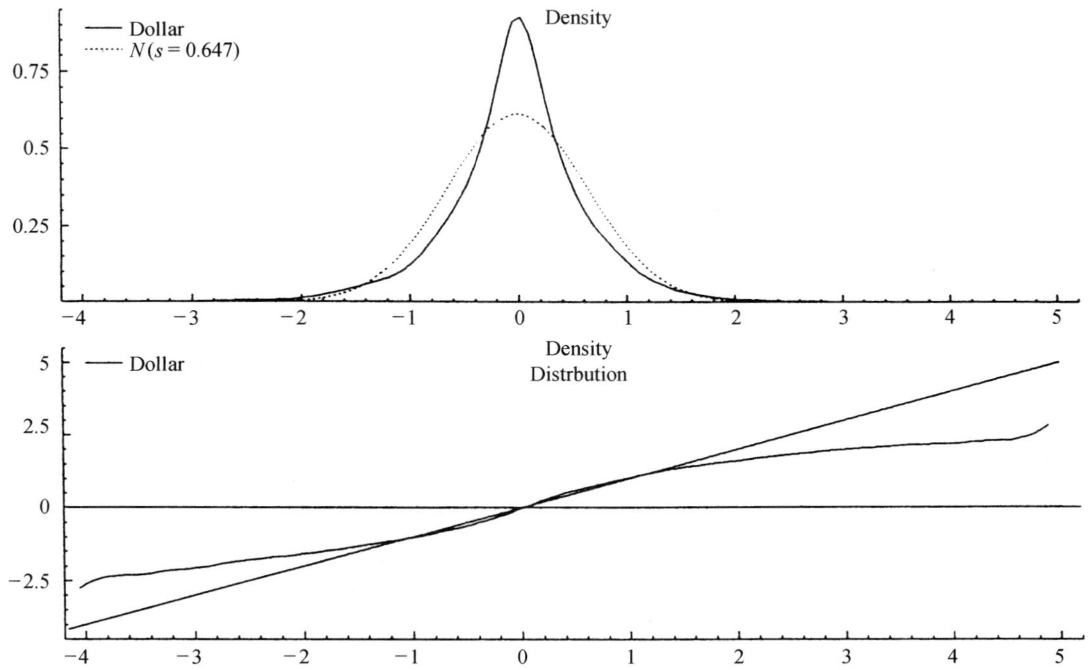

(c) Dollar/sterling exchange rate

Figure 5.1 (*cont.*)

of either normals or of a normal and a stable, or use some other distribution capable of modelling fat tails, for example, the Student-t or the double Weibull distribution (see Mittnik and Rachev, 1993a, and McDonald, 1996, for details and references). These alternatives will not, however, be pursued here, although they have undoubtedly contributed to our knowledge of the distributional behaviour of asset returns: see, in particular, Mittnik and Rachev (1993a, 1993b), and the references contained therein.

The symmetric about zero stable class of distributions is characterised by two parameters, a scale factor and the characteristic exponent, which indexes the distribution. (We restrict attention to symmetric about zero stable distributions so that we may more easily focus on the behaviour of the tails of the distributions. Allowing asymmetry about a non-zero location measure introduces two further parameters that merely complicate matters for the purposes at hand.) Most attention is focused on the characteristic exponent because, since closed-form density functions do not exist for most stable distributions, they are usually defined by their characteristic functions, which always exist.

Suppose $\{X_t\}_1^T$ is a strict white-noise zero mean process with probability distribution $F(X) = P(X < x)$. The characteristic function of X is defined as the Fourier-Stieltjes transform of $F(X)$

$$\varphi(\varsigma) = \int_{-\infty}^{+\infty} e^{i\varsigma x} \mathrm{d}F(X)$$

where ς is real (see Feller, 1966, page 473). The symmetric (about zero) stable characteristic function has the form

$$\varphi(\varsigma) = \exp(-\sigma^{\alpha} | \varsigma |^{\alpha})$$

where $0 < \alpha \leq 2$ is the characteristic exponent and σ is a scale parameter. Samorodnitsky and Taqqu (1994) refer to X being $S\alpha S$ (symmetric α-stable). The $N(0, 2)$ distribution is obtained when $\alpha = 2$ and the Cauchy distribution is obtained when $\alpha = 1$. Using the Fourier inversion formula provided by Feller (1966, page 482), the stable probability distribution becomes

$$\begin{aligned} F(X) &= \frac{1}{2\pi} \int_{-\infty}^{+\infty} \exp(-\sigma^{\alpha} | \varsigma |^{\alpha}) \exp(-i\varsigma X) \mathrm{d}\varsigma \\ &= \frac{1}{\pi} \int_{0}^{+\infty} \exp(-\sigma^{\alpha} | \varsigma |^{\alpha}) \cos(\varsigma X) \mathrm{d}\varsigma \end{aligned} \qquad (5.1)$$

As remarked above, when $\alpha = 2$ the distribution is normal and all moments are finite, whereas if $\alpha < 2$ all moments greater than α are infinite. This property produces the fat-tailed (relative to the normal) behaviour of stable distributions. A necessary and sufficient condition for a distribution to be fat-tailed is that of regular variation at infinity (Feller, 1966, chapter VIII.8). The stable $F(X)$ of equation (5.1) can be demonstrated to have this property

$$\lim_{s\to\infty} \frac{(1 - F(sX))}{(1 - F(s))} = X^{-\alpha}$$

which implies that the stable distribution displays a power declining tail, $X^{-\alpha}$, rather than an exponential decline as is the case with the normal. It is in this sense that α is also often referred to as the tail index.

Apart from its empirical usefulness, is there any theoretical justification for why the stable distribution should be an appropriate generating process for financial data? Mandelbrot (1963b, section IID) argues that such a justification arises from a generalisation of the Central Limit Theorem (CLT). This establishes that if the limiting distribution of an appropriately scaled sum of independent and identically distributed random variables exists then it must be a member of the stable class, *even if* these random variables have infinite variance. It thus differs from the usual CLT, which says that if the second moments are finite then the limiting distribution is normal. This result, for which a proof may be found in Feller (1966), generalises the moment requirements of the CLT and thus expands the set of limiting distributions. More importantly for our purposes, it also implies that if daily returns, say, follow a stable distribution then, since weekly, monthly and quarterly returns, for example, can be viewed as the sum of daily returns, they too will follow stable distributions having identical characteristic exponents. This is known as the stability or invariance under addition property of stable distributions. For more detailed technical discussion of stable distributions, see, for example, Mandelbrot (1963a, 1963b), Feller (1966), Brockwell and Davis (1991, chapter 13.3), Mittnik and Rachev (1993a, 1993b) and Samorodnitsky and Taqqu (1994). These references also deal with the correlation of stable processes over time: moving averages of a stable random variable are also stable, as long as certain conditions on the coefficients are satisfied. We are therefore not restricted to analysing uncorrelated series, and correlated series can be filtered in the usual ways, e.g., by fitting autoregressions.

Correlated stable variables may thus be able to explain a second stylised fact of returns, the volatility clustering that is so prevalent in financial data. The GARCH class of models discussed in chapter 4.4 can also, of course, exhibit volatility clustering, i.e., serial correlation of *conditional* variances. For example, the simple 'ARCH(1) with normal innovations' process for X_t is

$$X_t = U_t \sigma_t \tag{5.2}$$

where $U_t \sim NID(0, 1)$ and

$$\sigma_t^2 = \omega + \beta X_{t-1}^2 \tag{5.3}$$

Equations (5.2) and (5.3) can be written as

$$X_t^2 = \omega U_t^2 + \beta U_t^2 X_{t-1}^2 = B_t + A_t X_{t-1}^2 \tag{5.4}$$

say, thus demonstrating the volatility clustering property (X_t is serially uncorrelated but is *not* independent). The ARCH(1) process may also exhibit fat tails. De Haan *et al.* (1989) show that the X_t of (5.4) regularly varies at infinity and has a tail index ς defined implicitly by the equation

$$\Gamma\left(\frac{\varsigma + 1}{2}\right) = \pi^{1/2}(2\beta)^{-\varsigma/2}$$

where $\Gamma(\ )$ is the gamma function, as long as, amongst other things, $\beta < \bar{\beta} = 2e^{\upsilon} \approx 3.56856$, where υ is Euler's constant. From Groenendijk *et al.* (1995, figure 1), we have that $\varsigma = 2$ at $\beta = 1$, $\varsigma = \infty$ at $\beta = 0$, and $\varsigma = 0.00279$ at $\beta = \bar{\beta}$. It thus follows that, in terms of tail behaviour, the stable and ARCH models partially overlap. At $\beta = 0$ and 1 ($\varsigma = \infty$ and 2) the two models have normal tails, while for $1 < \beta < \bar{\beta}$ the tail indices can be equal. But for $0 < \beta < 1$, $\varsigma > 2$, X_t is covariance stationary, has finite variance and there is no stable counterpart, whereas for $\varsigma < 0.00279$ there is no ARCH counterpart. Tail behaviour can therefore only discriminate between the two classes of models in the regions where they do not overlap.

5.3 Determining the tail shape of a returns distribution

If $\alpha < 2$ then, through the property of regular variation at infinity, the tails of a stable process are a function of α and display a power decline. In fact, they follow an asymptotic Pareto distribution, so that

$$P(X > x) = P(X < -x) = C^{\alpha} x^{-\alpha}, \quad x > 0$$

where C is a finite and positive parameter measuring dispersion. However, as we have seen for the GARCH process, the tail index ζ may be defined for distributions other than the stable, and for these the index will not equal the characteristic exponent, although it will determine the maximal finite exponent, i.e., the tail index is such that $E(|X|^k) < \infty$ for all $0 \leq k < \zeta$. If $\zeta < 2$ then the variance of X is infinite and X may be characterised as being generated by a stable distribution for which $\alpha = \zeta$. If $\zeta \geq 2$, the variance of X is finite, but the distribution is not necessarily normal and may thus still have fat tails: for example, it may be Student-t, in which case ζ defines the degrees of freedom. Distributions such as the normal and the power exponential possess all moments and for these ζ is infinite and they may be described as being thin tailed.

For fat-tailed distributions other than the stable, and which also have the property of regular variation at infinity, tail behaviour will also be asymptotically Pareto (this will typically be the case for return distributions: see the arguments in Koedijk *et al.*, 1990, for example). Loretan and Phillips (1994) formalise this by defining the tail behaviour of the distribution of X to take the form

$$
\begin{aligned}
P(X > x) &= C^{\zeta} x^{-\zeta}(1 + \zeta_R(x)), \quad x > 0 \\
P(X < -x) &= C^{\zeta} x^{-\zeta}(1 + \zeta_L(x)), \quad x > 0
\end{aligned}
$$

where $\zeta_i \to 0$ $(i = R, L)$ as $x \to \infty$. The parameters C and ζ can be estimated using order statistics. If $X_{(1)} \leq X_{(2)} \leq \cdots \leq X_{(T)}$ are the order statistics of $\{X_t\}_1^T$ in ascending order, then ζ can be estimated by

$$
\begin{aligned}
\hat{\zeta} &= \left(s^{-1} \sum_{j=1}^{s} \log X_{(T-j+1)} - \log X_{(T-s)} \right)^{-1} \\
&= \left(s^{-1} \sum_{j=1}^{s} \left(\log X_{(T-j+1)} - \log X_{(T-s)} \right) \right)^{-1}
\end{aligned}
$$

$\hat{\zeta}$ is related to the simpler estimator proposed by de Haan and Resnick (1980) and modified by Groenendijk *et al.* (1995), being approximately a weighted average of their estimator

$$
\left(\frac{\log X_{(T-j+1)} - \log X_{(T-s)}}{\log(s/j)} \right)^{-1}
$$

evaluated at different values of $j < s$. An estimate of the scale dispersion parameter is

$$\hat{C} = (s/T)X_{(T-s)}^{\hat{\zeta}}$$

Hill (1975) is the original reference for these estimators, which are conditional ML estimators, while Hall (1982) provides their asymptotic theory. To make these estimators operational, the order statistic truncation number $s = s(T)$ must be selected. Although we require that $s(T) \rightarrow \infty$ as $T \rightarrow \infty$, various approaches have been taken in empirical applications with a finite sample. Typically $\hat{\zeta}$ is computed for different values of s, selecting an s in the region over which $\hat{\zeta}$ is more or less constant. Koedijk *et al.* (1990) use Monte Carlo simulation to choose s such that the MSE of $\hat{\zeta}$ is minimised, while Loretan and Phillips (1994) suggest that s should not exceed $0.1T$. Phillips *et al.* (1996), following Hall and Welsh (1985), deduce an 'optimal' choice of $s(T)$ using the asymptotic theory of Hall (1982), from which the MSE of the limit distribution of $\hat{\zeta}$ is minimised by choosing $s(T) = [\lambda T^{2/3}]$, where λ is estimated adaptively by

$$\hat{\lambda} = \left|\hat{\zeta}_1/2^{1/2}(T/s_2)(\hat{\zeta}_1 - \hat{\zeta}_2)\right|^{2/3}$$

Here $\hat{\zeta}_1$ and $\hat{\zeta}_2$ are preliminary estimates of ζ using data truncations $s_1 = [T^\sigma]$ and $s_2 = [T^\tau]$, respectively, where $0 < \sigma < 2/3 < \tau < 1$. Phillips *et al.* (1996) recommend setting $\sigma = 0.6$ and $\tau = 0.9$. Note that, as defined, these estimates pertain to the right or upper tail of the distribution of X; to estimate the parameters of the left or lower tail, we simply multiply the order statistics by -1 and repeat the calculations. We can also estimate a single pair of ζ and C estimates by redoing the calculations with absolute values of the order statistics.

Confidence intervals and hypothesis tests for ζ and C can be calculated using the results, from Hall (1982), that asymptotically

$$s^{1/2}(\hat{\zeta} - \zeta) \sim N(0, \zeta^2)$$

and

$$s^{1/2}(\log(T/s))^{-1}\left(\hat{C}_s - C\right) \sim N(0, C^2)$$

An hypothesis of particular interest is that of $H_0 : \zeta < 2$ against the alternative $H_1 : \zeta \geq 2$, since from the parameter's definition, $\zeta = 2$ divides off finite variance distributions, e.g., the Student-t and the ARCH process, from infinite variance distributions.

Constancy of the estimated tail indexes can be examined by using the following useful result. Suppose that we obtain estimates $\hat{\zeta}^{(1)}$ and $\hat{\zeta}^{(2)}$ from two independent samples. The statistic

$$\left(\frac{\zeta^{(1)}}{\hat{\zeta}^{(1)}} - 1\right)^2 s_1 + \left(\frac{\zeta^{(2)}}{\hat{\zeta}^{(2)}} - 1\right)^2 s_2$$

where $\zeta^{(1)}$ and $\zeta^{(2)}$ are hypothesised values of the tail index in the two samples, is then asymptotically distributed as χ_2^2. Thus, constancy of the tail index can be assessed in the following way. Suppose the null hypothesis is $H_{0,\alpha} : \zeta^{(1)} = \zeta^{(2)} = \zeta$ and we wish to test at the 5 per cent significance level. Solving the quadratic equation

$$\left(\frac{\zeta}{\hat{\zeta}^{(1)}} - 1\right)^2 s_1 + \left(\frac{\zeta}{\hat{\zeta}^{(2)}} - 1\right)^2 s_2 - \chi_{2,.05}^2 = 0$$

will then provide the upper and lower bounds for the tail indexes that are consistent with the null. An alternative parameter constancy test is proposed by Loretan and Phillips (1994): if $\hat{\tau}_\zeta = \hat{\zeta}^{(1)} - \hat{\zeta}^{(2)}$ then the statistic

$$V_\zeta = \frac{\hat{\tau}_\zeta^2}{\left(\frac{\hat{\zeta}^{(1)^2}}{s_1} + \frac{\hat{\zeta}^{(2)^2}}{s_2}\right)}$$

is asymptotically distributed as χ_1^2. A similar statistic is available to test $H_{0,C} : C^{(1)} = C^{(2)} = C$ using $\hat{\tau}_C = \hat{C}^{(1)} - \hat{C}^{(2)}$, and these can be used to assess whether the parameters are equal across the right and left tails of the distribution as well as across time periods.

However, there is some evidence, provided by McCulloch (1997), that $\hat{\zeta}$ is an upwardly biased estimate of the true value ζ when the distribution really is stable, so that these testing procedures should be used with considerable care.

Given an estimate of the tail index ζ, extreme return levels that are only rarely exceeded can be established by extrapolating the empirical distribution function outside the sample domain, and this can be useful for analysing 'safety first' portfolio selection strategies (see Jansen and de

Vries, 1991, and de Haan *et al.*, 1994). A consistent estimate of the 'excess level' $\hat{x}_p$, for which

$$P(X_1 \leq \hat{x}_p, X_2 \leq \hat{x}_p, \cdots, X_k \leq \hat{x}_p) = 1 - p$$

for small p and given k, is given by

$$\hat{x}_p = \frac{(kr/pT)^{\hat{\gamma}}}{1 - 2^{-\hat{\gamma}}} \left(X_{(T-r)} - X_{(T-2r)} \right) + X_{(T-r)} \tag{5.5}$$

where $\hat{\gamma} = \hat{\zeta}^{-1}$, $r = s/2$, k is the time period considered and p is the 'probability of excess' (see Dekkers and de Haan, 1989). This equation can be 'inverted' to obtain the probability $\hat{p}$ of sustaining a loss of x_p.

5.4 Empirical evidence on tail indices

A number of papers have investigated the tail behaviour of the empirical distribution of foreign exchange rate returns and, as well as assessing how fat-tailed returns are, they also investigate the stability of the distributions across different regimes (see Koedijk, Schafgans and de Vries, 1990, Hols and de Vries, 1991, Koedijk and Kool, 1992, Koedijk, Stork and de Vries, 1992, and Loretan and Phillips, 1994). The general finding from these papers is that exchange rate returns are fat tailed but with $\zeta < 4$ and, during a variety of fixed exchange rate regimes, have tail indices that are in the region $1 \leq \zeta \leq 2$. For floating rate regimes, however, ζ tends to exceed 2, which is interpreted as suggesting that a float lets exchange rates adjust more smoothly than regimes that involve some amount of fixity. It would also appear that ζ is stable across tails.

Jansen and de Vries (1991), Loretan and Phillips (1994) and de Haan *et al.* (1994) estimate tail indices for US stock and bond market returns, finding that estimates lie in the region $2 < \zeta < 4$, so that, although the distributions are fat tailed, they appear to be characterised by finite variances. Again, estimates of ζ for stock returns are stable across tails and across subperiods. As McCulloch (1997) points out though, even $\hat{\zeta}$ values well in excess of 2 could still be consistent with true values of ζ less than 2, so these results, while confirming the fat-tailed nature of the returns distributions, cannot be interpreted as conclusively ruling out infinite variances.

Estimates of tail indices for our three series are shown in table 5.2. All return distributions have estimated tail indices (for the 'optimal' setting of the truncation lag) lying in the region $2 < \zeta < 4$, with the left tail

Table 5.2. *Point estimates of tail indices*

s	Left tail		Right tail		Both tails	
			FT 30			
25	3.167	(0.633)	3.598	(0.720)	4.377	(0.875)
50	3.138	(0.444)	2.847	(0.403)	3.253	(0.460)
75	3.135	(0.362)	3.028	(0.350)	3.357	(0.385)
100	3.305	(0.330)	3.113	(0.311)	3.082	(0.308)
320	2.937	(0.164)	2.922	(0.163)	3.111	(0.174)
$\hat{s}$	2.887[298]	(0.345)	2.918[317]	(0.277)	3.024[405]	(0.150)
			S&P 500			
25	3.192	(0.638)	4.272	(0.854)	4.445	(0.889)
50	3.983	(0.563)	3.062	(0.433)	3.917	(0.554)
75	3.269	(0.373)	3.246	(0.375)	3.672	(0.424)
100	2.966	(0.297)	3.040	(0.304)	3.554	(0.355)
320	2.809	(0.157)	2.625	(0.147)	2.925	(0.163)
$\hat{s}$	2.749[335]	(0.150)	2.574[365]	(0.135)	2.783[474]	(0.128)
			Dollar/sterling			
25	3.967	(0.793)	4.200	(0.840)	4.461	(0.892)
50	3.672	(0.519)	3.559	(0.503)	4.269	(0.604)
75	3.421	(0.395)	3.547	(0.410)	3.825	(0.442)
100	3.046	(0.305)	3.477	(0.348)	3.615	(0.362)
200	2.673	(0.189)	2.971	(0.210)	3.107	(0.220)
$\hat{s}$	2.716[161]	(0.214)	2.867[161]	(0.226)	3.079[204]	(0.216)

Note: $\hat{s}$: optimal estimate of s using $\sigma = 0.6$ and $\tau = 0.9$. Actual value of $\hat{s}$ reported in [ ] in each column. Standard errors are shown in parentheses.

indices usually being a little smaller than the right, although not significantly so on the basis of the V_ζ test for constancy across tails (not reported).

Figure 5.2 plots the left tail shapes of the empirical distribution functions of the returns in double-logarithmic coordinates, i.e., it plots $\log_{10}(P(X < -x))$ against $\log_{10} x$ for $x > 0$. In these coordinates the Pareto distribution, for which $P(X < -x) = Dx^{-\zeta}$, where $D = C^{\zeta}$, appears as a straight line with a slope of $-\zeta$. Straight lines of slopes -2 and -4 are graphed against the empirical tails to facilitate comparison: the former line because it divides off finite variance distributions from ones with infinite variance, the latter line because the value $\zeta = 4$ is an important dividing point when testing whether a series is covariance stationary, as is

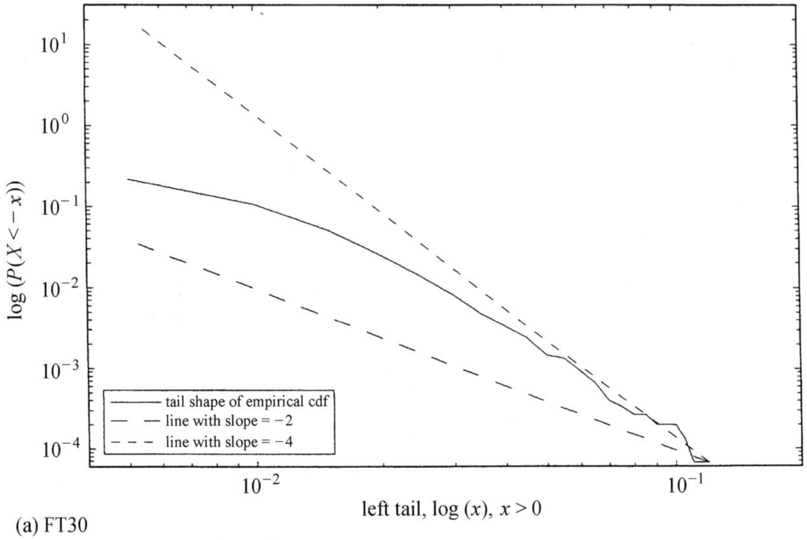

(a) FT30

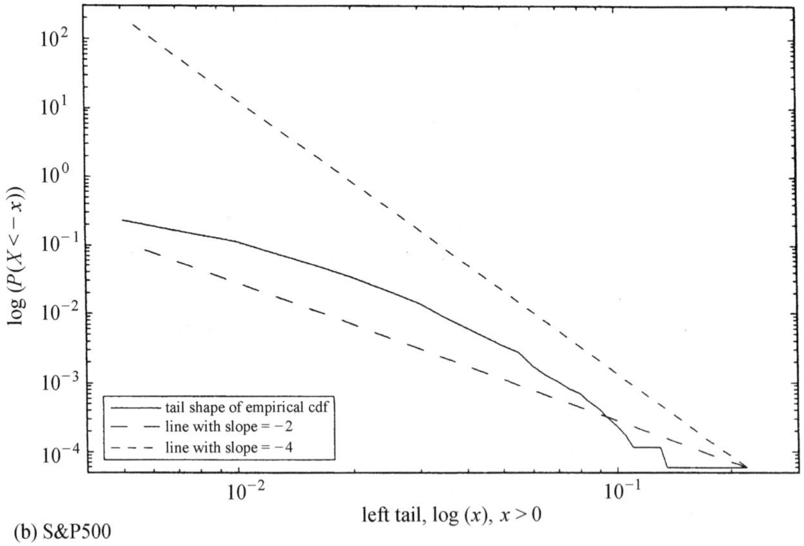

(b) S&P500

Figure 5.2 Tail shapes of return distributions

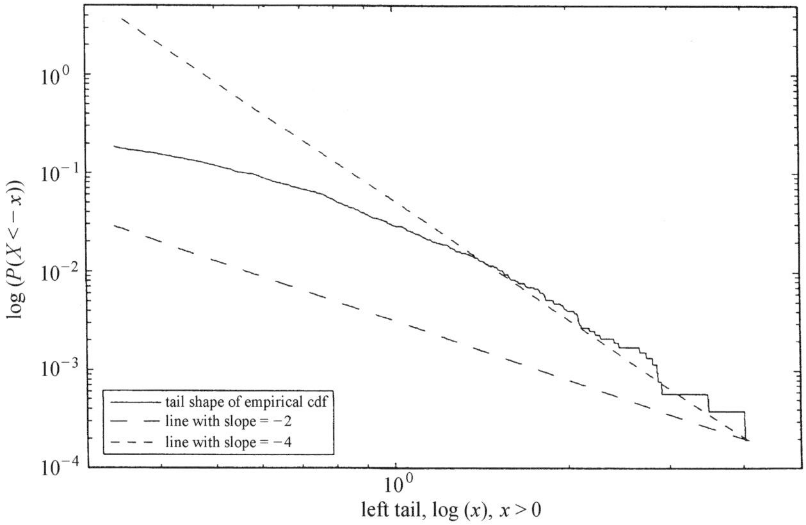

(c) Dollar/sterling exchange rate

Figure 5.2 (*cont.*)

discussed in the forthcoming section. These again make it clear that the return distributions are certainly fat tailed, but there appears to be little support for them following a stable distribution and thus having an infinite variance.

Stability of the tail indices was examined by splitting the sample periods in half and computing the V_ζ statistics. These are shown in table 5.3 along with subsample estimates of the tail indices. Only for the right tail of the S&P 500 distribution is there strong evidence of non-constancy. For the FT30 and exchange rate distributions, the estimated tail indices seem to be very similar, and certainly there is no evidence of the subperiod estimates coming close to 2.

Estimates of extreme levels can also be calculated using the formula (5.5) and some calculations are shown in table 5.4. For example, the probability that *within a given year* the FT30 will experience a one *day* fall of more than 20 per cent is 0.009, i.e., about once in every 110 years, but for the S&P 500 this probability is 0.02, about once every 50 years. On the other hand, the probability of the dollar/sterling exchange rate experiencing a one day fall of 20 per cent within a given year, which is certainly outside the observed sample range, is 0.00325 – once every 300 years!

Table 5.3. *Tail index stability tests*

		First half		Second half		
		$\hat{\zeta}$	$\hat{s}$	$\hat{\zeta}$	$\hat{s}$	V_{ζ}
FT30	left	2.78	200	2.99	201	0.53
	right	2.97	200	3.09	203	0.16
S&P500	left	3.09	207	3.35	208	0.64
	right	2.48	236	3.48	219	12.41
Dollar/	left	2.37	105	3.07	100	3.37
sterling	right	2.75	100	3.18	100	0.73

Table 5.4. *Lower-tail probabilities*

Return	Probability	Return	Probability
		FT30	
−0.200	0.00906	−0.193	0.0100
−0.300	0.00280	−0.246	0.0050
−0.400	0.00122	−0.428	0.0010
−0.500	0.00064	−0.950	0.0001

Note: Calculated using $k = 260$, $\hat{s} = 298$, $\hat{\zeta} = 2.887$.

Return	Probability	Return	Probability
		S&P500	
−0.200	0.02019	−0.258	0.0100
−0.300	0.00665	−0.333	0.0050
−0.400	0.00302	−0.598	0.0010
−0.500	0.00164	−1.383	0.0001

Note: Calculated using $k = 260$, $\hat{s} = 335$, $\hat{\zeta} = 2.749$.

Return	Probability	Return	Probability
		Dollar/sterling	
−0.200	0.00325	−0.132	0.0100
−0.300	0.00109	−0.171	0.0050
−0.400	0.00050	−0.310	0.0010
−0.500	0.00027	−0.725	0.0001

Note: Calculated using $k = 260$, $\hat{s} = 161$, $\hat{\zeta} = 2.716$.

5.5 Testing for covariance stationarity

As we have seen, the assumption of covariance stationarity, that the unconditional variance and covariances do not depend on time, is central to much of time series econometrics. This assumed constancy of second moments is, however, rarely implied by models of optimising behaviour, which are typically formulated in terms of restrictions on the *conditional* moments, as in the efficient markets hypothesis, or in terms of relationships between conditional moments, as in the CAPM. In financial markets we might reasonably expect that unconditional second moments would not remain constant over long periods of time: for example, information and technology are subject to temporal evolution and can be hypothesised to affect the unconditional variance of assets.

Nevertheless, the assumption of covariance stationarity is a convenient one to make and is frequently employed. For example, a GARCH X_t will be covariance stationary as long as certain conditions are met on the specification of the *conditional* variance. As we demonstrated in chapter 4, for the ARCH(1) process, $\beta < 1$ is required, while general conditions for a GARCH process are given in Bougerol and Picard (1992). Notwithstanding the wide popularity of GARCH models, however, there has accumulated considerable empirical evidence to suggest that *unconditional* second moments of returns data tend not to be constant, thus throwing into doubt the assumption of covariance stationarity. Mandelbrot (1963a), in arguing that returns had infinite unconditional variance, proposed examining the recursive estimates

$$\hat{\mu}_{2,t} = t^{-1} \sum_{j=1}^{t} X_j^2, \qquad t = 1, 2, \ldots, T$$

If $\hat{\mu}_{2,t}$ converges to a constant as T increases, covariance stationarity would seem to be a reasonable assumption, whereas if it wanders around then an infinite variance might be suggested (see also Granger and Orr, 1972). Pagan and Schwert (1990b) remark that this idea is equivalent to the cumulative sum of squares test of Brown, Durbin and Evans (1975), but they point out that it assumes that the maintained distribution is normal, which is obviously inappropriate when dealing with series of returns. Pagan and Schwert thus propose using

$$\psi(r) = (T\hat{\upsilon})^{-1/2} \sum_{j=1}^{[Tr]} \left(X_j^2 - \hat{\mu}_{2,T}\right)$$

where $0 < r < 1$ and

$$\hat{\nu}^2 = \hat{\gamma}_0 + 2\sum_{j=1}^{l} (1 - j/(l+1))\hat{\gamma}_j$$

is a kernel-based estimate of the 'long-run' variance of X_t^2, using the covariances $\hat{\gamma}_0, \ldots, \hat{\gamma}_l$ of the series. This statistic is a studentised version of the cumulative sum of squares statistic, since it standardises the partial sums by a sample-based estimate of ν^2 rather than its expected value under normality. Inference about $\psi(r)$ depends crucially on the value taken by the tail index ζ of the distribution of X. For $\zeta > 4$ and $T \to \infty$, Loretan and Phillips (1994) show that $\psi(r)$ converges weakly to a Brownian bridge (a tied-down Brownian motion: see chapter 3.1.6), making the probability that $\psi(r) < c$ equal to the probability that a $N(0, r(1-r))$ random variable is less than c.

For $\zeta < 4$, however, $\psi(r)$ converges to a standardised tied-down stable process. Critical values thus depend in a complicated fashion on ζ and are tabulated in Loretan and Phillips (1994, table 2). For example, for $\zeta > 4$, the 5 per cent critical value of $\psi(0.9)$ is 0.49, whereas for $\zeta = 2.1$ it is 0.27; however, while the $\zeta < 4$ 5 per cent critical value of $\psi(0.1)$ is also 0.49 because of the symmetry of the limit distribution, for $\zeta = 2.1$ it is 0.66. Moreover, the test has decreasing power as ζ tends to 2 from above, since its rate of divergence from the null becomes much slower because of the presence of increasing amounts of outliers. For $\zeta \leq 2$ the test is inconsistent, which is hardly surprising as in this case variances are infinite anyway.

The entire sequence of $\psi(r)$ values may also be investigated by considering scalar-valued test statistics, for example, $\sup_r(\psi(r))$, $\inf_r(\psi(r))$ and $R = \sup_r(\psi(r)) - \inf_r(\psi(r))$, the latter in fact being identical to Lo's (1991) modified rescaled range statistic discussed in chapter 3.4. Again, critical values for these statistics are provided in Loretan and Phillips (1994). While we have assumed throughout this section that X_t is strict white noise or, more generally, that it may be generated as the independent and identically distributed innovations from an autoregression of an observed series, the above propositions do not depend crucially on this assumption, which may be relaxed considerably. What matters for the purposes of testing for constancy of the unconditional variance is the value taken by the maximal finite moment of X_t, ζ, and in particular whether it exceeds 4 or not.

Figure 5.3 provides plots of the $\psi(r)$ sequences for the three return series. As has been found, all series have tail indices in the range $2 < \zeta < 4$. Ninety five per cent critical values for $\sup_r(\psi(r))$ decrease from 1.224 for $\zeta > 4$ to 0.98 for $\zeta = 2.1$, the negatives of these values being the corresponding critical values for $\inf_r(\psi(r))$. Appropriate critical

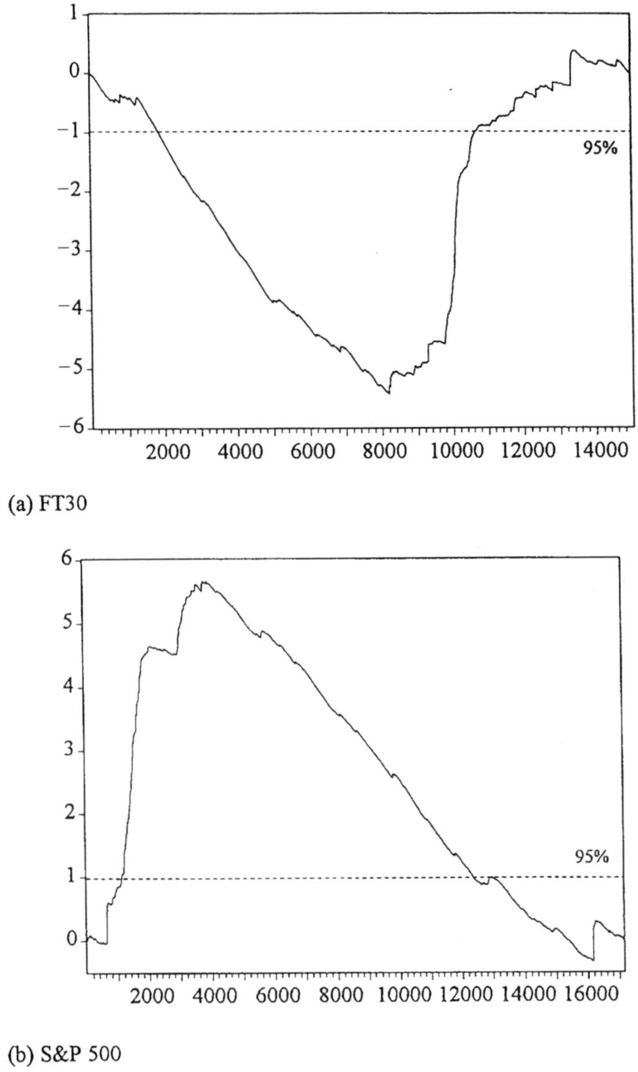

Figure 5.3 Cumulative sum of squares plots

values are superimposed on each of the plots. Before computing the statistics, however, the return series were pre-filtered using an autoregression to remove a non-zero mean and any serial correlation. Table 5.5 shows values of $\sup_r(\psi(r))$, $\inf_r(\psi(r))$, and the range statistic R, and these confirm the evidence against covariance stationarity.

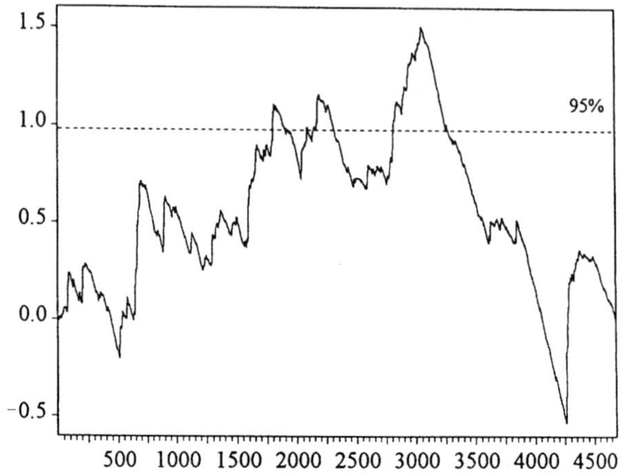

(c) Dollar/sterling exchange rate

Figure 5.3 (*cont.*)

5.6 Modelling the central part of returns distributions

We have concentrated attention so far on the tail shape of returns distributions as, until recently, there had been little discussion of the shape of the central part of such distributions. This lack of attention is a little surprising, given that returns distributions are typically characterised by being highly 'peaked' as well as being too fat tailed. Mantegna and Stanley (1995) consider fitting stable distributions to the central part of a return distribution. They do this by utilising the property of invariance under addition and studying the 'probability of return' $P(X_t(k) = 0)$, where $X_t(k) = \sum_{i=0}^{k} X_{t-i}$ is the k-period non-overlapping return, for different values of k. For a stable distribution, we have

Table 5.5. *Cumulative sum of squares tests of covariance stationarity*

	$\sup_r(\psi(r))$	$\inf_r(\psi(r))$	R
*FT*30	0.39	−5.44*	5.83*
*S&P*500	5.60*	−0.35	5.95*
Dollar/sterling	1.63	−0.58	2.21*

Note: *Denotes significance at 1% level for all values of $\zeta > 2$.

$$P(X_t(k) = 0) = \frac{\Gamma(1/\alpha)}{\pi\alpha(\gamma k)^{1/\alpha}}$$

Mantegna and Stanley suggest estimating α as (minus) the inverse of the slope estimate in a logarithmic regression of $P(X_t(k) = 0)$ on k. This procedure is followed here, but it requires an estimate of the probability of return for each value of k. This probability may be estimated as the frequency of $-x < X_t(k) \leq x$, where the value of x is chosen to be a suitably small number depending on the scale of the observed returns and the range of k values is chosen to reflect the length and frequency of the series.

The results from this regression procedure are shown in table 5.6, and all three return series have characteristic exponents that are below 2. Of particular interest is the estimate of α for the S&P500. Mantegna and Stanley (1995) used transactions data on this index for the six-year period from 1984 to 1989 and obtained an estimate of 1.40. With daily data over 64 years, we obtain $\hat{\alpha} = 1.42$: a remarkable confirmation of the invariance property of stable distributions.

Mantegna and Stanley remark on the tightness of the stable fit for values within about six standard deviations of zero, outside of which the tails of the distribution seem to follow an exponential, rather than a stable, decline. This is consistent with our findings: the central part of a returns distribution seems to follow a stable law, while the tails undergo an exponential decline so that the variance of the distribution is finite. That the centre is a stable distribution may well be surprising to some data analysts, for 'Winsor's principle' suggests that the middle of most distributions are normally distributed. We provide supporting evidence for this central non-normality in the next section, but we also note that the finding is consistent with theoretical results on truncated stable distributions, known as truncated Lévy Flights (Mantegna and Stanley, 1994, Shlesinger, 1995).

Table 5.6. *Estimates of characteristic exponents from the central part of distributions*

	Slope	$\hat{\alpha}$	R^2
*FT*30	−0.636	1.573	0.993
*S&P*500	−0.703	1.423	0.980
Dollar/sterling	−0.617	1.620	0.935

5.7 Data analytic modelling of skewness and kurtosis

So far in this chapter we have concentrated on the fat-tailed and highly peaked characteristics of return distributions and ignored, both theoretically and empirically, the possibility that the distributions may exhibit some degree of skewness. Skewness is important both because of its impact on portfolio choice and because kurtosis is not independent of skewness, so that the latter may 'induce' the former. Skewness measures for our series were reported in table 5.1: all are negative and significantly different from zero on using the fact that $\sqrt{(T/6)} \cdot skew \sim N(0, 1)$. We investigate skewness further by constructing plots using the order statistics introduced earlier. The median can be defined as $X_{med} = X_{([T/2])}$. For a symmetric distribution, the order statistics $X_{(p)}, X_{(T-p)}, \ p < [T/2]$, are equidistant from the median, i.e.

$$X_{(T-p)} - X_{med} = X_{med} - X_{(p)}$$

so that a plot of the upper-order statistics $X_{(T-p)}$ against the lower statistics $X_{(p)}$ should be linear with a slope of -1 if the distribution is symmetric.

Figure 5.4 shows these 'upper–lower' plots, which suggest that the distributions are symmetric over a wide range of values, with asymmetry

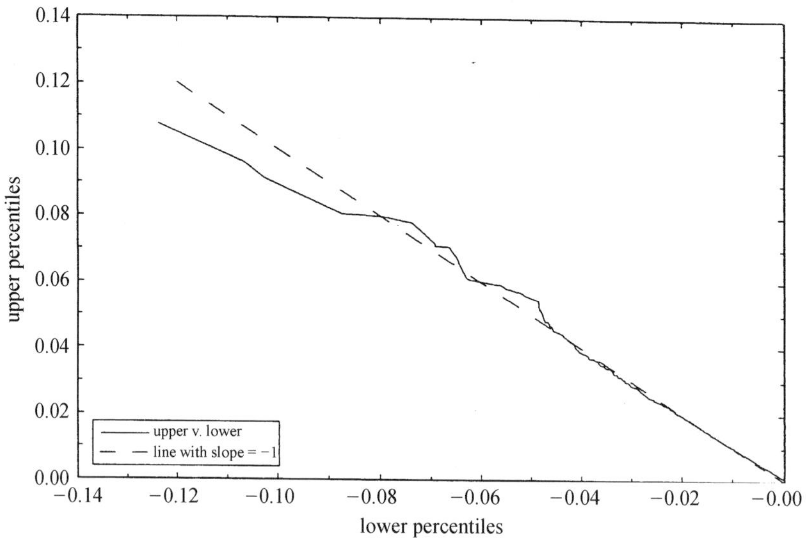

(a) FT30

Figure 5.4 'Upper-lower' symmetry plots

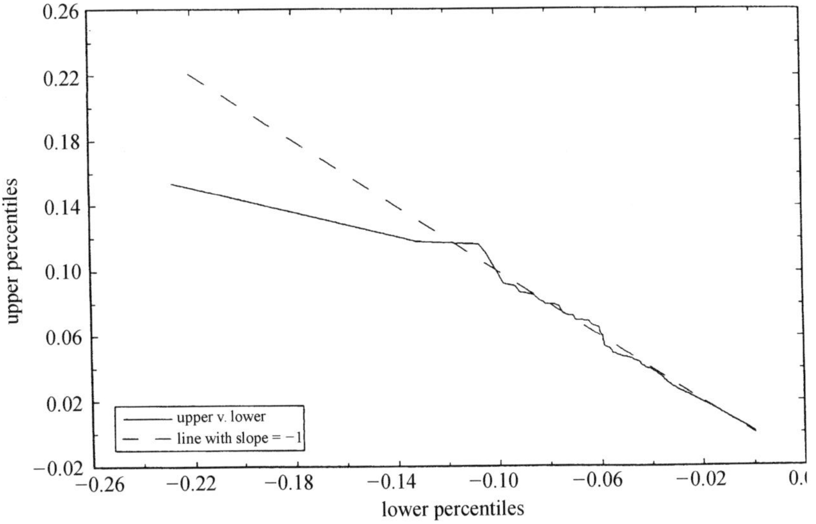

(b) S&P 500

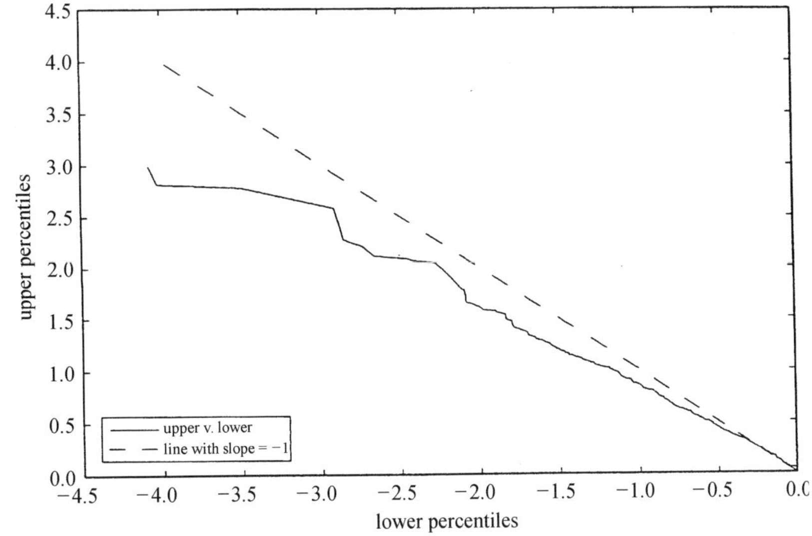

(c) Dollar/sterling exchange rate

Figure 5.4 (*cont.*)

only appearing in the tails of the distributions. Interestingly, the asymmetry is characterised by negative skewness, so that there is a greater probability of large falls in price than large increases. This is what we would expect from our knowledge of the episodic nature of market 'crashes', but is not what would be expected from three-moment portfolio analysis, in which investors should have a preference for positive skewness, for they should prefer portfolios with a larger probability of very large payoffs.

Badrinath and Chatterjee (1988, 1991) and Mills (1995) analyse skewness and kurtosis in returns distributions by fitting g, h and $g \times h$ distributions (see Tukey, 1977, and Hoaglin, 1985). These distributions are non-linear transformations of the normal. A g-distributed random variable Y_g is defined as

$$Y_g = A + Bg^{-1}(\exp(gZ) - 1)$$

where $Z \sim N(0, 1)$, and is thus a shifted log-normal random variable bounded by $-g^{-1}$. An h-distributed random variable is defined as

$$Y_h = A + BZ\exp\left(hZ^2/2\right)$$

A positive h will produce thicker tails than the normal. The $g \times h$ distribution is obtained by multiplying together the g and h distributions. In these definitions g and h are assumed to be constant, but Hoaglin (1985) allows them to be polynomial functions of Z^2 and also recommends that different functions be allowed for the two tails of the distribution. Details of how to fit these distributions may be found in the above references, and Mills (1995), for example, finds that the post-1987 Crash FTSE indices are characterised by positive skewness and different levels of excess kurtosis in the two tails, the right tail being thicker than the left. Badrinath and Chatterjee (1988) also find that the right tail of the New York market returns distribution is thicker than the left, and both studies conclude that the central part of the distribution behaves differently to the tails, as we have found here using different techniques.

5.8 Distributional properties of absolute returns

Granger and Ding (1995a) and Mills (1996a, 1997a) investigate the distributional properties of absolute daily returns, the usefulness of such a transformation for measuring risk being discussed in Granger and Ding (1995b). The use of absolute returns is suggested by the decomposition

$$X_t = |X_t| \cdot \operatorname{sign} X_t \tag{5.6}$$

where

$$\operatorname{sign} X_t = \begin{cases} 1 \text{ if } X_t > 0 \\ 0 \text{ if } X_t = 0 \\ -1 \text{ if } X_t < 0 \end{cases}$$

Granger and Ding (1995a) suggest three distributional properties related to the decomposition (5.6): (i), $|X_t|$ and sign X_t are independent, which will be the case if the conditional distributions $|X_t||(\text{sign } X_t = 1)$ and $|X_t| |(\text{sign } X_t = -1)$ are the same; (ii), the mean and variance of $|X_t|$ are equal; and (iii), the marginal distribution of $|X_t|$ is exponential after outlier reduction. This will be the case if both conditional distributions are exponential. Note that an exponential distribution with parameter ε has both mean and variance equal to ε, a skewness of 2 and a kurtosis of 9.

Granger and Ding (1995a) show that all three properties hold for the S&P500 series, which we confirm here in table 5.7, which reports conditional means and standard deviations of the absolute returns of the S&P500, the FT30, and the dollar/sterling exchange rate. We use both the original observations and 'outlier reduced' data: this was produced by replacing any observation greater than four times the standard deviation (S.D.) by the 4S.D. value having the same sign. We also report the ratio of these statistics plus skewness and kurtosis measures. For each series, these quantities are shown conditionally for $X_t > 0$ and $X_t < 0$ (denoted as $+$ and $-$), together with the frequencies (given in the row labelled 'Prob') of those signs occuring. The number of outliers reduced in each subsample are also reported.

For the two stock returns series there is evidence of asymmetry, in that $\text{Prob}(X_t > 0)$ exceeds $\text{Prob}(X_t < 0)$, which obviously reflects their underlying secular drift. The estimated conditional means and standard deviations of the outlier adjusted series are approximately equal, and the skewness and kurtosis measures are close to 2 and 9 respectively. This suggests that the marginal distributions of the outlier adjusted series are fairly well approximated by an exponential distribution. While formal testing of this hypothesis is inappropriate, as the series are not independent and identically distributed, it is interesting to note that very similar findings have been observed for the post-1987 Crash data on the London

Table 5.7. *Properties of marginal return distributions.*

	Observed		Outlier adjusted	
	+	–	+	–
		FT30		
Prob	0.50	0.44	–	–
Mean × 100	0.69	0.73	0.68	0.71
S.D. × 100	0.74	0.78	0.66	0.70
Mean/S.D.	0.93	0.93	1.02	1.01
Skewness	3.55	3.55	2.10	2.01
Kurtosis	26.87	28.76	8.77	8.13
Outliers	–	–	95	50
		S&P 500		
Prob	0.52	0.46	–	–
Mean × 100	0.72	0.73	0.71	0.76
S.D. × 100	0.85	0.94	0.74	0.81
Mean/S.D.	0.86	0.82	0.96	0.93
Skewness	4.30	4.82	2.49	2.30
Kurtosis	37.97	59.13	11.13	9.45
Outliers	–	–	138	74
		Dollar/Sterling		
Prob	0.46	0.45	–	–
Mean × 100	0.35	0.40	0.35	0.39
S.D. × 100	0.32	0.40	0.31	0.37
Mean/S.D.	1.10	0.99	1.14	1.06
Skewness	2.29	1.94	2.14	1.96
Kurtosis	12.29	8.21	9.24	7.46
Outliers	–	–	36	23

FTSE 100 and Mid 250 (Mills, 1997a). For the exchange rate series, there is much less evidence of asymmetry, with '+' and '–' frequencies being almost equal. Again the outlier adjusted means and standard deviations are almost equal and the skewness and kurtosis measures are close to 2 and 9. For all series the first property, that $|X_t|$ and sign X_t are independent, is confirmed using a Kolmogorov–Smirnov test. It would thus appear that the properties of absolute returns suggested by Granger and Ding (1995a) do indeed hold for this further selection of speculative price series (but see Rydén, Teräsvirta and Åsbrink, 1998, for further research in this area).

Granger and Ding (1995a) argue that, if $|X_t|$ is exponential, then it is reasonable to expect that the pair $|X_t|$, $|X_{t-k}|$ will be jointly exponential. This joint distribution has the properties that the marginal distributions are each exponential and that the conditional mean $E(|X_t|\,||X_{t-k}|)$ is a linear function of $|X_{t-k}|$. This suggests that linear regressions of absolute returns on lagged absolute returns may have some predictive power, although the results presented by Granger and Ding (1995a) and Mills (1996a, 1997a) show that any predictability is quite weak.

5.9 Summary and further extensions

We have surveyed a wide range of techniques for modelling the distribution of financial returns, illustrating each of them with stock and foreign exchange market data. The 'stylised facts' that come out of both our own empirical analysis and of the others surveyed here may be summarised thus. Returns are certainly not normally distributed but are characterised by fat tails and peakedness, both of which are unsurprising, and negative skewness, which is rather more surprising. However, it is only in the tails that skewness appears, with much of the distribution being symmetric. Although symmetric, this central part of the distribution is not normal, but tends to approximate a stable distribution. The tails, however, are not stable but are exponentially declining, being consistent with a finite variance. While having a finite variance, returns do not generally appear to have a constant (unconditional) variance, or indeed covariances – covariance stationarity is rejected for all series. Absolute returns, when adjusted for outliers, approximate to an exponential distribution.

These stylised facts suggest two broad areas of further research. The breakdown of covariance stationarity over all but the shortest of sample periods casts doubt on the validity and empirical accuracy of models that assume that the unconditional variance is constant, e.g., ARCH models. This suggests that extensions to time series models which explicitly incorporate error distributions that can effectively model outlier activity and time varying unconditional variances would be very useful.

The possibility that time series may have infinite variance has been taken into account for certain procedures discussed in earlier chapters. Phillips (1990) considers unit root tests under the assumption of infinite variance errors and shows that the non-parametric tests of chapter 3.1.4 continue to operate without any modification. Runde (1997) shows that the asymptotic distribution of the Box–Pierce Q^* statistic, introduced in example 2.1, is no longer χ^2 under an infinite variance assumption.

Rather than using Q^*, he proposes scaling it by the factor $T^{(2-\alpha)/\alpha} \big/ (\log T)^{2\alpha}$, and provides simulated critical values for the new statistic. Scaling by this factor will reduce the size of the statistic for typical situations, e.g., $T \leq 10{,}000$ and $\alpha > 1.5$. Some advances have been made in combining infinite variances with both short and long memory ARMA processes (Cioczek-Georges and Taqqu, 1995, and Kokoszka and Taqqu, 1994, 1996), but further research is clearly required.

It is also important that theoretical models of rational economic behaviour continue to be developed which can explain the outlier activity that leads to these common and distinctive distributional properties of financial returns. Some extensions of this type are discussed in McCulloch (1996), for example. Related to this, it is clear that evaluations of models should not rely on tests that are based on normal approximations. For example, trading rules should not be evaluated using tests that assume normal, stationary, and time-independent distributions. The use of bootstrap methodology (see Efron and Tibshirani, 1993) is one possibility and two examples are Brock, Lakonishok and LeBaron (1992) and Mills (1997b).

6 Regression techniques for non-integrated financial time series

The analysis of the general linear regression model forms the basis of every standard econometrics text and we see no need to repeat such a development here. Models relating to financial time series, however, often cannot be analysed within the basic framework of ordinary least squares regression, or even its extensions incorporating generalised least squares or instrumental variables techniques. This chapter thus develops a general theory of regression, based on the work of Hansen (1982), White (1984) and White and Domowitz (1984), that builds upon the univariate time series techniques of the previous chapters and is applicable to many, but by no means all, of the regression problems that arise in the analysis of the relationships between financial time series.

Section 1 thus sets out the basic dynamic linear regression model, while section 2 incorporates ARCH error effects into the framework. Misspecification testing is the topic of section 3, and section 4 discusses robust estimation techniques and generalised method of moments estimation, which may be used when the standard assumptions of regression are found to be invalid. The multivariate linear regression model is briefly introduced in section 5. This paves the way for more general multivariate regression techniques and the remaining sections of the chapter deal with vector autoregressions and its various extensions, including a discussion of the concepts of exogeneity and causality.

6.1 Regression models

6.1.1 Regression with non-integrated time series

We now extend our modelling techniques to consider relationships between a group of time series $\{\mathbf{z}_t\}$. We begin by analysing the simplest case in which a *single* variable y_t is postulated to be a (linear) function of past values of itself and present and past values of a vector of other variables $\mathbf{x}_t' = (x_{1t}, \ldots, x_{kt})$. Here $\mathbf{z}_t = (y_t, \mathbf{x}_t')'$ and, for the observed realisation $\{\mathbf{z}_t\}_1^T$, the model can be written as

$$y_t = \alpha_0 + \sum\nolimits_{i=1}^{m} \alpha_i y_{t-i} + \sum\nolimits_{i=0}^{m} \boldsymbol{\beta}_i \mathbf{x}_{t-i} + u_t, \quad m+1 \leq t \leq T \quad (6.1)$$

or

$$y_t = \mathbf{X}_t \boldsymbol{\beta} + u_t$$

In matrix form, we have

$$\mathbf{y} = \mathbf{X}\boldsymbol{\beta} + \mathbf{u} \quad (6.2)$$

where

$$\mathbf{y} = (y_{m+1}, \ldots, y_t)'$$
$$\mathbf{X} = (\mathbf{X}_{m+1}, \ldots, \mathbf{X}_T)'$$
$$\mathbf{X}_t = (1, y_{t-1}, \ldots, y_{t-m}, \mathbf{x}_t', \ldots, \mathbf{x}_{t-m}')$$
$$\mathbf{u} = (u_{m+1}, \ldots, u_T)'$$
$$\boldsymbol{\beta} = (\alpha_0, \alpha_1, \ldots, \alpha_m, \boldsymbol{\beta}_0, \ldots, \boldsymbol{\beta}_m)'$$
$$\boldsymbol{\beta}_i = (\boldsymbol{\beta}_{i1}, \ldots, \boldsymbol{\beta}_{ik}), \quad i = 0, \ldots, m$$

To estimate the parameters of interest, contained in the vector $\boldsymbol{\beta}$, certain assumptions are needed about $\{\mathbf{z}_t\}_1^T$ and the error process $\{u_t\}_1^T$. We begin by assuming that $\{\mathbf{z}_t\}_1^T$ is a normally distributed (weakly) stationary stochastic process. Noting that $\mathbf{z}_t$ is $k+1$ dimensional, extension of the stationarity requirements for a univariate series given in chapter 2.1 to this multivariate setting yields

$$E(\mathbf{z}_t) = \boldsymbol{\mu} = (\mu_y, \mu_1, \ldots, \mu_k)$$

and

$$Cov(\mathbf{z}_t, \mathbf{z}_s) = E(\mathbf{z}_t - \boldsymbol{\mu})(\mathbf{z}_{t-|t-s|} - \boldsymbol{\mu}) = \boldsymbol{\Gamma}(|t-s|), \quad 1 \leq t, s \leq T$$

so that the $\mathbf{z}_t$s have identical means and variances and their temporal covariances depend only on the absolute value of the time difference between them. Note, however, that the assumption of stationarity alone is not sufficient to obtain an operational model of the form (6.1). This is because the non-zero covariances allow dependence between, for example, $\mathbf{z}_1$ and $\mathbf{z}_T$, implying that the lag length m in (6.1) should strictly be set at $t-1$, so that the number of unknown parameters in the model increases with T. We thus need to restrict the form of the dependence in $\{\mathbf{z}_t\}_1^T$ and, to this end, the following concepts are important (see White, 1984, and Spanos, 1986, for detailed formal discussion): $\mathbf{z}_t$ is said to be *asymptotically independent* if

$$\boldsymbol{\Gamma}(\tau) \rightarrow 0 \text{ as } \tau = |t-s| \rightarrow \infty$$

and *ergodic* if

$$\lim_{T\rightarrow\infty}\left(\frac{1}{T}\sum_{\tau=1}^{T}\boldsymbol{\Gamma}(\tau)\right) = 0$$

It is conventional to make either the assumption of asymptotic independence or the somewhat weaker assumption of ergodicity (cf. the univariate development in chapter 2), and this allows us to restrict the *memory* of the process $\{\mathbf{z}_t\}_1^T$ and hence to fix the maximum lag at an appropriate value, say m, in (6.1). The error $\{u_t\}_1^T$ is defined formally as

$$u_t = y_t - E\left(y_t|\mathbf{y}_{t-1}^0, \mathbf{x}_t^0\right)$$

where

$$\mathbf{y}_{t-1}^0 = (y_{t-1}, y_{t-2}, \ldots, y_1)$$

and

$$\mathbf{x}_t^0 = (\mathbf{x}_t, \mathbf{x}_{t-1}, \ldots, \mathbf{x}_1)$$

We assume that it satisfies the following properties

$$E(u_t) = E\left(u_t|\mathbf{y}_{t-1}^0, \mathbf{x}_t^0\right) = 0$$

$$E(u_t u_s) = E\left\{E\left(u_t u_s|\mathbf{y}_{t-1}^0, \mathbf{x}_t^0\right)\right\} = \begin{cases} \sigma^2 & t = s \\ 0 & t > s \end{cases}$$

These two properties define u_t to be a martingale difference relative to the 'history' $\left(\mathbf{y}_{t-1}^0, \mathbf{x}_t^0\right)$ and to have a finite variance, i.e., that it is an *innovation* process. Note that the assumption of asymptotic independence implies that the roots of the polynomial $z^m - \sum_1^m \alpha_i z^{m-i} = 0$ are all less than unity in absolute value.

Assuming $\mathbf{X}$ to be of full rank $K = (m+1)(k+1)$, so that $\mathbf{X}'\mathbf{X}$ is non-singular, and u_t to be $NID(0, \sigma^2)$, the LS (and approximate ML) estimator of $\boldsymbol{\beta}$ obtained using the sample $\{\mathbf{z}_t\}_1^T$ is

$$\hat{\boldsymbol{\beta}}_T = (\mathbf{X}'\mathbf{X})^{-1}\mathbf{X}'\mathbf{y}$$

while the LS and approximate ML estimators of σ^2 are

$$\hat{\sigma}^2 = (T-m)^{-1}\hat{\mathbf{u}}'\hat{\mathbf{u}}$$

and

$$\tilde{\sigma}^2 = T^{-1}\hat{\mathbf{u}}'\hat{\mathbf{u}}$$

respectively, where $\hat{\mathbf{u}} = \mathbf{y} - \mathbf{X}\hat{\boldsymbol{\beta}}_T$ is the regression residual vector (the ML estimators are said to be approximate because the initial conditions involving the observations $y_1, \ldots, y_m$ are ignored). Since u_t is not independent of future y_ts, $E(\mathbf{X}'\mathbf{u}) \neq \mathbf{0}$, and so $\hat{\boldsymbol{\beta}}_T$ is a biased estimator of $\boldsymbol{\beta}$

$$E\left(\hat{\boldsymbol{\beta}}_T - \boldsymbol{\beta}\right) = E\left((\mathbf{X}'\mathbf{X})^{-1}\mathbf{X}'\mathbf{u}\right) \neq \mathbf{0}$$

However, assuming $\mathbf{G}_T = E(\mathbf{X}'\mathbf{X}/T)$ to be uniformally positive definite and since $E(\mathbf{X}_t'u_t) = \mathbf{0}$ then, under certain conditions concerning the magnitude of $E(\mathbf{X}'\mathbf{X})$, $\hat{\boldsymbol{\beta}}_T$ can be shown to be a *strongly consistent* estimator of $\boldsymbol{\beta}$, as indeed is $\hat{\sigma}_T^2$ of σ^2. The estimators are also *asymptotically normal*

$$\mathbf{G}_T^{-\frac{1}{2}} T^{\frac{1}{2}}\left(\hat{\boldsymbol{\beta}}_T - \boldsymbol{\beta}\right) \overset{a}{\sim} N(\mathbf{0}, \mathbf{I})$$
$$T^{\frac{1}{2}}\left(\hat{\sigma}_T^2 - \sigma^2\right) \overset{a}{\sim} N\left(\mathbf{0}, 2\sigma^4\right)$$

(for formal derivations of these results, see, for example, White, 1984, and Spanos, 1986). $\mathbf{G}_T$ can be consistently estimated in this case as $\sigma_T^2(\mathbf{X}'\mathbf{X})^{-1}$, this being the conventional formula in LS regression.

These results can be extended to allow both $\mathbf{z}_t$ and u_t to exhibit time dependence and heterogeneity simultaneously. Specifically, the memory requirement can be relaxed from that of stationarity and asymptotic independence (or ergodicity) to one of *strong mixing*, as discussed in chapter 3.1.4 (see conditions (3.10)). White (1984, exercise 3.51 and theorem 4.25) provides a formal statement of the required conditions and shows that, in these circumstances, $\hat{\boldsymbol{\beta}}_T$ is still consistent and asymptotically normal, although we now have

$$\mathbf{D}_T^{-\frac{1}{2}} T^{\frac{1}{2}}\left(\hat{\boldsymbol{\beta}}_T - \boldsymbol{\beta}\right) \overset{a}{\sim} N(\mathbf{0}, \mathbf{I})$$

where

$$\mathbf{D}_T = (\mathbf{X}'\mathbf{X}/T)^{-1}\hat{\mathbf{V}}_T(\mathbf{X}'\mathbf{X}/T)^{-1}$$

$\hat{\mathbf{V}}_T$ is an estimate of $\mathbf{V}_T = E(\mathbf{X}'\mathbf{u}\mathbf{u}'\mathbf{X}/T)$, which can be expressed in terms of individual observations as

$$\begin{aligned}\mathbf{V}_T &= E\left(T^{-1}\sum_{t=1}^{T}\mathbf{X}_t' u_t u_t' \mathbf{X}_t\right) = T^{-1}\sum_{t=1}^{T} E(\mathbf{X}_t' u_t u_t' \mathbf{X}_t)\\ &\quad + T^{-1}\sum_{\tau=1}^{T-1}\sum_{t=\tau+1}^{T} E(\mathbf{X}_t' u_t u_{t-\tau}' \mathbf{X}_{t-\tau} + \mathbf{X}_{t-\tau}' u_{t-\tau} u_t' \mathbf{X}_t)\\ &= T^{-1}\sum_{t=1}^{T} V(\mathbf{X}_t' u_t) + T^{-1}\sum_{\tau=1}^{T-1}\sum_{t=\tau+1}^{T} (Cov(\mathbf{X}_t' u_t, \mathbf{X}_{t-\tau}' u_{t-\tau})\\ &\quad + Cov(\mathbf{X}_{t-\tau}' u_{t-\tau}, \mathbf{X}_t' u_t))\end{aligned}$$

thus revealing that $\mathbf{V}_T$ is the average of the variances of $\mathbf{X}_t' u_t$ plus a term that takes account of the covariance between $\mathbf{X}_t' u_t$ and $\mathbf{X}_{t-\tau}' u_{t-\tau}$ for all t and τ. With our mixing assumptions, the covariance between $\mathbf{X}_t' u_t$ and $\mathbf{X}_{t-\tau}' u_{t-\tau}$ goes to zero as $\tau \to \infty$, and hence $\mathbf{V}_T$ can be approximated by

$$\begin{aligned}\tilde{\mathbf{V}}_T &= T^{-1}\sum_{t=1}^{T} E(\mathbf{X}_t' u_t u_t' \mathbf{X}_t)\\ &\quad + T^{-1}\sum_{\tau=1}^{n}\sum_{t=\tau+1}^{T} E(\mathbf{X}_t' u_t u_{t-\tau}' \mathbf{X}_{t-\tau} + \mathbf{X}_{t-\tau}' u_{t-\tau} u_t' \mathbf{X}_t)\end{aligned} \tag{6.3}$$

for some value n, because the neglected terms (those for which $n < \tau \leq T$) will be small in absolute value if n is sufficiently large. Note, however, that if n is simply kept fixed as T grows, then the number of neglected terms grows, and may grow in such a way that the sum of these terms does not remain negligible. The estimator $\hat{\mathbf{V}}_T$, obtained by replacing u_t by $\hat{u}_t$ in (6.3), will then be a consistent estimator of $\tilde{\mathbf{V}}_T$ (and hence of $\mathbf{V}_T$) if n does not grow too fast as T grows: specifically, we must ensure that n grows more slowly than $T^{\frac{1}{3}}$. Unfortunately, although it is consistent, $\hat{\mathbf{V}}_T$ need not be positive semi-definite in small samples. For this reason, we may use the Newey and West (1987) modified estimator, first introduced in chapter 3.1.4 and defined here as

$$\begin{aligned}\hat{\mathbf{V}}_T = T^{-1}\sum_{t=1}^{T}(\mathbf{X}_t'\hat{u}_t\hat{u}_t'\mathbf{X}_t) + T^{-1}\sum_{\tau=1}^{n}(1-(\tau/(n+1)))\\ \times\sum_{t=\tau+1}^{T}\left(\mathbf{X}_t'\hat{u}_t\hat{u}_{t-\tau}'\mathbf{X}_{t-\tau}+\mathbf{X}_{t-\tau}'\hat{u}_{t-\tau}\hat{u}_t'\mathbf{X}_t\right)\end{aligned} \quad (6.4)$$

6.1.2 Hypothesis testing

As is traditional, we consider hypotheses that can be expressed as linear combinations of the parameters in $\boldsymbol{\beta}$

$$\mathbf{R}\boldsymbol{\beta} = \mathbf{r}$$

where $\mathbf{R}$ and $\mathbf{r}$ are a matrix and a vector of known elements, both of row dimension q, that specify the q hypotheses of interest.

Several different approaches can be taken in computing a statistic to test the null hypothesis $\mathbf{R}\boldsymbol{\beta} = \mathbf{r}$ against the alternative $\mathbf{R}\boldsymbol{\beta} \neq \mathbf{r}$: we will consider here the use of Wald, Lagrange Multiplier and (quasi-)likelihood ratio statistics. Although the approaches to forming the test statistics differ, in each case an underlying asymptotic normality property is exploited to obtain a statistic which is asymptotically distributed as χ^2. Detailed development of the theory of hypothesis testing using these approaches may be found in Godfrey (1988).

The Wald statistic allows the simplest analysis, although it may not be the easiest to compute. Its motivation is the observation that, when the null hypothesis is correct, $\mathbf{R}\hat{\boldsymbol{\beta}}_T$ should be close to $\mathbf{R}\boldsymbol{\beta} = \mathbf{r}$, so that a value of $\mathbf{R}\hat{\boldsymbol{\beta}}_T - \mathbf{r}$ far from zero should be viewed as evidence against the null hypothesis. To tell how far from zero $\mathbf{R}\hat{\boldsymbol{\beta}}_T - \mathbf{r}$ must be before we reject the null hypothesis, we need to determine its asymptotic distribution. White (1984) shows that, if the rank of $\mathbf{R}$ is $q \leq K$, then the Wald statistic is

$$W_T = T\left(\mathbf{R}\hat{\boldsymbol{\beta}}_T - \mathbf{r}\right)'\hat{\boldsymbol{\Omega}}_T^{-1}\left(\mathbf{R}\hat{\boldsymbol{\beta}}_T - \mathbf{r}\right) \overset{a}{\sim} \chi_q^2 \tag{6.5}$$

where

$$\hat{\boldsymbol{\Omega}}_T = \mathbf{R}\mathbf{D}_T\mathbf{R}' = \mathbf{R}(\mathbf{X}'\mathbf{X}/T)^{-1}\hat{\mathbf{V}}_T(\mathbf{X}'\mathbf{X}/T)^{-1}\mathbf{R}'$$

This version of the Wald statistic is useful regardless of the presence of heteroskedasticity or serial correlation in the error $\mathbf{u}$ because a consistent estimator $\hat{\mathbf{V}}_T$ is used to construct $\hat{\boldsymbol{\Omega}}_T$. In the special case where $\mathbf{u}$ is white noise, $\hat{\mathbf{V}}_T$ can be consistently estimated by $\hat{\sigma}_T^2(\mathbf{X}'\mathbf{X}/T)$, and the Wald statistic then has the form

$$W_T = T\left(\mathbf{R}\hat{\boldsymbol{\beta}}_T - \mathbf{r}\right)'\left(\mathbf{R}((\mathbf{X}'\mathbf{X})/T)^{-1}\mathbf{R}'\right)^{-1}\left(\mathbf{R}\hat{\boldsymbol{\beta}}_T - \mathbf{r}\right)\Big/\hat{\sigma}_T^2$$

which is simply q times the standard F-statistic for testing the hypothesis $\mathbf{R}\boldsymbol{\beta} = \mathbf{r}$. The validity of the asymptotic χ_q^2 distribution for this statistic, however, depends crucially on the consistency of the estimator $\hat{\sigma}_T^2(\mathbf{X}'\mathbf{X}/T)$ for $\mathbf{V}_T$: if this $\hat{\mathbf{V}}_T$ is not consistent for $\mathbf{V}_T$, the asymptotic distribution of this form for W_T is not χ_q^2 and hence failure to take account of serial correlation and heterogeneity in the errors will lead to inferences being made using an incorrect distribution.

The Wald statistic is the most convenient test to use when the restrictions $\mathbf{R}\boldsymbol{\beta} = \mathbf{r}$ are not easy to impose in estimating $\boldsymbol{\beta}$. When these restrictions can be imposed easily, the Lagrange Multiplier statistic is more convenient to compute. The motivation for the LM statistic is that a constrained LS estimator can be obtained by solving the first-order condition of the Lagrangian expression

$$L = (\mathbf{y} - \mathbf{X}\boldsymbol{\beta})'(\mathbf{y} - \mathbf{X}\boldsymbol{\beta})/T + (\mathbf{R}\boldsymbol{\beta} - \mathbf{r})'\lambda$$

The Lagrange multipliers λ give the shadow price of the constraint and should therefore be small when the constraint is valid and large otherwise. The LM test can thus be thought of as testing the hypothesis that $\lambda = 0$. Solving the first-order conditions for λ yields

$$\ddot{\lambda}_T = 2\left(\mathbf{R}(\mathbf{X}'\mathbf{X}/T)^{-1}\mathbf{R}'\right)^{-1}\left(\mathbf{R}\hat{\boldsymbol{\beta}}_T - \mathbf{r}\right)$$

so that $\ddot{\lambda}_T$ is simply a non-singular transformation of $\mathbf{R}\hat{\boldsymbol{\beta}}_T - \mathbf{r}$. Also provided by solving the first-order conditions is the constrained LS estimator $\ddot{\boldsymbol{\beta}}_T$, given by

$$\ddot{\boldsymbol{\beta}}_T = \hat{\boldsymbol{\beta}}_T - \left(\mathbf{X}'\mathbf{X}/T\right)^{-1}\mathbf{R}'\ddot{\lambda}_T/2$$

from which can be calculated the constrained estimator of σ^2

$$\ddot{\sigma}^2 = (T - m)\ddot{\mathbf{u}}'\mathbf{u}$$

where $\ddot{\mathbf{u}} = \mathbf{y} - \mathbf{X}\ddot{\boldsymbol{\beta}}_T$ are the residuals from the constrained regression. The LM test statistic is then defined as

$$LM_T = T\ddot{\lambda}_T'\boldsymbol{\Lambda}_T\ddot{\lambda}_T \overset{a}{\sim} \chi_q^2 \tag{6.6}$$

where

$$\boldsymbol{\Lambda}_T = 4\left(\mathbf{R}\left(\mathbf{X}'\mathbf{X}/T\right)^{-1}\mathbf{R}'\right)^{-1}\mathbf{R}\left(\mathbf{X}'\mathbf{X}/T\right)^{-1}\ddot{\mathbf{V}}_T\left(\mathbf{X}'\mathbf{X}/T\right)^{-1}$$
$$\times\, \mathbf{R}'\left(\mathbf{R}\left(\mathbf{X}'\mathbf{X}/T\right)^{-1}\mathbf{R}'\right)^{-1}$$

$\ddot{\mathbf{V}}_T$ being computed from the constrained regression. Note that the Wald and LM statistics (6.5) and (6.6) would be identical if $\hat{\mathbf{V}}_T$ were used in place of $\ddot{\mathbf{V}}_T$ and, indeed, the two statistics are asymptotically equivalent.

As we have seen, when the errors u_t are $NID(0, \sigma^2)$, the LS estimator $\hat{\boldsymbol{\beta}}_T$ is also the ML estimator. When this is not the case, $\hat{\boldsymbol{\beta}}_T$ is said to be a QML estimator. When $\hat{\boldsymbol{\beta}}_T$ is the ML estimator, hypothesis tests can be based on the *log likelihood ratio* (LR)

$$LR_T = \log\left(L(\ddot{\boldsymbol{\beta}}_T, \ddot{\sigma}_T)\Big/L\left(\hat{\boldsymbol{\beta}}_T, \hat{\sigma}_T\right)\right)$$

where

$$L(\boldsymbol{\beta}, \sigma) = \exp\left(-T\log\sqrt{2\pi} - T\log\sigma - \tfrac{1}{2}\sum_{t=m+1}^{T}(y_t - \mathbf{X}_t\boldsymbol{\beta})^2\Big/\sigma^2\right)$$

is the sample likelihood based on the normality assumption. Simple algebra yields the following alternative form of the statistic

$$LR_T = (T/2)\log\left(\hat{\sigma}_T^2/\ddot{\sigma}_T^2\right)$$

and it can be shown that $-2LR_T$ is asymptotically equivalent to the Wald statistic (6.5) and thus has a χ_q^2 distribution asymptotically, *provided* that

$\hat{\sigma}_T^2(\mathbf{X}'\mathbf{X}/T)$ is a consistent estimator of $\mathbf{V}_T$. If this is not true, then $-2LR_T$ is not asymptotically χ_q^2.

So far we have considered linear hypotheses of the form $\mathbf{R}\boldsymbol{\beta} = \mathbf{r}$. In general, non-linear hypotheses can be conveniently represented as

$$H_0 : \mathbf{s}(\boldsymbol{\beta}) = \mathbf{0}$$

where $\mathbf{s}$ is a continuously differentiable function of $\boldsymbol{\beta}$. Just as with linear restrictions, we can construct a Wald test based on the asymptotic distribution of $\mathbf{s}(\hat{\boldsymbol{\beta}}_T)$, we can construct an LM test, or we can form a log likelihood ratio. Assuming that the rank of $\Delta\mathbf{s}(\boldsymbol{\beta}) = q \leq K$, where $\Delta\mathbf{s}$ is the gradient (derivative) of $\mathbf{s}$, then under $H_0 : \mathbf{s}(\boldsymbol{\beta}) = \mathbf{0}$, the Wald and LM test statistics are given by equations (6.5) and (6.6) with $\mathbf{s}(\hat{\boldsymbol{\beta}}_T)$ and $\Delta\mathbf{s}(\hat{\boldsymbol{\beta}})_T$ replacing $\mathbf{R}\hat{\boldsymbol{\beta}}_T - \mathbf{r}$ and $\mathbf{R}$, respectively, in (6.5) and $\mathbf{s}(\ddot{\boldsymbol{\beta}}_T)$ and $\Delta\mathbf{s}(\ddot{\boldsymbol{\beta}}_T)$ similarly replacing these terms in (6.6).

6.1.3 Instrumental variable estimation

We have so far considered only (ordinary) LS estimation of the model (6.1). If the assumption $E(\mathbf{X}_t'u_t) = \mathbf{0}$ does not hold, but a set of l instrumental variables (IVs), say $\mathbf{W}_t = (w_{1t}, \ldots, w_{lt})$, are available such that $E(\mathbf{W}_t'u_t) = \mathbf{0}$ and $E(\mathbf{W}'\mathbf{X}/T)$ has uniformly full column rank, then we can form the IV estimator

$$\tilde{\boldsymbol{\beta}}_T = \left(\mathbf{X}'\mathbf{W}\hat{\mathbf{P}}_T\mathbf{W}'\mathbf{X}\right)^{-1}\mathbf{X}'\mathbf{W}\hat{\mathbf{P}}_T\mathbf{W}'\mathbf{y}$$

where $\mathbf{W} = (\mathbf{W}_{m+1}, \ldots, \mathbf{W}_T)$ and $\hat{\mathbf{P}}_T$ is a symmetric $l \times l$ positive definite norming matrix. For example, with $\mathbf{W} = \mathbf{X}$ and $\hat{\mathbf{P}}_T = (\mathbf{W}'\mathbf{W}/T)^{-1}$, $\tilde{\boldsymbol{\beta}}_T = \hat{\boldsymbol{\beta}}_T$, while for any $\mathbf{W}$, choosing $\hat{\mathbf{P}}_T = (\mathbf{W}'\mathbf{W}/T)^{-1}$ yields the *two-stage least squares* estimator. Analogous to the results for the LS estimator, if $\mathbf{W}_t$ is also mixing, then $\tilde{\boldsymbol{\beta}}_T$ is strongly consistent and

$$\mathbf{D}_T^{-\frac{1}{2}}T^{\frac{1}{2}}\left(\tilde{\boldsymbol{\beta}}_T - \boldsymbol{\beta}\right) \stackrel{a}{\sim} N(\mathbf{0}, \mathbf{I})$$

where now

$$\mathbf{D}_T = \left(\mathbf{X}'\mathbf{W}\hat{\mathbf{P}}_T\mathbf{W}'\mathbf{X}/T^2\right)^{-1}(\mathbf{X}'\mathbf{W}/T)\hat{\mathbf{P}}_T\hat{\mathbf{V}}_T\hat{\mathbf{P}}_T(\mathbf{W}'\mathbf{X}/T)$$
$$\times\left(\mathbf{X}'\mathbf{W}\hat{\mathbf{P}}_T\mathbf{W}'\mathbf{X}/T^2\right)^{-1}$$

So far we have let $\hat{\mathbf{P}}_T$ be any positive definite matrix. By choosing $\hat{\mathbf{P}}_T = \hat{\mathbf{V}}_T^{-1}$, however, an *asymptotically efficient* estimator is obtained for the class of IV estimators with given instrumental variables $\mathbf{W}$, i.e.

$$\boldsymbol{\beta}_T^* = \left(\mathbf{X}'\mathbf{W}\hat{\mathbf{V}}_T^{-1}\mathbf{W}'\mathbf{X}\right)^{-1}\mathbf{X}'\mathbf{W}\hat{\mathbf{V}}_T^{-1}\mathbf{W}'\mathbf{y}$$

is asymptotically efficient within the class of IV estimators $\tilde{\boldsymbol{\beta}}_T$.

How should we choose the set of instruments $\mathbf{W}_t$? It can be shown that the asymptotic precision of the IV estimator cannot be worsened by including additional instruments. There are situations, however, when nothing is gained by adding an additional instrument: this is when the additional instrument is uncorrelated with the residuals of the regression of $\mathbf{X}$ on the already included instruments.

When serial correlation or heteroskedasticity of unknown form is present in (6.1), there may, in fact, be no limit to the number of instrumental variables available for improving the efficiency of the IV estimator: functions of $\mathbf{X}$ and $\mathbf{W}$ are possible instruments. In the absence of serial correlation or heteroskedasticity, however, it is possible to specify precisely a finite set of instruments that yield the greatest possible efficiency: they will be those functions of $\mathbf{W}_t$ that appear in the conditional expectation of $\mathbf{X}_t$ given $\mathbf{W}_t$.

6.1.4 Generalised methods of moments estimation

Suppose we have a general, possibly non-linear, model which we can write as $u_t = f(y_t, \mathbf{X}_t, \boldsymbol{\theta})$, where $\boldsymbol{\theta}$ is an $s \times 1$ vector of parameters and u_t can be both serially correlated and heteroskedastic. Our model tells us only that there is some true set of parameters $\boldsymbol{\theta}_0$ for which u_t is orthogonal to a set of instruments $\mathbf{W}_t$, so that

$$E(\mathbf{W}_t u_t) = E(\mathbf{W}_t f(y_t, \mathbf{X}_t, \boldsymbol{\theta}_0)) = E(\mathbf{m}(y_t, \mathbf{X}_t, \mathbf{W}_t, \boldsymbol{\theta}_0)) = \mathbf{0}$$

The estimation technique known as generalised methods of moments (GMM: Hansen, 1982) focuses on these orthogonality conditions: see Hamilton (1994, chapter 14) and Campbell, Lo and MacKinlay (1997, appendix) for detailed treatments and Johnston and DiNardo (1997, chapter 10) for a textbook discussion.

If we define a vector $\mathbf{m}_T(\boldsymbol{\theta})$ containing the sample averages of the elements of $\mathbf{m}(\ )$

$$\mathbf{m}_T(\boldsymbol{\theta}) = T^{-1}\sum_{t=1}^{T} \mathbf{m}(y_t, \mathbf{X}_t, \mathbf{W}_t, \boldsymbol{\theta})$$

GMM minimises the quadratic form $\mathbf{m}_T(\boldsymbol{\theta})'\mathbf{A}_T\mathbf{m}_T(\boldsymbol{\theta})$, where $\mathbf{A}_T$ is a weighting matrix, leading to the first-order condition

$$\mathbf{M}_T\left(\hat{\boldsymbol{\theta}}_T\right)'\mathbf{A}_T\mathbf{M}_T\left(\hat{\boldsymbol{\theta}}_T\right) = \mathbf{0}$$

where $\mathbf{M}_T(\boldsymbol{\theta}) = \partial\mathbf{m}_T(\boldsymbol{\theta})/\partial\boldsymbol{\theta}$.

The asymptotic distribution of $\hat{\theta}_T$ is

$$\mathbf{D}_{\mathrm{M},T}^{-\frac{1}{2}}T^{\frac{1}{2}}\left(\hat{\boldsymbol{\theta}}_T - \boldsymbol{\theta}_0\right) \overset{a}{\sim} N(\mathbf{0}, \mathbf{I})$$

where

$$\mathbf{D}_{\mathrm{M},T} = \left(\mathbf{M}_T'\mathbf{A}_T\mathbf{M}_T\right)^{-1}\mathbf{M}_T'\mathbf{W}\hat{\mathbf{V}}_{\mathrm{M},T}\mathbf{W}\mathbf{M}\left(\mathbf{M}_T'\mathbf{A}_T\mathbf{M}_T\right)^{-1}$$

$\hat{\mathbf{V}}_{\mathrm{M},T}$ being defined analogously to $\hat{\mathbf{V}}_T$ in (6.4). As in the IV case discussed in section 6.1.3, an asymptotically efficient estimator of $\hat{\boldsymbol{\theta}}_T$ is obtained by choosing the weighting matrix as $\mathbf{A}_T = \hat{\mathbf{V}}_{\mathrm{M},T}^{-1}$. When $f(y_t, \mathbf{X}_t, \boldsymbol{\theta})$ is linear then it is straightforward to show that the GMM estimator is the IV estimator and, if $\mathbf{W} = \mathbf{X}$, it is the LS estimator.

Example 6.1 Forward exchange rates as optimal predictors of future spot rates

An important illustration of these estimation techniques is found in the analysis of foreign exchange markets, where the efficient markets hypothesis becomes the proposition that the expected rate of return to speculation in the forward market, conditioned on available information, is zero. Hansen and Hodrick (1980) test this 'simple' efficiency hypothesis in the following way. Let s_t and $f_{t,k}$ be the logarithms of the spot exchange rate and the k-period forward rate determined at time t, respectively. Since $s_{t+k} - f_{t,k}$ is an approximate measure of the rate of return to speculation, the simple efficient markets hypothesis is that

$$f_{t,k} = E\left(s_{t+k}|\Phi_t\right)$$

where Φ_t is the information set available at time t. This implies that the speculative rate of return $y_{t+k} = s_{t+k} - f_{t,k}$ should be uncorrelated with information available at time t: for example, in the regression of the return on a constant and two lagged returns

$$y_{t+k} = \alpha_0 + \alpha_1 y_t + \alpha_2 y_{t-1} + u_{t+k}$$

the α_i, $i = 0, 1, 2$, should all be zero. Assuming that s_t and $f_{t,k}$, and hence y_t, are mixing and that $E(y_{t-j}u_{t+k}) = 0$ for $j \geq 0$, which is easily verified, LS estimation provides consistent estimates of the α_is. However, in the present circumstances, the forecast error $u_{t+k} = y_{t+k} - E(y_{t+k}|\Phi_t)$ will be serially correlated, so that the usual estimated covariance matrix will be inconsistent.

This serial correlation arises from the fact that the realised values of the spot exchange rate $s_{t+1}, s_{t+2}, \ldots, s_{t+k}$ are not known when the forward rate $f_{t,k}$ is set at time t, so that the corresponding k-period ahead forecast errors $u_{t+k-j} = s_{t+k-j} - f_{t-j,k}, j = 1, 2, \ldots, k-1$, are not observable. Since $u_{t+1}, u_{t+2}, \ldots, u_{t+k-1}$ are not part of the available information set, we cannot rule out the possibility that $E(u_{t+k}|u_{t+k-j}) \neq 0, 1 \leq j \leq k-1$, or that

$$Cov(u_{t+k}, u_{t+k-j}) \neq 0, \qquad j = 1, 2, \ldots, k-1$$

On the other hand, the preceding k-period forecast errors u_{t+k-j} for $j \geq k$ *are* observable. Efficiency thus requires $E(u_{t+k}|u_{t+k-j}) = 0, j \geq k$, and hence

$$Cov(u_{t+k}, u_{t+k-j}) = 0, \qquad j \geq k$$

With our mixing assumptions concerning s_t and $f_{t,k}$, $u_{t+k} = s_{t+k} - f_{t,k}$ will also be mixing, and combining the above covariances shows that the forecast errors can be thought of as being generated by an MA($k-1$) process.

Can we use generalised least squares procedures to make inferences about the α_is? The answer is no, because such techniques require the regressors to be *strictly exogenous*, which means that $E(u_{t+k}|\ldots, y_{t-1}, y_t, y_{t+1}, \ldots) = 0$, i.e., that future y values would be useless in determining the optimal forecast for y_{t+k} (strict, and other forms of, exogeneity are formally discussed in section 6.5). This is clearly inappropriate since such values would provide useful information for forecasting future rates of return. The use of regressors that are not strictly exogenous renders generalised LS techniques inconsistent, because the transformation used to eliminate the serial correlation in the residuals makes the transformed residuals for some particular period linear combinations of the original residuals and their lagged values. These in turn are likely to be correlated with the transformed data for the same period, since these include current values of the variables in the information set.

One way of avoiding these difficulties is to choose the sampling interval to equal the forecast interval, i.e., to set $k = 1$, in which case the forecast errors will be serially uncorrelated. This procedure of using *non-overlapping* data clearly does not make use of all the available information: $T(1 - k^{-1})$ observations are sacrificed. In the present application weekly observations are typically used with k set at 13 (three-month forward exchange rates readily being available). Using non-overlapping data, i.e., sampling only every thirteen weeks, would thus throw away over 90 per cent of the available observations.

The complete data set can be used if we adjust the covariance matrix of $\hat{\boldsymbol{\beta}} = (\hat{\alpha}_0, \hat{\alpha}_1, \hat{\alpha}_2)'$ in the appropriate fashion. As we have shown, a consistent covariance matrix is

$$\mathbf{D}_T = (\mathbf{X}'\mathbf{X}/T)^{-1}\hat{\mathbf{V}}_T(\mathbf{X}'\mathbf{X}/T)^{-1}$$

where now the columns making up the $\mathbf{X}$ matrix contain a constant and the two lagged values of y_{t+k}. In this application we have available an explicit expression for $\hat{\mathbf{V}}_T$, namely $\hat{\mathbf{V}}_T = T^{-1}\mathbf{X}'\hat{\boldsymbol{\Theta}}\mathbf{X}$ where, from the fact that the residuals $\hat{u}_{t+k}$ follow an MA($k-1$) process, the elements of the $T \times T$ symmetric matrix $\hat{\boldsymbol{\Theta}}$ have the form

$$\hat{\Theta}_{i,i+j} = R(j), \quad i = 1, 2, \ldots, T-k+1, \quad j = 0, 1, \ldots, k-1$$
$$\hat{\Theta}_{i+j,i} = \hat{\Theta}_{i,i+j}$$

where

$$R(j) = T^{-1}\sum_{t=j+1}^{T} \hat{u}_{t+k}\hat{u}_{t+k-j}$$

and $\hat{\Theta}_{i,j} = 0$ otherwise, i.e., $\hat{\boldsymbol{\Theta}}$ is 'band diagonal', the band width being $2k - 1$.

The hypothesis of market efficiency is $\boldsymbol{\beta} = \mathbf{0}$ and, in the framework of section 6.1.2, $\mathbf{R} = \mathbf{I}_3, \mathbf{r} = \mathbf{0}$ and $\hat{\boldsymbol{\Omega}}_T = \mathbf{D}_T$. The Wald statistic, for example, for testing this hypothesis takes the form

$$W_T = T\hat{\boldsymbol{\beta}}_T'\mathbf{D}_T^{-1}\hat{\boldsymbol{\beta}}_T \overset{a}{\sim} \chi_3^2$$

Hansen and Hodrick (1980) estimate regressions of this type for weekly data on spot and three month ($k = 13$) forward exchange rates for seven currencies (expressed in US cents per unit of foreign currency) from

March 1973 to January 1979, and for three currencies relative to the UK pound sterling for certain episodes after the First World War, in this case using one-month ($k = 4$) forward rates. Their findings indicate that the simple efficiency hypothesis is 'suspect' in both periods, but they offer a variety of reasons why this may be so, emphasising that rejection of the hypothesis $\boldsymbol{\beta} = \mathbf{0}$ cannot necessarily be identified with inefficiency in the foreign exchange market, as certain intertemporal asset allocation and risk considerations are ignored in this formulation of the efficient markets hypothesis.

6.2 ARCH-in-mean regression models

The estimation techniques developed above are applicable when little is known about the structure of the serial correlation and heteroskedasticity present in the errors in model (6.1). On certain occasions, however, it may be possible to specify the form of these departures from white noise, and a specification that has proved to be particularly useful in financial applications is the *(G)ARCH-in-Mean* [(G)ARCH-M] model proposed by Engle, Lilien and Robbins (1987) and employed by, for example, Domowitz and Hakkio (1985) for examining risk premia in the foreign exchange market and by French, Schwert and Stambaugh (1987) to model stock return volatility. Bollerslev, Chou and Kroner (1992) provide many further references to GARCH-M applications in finance, these often being attempts to model the linear relationship that emerges as a consequence of the intertemporal CAPM of Merton (1973, 1980).

The GARCH-M model extends the GARCH model developed in chapter 4.4 to the regression framework of equation (6.1)

$$y_t = \alpha_0 + \sum_{i=1}^{m} \alpha_i y_{t-i} + \sum_{i=0}^{m} \boldsymbol{\beta}_i \mathbf{x}_{t-i} + \delta\sigma_t^{\lambda} + u_t \tag{6.7}$$

$$u_t = \varepsilon_t - \sum_{i=1}^{n} \theta_i \varepsilon_{t-i} \tag{6.8}$$

$$E\left(\varepsilon_t^2 | \Phi_{t-1}\right) = \sigma_t^2 = \gamma_0 + \sum_{i=1}^{p} \gamma_i \varepsilon_{t-i}^2 + \sum_{i=1}^{q} \phi_i \sigma_{t-i}^2 + \vartheta\xi_t \tag{6.9}$$

Here we allow the serially correlated errors u_t to be modelled as an MA(n) process (equation (6.8)), and the conditional variance σ_t^2 (conditional upon the information set at time $t-1$, Φ_{t-1}) both enters the 'mean' equation (6.7) and depends itself (equation (6.9)) upon a vector of explanatory variables ξ_t. Typically, λ is set at one or two, so that either the conditional standard deviation or variance is included in the mean equation. Under the assumption that the ε_t are $NID(0, \sigma^2)$, QML estimates of the GARCH-M model given by equations (6.7)–(6.9) can be obtained by maximising the likelihood function using, for example, the BHHH algorithm analogous to that discussed in chapter 4.4.4. There are some complications, however. For example, the information matrix is no longer block diagonal, so that all parameters must be estimated simultaneously, unlike the case discussed previously where the block diagonality of the information matrix allowed estimates of the parameters of the mean and conditional variance equations to be obtained from separate iterations.

If it is preferred, the alternative assumption that the ε_t follow a standardised t-distribution may be employed to allow more adequate modelling of the fat tails often found in the observed unconditional distributions of financial time series. Baillie and Bollerslev (1989), for example, provide the relevant expression for the log-likelihood function.

Example 6.2 Stock returns and volatility

Recalling the GARCH models fitted to the daily returns of the S&P 500 index in example 4.3, we now fit a GARCH-M model of the form (with the return series now denoted y_t)

$$y_t = \alpha_0 + \delta\sigma_t + u_t$$

$$u_t = \varepsilon_t - \theta_1\varepsilon_{t-1}$$

$$E(\varepsilon_t^2|\Phi_{t-1}) = \sigma_t^2 = \gamma_0 + \gamma_1\varepsilon_{t-1}^2 + \phi_1\sigma_{t-1}^2 + \phi_2\sigma_{t-2}^2$$

i.e., the conditional standard deviation is included as a regressor in the mean equation of the previously fitted MA(1)–GARCH(1,2) model. QML estimation produced the following model, with robust t-statistics in parentheses and the insignificant constant excluded from the mean equation

$$\underset{}{y_t} = \underset{(7.01)}{0.0695\sigma_t} + \varepsilon_t - \underset{(17.1)}{0.148\varepsilon_{t-1}}$$

$$\sigma_t^2 = \underset{(6.17)}{1.20 \times 10^{-6}} + \underset{(7.90)}{0.139\varepsilon_{t-1}^2} + \underset{(3.60)}{0.502\sigma_{t-1}^2} + \underset{(2.83)}{0.357\sigma_{t-2}^2}$$

$$LogL = 56833$$

The inclusion of σ_t in the returns equation is an attempt to incorporate a measure of risk into the returns generating process and is an implication of the 'mean-variance hypothesis' underlying many theoretical asset pricing models, such as the intertemporal CAPM discussed above. Under this hypothesis, δ should be positive, and this is found to be the case, so that large values for the conditional variance are expected to be associated with large returns. The MA(1) error may capture the effect of non-synchronous trading and is highly significant. As before, the GARCH parameters sum to almost unity, indicating IGARCH behaviour and high persistence in the conditional variance. Similar models have been estimated by French, Schwert and Stambaugh (1987) for daily *excess* returns, defined to be the market return minus the risk-free interest rate.

Example 6.3 Conditional variance and the risk premium in the foreign exchange market

The evidence provided by Hansen and Hodrick (1980) for the rejection of the 'simple' efficiency hypothesis in foreign exchange markets, which was discussed in example 6.1, found that rejection was often due to the intercept α_0 being non-zero. This finding could be regarded as evidence of a risk premium, the presence of which would allow the forward rate to be a biased predictor of the future spot rate without sacrificing the notion of market efficiency. Of course, for this to be plausible, we must have an empirically tractable theory of a risk premium, for without such a theory there is no way of empirically distinguishing between an inefficient market and a, perhaps time-varying, risk premium.

Although several theoretical models have been proposed that generate a risk premium in the foreign exchange market, it has been found to be extremely difficult to translate them into testable econometric models and, consequently, their empirical performance provides only weak support for a time-varying risk premium. Domowitz and Hakkio (1985) therefore present a GARCH-M generalisation of the model used in example 6.1 to investigate the possible presence of a risk premium that depends on the conditional variance of the forecast errors. From example 6.1, the efficiency hypothesis states that the forward rate at time t, $f_{t,1}$, is an unbiased predictor of the future spot rate, s_{t+1}, where, as before, logarithms are used, but where we now set the forecast period at $k = 1$ for convenience. Thus

$$s_{t+1} - f_{t,1} = u_{t+1}$$

where u_{t+1} is the one-period forecast error, which should be zero mean white noise under the efficiency hypothesis. This can equivalently be written as

$$\Delta s_{t+1} = \left(f_{t,1} - s_t\right) + u_{t+1}$$

which is then regarded as a restricted case of the GARCH-M model of equations (6.7)–(6.9) with $y_t = \Delta s_t$ and $\mathbf{x}_t = \left(f_{t-1,1} - s_{t-1}\right)$: the restrictions being $m = n = 0$, so that no lagged ys or $\mathbf{x}$s appear in the equation for y_t and that the forecast error is serially uncorrelated; and $\beta_0 = 1$, so that forecasts are unbiased. Maintaining $\beta_0 = 1$ and u_t to be white noise, then $\alpha_0 \neq 0$ and $\delta = 0$ implies a non-zero but constant risk premium, while $\alpha_0 \neq 0$ and $\delta \neq 0$ implies a time-varying risk premium.

The risk premium is given by $\alpha_0 + \delta\sigma_t^2$ (assuming $\lambda = 2$ for convenience) and thus any change in it is due solely to changes in the conditional variance σ_t^2: it can, nevertheless, be positive or negative and can switch signs, depending on the values of α_0 and δ. For example, if $\alpha_0 \neq 0$ and $\delta \neq 0$, then for small forecast errors the risk premium will be negative (long positions in foreign currency require an expected loss), while for large forecast errors the risk premium may turn positive (long positions in forward foreign currency require an expected profit).

The model was fitted, with σ_t^2 assumed to follow an ARCH(4) process, to non-overlapping monthly data from June 1973 to August 1982 for five exchange rates *vis-á-vis* the US dollar: the UK, France, Germany, Japan and Switzerland. The null hypothesis of no risk premium ($\alpha_0 = 0$, $\beta_0 = 1$, and $\delta = 0$) could be rejected for the UK and Japan, but not for France, Germany or Switzerland, although for this last currency it is only because the standard error of $\hat{\beta}_0$ is so large that the null cannot be rejected, for the point estimate of β_0 is -1.092!

6.3 Misspecification testing

The regression techniques developed in section 6.1 are based on the assumption that the model (6.1) is correctly specified, i.e., that the assumptions underlying the model are valid. If they are not, then some of the techniques can be invalidated. It is thus important to be able to test these assumptions: such tests are known as *misspecification tests* and we begin their development by rewriting (6.1) as

$$\begin{aligned} y_t &= \alpha_0 + \boldsymbol{\beta}_0\mathbf{x}_t + \sum_{i=1}^{m}\left(\alpha_i y_{t-i} + \boldsymbol{\beta}_i\mathbf{x}_{t-i}\right) + u_t \\ &= \alpha_0 + \boldsymbol{\beta}_0\mathbf{x}_t + \sum_{i=1}^{m}\boldsymbol{\beta}_i^*\mathbf{z}_{t-i} + u_t \end{aligned} \tag{6.10}$$

where $\boldsymbol{\beta}_i^* = \left(\alpha_i, \boldsymbol{\beta}_i\right)$, so that $\boldsymbol{\beta} = \left(\boldsymbol{\beta}_0^*, \boldsymbol{\beta}_1^*, \ldots, \boldsymbol{\beta}_m^*\right)$.

6.3.1 Choosing the maximum lag, m

The estimation theory developed in section 6.1 is based on the assumption that the maximum lag, m, is known. If this is so, then the assumption of mixing, which lets the errors u_t exhibit both serial correlation and heterogeneity, still allows the LS estimate $\hat{\boldsymbol{\beta}}_T$ to be consistent and asymptotically normal, although the associated covariance matrix is $\mathbf{D}_T = (\mathbf{X}'\mathbf{X}/T)^{-1}\hat{\mathbf{V}}_T(\mathbf{X}'\mathbf{X}/T)^{-1}$, where the expression for $\hat{\mathbf{V}}_T$ is given by equation (6.4). If m is chosen to be larger than its optimum but unknown value m^*, $\hat{\boldsymbol{\beta}}_T$ will still be consistent and asymptotically normal, but multicollinearity problems will often arise. This is because as m increases, the same observed data $\{\mathbf{z}_t\}_1^T$ are required to provide more and more information about an increasing number of unknown parameters.

If, on the other hand, m is chosen to be 'too small', then the omitted lagged $\mathbf{z}_t$s will form part of the error term. If we assume that for the correct lag length m^*, u_t is a martingale difference, then the error term in the misspecified model will no longer be non-systematic relative to $(\mathbf{y}_{t-1}^0, \mathbf{x}_t^0)$ and hence will not be a martingale difference. This has the implication that $\hat{\boldsymbol{\beta}}_T$ and $\hat{\sigma}_T$ are no longer consistent or asymptotically normal and because of this it is important to be able to test for $m < m^*$. Given that the 'true' model is

$$y_t = \alpha_0 + \boldsymbol{\beta}_0 \mathbf{x}_t + \sum_{i=1}^{m^*} \boldsymbol{\beta}_i^* \mathbf{z}_{t-i} + u_t$$

the error term in the misspecified model can be written as

$$u_t^* = u_t + \sum_{i=m+1}^{m^*} \boldsymbol{\beta}_i^* \mathbf{z}_{t-i}$$

This implies that $m < m^*$ can be tested using the null hypothesis $H_0 : \boldsymbol{\beta}_{m+1}^* = \ldots = \boldsymbol{\beta}_{m^*}^* = \mathbf{0}$. The Wald statistic for testing this null against the alternative that at least one of the vectors $\boldsymbol{\beta}_i^*$, $m+1 \leq i \leq m^*$, is non-zero is $(m^* - m)(k+1)$ times the standard F-statistic based on a comparison of the residual sums of squares from the regressions with the maximum lag length set at m and m^* respectively. The asymptotically equivalent LM statistic can be computed as $T \cdot R^2$ from the auxiliary regression of $\hat{u}_t^*$ on $\mathbf{x}_t, \mathbf{z}_{t-1}, \ldots, \mathbf{z}_{t-m^*}$, where $\hat{u}_t^*$ are the residuals from the estimation of (6.10). Both the Wald and LM tests will be asymptotically χ_q^2, where $q = (m^* - m)(k+1)$.

The above analysis has assumed that, for the correct lag length m^*, u_t is a martingale difference. One consequence of incorrectly setting m to be less than m^* is that the residuals from the regression (6.10) will be serially correlated. An alternative LM test is $T \cdot R^2$ from the regression of $\hat{u}_t^*$ on $\mathbf{x}_t, \mathbf{z}_{t-1}, \ldots, \mathbf{z}_{t-m^*}$ and $\hat{u}_{t-1}^*, \ldots, \hat{u}_{t-m+m^*}^*$, which will be asymptotically $\chi^2_{m^*-m}$. This is strictly a test of residual serial correlation, and only an indirect test of lag length specification, but it points to the difficulty of distinguishing whether residual serial correlation is a consequence of an incorrect (too small) setting of the lag length m, or whether m is correct but, nevertheless, the error term is serially correlated. As we have seen, in the former case $\hat{\boldsymbol{\beta}}_T$ will be inconsistent, whereas in the latter it will be consistent and asymptotically normal. For detailed discussion of this important distinction, see Spanos (1986).

6.3.2 *Testing for normality, linearity and homoskedasticity*

Although the assumption that the errors in (6.10) are normally distributed is not a crucial one in the context of the asymptotic theory developed in section 6.1, its invalidity can have an important effect on LS estimates in finite samples and, since chapter 5 has shown that many financial time series are observed to be non-normal, it is important to examine this normality assumption in regression applications. A popular test proposed by Jarque and Bera (1980) measures departures from normality in terms of the third and fourth moments, i.e., the skewness and kurtosis, of the residuals $\hat{u}_t$ from estimation of (6.10). Letting μ_3 and μ_4 be the third and fourth (central) moments of u_t, and defining $m_3 = \left(\mu_3/\sigma^3\right)$ and $m_4 = \left(\mu_4/\sigma^4\right)$ to be the moment measures of skewness and kurtosis, respectively, estimators of these measures are given by

$$\hat{m}_i = \left(T^{-1}\sum \hat{u}_t^i\right)\Big/\left(T^{-1}\sum \hat{u}_t^2\right)^{i/2}, \qquad i = 3, 4$$

The asymptotic distributions of these estimators under the null hypothesis of normality are

$$T^{\frac{1}{2}}\hat{m}_3 \overset{a}{\sim} N(0, 6)$$
$$T^{\frac{1}{2}}(\hat{m}_4 - 3) \overset{a}{\sim} N(0, 24)$$

and, since they are also asymptotically independent, the squares of their standardised forms can be added to obtain

$$\frac{T}{6}\hat{m}_3^2 + \frac{T}{24}(\hat{m}_4 - 3)^2 \overset{a}{\sim} \chi_2^2$$

so that large values of this statistic would flag significant departures from normality.

The model (6.10) assumes that the conditional mean $E(y_t|\mathbf{y}_{t-1}^0, \mathbf{x}_t^0)$ is linear in $\mathbf{X}_t$. To test this assumption we may consider the null hypothesis

$$H_0 : \mu_{yt} = E(y_t|\mathbf{y}_{t-1}^0, \mathbf{x}_t^0) = \mathbf{X}_t\boldsymbol{\beta}$$

which needs to be tested against the non-linear alternative

$$H_1 : \mu_{yt} = h(\mathbf{X}_t)$$

If $h(\cdot)$ is assumed to take the form

$$h(\mathbf{X}_t) = \mathbf{X}_t\Xi + c_2\mu_{yt}^2 + c_3\mu_{yt}^3 + \ldots + c_n\mu_{yt}^n$$

then Ramsey's (1969) RESET test for linearity is based on testing $H_0 : c_2 = c_3 = \ldots = c_n = 0$ against $H_1 : c_i \neq 0, i = 2, \ldots, n$. Its LM version is based on the auxiliary regression of $\hat{u}_t$ on $\mathbf{x}_t, \mathbf{z}_{t-1}, \ldots, \mathbf{z}_{t-m}$ and $\hat{\mu}_{yt}^2, \ldots, \hat{\mu}_{yt}^n$, where $\hat{\mu}_{yt} = \hat{y}_t = \mathbf{X}_t\hat{\boldsymbol{\beta}}_T$, so that $T \cdot R^2$ is asymptotically distributed as χ_n^2. If non-linearities are encountered then non-linear regression techniques will be required: these are developed in White and Domowitz (1984) and analysed in detail in Gallant and White (1988).

To test for departures from homoskedasticity (assuming no serial correlation), we may consider constructing a test based on the difference

$$(\mathbf{X}'\boldsymbol{\Omega}\mathbf{X}) - \sigma^2(\mathbf{X}'\mathbf{X})$$

where $\boldsymbol{\Omega} = \mathrm{diag}(\sigma_{m+1}^2, \sigma_{m+2}^2, \ldots, \sigma_T^2)$. This can be expressed in the form

$$\sum_{t=m+1}^{T} \left(E(u_t^2) - \sigma^2\right)\mathbf{X}_t\mathbf{X}_t'$$

and a test for heteroskedasticity could be based on the statistic

$$T^{-1}\sum_{t=m+1}^{T} (\hat{u}_t^2 - \hat{\sigma}_T^2)\mathbf{X}_t\mathbf{X}_t'$$

Given that this is symmetric, we can express the $\frac{1}{2}K(K-1)$, where again $K=(m+1)(k+1)$, different elements in the form

$$T^{-1}\sum_{t=m+1}^{T}\left(\hat{u}_t^2-\hat{\sigma}_T^2\right)\boldsymbol{\Psi}_t \tag{6.11}$$

where

$$\boldsymbol{\Psi}_t=(\psi_{1t},\psi_{2t},\ldots,\psi_{Jt})', \qquad \psi_{lt}=x_{it}x_{jt},$$
$$i\geq j, i,j=2,\ldots,k, \quad l=1,2,\ldots,J, \quad J=\tfrac{1}{2}K(K-1)$$

the x_{it} being columns of $\mathbf{X}_t$. Although a test statistic can be based on (6.11), an asymptotically equivalent LM test (White, 1980) is the $T\cdot R^2$ statistic computed from the auxiliary regression of $\hat{u}_t^2$ on a constant and $\psi_{1t},\ldots,\psi_{Jt}$, which is asymptotically distributed as χ_J^2. Note, however, that the constant in the original regression (6.10) should not be involved in defining the ψ_{lt}s in the auxiliary regression, since the inclusion of such regressors would lead to perfect multicollinearity.

This test, of course, does not propose any alternative form of heteroskedasticity. If such information is available – for example, that the errors follow an ARCH process – then tests specifically tailored to the alternative can be constructed. In the ARCH case the appropriate LM test is $T\cdot R^2$ from the regression of $\hat{u}_t^2$ on a constant and lags of $\hat{u}_t^2$ (cf. the testing of ARCH in chapter 4.4.5).

6.3.3 Parameter stability

Throughout this analysis we have assumed that the parameter vector $\boldsymbol{\beta}$ is *time invariant*. Evidence has accumulated that this may be a rather heroic assumption in many regression applications in finance: see, for example, the references and results in Coutts, Roberts and Mills (1997). Parameter instability may occur in many different forms and testing for departures from parameter time invariance is not straightforward. One approach is to use *recursive* and *rolling* estimates of the parameters to assess stability. Recursive least squares estimates the parameters over an increasing sequence of samples $m+1,\ldots,t$, $\tau+m+k+1<t\leq T$, yielding the recursive estimates $\hat{\boldsymbol{\beta}}^{(t)}$ for $t=\tau+m+k+1,\ldots,T$, where τ is chosen to provide an adequate number of degrees of freedom when starting the recursion. Note that, by definition, $\hat{\boldsymbol{\beta}}^{(T)}=\hat{\boldsymbol{\beta}}_T$. The *recursive residuals* are defined as $v_t=u_{t|t-1}/f_t$, where the *prediction error* $u_{t|t-1}$ is defined as

$$u_{t|t-1} = y_t - \mathbf{X}_{t-1}\hat{\boldsymbol{\beta}}^{(t-1)}$$

and

$$f_t^2 = 1 + \mathbf{X}_t'\left(\mathbf{X}_{(t-1)}'\mathbf{X}_{(t-1)}\right)^{-1}\mathbf{X}_t$$

where $\mathbf{X}_{(t)} = \left(\mathbf{X}_{m+1}, \ldots, \mathbf{X}_t\right)$.

Subsample estimates may also be constructed: these may be denoted as $\hat{\boldsymbol{\beta}}^{(t_1,t_2)}$ when the estimation period is from t_1 to t_2. When the estimation period is sequentially incremented by one observation, then sequences of rolling regressions with estimation window $t_1 - t_2 + 1$ are obtained.

All these estimates may be used to examine whether the parameters of (6.10) are stable. Plots of the recursive and rolling regression coefficients are simple to construct and are often very informative, but there are also a range of formal test statistics available. For example, the cumulative sum of squares (CUSUMSQ) statistic, defined as

$$S_t = \sum\nolimits_{i=\tau_1}^{t} \nu_i^2 \Big/ \sum\nolimits_{i=\tau_1}^{T} \nu_i^2, \qquad \tau_1 = \tau + m + k + 2$$

(Brown, Durbin and Evans, 1975), provides a simple test of parameter stability. If S_t lies outside the range $c_0 \pm t/(T-2)$, where c_0 depends on the chosen level of significance, then there is evidence of some form of parameter instability. Edgerton and Wells (1994) have recently provided a range of critical values for the statistic, as well as an algorithm for calculating probability values. Although Krämer and Ploberger (1990) highlighted the poor power properties of the CUSUMSQ test against structural change, it does have good properties against heteroskedasticity. This is important here, because if the parameters of (6.10) are time varying but are estimated as being constant, as is implied by LS, then the residuals will be heteroskedastic. Thus a test for heteroskedasticity may also be interpreted as a test for parameter constancy. Similarly, parameter instability may also lead to serial correlation in the recursive residuals, so that portmanteau statistics may be calculated using the ν_t.

Ploberger, Krämer and Kontrus (1989) considered a test based on recursive coefficients rather than on recursive residuals. Their *fluctuation* test is defined as

$$\max\left(\frac{t}{\hat{\sigma}T}\left\|\left(\mathbf{X}'\mathbf{X}\right)^{\frac{1}{2}}\left(\hat{\beta}^{(t)} - \hat{\beta}_T\right)\right\|\right)$$

and critical values are provided in their table 1.

Following Dufour (1982), the recursive residuals can also be used to explore parameter instability within an auxiliary regression framework. For example, regressing ν_t on $\mathbf{x}_t$ provides a general exploratory test, whereas regressing ν_t on sets of dummy variables defined to represent periods of possible instability provides more specific tests of parameter constancy. If specific break points are hypothesised, then versions of the traditional Chow (1960) test may be computed: for details see, for example, Hendry and Doornik (1996). A test that may be used without selecting explicit break points is that proposed by Hansen (1992), which is discussed in Johnston and DiNardo (1997, chapter 4). We emphasise that the tests discussed here are by no means exhaustive, having been chosen primarily because of their popularity and ease of computation (which are certainly not independent choices, of course). Many other tests have been proposed in recent years: Chu, Hornik and Kuan (1995), for example, have provided new tests and references to others.

Example 6.4 Testing the CAPM

The CAPM is an important asset pricing theory in financial economics and has been the subject of considerable econometric research. An excellent exposition of the derivation of the model which, as we have noted earlier, postulates a linear relationship between the expected risk and return of holding a portfolio of financial assets, can be found in Berndt (1991, chapter 2), who also considers many of the econometric issues involved in the empirical implementation of the model.

The simple linear relationship between a small portfolio's return, r_p, and its associated risk, measured by the standard deviation of returns, σ_p, can be written as

$$r_p - r_f = \left(\sigma_p/\sigma_m\right) \cdot \left(r_m - r_f\right) \tag{6.12}$$

where r_m and σ_m are the returns on the overall market portfolio and the standard deviation of such returns, respectively, and r_f is the return on a risk-free asset. The term $r_p - r_f$ is thus the risk premium for portfolio p, while $r_m - r_f$ is the overall market's risk premium. Denoting these risk premia as y and x, respectively, letting $\beta = \sigma_p/\sigma_m$, and adding an intercept term α and a stochastic error term u, the latter reflecting the effects of specific (unsystematic) and diversifiable risk, the CAPM becomes the simple linear regression

$$y = \alpha + \beta x + u \tag{6.13}$$

The LS estimate of the slope coefficient β is $\hat{\beta} = Cov(x, y)/V(x)$, which is equivalent to σ_{pm}/σ_m^2, where σ_{pm} is the covariance between portfolio p and the market portfolio: this is known as the 'investment beta' for portfolio p and measures the sensitivity of the return on the portfolio to variation in the returns on the market portfolio. Portfolios having $\hat{\beta}$s in excess of unity are thus relatively risky, while those with $\hat{\beta}$s less than unity are much less sensitive to market movements.

LS estimation of the CAPM regression from observed time series $\{y_t, x_t\}_1^T$ is, of course, trivial. However, in this time series context the underlying CAPM theory requires certain assumptions to hold. Specifically, we must assume that the risk premia are stationary, normally distributed and serially uncorrelated, in which case the error process $\{u_t\}_1^T$ will be *NID*. Note also that the intercept α has been included without any justification, for it does not appear in the original CAPM expression (6.12). The CAPM theory thus provides the testable hypothesis $\alpha = 0$, along with the following implications: the residuals of the regression (6.13) should be serially uncorrelated, homoskedastic and normal, the systematic relationship between y and x should be linear, and the estimate of β should be time invariant.

The empirical performance of the CAPM was investigated using the data set provided by Berndt (1991, chapter 2), which contains monthly returns from January 1978 to December 1987 on seventeen US companies plus a monthly risk-free return. Treating each companies' risk premia, calculated as the difference between the company return and the risk-free return, as a separate portfolio enabled seventeen CAPM regressions of the form (6.13) to be estimated and these are reported in table 6.1.

Only three of the estimated regressions survive the battery of misspecification tests unscathed: those for CONED, DELTA and MOTOR (see Berndt for the actual companies associated with these variable names). Little evidence of serial correlation or non-linearity is found in the residuals, but rather more evidence of heteroskedasticity, non-normality and parameter non-constancy is encountered. Standard errors calculated using (6.3) have a tendency to be larger than their OLS counterparts for betas, but smaller for intercepts, although the differences are usually quite small. Those regressions which exhibited significant ARCH were estimated with GARCH errors, but little change was found in the coefficients of the mean equation. GARCH-M extensions were found to be unnecessary in all cases.

Table 6.1. *Estimates of the CAPM regression (6.13)*

Company	$\hat{\alpha}$	$\hat{\beta}$	R^2	*dw*	*NONLIN*	*NORM*	*HET*	*ARCH*	*CHOW*
BOISE	0.0031	0.94							
	(0.0068)	(0.10)	0.43	2.17	2.95	4.72	9.57*	8.69*	2.69
	[0.0053]	[0.13]							
CITCRP	0.0025	0.67							
	(0.0062)	(0.09)	0.32	1.84	0.40	1.20	10.33*	2.50	6.44*
	[0.0058]	[0.14]							
CONED	0.0110	0.09							
	(0.0046)	(0.07)	0.02	2.15	0.74	1.12	0.20	5.04	0.05
	[0.0036]	[0.06]							
CONTIL	−0.0132	0.73							
	(0.0131)	(0.19)	0.11	2.07	0.45	2245*	0.37	0.06	2.56
	[0.0128]	[0.24]							
DATGEN	−0.0067	1.03							
	(0.0098)	(0.14)	0.31	2.08	7.20*	5.03	3.21	0.15	1.89
	[0.0094]	[0.19]							
DEC	0.0068	0.85							
	(0.0074)	(0.11)	0.34	2.14	0.72	9.23*	0.66	16.03*	5.67
	[0.0066]	[0.13]							
DELTA	0.0014	0.49							
	(0.0083)	(0.12)	0.12	1.99	0.01	2.55	0.43	2.46	3.67
	[0.0082]	[0.15]							
GENMIL	0.0078	0.27							
	(0.0058)	(0.08)	0.08	2.08	0.14	2.64	0.94	2.16	14.90*
	[0.0050]	[0.10]							

Table 6.1 *Continued*

Company	$\hat{\alpha}$	$\hat{\beta}$	R^2	*dw*	*NONLIN*	*NORM*	*HET*	*ARCH*	*CHOW*
GERBER	0.0051	0.63							
	(0.0071)	(0.10)	0.24	2.25	8.38*	7.14*	0.27	1.72	6.62*
	[0.0065]	[0.11]							
IBM	−0.0005	0.46							
	(0.0046)	(0.07)	0.28	1.88	0.06	1.14	0.17	3.06	6.68*
	[0.0054]	[0.07]							
MOBIL	0.0042	0.72							
	(0.0059)	(0.09)	0.37	2.09	0.55	34.6*	6.93*	1.68	0.29
	[0.0051]	[0.09]							
MOTOR	0.0069	0.10							
	(0.0083)	(0.12)	0.01	1.86	0.90	2.23	0.97	0.73	2.05
	[0.0077]	[0.10]							
PANAM	−0.0086	0.74							
	(0.0112)	(0.16)	0.15	2.21	0.51	10.9*	2.52	4.46	0.14
	[0.0103]	[0.15]							
PSNH	−0.0126	0.21							
	(0.0100)	(0.15)	0.02	1.88	0.25	92.5*	1.64	10.46*	0.03
	[0.0105]	[0.10]							
TANDY	0.0107	1.05							
	(0.0097)	(0.14)	0.32	1.89	3.27	6.13*	2.76	0.66	0.13
	[0.0100]	[0.14]							

Table 6.1 *Continued*

Company	$\hat{\alpha}$	$\hat{\beta}$	R^2	*dw*	*NONLIN*	*NORM*	*HET*	*ARCH*	*CHOW*
TEXACO	0.0007	0.61							
	(0.0062)	(0.09)	0.28	2.02	0.00	127.5*	2.59	3.10	0.14
	[0.0049]	[0.10]							
WEYER	−0.0031	0.82							
	(0.0059)	(0.09)	0.43	2.29*	1.76	1.44	15.07*	9.97*	9.88*
	[0.0046]	[0.10]							
Asymptotic distribution					χ_1^2	χ_2^2	χ_2^2	χ_3^2	χ_2^2
Critical 0.05 value				1.72	3.84	5.99	5.99	7.81	5.99
				2.28					

Notes:
*: Significant at 0.05 level.
(. . .): Conventional standard error; [. . .]: Newey–West (1987) standard error from (6.3).
dw: Durbin–Watson statistic.
NONLIN: Ramsey's (1969) RESET test for functional form, calculated from the regression of $\hat{u}_t$ on x_t and $\hat{y}_t^2$.
NORM: Jarque–Bera (1980) test for normality.
HET: Test for heteroskedasticity, calculated from the regression of $\hat{u}_t^2$ on a constant, $\hat{y}_t$ and $\hat{y}_t^2$.
CHOW: Chow's (1960) test for coefficient stability: break point taken to be December 1984.

Example 6.5 Further modelling of the *FTA All Share* index

In example 2.6 we fitted an AR(3) process to the logarithmic changes of the *FTA All Share* index, which we now denote as Δp_t. Mills (1991a) finds evidence that Δp_t is related to the logarithmic changes in long interest rates and dividends, and we therefore investigate the extended regression model

$$\Delta p_t = \alpha_0 + \sum\nolimits_{i=1}^{3} \alpha_i \Delta p_{t-i} + \sum\nolimits_{i=0}^{3} \beta_{1i} \Delta r20_{t-i} + \sum\nolimits_{i=0}^{3} \beta_{2i} \Delta d_{t-i} + u_t \qquad (6.14)$$

Here $r20_t$ and d_t are the logarithms of 20-year gilts and the dividend index, respectively, so that $k = 2$, and the lag length is set at $m = 3$, although this could be selected using an information criterion, by an obvious extension to the discussion in example 2.3. Unit root tests confirm that both series are $I(1)$, hence their appearance in first-differenced form. Estimates of this model are presented in table 6.2, where it is seen that many of the coefficients are insignificant, particularly when measured against the 'Newey–West' standard errors, computed using (6.4) with $n = 5$. The following set of hypotheses were therefore tested

Table 6.2. *Estimates of the All Share regression (6.14)*

1	Δp_{-1}	Δp_{-2}	Δp_{-3}	$\Delta r20$	$\Delta r20_{-1}$	$\Delta r20_{-2}$	$\Delta r20_{-3}$
0.0075	0.055	−0.174	0.122	−0.471	−0.179	0.058	−0.038
(0.0040)	(0.054)	(0.053)	(0.054)	(0.095)	(0.101)	(0.102)	(0.095)
[0.0036]	[0.054]	[0.080]	[0.077]	[0.145]	[0.136]	[0.115]	[0.087]

Δd	Δd_{-1}	Δd_{-2}	Δd_{-3}	R^2	$\hat{\sigma}$	W_{372}
0.504	−0.007	0.063	−0.462			
(0.212)	(0.212)	(0.212)	(0.213)	0.149	0.0572	3.72
[0.246]	[0.175]	[0.175]	[0.192]			

Notes:
(…): Conventional standard error. […]: Newey–West standard error.
W_{372} is the Wald statistic (6.5) computed using $T = 372$ observations. There are $q = 7$ restrictions, and hence it is asymptotically distributed as χ^2_7, the 5% critical value being 14.07.

$$\alpha_1 = \beta_{11} = \beta_{12} = \beta_{13} = \beta_{21} = \beta_{22} = 0,$$
$$\beta_{20} + \beta_{23} = 0$$

the final restriction also being suggested by the estimated coefficients. The Wald statistic reported in table 6.2 shows that this joint hypothesis cannot be rejected, the associated marginal significance level being 0.86, and estimation of the restricted equation yields

$$\begin{aligned}\Delta p_t = & \underset{[0.0033]}{0.0084} - \underset{[0.049]}{0.144}\,\Delta p_{t-2} + \underset{[0.049]}{0.117}\,\Delta p_{t-3} \\ & - \underset{[0.088]}{0.545}\,\Delta r20_t + \underset{[0.158]}{0.488}\,(\Delta d_t - \Delta d_{t-3})\end{aligned}$$

$$R^2 = 0.137 \quad \hat{\sigma} = 0.0571$$

The current change in the gilt yield enters negatively, reflecting the well-known trade-off between the equity and gilt markets in the UK. Noting that the dividend regressor can be expressed as $\Delta(d_t - d_{t-3})$, this implies that the current change in *quarterly* dividend growth is positively related to the growth of stock prices, this probably being a consequence of typical dividend payment dates being every quarter.

The additional regressors reduce the residual standard error somewhat over the univariate model (see example 2.6) but, as both contain contemporaneous terms, they are of little use in forecasting and, of course, beg the question of whether they can be regarded as exogenous, a question we return to later.

6.4 Robust estimation

As we have seen from the above examples and from the variety of results presented in, for example, Coutts, Mills and Roberts (1994) and Mills and Coutts (1996), non-normality of residuals may be a common occurrence, being typically caused by the presence of some abnormally large outliers. Non-normality, per se, may not have important consequences theoretically, for, although LS estimators are no longer asymptotically efficient, they nevertheless remain unbiased and consistent and standard hypothesis tests are still asymptotically χ^2. However, the power of such tests can be extremely sensitive to departures from normality and can lack robustness, in the sense that the finite sample distribution can be altered dramatically when the distribution of the error is altered only slightly (see Koenker, 1982).

Moreover, if the error variance is infinite, LS estimators lose their minimum variance property and, since it is then impossible to obtain a meaningful estimate of the variance, conventional hypothesis tests can be very misleading. The strong likelihood of non-normal, and possibly infinite variance, errors has therefore led to the development of alternative estimation procedures which, relative to LS, place less weight on outliers, and these are generally known as *robust* estimators.

A wide variety of robust estimators have been proposed, and we will concentrate here on methods based on regression *quantiles*: for financial applications see, for example, Tomczyk and Chatterjee (1984), Chan and Lakonishok (1992) and Mills and Coutts (1996). The regression quantile family of estimators is based on minimising the criterion function

$$\sum_t \rho_\theta(u_t)$$

where, for $0 < \theta < 1$

$$\rho_\theta(u_t) = \begin{cases} \theta|u_t| & \text{if } u_t \geq 0 \\ (1-\theta)|u_t| & \text{if } u_t < 0 \end{cases}$$

Since $\rho_\theta(u_t)$ is a weighted sum of the absolute values of the residuals, outliers are given less importance than under a squared residual criterion. When $\theta = 0.5$, the least absolute errors (LAE) estimator is obtained, whereas, more generally, large (small) values of θ attach a heavy penalty to observations with large positive (negative) residuals. For example, for a given value of θ, a bivariate regression line passes through at least two observations, with at most $T\theta$ observations lying below the line and at least $(T-2)\theta$ observations lying above it.

Varying θ between 0 and 1 yields a set of 'regression quantile' estimators $\hat{\beta}(\theta)$: for example, the LAE estimator is $\hat{\beta}(0.5)$. The effect of large outlying observations will tend to be concentrated in the regression quantiles corresponding to extreme values of θ, while the behaviour of the sample observations will determine how the regression quantiles change as θ varies. Consequently, a variety of estimators have been proposed that combine several regression quantiles: for example, the trimean (TRM)

$$\hat{\beta}_{TRM} = 0.25\hat{\beta}(0.25) + 0.5\hat{\beta}(0.5) + 0.25\hat{\beta}(0.75)$$

The regression quantiles can also be combined in the form of a *trimmed* regression quantile estimator (TRQ)

$$\hat{\beta}_\phi = (1-2\phi)^{-1} \int_\phi^{1-\phi} \hat{\beta}(\theta)\mathrm{d}\theta$$

where $0 < \phi < 0.5$. This estimator is obtained by computing $\hat{\beta}(\phi)$ and $\hat{\beta}(1-\phi)$, excluding all observations lying on or below the ϕth regression quantile line and all those lying above the $(1-\phi)$th quantile line, and applying OLS to the remaining observations. It can thus be interpreted as a 'trimmed least squares' estimator (Ruppert and Carroll, 1980). All these estimators can be shown to produce asymptotically normal estimators of β, with appropriate covariance matrices given in, for example, Judge *et al.* (1985, chapter 20), where a detailed treatment of robust estimators in econometrics in general can be found.

Example 6.6 Robust estimation of the CAPM

The eight CAPM regressions found to have significant non-normality in example 6.4 were reestimated using four robust techniques: LAE, TRM, and TRQ with the trimming parameter set at $\phi = 0.1$ and 0.2. These estimates, along with the OLS estimates for comparison, are reported in table 6.3. In seven of the models, the robust beta estimators are consistently smaller than the OLS, while for the eighth, that of PSNH, the standard errors are sufficiently smaller to render the estimates significant. A similar pattern occurs for the estimates of α: for all except PSNH the robust estimates are smaller than the OLS. Moreover, some of the estimates even become significantly different from zero. Interestingly, only for PSNH are the OLS residuals negatively skewed. These findings are consistent with, for example, Mills and Coutts (1996), who also found that robust beta estimates for the industry baskets of the London Stock Exchange's *350* index were smaller than their OLS counterparts.

6.5 The multivariate linear regression model

An immediate extension of the regression model (6.1) is to replace the 'dependent' variable y_t by a vector, say $\mathbf{y}_t = (y_{1t}, \ldots, y_{nt})'$, so that we now have the *multivariate (dynamic) regression model*

$$\mathbf{y}_t = \mathbf{C} + \sum\nolimits_{i=1}^{m} \mathbf{A}_i'\mathbf{y}_{t-i} + \sum\nolimits_{i=0}^{m} \mathbf{B}_i'\mathbf{x}_{t-i} + \mathbf{u}_t, \quad m+1 \leq t \leq T \tag{6.15}$$

where $\mathbf{C}$ is an $n \times 1$ vector of constants, $\mathbf{A}_1, \ldots, \mathbf{A}_m$ are $n \times n$ matrices of lag coefficients, $\mathbf{B}_0, \mathbf{B}_1, \ldots, \mathbf{B}_m$ are $k \times n$ coefficient matrices, and $\mathbf{u}_t$ is an $n \times 1$ vector of errors having the properties

Table 6.3. *Robust estimates of the CAPM regression*

	CONTIL		DEC	
	$\hat{\alpha}$	$\hat{\beta}$	$\hat{\alpha}$	$\hat{\beta}$
OLS	−0.013 (0.013)	0.73 (0.19)	0.007 (0.007)	0.85 (0.11)
LAE	−0.013 (0.008)	0.67 (0.11)	0.007 (0.009)	0.74 (0.13)
TRM	−0.017 (0.004)	0.66 (0.05)	0.005 (0.004)	0.77 (0.06)
TRQ($\phi = 0.1$)	−0.018 (0.007)	0.62 (0.11)	0.005 (0.007)	0.71 (0.10)
TRQ ($\phi = 0.2$)	−0.017 (0.008)	0.63 (0.11)	0.004 (0.008)	0.78 (0.11)
	GERBER		MOBIL	
	$\hat{\alpha}$	$\hat{\beta}$	$\hat{\alpha}$	$\hat{\beta}$
OLS	0.005 (0.007)	0.63 (0.10)	0.004 (0.006)	0.72 (0.09)
LAE	−0.008 (0.009)	0.57 (0.14)	0.004 (0.007)	0.59 (0.10)
TRM	−0.001 (0.004)	0.57 (0.06)	0.003 (0.003)	0.63 (0.04)
TRQ ($\phi = 0.1$)	−0.001 (0.007)	0.58 (0.10)	0.002 (0.006)	0.64 (0.08)
TRQ ($\phi = 0.2$)	−0.002 (0.007)	0.58 (0.10)	0.002 (0.006)	0.60 (0.09)
	PANAM		PSNH	
	$\hat{\alpha}$	$\hat{\beta}$	$\hat{\alpha}$	$\hat{\beta}$
OLS	−0.009 (0.011)	0.74 (0.16)	−0.013 (0.010)	0.21 (0.15)
LAE	−0.019 (0.009)	0.60 (0.13)	−0.007 (0.006)	0.21 (0.09)
TRM	−0.013 (0.006)	0.68 (0.08)	−0.009 (0.005)	0.24 (0.07)
TRQ($\phi = 0.1$)	−0.010 (0.011)	0.65 (0.16)	−0.008 (0.008)	0.19 (0.11)
TRQ($\phi = 0.2$)	−0.012 (0.010)	0.65 (0.14)	−0.008 (0.006)	0.24 (0.09)
	TANDY		TEXACO	
	$\hat{\alpha}$	$\hat{\beta}$	$\hat{\alpha}$	$\hat{\beta}$
OLS	0.011 (0.010)	1.05 (0.14)	0.001 (0.006)	0.61 (0.09)
LAE	0.004 (0.013)	0.96 (0.18)	−0.002 (0.006)	0.54 (0.09)
TRM	0.008 (0.005)	0.94 (0.08)	−0.002 (0.003)	0.58 (0.05)
TRQ ($\phi = 0.1$)	0.007 (0.010)	0.99 (0.14)	−0.002 (0.005)	0.55 (0.08)
TRQ ($\phi = 0.2$)	0.008 (0.010)	0.95 (0.15)	−0.002 (0.005)	0.57 (0.07)

Notes: All computations were carried out using SHAZAM 7.0 (Shazam, 1993). ( ) denotes standard error, computed using the formulae in SHAZAM (1993, chapter 23).

$$E(\mathbf{u}_t) = E\left(\mathbf{u}_t \middle| \mathbf{Y}_{t-1}^0, \mathbf{x}_t^0\right) = \mathbf{0}$$

and

$$E\left(\mathbf{u}_t\mathbf{u}_s'\right) = E\left(\mathbf{u}_t\mathbf{u}_s' \middle| \mathbf{Y}_{t-1}^0, \mathbf{x}_t^0\right) = \begin{cases} \mathbf{\Omega} & t = s \\ \mathbf{0} & t \neq s \end{cases}$$

where

$$\mathbf{Y}_{t-1}^0 = \left(\mathbf{y}_{t-1}, \mathbf{y}_{t-2}, \ldots, \mathbf{y}_1\right)$$

In matrix form, we have

$$\mathbf{Y} = \mathbf{X}^*\mathbf{B} + \mathbf{U}$$

where

$$\begin{aligned} \mathbf{Y} &= \left(\mathbf{y}_{m+1}, \ldots, \mathbf{y}_T\right)' \\ \mathbf{X}^* &= \left(\mathbf{X}_{m+1}^*, \ldots, \mathbf{X}_T^*\right)' \\ \mathbf{X}_t^* &= \left(\mathbf{1}, \mathbf{y}_{t-1}, \ldots, \mathbf{y}_{t-m}, \mathbf{x}_t, \ldots, \mathbf{x}_{t-m}\right) \\ \mathbf{U} &= \left(\mathbf{u}_{m+1}, \ldots, \mathbf{u}_T\right)' \end{aligned}$$

and

$$\mathbf{B} = \left(\mathbf{C}', \mathbf{A}_1', \ldots, \mathbf{A}_m', \mathbf{B}_0', \ldots, \mathbf{B}_m'\right)$$

The estimation theory for this model is basically a multivariate extension of that developed for the univariate case ($n = 1$) above. For example, the LS and (approximate) ML estimator of $\mathbf{B}$ is

$$\hat{\mathbf{B}} = \left(\mathbf{X}^{*\prime}\mathbf{X}^*\right)^{-1}\mathbf{X}^{*\prime}\mathbf{Y}$$

while the ML estimator of $\mathbf{\Omega}$ is

$$\hat{\mathbf{\Omega}} = T^{-1}\hat{\mathbf{U}}'\hat{\mathbf{U}}, \qquad \hat{\mathbf{U}} = \mathbf{Y} - \mathbf{X}^{*\prime}\hat{\mathbf{B}}$$

Spanos (1986, chapter 24) considers this model in some detail, presenting misspecification tests that are essentially multivariate extensions of those outlined in section 6.3.

Example 6.7 Multivariate tests of the CAPM

Since the publication of Gibbons (1982), multivariate tests of the CAPM have been the subject of considerable research: for a detailed treatment, see Campbell, Lo and MacKinlay (1997, chapter 5). The multivariate CAPM can be analysed empirically within the framework of the multivariate regression model. By letting $\mathbf{y}_t$ be the vector of n excess asset returns at time t and x_t be the excess market return at time t, the model can be written as

$$\mathbf{y}_t = \mathbf{C} + \mathbf{B}x_t + \mathbf{u}_t$$

where $\mathbf{C}$ and $\mathbf{B}$ are $n \times 1$ vectors of parameters and the error $\mathbf{u}_t$ is assumed to have the properties of the error in equation (6.15). The CAPM imposes the n restrictions that the intercepts in each asset return equation are zero, i.e., $\mathbf{C} = \mathbf{0}$. MacKinlay (1987, see also Gibbons, Ross and Shanken, 1989) shows that this hypothesis can be tested using the statistic

$$J = \frac{(T-n-1)T}{(T-2)n}\left(1 + \frac{\bar{x}^2}{s_x^2}\right)^{-1} \mathbf{C}'\hat{\boldsymbol{\Omega}}^{-1}\mathbf{C}$$

Under $H_0 : \mathbf{C} = \mathbf{0}$, J is distributed as F with n and $T-n-1$ degrees of freedom.

The $n = 17$ assets considered separately in example 6.4 were reexamined in this multivariate framework. Of course, since the same (single) regressor appears in each equation, slope and intercept estimates are the same as the single equation OLS estimates. A test of $\mathbf{C} = \mathbf{0}$ produces a J value of 0.71, with an associated marginal significance level of 0.79. Not surprisingly, given the intercept estimates reported in table 6.1, we cannot reject the null that all the intercepts are zero, in accordance with the predictions of the CAPM, although we should emphasise that none of the misspecifications uncovered in the individual asset models in example 6.4 have been tackled here.

6.6 Vector autoregressions

6.6.1 Concepts of exogeneity and causality

Throughout the various forms of regression models encountered so far in this chapter we have made the assumption that $\mathbf{y}_t$ is a function of past values of itself and present and past values of $\mathbf{x}_t$. More precisely, we have been assuming that $\mathbf{x}_t$ is *weakly exogenous*: the stochastic structure of $\mathbf{x}_t$ contains no information that is relevant for the estimation of the parameters of interest, $\mathbf{B}$ and $\mathbf{\Omega}$. Formally, $\mathbf{x}_t$ will be weakly exogenous if, when the joint distribution of $\mathbf{z}_t = (\mathbf{y}_t', \mathbf{x}_t')'$, conditional on the past, is factorised as the conditional distribution of $\mathbf{y}_t$ given $\mathbf{x}_t$ times the marginal distribution of $\mathbf{x}_t$; (a) the parameters of these conditional and marginal distributions are not subject to cross-restrictions, and (b) the parameters of interest can be uniquely determined from the parameters of the conditional model alone. Under these conditions $\mathbf{x}_t$ may be treated 'as if' it were determined outside the conditional model for $\mathbf{y}_t$. For more details on weak exogeneity, see Engle, Hendry and Richard (1983), Engle and Hendry (1993) and Hendry (1995). Engle and Hendry (1993) extend weak exogeneity to that of *superexogeneity*: $\mathbf{x}_t$ will be superexogenous if it is weakly exogenous for $\mathbf{B}$ and $\mathbf{\Omega}$ and if the parameters of the conditional distribution of $\mathbf{y}_t$ are *invariant* to interventions that affect the marginal distribution of $\mathbf{x}_t$.

While the weak exogeneity of $\mathbf{x}_t$ allows efficient estimation of $\mathbf{B}$ and $\mathbf{\Omega}$ without any reference to the stochastic structure of $\mathbf{x}_t$, the marginal distribution of $\mathbf{x}_t$, while not containing $\mathbf{y}_t$, will contain $\mathbf{Y}_{t-1}^0$, and the possible presence of lagged **y**s can lead to problems when attempting to forecast $\mathbf{y}_t$. In order to be able to treat $\mathbf{x}_t$ as given when forecasting $\mathbf{y}_t$, we need to ensure that no *feedback* exists from $\mathbf{Y}_{t-1}^0$ to $\mathbf{x}_t$: the absence of such feedback is equivalent to the statement that $\mathbf{y}_t$ *does not Granger-cause* $\mathbf{x}_t$. Weak exogeneity supplemented with Granger non-causality is called *strong exogeneity*.

Unlike weak exogeneity, Granger non-causality is directly testable (the original reference to this concept of causality is Granger, 1969). To investigate such tests, and to relate Granger non-causality to yet another concept of exogeneity, we need to introduce the *dynamic structural equation model* (DSEM) and the *vector autoregressive* (VAR) process. The DSEM extends the multivariate regression model in two directions: first, by allowing 'simultaneity' between the 'endogenous' variables in $\mathbf{y}_t$ and, second, by explicitly considering the process generating the 'exogenous' variables $\mathbf{x}_t$. We thus have (in this and the subsequent sub-section constant terms are omitted for simplicity of notation)

$$\mathbf{A}_0\mathbf{y}_t = \sum\nolimits_{i=1}^{m} \mathbf{A}_i\mathbf{y}_{t-i} + \sum\nolimits_{i=0}^{m} \mathbf{B}_i\mathbf{x}_{t-i} + \mathbf{u}_{1t} \tag{6.16}$$

and

$$\mathbf{x}_t = \sum\nolimits_{i=1}^{m} \mathbf{C}_i\mathbf{x}_{t-i} + \mathbf{u}_{2t} \tag{6.17}$$

The simultaneity of the model is a consequence of $\mathbf{A}_0 \neq \mathbf{I}_n$. The errors $\mathbf{u}_{1t}$ and $\mathbf{u}_{2t}$ are assumed to be jointly dependent processes, which could be serially correlated but will be assumed here to be white noise: see Mills (1990, chapter 14) and, in particular, Lütkepohl (1991) for a more general development. The identification conditions for the set of *structural* equations (6.16) are summarised in Hendry, Pagan and Sargan (1984), while (6.17) shows that $\mathbf{x}_t$ is generated by an mth order VAR process, in which current values of $\mathbf{x}$ are functions of m past values of $\mathbf{x}$ *only*.

If, in the DSEM (6.17), $E(\mathbf{u}_{1t}\mathbf{x}_{t-s}) = \mathbf{0}$ for *all* s, $\mathbf{x}_t$ is said to be *strictly* exogenous. Strict exogeneity is useful because no information is lost by limiting attention to distributions conditional on $\mathbf{x}_t$, which will usually result in considerable simplifications in statistical inference: for example, IV techniques may be used in the presence of serially correlated disturbances. A related concept is that of a variable being *predetermined*: a variable is predetermined if all its current and past values are independent of the current error $\mathbf{u}_{1t}$. If $\mathbf{x}_t$ is strictly exogenous, then it will also be predetermined, while if $E(\mathbf{u}_{1t}\mathbf{y}_{t-s}) = \mathbf{0}$ for $s > 0$, then $\mathbf{y}_{t-s}$ will be predetermined as well.

In many cases, strictly exogenous variables will also be weakly exogenous in DSEMs, although one important class of exceptions is provided by rational expectations variables, in which behavioural parameters are generally linked to the distributions of exogenous variables. Similarly, predetermined variables will usually be weakly exogenous, except again in the case where there are cross-restrictions between behavioural parameters and the parameters of the distribution of the predetermined variables.

Strict exogeneity can be tested in DSEMs by using the *final form*, in which each endogenous variable is expressed as an infinite distributed lag of the exogenous variables

$$\mathbf{y}_t = \sum\nolimits_{i=0}^{\infty} \mathbf{J}_i \mathbf{x}_{t-i} + \mathbf{e}_t$$

where the $\mathbf{J}_i$ matrices are functions of the $\mathbf{A}_i$s and $\mathbf{B}_i$s and where $\mathbf{e}_t$ is a stochastic process possessing a VAR representation and having the property that $E(\mathbf{e}_t\mathbf{x}_{t-s}) = \mathbf{0}$ for all s. Geweke (1978) proves that, in the regression of $\mathbf{y}_t$ on *all* current, lagged, and future values of $\mathbf{x}_t$

$$\mathbf{y}_t = \sum\nolimits_{i=-\infty}^{\infty} \mathbf{K}_i \mathbf{x}_{t-i} + \mathbf{e}_t \tag{6.18}$$

there will exist a DSEM relating $\mathbf{x}_t$ and $\mathbf{y}_t$ in which $\mathbf{x}_t$ is strictly exogenous if, and only if, the coefficients on *future* values of $\mathbf{x}_t$, i.e., $\mathbf{x}_{t-s}$, $s < 0$, are all equal to zero. An equivalent test is based on the regression

$$\mathbf{x}_t = \sum_{i=1}^{\infty} \mathbf{E}_{2i}\mathbf{x}_{t-i} + \sum_{i=1}^{\infty} \mathbf{F}_{2i}\mathbf{y}_{t-i} + \mathbf{w}_t \tag{6.19}$$

in which $E(\mathbf{y}_{t-s}\mathbf{w}_t') = \mathbf{0}$ for all t and $s > 0$. Geweke proves that $\mathbf{x}_t$ will be strictly exogenous in a DSEM relating $\mathbf{x}_t$ and $\mathbf{y}_t$ if, and only if, the coefficient matrices $\mathbf{F}_{2i}$, $i = 1, 2, \ldots$, are all zero.

Strict exogeneity is intimately related to Granger non-causality. Indeed, the two tests for strict exogeneity of $\mathbf{x}_t$ above can also be regarded as tests for $\mathbf{y}_t$ not Granger-causing $\mathbf{x}_t$. The two concepts are *not* equivalent, however. As Geweke (1984) points out, if $\mathbf{x}_t$ is strictly exogenous in the DSEM (6.16), then $\mathbf{y}_t$ does not Granger-cause $\mathbf{x}_t$, where $\mathbf{y}_t$ is endogenous in that model. However, if $\mathbf{y}_t$ does not Granger-cause $\mathbf{x}_t$, then there exists *a* DSEM with $\mathbf{y}_t$ endogenous and $\mathbf{x}_t$ strictly exogenous, in the sense that there will exist systems of equations formally similar to (6.16), *but* none of these systems necessarily satisfy the overidentifying restrictions of the specific model. This implies that tests for the absence of a causal ordering can be used to refute the strict exogeneity specification in a given DSEM, but such tests cannot be used to establish it.

Furthermore, as we have already discussed, statistical inference may be carried out conditionally on a subset of variables that are not strictly exogenous: all that we require is that they be weakly exogenous. Thus, unidirectional Granger causality is neither necessary nor sufficient for inference to proceed conditional on a subset of variables.

6.6.2 Tests of Granger causality

To develop operational tests of Granger causality, we now consider the $g = n + k + r$ dimensional vector $\mathbf{z}_t = (\mathbf{y}_t', \mathbf{x}_t', \mathbf{r}_t')'$, which we assume has the following mth-order VAR representation: see, for example, Sims (1980)

$$\mathbf{z}_t = \sum_{i=1}^{m} \mathbf{\Pi}_i \mathbf{z}_{t-i} + \mathbf{v}_t \tag{6.20}$$

where

$$E(\mathbf{v}_t) = E(\mathbf{v}_t | \mathbf{Z}_{t-1}^0) = \mathbf{0}$$

$$E(\mathbf{v}_t\mathbf{v}_s') = E(\mathbf{v}_t\mathbf{v}_s' | \mathbf{Z}_{t-1}^0) = \begin{cases} \mathbf{\Sigma}_{\mathbf{v}}, & t = s \\ \mathbf{0}, & t \neq s \end{cases}$$

and

$$\mathbf{Z}_{t-1}^0 = (\mathbf{z}_{t-1}, \mathbf{z}_{t-2}, \ldots, \mathbf{z}_1)$$

The VAR of equation (6.20) can be partitioned as (the r equations modelling $\mathbf{r}_t$ may be ignored here)

$$\mathbf{y}_t = \sum_{i=1}^{m} \mathbf{C}_{2i}\mathbf{x}_{t-i} + \sum_{i=1}^{m} \mathbf{D}_{2i}\mathbf{y}_{t-i} + \sum_{i=1}^{m} \mathbf{G}_{1i}\mathbf{r}_{t-i} + \mathbf{v}_{1t} \qquad (6.21)$$

$$\mathbf{x}_t = \sum_{i=1}^{m} \mathbf{E}_{2i}\mathbf{x}_{t-i} + \sum_{i=1}^{m} \mathbf{F}_{2i}\mathbf{y}_{t-i} + \sum_{i=1}^{m} \mathbf{G}_{2i}\mathbf{r}_{t-i} + \mathbf{v}_{2t} \qquad (6.22)$$

where $\mathbf{v}_t' = \left(\mathbf{v}_{1t}', \mathbf{v}_{2t}'\right)$ and where $\boldsymbol{\Sigma}_{\mathbf{v}}$ is correspondingly partitioned as

$$\boldsymbol{\Sigma}_{\mathbf{v}} = \begin{pmatrix} \boldsymbol{\Sigma}_{11} & \boldsymbol{\Sigma}_{12} \\ \boldsymbol{\Sigma}_{12} & \boldsymbol{\Sigma}_{22} \end{pmatrix}$$

Here $\boldsymbol{\Sigma}_{ij} = E\left(\mathbf{v}_{it}\mathbf{v}_{jt}'\right)$, $i, j = 1, 2$, so that although the vectors $\mathbf{v}_{1t}$ and $\mathbf{v}_{2t}$ are each serially uncorrelated, they can be correlated with each other contemporaneously, although at no other lag. Given equations (6.21) and (6.22), $\mathbf{x}$ *does not Granger-cause* $\mathbf{y}$ if, and only if, $\mathbf{C}_{2i} \equiv \mathbf{0}$, for all i. An equivalent statement of this proposition is that $\left|\boldsymbol{\Sigma}_{11}\right| = \left|\boldsymbol{\Sigma}_1\right|$, where $\boldsymbol{\Sigma}_1 = E\left(\mathbf{w}_{1t}\mathbf{w}_{1t}'\right)$, obtained from the 'restricted' regression

$$\mathbf{y}_t = \sum_{i=1}^{m} \mathbf{C}_{1i}\mathbf{y}_{t-i} + \sum_{i=1}^{m} \mathbf{G}_{3i}\mathbf{r}_{t-i} + \mathbf{w}_{1t} \qquad (6.23)$$

Similarly, $\mathbf{y}$ *does not Granger-cause* $\mathbf{x}$ if, and only if, $\mathbf{F}_{2i} \equiv \mathbf{0}$, for all i or, equivalently, that $\left|\boldsymbol{\Sigma}_{22}\right| = \left|\boldsymbol{\Sigma}_2\right|$, where $\boldsymbol{\Sigma}_2 = E\left(\mathbf{w}_{2t}\mathbf{w}_{2t}'\right)$, obtained from the regression

$$\mathbf{x}_t = \sum_{i=1}^{m} \mathbf{E}_{1i}\mathbf{x}_{t-i} + \sum_{i=1}^{m} \mathbf{G}_{4i}\mathbf{r}_{t-i} + \mathbf{w}_{2t} \qquad (6.24)$$

If the system (6.21)–(6.22) is premultiplied by the matrix

$$\begin{bmatrix} \mathbf{I}_n & -\boldsymbol{\Sigma}_{12}\boldsymbol{\Sigma}_{22}^{-1} \\ -\boldsymbol{\Sigma}_{12}'\boldsymbol{\Sigma}_{11}^{-1} & \mathbf{I}_k \end{bmatrix}$$

then the first n equations of the new system can be written as

$$\mathbf{y}_t = \sum_{i=0}^{m} \mathbf{C}_{3i}\mathbf{x}_{t-i} + \sum_{i=1}^{m} \mathbf{D}_{3i}\mathbf{y}_{t-i} + \sum_{i=1}^{m} \mathbf{G}_{5i}\mathbf{r}_{t-i} + \boldsymbol{\omega}_{1t} \qquad (6.25)$$

where the error $\boldsymbol{\omega}_{1t} = \mathbf{v}_{1t} - \boldsymbol{\Sigma}_{12}\boldsymbol{\Sigma}_{22}^{-1}\mathbf{v}_{2t}$, since it is uncorrelated with $\mathbf{v}_{2t}$, is also uncorrelated with $\mathbf{x}_t$. Similarly, the last k equations can be written as

$$\mathbf{x}_t = \sum\nolimits_{i=1}^{m} \mathbf{E}_{3i}\mathbf{x}_{t-i} + \sum\nolimits_{i=0}^{m} \mathbf{F}_{3i}\mathbf{y}_{t-i} + \sum\nolimits_{i=1}^{m} \mathbf{G}_{6i}\mathbf{r}_{t-i} + \omega_{2t} \qquad (6.26)$$

Denoting $\boldsymbol{\Sigma}_{\omega i} = E(\omega_{it}\omega_{it}'), i = 1, 2,$ there is *instantaneous causality* between $\mathbf{y}$ and $\mathbf{x}$ if, and only if, $\mathbf{C}_{30} \neq \mathbf{0}$ and $\mathbf{E}_{30} \neq \mathbf{0}$ or, equivalently, if $|\boldsymbol{\Sigma}_{11}| > |\boldsymbol{\Sigma}_{\omega 1}|$ and $|\boldsymbol{\Sigma}_{22}| > |\boldsymbol{\Sigma}_{\omega_2}|$.

Tests of Granger causality can be constructed once estimates of the various covariance matrices have been obtained. Consistent and efficient estimates of the parameters of the regressions (6.21)–(6.26) are given by LS, so that the following matrices can be formed

$$\hat{\boldsymbol{\Sigma}}_i = (T-m)^{-1} \sum_{t=m+1}^{T} \hat{\mathbf{w}}_{it}\hat{\mathbf{w}}_{it}'$$

$$\hat{\boldsymbol{\Sigma}}_{ii} = (T-m)^{-1} \sum_{t=m+1}^{T} \hat{\mathbf{v}}_{it}\hat{\mathbf{v}}_{it}'$$

$$\hat{\boldsymbol{\Sigma}}_{\omega i} = (T-m)^{-1} \sum_{t=m+1}^{T} \hat{\omega}_{it}\hat{\omega}_{it}'$$

for $i = 1, 2,$ where $\hat{\mathbf{w}}_{it}$ is the vector of LS residuals corresponding to the error vector $\mathbf{w}_{it}$, etc. The LR test statistic of the null hypothesis H_{01} : $\mathbf{C}_{2i} = \mathbf{0}$ for all i ($\mathbf{x}$ does not Granger-cause $\mathbf{y}$) is

$$LR_1 = (T-m)\log\left(\left|\hat{\boldsymbol{\Sigma}}_1\right| \Big/ \left|\hat{\boldsymbol{\Sigma}}_{11}\right|\right) \sim \chi^2_{nkm}$$

Similarly, the null that $\mathbf{y}$ does not Granger cause $\mathbf{x}$, $H_{02} : \mathbf{F}_{2i} = \mathbf{0}$, is tested by

$$LR_2 = (T-m)\log\left(\left|\hat{\boldsymbol{\Sigma}}_2\right| \Big/ \left|\hat{\boldsymbol{\Sigma}}_{22}\right|\right) \sim \chi^2_{nkm}$$

while the null that there is no instantaneous causality between $\mathbf{y}$ and $\mathbf{x}$, $H_{03} : \mathbf{C}_{30} = \mathbf{E}_{30} = \mathbf{0}$, is tested by

$$\begin{aligned} LR_3 &= (T-m)\log\left(\left|\hat{\boldsymbol{\Sigma}}_1\right| \Big/ \left|\hat{\boldsymbol{\Sigma}}_{\omega 1}\right|\right) \\ &= (T-m)\log\left(\left|\hat{\boldsymbol{\Sigma}}_2\right| \Big/ \left|\hat{\boldsymbol{\Sigma}}_{\omega 2}\right|\right) \sim \chi^2_{nk} \end{aligned}$$

Since these are tests of nested hypotheses, they are asymptotically independent. All three restrictions can be tested at once since

$$LR_1 + LR_2 + LR_3 \sim \chi^2_{nk(2m+1)}$$

Wald and LM statistics may be constructed in analogous fashion. Although various other tests of causality have been proposed, they tend to require considerably more computation and, in any event, simulation studies carried out by a variety of authors reach a consensus that inference should be carried out using the procedures detailed above, these being found to combine the greatest reliability with computational ease.

6.6.3 Determining the order of a VAR

These tests of causality assume that the order m of the underlying VAR is known. In practice, of course, m will be unknown and must be determined empirically. A traditional tool for determining the order is to use a sequential testing procedure. If we have the g-dimensional VAR given by (6.20), from which the ML estimate of $\boldsymbol{\Sigma}_{\mathbf{v}}$ is

$$\hat{\boldsymbol{\Sigma}}_{\mathbf{v},m} = T^{-1}\hat{\mathbf{V}}_m\hat{\mathbf{V}}'_m$$

where $\hat{\mathbf{V}}_m = (\hat{\mathbf{v}}_{m+1}, \ldots, \hat{\mathbf{v}}_T)$ is the matrix of residuals obtained by LS estimation of the mth-order VAR [VAR(m)], then, for example, the LR statistic for testing m against l, $l < m$, is

$$LR(m,l) = (T - gm)\log\left(\left|\hat{\boldsymbol{\Sigma}}_{\mathbf{v},l}\right| \Big/ \left|\hat{\boldsymbol{\Sigma}}_{\mathbf{v},m}\right|\right) \sim \chi^2_{g^2(m-l)}$$

This uses the scaling factor $T - gm$ rather than T to account for possible small-sample bias in the statistic.

Other procedures are based upon minimising some objective function and are essentially multivariate analogs of those discussed in example 2.3. The objective function that is most favoured is the multivariate *BIC* criterion, defined here as

$$BIC(m) = \log\left|\hat{\boldsymbol{\Sigma}}_{\mathbf{v},m}\right| + g^2 mT^{-1}\log T, \qquad m = 0, 1, \ldots, m^*$$

where m^* is the *maximum* order considered. This can be shown to provide a consistent estimate of the correct lag order and Lütkepohl (1985) finds that it also chooses the correct order most often, and the resulting VAR models provide the best forecasts, in a Monte Carlo comparison of objective functions.

After a tentative model has been specified using one of these procedures, checks on its adequacy may be carried out. These are analogous to the diagnostic checks used for univariate models and might involve overfitting and testing the significance of the extra parameters, plotting standardised residuals against time and analysing the estimated cross-correlation matrices of the residual series. Multivariate portmanteau and LM statistics are also available, but with vector time series there is probably no substitute for detailed inspection of the residual correlation structure for revealing subtle relationships which may indicate important directions for model improvement.

6.7 Variance decompositions, innovation accounting and structural VARs

A concise representation of the VAR(m) model is obtained by using lag operator notation

$$\mathbf{\Pi}(B)\mathbf{z}_t = \mathbf{v}_t$$

where

$$\mathbf{\Pi}(B) = \mathbf{I} - \mathbf{\Pi}_1 B - \mathbf{\Pi}_2 B^2 - \ldots - \mathbf{\Pi}_m B^m$$

Analogous to the univariate case, the vector MA representation of $\mathbf{z}_t$ is

$$\mathbf{z}_t = \mathbf{\Pi}^{-1}(B)\mathbf{v}_t = \mathbf{\Psi}(B)\mathbf{v}_t = \mathbf{v}_t + \sum\nolimits_{i=1}^{\infty} \mathbf{\Psi}_i \mathbf{v}_{t-i} \qquad (6.27)$$

where

$$\mathbf{\Psi}_i = \sum\nolimits_{j=1}^{i} \mathbf{\Pi}_j \mathbf{\Psi}_{i-j}, \qquad \mathbf{\Psi}_0 = \mathbf{I}_n$$

In this set up, no distinction is made between endogenous and (strictly) exogenous variables, so the $\mathbf{\Psi}_i$ matrices can be interpreted as the *dynamic multipliers* of the system, since they represent the model's response to a unit shock in each of the variables. The response of z_i to a unit shock in z_j (i.e., to v_{jt} taking the value unity, where v_{jt} is the jth element of $\mathbf{v}_t$) is therefore given by the sequence, known as the *impulse response function*

$$\Psi_{ij,1}, \Psi_{ij,2}, \ldots$$

where $\Psi_{ij,k}$ is the ijth element of the matrix $\mathbf{\Psi}_k$. If a variable, or block of variables, are strictly exogenous, then the implied zero restrictions ensure that these variables do not react to a shock to any of the endogenous variables. Recall, however, that $E(\mathbf{v}_t\mathbf{v}_t') = \mathbf{\Sigma}_\mathbf{v}$, so that the components of $\mathbf{v}_t$ are contemporaneously correlated. If these correlations are high, simulation of a shock to z_j, while all other components of $\mathbf{z}_t$ are held constant, could be misleading, as there is no way of separating out the response of z_i to z_j from its response to other shocks that are correlated with v_{jt}.

However, if we define the lower triangular matrix $\mathbf{S}$ such that $\mathbf{SS}' = \mathbf{\Sigma}_\mathbf{v}$ and $\mathbf{n}_t = \mathbf{S}^{-1}\mathbf{v}_t$, then $E(\mathbf{n}_t\mathbf{n}_t') = \mathbf{I}_g$, so that the transformed shocks $\mathbf{n}_t$ are orthogonal to each other. We can then renormalise the MA representation (6.27) into the *recursive* form

$$\mathbf{z}_t = \sum\nolimits_{i=0}^{\infty} (\mathbf{\Psi}_i\mathbf{S})(\mathbf{S}^{-1}\mathbf{v}_{t-i}) = \sum\nolimits_{i=0}^{\infty} \mathbf{\Psi}_i^O \mathbf{n}_{t-i}$$

where $\mathbf{\Psi}_i^O = \mathbf{\Psi}_i\mathbf{S}^{-1}$ (so that $\mathbf{\Psi}_0^O = \mathbf{\Psi}_0\mathbf{S}^{-1}$ is lower triangular). The impulse response function of z_i to a unit shock in z_j is then given by the sequence

$$\Psi_{ij,0}^O,\ \Psi_{ij,1}^O,\ \Psi_{ij,2}^O, \ldots$$

where each impulse response can be written compactly as

$$\Psi_{ij,h}^O = \mathbf{e}_j'\mathbf{\Psi}_h\mathbf{S}\mathbf{e}_i \tag{6.28}$$

where $\mathbf{e}_i$ is the $n \times 1$ selection vector containing unity as the ith element and zeros elsewhere. This sequence is known as the *orthogonalised impulse response function.*

The uncorrelatedness of the $\mathbf{n}_t$s allows the error variance of the H-step ahead forecast of z_i to be decomposed into components accounted for by these shocks, or innovations: hence the phrase coined by Sims (1981) for this technique, that of *innovation accounting*. In particular, the proportion of the H-step ahead forecast error variance of variable i accounted for by the orthogonalised innovations to z_j is given by

$$V_{ij,h}^O = \frac{\sum_{h=0}^{H} (\Psi_{ij,h}^O)^2}{\sum_{h=0}^{H} \mathbf{e}_i'\mathbf{\Psi}_h\mathbf{\Sigma}_\mathbf{v}\mathbf{\Psi}_h'\mathbf{e}_i} = \frac{\sum_{h=0}^{H} (\mathbf{e}_i'\mathbf{\Psi}_h\mathbf{S}\mathbf{e}_j)^2}{\sum_{h=0}^{H} \mathbf{e}_i'\mathbf{\Psi}_h\mathbf{\Sigma}_\mathbf{v}\mathbf{\Psi}_h'\mathbf{e}_i}$$

For large H, this *orthogonalised forecast error variance decomposition* allows the isolation of those relative contributions to variability that are, intuitively, 'persistent' (for further details of this technique, see, for example, Doan, Litterman and Sims, 1984). The technique does, however, have an important disadvantage: the choice of the $\mathbf{S}$ matrix is not unique, so that different choices (for example, different orderings of the variables) will alter the $\Psi_{ij,k}^{O}$ coefficients and hence the impulse response functions and variance decompositions. The extent of these changes will depend upon the size of the contemporaneous correlations between the components of the $\mathbf{v}_t$ vector. This non-invariance property has generated much detailed analysis and criticism of the variance decomposition methodology, focusing on the inability of VARs to be regarded as 'structural' in the traditional econometric sense, so that shocks cannot be uniquely identified with a particular variable unless prior identifying assumptions are made, without which the computed impulse response functions and variance decompositions would be invalid.

To make this point more concrete, suppose we have a (first-order) DSEM but, in keeping with the general philosophy of VARs, no variables are considered to be exogenous, at least *a priori*, i.e.

$$\mathbf{A}_0\mathbf{y}_t = \mathbf{A}_1\mathbf{y}_{t-1} + \mathbf{B}\mathbf{u}_t \tag{6.29}$$

We also assume that the structural errors $\mathbf{u}_t$ have zero cross-correlation: hence

$$E\left(\mathbf{u}_t\mathbf{u}_s'\right) = \begin{cases} \mathbf{\Sigma}_\mathbf{u}, & t = s \\ \mathbf{0}, & t \neq s \end{cases}$$

and $\mathbf{\Sigma}_\mathbf{u}$ is diagonal. The diagonal elements of $\mathbf{A}_0$ and $\mathbf{B}$ are normalised to unity, thus associating each structural equation with a natural left-hand side variable and with a particular structural error. Contemporaneous interactions are captured by non-zero off-diagonal elements in these matrices; $\mathbf{A}_0$ capturing interactions between the variables, $\mathbf{B}$ modelling the direct effects of disturbances on variables other than those appearing on the left-hand side of the structural equations.

Premultiplying (6.29) by $\mathbf{A}_0^{-1}$ obtains the VAR (6.20) with $m = 1$, $\mathbf{\Pi}_1 = \mathbf{A}_0^{-1}\mathbf{A}_1$ and $\mathbf{A}_0\mathbf{v}_t = \mathbf{B}\mathbf{u}_t$. The VAR is thus seen to be the *reduced form* of the DSEM and the VAR error $\mathbf{v}_t$ is a linear combination of the errors of the DSEM. It is this fact that makes the interpretation of impulse response functions and variance decompositions potentially ambiguous. Recall that $\Psi_{ij,k}$ measures the response of z_i to a unit shock in z_j after k periods. But a shock to z_j, given by the jth element of $\mathbf{v}_t$, is now seen to be made up of all the *structural* innovations $\mathbf{u}_t$ and hence, in the absence of further information, could have been the consequence of a shock to *any* of the variables in the DSEM. The recursive triangularisation introduced above implies $\mathbf{v}_t = \mathbf{S}\mathbf{n}_t$, so the recursive innovations and the structural innovations will only coincide if $\mathbf{S} = \mathbf{A}_0^{-1}\mathbf{B}$, which will be satisfied if the

DSEM itself has the same lower triangular structure, i.e., if **B** is diagonal and $\mathbf{A}_0$ lower triangular.

Numerous authors have argued that these assumptions have no particular economic rationale – that they are *atheoretical*, using the term of Cooley and LeRoy (1985). This has led to the development of other sets of identifying restrictions that are based more explicitly on economic considerations. Bernanke (1986) and Blanchard (1989), for example, impose alternative sets of restrictions on $\mathbf{A}_0$ and **B** that in effect constrain the short-run impact of shocks to **z**, while Blanchard and Quah (1989) exploit a different set of restrictions which constrain the long-run effects of shocks to **z** and thus impose restrictions across $\mathbf{A}_0$, $\mathbf{A}_1$ and **B**. Swanson and Granger (1997) present a method that combines both prior economic knowledge and statistical analysis of the VAR residuals.

An alternative approach has been proposed by Pesaran and Shin (1997), extending the work of Koop, Pesaran and Potter (1996). This proposes using *generalised impulse responses* as a means of circumventing the dependence of the orthogonalised responses to the ordering of the variables. The generalised impulse response is defined by replacing **S** in (6.28) with $\sigma_{ii}^{-1/2}\boldsymbol{\Sigma}_{\mathbf{v}}$, where σ_{ii} is the ith diagonal element of $\boldsymbol{\Sigma}_{\mathbf{v}}$

$$\psi^G_{ij,h} = \sigma_{ii}^{-1/2}\mathbf{e}_j\boldsymbol{\Psi}_h\boldsymbol{\Sigma}_{\mathbf{v}}\mathbf{e}_i$$

thus leading to the *generalised forecast error variance decomposition*

$$V^G_{ij,h} = \frac{\sum_{h=0}^{H}\left(\psi^G_{ij,h}\right)^2}{\sum_{h=0}^{H}\mathbf{e}_i'\boldsymbol{\Psi}_h\boldsymbol{\Sigma}_{\mathbf{v}}\boldsymbol{\Psi}_h'\mathbf{e}_i} = \frac{\sigma_{ii}^{-1}\sum_{h=0}^{H}\left(\mathbf{e}_i'\boldsymbol{\Psi}_h\boldsymbol{\Sigma}_{\mathbf{v}}\mathbf{e}_j\right)^2}{\sum_{h=0}^{H}\mathbf{e}_i'\boldsymbol{\Psi}_h\boldsymbol{\Sigma}_{\mathbf{v}}\boldsymbol{\Psi}_h'\mathbf{e}_i}$$

The generalised impulse responses are invariant to the ordering of the variables, are unique and fully take into account the historical patterns of correlations observed amongst the different shocks. The orthogonalised and generalised impulse responses will only coincide if $\boldsymbol{\Sigma}_{\mathbf{v}}$ is diagonal, and in general are only the same for $j = 1$ (Pesaran and Shin, 1997).

Methods of computing standard errors of the impulse response functions in the above situations are discussed in detail in Hamilton (1994, chapter 11.7).

or

$$\mathbf{\Phi}(B)\mathbf{z}_t = \mathbf{\Theta}(B)\mathbf{v}_t$$

where

$$\mathbf{\Phi}(B) = \mathbf{I} - \mathbf{\Phi}_1 B - \ldots - \mathbf{\Phi}_p B^p$$

and

$$\mathbf{\Theta}(B) = \mathbf{I} - \mathbf{\Theta}_1 B - \ldots - \mathbf{\Theta}_q B^q$$

which, of course, admits a VAR(∞) representation with $\mathbf{\Pi}(B) = \mathbf{\Theta}^{-1}(B)\mathbf{\Phi}(B)$. The presence of a vector MA component unfortunately complicates analysis somewhat, and vector ARMA models are now rarely used. Details of such models, including estimation methods and model-building techniques, may be found in, for example, Mills (1990, chapter 14) and Lütkepohl (1991).

Example 6.8 The interaction of equity and bond markets in the UK

The example that is used to illustrate VAR modelling brings together four series that have been used in previous examples. These are the *FTA All Share* index and associated dividend index, first introduced in example 2.6, and the series on 20 year UK gilts and 91 day Treasury bills, used to construct the spread in example 2.2. Previous examples have shown that the logarithms are all $I(1)$, so that the first-differences, Δp, Δd, Δrs and $\Delta r20$, are individually stationary and hence suitable for modelling in a VAR framework. The first three series were analysed within a single equation framework modelling Δp in example 6.5. The sample period is January 1965 to December 1995, so that $T = 372$. Thus $g = 4$ and $\mathbf{z}_t = (\Delta p_t, \Delta d_t, \Delta rs_t, \Delta r20_t)$. Table 6.4 presents *BIC* values for lags $m = 0, 1, \ldots, 12$, along with LR statistics for testing m against $m - 1$, beginning at $m = 12$. The minimum *BIC* is found at $m = 2$, whereas the first significant LR statistic, using the 5 per cent level for each test, is at $m = 6$. Diagnostic checks on the sets of residuals, however, found that the residuals from the dividend equation when $m = 2$ were autocorrelated, with significant autocorrelations at lags 3 and 6, a consequence of the seasonality induced into the index through quarterly dividend payments. Setting $m = 6$ revealed no residual autocorrelation, and this order of VAR was therefore selected. Summary statistics for the VAR(6) are shown in table 6.5, along with the estimated contemporaneous residual correlation matrix.

Table 6.4. *BIC values and LR statistics for determining the order of the VAR in example 6.8*

m	$BIC(m)$	$LR(m, m-1)$
0	−26.761	94.92
1	−26.962	22.19
2	−26.965†	19.05
3	−26.954	2.15
4	−26.895	10.86
5	−26.864	29.64*
6	−26.885	11.98
7	−26.858	25.05
8	−26.863	13.12
9	−26.840	13.50
10	−26.814	8.28
11	−26.776	11.24
12	−26.748	–

$LR(m, m-1) \sim \chi^2_{16}$, $\chi^2_{16,0.05} = 26.30$
†: minimum *BIC*; *: first significant *LR* statistic

Table 6.5 *Summary statistics for the VAR(6) of example 6.8*

	R^2	*s.e.*	$Q(12)$
Δp	0.11	0.060	9.7
Δd	0.11	0.014	7.5
Δrs	0.19	0.059	7.5
$\Delta r20$	0.17	0.032	3.0

Contemporaneous residual correlation matrix

	Δp	Δd	Δrs	$\Delta r20$
Δp	1			
Δd	0.10	1		
Δrs	−0.14	0.08	1	
$\Delta r20$	−0.25	−0.03	0.45	1

Two sets of Granger causality tests are computed for illustration. The first set uses $\mathbf{y}_t = (\Delta p_t, \Delta d_t)$, $\mathbf{x}_t = (\Delta rs_t, \Delta r20_t)$ and $\mathbf{r}_t$ null, so that $n = k = 2$ and $r = 0$. This tests whether the equity market 'as a whole' Granger causes the bond market and vice versa. The second set defines $\mathbf{y}_t = \Delta p_t$, $\mathbf{x}_t = \Delta r20_t$ and $\mathbf{r}_t = (\Delta d_t, \Delta rs_t)$, so that $n = k = 1$ and $r = 2$, and looks at the causal patterns between equity prices and gilt yields alone. From the first set of statistics shown in table 6.6, the equity market Granger causes the bond market, but there is no evidence of feedback, although there is instantaneous causality. With attention focused on just equity prices and gilt yields, there is more evidence of feedback, the p-value of the test of $\Delta r20$ not Granger-causing Δp being only 0.06.

Three variance decompositions are reported in table 6.7. The first (denoted I) uses the ordering defining $\mathbf{z}$, while the second (II) reverses this, i.e., $\Delta r20$, Δrs, Δd, Δp. The third (III) is the generalised variance decomposition. Own innovations have the major weight in the decompositions, but many of the other weights are significant (the standard errors attached to the decomposition values are all smaller than 0.1).

Because Δd is effectively contemporaneously uncorrelated with the other three variables, a change in ordering has little impact on its role in the variance decomposition, which is very small apart from on its own decomposition. This is not the case for the others, where major shifts in weights are found when the ordering is changed. In the absence of any structural model suggesting a theoretical ordering, there is no way of establishing which of the variance decompositions is appropriate, although the order invariant generalised variance decomposition (case III) offers obvious advantages. Focusing on this, it is seen that there are quantitatively important feedbacks between Δp and $\Delta r20$ and between $\Delta r20$ and Δrs.

Table 6.6. *Granger causality tests*

	(i) $\mathbf{y} = (\Delta p, \Delta d)$, $\mathbf{x} = (\Delta rs, \Delta r20)$			(ii) $\mathbf{y} = (\Delta p)$, $\mathbf{x} = (\Delta r20)$		
	χ^2	*df*	*p*-value	χ^2	*df*	*p*-value
LR_1	25.15	24	0.40	11.89	6	0.06
LR_2	38.21	24	0.03	26.41	6	0.00
LR_3	27.68	4	0.00	23.43	1	0.00

Table 6.7 *Variance decompositions*

		Explained by											
		Δp			Δd			Δrs			$\Delta r20$		
	h	I	II	III	I	II	III	I	II	III	I	II	III
Δp	0	100	92.6	91.5	0	1.0	1.0	0	0.1	1.7	0	6.3	5.8
	3	96.2	88.6	88.0	1.3	1.9	1.9	0	0.6	1.9	2.5	8.9	8.2
	6	94.0	87.1	86.6	2.4	2.7	2.7	0.2	0.8	2.1	3.3	9.3	8.6
	9	94.0	87.0	86.6	2.4	2.8	2.7	0.2	0.9	2.1	3.4	9.3	8.6
	12	93.9	87.0	86.6	2.4	2.8	2.7	0.2	0.9	2.1	3.5	9.3	8.6
Δd	0	1.1	0	1.1	98.9	98.9	98.3	0	1.0	0.6	0	0.1	0
	3	1.8	0.6	1.8	96.8	96.8	95.9	1.3	2.2	1.8	0	0.5	0.5
	6	2.3	0.9	2.3	94.6	94.4	94.1	1.9	3.5	2.4	1.2	1.2	1.2
	9	2.3	0.9	2.3	94.2	94.0	93.8	2.2	3.9	2.7	1.2	1.2	1.2
	12	2.3	0.9	2.3	94.1	93.9	93.7	2.3	4.0	2.8	1.2	1.2	1.2
Δrs	0	1.9	0	1.5	0.8	0	0.5	97.2	79.5	81.3	0	20.5	16.7
	3	3.8	0.6	3.0	2.1	1.0	1.3	90.7	70.8	74.1	3.4	27.6	21.6
	6	4.2	1.5	3.3	2.4	1.3	1.5	89.5	69.1	73.0	4.0	28.1	22.2
	9	4.2	1.5	3.3	2.4	1.3	1.5	89.4	69.1	73.0	4.0	28.1	22.2
	12	4.2	1.5	3.3	2.4	1.4	1.5	89.4	69.1	73.0	4.0	28.1	22.2
$\Delta r20$	0	6.3	0	5.0	0	0	0.1	18.0	0	16.1	75.7	100	78.8
	3	14.3	6.0	11.3	1.1	0.8	0.6	15.5	0.3	14.6	69.1	92.9	73.5
	6	14.5	6.4	11.5	1.5	1.2	0.9	15.7	0.4	14.7	68.3	92.0	72.9
	9	14.6	6.5	11.6	1.5	1.2	0.9	15.7	0.5	14.7	68.1	91.9	72.8
	12	14.6	6.5	11.6	1.5	1.2	1.0	15.7	0.5	14.7	68.1	91.8	72.7

7 Regression techniques for integrated financial time series

Chapter 6 has developed regression techniques for modelling relationships between *non-integrated* time series. As we have seen in earlier chapters, however, many financial time series are integrated, often able to be characterised as $I(1)$ processes, and the question thus arises as to whether the presence of integrated variables affects our standard regression results and conventional procedures of inference.

To this end, section 1 investigates this question through the analysis of spurious regressions between integrated time series. This leads naturally on to the concept of cointegration, which is introduced in section 2. Testing for cointegration in regression models is discussed in section 3 and the estimation of cointegrating regressions is the subject material of section 4. Section 5 considers VARs containing integrated and, possibly, cointegrated variables, which enables us to develop the vector error correction model (VECM) framework. Causality testing in VECMs is discussed in section 6 and alternative estimation methods in section 7. Finally, impulse response functions are analysed within a VECM framework in section 8.

7.1 Spurious regression

We begin by considering the simulation example analysed by Granger and Newbold (1974) in an important article examining some of the likely empirical consequences of nonsense, or *spurious*, regressions in econometrics. They consider a situation in which y_t and x_t are generated by the *independent* random walks

$$y_t = y_{t-1} + v_t, \quad x_t = x_{t-1} + w_t, \quad t = 1, 2, \ldots$$

where v_t and w_t are independent white noises. The regression of y_t on a constant and x_t is then considered

$$y_t = \hat{\alpha}_T + \hat{\beta}_T x_t + \hat{u}_t, \quad t = 1, 2, \ldots, T \tag{7.1}$$

With $T = 50$, $y_0 = x_0 = 100$ and v_t and w_t drawn from independent $N(0, 1)$ distributions, Granger and Newbold report a rejection rate of 76 per cent when testing the (correct) null hypothesis that $\beta = 0$ in the regression (7.1) using the conventional t-statistic for assessing the significance of $\hat{\beta}_T$. Moreover, when five independent random walks are included as regressors in a multiple regression, the rejection rate of a conventional F-statistic testing that the coefficient vector is zero rises to 96 per cent. For regressions involving independent ARIMA(0,1,1) series the corresponding rejection rates are 64 per cent and 90 per cent, and Granger and Newbold thus conclude that conventional significance tests are seriously biased towards rejection of the null hypothesis of no relationship, and hence towards acceptance of a *spurious* relationship, when the series are generated as statistically independent integrated processes.

Moreover, such regression results are frequently accompanied by large R^2 values and highly autocorrelated residuals, as indicated by very low Durbin–Watson (dw) statistics. These findings led Granger and Newbold (1974) to suggest that, in the joint circumstances of a high R^2 and a low dw statistic (a useful rule being $R^2 > dw$), regressions should be run on the first differences of the variables. Further empirical evidence in favour of first differencing in regression models is provided by Granger and Newbold (1986, pp. 205–15) and Plosser and Schwert (1978).

These essentially empirical conclusions have since been given an analytical foundation by Phillips (1986), who makes much weaker assumptions about the innovations $\xi_t = (v_t, w_t)'$ than those made above. In fact, Phillips assumes that ξ_t follows a multivariate version of the conditions (3.10) used to develop non-parametric unit root tests and also employed in the (stationary) regression framework of chapter 6.1, i.e.

$E(\xi_t) = 0$ for all t; (7.2a)

$\sup_{i,t} E\left(|\xi_{it}|^{\beta}\right) < \infty$ for some $\beta > 2$, $i = 1, 2$ ($\xi_{1t} = v_t, \xi_{2t} = w_t$); (7.2b)

$\boldsymbol{\Sigma}_S = \lim_{T\to\infty} T^{-1} E(\mathbf{S}_T \mathbf{S}_T')$ exists and is positive definite, where $\mathbf{S}_T = \sum_{t=1}^{T} \xi_t$; (7.2c)

ξ_t is strong mixing. (7.2d)

In the special case when v_t and w_t are independent, the 'long-run' covariance matrix $\boldsymbol{\Sigma}_S$ is

$$\boldsymbol{\Sigma}_S = \begin{bmatrix} \sigma_v^2 & 0 \\ 0 & \sigma_w^2 \end{bmatrix}$$

where

$$\sigma_v^2 = \lim_{T\to\infty} T^{-1}E(P_T^2), \qquad \sigma_w^2 = \lim_{T\to\infty} T^{-1}E(Q_T^2)$$

and

$$P_t = \sum\nolimits_{j=1}^{t} v_j, \qquad Q_t = \sum\nolimits_{j=1}^{t} w_j, \qquad P_0 = Q_0 = 0$$

Phillips (1986) shows that, under these conditions, suitably standardised sample moments of the sequences $\{y_t\}_1^\infty$ and $\{x_t\}_1^\infty$ converge weakly to appropriately defined functionals of Brownian motion, rather than to constants as in the non-integrated regressor case discussed in chapter 6, which assumes that y_t and x_t are, for example, ergodic. As a consequence, the standard distributional results of least squares regression break down, since they are based on the ratios of sample moments converging to constants. While not providing too great a level of rigour, a sketch of the derivation of this crucial result is nonetheless illuminating. We begin by noting that we may write $y_t = P_t + y_0$ and $x_t = Q_t + x_0$, where the initial conditions y_0 and x_0 can either be constants or can have certain specified distributions, from which we construct the standardised sums (recall the development in chapter 3.1.2)

$$\begin{aligned} &Y_T(r) = T^{-1/2}\sigma_v^{-1}P_{[rT]} = T^{-1/2}\sigma_v^{-1}P_{j-1}, \\ &X_T(r) = T^{-1/2}\sigma_w^{-1}Q_{[rT]} = T^{-1/2}\sigma_w^{-1}Q_{j-1}, \\ &(j-1)/T \le r < j/T, \qquad j = 1, \ldots, T \end{aligned}$$

Using the more general partial sum process $\boldsymbol{S}_t$, we can also construct

$$\boldsymbol{Z}_T(r) = T^{-1/2}\boldsymbol{\Sigma}_S^{-1/2}\boldsymbol{S}_{[rT]} = T^{-1/2}\boldsymbol{\Sigma}_S^{-1/2}\boldsymbol{S}_{j-1}$$

where $\boldsymbol{\Sigma}_S^{1/2}$ is the positive definite square root of $\boldsymbol{\Sigma}_S$. Phillips (1987c) proves that, as $T \to \infty$, $\boldsymbol{Z}_T(r)$ converges weakly to the vector Brownian motion $\boldsymbol{Z}(r)$, i.e.

$$\boldsymbol{Z}_T(r) \Rightarrow \boldsymbol{Z}(r)$$

From the properties of Brownian motion, $\boldsymbol{Z}(r)$ is *multivariate* normal, with independent increments (so that $\boldsymbol{Z}(s)$ is independent of $\boldsymbol{Z}(r) - \boldsymbol{Z}(s)$ for $0 < s < r \le 1$) and with independent elements (so that the ith element $Z_i(r)$ is independent of the jth element $Z_j(r)$, $i \ne j$).

When the sequences v_t and w_t are independent

$$\boldsymbol{Z}_T(r) = \begin{bmatrix} Y_T(r) \\ X_T(r) \end{bmatrix}, \qquad \boldsymbol{Z}(r) = \begin{bmatrix} V(r) \\ W(r) \end{bmatrix}$$

and hence

$$Y_T(r) \Rightarrow V(r), \qquad X_T(r) \Rightarrow W(r)$$

as $T \to \infty$, where $V(r)$ and $W(r)$ are independent Brownian motions. Phillips (1986) then shows the following results

(i) $$\hat{\beta}_T \Rightarrow \frac{\sigma_v \sigma_w^{-1}\left(\int_0^1 V(r)W(r)\mathrm{d}r - \int_0^1 V(r)\mathrm{d}r \int_0^1 W(r)\mathrm{d}r\right)}{\int_0^1 W(r)^2\mathrm{d}r - \left(\int_0^1 W(r)\mathrm{d}r\right)^2} = \sigma_v \sigma_w^{-1} \frac{\varsigma_{VW}}{\varsigma_{WW}}$$

(ii) $$T^{-1/2} t_{\hat{\beta}_T} \Rightarrow \frac{\varsigma_{VW}}{\left(\varsigma_{VV}\varsigma_{WW} - \varsigma_{VW}\right)^{1/2}}$$

(iii) $$R^2 \Rightarrow \frac{\varsigma_{VW}^2}{\varsigma_{VV}\varsigma_{WW}}$$

(iv) $$dw \xrightarrow{p} 0$$

where we use the notation $\varsigma_{ab} = \int_0^1 a(r)b(r)\mathrm{d}r - \int_0^1 a(r)\mathrm{d}r \int_0^1 b(r)\mathrm{d}r$.

As Phillips (1986) remarks, these analytical findings go a long way towards explaining the Monte Carlo findings reported by Granger and Newbold (1974). Result (i) shows that, in contrast to the usual results of regression theory, $\hat{\beta}_T$ and, similarly, $\hat{\alpha}_T$, do not converge in probability to constants as $T \to \infty$. $\hat{\beta}_T$ has a non-degenerate limiting distribution, so that different arbitrary large samples will yield randomly differing estimates of β. The distribution of $\hat{\alpha}_T$ (not shown) actually diverges, so that estimates are likely to get farther and farther away from the true value of zero as the sample size increases. Thus the uncertainty about the regression (7.1) stemming from its spurious nature persists asymptotically in these limiting distributions, being a consequence of the sample moments of y_t and x_t (and their joint sample moments) not converging to constants but, upon appropriate standardisation, converging weakly to random variables.

Result (ii) shows that the conventional t-ratio on $\hat{\beta}_T$ (and similarly for $\hat{\alpha}_T$) does not have a t-distribution, and indeed does not have any limiting distribution, diverging as $T \to \infty$ so that there are *no* asymptotically correct values for these tests. We should thus expect the rejection rate when these tests are based on a critical value delivered from conventional asymptotics (such as 1.96) to continue to increase with sample size, and this is consistent with the findings of Granger and Newbold.

Results (iii) and (iv) show that R^2 has a non-degenerate limiting distribution and that dw converges in probability to zero as $T \to \infty$. Low values for dw and moderate values of R^2 are therefore to be expected in spurious regressions such as (7.1) with data generated by integrated processes, again confirming the simulation findings reported by Granger and Newbold.

These results are easily extended to multiple regressions of the form

$$y_t = \hat{\alpha}_T + \hat{\boldsymbol{\beta}}'_T \mathbf{x}_t + \hat{u}_t \tag{7.3}$$

where $\mathbf{x}_t = (x_{1t}, \ldots, x_{kt})'$ is a vector of $I(1)$ processes. Phillips (1986) shows that analogous results to (i)–(iv) above hold for (7.3) and, in particular, that the distribution of the customary F-statistic for testing a set of linear restrictions on $\boldsymbol{\beta}$ diverges as $T \to \infty$ and so there are no asymptotically correct critical values for this statistic either. Moreover, the divergence rate for the F-statistic is greater than that for individual t-tests, so in a regression with many regressors, therefore, we might expect a noticeably greater rejection rate for a 'block' F-test than for individual t-tests or for a test with fewer regressors, and this is again consistent with the results reported by Granger and Newbold.

We should emphasise that, although the derivation of the asymptotic results has assumed independence of y_t and $\mathbf{x}_t$, so that the true values of α and $\boldsymbol{\beta}$ are zero, this is not crucial to the major conclusions. Although the correlation properties of the time series do have quantitative effects on the limiting distributions, these being introduced via the parameters of the limiting covariance matrix $\boldsymbol{\Sigma}_S$ in the bivariate regression analysed in detail above, such effects do not interfere with the main qualitative results: viz. that $\hat{\alpha}_T$ and $\hat{\boldsymbol{\beta}}_T$ do not converge in probability to constants, that the distributions of F- and t-statistics diverge as $T \to \infty$, and that dw converges in probability to zero whereas R^2 has a non-degenerate limiting distribution as $T \to \infty$. Hamilton (1994, chapter 18.3) provides a detailed treatment of the spurious multiple regression model.

A Monte Carlo simulation similar to that of Granger and Newbold (1974) enables us to interpret these results in a perhaps more transparent fashion. The independent random walks y_t and x_t were generated for a sample now of size $T = 1000$, with v_t and w_t again drawn from independent $N(0, 1)$ populations and $y_0 = x_0 = 0$, using 10,000 iterations. Figures 7.1 to 7.4 present the density functions of $\hat{\beta}_{1000}$, its associated t-ratio, and the R^2 and dw statistics. The distribution of $\hat{\beta}_{1000}$ is almost normally distributed (a central limit theorem does, in fact, hold as the simulations use independent replications). Although the sample mean is −0.0052, the sample standard deviation is 0.635, confirming that, for large T, the distribution does not converge to a constant and different samples produce very different estimates of β, the range of estimates being approximately ±3.0. The distribution of the t-ratio, shown in figure 7.2, is again normal but with a standard deviation of 23.62. The 5 per cent critical values from this distribution are ±48.30, while using ±1.96 would entail a rejection rate of 93.4 per cent. The distribution of the R^2 statistic has a mean of 0.24, a standard deviation of 0.23 and a maximum value of 0.94, while that for the dw statistic has a mean of 0.018, a standard deviation of 0.011, and a maximum value of only 0.10. (Note that the smoothing involved in constructing the density functions leads to negative values in the left-hand tails of these two distributions: the actual minimum sample values of R^2 and dw are, of course, positive, although extremely small, being 0.0008 for dw and of the order of 10^{-10} for R^2.) Both sampling distributions thus illustrate the theoretical predictions of Phillips' (1986) analysis.

It should be emphasised that, in the general set up discussed here, where both y_t and $\mathbf{x}_t$ are $I(1)$ processes, the error, u_t, since it is by defini-

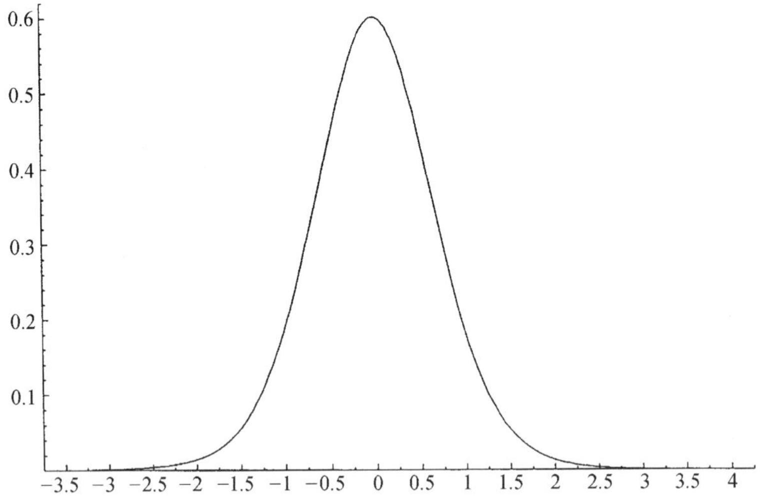

Figure 7.1 Simulated frequency distributions of $\hat{\beta}_{1000}$

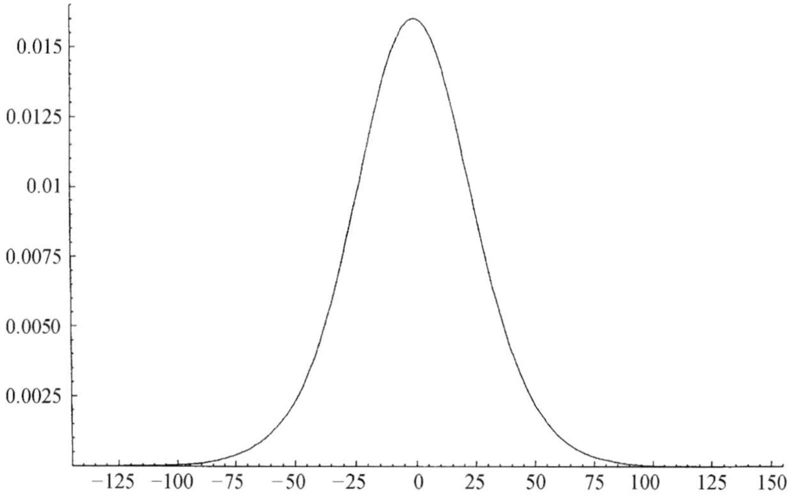

Figure 7.2 Simulated frequency distribution of the t-ratio of $\hat{\beta}_{1000}$

tion a linear combination of $I(1)$ processes, will also be integrated, unless a special restriction, to be discussed subsequently, holds. Moreover, the usual respecification of the model to include y_{t-1} as an additional regressor on the finding of a very low dw value will have pronounced consequences: the estimated coefficient on y_{t-1} will converge to unity, while

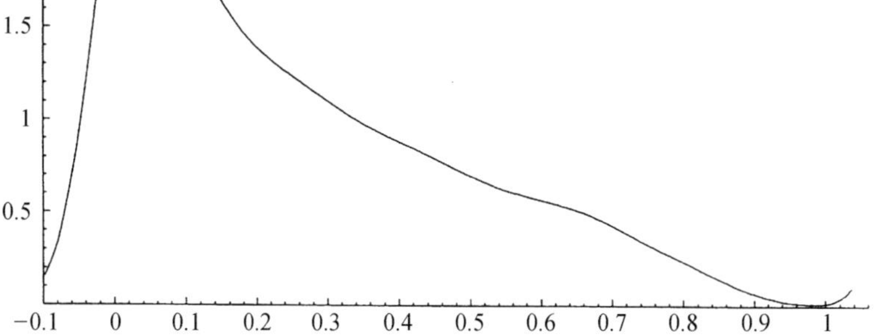

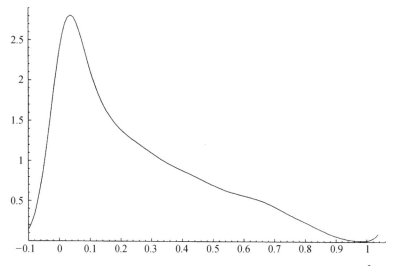

Figure 7.3 Simulated frequency distribution of the spurious regression R^2

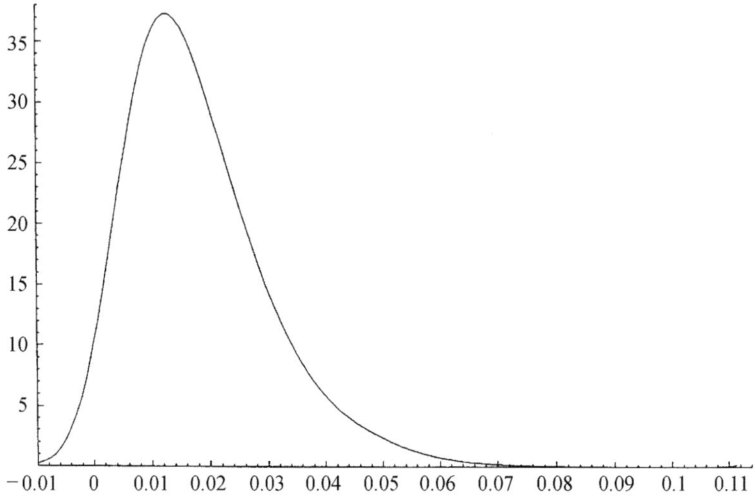

Figure 7.4 Simulated frequency distribution of the spurious regression *dw*

that on the integrated regressor(s) will converge to zero, thus highlighting the spurious nature of the static regression.

Indeed, the spurious nature of the regression is, in fact, a consequence of the error being $I(1)$. Achieving a stationary, or $I(0)$, error is usually a minimum criterion to meet in econometric modelling, for much of the focus of recent developments in the construction of dynamic regression models has been to ensure that the error is not only $I(0)$ but white noise. Whether the error in a regression between integrated variables is stationary is thus a matter of considerable importance.

7.2 Cointegrated processes

As we have just remarked, a linear combination of $I(1)$ processes will usually also be $I(1)$. In general, if y_t and x_t are both $I(d)$, then the linear combination

$$u_t = y_t - ax_t \tag{7.4}$$

will usually be $I(d)$. It is possible, however, that u_t may be integrated of a lower order, say $I(d - b)$, where $b > 0$, in which case a special constraint operates on the long-run components of the two series. If $d = b = 1$, so that y_t and x_t are both $I(1)$ and dominated by 'long wave' components, u_t will be $I(0)$, and hence will not have such components: y_t and ax_t must therefore have long-run components that cancel out to produce u_t. In such circumstances, y_t and x_t are said to be *cointegrated*; we emphasise that it will *not* generally be true that there will exist such an a which makes $u_t \sim I(0)$ or, in general, $I(d-b)$.

The idea of cointegration can be related to the concept of *long-run equilibrium*, which we may illustrate by the bivariate relationship

$$y_t = ax_t$$

or

$$y_t - ax_t = 0$$

Thus u_t given by (7.4) measures the extent to which the 'system' is out of equilibrium, and can therefore be termed the 'equilibrium error'. Assuming that $d = b = 1$, so that y_t and x_t are both $I(1)$, the equilibrium error will then be $I(0)$ and u_t will rarely drift far from zero, and will often cross the zero line. In other words, equilibrium will occasionally occur, at least to a close approximation, whereas if y_t and x_t are not cointegrated, so that $u_t \sim I(1)$, the equilibrium error will wander widely and zero-crossings would be very rare, suggesting that under these circumstances the concept of equilibrium has no practical implications.

How is the concept of cointegration linked with the analysis of spurious regressions? Condition (7.2c) on the innovation sequence ξ_t requires that the limiting covariance matrix $\boldsymbol{\Sigma}_S$ is non-singular. If we allow $\boldsymbol{\Sigma}_S$ to be singular, the asymptotic theory yielding the results (i)–(iv) no longer holds. In general, we have

$$\boldsymbol{\Sigma}_S = \begin{bmatrix} \sigma_v^2 & \sigma_{vw} \\ \sigma_{vw} & \sigma_w^2 \end{bmatrix}$$

so that for $\boldsymbol{\Sigma}_S$ to be singular, we require $|\boldsymbol{\Sigma}_S| = \sigma_v^2\sigma_w^2 - \sigma_{vw}^2 = 0$. This implies that $\boldsymbol{\Sigma}_S\gamma = \mathbf{0}$, where $\gamma' = (1, -a)$ and $a = \sigma_{vw}/\sigma_w^2$. Singularity of $\boldsymbol{\Sigma}_S$ is a necessary condition for y_t and x_t to be cointegrated (Phillips, 1986; Phillips and Ouliaris, 1990), since in this case $|\boldsymbol{\Sigma}_S| = 0$ implies that the 'long-run' correlation between the innovations v_t and w_t, given by $\rho_{vw} = \sigma_{vw}/\sigma_v\sigma_w$, is unity. For values of ρ less than unity, y_t and x_t are not cointegrated, and when $\rho_{vw} = 0$, so that v_t and w_t are independent, we have Granger and Newbold's (1974) spurious regression.

What differences to the asymptotic regression theory for integrated regressors result when y_t is cointegrated with x_t? Since the equilibrium error u_t can be regarded as the error term in the regression of y_t on x_t, we may consider first the model

$$y_t = \beta x_t + u_t \tag{7.5a}$$

where

$$x_t = \pi + x_{t-1} + w_t \tag{7.5b}$$

and where u_t and w_t are contemporaneously correlated white noise, i.e., $E(u_t w_t) = \sigma_{uw}$.

The OLS estimator of β is

$$\hat{\beta}_T = \left(\sum_{t=1}^T x_t y_t\right)\left(\sum_{t=1}^T x_t^2\right)^{-1} = \beta + \left(\sum_{t=1}^T x_t u_t\right)\left(\sum_{t=1}^T x_t^2\right)^{-1}$$

Now, if $\pi = 0$, then, since $x_t \sim I(1)$, $\sum_{t=1}^T x_t^2$ needs to be scaled by T^{-2} for it to converge to a finite value, whereas $\sum_{t=1}^T x_t u_t$ just requires scaling by T^{-1} for it to converge to a finite value (see chapter 3.1.2). Thus

$$T\left(\hat{\beta}_T - \beta\right) = \left(T^{-1}\sum_{t=1}^T x_t u_t\right)\left(T^{-2}\sum_{t=1}^T x_t^2\right)^{-1}$$

converges to zero, i.e., $\hat{\beta}_T$ converges to β at the rate T. Contrast this with the standard regression case when $x_t \sim I(0)$: now $\sum_{t=1}^T x_t^2$ only needs scaling by T^{-1} and we have

$$T^{1/2}\left(\hat{\beta}_T - \beta\right) = \left(T^{-1/2}\sum_{t=1}^T x_t u_t\right)\left(T^{-1}\sum_{t=1}^T x_t^2\right)^{-1}$$

i.e., $\hat{\beta}_T$ converges to β at the rate $T^{1/2}$. The faster rate of convergence under cointegration is known as the *super-consistency* property (Stock, 1987) and implies that, even though $E(x_t u_t)$ may be non-zero through σ_{uw} being non-zero, there is no asymptotic endogeneity bias. However, although $\hat{\beta}_T$ is super-consistent, it is not necessarily asymptotically unbiased or normally distributed. To obtain the limiting distribution of $\hat{\beta}_T$ and its t-ratio, we condition u_t on w_t through

$$u_t = \gamma w_t + v_t, \qquad \gamma = \sigma_{uw}/\sigma_w^2, \qquad \sigma_v^2 = \sigma_u^2 - \sigma_{uw}^2/\sigma_w^2 \tag{7.6}$$

so that a non-zero contemporaneous correlation between the innovations u_t and w_t, and hence endogeneity between y_t and x_t, may be incorporated. The limiting distribution of $\hat{\beta}_T - \beta$ can then be written

$$T\left(\hat{\beta}_T - \beta\right) \Rightarrow (\gamma/2)\left(W(1)^2+1\right)\left(\int_0^1 W(r)^2 \mathrm{d}r\right)^{-1} + \left((\sigma_u/\sigma_w)^2 - \gamma^2\right) N(0,1)$$

while that of the t-ratio is

$$t_{\hat{\beta}_T} \Rightarrow (\rho_{uw}/2)\left(W(1)^2+1\right)\left(\int_0^1 W(r)^2 \mathrm{d}r\right)^{-1/2} + \left(1-\rho_{uw}^2\right)^{1/2} N(0,1)$$

where $\rho_{uw} = \sigma_{uw}/\sigma_u\sigma_w$. In general, therefore, these limiting distributions will not have standard normal distributions unless $\gamma = \rho_{uw} = 0$, which is the condition for strong exogeneity of x_t. When this condition does not hold, the first terms in the limiting distributions gives rise to 'second-order' endogeneity bias (Phillips and Hansen, 1990), which, although asymptotically negligible in estimating β because of super-consistency, can be important in finite samples.

These theoretical results can also be demonstrated via Monte Carlo simulation. The model given by (7.5) was used with $\beta = \pi = 0$ and with the settings $\sigma_w^2 = \sigma_v^2 = 1$ and $\sigma_{uw} = 0.75$, so that $\gamma = 0.75$ and $\rho_{uw} = 0.57$. With once again $T = 1000$ and 10,000 iterations, figure 7.5 shows the simulated frequency distribution of $\hat{\beta}_{1000}$. The sample mean is 0.0028 and 95 per cent of the estimates lie in the interval (−0.0016, 0.0093), reflecting the super-consistency property. However, this interval also shows the skewness of the distribution, i.e., the presence of second-order endogeneity bias caused by the lack of strong exogeneity of x_t. Figure 7.6 shows the simulated t-ratio. Since γ is non-zero, the distribution will not be standard normal: although normal in shape, it is centered on 0.994 with a standard deviation of 0.884.

Figures 7.7–7.9 show the results of three related simulations. Figure 7.7 shows the simulated frequency distribution of the slope coefficient of the regression of y_t on x_t when x_t is generated by the stationary AR(1) process $x_t = 0.5x_{t-1} + w_t$ rather than the random walk of (7.5b), but where all other settings remain the same. The endogeneity bias is now readily apparent, with the distribution, although normal, having a mean of 0.565 and a standard deviation of 0.035. Figure 7.8 shows the simulated frequency distribution of the slope coefficient in the same stationary regression but where now $\sigma_{uw} = 0$, so that there is no endogeneity:

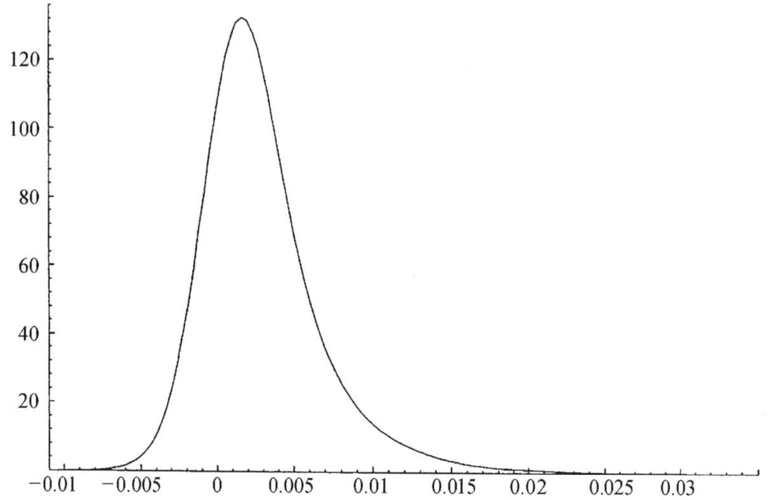

Figure 7.5 Simulated frequency distribution of $\hat{\beta}_{1000}$ from the cointegrated model with endogenous regressor.

consequently, the distribution is centered on zero. Finally, figure 7.9 shows the frequency distribution of $\hat{\beta}_{1000}$ from the cointegrated model but with $\sigma_{uw} = 0$. With no endogeneity, the distribution is normal, as compared to figure 7.5, but has a standard error of 0.0035, thus reflecting

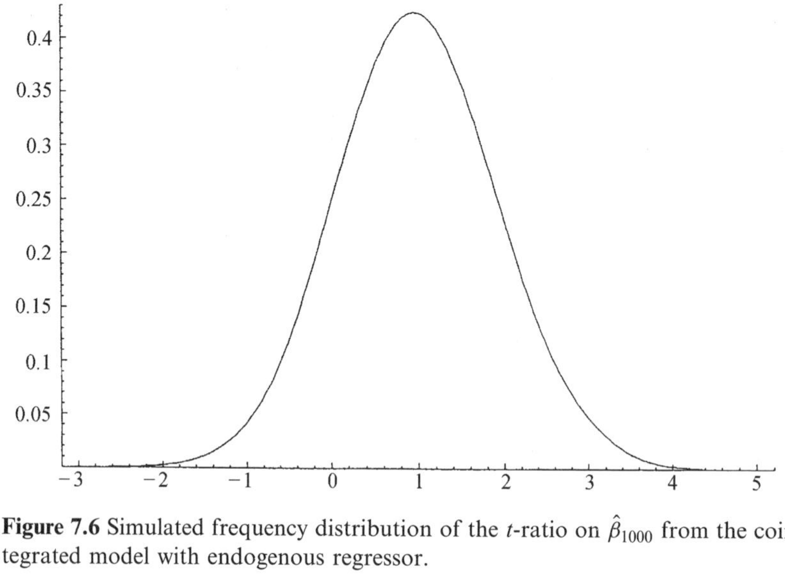

Figure 7.6 Simulated frequency distribution of the t-ratio on $\hat{\beta}_{1000}$ from the cointegrated model with endogenous regressor.

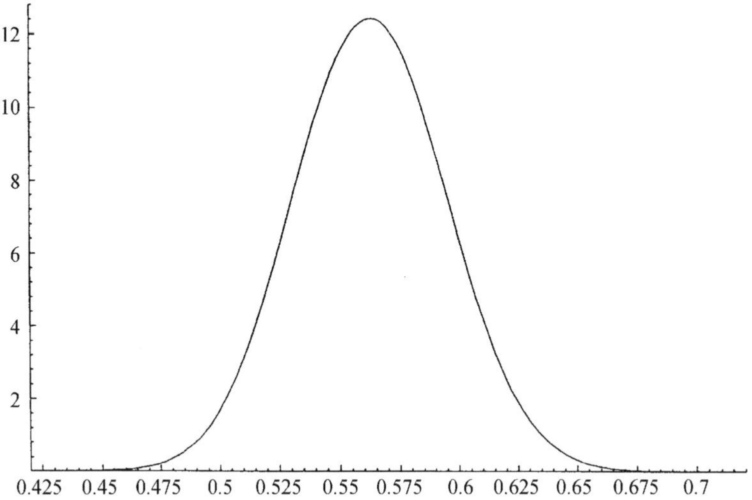

Figure 7.7 Simulated frequency distribution of the slope coefficient from the stationary model with endogeneity.

the super-consistency property of cointegrated regressions when compared to its stationary counterpart in figure 7.8.

The assumption made in all these simulations, that x_t is without drift ($\pi = 0$), is not innocuous, however, for when x_t contains a drift

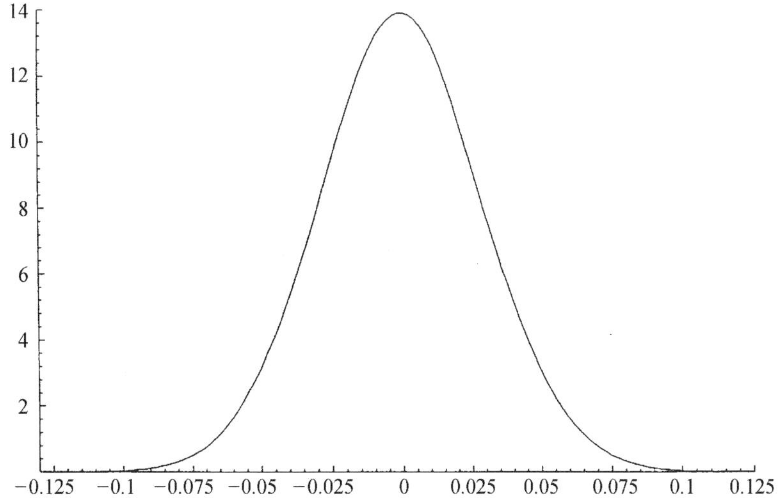

Figure 7.8 Simulated frequency distribution of the slope coefficient from the stationary model without endogeneity.

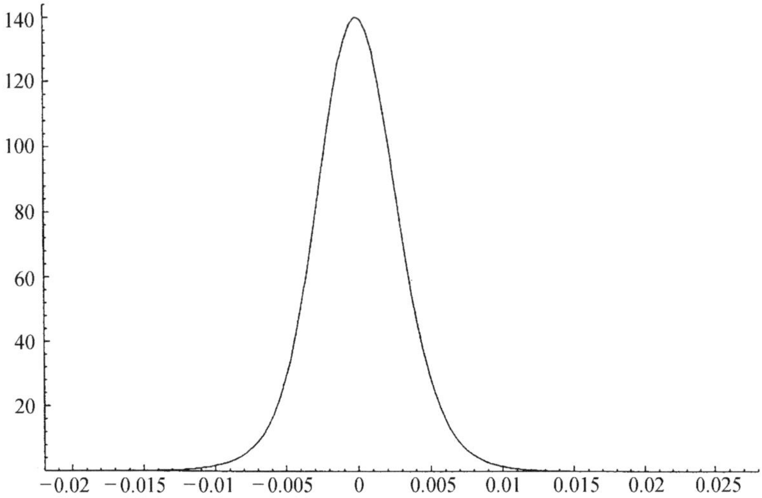

Figure 7.9 Simulated frequency distribution of the t-ratio on $\hat{\beta}_{1000}$ from the cointegrated model with exogenous regressor.

$$x_t = t\pi + \sum_{j=1}^{t} w_j = t\pi + Q_t$$

and we need to consider

$$T^{-3/2} \sum_{t=1}^{T} x_t u_t = \pi T^{-3/2} \sum_{t=1}^{T} t u_t + T^{-3/2} \sum_{t=1}^{T} u_t Q_t$$

and

$$T^{3/2}\left(\hat{\beta}_T - \beta\right) = \left(T^{-3/2} \sum_{t=1}^{T} x_t u_t\right)\left(T^{-3} \sum_{t=1}^{T} x_t^2\right)^{-1}$$

West (1988) shows that the probability limits of $T^{-3/2} \sum_{t=1}^{T} u_t Q_t$ and $T^{-3} \sum_{t=1}^{T} x_t^2$ are zero and $\pi^2/3$ respectively, and that $\pi T^{-3/2} \sum_{t=1}^{T} t u_t$ is normally distributed with mean zero and variance $\pi^2 \sigma_u^2/3$. Hence

$$T^{3/2}\left(\hat{\beta}_T - \beta\right) \Rightarrow N\left(0, 3\sigma_u^2/\pi^2\right)$$

so that in these circumstances asymptotic normality does hold, irrespective of whether there is endogeneity or not. Thus, consider the model (7.5) with $\pi = 1$ and again $\sigma_w^2 = \sigma_v^2 = 1$ and $\sigma_{uw} = 0.75$. Since $\sigma_u^2 = 1.75$ and $\beta = 0$, $\hat{\beta}_{1000}$ should be normally distributed with mean zero and standard deviation 0.000072. Figure 7.10 shows the simulated frequency distribution of $\hat{\beta}_{1000}$, which is indeed approximately normally distributed with a sample mean of zero and a standard deviation of 0.000069, and should be compared with the skewed distribution for $\hat{\beta}_{1000}$ that results from the absence of drift, shown in figure 7.5.

In general we may consider regressions of the form (7.5) but with a vector of $I(1)$, rather than random walk, regressors $\mathbf{x}_t$ which may contain drifts, and with $u_t \sim I(0)$ rather than white noise, so that the sequence $\mathbf{e}_t' = (u_t, w_t)$ of joint innovations may be assumed to satisfy the conditions (7.2). When the regressor vector $\mathbf{x}_t$ is without drift, Phillips and Durlauf (1986) show that super-consistency again holds for the OLS estimator $\hat{\boldsymbol{\beta}}_T$ of the coefficient vector $\boldsymbol{\beta}$. They then go on to consider testing general linear hypotheses of the type considered in chapter 6.1.2. The limiting distribution of the Wald statistic (6.5), which is chi-square for non-integrated regressors, now contains nuisance parameters even if u_t is white noise, and is non-normal and asymmetric.

When some of the regressors have drifts, Park and Phillips (1988) show that super-consistency of $\hat{\boldsymbol{\beta}}_T$ again results. However, unlike when there is just a single regressor, the limiting distribution of $T(\hat{\boldsymbol{\beta}}_T - \boldsymbol{\beta})$ is both non-

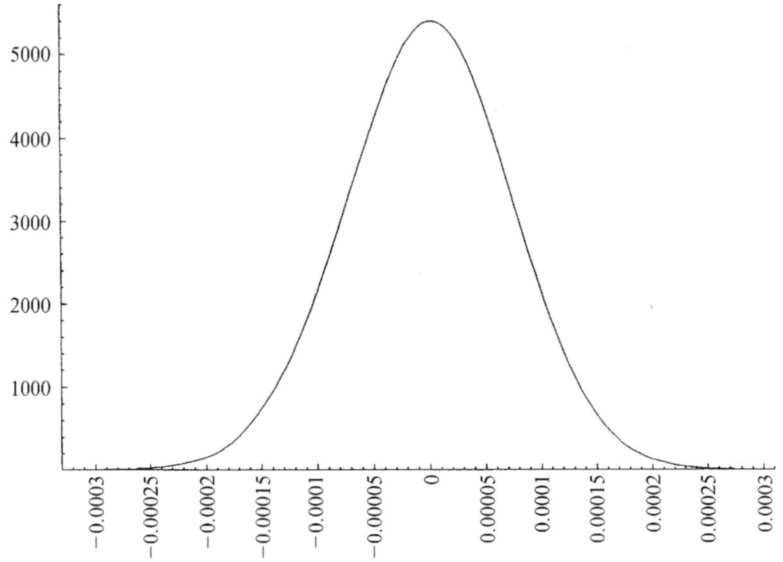

Figure 7.10 Simulated frequency distribution of $\hat{\beta}_{1000}$ from the cointegrated model with endogenous regressor and drift.

normal and singular, since the regressors will be perfectly correlated asymptotically. This is because an $I(1)$ variable with drift can always be expressed as the sum of a time trend and an $I(1)$ variable without drift, e.g.,

$$\Delta x_t = \pi + w_t = x_0 + \pi t + \Delta \tilde{x}_t, \quad \Delta \tilde{x}_t = w_t$$

so that the correlation between two such variables will be dominated by their trends rather than by the driftless $I(1)$ components. This suggests that these variables should be detrended and a time trend added to (7.5a). The estimator of the coefficient of the trend will be asymptotically normal, while the estimators of the coefficients on their 'driftless' components will have the non-standard distribution discussed above. That normality occurs when there is just one regressor may be explained by noting that the non-zero drift π imparts a trend into the regression. It is the trend coefficient, $\pi\beta$, that is asymptotically normal and this allows the result on $\hat{\beta}_T$ to follow. When there are two or more integrated regressors with drifts, the trend coefficient becomes a linear combination of the different drifts, and only this combination can be identified and is asymptotically normal. The vector $\hat{\boldsymbol{\beta}}_T$ can only be estimated by the coefficients on driftless $I(1)$ regressors and this will have the non-standard limiting distribution. If all the regressors are strongly exogeneous, $\hat{\boldsymbol{\beta}}_T$ will once again be asymptotically normal on appropriate standardisation.

If a time trend is included as an additional regressor in (7.5a) then Park and Phillips (1988) show that the asymptotic results for the least squares estimators remain valid, although the estimator of the coefficient on the time trend depends on π. Furthermore, if additional stationary regressors are included in (7.5a) then their coefficients will be asymptotically normal.

7.3 Testing for cointegration in regression

Given the crucial role that cointegration plays in regression models with integrated variables, it is important to test for its presence. A number of tests have been proposed that are based on the residuals from the *cointegrating regression*

$$\hat{u}_t = y_t - \hat{\alpha}_T - \hat{\boldsymbol{\beta}}_T \mathbf{x}_t \tag{7.7}$$

Such residual-based procedures seek to test a null hypothesis of *no* cointegration by using unit root tests applied to $\hat{u}_t$. Perhaps the simplest test to use is the usual Durbin–Watson *dw* statistic but, since the null is that $\hat{u}_t$

is $I(1)$, the value of the test statistic under the null is $dw = 0$, with rejection in favour of the $I(0)$ alternative occurring for values of dw *greater* than zero (Sargan and Bhargava, 1983, Bhargava, 1986). As is well known, the conventional critical values of the dw statistic depend upon the underlying processes generating the observed data, and Engle and Granger (1987) and Phillips and Ouliaris (1988) provide critical values, for various sample sizes and generating processes, in the 'non-standard' case considered here. Unfortunately, there are several difficulties associated with this simple test: under the no cointegration null the asymptotic distribution of dw depends on nuisance parameters such as the correlations among $\Delta \mathbf{x}_t$; the critical value bounds diverge as the number of regressors increases, becoming so wide as to have no practical value for inference; and the statistic assumes that under the null u_t is a random walk, and under the alternative u_t is a stationary AR(1) process. If this actually is the case, then Bhargava (1986) shows that dw has excellent power properties, but the critical bounds will not be correct if there is higher-order residual autocorrelation.

Engle and Granger (1987) thus prefer to use the t-ratio on $\hat{u}_{t-1}$ from the regression of $\Delta\hat{u}_t$ on $\hat{u}_{t-1}$ and lagged values of $\Delta\hat{u}_t$, in a manner analogous to the unit root testing approach for an observed series discussed in chapter 3 (see, for example, equation (3.8)). The problem here is that, since $\hat{u}_t$ is derived as a residual from a regression in which the cointegrating vector is estimated, and since if the null of non-cointegration was true such a vector would not be identified, using the τ_μ critical values would reject the null too often, because least squares will seek the cointegrating vector which minimises the residual variance and hence is most likely to result in a stationary residual series. Moreover, an additional factor that influences the distribution of the t-ratio is the number of regressors contained in $\mathbf{x}_t$. Critical values are again available from many sources (see, for example, Hamilton, 1994, table B.9, and Banerjee *et al.*, 1993, table 7.1). For example, the large T 5 per cent, 2.5 per cent and 1 per cent critical values when $\mathbf{x}_t = x_t$ are -3.37, -3.64 and -3.96.

As with conventional unit roots tests, more extensive critical values than those given in standard tables are available in most econometric packages, again obtained using the response surfaces computed by MacKinnon (1991). For example, when $\mathbf{x}_t = x_t$, so that there are $n = 2$ variables in $(y_t, \mathbf{x}_t)$, the 1 per cent critical values, denoted $C_{.01}(T)$, are calculated using

$$C_{.01}(T) = -3.900 - 10.534T^{-1} - 30.03T^{-2}$$

MacKinnon (1996) can be consulted for details of how to obtain p-values for a wide range of sample sizes. As with the conventional unit root tests, different sets of critical values are to be used if there is either no constant in the cointegrating regression or if there is both a constant and trend (corresponding to the τ and τ_τ variants). Non-parametric variants may also be constructed (see Phillips and Ouliaris, 1990).

Tests may also be derived using the *error correction model* (ECM) representation of a cointegrated system. Consider again the model given by (7.5) and (7.6) with $\pi = 0$ and where u_t is now generated by a stationary AR(1) process

$$\begin{aligned} y_t - \beta x_t &= u_t \\ u_t &= \rho u_{t-1} + \varepsilon_{1t}, \quad |\rho| < 1 \\ \Delta x_t &= w_t \\ u_t &= \gamma w_t + \nu_t \end{aligned} \tag{7.8}$$

This can be written as

$$\begin{aligned} \Delta y_t - \beta \Delta x_t &= (\rho - 1) y_{t-1} - \beta(\rho - 1) x_{t-1} + \varepsilon_{1t} \\ \Delta y_t - \gamma \Delta x_t &= \varepsilon_{2t} \end{aligned}$$

where $\varepsilon_{2t} = \nu_t + \beta w_t - u_{t-1}$. Thus

$$\begin{bmatrix} \Delta y_t \\ \Delta x_t \end{bmatrix} = \begin{bmatrix} 1 & -\beta \\ 1 & -\gamma \end{bmatrix}^{-1} \begin{bmatrix} (\rho - 1) y_{t-1} - \beta(\rho - 1) x_{t-1} + \varepsilon_{1t} \\ \varepsilon_{2t} \end{bmatrix}$$

or

$$\begin{bmatrix} \Delta y_t \\ \Delta x_t \end{bmatrix} = (\beta - \gamma)^{-1} \begin{bmatrix} \gamma(1 - \rho) y_{t-1} - \gamma\beta(1 - \rho) x_{t-1} \\ (1 - \rho) y_{t-1} - \beta(1 - \rho) x_{t-1} \end{bmatrix} + \begin{bmatrix} \zeta_{1t} \\ \zeta_{2t} \end{bmatrix}$$

where

$$\begin{bmatrix} \zeta_{1t} \\ \zeta_{2t} \end{bmatrix} = (\beta - \gamma)^{-1} \begin{bmatrix} \beta\varepsilon_{2t} - \gamma\varepsilon_{1t} \\ \varepsilon_{2t} - \varepsilon_{1t} \end{bmatrix}$$

which leads to the ECM representation

$$\begin{aligned} \Delta y_t &= \delta\gamma(y_{t-1} - \beta x_{t-1}) + \zeta_{1t} = \delta\gamma u_{t-1} + \zeta_{1t} = \theta_1 u_{t-1} + \zeta_{1t} \\ \Delta x_t &= \delta(y_{t-1} - \beta x_{t-1}) + \zeta_{2t} = \delta u_{t-1} + \zeta_{2t} = \theta_2 u_{t-1} + \zeta_{2t} \end{aligned} \tag{7.9}$$

where we let $\delta = (\beta - \gamma)^{-1}(1 - \rho)$. From the ECM representation (7.9), δ is non-zero if and only if ρ is not equal to 1, but $\rho = 1$ is the condition that ensures that *both* u_t and w_t are random walks, in which case y_t and x_t *cannot* be cointegrated, i.e., if $\rho = 1$ there does not exist a β that makes the linear combination of y_t and x_t stationary. The tests discussed above investigate the null hypothesis $\rho = 1$ using the residuals from the cointegrating regression (7.7), but an alternative is to test either of the nulls $\theta_1 = 0$ and $\theta_2 = 0$, or the joint null $\theta_1 = \theta_2 = 0$, which would be more efficient given that the cross-equation restriction in (7.8) implies that the *error correction* u_{t-1} enters both equations of the ECM. There is a problem, however: since β is unknown, it must be estimated from the data. But if $\rho = 1$ is valid, β is unidentified and the ECM (7.9) is invalid. Only if y_t and x_t are cointegrated can β be estimated from the cointegrated regression, but a test must be based upon the distribution of the statistic assuming that the null is true.

A solution to this problem may be found by rewriting the error correction equation for y_t, say, as

$$\Delta y_t = \theta_1(y_{t-1} - x_{t-1}) + dx_{t-1} + \zeta_{1t}$$

where $d = \theta_1(1 - \beta)$, so that a test of $\theta_1 = 0$ can be based on its associated t-ratio and tests of $\theta_2 = 0$ and $\theta_1 = \theta_2 = 0$ can be constructed analogously. However, this statistic will not be asymptotically normal and Banerjee *et al.* (1993, table 7.6) provide fractiles for the simulated distribution for various sample sizes: they are slightly closer to zero than those of the corresponding residual unit root test.

How powerful are these tests of cointegration? Banerjee *et al.* (1993) investigate power by conducting a Monte Carlo experiment using two alternative data generating processes for y_t and x_t. The first is the model (7.8), where we rewrite the equation for y_t as

$$y_t = \rho y_{t-1} + \beta x_t - \beta\rho x_{t-1} + \varepsilon_{1t}$$

The second is the general dynamic model

$$y_t = \alpha_1 y_{t-1} + \alpha_2 x_t + \alpha_3 x_{t-1} + u_t$$

from which the first model is obtained by imposing the 'common factor' restriction $\alpha_1\alpha_2 + \alpha_3 = 0$. Banerjee *et al.* (1993) find that the t-ratio test performs better than the unit root test in the absence of a common factor.

Example 7.1 Cointegration and the market model: an example of testing for cointegration
The market model is typically defined as

$$r_{p,t} = \alpha + \beta_0 r_{m,t} + u_t$$

using the notation introduced in example 6.4 (in contrast to the CAPM analysed there, the actual returns on a stock or small portfolio in period t, $r_{p,t}$, and on the corresponding market return, $r_{m,t}$, are used rather than excess returns). If we assume that either dividends are reinvested or that they are ignored completely, then the returns will typically be calculated as

$$r_{p,t} = \Delta y_t \qquad r_{m,t} = \Delta x_t$$

where y_t and x_t are the logarithms of the stock price and market index respectively. If y_t and x_t are $I(1)$ then such a specification would be appropriate if the two series were *not* cointegrated: if they were cointegrated then the market model would be misspecified in that an error correction term $y_{t-1} - \beta x_{t-1}$ would be required as an additional regressor.

We illustrate the possibility of cointegration within the market model by using several examples taken from a data set that has been extensively analysed by Mills (1996b) and Coutts, Roberts and Mills (1997). This data set contains weekly observations on the London Stock Exchange *FTSE 100* index and on the prices of the 56 companies that remained constituents of the index throughout the first ten years of its existence, January 1984 to December 1993, so that $T = 521$. The relationships between the (logarithmic) prices of three of these companies, Courtaulds (CTLD), Prudential (PRU) and Legal & General (LGEN), and the *FTSE 100* are analysed in a sequence of examples. (Unit root tests confirm that all are $I(1)$, although the *FTSE 100* is only marginally so: the possibility that it is $I(0)$ – more precisely, trend stationary – will be taken into account in a later example.)

Table 7.1 presents the three cointegration test statistics discussed above for each of the three series. There is no evidence of cointegration between CTLD and the *FTSE 100*, little evidence of cointegration for PRU, but it appears that LGEN is cointegrated with the *FTSE 100*. Figure 7.11 plots each of the three series against the *FTSE 100* and the lack of cointegration between CTLD and the market index is readily apparent. There is much more evidence of common trends in the other two plots, but it would be difficult to ascertain whether cointegration does in fact exist from the plots alone, thus emphasising the need for formal testing procedures.

Table 7.1. *Market model cointegration test statistics*

	dw	*C*	*t*
CTLD	0.05	−1.38	−2.40
PRU	0.24*	−2.92	−3.03
LGEN	0.14*	−3.47*	−3.71*

Notes: *dw* is the Durbin–Watson statistic from the cointegrating regression. *C* is the unit root test on the cointegrating residuals. *t* is the *t*-ratio from the error correction model. * denotes significance at the 5% level: critical values are, approximately, 0.14 for *dw* and −3.42 for *C* and *t*.

7.4 Estimating cointegrating regressions

As we have seen, OLS estimation of the cointegrating regression produces estimates that, although superconsistent, are nevertheless biased even in large samples (recall figure 7.5, which showed a biased sampling distribution of $\hat{\beta}_{1000}$ when there was endogeneity between y_t and x_t: autocorrelation in u_t will exacerbate the situation further).

A general setup that allows for both contemporaneous correlation and autocorrelation is the 'triangular' system

$$y_t = \boldsymbol{\beta}\mathbf{x}_t + u_t \tag{7.10}$$

$$\Delta\mathbf{x}_t = \mathbf{w}_t$$

We assume that $\mathbf{u}_t' = (u_t, \mathbf{w}_t')$ satisfies the conditions (7.2). With $\boldsymbol{S}_T = \sum_{t=1}^{T}\mathbf{u}_t$ then, for $r \in [0, 1]\boldsymbol{U}_T(r) = T^{-1/2}\boldsymbol{S}_{[Tr]} \Rightarrow \boldsymbol{U}(r) = (U_1(r)', \boldsymbol{U}_2(r)')'$, where $\boldsymbol{U}(r)$ is $(1+k)$ vector Brownian motion, partitioned conformably with $\mathbf{u}_t$, and having long-run covariance matrix $\boldsymbol{\Sigma}_S$, defined as

$$\boldsymbol{\Sigma}_S = \lim_{T\to\infty} T^{-1}E(\boldsymbol{S}_T\boldsymbol{S}_T') = \lim_{T\to\infty} T^{-1}\sum_{t=1}^{T}\sum_{s=1}^{T}E(\mathbf{u}_t\mathbf{u}_s')$$

Since this is the sum of all covariances of $\mathbf{w}_t$ and $\mathbf{w}_s$, it can be decomposed into a contemporaneous variance and sums of autocovariances

$$\boldsymbol{\Sigma}_S = \boldsymbol{\Lambda}_0 + \boldsymbol{\Lambda} + \boldsymbol{\Lambda}$$

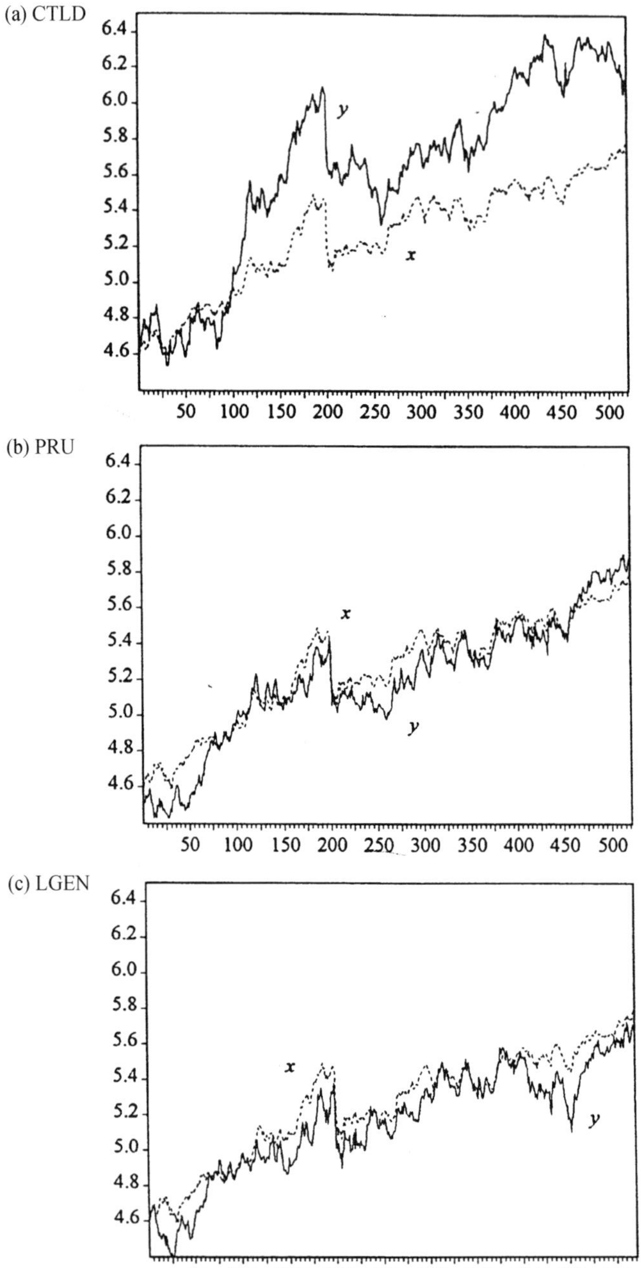

Figure 7.11 Stock prices and the *FTSE 100*

where $\mathbf{\Lambda}_0 = E(\mathbf{w}_0\mathbf{w}_0')$ and $\mathbf{\Lambda} = \sum_{t=1}^{\infty} E(\mathbf{w}_0\mathbf{w}_t')$. For convenience, we partition $\mathbf{\Sigma}_S$ as

$$\mathbf{\Sigma}_S = \begin{bmatrix} \Sigma_{11} & \mathbf{\Sigma}_{21}' \\ \mathbf{\Sigma}_{21} & \mathbf{\Sigma}_{22} \end{bmatrix}$$

with $\mathbf{\Lambda}_0$ and $\mathbf{\Lambda}$ partitioned similarly (note that Σ_{11} is a scalar).

Park and Phillips (1988) show that the limiting distribution of $\hat{\boldsymbol{\beta}}_T$ is

$$T\left(\hat{\boldsymbol{\beta}}_T - \boldsymbol{\beta}\right) \Rightarrow \left(\int_0^1 \boldsymbol{U}_2(r)\boldsymbol{U}_2(r)'\mathrm{d}r\right)^{-1}\left(\int_0^1 \boldsymbol{U}_2(r)\mathrm{d}U_1(r)' + \mathbf{\Delta}_{21}\right)$$

where $\mathbf{\Delta}_{21} = \mathbf{\Sigma}_{21} + \mathbf{\Lambda}_{21}$. It is this term that introduces the second-order bias and, of course, arises because of the contemporaneous and serial dependence of the regressors. Phillips and Hansen (1990) have proposed a modification to OLS that eliminates this bias. Define

$$y_t^+ = y_t - \hat{\mathbf{\Sigma}}_{12}\hat{\mathbf{\Sigma}}_{22}^{-1}\Delta\mathbf{x}_t$$

which uses any consistent estimator $\hat{\mathbf{\Sigma}}_S$ of $\mathbf{\Sigma}_S$. The fully-modified OLS (FM-OLS) estimator is defined as

$$\hat{\boldsymbol{\beta}}_T^+ = \left(\sum\nolimits_{t=1}^{T} y_t^+\mathbf{x}_t' - T\hat{\boldsymbol{\delta}}^+\right)\left(\sum\nolimits_{t=1}^{T} \mathbf{x}_t\mathbf{x}_t'\right)^{-1}$$

where

$$\hat{\boldsymbol{\delta}}^+ = \left(\mathbf{I} - \hat{\mathbf{\Sigma}}_{12}\hat{\mathbf{\Sigma}}_{22}^{-1}\right)\hat{\mathbf{\Delta}}_2$$

$\hat{\mathbf{\Delta}}_2$ being a consistent estimator of $\mathbf{\Delta}_2 = \sum_{t=0}^{\infty} E(\mathbf{w}_0\mathbf{u}_t')$. The limiting distribution of the FM-OLS estimator is

$$T\left(\hat{\boldsymbol{\beta}}_T^+ - \boldsymbol{\beta}\right) \Rightarrow \left(\int_0^1 \boldsymbol{U}_2(r)\boldsymbol{U}_2(r)'\mathrm{d}r\right)^{-1}\left(\int_0^1 \boldsymbol{U}_2(r)\mathrm{d}U_{1.2}(r)'\right)$$

where $U_{1.2}(r)$ is independent of $\boldsymbol{U}(r)$. The use of y_t^+ corrects for long-run simultaneity, whilst incorporating $\hat{\boldsymbol{\delta}}^+$ accounts for any residual autocorrelation. This allows conventional chi square asymptotics to be used for inference. For example, the null $\mathbf{R}\boldsymbol{\beta} = \mathbf{r}$ may be tested by constructing the *modified* Wald statistic (cf. equation (6.5))

$$W_T^+ = T\left(\mathbf{R}\hat{\boldsymbol{\beta}}_T^+ - \mathbf{r}\right)'\left[\mathbf{R}(\mathbf{X}'\mathbf{X}/T)^{-1}\hat{\mathbf{V}}_T^+(\mathbf{X}'\mathbf{X}/T)^{-1}\mathbf{R}'\right]^{-1}\left(\mathbf{R}\hat{\boldsymbol{\beta}}_T^+ - \mathbf{r}\right)$$

where $\hat{\mathbf{V}}_T^+ = \hat{\Sigma}_{11} - \hat{\boldsymbol{\Sigma}}_{12}\hat{\boldsymbol{\Sigma}}_{22}^{-1}\hat{\boldsymbol{\Sigma}}_{12}$ and $\mathbf{X}$ is as defined in (6.2). For $\hat{\boldsymbol{\Sigma}}_S$ we may use the Newey–West estimator (6.4).

Several other estimators have been proposed that correct for both correlation between u_t and $\mathbf{w}_t$ and autocorrelation in u_t. The approaches of Saikkonen (1991), Phillips and Loretan (1991), Stock and Watson (1993) and Banerjee, Dolado and Mestre (1998) all suggest augmenting (7.10) with leads and lags of $\Delta\mathbf{x}_t$ when there is correlation between u_t and $\mathbf{w}_t$, i.e., estimating

$$y_t = \boldsymbol{\beta}\mathbf{x}_t + \sum\nolimits_{s=-p}^{p} \gamma_s \Delta\mathbf{x}_{t-s} + u_t \tag{7.11}$$

where p is chosen such that the correlation between u_t and $\mathbf{w}_t$ is zero for $|s| > p$. If $\mathbf{x}_t$ is strongly exogeneous, so that u_t does not Granger-cause $\mathbf{w}_t$, then the leads of $\Delta\mathbf{x}_t$ will not be required ($\gamma_s = 0,\ s < 0$). Autocorrelation in u_t may be captured by assuming that u_t follows an AR(p) process and estimating (7.11) by generalised least squares, by including lags of Δy_t as additional regressors

$$y_t = \boldsymbol{\beta}\mathbf{x}_t + \sum\nolimits_{s=-p}^{p} \gamma_s \Delta\mathbf{x}_{t-s} + \sum\nolimits_{s=1}^{p} \delta_s \Delta y_{t-s} + u_t \tag{7.12}$$

or by including lagged values of the equilibrium error $y_t - \boldsymbol{\beta}\mathbf{x}_t$

$$y_t = \boldsymbol{\beta}\mathbf{x}_t + \sum\nolimits_{s=-p}^{p} \gamma_s \Delta\mathbf{x}_{t-s} + \sum\nolimits_{s=1}^{p} \theta_s (y_{t-s} - \boldsymbol{\beta}\mathbf{x}_{t-s}) + u_t \tag{7.13}$$

in which case NLS estimation will be required. Note that an equivalent form of (7.13) is the ECM

$$\Delta y_t = \sum\nolimits_{s=-p}^{p} \gamma_s^* \Delta\mathbf{x}_{t-s} + \sum\nolimits_{s=1}^{p} \theta_s^* (y_{t-s} - \boldsymbol{\beta}\mathbf{x}_{t-s}) + u_t \tag{7.14}$$

where $\gamma_0^* = \gamma_0 + \boldsymbol{\beta}$, $\theta_0^* = \theta_0 - 1$ and $\gamma_s^* = \gamma_s$ and $\theta_s^* = \theta_s$ for $s \neq 0$. While all these estimators can be shown to be asymptotically efficient, Phillips and Loretan (1991) point out that the NLS estimator of (7.13), or equivalently (7.14), has an important advantage over OLS estimation of (7.12). This is because, since both y_t and $\mathbf{x}_t$ are $I(1)$

$$y_{t-s} = \sum\nolimits_{i=s}^{t-1} \Delta y_{t-i}, \qquad \mathbf{x}_{t-s} = \sum\nolimits_{i=s}^{t-1} \Delta\mathbf{x}_{t-i}$$

if we set initial conditions $y_0 = \mathbf{x}_0 = 0$. Substituting these partial sums into (7.13) will produce (7.12) but with the lag length p set equal to $t - 1$. Moreover, the lag coefficients will not, in general, decay as the lag increases because the partial sums imply unit weights for individual innovations. Thus, in order to model short-run dynamics using the variables Δy_{t-s} and $\Delta \mathbf{x}_{t-s}$, it is necessary to include all lags because of this shock persistence, which is quite impractical in empirical applications and cannot be justified in theory, where lag truncation arguments are needed to develop the asymptotics.

Example 7.2 Estimating a cointegrated market model

Example 7.1 found strong evidence in favour of cointegration between LGEN and the *FTSE 100* index, and this example considers the various estimators of the cointegration parameter that result from taking different approaches to dynamic modelling. Estimation of the static cointegrating regression by OLS obtains

$$y_t = \underset{(0.063)}{-\ 0.036} + \underset{(0.012)}{0.988}\ x_t + \hat{u}_t$$

Of course, the standard errors shown in parentheses cannot be used for inference, but estimation by FM-OLS, using $n = [521]^{1/3} = 8$ lags in the Newey–West estimator of $\mathbf{\Sigma}_S$, produces almost identical parameter estimates but considerably larger standard errors

$$y_t = \underset{(0.358)}{-\ 0.044} + \underset{(0.067)}{0.988}\ x_t + \hat{u}_t$$

In investigating the alternative dynamic estimators, we first ascertain whether x is strongly exogenous. Using four lags, the hypothesis that y does not Granger-cause x has a p-value of 0.58, and the inclusion of four leads of $\Delta \mathbf{x}_t$ in (7.11), after estimation by GLS, are only jointly significant at the 0.34 level. A parsimonious GLS estimated model is

$$y_t = \underset{(0.284)}{-\ 0.165} + \underset{(0.053)}{1.011}\ x_t + \underset{(0.051)}{0.103}\ \Delta x_t + \hat{u}_t$$

$$\hat{u}_t = \underset{(0.034)}{0.819}\ \hat{u}_{t-1} + \underset{(0.034)}{0.123}\ \hat{u}_{t-3} + \hat{a}_t$$

which has an equation standard error of 3.18 per cent. Attempts to fit a model of the form (7.12) were unsuccessful, for the reasons discussed above: the lag coefficients failed to die out, remaining significant at high lags, and the error term could not be reduced to white noise – exactly the problems that should be produced by the shock persistence caused by the unit roots in the system. Fitting models of the form (7.13/7.14) was successful, however, yielding

$$\begin{aligned} y_t = &- \underset{(0.023)}{0.005} + \underset{(0.075)}{0.997}\ x_t + \underset{(0.093)}{0.110}\ \Delta x_t \\ &+ \underset{(0.034)}{0.815}\ (y_{t-1} - 0.997x_{t-1}) + \underset{(0.034)}{0.128}\ (y_{t-3} - 0.997x_{t-3}) + \hat{u}_t \end{aligned}$$

which has an equation standard error of 3.03 per cent. All the models suggest that $\beta = 1$ and imposing this restriction leads to

$$\begin{aligned} y_t - x_t = &- \underset{(0.002)}{0.006} + \underset{(0.056)}{0.107}\ \Delta x_t + \underset{(0.034)}{0.815}\ (y_{t-1} - x_{t-1}) \\ &+ \underset{(0.034)}{0.128}\ (y_{t-3} - x_{t-3}) + \hat{u}_t \end{aligned}$$

Thus the *price relative*, $y_t - x_t$, plotted in figure 7.12, is stationary, following an autoregressive process with one large root (0.943) and a pair of complex roots, and it is positively related to the current change in the market index.

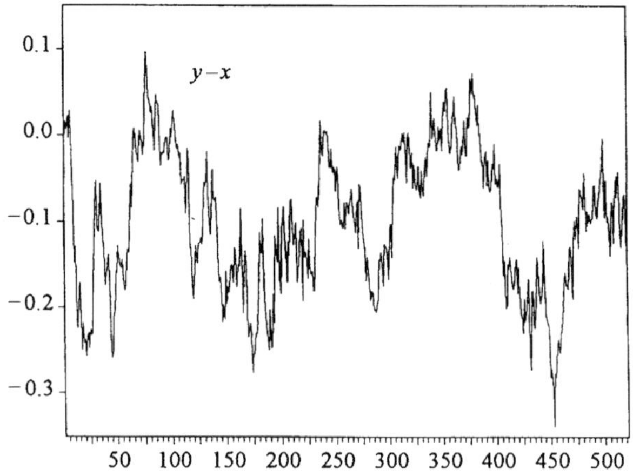

Figure 7.12 LGEN relative to the *FTSE 100*

7.5 VARs with integrated variables

7.5.1 VARs with I(1) variables

Consider again the VAR(m) process introduced in chapter 6.6

$$\mathbf{\Pi}(B)\mathbf{z}_t = \boldsymbol{\mu} + \mathbf{v}_t \tag{7.15}$$

where $\mathbf{z}_t$, assumed to be $I(1)$, and $\mathbf{v}_t$ are both $n \times 1$ vectors, conditions (6.20) hold

$$\mathbf{\Pi}(B) = \mathbf{I}_n - \sum\nolimits_{i=1}^{m} \mathbf{\Pi}_i B^i \tag{7.16}$$

and where we have introduced an $n \times 1$ vector of constants, $\boldsymbol{\mu}$. Assuming $m > 1$, the matrix polynomial $\mathbf{\Pi}(B)$ can always be written as

$$\mathbf{\Pi}(B) = (\mathbf{I}_n - \mathbf{\Pi}B) - \mathbf{\Phi}(B)B(1 - B)$$

where

$$\mathbf{\Pi} = \sum\nolimits_{i=1}^{m} \mathbf{\Pi}_i$$

and

$$\mathbf{\Phi}(B) = \sum\nolimits_{i=1}^{m-1} \mathbf{\Phi}_i B^{i-1}, \qquad \mathbf{\Phi}_i = -\sum\nolimits_{j=i+1}^{m} \mathbf{\Pi}_j$$

The $\mathbf{\Phi}_i$ can be obtained recursively from $\mathbf{\Phi}_1 = -\mathbf{\Pi} + \mathbf{\Pi}_1$ as $\mathbf{\Phi}_i = \mathbf{\Phi}_{i-1} + \mathbf{\Pi}_i$, $i = 2, \ldots, m-1$. With this decomposition of $\mathbf{\Pi}(B)$, (7.15) can always be written as

$$\mathbf{z}_t = \mathbf{\Phi}(B)\Delta\mathbf{z}_{t-1} + \boldsymbol{\mu} + \mathbf{\Pi}\mathbf{z}_{t-1} + \mathbf{v}_t \tag{7.17}$$

or

$$\Delta\mathbf{z}_t = \mathbf{\Phi}(B)\Delta\mathbf{z}_{t-1} + \boldsymbol{\mu} + \mathbf{A}\mathbf{z}_{t-1} + \mathbf{v}_t \tag{7.18}$$

where

$$\mathbf{A} = \mathbf{\Pi} - \mathbf{I}_n = -\mathbf{\Pi}(1)$$

We consider first the case where

$$\boldsymbol{\Pi} = \mathbf{I}_n \tag{7.19}$$

so that $\mathbf{A} = \mathbf{0}$ and $\Delta\mathbf{z}_t$ follows the VAR($m-1$) process

$$\Delta\mathbf{z}_t = \boldsymbol{\Phi}(B)\Delta\mathbf{z}_{t-1} + \boldsymbol{\mu} + \mathbf{v}_t \tag{7.20}$$

$\boldsymbol{\Pi} = \mathbf{I}_n$ implies that

$$|\mathbf{A}| = \left|\boldsymbol{\Pi}_1 + \ldots + \boldsymbol{\Pi}_m - \mathbf{I}_n\right| = 0 \tag{7.21}$$

in which case the VAR (7.15) is said to contain *at least one* unit root. Note, however, that (7.21) does not necessarily imply (7.19), and it is this fact that leads to cointegrated or reduced rank VARs, as we shall see later.

Consider OLS estimation of the levels VAR (7.15) and the differenced VARs (7.17) and (7.18) under the assumption that none of the variables making up $\mathbf{z}_t$ contain drifts, so that $\boldsymbol{\mu} = \mathbf{0}$, although constants are included in the estimated regressions. The fitted values from (7.15) and (7.17) will be the same, because the $\hat{\boldsymbol{\Pi}}_i$ are linked to the $\hat{\boldsymbol{\Phi}}_i$ by

$$\begin{aligned}
\hat{\boldsymbol{\Pi}}_1 &= \hat{\boldsymbol{\Pi}} + \hat{\boldsymbol{\Phi}}_1 \\
\hat{\boldsymbol{\Pi}}_i &= \hat{\boldsymbol{\Phi}}_i - \hat{\boldsymbol{\Phi}}_{i-1}, \quad i = 2, 3, \ldots, m-1 \\
\hat{\boldsymbol{\Pi}}_m &= -\hat{\boldsymbol{\Phi}}_{m-1}
\end{aligned}$$

Now, from Hamilton (1994, chapter 18.2), the $\hat{\boldsymbol{\Phi}}_i$ converge to $\boldsymbol{\Phi}_i$ at rate $T^{1/2}$, and $T^{1/2}(\hat{\boldsymbol{\Phi}}_i - \boldsymbol{\Phi}_i)$ is asymptotically normal. Since the $\hat{\boldsymbol{\Pi}}_i$, $i > 2$, are linear combinations of the $\hat{\boldsymbol{\Phi}}_i$, $T^{1/2}(\hat{\boldsymbol{\Pi}}_i - \boldsymbol{\Pi}_i)$, $i > 2$, is also asymptotically normal. $\hat{\boldsymbol{\Pi}}$, on the other hand, converges to $\boldsymbol{\Pi}$ at rate T and, although its asymptotic distribution is non-normal, this faster rate of convergence ensures that $\hat{\boldsymbol{\Pi}}_1 = \hat{\boldsymbol{\Pi}} + \hat{\boldsymbol{\Phi}}_1$ also converges at rate $T^{1/2}$ to an asymptotic normal, as the speed of convergence is determined by the coefficients with the slower rate. Hence, if the VAR is estimated in levels, then even though it contains a unit root, conventional t- and F-tests involving a linear combination other than $\boldsymbol{\Pi} = \boldsymbol{\Pi}_1 + \ldots + \boldsymbol{\Pi}_m$ have usual asymptotic distributions. For example, tests for determining the order of the VAR, since they will not involve $\boldsymbol{\Pi} = \boldsymbol{\Pi}_1 + \ldots + \boldsymbol{\Pi}_m$, will have usual χ^2 distributions. On the other hand, Granger-causality tests will involve coefficients of $\boldsymbol{\Pi}$ and will typically not have limiting χ^2 distributions.

If there is a drift in $\mathbf{z}_t$ then the above results still hold, unlike the univariate case where a single regressor with drift makes *all* coefficients asymptotically normal and *all* F-tests asymptotically χ^2.

7.5.2 VARs with cointegrated variables

Let us now reconsider the case when (7.21) holds, so that $\mathbf{A}$ is singular, $|\mathbf{A}| = 0$, but $\mathbf{A} \neq \mathbf{0}$ and $\mathbf{\Pi} \neq \mathbf{I}_n$. Being singular, $\mathbf{A}$ will thus have reduced rank, say r, where $0 < r < n$. In such circumstances, $\mathbf{A}$ can be expressed as the product of two $n \times r$ matrices $\boldsymbol{\beta}$ and $\boldsymbol{\alpha}$, both of full column rank r, i.e., $\mathbf{A} = \boldsymbol{\beta}\boldsymbol{\alpha}'$. To see this, note that $\boldsymbol{\alpha}'$ is the matrix containing the r linearly independent rows of $\mathbf{A}$, so that $\mathbf{A}$ must be able to be written as a linear combination of $\boldsymbol{\alpha}'$: $\boldsymbol{\beta}$ must then be the matrix of coefficients that are needed to be able to do this. These r linearly independent rows of $\mathbf{A}$ contained as the rows of $\boldsymbol{\alpha}' = (\boldsymbol{\alpha}_1, \ldots, \boldsymbol{\alpha}_r)'$ are known as the *cointegrating vectors* and $\mathbf{A}$ will contain only $n - r$ unit roots, rather than the n unit roots that it will contain if $\mathbf{A} = \mathbf{0}$, which will be the case if $r = 0$.

Why are the rows of $\boldsymbol{\alpha}'$ known as cointegrating vectors? Substituting $\mathbf{A} = \boldsymbol{\beta}\boldsymbol{\alpha}'$ into equation (7.18) yields

$$\Delta \mathbf{z}_t = \mathbf{\Phi}(B)\Delta \mathbf{z}_{t-1} + \boldsymbol{\mu} + \boldsymbol{\beta}\boldsymbol{\alpha}'\mathbf{z}_{t-1} + \mathbf{v}_t$$

The assumption that $\mathbf{z}_t$ is $I(1)$ implies that, since $\Delta \mathbf{z}_t$ must then be $I(0)$, $\boldsymbol{\alpha}'\mathbf{z}_t$ must also be $I(0)$ for both sides of the equation to 'balance'. In other words, $\boldsymbol{\alpha}'$ is a matrix whose rows, when post-multiplied by $\mathbf{z}_t$, produce stationary linear combinations of $\mathbf{z}_t$, i.e., the r linear combinations $\boldsymbol{\alpha}_1\mathbf{z}_t, \ldots, \boldsymbol{\alpha}_r\mathbf{z}_t$ are all stationary.

Thus, if $\mathbf{z}_t$ is cointegrated with cointegrating rank r, then it can be represented as the *vector error correction model* (VECM)

$$\Delta \mathbf{z}_t = \mathbf{\Phi}(B)\Delta \mathbf{z}_{t-1} + \boldsymbol{\mu} + \boldsymbol{\beta}\mathbf{e}_{t-1} + \mathbf{v}_t \tag{7.22}$$

where $\mathbf{e}_t = \boldsymbol{\alpha}'\mathbf{z}_t$ are the r stationary *error corrections*. This is known as Granger's Representation Theorem (Engle and Granger, 1987) and a detailed proof can be found in, for example, Banerjee *et al.* (1993, chapter 5.3), where various additional technical conditions are discussed.

Several additional points are worth mentioning. The parameters $\boldsymbol{\alpha}$ and $\boldsymbol{\beta}$ are not uniquely identified, since for any non-singular $r \times r$ matrix ξ, the products $\boldsymbol{\beta}\boldsymbol{\alpha}'$ and $\boldsymbol{\beta}\xi(\xi^{-1}\boldsymbol{\alpha}')$ will both equal $\mathbf{A}$. If $r = 0$ then we have already seen that the model becomes a VAR$(m-1)$ in the first differences $\Delta \mathbf{z}_t$. If $r = n$, on the other hand, $\mathbf{A}$ is of full rank, is non-singular, and $\mathbf{z}_t$ will contain *no* unit roots, i.e., $\mathbf{z}_t$ is in fact $I(0)$ and a VAR(m) in the levels is appropriate from the outset: we are then in the framework of chapter 6.6. The error corrections $\mathbf{e}_t$, although stationary, are not restricted to having zero mean, so that, as (7.22) stands, growth in $\mathbf{z}_t$ can come about via both the error correction $\mathbf{e}_t$ and the autonomous drift component $\boldsymbol{\mu}$. Note, however, that without loss of generality, $\boldsymbol{\mu}$ can be written as $\boldsymbol{\mu} = \boldsymbol{\beta}\gamma + \boldsymbol{\beta}_\perp\gamma^*$, where $\boldsymbol{\beta}_\perp$ is an $n \times (n-r)$ matrix known as the *orthogonal complement* of $\boldsymbol{\beta}$, defined such that $\boldsymbol{\beta}_\perp\boldsymbol{\beta} = \mathbf{0}$. Note that since, for example, $\boldsymbol{\beta}'\boldsymbol{\mu} = \boldsymbol{\beta}'\boldsymbol{\beta}\gamma + \boldsymbol{\beta}'\boldsymbol{\beta}_\perp\gamma^* = \boldsymbol{\beta}'\boldsymbol{\beta}\gamma$, we have $\gamma = (\boldsymbol{\beta}'\boldsymbol{\beta})^{-1}\boldsymbol{\beta}'\boldsymbol{\mu}$ and $\gamma^* = (\boldsymbol{\beta}_\perp{}'\boldsymbol{\beta}_\perp)^{-1}\boldsymbol{\beta}_\perp'\boldsymbol{\mu}$, so that geometrically $\boldsymbol{\mu}$ has been decomposed in the directions of γ and γ^*. The VECM (7.22) can then be written as

$$\Delta\mathbf{z}_t = \boldsymbol{\Phi}(B)\Delta\mathbf{z}_{t-1} + \boldsymbol{\beta}_\perp\gamma^* + \boldsymbol{\beta}(\gamma + \mathbf{e}_{t-1}) + \mathbf{v}_t \qquad (7.23)$$

so that if the condition $\boldsymbol{\beta}_\perp\gamma^* = \mathbf{0}$ holds, i.e., that $\boldsymbol{\mu} = \boldsymbol{\beta}\gamma$, then the constant enters the system only via the error correction term. How the constant is treated is important in determining the appropriate estimation procedure and the set of critical values used for inference. An important extension is when a linear trend is included in the VAR

$$\boldsymbol{\Pi}(B)\mathbf{z}_t = \boldsymbol{\mu}_0 + \boldsymbol{\mu}_1 t + \mathbf{v}_t \qquad (7.24)$$

Here we can write $\boldsymbol{\mu}_i = \boldsymbol{\beta}\gamma_i + \boldsymbol{\beta}_\perp\gamma_i^*$, $i = 0, 1$, and the counterpart to (7.23) becomes

$$\begin{aligned}\Delta\mathbf{z}_t = &\boldsymbol{\Phi}(B)\Delta\mathbf{z}_{t-1} + \boldsymbol{\beta}_\perp(\gamma_0^* + \gamma_1^* t)\\ &+ \boldsymbol{\beta}(\gamma_0 + \gamma_1 + \gamma_1(t-1) + \mathbf{e}_{t-1}) + \mathbf{v}_t\end{aligned} \qquad (7.25)$$

In this case the constant and trend will be restricted to the error correction if $\boldsymbol{\mu}_i = \boldsymbol{\beta}\gamma_i$, $i = 0, 1$, i.e., we define the 'trend included' error correction as $\mathbf{e}_t^* = \mathbf{e}_t + \gamma_0 + \gamma_1 t$. Further implications of the presence of a linear trend are best analysed by introducing the infinite-order vector polynomial $\mathbf{C}(B)$, defined such that $\mathbf{C}(B)\boldsymbol{\Pi}(B) = (1-B)\mathbf{I}_n$, and which can be written, analogously to $\boldsymbol{\Pi}(B)$, as

$$\begin{aligned}\mathbf{C}(B) &= \mathbf{I}_n + \mathbf{C}B + (\mathbf{C}_1^*B + \mathbf{C}_2^*B^2 + \ldots)(1-B)\\ &= \mathbf{I}_n + \mathbf{C} + (\mathbf{C}_0^* + \mathbf{C}_1^*B + \mathbf{C}_2^*B^2 + \ldots)(1-B)\\ &= \mathbf{I}_n + \mathbf{C} + \mathbf{C}^*(B)(1-B)\\ &= \mathbf{C}(1) + \mathbf{C}^*(B)(1-B)\end{aligned}$$

where the matrices $\mathbf{C}_0, \mathbf{C}_1, \ldots,$ are given by the recursions

$$\mathbf{C}_i = \sum_{j=1}^{m} \mathbf{C}_{i-j}\boldsymbol{\Pi}_j, \; i > 0, \quad \mathbf{C}_0 = \mathbf{I}_n$$

and where

$$\mathbf{C} = \sum_{i=1}^{\infty} \mathbf{C}_i = \mathbf{C}(1) - \mathbf{I}_n$$
$$\mathbf{C}_0^* = -\mathbf{C}$$

and

$$\mathbf{C}_i^* = \mathbf{C}_{i-1}^* + \mathbf{C}_i\,, \quad i > 0$$

Equation (7.24) can then be written as

$$\begin{aligned}\Delta\mathbf{z}_t &= \mathbf{C}(B)\big(\boldsymbol{\mu}_0 + \boldsymbol{\mu}_1 t + \mathbf{v}_t\big)\\ &= (\mathbf{C}(1) + \mathbf{C}^*(1-B))\big(\boldsymbol{\mu}_0 + \boldsymbol{\mu}_1 t\big) + \mathbf{C}(B)\mathbf{v}_t\\ &= \mathbf{C}(1)\boldsymbol{\mu}_0 + \mathbf{C}^*(1)\boldsymbol{\mu}_1 + \mathbf{C}(1)\boldsymbol{\mu}_1 t + \mathbf{C}(B)\mathbf{v}_t\\ &= \mathbf{b}_0 + \mathbf{b}_1 t + \mathbf{C}(B)\mathbf{v}_t\end{aligned}$$

where

$$\mathbf{b}_0 = \mathbf{C}(1)\boldsymbol{\mu}_0 + \mathbf{C}^*(1)\boldsymbol{\mu}_1$$

and

$$\mathbf{b}_1 = \mathbf{C}(1)\boldsymbol{\mu}_1$$

In levels, this becomes

$$\begin{aligned}\mathbf{z}_t &= \mathbf{z}_0 + \mathbf{b}_0 t + \mathbf{b}_1\frac{t(t+1)}{2} + \mathbf{C}(B)\sum_{s=1}^{t}\mathbf{v}_s\\ &= \mathbf{z}_0 + \mathbf{b}_0 t + \mathbf{b}_1\frac{t(t+1)}{2} + (\mathbf{C}(1) + \mathbf{C}^*(1-B))\sum_{s=1}^{t}\mathbf{v}_s\\ &= \mathbf{z}_0 + \mathbf{b}_0 t + \mathbf{b}_1\frac{t(t+1)}{2} + \mathbf{C}(1)\mathbf{s}_t + \mathbf{C}^*(B)(\mathbf{v}_t - \mathbf{v}_0)\\ &= \mathbf{z}_0^* + \mathbf{b}_0 t + \mathbf{b}_1\frac{t(t+1)}{2} + \mathbf{C}(1)\mathbf{s}_t + \mathbf{C}^*(B)\mathbf{v}_t\end{aligned} \tag{7.26}$$

where

$$\mathbf{z}_0^* = \mathbf{z}_0 - \mathbf{C}^*(B)\mathbf{v}_0, \qquad \mathbf{s}_t = \sum_{s=1}^{t}\mathbf{v}_s$$

The inclusion of a linear trend in the VAR (7.24) implies a *quadratic* trend in the levels equation (7.26). Furthermore, since $\mathbf{b}_1 = \mathbf{C}(1)\boldsymbol{\mu}_1$, this quadratic trend will only disappear if $\mathbf{C}(1) = \mathbf{0}$. Recall that $\mathbf{C}(1)\boldsymbol{\Pi}(1) = \mathbf{0}$, so that $\mathbf{C}(1) = \mathbf{0}$ requires that $\boldsymbol{\Pi}(1) = -\mathbf{A} \neq \mathbf{0}$.

This will be the case only if $\mathbf{\Pi}(B)$ does not contain the factor $(1 - B)$, i.e., that $\mathbf{z}_t$ is $I(0)$, which has been ruled out by assumption and implies that $\mathbf{A}$ is of full rank n. If $\mathbf{\Pi}(1) = \mathbf{0}$, so that $\mathbf{A} = \mathbf{0}$, is of rank zero and contains n unit roots, then there is no cointegration and $\mathbf{C}(1)$, and hence $\mathbf{b}_1$, are unconstrained. In the general case, where the rank of $\mathbf{A}$ is r, it then follows that the rank of $\mathbf{C}(1)$ is $n - r$ (see Banerjee *et al.*, 1993, chapter 5.3.1). The rank of $\mathbf{b}_1$, and hence the number of independent quadratic deterministic trends, is thus also equal to $n - r$, and will therefore decrease as the cointegrating rank r increases. Without the restriction on the trend coefficient $\mathbf{b}_1$, the solution (7.26) will have the property that the nature of the trend in $\mathbf{z}_t$ will vary with the number of cointegrating vectors.

To avoid this unsatisfactory outcome, the restriction $\mathbf{b}_1 = \mathbf{C}(1)\boldsymbol{\mu}_1 = \mathbf{0}$ may be imposed, in which case the solution for $\mathbf{z}_t$ will contain only linear trends, irrespective of the value of r. The choice of r then determines the split between the number of independent linear deterministic trends, r, and the number of stochastic trends, $n - r$, in the model.

$\mathbf{C}(1)$ can be shown (see, for example, Banerjee *et al.*, 1993, chapter 5.3.1) to have the representation

$$\mathbf{C}(1) = \boldsymbol{\alpha}_\perp \left(\boldsymbol{\beta}'_\perp (\mathbf{I}_n - \mathbf{\Phi}(1))\boldsymbol{\alpha}_\perp\right)^{-1} \boldsymbol{\beta}'_\perp$$

so that the cointegrating vectors $\boldsymbol{\alpha}'\mathbf{z}_t$ have a linear but not a quadratic trend: since $\boldsymbol{\alpha}'\boldsymbol{\alpha}_\perp = \mathbf{0}$, $\boldsymbol{\alpha}'\mathbf{C}(1) = \mathbf{0}$ and

$$\boldsymbol{\alpha}'\mathbf{z}_t = \boldsymbol{\alpha}'\mathbf{z}_0^* + \boldsymbol{\alpha}'\mathbf{C}^*(1)\boldsymbol{\mu}_1 t + \boldsymbol{\alpha}'\mathbf{C}^*(B)\mathbf{v}_t \tag{7.27}$$

Note also that

$$\begin{aligned}\mathbf{C}(1)\boldsymbol{\mu}_1 &= \boldsymbol{\alpha}_\perp \left(\boldsymbol{\beta}'_\perp (\mathbf{I}_n - \mathbf{\Phi}(1))\boldsymbol{\alpha}_\perp\right)^{-1} \boldsymbol{\beta}'_\perp \boldsymbol{\mu}_1 \\ &= \boldsymbol{\alpha}_\perp \left(\boldsymbol{\beta}'_\perp (\mathbf{I}_n - \mathbf{\Phi}(1))\boldsymbol{\alpha}_\perp\right)^{-1} \boldsymbol{\beta}'_\perp \boldsymbol{\beta}\gamma_1 = \mathbf{0}\end{aligned}$$

so that $\mathbf{b}_1 = \mathbf{0}$ in (7.26) and $\boldsymbol{\mu}_1 = \boldsymbol{\beta}\gamma_1$ in (7.24) are equivalent restrictions. This restriction may be imposed by setting $\boldsymbol{\mu}_1 = \mathbf{Ac}$, where $\mathbf{c}$ is an $n \times 1$ vector of unknown coefficients. In this case $\mathbf{b}_1 = \mathbf{C}(1)\mathbf{Ac} = -\mathbf{C}(1)\mathbf{\Pi}(1)\mathbf{c} = \mathbf{0}$ in (7.26). Furthermore, since $\mathbf{C}^*(1)\mathbf{A} = \mathbf{I}_n$ (see Pesaran and Shin, 1996), $\boldsymbol{\alpha}'\mathbf{C}^*(1)\boldsymbol{\mu}_1 = \boldsymbol{\alpha}'\mathbf{C}^*(1)\mathbf{Ac} = \boldsymbol{\alpha}'\mathbf{c}$, so that (7.27) becomes

$$\boldsymbol{\alpha}'\mathbf{z}_t = \boldsymbol{\alpha}\mathbf{z}_0^* + \boldsymbol{\alpha}'\mathbf{c}t + \boldsymbol{\alpha}'\mathbf{C}^*(B)\mathbf{v}_t$$

The cointegrating vectors will not contain linear trends if $\boldsymbol{\alpha}'\mathbf{c} = \mathbf{0}$, and these are known as the 'co-trending' restrictions.

7.5.3 Estimation of VECMs and tests of the cointegrating rank

ML estimation of the VECM (7.22) is discussed in many texts: see, for example, Banerjee *et al.* (1993, chapter 8.2), Hamilton (1994, chapter 20.2), and Johansen (1995, chapter 6), and routines are available in most econometrics packages. Without going into unnecessary details for our purposes, ML estimates are obtained in the following way. Consider (7.22) written as

$$\Delta\mathbf{z}_t = \boldsymbol{\mu} + \sum\nolimits_{i=1}^{m-1} \boldsymbol{\Phi}_i \Delta\mathbf{z}_{t-i} + \boldsymbol{\beta\alpha}'\mathbf{z}_{t-1} + \mathbf{v}_t \qquad (7.28)$$

The first step is to estimate (7.28) under the restriction $\boldsymbol{\beta\alpha}' = \mathbf{0}$. As this is simply a VAR($m-1$) in $\Delta\mathbf{z}_t$, OLS estimation will yield the set of residuals $\hat{\mathbf{v}}_t$, from which is calculated the sample covariance matrix

$$\mathbf{S}_{00} = T^{-1}\sum\nolimits_{t=1}^{T} \hat{\mathbf{v}}_t\hat{\mathbf{v}}_t'$$

The second step is to estimate the multivariate regression

$$\mathbf{z}_{t-1} = \boldsymbol{\kappa} + \sum\nolimits_{i=1}^{m-1} \boldsymbol{\Xi}_i \Delta\mathbf{z}_{t-i} + \mathbf{u}_t$$

and use the OLS residuals $\hat{\mathbf{u}}_t$ to calculate the covariance matrices

$$\mathbf{S}_{11} = T^{-1}\sum\nolimits_{t=1}^{T} \hat{\mathbf{u}}_t\hat{\mathbf{u}}_t'$$

and

$$\mathbf{S}_{10} = T^{-1}\sum\nolimits_{t=1}^{T} \hat{\mathbf{u}}_t\hat{\mathbf{v}}_t' = \mathbf{S}_{01}'$$

In effect, these two regressions partial out the effects of $(\Delta\mathbf{z}_{t-1}, \ldots, \Delta\mathbf{z}_{t-m+1})$ from $\Delta\mathbf{z}_t$ and $\mathbf{z}_{t-1}$, leaving us to concentrate on the relationship between $\Delta\mathbf{z}_t$ and $\mathbf{z}_{t-1}$, which is parameterised by $\boldsymbol{\beta\alpha}'$. $\boldsymbol{\alpha}$ is then estimated by the r linear combinations of $\mathbf{z}_{t-1}$ which have the largest squared partial correlations with $\Delta\mathbf{z}_t$: this is known as a *reduced rank* regression.

More precisely, this procedure maximises the likelihood of (7.28) by solving a set of equations of the form

$$\left(\lambda_i \mathbf{S}_{11} - \mathbf{S}_{10}\mathbf{S}_{00}^{-1}\mathbf{S}_{01}\right)\upsilon_i = \mathbf{0} \tag{7.29}$$

where $\hat{\lambda}_1 > \hat{\lambda}_2 > \cdots > \hat{\lambda}_n$ are the set of eigenvalues and $\mathbf{V} = (\upsilon_1, \upsilon_2, \ldots, \upsilon_n)$ is the set of associated eigenvectors, subject to the normalisation

$$\mathbf{V}'\mathbf{S}_{11}\mathbf{V} = \mathbf{I}_n$$

The ML estimate of $\boldsymbol{\alpha}$ is then given by the eigenvectors corresponding to the r largest eigenvalues

$$\hat{\boldsymbol{\alpha}} = (\upsilon_1, \upsilon_2, \ldots, \upsilon_r)$$

and the ML estimate of $\boldsymbol{\beta}$ is then given by

$$\hat{\boldsymbol{\beta}} = \mathbf{S}_{01}\hat{\boldsymbol{\alpha}}$$

which is equivalent to the estimate of $\boldsymbol{\beta}$ that would be obtained by substituting $\hat{\boldsymbol{\alpha}}$ into (7.28) and estimating by OLS, which also provides ML estimates of the remaining parameters in the model.

This procedure can be straightforwardly adapted when a linear trend is included in (7.28) and when the various restrictions are placed upon the intercept and trend coefficients: this involves adjusting the first- and second-step regressions to accommodate the alterations (Pesaran and Pesaran, 1997, chapter 19.7, conveniently list the alternative setups).

Of course, ML estimation is based upon a known value of the cointegrating rank, r, and in practice this value will be unknown. Fortunately, the set of equations (7.29) also provides a method of determining the value of r. If $r = n$ and $\mathbf{A}$ is unrestricted, the maximised log likelihood is given by (Banerjee *et al.*, 1993, chapter 8.3)

$$L(n) = K - (T/2)\sum\nolimits_{i=1}^{n} \log(1 - \lambda_i)$$

where $K = -(T/2)\left(n(1 + \log 2\pi) + \log\left|\mathbf{S}_{00}\right|\right)$. For a given value of $r < n$, only the first r eigenvalues should be positive, and the restricted log likelihood is

$$L(r) = K - (T/2)\sum\nolimits_{i=1}^{r} \log(1 - \lambda_i)$$

A likelihood ratio test of the hypothesis that there are r cointegrating vectors against the alternative that there are n is thus given by

$$\eta_r = 2(L(n) - L(r)) = -T\sum\nolimits_{i=r+1}^{n} \log(1 - \lambda_i)$$

This is known as the *trace* statistic and testing proceeds in sequence from $\eta_0, \eta_1, \ldots, \eta_{n-1}$. A cointegrating rank of r is selected if the *last* significant statistic is η_{r-1}, which thereby rejects the hypothesis of $n - r + 1$ unit roots in **A**. The trace statistic measures the 'importance' of the adjustment coefficients $\boldsymbol{\beta}$ on the eigenvectors to be potentially omitted. An alternative test of the significance of the largest eigenvalue is

$$\zeta_r = -T\log\left(1 - \lambda_{r+1}\right), \quad r = 0, 1, \ldots, n - 1$$

which is known as the *maximal-eigenvalue* or *λ-max* statistic. Both η_r and ζ_r have non-standard limiting distributions which are functionals of multivariate Brownian motions, and are generalisations of the Dickey–Fuller distributions discussed in chapter 3. Although there are no analytical forms for the distributions, critical values can be obtained by Monte Carlo simulation. The limiting distributions depend on n and on the restrictions imposed on the behaviour of the trends appearing in the VECM. For example, if $\boldsymbol{\mu}$ in (7.28) is replaced by $\boldsymbol{\mu}_0 + \boldsymbol{\mu}_1 t$, then both the ML estimation and testing procedures outlined above need to be amended to take into account both the presence of a linear trend and the various possible restrictions that could be placed on $\boldsymbol{\mu}_0$ and $\boldsymbol{\mu}_1$ (see, for example, Johansen, 1995, chapters 6 and 15, for extended discussion).

For this modelling framework to become operational, we have to determine the lag order m, the trend order l and the reduced (cointegrating) rank r. By trend order we mean that if $l = 1$ then the linear trend model is appropriate, if $l = 0$ then only a constant is included, while if not even a constant is required we set $l = -1$ by convention. Typically, m and l are first determined using either an information criterion or a sequence of likelihood ratio or Wald tests and, conditional on these settings, r is then determined by the sequence of trace or λ-max tests. However, in empirical applications, the choice of r is frequently sensitive to the choice of m and l and the trend restrictions.

A further problem is that the trace and λ-max tests rely on critical values drawn from limiting distributions, and these have been shown to have rather unreliable finite sample performance: see, inter alia, Reimers (1992), Haug (1996), Ho and Sørensen (1996) and Toda (1994, 1995). Indeed, Reinsel and Ahn (1992) and Reimers (1992) have suggested using the factor $T - nm$ rather than T, as this seems to provide a better approximation to the limit distribution in finite samples, since the conventional statistic tends to over-reject true nulls in small samples.

Given these complications, it is thus appealing to consider whether we can select jointly the cointegrating rank, the lag length and the appropriate restriction on the trend component. One possibility for doing this is to use information criteria to select between all possible models, as suggested by Lütkepohl (1991, chapter 11.4); see also Mills (1998). For example, if we denote the set of models to be considered as VECM(m, l, r), we could select that model which minimises $BIC(m, l, r)$ as defined in chapter 6.6.

Example 7.3 Cointegration in the UK financial markets

In example 6.8 we analysed the vector $(\Delta p_t, \Delta d_t, \Delta rs_t, \Delta r20_t)$ by implicitly assuming that there was no cointegration between the series. We now investigate whether the appropriate relationship between these four series is, in fact, a VECM in $\mathbf{z}_t = (p_t, d_t, rs_t, r20_t)$, although we do this using a slightly shorter sample period, January 1969 to December 1995. With T thus equal to 324, we follow Saikkonen and Lütkepohl (1996) and set the maximum order of m to be considered as the integer part of $T^{1/3}$, i.e., we set $m = 6$.

Figure 7.13(a) plots BIC values for $1 \leq m \leq 6$ and $-1 \leq l \leq 1$ and these show that setting $l = 1$, so that a linear trend is included, produces values of BIC that are smaller than other settings of l. (For ease of interpretation, we plot $BIC^* = -(BIC + f)$, where f is a suitably defined constant, so that we are searching for the *maximum* BIC^*.) Conditional upon $m = 2$ and $l = 1$, figure 7.13(b) plots BIC values for $0 \leq r \leq 4$ with the cointegrating vector allowed to have both a trend and a constant or just a constant, from which it is seen that the VECM(2,1,2) model is selected with the trend allowed to enter the error correction. (This model, in fact, also produces the minimum BIC over all possible models investigated.) The BICs were computed automatically for alternative settings of m and l (with and without trend restrictions) using *EVIEWS*, which makes this a simple strategy to implement.

Table 7.2 presents the sequence of trace statistics and associated eigenvalues conditional upon $m = 2$ and $l = 1$. Employing a 5 per cent significance level, this suggests that $r = 1$, irrespective of whether the cointegrating vector contains both a trend and a constant or just a constant. We should note, however, that the statistics testing the null $r = 1$ are very close to their 5 per cent critical values and, since Banerjee *et al.* (1993, chapter 8.5.3) warn against omitting cointegrating vectors in these circumstances, this perhaps points in favour of the model selected by BIC. Nevertheless, in either case there is clear evidence of cointegration, implying that using a VAR in the first differences to model $\mathbf{z}_t$ constitutes a misspecification.

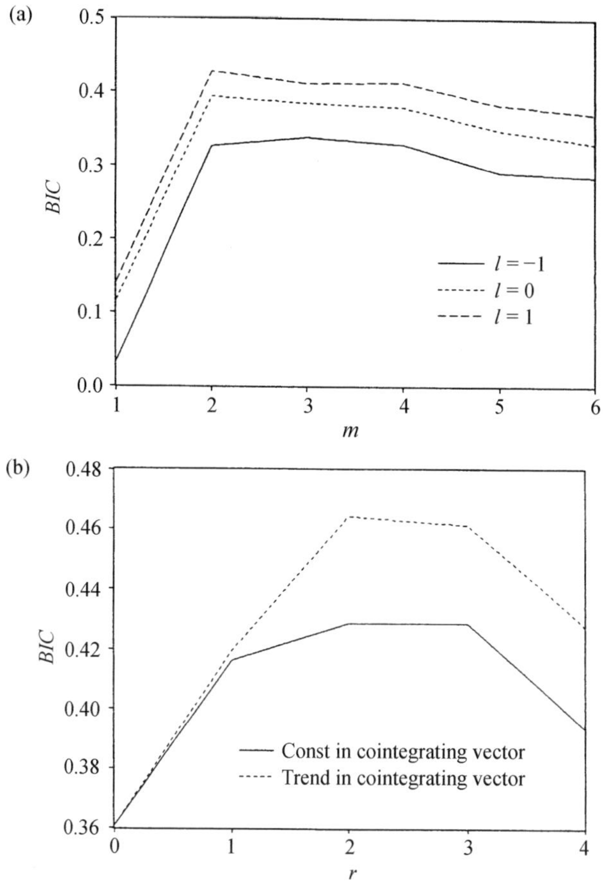

Figure 7.13 Determining VECM(m, l, r) using BIC

With $r = 2$ and a trend included in the cointegrating vector, the ML estimation procedure produces

$$\hat{\boldsymbol{\alpha}}' = \begin{bmatrix} 0.275 & -0.761 & 0.277 & -0.079 \\ 0.400 & 0.039 & -0.283 & 0.845 \end{bmatrix}$$

but, as we remarked earlier, these estimates are not unique, so that the question of how they can be interpreted arises. This is now discussed within the context of identification of VECMs.

Table 7.2. *Cointegrating rank test statistics*

r	η_r	λ_r	$\eta_{r,0.05}$
(a) Trend and constant in cointegrating vector: $\boldsymbol{\mu}_1 = \boldsymbol{\beta}\gamma_1$			
$=0$	73.62	0.0941	62.99
≤ 1	41.62	0.0813	42.44
≤ 2	14.13	0.0366	25.32
≤ 3	2.05	0.0063	12.25
(b) Constant only in cointegrating vector: $\boldsymbol{\mu}_1 = \mathbf{0}$, $\boldsymbol{\mu}_0 = \boldsymbol{\beta}\gamma_0$			
$=0$	56.84	0.0871	47.21
≤ 1	27.33	0.0470	29.68
≤ 2	11.73	0.0351	15.41
≤ 3	0.16	0.0049	3.76

7.5.4 Identification of VECMs

The assumption that the rank of $\mathbf{A}$ is r implicitly imposes $(n - r)^2$ restrictions on its n^2 coefficients, leaving $n^2 - (n-r)^2 = 2nr - r^2$ free parameters. The two $n \times r$ matrices $\boldsymbol{\alpha}$ and $\boldsymbol{\beta}$ involve $2nr$ parameters, so that identifying $\mathbf{A} = \boldsymbol{\beta}\boldsymbol{\alpha}'$ requires a total of r^2 restrictions. If the identifying restrictions are imposed only on $\boldsymbol{\alpha}$, are linear and if there are *no* cross-cointegrating vector restrictions, then they can be written for the ith cointegrating vector as

$$\mathbf{R}_i\boldsymbol{\alpha}_i = \mathbf{a}_i \tag{7.30}$$

where $\mathbf{R}_i$ and $\mathbf{a}_i$ are an $r \times n$ matrix and an $r \times 1$ vector respectively. A necessary and sufficient condition for $\boldsymbol{\alpha}$ to be uniquely identified is that the rank of each $\mathbf{R}_i\boldsymbol{\alpha}_i$ is r, while the necessary condition is that there must be r restrictions placed on each of the r cointegrating vectors. The more general case of non-linear and cross-vector restrictions is discussed in Pesaran and Shin (1996). Note that identification of $\boldsymbol{\alpha}$, and hence $\mathbf{A}$, is achieved solely through restrictions on $\boldsymbol{\alpha}$ itself: long-run relationships cannot be identified through restrictions on the short-run dynamics, i.e., the $\boldsymbol{\Phi}_i$ coefficients in (7.28) can be estimated freely.

If the number of restrictions that are imposed on $\boldsymbol{\alpha}$ is k, then $k = r^2$ constitutes *exact identification*. The imposition of r restrictions on each of the r cointegrating vectors does not alter the likelihood $L(r)$, so that while their imposition enables a unique estimate of $\boldsymbol{\alpha}$ to be obtained, the validity of the restrictions cannot be tested. Typically r restrictions are obtained by normalisation, and if $r = 1$ then this is all that is required. For $r > 1$, a further $r^2 - r$ restrictions are required ($r - 1$ on each equation), and this forms the basis for Phillips' (1991) *triangular representation*. This writes $\boldsymbol{\alpha}$ as

$$\boldsymbol{\alpha}' = \begin{bmatrix} \mathbf{I}_r & -A \end{bmatrix}$$

where A is an $r \times (n - r)$ matrix. The r^2 just-identifying restrictions are thus made up of r normalisations and $r^2 - r$ zero restrictions, corresponding to solving $\boldsymbol{\alpha}'\mathbf{z}_t$ for the first r components of $\mathbf{z}_t$.

When $k > r^2$, there are $k - r^2$ *overidentifying* restrictions. ML estimation subject to the restrictions (7.30) is discussed in, for example, Pesaran and Pesaran (1997). If $L(r : p)$ denotes the log likelihood after the imposition of the $p = k - r^2$ overidentifying restrictions, then the validity of these restrictions can be tested using the likelihood ratio statistic

$$2(L(r) - L(r : p)) \overset{a}{\sim} \chi^2_p$$

Restrictions can also be imposed on $\boldsymbol{\beta}$ and may link both $\boldsymbol{\alpha}$ and $\boldsymbol{\beta}$. The identification, estimation and testing of very general sets of restrictions is discussed in Doornik and Hendry (1997) and programmed in their *PcFiml 9.0*.

7.5.5 *Exogeneity in VECMs*

In the previous subsection we considered hypotheses about the cointegrating matrix $\boldsymbol{\alpha}$. We now consider hypotheses concerning the adjustment factors $\boldsymbol{\beta}$. Suppose, as in chapter 6.6, we again make the partition $\mathbf{z}_t = \left(\mathbf{y}_t', \mathbf{x}_t'\right)'$ and now write the VECM as

$$\Delta\mathbf{y}_t = \sum\nolimits_{i=1}^{m-1} \boldsymbol{\Phi}_{1i}\Delta\mathbf{z}_{t-i} + \boldsymbol{\beta}_1\boldsymbol{\alpha}'\mathbf{z}_{t-1} + \mathbf{T}_1 + \mathbf{v}_{1t} \tag{7.31}$$

$$\Delta\mathbf{x}_t = \sum\nolimits_{i=1}^{m-1} \boldsymbol{\Phi}_{2i}\Delta\mathbf{z}_{t-i} + \boldsymbol{\beta}_2\boldsymbol{\alpha}'\mathbf{z}_{t-1} + \mathbf{T}_2 + \mathbf{v}_{2t} \tag{7.32}$$

where

$$\boldsymbol{\Phi}_i = \begin{bmatrix} \boldsymbol{\Phi}_{1i} \\ \boldsymbol{\Phi}_{2i} \end{bmatrix} \quad i = 1, \ldots, m-1, \quad \boldsymbol{\beta} = \begin{bmatrix} \boldsymbol{\beta}_1 \\ \boldsymbol{\beta}_2 \end{bmatrix},$$

$$\mathbf{T}_j = \boldsymbol{\mu}_{0j} + \boldsymbol{\mu}_{1j}t, \quad j = 1, 2$$

and where $\mathbf{v}_t$ and its covariance matrix $\boldsymbol{\Sigma}_v$ are partitioned as in chapter 6.6.2. Premultiplying (7.32) by $\boldsymbol{\omega} = \boldsymbol{\Sigma}_{12}\boldsymbol{\Sigma}_{22}^{-1}$ and subtracting the result from (7.31) yields the conditional model for $\Delta\mathbf{y}_t$

$$\Delta\mathbf{y}_t = \boldsymbol{\omega}\Delta\mathbf{x}_t + \sum_{i=1}^{m-1} \tilde{\boldsymbol{\Phi}}_{1i}\Delta\mathbf{z}_{t-i} + (\boldsymbol{\beta}_1 - \boldsymbol{\omega}\boldsymbol{\beta}_2)\boldsymbol{\alpha}'\mathbf{z}_{t-1} + \tilde{\mathbf{T}}_1 + \tilde{\mathbf{v}}_{1t} \qquad (7.33)$$

where $\tilde{\boldsymbol{\Phi}}_{1i} = \boldsymbol{\Phi}_{1i} - \boldsymbol{\omega}\boldsymbol{\Phi}_{2i}$, $\tilde{\mathbf{T}}_1 = \mathbf{T}_1 - \boldsymbol{\omega}\mathbf{T}_2$ and $\tilde{\mathbf{v}}_{1t} = \mathbf{v}_{1t} - \boldsymbol{\omega}\mathbf{v}_{2t}$, with covariance matrix $\boldsymbol{\Sigma}_{11.2} = \boldsymbol{\Sigma}_{11} - \boldsymbol{\Sigma}_{12}\boldsymbol{\Sigma}_{22}^{-1}\boldsymbol{\Sigma}_{12}'$. $\boldsymbol{\alpha}$ enters both the conditional model (7.33) and the marginal model (7.32) unless $\boldsymbol{\beta}_2 = \mathbf{0}$. This is the condition for $\mathbf{x}_t$ to be weakly exogenous for $(\boldsymbol{\alpha}, \boldsymbol{\beta}_1)$, in which case the ML estimates of these parameters can be calculated from the conditional model alone (Johansen, 1995, theorem 8.1).

Example 7.4 Identifying the cointegrating vectors and testing for weak exogeneity

Given that we have found two cointegrating vectors in example 7.3, we now wish to uniquely identify them and, in so doing, see if we can provide them with an economic interpretation. Mills (1991a) discusses the equilibrium relationship often thought to hold between the equity and gilt markets: that the gilt and dividend yields should be in constant proportion to each other. In terms of our VECM, this implies that one of the cointegrating vectors should take the form

$$e_{1t}^* = p_t - d_t + r20_t + \gamma_{10}$$

This places four restrictions, and hence two overidentifying restrictions, on the first cointegrating vector $\alpha_1 : \alpha_{11} = 1,\ \alpha_{12} = -1,\ \alpha_{13} = 0,\ \alpha_{14} = 1$ (the trend is also excluded). The second equilibrium relationship might involve the spread between the interest rates

$$e_{2t}^* = rs_t - r20_t + \alpha_{22}d_t + \gamma_{20} + \gamma_{21}t$$

where we also place a zero restriction on p_t, i.e., $\alpha_{21} = 0$, $\alpha_{23} = 1$, $\alpha_{24} = -1$. With only the just-identifying restrictions $\alpha_{11} = \alpha_{23} = 1$ and $\alpha_{21} = \alpha_{13} = 0$ imposed, we obtain the triangular representation

$$e_{1t}^* = p_t - \underset{(0.251)}{1.233}\, d_t + \underset{(0.134)}{1.267}\, r20_t - \underset{(0.554)}{5.587} + \underset{(0.00224)}{0.00265}\, t$$

and

$$e_{2t}^* = rs_t - \underset{(0.171)}{1.187}\, r20_t - \underset{(0.319)}{1.907}\, d_t + \underset{(0.706)}{4.128} + \underset{(0.0029)}{0.0159}\, t$$

Imposition of the further identifying restrictions yields, with the additional data-based restriction that the coefficient on d_t in e^*_{2t} is $\alpha_{22} = -2$

$$e^*_{1t} = p_t - d_t + r20_t - \underset{(0.028)}{5.363}$$

$$e^*_{2t} = rs_t - r20_t - 2d_t + \underset{(0.818)}{3.873} + \underset{(0.0004)}{0.0170}\, t$$

A likelihood ratio test of the set of overidentifying restrictions produces the statistic $\chi^2_5 = 3.67$, with a p-value of 0.60, so that the set of restrictions are accepted.

Figure 7.14 plots the two error corrections and both are seen to be stationary. The first implies the long-run equilibrium $p_t = 5.363 + d_t - r20_t$ or, in terms of the levels, P_t, D_t and $R20_t$, it implies that the ratio

$$R20_t/(D_t/P_t)$$

is stationary. Since D_t/P_t is the dividend yield, in equilibrium the gilt yield and the dividend yield are in constant proportion to each other. Since deviations from this equilibrium are stationary, divergences from this ratio can only be temporary. This ratio was, in fact, exactly the decomposition used by investment analysts of the 1950s and early 1960s to analyse movements in equity prices and was termed by them the *confidence factor* (see Mills, 1991a). Note that extreme values of the factor are observed in 1974 and 1987, both periods of great upheaval in the UK equity market, but even here there is a marked tendency to move back towards equilibrium.

The second error correction is a little more difficult to interpret. Concentrating on $e_{2t} = rs_t - r20_t - 2d_t$, note that this can be written as

$$\begin{aligned} e_{2t} &= rs_t + r20_t - 2(d_t - p_t) - 2(r20_t + p_t) \\ &= 2(g_t - (r20_t + p_t)) \end{aligned}$$

where

$$g_t = \tfrac{1}{2}(rs_t - (d_t - p_t) + (r20_t - (d_t - p_t)))$$

is the (logarithm of) the geometric mean of the yields in the two money markets relative to the equity market. This error correction can thus be

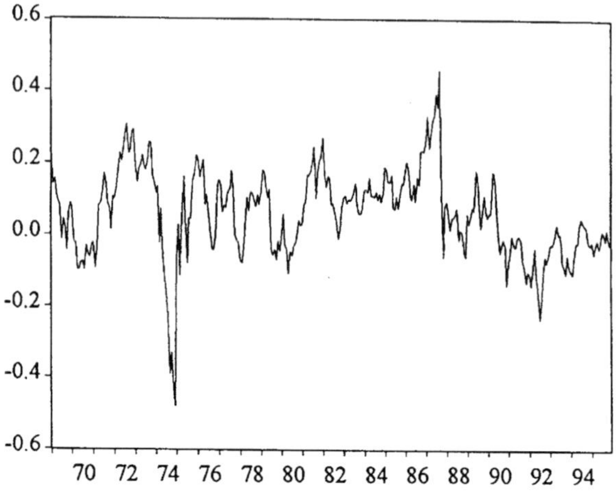

(a) Error correction e_1^*: the 'Confidence' factor

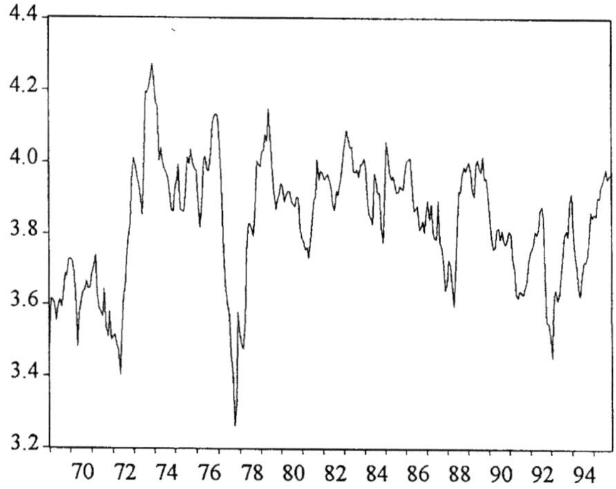

(b) Error correction e_2^*: the interest rate spread

Figure 7.14 Estimated error corrections

interpreted as a measure of the relative money market yield scaled by the levels of the equity and gilt markets. The presence of a linear trend in the estimated error correction shows that this relationship has altered deterministically over time.

The estimated 'loading factor' or 'adjustment' matrix is, with standard errors shown in parentheses

$$\hat{\beta} = \begin{bmatrix} -0.054 & -0.007 \\ (0.018) & (0.004) \\ 0.013 & 0.000 \\ (0.003) & (0.001) \\ -0.020 & 0.010 \\ (0.017) & (0.004) \\ 0.004 & -0.006 \\ (0.010) & (0.002) \end{bmatrix}$$

Although some of the coefficients are insignificant, each row contains at least one significant coefficient. It would therefore seem that $\boldsymbol{\beta}$ cannot therefore be partitioned as $\boldsymbol{\beta} = \begin{bmatrix} \boldsymbol{\beta}_1 & \mathbf{0} \end{bmatrix}'$ and the VECM cannot be partitioned as (7.31)–(7.32), so that no variable in $\mathbf{z}_t$ is weakly exogenous and analysis should continue with the complete model. However, a test of $\beta_{41} = \beta_{42} = 0$ cannot reject this joint null hypothesis (the statistic is $\chi_2^2 = 4.20$, with a p-value of 0.122), so it is possible that $r20$ may be weakly exogenous with respect to $\boldsymbol{\alpha}$ and $\boldsymbol{\beta}_1, \boldsymbol{\beta}_2, \boldsymbol{\beta}_3$.

7.5.6 Structural VECMs

Following Johansen and Juselius (1994), a 'structural VECM' may be written as (abstracting from deterministic components)

$$\boldsymbol{\Gamma}_0 \Delta \mathbf{z}_t = \sum\nolimits_{i=1}^{m-1} \boldsymbol{\Gamma}_i \Delta \mathbf{z}_{t-i} + \boldsymbol{\Omega}\boldsymbol{\alpha}' \mathbf{z}_{t-1} + \boldsymbol{\nu}_t \tag{7.34}$$

which is related to the 'reduced form' VECM

$$\Delta \mathbf{z}_t = \sum\nolimits_{i=1}^{m-1} \boldsymbol{\Phi}_i \Delta \mathbf{z}_{t-i} + \boldsymbol{\beta}\boldsymbol{\alpha}' \mathbf{z}_{t-1} + \mathbf{v}_t \tag{7.35}$$

through

$$\boldsymbol{\Gamma}_i = \boldsymbol{\Gamma}_0 \boldsymbol{\Phi}_i, \quad \boldsymbol{\Gamma}_0 \boldsymbol{\beta} = \boldsymbol{\Omega}, \quad \boldsymbol{\nu}_t = \boldsymbol{\Gamma}_0 \mathbf{v}_t$$

so that

$$E(\boldsymbol{\nu}_t \boldsymbol{\nu}_t') = \boldsymbol{\Sigma}_\nu = \boldsymbol{\Gamma}_0 \boldsymbol{\Sigma}_{\mathbf{v}} \boldsymbol{\Gamma}_0'$$

Note that in this framework we are assuming that the cointegrating vectors have already been identified, so that identification of the 'short-run' structure, the parameters $\boldsymbol{\Gamma}_0, \boldsymbol{\Gamma}_1, \ldots, \boldsymbol{\Gamma}_{m-1}, \boldsymbol{\Omega}$, is carried out conditionally upon the form of $\boldsymbol{\alpha}$. This can be done using conventional methods and will typically proceed in an exploratory fashion, as little is usually known a priori about the short-run structure (see Johansen and Juselius, 1994).

Identification in the traditional econometric simultaneous equations framework requires an a priori partitioning of the variables into endogenous and exogenous categories, i.e., as $\mathbf{z}_t = (\mathbf{y}_t', \mathbf{x}_t')'$. Wickens (1996) and Hsiao (1997) analyse the identification of such cointegrated simultaneous equation systems. Their analysis highlights the difference between the two approaches. In the structural approach, the presence or absence of cointegration is presumed in the structure of the model, along with the endogenous–exogenous classification of the variables. In the 'time series' approach, hypotheses about cointegration and exogeneity are determined by the data, so that although less prior information is needed than in the structural approach, the data are required to be more informative so as to allow reliable inferences to be made.

Example 7.5 An estimated structural VECM

Table 7.3 presents the unrestricted ML estimates of the VECM(2,1,2) model selected in example 7.3, although the model is estimated conditionally upon the identified cointegrating vectors of example 7.4.

Table 7.3. *Unrestricted estimates of VECM(2,1,2) model*

	$\boldsymbol{\Phi}_1$				$\boldsymbol{\beta}$			
	Δp_{t-1}	Δrs_{t-1}	Δd_{t-1}	$\Delta r20_{t-1}$	$e^*_{1,t-1}$	$e^*_{2,t-1}$	$\boldsymbol{\beta}_\perp \gamma^*_0$	$\hat{\sigma}$
Δp_t	0.161	0.111	0.136	−0.224	−0.115	0.003	0.0109	6.05%
	[2.72]	[1.78]	[0.45]	[1.95]	[3.98]	[0.14]	[1.29]	
Δrs_t	−0.117	0.274	0.437	0.263	0.035	−0.051	0.0143	5.85%
	[2.05]	[4.54]	[1.49]	[2.36]	[1.25]	[2.59]	[1.74]	
Δd_t	−0.007	0.007	0.159	−0.002	0.011	0.013	0.0008	1.07%
	[0.64]	[0.60]	[2.95]	[0.10]	[2.19]	[3.70]	[0.53]	
$\Delta r20_t$	−0.144	−0.036	0.258	0.239	−0.009	0.004	−0.0021	3.29%
	[4.49]	[1.05]	[1.56]	[3.81]	[0.57]	[0.35]	[0.46]	

$$\boldsymbol{R} = \begin{bmatrix} 1 & & & \\ 0.03 & 1 & & \\ -0.17 & 0.01 & 1 & \\ -0.29 & -0.01 & 0.48 & 1 \end{bmatrix} \qquad |\hat{\boldsymbol{\Sigma}}_{\mathbf{v}}| = 1.010 \times 10^{-12}$$

$\boldsymbol{R}$ is the matrix of contemporaneous residual correlations.

The following estimated structural form was obtained by imposing various data acceptable coefficient restrictions (a likelihood ratio test of the 17 imposed restrictions yields a χ^2 statistic of 11.38, as $|\hat{\Sigma}_v| = 1.05 \times 10^{-12}$)

$$\Delta p_t = \underset{[3.73]}{0.0131} - \Delta r20_t - \underset{[4.50]}{0.108}\, e^*_{1,t-1}, \hat{\sigma} = 5.99\%$$

$$\Delta rs_t = \underset{[3.22]}{0.023} - \underset{[3.97]}{0.460}(\Delta p_t - \Delta r20_t) + \underset{[6.36]}{0.316}\, \Delta rs_{t-1} - \underset{[3.19]}{0.053}\, e^*_{2,t-1}, \ \hat{\sigma} = 5.70\%$$

$$\Delta d_t = \underset{[3.15]}{0.166}\, \Delta d_{t-1} + \underset{[9.84]}{0.014}\left(e^*_{1,t-1} + e^*_{2,t-1}\right), \hat{\sigma} = 1.07\%$$

$$\Delta r20_t = -\underset{[4.94]}{0.147}\, \Delta p_{t-1} + \underset{[3.68]}{0.194}\, \Delta r20_{t-1}, \hat{\sigma} = 3.29\%$$

As well as zero restrictions, three further restrictions have been imposed: an implied dependent variable of $\Delta(p_t + r20_t)$ in the first equation, so that the equity and gilt markets change contemporaneously in equal and opposite directions; equal and opposite coefficients on Δp_t and $\Delta r20_t$ in the *rs* equation; and equality of coefficients on the two error corrections in the *d* equation.

The error corrections appear in all but the *r*20 equation, but as this contains Δp_{t-1} as a regressor, no variable is weakly exogenous for the parameters in any of the four equations. Indeed, this is the only case when a lagged variable, other than a dependent variable, appears in an equation, thus demonstrating the importance of the cointegration framework in establishing the presence of the error corrections: without the information contained in the cointegration properties of the data, only a small part of the variation of the data would have been explained and few interesting regularities would have been uncovered.

7.6 Causality testing in VECMs

Tests of hypotheses about $\boldsymbol{\alpha}$ and $\boldsymbol{\beta}$ also appear when questions of causality arise in VECMs. Consider again the partition used in chapter 6.6.2, $\mathbf{z}_t = \left(\mathbf{y}'_t, \mathbf{x}'_t, \mathbf{r}'_t\right)'$, where the dimensions of the three vectors are n_1, n_2 and $n_3 = n - n_1 - n_2$ and $\boldsymbol{\Phi}_i$ and $\mathbf{A} = \boldsymbol{\beta}\boldsymbol{\alpha}'$ are partitioned conformably. The null hypothesis that $\mathbf{x}$ does not Granger cause $\mathbf{y}$ can then be formulated as

$$H_0 : \mathbf{\Phi}_{1,12} = \cdots = \mathbf{\Phi}_{m-1,12} = \mathbf{0}, \mathbf{A}_{12} = \mathbf{0}$$

where $\mathbf{\Phi}_{i,12}$ and $\mathbf{A}_{12}$ are appropriate $n_1 \times n_2$ submatrices of $\mathbf{\Phi}_i$ and $\mathbf{A}$, respectively. However, causality tests are often constructed from the OLS estimates of the VAR, which implicitly use an unrestricted estimate of $\mathbf{\Pi}$. Toda and Phillips (1993, 1994), by extending the analysis of Sims, Stock and Watson (1990), conclude that, when cointegration is present, i.e., when $\mathbf{A}_{12} = \boldsymbol{\beta}_1 \boldsymbol{\alpha}_2'$, where $\boldsymbol{\beta}_1$ and $\boldsymbol{\alpha}_2$ are conformable partitions of $\boldsymbol{\beta}$ and $\boldsymbol{\alpha}$, standard Wald tests of causality constructed using an unrestricted estimate of $\mathbf{A}$ are only distributed asymptotically as χ^2 if $\boldsymbol{\alpha}_2$ is of rank n_2. If this rank condition fails, the limit distribution involves a mixture of a χ^2 and a non-standard distribution which involves nuisance parameters. Unfortunately, since we require knowledge of the cointegration properties of the system, which are not available from just estimation of the 'levels' VAR, there is no valid statistical basis for ascertaining whether this rank condition actually holds.

If there is no cointegration, then the Wald statistic for causality again has a non-standard limit distribution, although in this case it is free of nuisance parameters, so that critical values can be tabulated conveniently. However, if it is known that the system is $I(1)$ with no cointegration, so that $\mathbf{A} = \mathbf{0}$, then of course we have a VAR in the differences $\Delta\mathbf{z}_t$, and causality tests in such models do have χ^2 distributions, for we are back in the framework of chapter 6.6. Toda and Phillips (1993) argue that such tests are likely to have higher power than tests from the levels VAR as they take account of the unit root constraint $\mathbf{A} = \mathbf{0}$, while the latter tests contain redundant parameter restrictions.

When we have cointegration, causality tests should optimally be constructed from the VECM, in which we know the value of the cointegrating rank r. In such models, it is often natural to refer to the first half of the hypothesis H_0 as 'short-run non-causality' and the second half as 'long-run non-causality'. It is testing for long-run non-causality in VECMs that gives rise to difficulties. Toda and Phillips (1993, 1994) show that the standard Wald statistic for testing H_0 will only have an asymptotically valid χ^2 distribution if either the rank of $\boldsymbol{\alpha}_2$ is n_2 or the rank of $\boldsymbol{\beta}_1$ is n_1, in which case the statistic will be asymptotically distributed as $\chi^2_{n_1 n_2 m}$ (Toda and Phillips, 1993, theorem 3).

Before we can apply these conventional χ^2 asymptotics, we need to test whether either of the two rank conditions actually hold. This can be done using the ML estimates of these matrices, after which causality tests can then be carried out. However, the Wald statistics required are extremely difficult to construct and the testing sequence is complicated, as the papers by Toda and Phillips show. Because of the complexity of this procedure, and because it requires prior knowledge of r (which typically can only be obtained by pretests), it would be useful if alternative, simpler, strategies were available.

A more straightforward procedure has been proposed by Toda and Yamamoto (1995) (see also Saikkonen and Lütkepohl, 1996). Suppose we consider the levels VAR(m) model again but now augment the order by one, i.e., we fit a VAR($m+1$). The non-causality hypothesis can now be tested by a conventional Wald statistic, because the additional lag, for which $\mathbf{\Phi}_{m,12} = \mathbf{0}$ by assumption, allows standard asymptotic inference to be used once again. Under the assumption here that the elements of $\mathbf{z}_t$ are at most $I(1)$, the inclusion of one additional lag in the estimated model suffices. For general orders of integration, a VAR($m + d_{\max}$) should be fitted, where $d_{\max}$ is the maximum order of integration of the components. It is thus not necessary to know precisely the orders of integration or the cointegration rank. It is not surprising, then, that this approach is less powerful than the Toda and Phillips approach and it is also inefficient, as the order of the VAR is intentionally set too large (see the discussion in Stock, 1997). However, if the number of variables in the VAR is relatively small and the lag order is quite large, adding an additional lag might lead to only minor inefficiencies, while the pretest biases associated with cointegration tests may be more serious. Given the ease with which the tests can be constructed, this 'lag augmentation' VAR (LA-VAR) approach should be seriously considered, particularly as Monte Carlo evidence presented by Yamada and Toda (1998) show that it has excellent performance in terms of size stability when testing for Granger causality.

7.7 Fully modified VAR estimation

As we have seen, the long-run matrix $\mathbf{A}$, or equivalently $\mathbf{\Pi}$, contains the information about the non-stationarity and cointegration properties of $\mathbf{z}_t$ and, as such, is often the focus of primary attention in empirical research. An estimate of $\mathbf{A}$ can easily be obtained by OLS regression but, as Phillips (1995) shows, such an estimate has poor properties when non-stationarities are present. For example, OLS estimates of any cointegrating relations have limit distributions that are shifted away from the true parameters, even though the estimates are consistent (they are asymptotically second-order biased although first-order unbiased). This is because cointegrating links between non-stationary series lead to endogeneities in the regressors appearing in levels VARs, and it is these endogeneities that produce the estimation biases, for which OLS is not designed to take account of, this argument being identical to that used for the single equation case discussed in section 7.2.

Phillips (1995) thus considers an alternative approach in which endogeneity corrections are made to the OLS regression formula for VARs. The potential advantage of this approach is that these corrections once again do not require advance knowledge of the value of r or an estimate of $\boldsymbol{\alpha}$. This approach, termed FM-VAR estimation, builds on the earlier work by Phillips and Hansen (1990) on FM-OLS regression that, as we have seen, provides optimal estimates of single cointegrating regressions. To define the FM-VAR estimator, it is convenient to rewrite

$$\mathbf{z}_t = \boldsymbol{\Phi}(B)\Delta\mathbf{z}_{t-1} + \boldsymbol{\Pi}\mathbf{z}_{t-1} + \mathbf{v}_t$$

as

$$\mathbf{z}_t = \mathbf{F}\mathbf{w}_t + \mathbf{v}_t \tag{7.36}$$

where $\mathbf{w}_t = \left(\Delta\mathbf{z}_{t-1}, ..., \Delta\mathbf{z}_{t-m+1}, \mathbf{z}_{t-1}\right)$ and $\mathbf{F} = (\boldsymbol{\Phi}_1, ..., \boldsymbol{\Phi}_{m-1}, \boldsymbol{\Pi})$. The FM-VAR estimator of $\mathbf{F}$ is then defined as

$$\begin{aligned}\hat{\mathbf{F}}^{+} &= \left[\mathbf{Z}'\mathbf{W} - \hat{\boldsymbol{\Omega}}_{\mathbf{vz}}\hat{\boldsymbol{\Omega}}_{\mathbf{zz}}^{-1}\left(\Delta\mathbf{Z}_{-1}'\mathbf{Z}_{-1} - T\hat{\boldsymbol{\Delta}}_{\Delta\mathbf{z}\Delta\mathbf{z}}\right)\right]\left(\mathbf{W}'\mathbf{W}\right)^{-1} \\ &= \hat{\mathbf{F}} - \left[\hat{\boldsymbol{\Omega}}_{\mathbf{vz}}\hat{\boldsymbol{\Omega}}_{\mathbf{vv}}^{-1}\left(\Delta\mathbf{Z}_{-1}'\mathbf{Z}_{-1} - T\hat{\boldsymbol{\Delta}}_{\Delta\mathbf{z}\Delta\mathbf{z}}\right)\right]\left(\mathbf{W}'\mathbf{W}\right)^{-1}\end{aligned} \tag{7.37}$$

Here $\mathbf{Z}$, $\mathbf{Z}_{-1}$, $\mathbf{W}$, $\Delta\mathbf{Z}_{-1}$ are data matrices constructed from the variables in (7.36), e.g., $\mathbf{Z}' = (\mathbf{z}_1, ..., \mathbf{z}_T)$ and $\Delta\mathbf{Z}_{-1}' = (\Delta\mathbf{z}_0, \ldots, \Delta\mathbf{z}_{T-1})$. $\hat{\boldsymbol{\Delta}}_{\Delta\mathbf{z}\Delta\mathbf{z}}$, $\hat{\boldsymbol{\Omega}}_{\mathbf{vz}}$ and $\hat{\boldsymbol{\Omega}}_{\mathbf{vv}}$ are kernel estimates of various covariance matrices: see Phillips (1995), for example, for definitions of these matrices and kernel estimates.

$$\hat{\mathbf{F}} = \mathbf{Z}'\mathbf{W}\left(\mathbf{W}'\mathbf{W}\right)^{-1}$$

is the OLS estimator of $\mathbf{F}$, which is thus 'modified' to take into account the endogeneity brought about by the inclusion of the $I(1)$ regressor $\mathbf{Z}_{-1}$: see Phillips (1995) for technical details and extended discussion. A routine for computing the FM-VAR estimator within the GAUSS language is provided in Ouliaris and Phillips (1995).

If the VAR has a full set of unit roots ($r = 0$), $\hat{\mathbf{F}}^{+}$ is hyperconsistent, in the sense that its rate of convergence exceeds the usual order T rate, for all elements of the unit root matrix $\boldsymbol{\Pi} = \mathbf{I}_n$. If there are some stationary components in the VAR, then the corresponding FM estimates of these coefficients have the same asymptotic distribution as the OLS estimates of the levels VAR. When the VAR is a composite system, so that it has some unit roots and some cointegrated variables (i.e., $0 < r < n$), FM-VAR provides an optimal estimate of the cointegration matrix $\boldsymbol{\alpha}$ without requiring prior knowledge of, or pretesting for, the value of r. Any cointegrating relations are thus implicitly estimated as if ML estimation was being performed with the cointegrating rank known correctly.

Hypothesis tests on $\mathbf{F}$ that use the FM-VAR regression estimator $\hat{\mathbf{F}}^{+}$ may be constructed from the asymptotic approximation

$$T^{1/2}\left(\hat{\mathbf{F}}^{+} - \mathbf{F}\right) \sim N\left(0, \hat{\boldsymbol{\Sigma}}_{\mathbf{vv}} \otimes T\left(\mathbf{W}'\mathbf{W}\right)^{-1}\right)$$

Suppose that we wish to test the set of q restrictions

$$H_0 : \mathbf{R}\mathrm{vec}(\mathbf{F}) = \boldsymbol{r}$$

where $\mathbf{R}$ is of full row rank q. The Wald statistic of this hypothesis is

$$W_F^{+} = T\left(\mathbf{R}\mathrm{vec}(\hat{\mathbf{F}}^{+}) - \boldsymbol{r}\right)'\left[\mathbf{R}\left\{\hat{\boldsymbol{\Sigma}}_{\mathbf{vv}} \otimes T\left(\mathbf{W}'\mathbf{W}\right)^{-1}\right\}\mathbf{R}'\right]^{-1}\left(\mathbf{R}\mathrm{vec}(\hat{\mathbf{F}}^{+}) - \boldsymbol{r}\right)$$

Phillips (1995) shows that the χ_q^2 distribution is an upper bounding variate for this statistic, so that the usual χ^2 critical values can be used to construct tests that have conservative size.

In this framework, causality restrictions can be set up in the following way. As in section 7.3, suppose we wish to test whether $\mathbf{x}$ has no causal effect on $\mathbf{y}$. This imposes the restrictions $\boldsymbol{\Phi}_{1,12} = \cdots = \boldsymbol{\Phi}_{m-1,12} = \mathbf{0}$, $\mathbf{A}_{12} = \mathbf{0}$ which can be written as

$$H_0' : \mathbf{R}\mathrm{vec}(\mathbf{F}) = \mathbf{0}$$

where $\mathbf{R} = (\mathbf{S} \otimes \mathbf{S}_1)$, $\mathbf{S}$ and $\mathbf{S}_1$ being selection matrices defined as $\mathbf{S} = \mathbf{I}_m \otimes \left[\mathbf{0}_{n_1} \quad \mathbf{I}_{n_2} \quad \mathbf{0}_{n_3}\right]$ and $\mathbf{S}_1 = \left[\mathbf{I}_{n_1} \quad \mathbf{0}\right]$. The associated Wald statistic then has a χ_m^2 limit distribution.

Example 7.6 Causality tests using the LA-VAR and FM-VAR approaches

Causality tests using a VAR(2) model were constructed using the LA-VAR procedure. Since each series making up the VAR appears to be $I(1)$, a VAR(3) was actually fitted, leading to the causality test statistics shown in table 7.4(a) . At the 10 per cent significance level, causality is found only from *rs* to *d* and *r*20 to *rs*, but feedback is found between *r*20 and *p*. This relatively slight evidence of causal structures compared to the

Table 7.4. *Granger causality tests*

$\downarrow i \quad j \rightarrow$	p	rs	d	$r20$
(a) LA-VAR estimation				
p	–	4.23	0.27	10.33*
rs	3.57	–	4.41	11.19*
d	3.15	5.05*	–	0.10
$r20$	24.89*	2.54	4.28	–
(b) FM-VAR estimation				
p	–	1.51	20.92*	57.38*
rs	5.14*	–	4.75*	12.15*
d	19.86*	7.84*	–	8.73*
$r20$	14.73*	1.42	3.03	–

Notes: Statistics have a limiting χ_2^2 distribution. * denotes significance at 10% level.

patterns found in the structural model of example 7.5 may well be a consequence of the inefficiency of this 'augmented VAR' approach to causality testing.

Table 7.4(b) reports the Wald causality test statistics W_F^+ obtained from FM-VAR estimation and, while confirming the patterns found in the VAR(3) model, they also provide evidence of causality running from $r20$ to d and p to rs, and feedback between p and d and rs and d. This is in accordance with the simulation results of Yamada and Toda (1997, 1998), who find that FM-VAR tests of Granger causality tend to have higher power than LA-VAR tests, although their performance is very sensitive to parameter values and, in particular, to how the covariance matrices in (7.37) are estimated.

7.8 Impulse response asymptotics in non-stationary VARs

As we showed in chapter 6.7, the various impulse responses of the VAR are computed from the sequence of matrices

$$\mathbf{\Psi}_i = \sum\nolimits_{j=1}^{m} \mathbf{\Pi}_j \mathbf{\Psi}_{i-j}, \quad \mathbf{\Psi}_0 = \mathbf{I}_n$$

Their computation remains exactly the same in non-stationary VARs but, if $\mathbf{A} = -\sum_{j=1}^{m} \mathbf{\Pi}_j$ is of reduced rank, the elements of $\mathbf{\Psi}_i$ will not die out as i increases, and this leads to some analytical complications. Following Phillips (1998), we consider the behaviour of these impulse responses as the lead time $i \to \infty$, and the asymptotic behaviour of estimates of these quantities as $T \to \infty$.

In stationary VARs, where all the roots of the long-run multiplier matrix $\mathbf{A}$ lie outside the unit circle, the system's estimated impulse responses are $T^{1/2}$-consistent and, upon appropriate centring and scaling, have asymptotic normal distributions (see Lütkepohl, 1991, chapter 3.7): as $i \to \infty$, both $\boldsymbol{\Psi}_i$ and their estimates $\hat{\boldsymbol{\Psi}}_i$ tend to zero. For non-stationary VARs, where the $\boldsymbol{\Psi}_i$ do not necessarily die out as $i \to \infty$, Phillips (1998) shows that a very different limit theory holds for the impulse response estimates, which may be summarised thus (see also Stock, 1996):

(i) When there are unit roots in the system, the long horizon impulse responses estimated from a levels VAR by OLS are inconsistent, the limiting values of the estimated responses being random variables rather than the true impulse responses. The reason for this is that because these true impulse responses do not die out as the lead time increases, they carry the effects of the unit roots with them indefinitely. Since the unit roots are estimated with error, the effects of the estimation error persist in the limit as $T \to \infty$. The limiting distributions of $\hat{\boldsymbol{\Psi}}_i$ as $i \to \infty$ are asymmetric, so that confidence intervals for impulse responses will be as well. A similar result holds if FM-VAR estimation is used rather than OLS.

(ii) The limiting impulse responses in a cointegrated VAR model are non-zero only in those directions where the model is non-stationary and has unit roots, i.e., $\boldsymbol{\alpha}_{\perp}$. They are estimated consistently as long as the cointegrating rank is either known or is itself consistently estimated, either by an order selection method or by using classical likelihood ratio tests that are suitably modified to ensure that the size of the test goes to zero as the sample size goes to infinity. This is because in a reduced rank regression the matrix product $\boldsymbol{\beta}\boldsymbol{\alpha}'$ is estimated rather than $\mathbf{A}$, so that no unit roots are estimated (either explicitly or implicitly). Simulations reported by Phillips (1998) show that impulse responses are estimated accurately by such procedures. However, these consistent selection procedures will tend to mistakenly take roots that are close to unity as actually being unity, so that, rather than dying out, they will converge to non-zero constants. Furthermore, as Stock (1996) shows, in these circumstances prediction intervals will be undesirably wide.

Nevertheless, it is clear from these results that impulse responses for non-stationary VARs should not be computed from an unrestricted levels

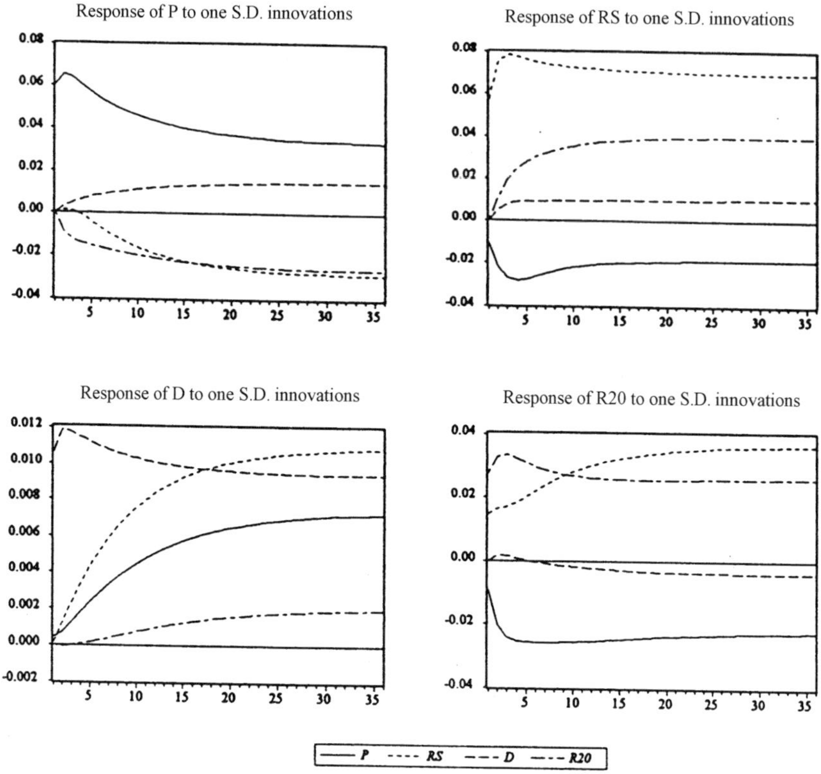

(a) VECM impulse responses

Figure 7.15 Estimated impulse response functions

VAR. Knowledge of the number of unit roots in the system is very important for obtaining accurate estimates, so it is important that the cointegrating rank is selected by a consistent method that works well in practice.

Example 7.7 Impulse responses from the VECM

The VECM(2,1,2) model arrived at in example 7.5 has an implied long-run matrix, given by $\hat{\boldsymbol{\beta}}\hat{\boldsymbol{\alpha}} + \mathbf{I}_4$, that has two unit roots (given by the two cointegrating vectors) and two real roots of 0.88 and 0.86. Consequently, impulse responses converge to non-zero constants, as shown in figure 7.15(a). Of particular interest is the long-run effect of d on p, which steadily accumulates over three years. This result was remarked upon in Mills (1991a) as being consistent with the views of

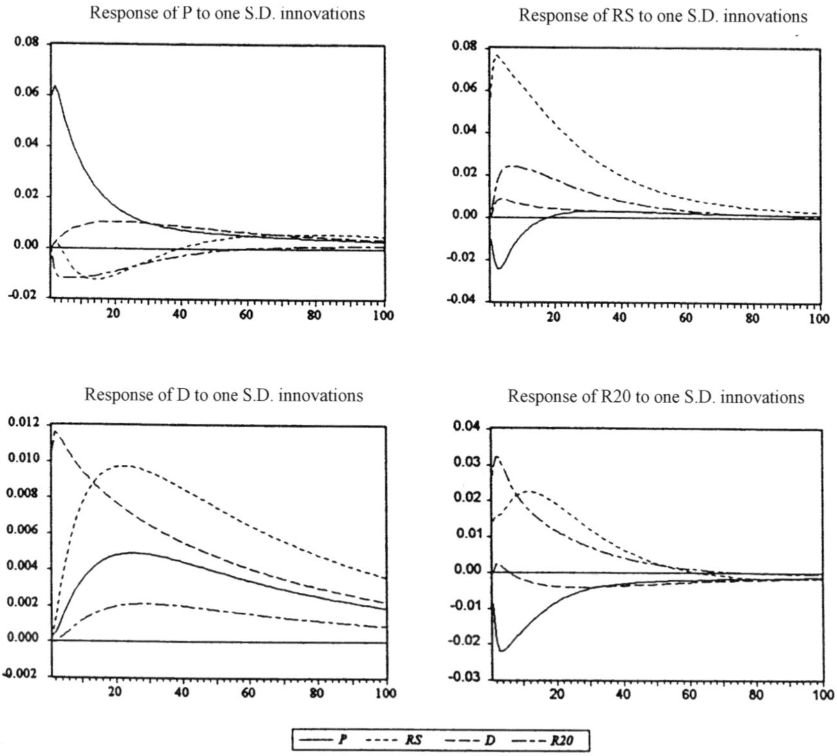

(b) OLS impulse responses

Figure 7.15 (*cont.*)

market professionals who believe that financial factors have only a short-run impact on equity prices, with dividends being the long-run driving force. All responses appear to have converged to their long-run values after three years.

OLS and FM-VAR estimation of the unrestricted VAR model provide four stationary roots, for $\hat{\mathbf{\Pi}}$ the roots are 0.99, 0.98, 0.89 and 0.86, while for $\hat{\mathbf{\Pi}}^+$ the roots are 0.99, 0.98, 0.94 and 0.82, so that all estimated impulse responses eventually decline to zero. Figure 7.15(b) shows this for the OLS impulse responses, but it is noticeable that the decline can be very slow, particularly for *d*. Nevertheless, the differences between the sets of responses in figure 7.15 are clearcut: even though the long-run matrices are almost identical, estimating the two unit roots as 0.99 and 0.98 produces major differences to the impulse responses.

8 Further topics in the analysis of integrated financial time series

In this chapter we investigate several further topics in the analysis of integrated time series. Section 1 looks again at the problem of testing for a single long-run relationship, and presents a technique that is applicable without requiring firm knowledge that the variables in the analysis are definitely $I(0)$ or $I(1)$. Section 2 moves back to the VECM framework and investigates the possibility that there may be common cycles, as well as common trends, in the data, while section 3 investigates techniques of extracting permanent and transitory components from the model. The links between present value models, excess volatility, rational bubbles and cointegration are examined in section 4. Section 5 considers non-linear extensions of cointegration and error correction models, and briefly discusses some recent techniques for introducing structural breaks and infinite variance errors into the cointegrating framework. It also looks at the issues involved in handling the very large, high frequency, data sets that result from analysing market micro-structures.

8.1 Testing for a single long-run relationship

Consider again the levels VAR of (7.24), now written as

$$\mathbf{z}_t = \boldsymbol{\mu}_0 + \boldsymbol{\mu}_1 t + \sum_{i=1}^{m} \boldsymbol{\Pi}_i \mathbf{z}_{t-i} + \mathbf{v}_t \tag{8.1}$$

where the elements of $\mathbf{z}_t$ are permitted to be either $I(0)$, $I(1)$ or cointegrated, along with the *unrestricted* VECM

$$\Delta\mathbf{z}_t = \boldsymbol{\mu}_0 + \boldsymbol{\mu}_1 t + \mathbf{A}\mathbf{z}_{t-1} + \sum_{i=1}^{m-1} \boldsymbol{\Phi}_i \Delta\mathbf{z}_{t-1} + \mathbf{v}_t \tag{8.2}$$

where

$$\mathbf{A} = \sum_{i=1}^{m} \boldsymbol{\Pi}_i - \mathbf{I}_n$$

and

$$\mathbf{\Phi}_i = -\sum\nolimits_{j=i+1}^{m} \mathbf{\Pi}_j, \quad i = 1, \ldots, m-1$$

are now referred to as the matrices of the long-run multipliers and the short-run dynamic coefficients respectively.

Consider now the partition $\mathbf{z}_t = (y_t, \mathbf{x}_t')'$, where y_t is scalar, and define the conformable partitions $\mathbf{v}_t = (\nu_{1t}, \mathbf{v}_{2t}')'$, and

$$\boldsymbol{\mu}_j = \begin{bmatrix} \mu_{j1} \\ \boldsymbol{\mu}_{j2} \end{bmatrix}, \; j = 0, 1, \quad \mathbf{A} = \begin{bmatrix} A_{11} & \mathbf{A}_{12} \\ \mathbf{A}_{21} & \mathbf{A}_{22} \end{bmatrix}, \quad \mathbf{\Phi}_i = \begin{bmatrix} \phi_{11,i} & \phi_{12,i} \\ \phi_{21,i} & \mathbf{\Phi}_{22,i} \end{bmatrix}$$

$$\mathbf{\Sigma}_{\mathbf{v}} = \begin{bmatrix} \sigma_{11} & \sigma_{12} \\ \sigma_{21} & \mathbf{\Sigma}_{22} \end{bmatrix}$$

This is similar to the partitioning used in chapter 7.5.5 to investigate weak exogeneity in VECMs, although here we do not assume that **A** is necessarily reduced rank. We do, though, assume that $\mathbf{A}_{21} = \mathbf{0}$, which ensures that there exists *at most* one (non-degenerate) long-run relationship between y_t and $\mathbf{x}_t$, irrespective of the order of integration of the $\mathbf{x}_t$ process. Equation (8.2) can then be written in terms of the *dependent* variable y_t and the forcing variables $\mathbf{x}_t$ as

$$\begin{aligned} \Delta y_t = \mu_{01} + \mu_{11} t + A_{11} y_{t-1} + \mathbf{A}_{12}\mathbf{x}_{t-1} + \sum\nolimits_{i=1}^{m-1} \phi_{11,i} \Delta y_{t-i} \\ + \sum\nolimits_{i=1}^{m-1} \boldsymbol{\phi}_{12,i} \Delta \mathbf{x}_{t-i} + \nu_{1t} \end{aligned} \tag{8.3}$$

$$\begin{aligned} \Delta \mathbf{x}_t = \boldsymbol{\mu}_{02} + \boldsymbol{\mu}_{12} t + \mathbf{A}_{22}\mathbf{x}_{t-1} + \sum\nolimits_{i=1}^{m-1} \boldsymbol{\phi}_{21,i} \Delta y_{t-i} \\ + \sum\nolimits_{i=1}^{m-1} \mathbf{\Phi}_{22,i} \Delta \mathbf{x}_{t-i} + \mathbf{v}_{2t} \end{aligned} \tag{8.4}$$

The contemporaneous correlation between ν_{1t} and $\mathbf{v}_{2t}$ can be characterised by the regression

$$\nu_{1t} = \boldsymbol{\omega}' \mathbf{v}_{2t} + \xi_t \tag{8.5}$$

where $\boldsymbol{\omega} = \mathbf{\Sigma}_{22}^{-1}\sigma_{21}$, $\{\xi_t\}$ is a $WN(0, \sigma_\xi^2)$ process with $\sigma_\xi^2 = \sigma_{11} - \sigma_{12}\,\mathbf{\Sigma}_{22}^{-1}\sigma_{21}$, and the $\{\xi_t\}$ and $\{\mathbf{v}_{2t}\}$ processes are uncorrelated by construction. Substituting (8.4) and (8.5) into (8.3) yields

$$\Delta y_t = a_0 + a_1 t + \phi y_{t-1} + \boldsymbol{\delta}'\mathbf{x}_{t-1} + \sum_{i=1}^{m-1} \psi_i \Delta y_{t-i} + \sum_{i=0}^{m-1} \boldsymbol{\varphi}_i \Delta \mathbf{x}_{t-i} + \xi_t \tag{8.6}$$

where

$$a_0 \equiv \mu_{01} - \boldsymbol{\omega}'\boldsymbol{\mu}_{02}, \quad a_1 \equiv \mu_{11} - \boldsymbol{\omega}'\boldsymbol{\mu}_{12}, \quad \phi \equiv A_{11}, \quad \boldsymbol{\delta} \equiv \mathbf{A}_{12}' - \mathbf{A}_{22}'\boldsymbol{\omega}$$
$$\psi_i \equiv \phi_{11,i} - \boldsymbol{\omega}'\boldsymbol{\phi}_{21,i}, \quad \boldsymbol{\varphi}_0 \equiv \boldsymbol{\omega}', \quad \boldsymbol{\varphi}_i \equiv \boldsymbol{\phi}_{12,i} - \boldsymbol{\omega}'\boldsymbol{\Phi}_{22,i}$$

It follows from (8.6) that if $\phi \neq 0$ and $\boldsymbol{\delta} \neq \mathbf{0}$ then there exists a long-run relationship between the levels of y_t and $\mathbf{x}_t$, given by

$$y_t = \theta_0 + \theta_1 t + \boldsymbol{\theta}'\mathbf{x}_t + \upsilon_t \tag{8.7}$$

where $\theta_0 \equiv -a_0/\phi, \theta_1 \equiv -a_1/\phi, \boldsymbol{\theta} \equiv -\boldsymbol{\delta}/\phi$ is the vector of long-run response parameters, and $\{\upsilon_t\}$ is a mean zero stationary process. If $\phi < 0$ then this long-run relationship is *stable* and (8.6) can be written in the ECM form

$$\Delta y_t = a_0 + a_1 t + \phi(y_{t-1} - \boldsymbol{\theta}'\mathbf{x}_{t-1}) + \sum_{i=1}^{m-1} \psi_i \Delta y_{t-i} + \sum_{i=0}^{m-1} \boldsymbol{\varphi}_i \Delta \mathbf{x}_{t-i} + \xi_t \tag{8.8}$$

If $\phi = 0$ in (8.8) then no long-run relationship exists between y_t and $\mathbf{x}_t$. However, a test for $\phi = 0$ runs into the difficulty that the long-run parameter vector $\boldsymbol{\theta}$ is no longer identified under this null, being present only under the alternative hypothesis. Consequently, Pesaran, Shin and Smith (1996) test for the absence of a long-run relationship, and avoid the lack of identifiability of $\boldsymbol{\theta}$, by examining the joint null hypothesis $\phi = 0$ *and* $\boldsymbol{\delta} = \mathbf{0}$ in the unrestricted ECM (8.6). Note that it is then possible for the long-run relationship to be *degenerate*, in that $\phi \neq 0$ but $\boldsymbol{\delta} = \mathbf{0}$, in which case the long-run relationship only involves y_t and possibly a linear trend.

Pesaran, Shin and Smith consider the conventional Wald statistic of the null $\phi = 0$ and $\boldsymbol{\delta} = \mathbf{0}$ and show that its asymptotic distribution involves the non-standard unit root distribution and depends on both the dimension and cointegration rank ($0 \leq r \leq k$) of the forcing variables $\mathbf{x}_t$. This cointegration rank is the rank of the matrix $\mathbf{A}_{22}$ appearing in (8.4). Pesaran, Shin and Smith obtain this asymptotic distribution in two polar cases: (i) when $\mathbf{A}_{22}$ is of full rank, in which case $\mathbf{x}_t$ is an $I(0)$ vector process, and (ii) when the $\mathbf{x}_t$ process is not mutually cointegrated ($r = 0$ and $\mathbf{A}_{22} = \mathbf{0}$) and hence is an $I(1)$ process. They point out that the critical values obtained from stochastically simulating these two distributions must provide lower and upper critical value bounds for all possible classifications of the forcing variables into $I(0)$, $I(1)$ and cointegrated processes. A *bounds procedure* to test for the existence of a long-run relationship within the unrestricted ECM (8.6) is thus as follows. If the Wald (or related F-) statistic falls below the lower critical value bound, then the null $\phi = 0$ and $\boldsymbol{\delta} = \mathbf{0}$ is not rejected, irrespective of the order of integration or cointegration rank of the variables. Similarly, if the statistics are greater than their upper critical value bounds, the null is rejected and we conclude that there is a long-run relationship between y_t and $\mathbf{x}_t$. If the statistics fall within the bounds, inference is inconclusive and detailed information about the integration–cointegration properties of the variables is then necessary in order to proceed further. It is the fact that we may be able to make firm inferences without this information, and thus avoid the severe pretesting problems usually involved in this type of analysis, that makes this procedure attractive in applied situations. Pesaran, Shin and Smith provide critical values for alternative values of k under two situations; Case 1: $a_0 \neq 0,\ a_1 = 0$ (with intercept but no trend in (8.6)), and Case 2: $a_0 \neq 0,\ a_1 \neq 0$ (with both intercept and trend in (8.6)).

Pesaran, Shin and Smith show that this testing procedure is consistent and that the approach is applicable in quite general situations. For example, equation (8.6) can be regarded as an autoregressive distributed lag (ARDL) model in y_t and $\mathbf{x}_t$ having all lag orders equal to m. Differential lag lengths can be used without affecting the asymptotic distribution of the test statistic.

Example 8.1 Is there a long-run market model?

In examples 7.1 and 7.2 we investigated whether there was cointegration between the LGEN stock price and the *FTSE 100* index on the assumption that the logarithms of both series were $I(1)$. As was remarked in example 7.1, the latter series is only marginally $I(1)$: its ADF test statistic is -3.38, which is close to the 5 per cent critical value of -3.42. We thus investigate the existence of a long-run relationship between the two series (denoted once again as y_t and x_t) using the testing technique outlined above, which does not require a definite classification of the integration properties of x_t. Estimating equation (8.6) with $m = 3$ produced a Wald test statistic of 11.86 for both Case 1 and Case 2, as the trend was found to be completely insignificant. With $k = 1$ as here, the 5 per cent significance level bounds for the Wald statistic for Case 1 are 9.87 and 11.53, so that the hypothesis of no long-run relationship is clearly rejected, irrespective of the order of integration of x_t.

Given this evidence in favour of a long-run relationship, we then fitted a parsimonious form of the ECM (8.8), obtaining

$$\Delta y_t = -\underset{(0.015)}{0.053}\left(y_{t-1} - \underset{(0.005)}{1.086}\; x_{t-1}\right) - \underset{(0.028)}{0.118}\,(\Delta y_{t-1} + \Delta y_{t-2})$$

$$+ \underset{(0.057)}{1.106}\;\Delta x_t + \underset{(0.063)}{0.151}\;\Delta x_{t-2}$$

How does this model, which has an equation standard error of 3.02 per cent, compare with the model fitted in example 7.2? That model, written in ECM form, is

$$\Delta y_t = -0.006 - 0.057(y_{t-1} - x_{t-1}) - 0.128(\Delta y_{t-1} + \Delta y_{t-2})$$

$$+ 1.107\Delta x_t + 0.128(\Delta x_{t-1} + \Delta x_{t-2})$$

There is thus a difference in the long-run response – 1.086 to 1 – and some differences in the short-run dynamics (as well as a constant being significant in the latter model). Written in levels, the two models are

$$\begin{aligned} y_t =& 1.106x_t - 1.048x_{t-1} + 0.151x_{t-2} - 0.151x_{t-3} + 0.829y_{t-1} \\ &+ 0.118y_{t-3} \end{aligned}$$

and

$$\begin{aligned} y_t =& 1.107x_t - 0.922x_{t-1} - 0.128x_{t-3} + 0.815y_{t-1} + 0.128y_{t-3} \\ &- 0.006 \end{aligned}$$

Figure 8.1 shows the impulse response functions calculated from the two models. It is seen that the impact effect is almost identical in the two models and that, after some initial fluctuations, both functions converge monotonically to long-run equilibrium, although the shapes are very different. Nevertheless, median lags are almost the same, being of the order of twelve months, so that convergence to equilibrium is rather slow.

8.2 Common trends and cycles

Consider again the VAR(m) process for the $I(1)$ vector $\mathbf{z}_t$

$$\mathbf{\Pi}(B)\mathbf{z}_t = \mathbf{v}_t$$

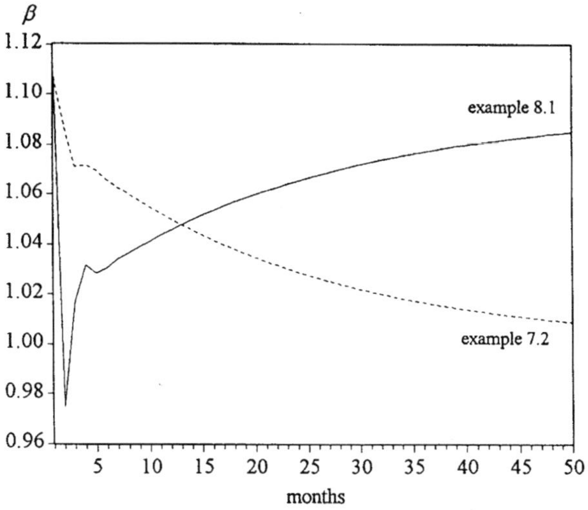

Figure 8.1 Impulse responses from the two market models

where, for simplicity, we exclude the constant and linear trend and set initial values $\mathbf{z}_0 = \mathbf{v}_0 = \mathbf{0}$. Analogous to the 'levels solution' (7.26), we then have

$$\mathbf{z}_t = \mathbf{C}(1)\mathbf{s}_t + \mathbf{C}^*(B)\mathbf{v}_t$$

If there is cointegration then $\mathbf{C}(1)$ is of reduced rank $k = n - r$ and can be written as the product $\boldsymbol{\gamma}\boldsymbol{\delta}'$, both of which have rank k. Thus, on defining

$$\boldsymbol{\tau}_t = \boldsymbol{\delta}'\mathbf{s}_t \qquad \mathbf{c}_t = \mathbf{C}^*(B)\mathbf{v}_t$$

we have the Stock and Watson (1988) 'common trends' representation

$$\begin{aligned} \mathbf{z}_t &= \boldsymbol{\gamma}\boldsymbol{\tau}_t + \mathbf{c}_t \\ \boldsymbol{\tau}_t &= \boldsymbol{\tau}_{t-1} + \boldsymbol{\delta}'\mathbf{v}_t \end{aligned} \tag{8.9}$$

which expresses $\mathbf{z}_t$ as a linear combination of $k = n - r$ random walks, the common trends $\boldsymbol{\tau}_t$, plus some stationary 'transitory' components $\mathbf{c}_t$. Equation (8.9) may be regarded as a multivariate extension of the Beveridge and Nelson (1981) decomposition introduced in chapter 3.2.1. As Wickens (1996) shows, $\boldsymbol{\delta}$ is not uniquely defined (cf. the argument concerning the cointegrating matrix $\boldsymbol{\alpha}$), so that these trends are also not uniquely defined without introducing additional identifying conditions.

In the same way that common trends appear in $\mathbf{z}_t$ when $\mathbf{C}(1)$ is of reduced rank, common cycles appear if $\mathbf{C}^*(B)$ is of reduced rank, since $\mathbf{c}_t = \mathbf{C}^*(B)\mathbf{v}_t$ is the cyclical component of $\mathbf{z}_t$. The presence of common cycles requires that there are linear combinations of the elements of $\mathbf{z}_t$ that do not contain these cyclical components, i.e., that there are a set of s linearly independent vectors, gathered together in the $n \times s$ matrix $\boldsymbol{\phi}$, such that

$$\boldsymbol{\phi}'\mathbf{c}_t = \boldsymbol{\phi}'\mathbf{C}^*(B)\mathbf{v}_t = \mathbf{0}$$

in which case

$$\boldsymbol{\phi}'\mathbf{z}_t = \boldsymbol{\phi}\,\gamma\boldsymbol{\tau}_t$$

Such a matrix will exist if all the $\mathbf{C}_i^*$ have less than full rank and if $\boldsymbol{\phi}'\mathbf{C}_i^* = \mathbf{0}$ for all i (see Vahid and Engle, 1993, and Engle and Issler, 1995).

Under these circumstances, we can write $\mathbf{C}_i^* = \mathbf{G}\tilde{\mathbf{C}}_i$ for all i, where $\mathbf{G}$ is an $n \times (n-s)$ matrix having full column rank and $\tilde{\mathbf{C}}_i$ may not have full rank. The cyclical component can then be written as

$$\mathbf{c}_t = \mathbf{G}\tilde{\mathbf{C}}(B)\mathbf{v}_t \equiv \mathbf{G}\tilde{\mathbf{c}}_t$$

so that the n-element cycle $\mathbf{c}_t$ can be written as linear combinations of an $(n-s)$-element cycle $\tilde{\mathbf{c}}_t$, thus leading to the common trend–common cycle representation

$$\mathbf{z}_t = \gamma\boldsymbol{\tau}_t + \mathbf{G}\tilde{\mathbf{c}}_t \tag{8.10}$$

The number, s, of linearly independent 'cofeature' vectors making up $\boldsymbol{\phi}$ can be at most $k = n - r$, and these will be linearly independent of the cointegrating vectors making up $\boldsymbol{\alpha}$ (Vahid and Engle, 1993, theorem 1). This is a consequence of the fact that $\boldsymbol{\phi}'\mathbf{z}_t$, being the vector of common trends, is $I(1)$, whereas $\boldsymbol{\alpha}'\mathbf{z}_t$, being the vector of error corrections, is $I(0)$.

An interesting special case of the representation (8.10) occurs when $r + s = n$. In these circumstances, $\mathbf{z}_t$ has the unique trend–cycle decomposition $\mathbf{z}_t = \mathbf{z}_t^\tau + \mathbf{z}_t^c$, where

$$\mathbf{z}_t^\tau = \boldsymbol{\Theta}_2\boldsymbol{\phi}'\mathbf{z}_t = \boldsymbol{\Theta}_2\boldsymbol{\phi}'\gamma\boldsymbol{\tau}_t$$

contains the stochastic trends and

$$\mathbf{z}_t^c = \boldsymbol{\Theta}_1\boldsymbol{\alpha}'\mathbf{z}_t = \boldsymbol{\Theta}_1\boldsymbol{\alpha}'\mathbf{c}_t$$

contains the cyclical component. Here

$$[\boldsymbol{\Theta}_1 \quad \boldsymbol{\Theta}_2] = \begin{bmatrix} \boldsymbol{\alpha}' \\ \boldsymbol{\phi}' \end{bmatrix}^{-1}$$

Note that $\mathbf{z}_t^c$ is a linear combination of the error correction terms $\mathbf{e}_t = \boldsymbol{\alpha}'\mathbf{z}_t$. Since both $\mathbf{z}_t^\tau$ and $\mathbf{z}_t^c$ are functions of $\boldsymbol{\alpha}$ and $\boldsymbol{\phi}$, they can easily be calculated as simple linear combinations of $\mathbf{z}_t$.

The common trend–common cycle representation (8.10) depends, of course, on the number of cointegrating and cofeature vectors, r and s, in the system. The number of cofeature vectors (common cycles) can be determined using the approach of Engle and Kozicki (1993), as extended by Vahid and Engle (1993) to the current context in which there may also be cointegration. The rank s of the cofeature matrix can be determined by calculating the test statistic

$$C(s) = -(T - m - 2)\sum\nolimits_{i=1}^{s} \log\left(1 - \ell_i^2\right)$$

where $\ell_1, \ldots, \ell_s$ are the s smallest squared canonical correlations between $\Delta\mathbf{z}_t$ and the set $(\Delta\mathbf{z}_{t-1}, \ldots, \Delta\mathbf{z}_{t-m+1}, \mathbf{e}_{t-1})$. Under the null hypothesis that the rank of $\boldsymbol{\phi}$ is at least s, this statistic has a χ^2 distribution with $s^2 + sn(m-1) + sr - sn$ degrees of freedom (Vahid and Engle, 1993). The canonical correlations may be computed using the procedure outlined in Hamilton (1994, chapter 20.1).

An equivalent representation is obtained by incorporating the s cofeature vectors, as well as the r cointegrating vectors, into the VECM representation

$$\Delta\mathbf{z}_t = \boldsymbol{\Phi}(B)\Delta\mathbf{z}_{t-1} + \boldsymbol{\beta}\mathbf{e}_{t-1} + \mathbf{v}_t \tag{8.11}$$

directly. Vahid and Engle (1993) point out that the cofeature matrix $\boldsymbol{\phi}$ is only identified up to an invertible transformation, as any linear combination of the columns of $\boldsymbol{\phi}$ will also be a cofeature vector. The matrix can therefore be rotated to have an s-dimensional identity sub-matrix

$$\boldsymbol{\phi} = \begin{bmatrix} \mathbf{I}_s \\ \boldsymbol{\phi}^*_{(n-s)\times s} \end{bmatrix}$$

$\boldsymbol{\phi}'\Delta\mathbf{z}_t$ can then be considered as s 'pseudo-structural form' equations for the first s elements of $\Delta\mathbf{z}_t$. The system can be completed by adding the unconstrained VECM equations for the remaining $n-s$ equations of $\Delta\mathbf{z}_t$ to obtain the system

$$\begin{bmatrix} \mathbf{I}_s & \boldsymbol{\phi}^{*\prime} \\ \mathbf{0}_{(n-s)\times s} & \mathbf{I}_{n-s} \end{bmatrix} \Delta\mathbf{z}_t = \begin{bmatrix} \mathbf{0}_{s\times(n(m-1)+r)} \\ \boldsymbol{\Phi}_1^* \ldots \boldsymbol{\Phi}_{m-1}^* \ \boldsymbol{\beta}^* \end{bmatrix} \begin{bmatrix} \Delta\mathbf{z}_{t-1} \\ \vdots \\ \Delta\mathbf{z}_{t-m+1} \\ \mathbf{e}_{t-1} \end{bmatrix} + \mathbf{v}_t \quad (8.12)$$

where $\boldsymbol{\Phi}_1^*$ contains the last $n-s$ rows of $\boldsymbol{\Phi}_1$, etc. Writing the restricted model in this way makes it clear why there are $s^2 + sn(m-1) + sr - sn$ degrees of freedom for the common feature test statistic $C(s)$. The unrestricted VECM (8.11) has $n(n(m-1)+r)$ parameters, whereas the pseudo-structural model (8.12) has $sn - s^2$ parameters in the first s equations and $(n-s)(n(m-1)+r)$ parameters in the $n-s$ equations which complete the system, so imposing $s^2 + sn(m-1) + sr - sn$ restrictions. The system (8.12) can be estimated by FIML or some other simultaneous equation estimation technique and a likelihood ratio statistic of the restrictions imposed by the s cofeature vectors can then be constructed, which will be equivalent to $C(s)$. Equivalently, the common cycle restrictions can be imposed directly on the VECM to yield

$$\Delta\mathbf{z}_t = \begin{bmatrix} -\boldsymbol{\phi}^{*\prime} \\ \mathbf{I}_{n-s} \end{bmatrix} \left[\boldsymbol{\Phi}_1^* \Delta\mathbf{z}_{t-1} + \ldots + \boldsymbol{\Phi}_m^* \Delta\mathbf{z}_{t-m+1} + \boldsymbol{\beta}^* \mathbf{e}_{t-1}\right] + \mathbf{v}_t \quad (8.13)$$

which is a reduced rank VECM. Note that if $m=1$ and $r=n-s$, the system will be just-identified and no test for common cycles is needed, for the system will necessarily have r common cycles. As the lag order m increases, so the system will generally become overidentified and tests for common cycles become necessary.

From (8.13), it is clear that the presence of s cofeature vectors implies that $\boldsymbol{\phi}'\Delta\mathbf{z}_t$ is independent of $\Delta\mathbf{z}_{t-1}, \ldots, \Delta\mathbf{z}_{t-m+1}$ and $\mathbf{e}_{t-1}$, and hence of all past values of $\mathbf{v}_t$. Vahid and Engle (1997) have subsequently generalised this approach to consider 'codependent' cycles. A codependent cycle of order q implies a linear combination of $\Delta\mathbf{z}_t$ that is independent of $\mathbf{v}_{t-j}$, $j > q$, so that a common cycle is a codependent cycle of order 0.

Example 8.2 Are there common cycles in the UK financial markets?

In example 7.3 we found that, in the VECM fitted to $\mathbf{z}_t = (p_t, d_t, rs_t, r20_t)$, there was $r=2$ cointegrating vectors and hence $k=2$ common trends. There can then be at most 2 common cycles. If s was 2, then the structural model (8.12) with $m = 2$ would take the form of two structural equations

$$\Delta p_t = -\phi_{13}^* \Delta rs_t - \phi_{14}^* \Delta r20_t + \nu_{1t}$$
$$\Delta d_t = -\phi_{23}^* \Delta rs_t - \phi_{24}^* \Delta r20_t + \nu_{2t}$$

say, and two unrestricted reduced form equations for the other two variables, Δrs_t and $\Delta r20_t$, which imposes a total of 8 restrictions. The restricted reduced form (8.13) replaces the above two structural equations with reduced form equations in which the coefficients are linear combinations of $\mathbf{\Phi}_1^*$ and $\boldsymbol{\beta}^*$, the weights being given by (minus) the $\boldsymbol{\phi}^*$ coefficients.

Table 8.1 provides the common feature test statistics, from which we see that s is zero, so that no common feature exists. The estimated common feature in the pseudo-structural model (8.13) with $s = 1$ takes the form, after the deletion of insignificant coefficients

$$\boldsymbol{\phi}_1 \Delta \mathbf{z}_t = \Delta p_t - 0.007 + 0.587 \Delta r20_t$$

However, a property of common features is that they should be orthogonal to past information. We find that $\boldsymbol{\phi}_1 \Delta \mathbf{z}_t$ is correlated with the 'confidence' error correction $e_{1,t-1}^*$, which thus explains the rejection of any common cycle in table 8.1 and implies that there is a codependent feature of order 1.

8.3 Estimating permanent and transitory components of a VECM

The presence of cointegration implies that the vector $\mathbf{z}_t$ may be thought of as being 'driven' by a smaller number of common trends or *permanent components* but, as we have seen, an important issue is whether such components can be identified. While there have been several identification schemes proposed, we focus here on achieving identification through the permanent-transitory decomposition of Gonzalo and Granger (1995). Consider again the VECM

Table 8.1. *Common cycle tests*

Null	$C(p, s)$	df	p-value
$s > 0$	19.85	3	0.000
$s > 1$	54.60	8	0.000

$$\Delta \mathbf{z}_t = \mathbf{\Phi}(B)\Delta \mathbf{z}_{t-1} + \boldsymbol{\beta}\boldsymbol{\alpha}'\mathbf{z}_{t-1} + \mathbf{v}_t \tag{8.14}$$

As in (8.10), $\mathbf{z}_t$ can be explained in terms of a smaller number, $k = n - r$, of $I(1)$ variables, which we now refer to generally as common factors and denote $\mathbf{f}_t$, plus some $I(0)$ components, denoted $\tilde{\mathbf{z}}_t$

$$\mathbf{z}_t = \mathbf{G}_1\mathbf{f}_t + \tilde{\mathbf{z}}_t \tag{8.15}$$

The first identification condition is that the common factors $\mathbf{f}_t$ are linear combinations of $\mathbf{z}_t$

$$\mathbf{f}_t = \mathbf{J}\mathbf{z}_t$$

so that

$$\tilde{\mathbf{z}}_t = (\mathbf{I}_n - \mathbf{G}_1\mathbf{J})\mathbf{z}_t = \mathbf{G}_2\boldsymbol{\alpha}'\mathbf{z}_t$$

for some appropriately defined matrix $\mathbf{G}_2$. The second identification condition is that $\tilde{\mathbf{z}}_t$ does not Granger-cause $\mathbf{G}_1\mathbf{f}_t$ in the long run: see Gonzalo and Granger (1995, definition 1) for further details and Granger and Lin (1995) for a formal definition of long-run Granger causality. This implies that, in the VAR representation of $(\Delta\mathbf{f}_t, \tilde{\mathbf{z}}_t)$

$$\begin{bmatrix} \mathbf{H}_{11}(B) & \mathbf{H}_{12}(B) \\ \mathbf{H}_{21}(B) & \mathbf{H}_{22}(B) \end{bmatrix} \begin{bmatrix} \Delta\mathbf{f}_t \\ \tilde{\mathbf{z}}_t \end{bmatrix} = \begin{bmatrix} \mathbf{u}_{1t} \\ \mathbf{u}_{2t} \end{bmatrix}$$

the total multiplier of $\Delta\mathbf{f}_t$ with respect to $\tilde{\mathbf{z}}_t$ is zero, i.e., $\mathbf{H}_{12}(1) = \mathbf{0}$. Now premultiplying (8.14) by $\mathbf{J}$, and noting that $\mathbf{J}\Delta\mathbf{z}_t = \Delta\mathbf{f}_t$ and $\boldsymbol{\alpha}'\mathbf{z}_t = \mathbf{G}_2^{-1}\tilde{\mathbf{z}}_t$, yields

$$\begin{bmatrix} \mathbf{I}_n - \mathbf{\Phi}(B) & \mathbf{J}\boldsymbol{\beta}\mathbf{G}_2^{-1}B \\ \mathbf{H}_{21}(B) & \mathbf{H}_{22}(B) \end{bmatrix} \begin{bmatrix} \Delta\mathbf{f}_t \\ \tilde{\mathbf{z}}_t \end{bmatrix} = \begin{bmatrix} \mathbf{J}\mathbf{v}_t \\ \mathbf{u}_{2t} \end{bmatrix}$$

so that the condition $\mathbf{H}_{12}(1) = \mathbf{0}$ is satisfied if $\mathbf{J} = \boldsymbol{\beta}'_\perp$ (recall that $\boldsymbol{\beta}'_\perp\boldsymbol{\beta} = \mathbf{0}$). Note that $\mathbf{J}\Delta\mathbf{z}_t$ then has the 'common feature' of not containing the error correction $\mathbf{e}_{t-1}$. Substituting these two identifying conditions into (8.15) yields

$$\mathbf{I}_n = \mathbf{G}_1\boldsymbol{\beta}'_\perp + \mathbf{G}_2\boldsymbol{\alpha}'$$

or

$$\begin{bmatrix} \mathbf{G}_1 \\ \mathbf{G}_2 \end{bmatrix} = [\boldsymbol{\beta}'_\perp, \boldsymbol{\alpha}']^{-1}$$

i.e.

$$\mathbf{G}_1 = \boldsymbol{\alpha}_\perp\left(\boldsymbol{\beta}'_\perp\boldsymbol{\alpha}_\perp\right)^{-1}, \quad \mathbf{G}_2 = \boldsymbol{\beta}\left(\boldsymbol{\alpha}'\boldsymbol{\beta}\right)^{-1}$$

The Gonzalo–Granger decomposition (8.14) and the Stock–Watson representation (8.9) are closely linked: the Stock–Watson common trend is the random walk component of the Gonzalo–Granger common factor $\mathbf{f}_t$ and, since they differ only by $I(0)$ components, they will be cointegrated.

The Gonzalo–Granger decomposition can be computed as long as we have available an estimate of $\boldsymbol{\beta}_\perp$, $\hat{\boldsymbol{\beta}}_\perp$ say, for then we have $\hat{\mathbf{f}}_t = \hat{\boldsymbol{\beta}}'_\perp\mathbf{z}_t$ and

$$\hat{\mathbf{G}}_1 = \left(\mathbf{I}_n - \hat{\mathbf{G}}_2\hat{\boldsymbol{\alpha}}'\right)\hat{\boldsymbol{\beta}}_\perp\left(\hat{\boldsymbol{\beta}}'_\perp\hat{\boldsymbol{\beta}}_\perp\right)^{-1}$$

where $\hat{\mathbf{G}}_2 = \hat{\boldsymbol{\beta}}\left(\hat{\boldsymbol{\alpha}}'\hat{\boldsymbol{\beta}}\right)^{-1}$. As Gonzalo and Granger (1995) point out, there is a duality between $\boldsymbol{\beta}_\perp$ and $\boldsymbol{\alpha}$, so that an estimate of $\boldsymbol{\beta}_\perp$ can be obtained by solving an eigenvalue problem that is related to that which provides the estimate of $\boldsymbol{\alpha}$. Gonzalo and Granger (1995, theorem 1) show that the ML estimator of $\boldsymbol{\beta}_\perp$ is obtained by solving the set of equations

$$\left(\lambda_i\mathbf{S}_{00} - \mathbf{S}_{01}\mathbf{S}_{11}^{-1}\mathbf{S}_{10}\right)\mathbf{m}_i = 0$$

which yields the same eigenvalues as solving (7.29) but the eigenvectors $\mathbf{M} = (\hat{\mathbf{m}}_1, \ldots, \hat{\mathbf{m}}_n)$ normalised such that $\mathbf{M}'\mathbf{S}_{00}\mathbf{M} = \mathbf{I}$. The estimate is then $\hat{\boldsymbol{\beta}}_\perp = \left(\hat{\mathbf{m}}_{r+1}, \ldots, \hat{\mathbf{m}}_n\right)$.

Example 8.3 A permanent and transitory decomposition of the UK financial markets

With the VECM(2,1,2) model, the four series will be functions of $k = 2$ common factors, which are given by

$$\begin{bmatrix} f_{1t} \\ f_{2t} \end{bmatrix} = \hat{\boldsymbol{\beta}}'_\perp\mathbf{z}_t = \begin{bmatrix} 8.086 & 45.736 & 11.092 & 10.171 \\ 10.535 & 23.343 & -1.375 & -16.333 \end{bmatrix} y_t$$

The permanent components are then given by

$$\mathbf{z}_t^p = \mathbf{G}_1\mathbf{f}_t = \mathbf{G}_1\hat{\boldsymbol{\beta}}'_\perp\mathbf{z}_t = \begin{bmatrix} 0.426 & 0.992 & -0.035 & -0.621 \\ 0.163 & 0.675 & 0.116 & 0.005 \\ -0.039 & 0.805 & 0.394 & 0.788 \\ -0.222 & -0.232 & 0.143 & 0.558 \end{bmatrix}\mathbf{z}_t$$

Figure 8.2 shows the permanent components of p and d superimposed on the actual series and the two (standardised) transitory components plotted together. The permanent components act essentially as trends, while the transitory components are almost mirror images of each other, the correlation between them being -0.67. Figure 8.3 shows the permanent components of rs and $r20$ superimposed on the actual series, and here there are pronounced and prolonged divergences between permanent and actual: in particular, note the large divergences for $r20$ in the early 1970s and for rs during the 1990s.

8.4 Present value models, excess volatility and cointegration

8.4.1 Present value models and the 'simple' efficient markets hypothesis

As remarked in chapter 1, present value models are extremely popular in finance as they are often used to formulate models of efficient markets. Written generally, a present value model for two variables, y_t and x_t, states that y_t is a linear function of the present discounted value of the expected future values of x_t

$$y_t = \phi(1-\delta)\sum_{i=0}^{\infty} \delta^{i+1} E\left(x_{t+i}\middle|\Phi_t\right) + c \tag{8.16}$$

where c, the constant, ϕ, the coefficient of proportionality, and δ, the constant discount factor, are parameters that may be known a priori or may need to be estimated. As usual, $E\left(x_{t+i}\middle|\Phi_t\right)$ is the expectation of x_{t+i} conditional on the information set available at time t, Φ_t.

A simple example of how (8.16) might arise is to consider an implication of the efficient markets hypothesis, that stock returns, r_t, are unforecastable. This can be formalised as $E\left(r_{t+1}\middle|\Phi_t\right) = r$, where r is a constant, sometimes referred to as the discount rate (see Shiller, 1981a, 1981b). If y_t is the beginning of period t stock price and x_t the dividend paid during the period, then

$$r_{t+1} = (y_{t+1} - y_t + x_t)/y_t$$

so that we can express y_t as the first-order rational expectations model of the form

$$y_t = \delta E\left(y_{t+1}\middle|\Phi_t\right) + \delta E\left(x_t\middle|\Phi_t\right) \tag{8.17}$$

where $\delta = 1/(1+r)$. This can be solved by recursive substitution to yield

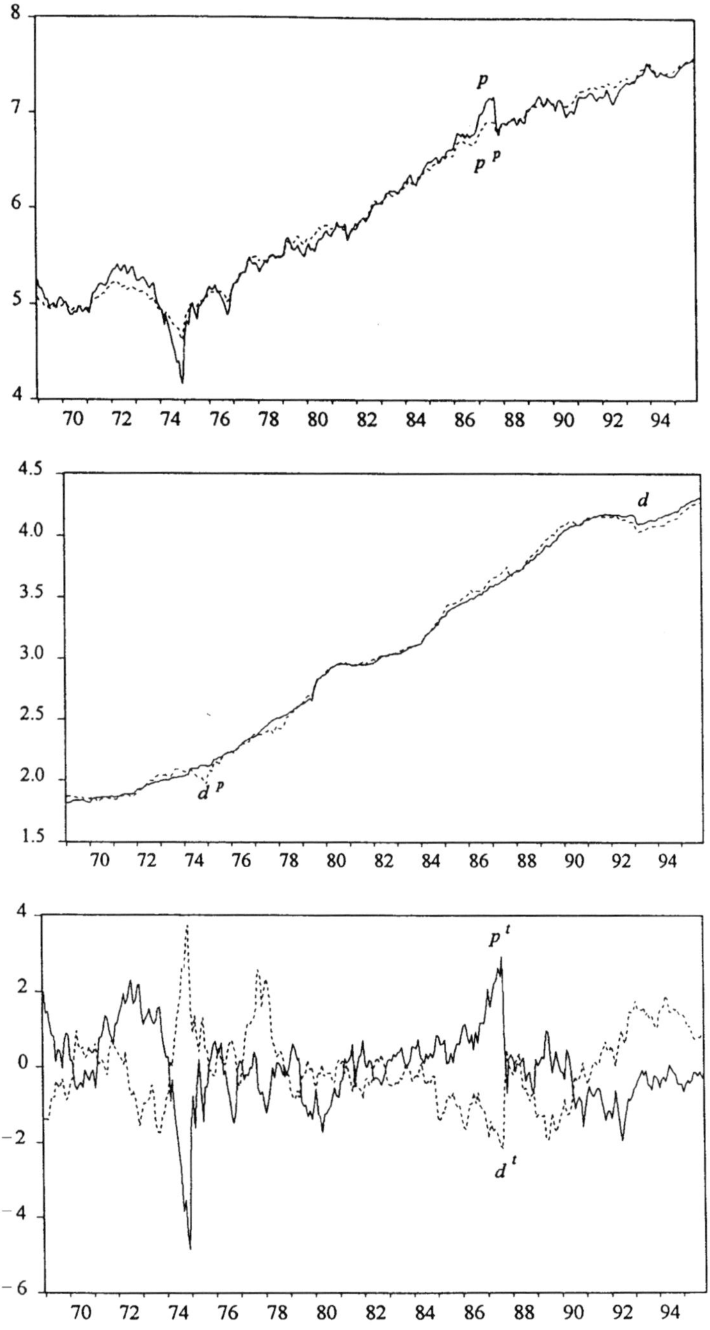

Figure 8.2 Permanent and transitory components of stock prices and dividends

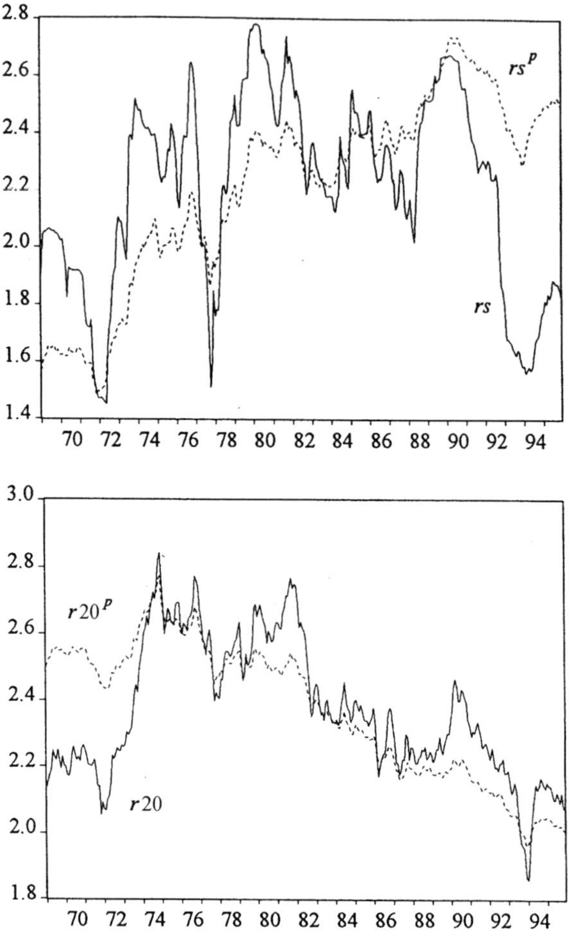

Figure 8.3 Interest rate permanent components

$$y_t = \sum_{i=0}^{n} \delta^{i+1} E\left(x_{t+i}|\Phi_t\right) + \delta^n E\left(y_{t+n}|\Phi_t\right) \tag{8.18}$$

If we impose the terminal (or transversality) condition that the second term in (8.18) goes to zero as $n \to \infty$, the present value relation (8.16) is obtained with $c = 0$ and $\phi = 1/(1-\delta) = (1+r)/r$.

Typically, y_t and x_t will be $I(1)$ processes, so Campbell and Shiller (1987, 1988a) consider subtracting $(\delta/(1-\delta))x_t$ from both sides of (8.18). On defining $\theta = \delta/(1-\delta) = 1/r$ and rearranging, we obtain a new variable, S_t, which Campbell and Shiller (1987) term the 'spread'

$$S_t = y_t - \theta x_t = \phi \sum\nolimits_{i=1}^{\infty} \delta^i E(\Delta x_{t+i} | \Phi_t) \tag{8.19}$$

If y_t and x_t are $I(1)$, then it follows from (8.19) that S_t must be $I(0)$, which in turn implies that y_t and x_t are cointegrated with cointegrating parameter θ. Consequently, S_t and Δx_t must together form a jointly covariance stationary process, which can be approximated in finite samples by a bivariate VAR(m) process

$$\begin{aligned} S_t &= \sum\nolimits_{i=1}^{m} a_i S_{t-i} + \sum\nolimits_{i=1}^{m} b_i \Delta x_{t-i} + \nu_{1t} \\ \Delta x_t &= \sum\nolimits_{i=1}^{m} c_i S_{t-i} + \sum\nolimits_{i=1}^{m} d_i \Delta x_{t-i} + \nu_{2t} \end{aligned} \tag{8.20}$$

It is convenient to rewrite (8.20) in *companion form*, i.e., as

$$\begin{bmatrix} S_t \\ S_{t-1} \\ \vdots \\ S_{t-m+1} \\ \Delta x_t \\ \Delta x_{t-1} \\ \vdots \\ \Delta x_{t-m+1} \end{bmatrix} = \begin{bmatrix} a_1 & \cdots & a_{m-1} & a_m & b_1 & \cdots & b_{m-1} & b_m \\ 1 & & & & & & & \\ & \ddots & & & & & & \\ & & 1 & 0 & & & & \\ c_1 & \cdots & c_{m-1} & c_m & d_1 & \cdots & d_{m-1} & d_m \\ & & & & 1 & & & \\ & & & & & \ddots & & \\ & & & & & & 1 & 0 \end{bmatrix} \begin{bmatrix} S_{t-1} \\ S_{t-2} \\ \vdots \\ S_{t-m} \\ \Delta x_{t-1} \\ \Delta x_{t-2} \\ \vdots \\ \Delta x_{t-m} \end{bmatrix} + \begin{bmatrix} \nu_{1t} \\ 0 \\ \vdots \\ 0 \\ \nu_{2t} \\ 0 \\ \vdots \\ 0 \end{bmatrix}$$

where blank elements are zero. This can be written more compactly, in an obvious notation, as

$$\mathbf{z}_t = \mathbf{\Pi} \mathbf{z}_{t-1} + \mathbf{v}_t \tag{8.21}$$

We can use the first-order formulation (8.21) to express the variant of the present value model presented as equation (8.19) in closed form solution, i.e., as a function of variables known to agents at the time expectations are formed. If we restrict the information set to consist only of current and lagged S_t and Δx_t, i.e., $\Phi_t^* = (S_t^0, \Delta x_t^0)$, using the notation introduced in chapter 6, then the conditional expectation of future values of $\mathbf{z}_t$, conditional on Φ_t^*, is

$$E(\mathbf{z}_{t+i} | \Phi_t^*) = \mathbf{\Pi}^i \mathbf{z}_t$$

Define $\mathbf{g}$ as a $(2m \times 1)$ selection vector with unity as the first element and zeros elsewhere, and $\mathbf{h}$ as another selection vector with unity as the $(m+1)$-th element and zeros elsewhere, so that $S_t = \mathbf{g}'\mathbf{z}_t$, $\Delta x_t = \mathbf{h}'\mathbf{z}_t$, and

$$E(\Delta x_{t+i}|\Phi_t^*) = E(\mathbf{h}'\mathbf{z}_{t+i}|\Phi_t^*) = \mathbf{h}'\mathbf{\Pi}^i\mathbf{z}_t$$

Equation (8.19) can then be written as

$$\mathbf{g}'\mathbf{z}_t = \theta\mathbf{h}'\left(\sum_{i=1}^{\infty} \delta^i\mathbf{\Pi}^i\right)\mathbf{z}_t = \theta\mathbf{h}'\delta\mathbf{\Pi}(\mathbf{I} - \delta\mathbf{\Pi})^{-1}\mathbf{z}_t \tag{8.22}$$

which is a closed-form variant of the present value model. The advantage of this formulation is that it imposes the model's restrictions on the coefficients of the VAR, since if (8.22) is to hold non-trivially, the following $2m$ restrictions must hold

$$\mathbf{g}' - \theta\mathbf{h}'\delta\mathbf{\Pi}(\mathbf{I} - \delta\mathbf{\Pi})^{-1} = \mathbf{0} \tag{8.23}$$

Although these restrictions appear complex and hard to interpret, for a given δ, and hence θ, they turn out to be equivalent to the following set of linear restrictions

$$\begin{aligned} &1 - \delta a_1 - \theta\delta c_1 = 0 \\ &a_i + \theta c_i = 0, i = 2, \ldots, m \\ &b_i + \theta d_i = 0, i = 2, \ldots, m \end{aligned} \tag{8.24}$$

These restrictions can be interpreted as follows. The present value model implies that, from (8.17)

$$E(y_t - \delta^{-1}y_{t-1} + x_{t-1}|\Phi_t^*) = 0 \tag{8.25}$$

or, equivalently

$$E(y_t|\Phi_t^*) = \delta^{-1}y_{t-1} - x_{t-1}$$

so that $\delta^{-1}y_{t-1} - x_{t-1}$ is an optimal predictor of y_t. Since

$$E(y_t|\Phi_t^*) = (1 + r)y_{t-1} - x_{t-1}$$

we also have that

$$E\big(\big((y_t - y_{t-1} + x_{t-1})/y_{t-1}\big)|\Phi_t^*\big) - r = 0$$

i.e., that excess expected returns are zero. In terms of S_t and Δx_t, this can be written as

$$E(S_t - \delta^{-1}S_{t-1} + \theta\Delta x_t | \Phi_t^*) = 0$$

or

$$E(S_t | \Phi_t^*) = \delta^{-1}S_{t-1} - \theta\Delta x_t \tag{8.26}$$

Using the VAR formulation (8.20), we have

$$\begin{aligned}E(S_t - \delta^{-1}S_{t-1} + \theta\Delta x_{t-1} | \Phi_t^*) = &\sum\nolimits_{i=1}^{m} (a_i + \theta c_i)S_{t-i} \\ &+ \sum\nolimits_{i=1}^{m} (b_i + \theta d_i)\Delta x_{t-i}\end{aligned}$$

which is identically equal to zero under the restrictions (8.24).

A further implication of the present value model for the VAR (8.20) is that S_t must Granger-cause Δx_t unless S_t is itself an *exact* linear function of $\{x_t^0\}$. This is because S_t is an optimal forecast of a weighted sum of future values of Δx_t conditional on Φ_t (recall equation (8.19)). S_t will therefore have incremental explanatory power for future Δx_t if agents have information useful for forecasting Δx_t beyond $\{x_t^0\}$: if not, they form S_t as an exact linear function of $\{x_t^0\}$.

Following Campbell and Shiller (1987), we can also use these restrictions to construct 'volatility tests' of the model. If the 'theoretical spread', S_t^*, is defined as

$$S_t^* = \phi \sum\nolimits_{i=1}^{\infty} \delta^i E(\Delta x_{t+i} | \Phi_t^*) = \theta \mathbf{h}' \delta \mathbf{\Pi} (\mathbf{I} - \delta \mathbf{\Pi})^{-1} \mathbf{z}_t$$

then, if the present value model is correct, we have from (8.19)

$$S_t^* = S_t$$

and hence

$$V(S_t^*) = V(S_t)$$

This equality provides a way of assessing the model informally by examining the comovement of $V(S_t^*)$ and $V(S_t)$. In particular, if the model is correct, the ratio $V(S_t)/V(S_t^*)$ should differ from unity only because of sampling error in the estimated coefficients of the VAR.

Campbell and Shiller (1987) also suggest a second volatility test in addition to this 'levels variance ratio'. Denoting the innovation associated with (8.26) as

$$\xi_t = S_t - \delta^{-1} S_{t-1} + \theta \Delta x_t$$

the 'theoretical innovation' can be defined analogously as

$$\xi_t^* = S_t^* - \delta^{-1} S_{t-1}^* + \theta \Delta x_t$$

Under the present value model, $\xi_t^* = \xi_t$ since $S_t^* = S_t$, so that the 'innovation variance ratio', $V(\xi_t)/V(\xi_t^*)$, should again be compared with unity.

The interpretation of (8.16) as the present value of a stock price given the future dividend stream relies on y_t and x_t being the *levels* of prices and dividends, respectively. If dividends grow at a constant rate $g < r$ then

$$E(x_{t+i}|\Phi_t) = (1+g)^i x_t$$

and

$$E(\Delta x_{t+i}|\Phi_t) = (1+g)^{i-1} g x_t$$

so that (8.19) becomes

$$S_t = \frac{(1+r)g}{r(r-g)} x_t \tag{8.27}$$

which is clearly no longer $I(0)$. However, since (8.27) implies that

$$y_t = \frac{(1+g)}{(r-g)} x_t = \frac{1}{(r-g)} x_{t+1} \tag{8.28}$$

the 'full spread'

$$Sf_t = y_t - \frac{(1+g)}{(r-g)} x_t = y_t - \frac{1}{(r-g)} x_{t+1}$$

will be $I(0)$. Equation (8.28) can be written as

$$\log(y_t) - \log(x_t) = \kappa$$

where $\kappa = (1+g)/(r-g)$, so that, when expressed in logarithms, prices and dividends are cointegrated with a unit cointegrating parameter. This representation leads to the 'dividend-ratio' form of the model developed in section 8.4.3.

8.4.2 *Rational bubbles*

These tests of the present value model have all been based on the assumption that the transversality condition in equation (8.18) holds, i.e., that

$$\lim_{n\to\infty} \delta^n E\left(y_{t+n}\middle|\Phi_t\right) = 0$$

If this is the case, then $y_t = y_t^f$, where y_t^f is the unique forward solution, often termed the 'market fundamentals' solution

$$y_t^f = \sum_{i=0}^{\infty} \delta^{i+1} E\left(x_{t+i}\middle|\Phi_t\right)$$

If this transversality condition fails to hold, however, there will be a family of solutions to (8.17): see, for example, Blanchard and Watson (1982), West (1987) and Diba and Grossman (1987, 1988). In such circumstances, any y_t that satisfies

$$y_t = y_t^f + B_t$$

where

$$E\left(B_{t+1}\middle|\Phi_t\right) = \delta^{-1} B_t = (1+r)B_t \tag{8.29}$$

is also a solution. B_t is known as a *speculative*, or *rational*, *bubble*, an otherwise extraneous event that affects y_t because everyone expects it to do so, i.e., it is a self-fulfilling expectation. An example of such a bubble is (see Blanchard and Watson, 1982, and West, 1987)

$$B_t = \begin{cases} \left(B_{t-1} - \bar{B}\right)/\pi\delta & \text{with probability } \pi \\ \bar{B}/(1-\pi)\delta & \text{with probability } 1-\pi \end{cases} \tag{8.30}$$

where $0 < \pi < 1$ and $\bar{B} > 0$ (other examples are provided by, for example, Hamilton, 1986). According to (8.30), strictly positive bubbles grow and burst, with the probability that the bubble bursts being $1 - \pi$. While the bubble floats it grows at rate $(\delta\pi)^{-1} = (1+r)/\pi > 1 + r$: investors in the asset thus receive an extraordinary return to compensate them for the capital loss that would have occurred had the bubble burst.

Equation (8.29) implies that the rational bubble has explosive conditional expectations, since

$$E\left(B_{t+i}\middle|\Phi_t\right) = (1+r)^i B_t$$

and $r > 0$. Thus, if y_t is the price of a freely disposable asset, say a stock, then a negative rational bubble ($B_t < 0$) cannot exist, because its existence would imply that y_t decreases without bound at the geometric rate $(1+r)$, so that it becomes negative at some finite time $t+i$. Negative rational bubbles are, at least theoretically, possible if y_t is an exchange rate, for this characterises a continual currency appreciation.

While positive bubbles are theoretically possible, Diba and Grossman (1987, 1988) discuss a number of conditions that must be met for their existence. Positive bubbles imply that asset holders might expect such a bubble to come to dominate y_t, which would then bear little relation to market fundamentals. Bubbles would only be empirically plausible if, despite explosive conditional expectations, the probability is small that a rational bubble becomes arbitrarily large. Moreover, for exchange rates a positive bubble would imply a continual devaluation of the currency, and this can be ruled out by an argument symmetric to that used above for a negative rational bubble in stock prices.

Diba and Grossman also show that, if a rational bubble does not exist at time t, then it cannot get started at any later date $t+i$, $i > 0$, and that if an existing rational bubble bursts, a new independent rational bubble cannot simultaneously start. Thus, if a rational bubble exists at time t, then it must have started at time $t = 0$ (the first date of trading of the asset), it has not burst, it will not restart if it bursts and, if it is a bubble in a stock price, the stock has been continuously overvalued relative to market fundamentals.

The presence of bubbles can be tested for by examining their implications for cointegration between various series. When $y_t = y^f_t$, so that no bubbles are present, equation (8.25) implies that

$$U_{t+1} = y_t - \delta\left(y_{t+1} + x_t\right)$$

must be $I(0)$ and, as we have already shown, the spread $S_t = y_t - \theta x_t$ must also be $I(0)$, so that y_t must be cointegrated with both x_t and $y_{t+1} + x_t$ (it must also be the case that Δy_t is $I(0)$). If, on the other hand, a bubble is present, so that $y_t = y^f_t + B_t$, the bubble must appear in both U_t and S_t. Since, by definition, B_t is non-stationary, these variables cannot be $I(0)$ and the cointegration relationships cannot hold.

Hamilton and Whiteman (1985) discuss these implications in more detail, showing that, if $x_t \sim I(d)$, then rational bubbles can only exist if $y_t \sim I(d+b)$, where $b > 0$. However, the finding that y_t is of a higher order of integration than x_t is not necessarily evidence in favour of bubbles. As Hamilton and Whiteman point out, such a finding might be explained by numerous other factors: what appears to be a bubble could have arisen instead from rational agents responding solely to fundamentals not observed by the modeller.

One further important drawback with tests of stationarity and cointegration is the question of power. Diba (1990), for example, argues that if $\bar{B}$ in (8.30) is sufficiently close to zero, the ensuing bubble would generate fluctuations in a finite sample that could not be distinguished from stationary behaviour. Meese (1986) provides both simulation and empirical evidence on exchange rate bubbles that is consistent with this.

Example 8.4 Testing stock market volatility

Campbell and Shiller (1987) employ the 'cointegration approach' to test the present value model for annual data on the real *S&P Composite* price index (y_t) and the associated dividend index (x_t) from 1871 to 1986. As a preliminary, unit root tests are needed to ensure that both y_t and x_t are $I(1)$: this was indeed found to be the case. Less conclusive evidence was presented that the spread was stationary, which would imply that y_t and x_t are cointegrated (in practice Campbell and Shiller use $SL_t = y_t - \theta x_{t-1}$ rather than S_t to avoid timing problems caused by the use of beginning-of-year stock prices and dividends paid within-year).

Nonetheless, assuming cointegration and using the cointegrating regression estimate of θ (an implied discount rate of 3.2 per cent), a second-order VAR was constructed for the bivariate (SL_t, Δx_t) process. The estimates suggested that dividend changes were highly predictable and there was strong evidence that the spread Granger-caused dividend changes, one implication of the present value model. The restrictions (8.24) could not be rejected at conventional significance levels, and neither were the two variance ratios significantly larger than unity.

Markedly different results were obtained, however, when the sample mean return was used to calculate a discount rate of 8.2 per cent. Now the restrictions (8.24) could be rejected at low significance levels and the two variance inequalities were sharply violated. Campbell and Shiller suggest that the implied discount rate of 3.2 per cent obtained from the cointegrating regression may be too low, which might be argued as being consistent with the argument that the cointegration parameter is estimating the discount rate κ^{-1} rather than r: nevertheless, although they prefer to use the higher discount rate of 8.2 per cent, which implies a 4.8 per cent growth in dividends and leads to excessive volatility, they do emphasise that the strength of the evidence depends sensitively on the assumed value of the discount rate.

Updating Mills (1993), we apply this technique to UK data on real stock prices and dividends, obtained by dividing the *FTA All Share* price and dividend series used in previous examples by the retail price index. The series are shown for the period January 1965 to December 1995 in figure 8.4. Following the Dickey and Pantula (1987) approach of chapter 3.1.8 to testing for more than one unit root, we confirm that both series are $I(1)$, thus ruling out the presence of rational bubbles.

Are the two series cointegrated? A unit root test on the residuals from the cointegrating regression of real prices on real dividends yields the statistic $C = -3.52$, which is significant at the 5 per cent level and, on estimating a VECM, a trace statistic $\eta_0 = 17.1$, which is significant at the 10 per cent level. Given this, albeit somewhat weak, evidence in favour of cointegration, we proceed by assuming that the series are cointegrated. The estimates of the cointegration parameter θ from the two approaches are 29.06 and 27.80, respectively, implying discount rates of 3.4 per cent and 3.6 per cent. Since the two estimates are so close to each other, we continue the analysis using just the former.

Fitting a fourth-order VAR of the form (8.11) leads to a Wald test statistic of the restrictions (8.24) taking the value $\chi_8^2 = 37.9$, which is clearly significant, thus rejecting the present value restrictions. A test of S_t Granger-causing Δx_t has a p-value of only 0.14, which is a violation of the present value model implication. The variance ratio inequalities are

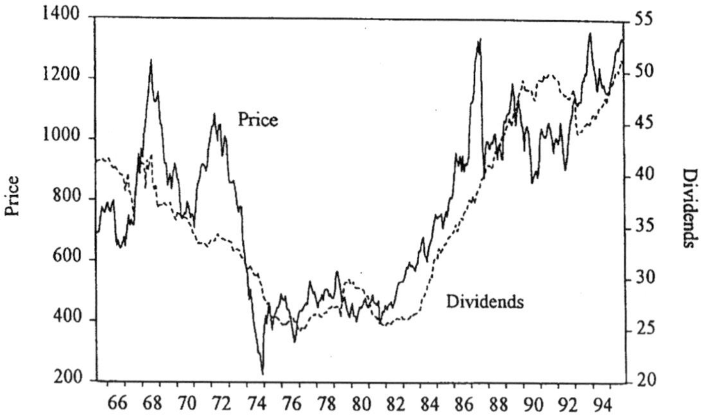

Figure 8.4 *FTA All Share* index: real prices and dividends (monthly 1965–95)

also sharply violated: $V(S_t)/V(S_t^*) = 17.2$ and $V(\xi_t)/V(\xi_t^*) = 5.3$. The implied excess volatility can readily be seen from figure 8.5, which plots S_t and S_t^*.

Example 8.5 Testing the expectations hypothesis of the term structure of interest rates

Shiller (1979) shows that the expectations hypothesis of the term structure of interest rates, that the current long rate is the weighted average of current and expected future short rates, can be put into the form of the present value model (8.16). In this framework, y_t is the current interest rate (the yield to maturity) on a long bond (strictly a perpetuity), x_t is the current one-period interest rate, θ is set to unity, δ is a parameter of linearisation, typically set equal to $(1+\bar{y})^{-1}$, and c is a liquidity premium unrestricted by the model.

The expectations hypothesis thus asserts that, if y_t and x_t are both $I(1)$, then the spread, $S_t = y_t - x_t$ (noting that $\theta = 1$), must be $I(0)$ and hence that y_t and x_t must be cointegrated with cointegrating vector $(1, -1)$. S_t and Δx_t then have the VAR representation (8.20) and the expectations hypothesis implies the restrictions given by equation (8.24), although the first of these can now be written as $a_1 + c_1 = 1 + \bar{y}$. Equation (8.25) now has the implication that the excess return on holding a long bond for one period, rather than a one-period bond, should be unpredictable.

Although this form of the expectations hypothesis is only strictly valid when the long rate is a perpetuity, it can still be used for bonds of finite,

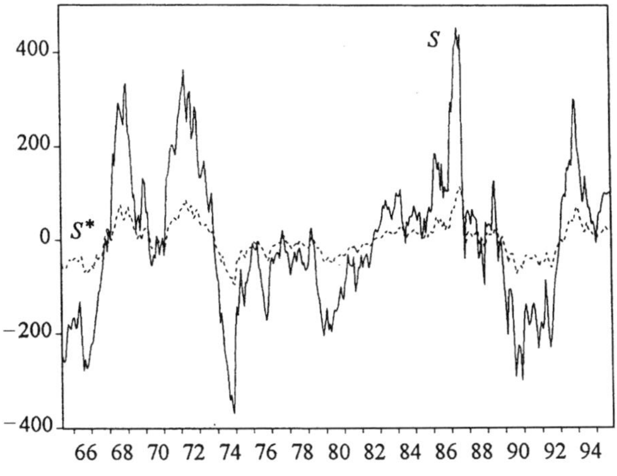

Figure 8.5 *FTA All Share* index: 'excess volatility' (monthly 1965–95)

but very long, life, e.g., twenty years. Campbell and Shiller (1987) thus test the model using monthly data on the yield on US Treasury twenty-year bonds and one-month Treasury bill rates for the period 1959 to 1983. Evidence is presented that the spread is stationary, but a test of the restrictions (8.24) rejects the expectations hypothesis very strongly. Nevertheless, the variance ratios are not significantly different from unity and the 'theoretical spread', S_t^*, is highly correlated with the actual spread, S_t. Campbell and Shiller interpret these conflicting findings as evidence that deviations from the present value model are only transitory and suggest that the model does, in fact, fit the data comparatively well.

Updating Mills (1991b), we consider here how the expectations hypothesis fits the UK interest rate data used in many previous examples. Because the short rate is the yield on 91 day (three-month) Treasury bills, we use quarterly, rather than monthly, data for the period 1952I to 1995IV, a total of $T = 176$ observations. The spread, shown in figure 8.6, is stationary, with an ADF test producing $\tau_\mu = -3.36$, which rejects a unit root at the 5 per cent level (note that we can carry out a unit root test directly on the spread, rather than test for cointegration between y_t and x_t, because the cointegration parameter is assumed to be $\theta = 1$ a priori).

A VAR(1) was then fitted to S_t and Δx_t, and imposing the two restrictions in (8.24) leads to the test statistic $\chi_2^2 = 12.39$, which is significant at the 0.5 per cent level. However, S_t Granger-causes Δx_t at the 2.5 per cent level and the variance ratio $V(S_t)/V(S_t^*)$ is only 3.9. The plot of the

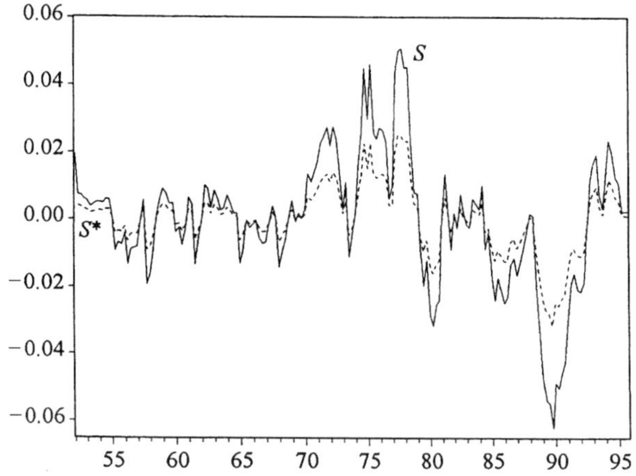

Figure 8.6 UK interest rate volatility (quarterly 1952–95)

theoretical spread S_t^*, also shown in figure 8.6, reveals that the two spreads move closely together, with the major divergence being in the late 1980s and early 1990s, when a succession of policy shocks inverted the yield curve, making the spread unusually negative. Apart from this period, the evidence in favour of using the present value model to analyse the setting of interest rates is surprisingly strong – indeed, it should be noted that in Mills (1991b), where the sample period ended in 1988, the restrictions could not be rejected and the variance ratio was in the region of 2.5.

8.4.3 The 'dividend-ratio model': a log-linear approximation to the present value model

As has been remarked on above, the present value model (8.16) when applied to stock prices is specified in terms of the levels of prices and dividends, and this may present statistical problems if these series grow exponentially. To incorporate such non-stationarity, Campbell and Shiller (1988c) focus attention on the *logarithmic* return. Recall the definition of the one-period return as, in this case

$$r_{t+1} = \left(P_{t+1} + D_t - P_t\right)/P_t = \left(P_{t+1} + D_t/P_t\right) - 1$$

Taking logarithms and using the approximation $r_{t+1} \cong \log\left(1 + r_{t+1}\right) = h_{1,t+1}$ yields

$$h_{1,t+1} = \log\left(P_{t+1} + D_t\right) - \log(P_t)$$

Campbell and Shiller examine the relationship between $h_{1,t+1}$ and the logarithms of dividends and prices, d_t and p_t. The relationship is non-linear, of course, but can be approximated as

$$h_{1,t+1} = k + \rho p_{t+1} + (1-\rho)d_t - p_t = k + \zeta_t - \rho\zeta_{t-1} + \Delta d_t \tag{8.31}$$

where $\zeta_t = d_{t-1} - p_t$ is the logarithmic 'dividend/price ratio' or dividend yield, ρ is the average of the ratio $P_t/(P_t + D_{t-1})$, and $k = -\log(\rho)$ $-(1-\rho)\log(1/\rho - 1)$: see Campbell and Shiller (1988b, 1988c) for details of the derivation of equation (8.31).

Equation (8.31) can be thought of as a difference equation relating ζ_t to ζ_{t-1}, Δd_t and $h_{1,t+1}$ and, on solving forwards and imposing the terminal condition that $\lim_{i\to\infty} \rho^i \zeta_{t+i} = 0$, we obtain

$$\zeta_t \cong \sum_{i=0}^{\infty} \rho^i \left(h_{1,t+i+1} - \Delta d_{t+i}\right) - \frac{k}{1-\rho} \tag{8.32}$$

As it stands, this equation has no economic content, since it simply says that ζ_t, the log dividend–price ratio, can be written as a discounted value of the differences between future returns and dividend growth rates discounted at the constant rate ρ, less a constant $k/(1-\rho)$. Suppose, however, that, as before, expected one-period returns are constant: $E\left(h_{1,t+1}|\Phi_t\right) = r$. Then, on taking conditional expectations of (8.32), we obtain

$$\zeta_t \cong -\sum_{i=0}^{\infty} \rho^i E\left(\Delta d_{t+i}|\Phi_t\right) + \frac{r-k}{1-\rho} \tag{8.33}$$

which expresses the log dividend–price ratio as a linear function of expected real dividend growth into the infinite future. The restrictions implicit in (8.33) can be tested using a framework analogous to that developed in section 8.4.2 above, noting that, in this context, ζ_t is the logarithmic counterpart of the spread $S_t = P_t - \theta D_t$. Thus we consider ζ_t and Δd_t to be generated by a VAR, which can be written in companion form as in equation (8.21) with $\mathbf{z}_t = (\zeta_t, \Delta d_t)'$. The implied solution to the present value model conditional on the restricted information set $\Phi_t^* = \left(\zeta_t^0, \Delta d_t^0\right)$ is then

$$\mathbf{g}'\mathbf{z}_t = -\mathbf{h}'\boldsymbol{\Pi}(\mathbf{I} - \rho\boldsymbol{\Pi})^{-1}\mathbf{z}_t$$

with the accompanying set of restrictions

$$\mathbf{g}' + \mathbf{h}'\boldsymbol{\Pi}(\mathbf{I} - \rho\boldsymbol{\Pi})^{-1} = \mathbf{0} \tag{8.34}$$

As with the analogous set (8.24), these restrictions imply that $E\left(h_{1,t+1}|\Phi_t^*\right) = 0$, so that returns are unpredictable. Moreover, as with the VAR of (8.21), a further implication of this model is that ζ_t should Granger-cause Δd_t.

Campbell and Shiller (1988c) argue that working with logarithms has certain advantages over the approach developed previously when testing the implications of the present value model for stock prices. One advantage is that it is easy to combine with individual log-linear models of prices and dividends which, as stressed by Kleidon (1986b), for example, are both more appealing on theoretical grounds and do appear to fit the data better than linear ones. A second advantage is that using the variables ζ_t and Δd_t mitigates measurement error problems that may occur when deflating nominal stock prices and dividends by some price index to obtain real variables.

The model has been extended in various ways. Campbell and Shiller (1988c) allow expected log returns to be given by the model $E(h_{1,t+1}|\Phi_t) = r + R_t$, where R_t is the real return on, for example, Treasury bills. In this case $R_{t+i} - \Delta d_{t+i}$ replaces $-\Delta d_{t+i}$ in equation (8.32) and $\mathbf{z}_t = (\zeta_t, R_t - \Delta d_t)'$ becomes the vector modelled as a VAR. Campbell and Shiller (1988b) focus attention on the j-period discounted return

$$h_{j,t} = \sum_{i=0}^{j-1} \rho^j h_{1,t+i}$$

which leads to the following set of restrictions on the VAR

$$\mathbf{g}'\left(\mathbf{I} - \rho^j \mathbf{\Pi}^j\right) + \mathbf{h}'\mathbf{\Pi}(\mathbf{I} - \rho\mathbf{\Pi})^{-1}\left(\mathbf{I} - \rho^j \mathbf{\Pi}^j\right) = 0$$

Although these restrictions are *algebraically* equivalent to those of (8.34) for all j, reflecting the fact that if one-period returns are unpredictable, then j-period returns must also be, and vice-versa, Wald tests may yield different results depending on which value of j is chosen. Nevertheless, the VAR framework confers yet another advantage in this setup: it needs to be estimated only once, as tests can be conducted for any j without reestimating the system.

Campbell and Shiller (1988b) also extend the VAR framework to incorporate a third variable, a long moving average of the earnings–price ratio, which is included as a potential predictor of stock returns. Campbell (1991), on the other hand, uses the model to analyse the unexpected component of returns, while Campbell and Shiller (1988a) concentrate on using the model to reinterpret the Marsh and Merton (1987) error-correction model of dividend behaviour in the context of a 'near-rational expectations' model in which dividends are persistent and prices are disturbed by persistent random noise.

Campbell and Shiller (1988b, 1988c) apply the dividend-ratio model to various data sets, including an updated Standard and Poor's. They find that the restrictions of the model tend to be rejected by the data and that the earnings variable is a powerful predictor of stock returns, particularly when returns are calculated over several years.

Example 8.6 The dividend-ratio model for UK equity prices

This model was applied to the UK data analysed in example 8.4. As a prerequisite, we require that ζ_t and Δd_t are stationary. Example 3.1 has shown that the presence of a unit root in the levels of the dividend yield can be rejected and a similar result occurs here for the logarithms:

an ADF test rejects a unit root at the 5 per cent level. That Δd_t is stationary has been reported in example 6.5. On fitting a VAR(3) to $\mathbf{z}_t = (\zeta_t, \Delta d_t)'$, we find that ζ_t does not Granger-cause Δd_t, the marginal significance level of the test being only 0.874.

A Wald test of the restrictions (8.34) is equivalent to a test that the coefficients in the regression of $h_{1,t+1}$ on lags of ζ_t and Δd_t are all zero, i.e., that returns are unforecastable. Computing $h_{1,t+1}$ using (8.31) with ρ estimated to be 0.954, yields the following regression

$$\begin{aligned} h_{1,t+1} = \underset{(0.044)}{0.069} + \underset{(0.055)}{0.171}\,\zeta_{t-1} - \underset{(0.081)}{0.286}\,\zeta_{t-2} + \underset{(0.055)}{0.123}\,\zeta_{t-3} \\ -\underset{(0.232)}{0.020}\,\Delta d_{t-1} + \underset{(0.231)}{0.362}\,\Delta d_{t-2} + \underset{(0.231)}{0.664}\,\Delta d_{t-3} \end{aligned}$$

The coefficients are jointly significant, rejecting the unforecastability null at the 0.1 per cent level and thus conclusively rejecting the dividend-ratio model for UK equity prices. Noting that the coefficients on the lags of ζ_t and Δd_t sum to approximately zero and unity respectively, the following restricted regression was obtained

$$h_{1,t+1} = \underset{(0.003)}{0.045} + \underset{(0.054)}{0.166}\,\Delta\zeta_{t-1} - \underset{(0.081)}{0.284}\,\Delta\zeta_{t-2} + \Delta d_{t-2} - \underset{(0.166)}{0.652}\,\Delta^2 d_{t-2}$$

thus showing that returns are in fact forecastable by past changes in the log dividend yield, past dividend growth, and the past *acceleration* in dividends, $\Delta^2 d_t$.

8.5 Generalisations and extensions of cointegration and error correction models

8.5.1 Non-linear generalisations

Given the tendency for financial time series to contain important non-linearities, it comes as no surprise that several models have been developed that generalise cointegration and error correction models in non-linear directions. These have taken two general forms: a linear cointegrating vector has been allowed to enter as a non-linear error correction, and the cointegrating relationship itself has been allowed to be non-linear. (Other extensions include the concept of fractional cointegration (Baillie and Bollerslev, 1993) and the use of non-linear stochastic trend models to define non-linear error corrections (Granger, Inoue and Morin, 1997).)

Granger and Swanson (1996) discuss examples of the former. Suppose we are modelling the $I(1)$ process $\mathbf{z}_t = (y_t, \mathbf{x}_t')'$ and there is the single cointegrating vector $e_t = \boldsymbol{\alpha}'\mathbf{z}_t$. Granger and Swanson suggest the simple non-linear error correction model in which, rather than e_{t-1} appearing, it is replaced by e_{t-1}^+ and e_{t-1}^-, defined as

$$e_{t-1}^+ = \begin{cases} e_{t-1} \text{ if } e_{t-1} \geq 0 \\ 0 \text{ otherwise} \end{cases}, \qquad e_{t-1}^- = e_{t-1} - e_{t-1}^+$$

A rather less 'ad hoc' generalisation follows from the interpretation of $\boldsymbol{\alpha}'\mathbf{z}_t = 0$ as an attractor or equilibrium, so that e_t is a measure of the extent to which the system is out of equilibrium. Thus, if the market 'prefers' e_t to be small, there must be costs associated with having non-zero values of e_t. The traditional approach is then to assume a quadratic cost function, in which case the linear error correction model is obtained (see Nickell, 1985). If the cost function is non-linear, perhaps because of transaction costs which prevent profitable arbitrage for small deviations from equilibrium, or because heterogeneity among arbitrageurs leads to differing transaction costs, then a non-linear error correction results, as, for example

$$g(\delta e_{t-1}) = (1 + \exp(-\delta e_{t-1}))^{-1} - \tfrac{1}{2}$$

Granger and Teräsvirta (1993), Yadav, Pope and Paudyal (1994), and Balke and Fomby (1997), for example, all consider threshold cointegration models, in which adjustment back towards equilibrium only takes place when the deviation from equilibrium exceeds a critical threshold. This could occur because fixed costs of adjustment may prevent continuous adjustment: in an efficient financial market, for example, the presence of transaction costs may create a band in which asset returns are free to diverge and in which arbitrage possibilities exist. These models are easily extended to incorporate a smooth transition from independence to cointegration. As an alternative, a bilinear error correction has been proposed by Peel and Davidson (1998), which may be more suitable for modelling time-varying risk premia that undergo abrupt changes.

There have also been various attempts to estimate non-linear error correction models using neural networks. For further discussion and examples, see Haefke and Helmenstein (1996) and Markellos (1997). The latter proposes a phase space analysis framework which, in the spirit of earlier work by Granger and Hallman (1991), relates cointegration and error correction to attractors through two new concepts, *equilibration* and *transient correction*. Equilibration requires the use of non-linear VARs defined in phase space, while testing procedures for equilibration are very similar to those used in standard cointegration analysis.

Example 8.7 Non-linear error correction in the UK financial markets

In examples 7.3 and 7.4 we uncovered evidence that, at least for the years 1969 to 1995, the error correction $e_t = p_t - d_t + r20_t + \gamma$ provides the link between the UK gilt and equity markets. Figure 8.7 provides a plot of this series (with $\gamma = -\bar{e}$) for the longer sample period of 1952 to 1995. It is clear that the series is non-stationary before 1969, probably because of various restrictions and controls that were imposed on interest rates and dividends during these years. This is confirmed by the estimated 'linear single equation ECM'

$$\Delta p_t = \underset{(0.002)}{0.006} + \underset{(0.126)}{0.269}\,\Delta d_t - \underset{(0.075)}{0.490}\,\Delta r20_t - \underset{(0.005)}{0.009}\,e_{t-1}$$

$$+ \underset{(0.043)}{0.071}\,\Delta p_{t-1} - \underset{(0.042)}{0.099}\,\Delta p_{t-2} + \underset{(0.042)}{0.095}\,\Delta p_{t-3}$$

in which the error correction is barely significant at the 10 per cent level. However, replacing e_{t-1} with e_{t-1}^{+} produces

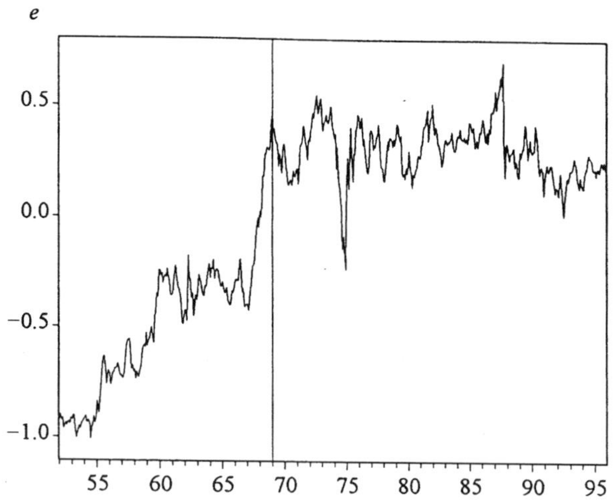

Figure 8.7 The error correction $e_t = p_t - d_t + r20_t + \gamma$ for 1952–95 (monthly)

$$\Delta p_t = \underset{(0.003)}{0.012} + \underset{(0.126)}{0.286}\ \Delta d_t - \underset{(0.074)}{0.497}\ \Delta r20_t - \underset{(0.013)}{0.034}\ e^+_{t-1}$$

$$+ \underset{(0.043)}{0.077}\ \Delta p_{t-1} - \underset{(0.042)}{0.093}\ \Delta p_{t-2} + \underset{(0.042)}{0.099}\ \Delta p_{t-3}$$

in which the non-linear error correction now enters significantly at the 1 per cent level, with all other parameter estimates remaining essentially unaltered. Using the cumulative logistic function $g(\delta e_{t-1})$ rather than e^+_{t-1} yields

$$\Delta p_t = \underset{(0.127)}{0.263}\ \Delta d_t - \underset{(0.075)}{0.491}\ \Delta r20_t - \underset{(0.005)}{0.012}\ g\left(\hat{\delta} e_{t-1}\right)$$

$$+ \underset{(0.043)}{0.071}\ \Delta p_{t-1} - \underset{(0.042)}{0.099}\ \Delta p_{t-2} + \underset{(0.042)}{0.095}\ \Delta p_{t-3}$$

where $\hat{\delta} = -2.82$ and, once again, this non-linear error correction is significant at the 1 per cent level. The within-sample fits of the three models are roughly the same, but on reestimating them over the shorter sample ending in 1990 and forecasting the remaining five years, we find that the two non-linear models produce smaller root mean squared forecast errors than the linear model.

8.5.2 Testing for cointegration with infinite variance errors and structural breaks

In chapter 5 we presented considerable evidence that returns distributions were usually fat tailed and may have infinite variance, and discussed briefly the impact of such an assumption on unit root tests for individual series. Caner (1998) considers the impact of infinite variance errors on both the residual-based tests of cointegration proposed by Phillips and Ouliaris (1990) and the VECM reduced rank likelihood tests associated with Johansen (1995). Assuming that the errors are stable, rather than normal, results in statistics that are functionals of stable processes rather than functionals of Brownian motion, and which depend on the value taken by the tail index as well as the number of variables in the system. Critical values are larger (in absolute value) than the conventional critical values, so that the size distortions induced by incorrectly assuming normality will lead to over-rejection of the null of no cointegration. However, Caner shows that these size distortions are only moderate for the residual-based tests, although they are more substantial for the trace and λ-max test statistics based on ML estimation of the VECM representation.

There have been several analyses looking at cointegration in the presence of structural shifts. Campos, Ericsson and Hendry (1996) consider the properties of several regression cointegration tests when one of the variables in the cointegrating relationship contains a structural break, finding that the break has little effect on the size of the tests but can affect their power when the data do not have a 'common factor', thus pointing towards the use of tests based on the ECM rather than on the cointegrating regression (recall chapter 7.3). Quintos and Phillips (1993) propose a recursive LM statistic to detect breaks in the cointegrating vector, while Quintos (1997) develops an extension of the fluctuation test, introduced in chapter 6.3.3, to examine both parameter and rank stability in VECMs. Other tests have been analysed by Gregory and Hansen (1996) and Gregory, Nason and Watt (1996).

Siklos and Granger (1997) look at the problem of structural breaks in cointegrating relationships from an alternative perspective: their argument is that an empirical finding of non-cointegration could be a consequence of external shocks or structural breaks which interrupt the underlying equilibrium relationship, perhaps for an extended period of time. This leads them to define the concept of *temporary cointegration*, in which the cointegrating relationship can be switched on or off depending on the nature of the policy regime that is in place.

8.5.3 Analysing large data sets

The availability of extremely large data sets containing high frequency, 'tic-by-tic', observations on prices in the foreign exchange and stock markets has led to great interest in using this type of data to answer questions concerning the understanding of market behaviour and micro market structure and to test economically interesting hypotheses over short time intervals. The econometric analysis of such time series raises many questions concerning the appropriate statistical approach to take when dealing with this type of data: for example, not all of the data are equally informative and decisions have to be taken about how much of the data should be used. The choice of time interval is important here and whether or not to use calendar time or 'economic' time, as emphasised by Dacarogna *et al.* (1993) and extended by Müller *et al.* (1997).

Goodhart and O'Hara (1997) provide a wide-ranging survey of many of the key issues in using high frequency financial data. Many of the techniques discussed in this book remain applicable, albeit with some modification and extension, to the analysis of a single, or a small group of, high frequency time series. For example, Andersen and Bollerslev (1997) and Daníelsson and de Vries (1997) present modified ARMA–ARCH volatility persistence models and techniques for tail index estimation, respectively. One feature of high frequency data is that the observations tend not to arrive at equally spaced time intervals. Engle and Russell (1997) and de Jong and Nijman (1997) thus develop extensions of GARCH and regression models to analyse financial data with this property. There are, however, data sets beginning to appear that contain large numbers of variables across both agents and time – 'mega panels'. Granger (1998) presents an extremely interesting discussion of some of the econometric and statistical issues that necessarily arise in the analysis of such data sets, although such analysis is clearly in its infancy (see also Wegman, 1995, for a more general statistical discussion).

Data appendix

The following series can be obtained from *http://lboro.ac.uk/departments/ec/cup/*

RS: 91 day Treasury Bill rate, monthly, March 1952 to December 1995 (526 observations).

R20: Yield on 20 Year UK Gilts, monthly, March 1952 to December 1995 (526 observations).

RSQ: 91 day Treasury Bill rate, quarterly, 1952Q1 to 1995Q4 (176 observations).

R20Q: Yield on 20 Year UK Gilts, quarterly, 1952Q1 to 1995Q4 (176 observations).

RSQREAL: Real 91 day Treasury Bill rate, quarterly, 1952Q1 to 1995Q3 (175 observations).

FTAPRICE: *FTA All Share* price index, monthly, January 1965 to December 1995 (372 observations).

FTADIV: *FTA All Share* dividend index, monthly, January 1965 to December 1995 (372 observations).

FTARET: *FTA All Share* nominal returns, monthly, January 1965 to December 1995 (372 observations).

RPI: UK Retail Price Index, monthly, January 1965 to December 1995 (372 observations).

EXCHD: Dollar/sterling exchange rate, daily, 1974 to 1994 (5192 observations).

EXCHQ: Dollar/sterling exchange rate, quarterly, 1972Q1 to 1996Q4 (100 observations).

S&P500: *S&P 500* index, annual, 1871 to 1997 (127 observations).

S&P500R: *S&P 500* real returns, annual 1872 to 1995 (124 observations).

S&P500D: *S&P 500* index, daily, 1928 to 1991 (17,054 observations).

FT30: *FT 30* index, daily, 1935 to 1994 (15,003 observations).

FTSE100: *FTSE 100* index, weekly, 1984 to 1993 (521 observations).

CTLD: Courtaulds share price, weekly, 1984 to 1993 (521 observations).
LGEN: Legal & General share price, weekly, 1984 to 1993 (521 observations).
PRU: Prudential share price, weekly, 1984 to 1993 (521 observations).

References

Agiakloglou, C. and Newbold, P. (1994), 'Lagrange Multiplier Tests for Fractional Difference', *Journal of Time Series Analysis*, 15, 253–62.

Agiakloglou, C., Newbold, P. and Wohar, M. (1992), 'Bias in an Estimator of the Fractional Difference Parameter', *Journal of Time Series Analysis*, 13, 235–46.

Akaike, H. (1974), 'A New Look at the Statistical Model Identification', *IEEE Transactions on Automatic Control*, AC-19, 716–23.

Andersen, T.G. and Bollerslev, T. (1997), 'Intraday Periodicity and Volatility Persistence in Financial Markets', *Journal of Empirical Finance*, 4, 115–58.

Bachelier, L. (1900), 'Théorie de la Spéculation', *Annales de l'Ecole Normale Superieure*, Series 3, 17, 21–86.

Badrinath, S.G. and Chatterjee, S. (1988), 'On Measuring Skewness and Elongation in Common Stock Distributions: The Case of the Market Index', *Journal of Business*, 61, 451–72.

(1991), 'A Data-Analytic Look at Skewness and Elongation in Common Stock Return Distributions', *Journal of Business and Economic Statistics*, 9, 223–33.

Bai, J. (1997), 'Estimating Multiple Breaks One at a Time', *Econometric Theory*, 13, 315–52.

Bai, J. and Perron, P. (1998), 'Estimating and Testing Linear Models with Multiple Structural Changes', *Econometrica*, 66, 47–78.

Baillie, R.T. (1996), 'Long Memory Processes and Fractional Integration in Econometrics', *Journal of Econometrics*, 73, 5–59.

Baillie, R.T. and Bollerslev, T. (1989), 'The Message in Daily Exchange Rates: a Conditional Variance Tale', *Journal of Business and Economic Statistics*, 7, 297–305.

(1992), 'Prediction in Dynamic Models with Time-Dependent Conditional Variances', *Journal of Econometrics*, 52, 91–113.

(1993), 'Cointegration, Fractional Cointegration and Exchange Rate Dynamics', *Journal of Finance*, 49, 737–45.

Baillie, R.T., Bollerslev, T. and Mikkelson, H.O. (1996), 'Fractionally Integrated Generalized Autoregressive Conditional Heteroskedasticity', *Journal of Econometrics*, 74, 3–30.

Balke, N.S. and Fomby, T.B. (1997), 'Threshold Cointegration', *International Economic Review*, 38, 627–45.

Banerjee, A., Dolado, J.J., Galbraith, J.W. and Hendry, D.F. (1993), *Co-integration, Error Correction and the Econometric Analysis of Non-Stationary Data*, Oxford: Oxford University Press.

Banerjee, A., Dolado, J.J. and Mestre, R. (1998), 'Error-Correction Mechanism Tests for Cointegration in a System Equation Framework', *Journal of Time Series Analysis*, 19, 267–83.

Banerjee, A., Lumsdaine, R.L. and Stock, J.H. (1992), 'Recursive and Sequential Tests of the Unit Root and Trend Break Hypothesis: Theory and International Evidence', *Journal of Business and Economic Statistics*, 10, 271–87.

Barnett, W.A., Gallant, A.R., Hinich, M.J., Jungeilges, J.A., Kaplan, D.T. and Jensen, M.J. (1996), 'An Experimental Design to Compare Tests of Nonlinearity and Chaos', in W.A. Barnett, A.P. Kirman and M. Salmon (eds.), *Nonlinear Dynamics and Economics*, Cambridge University Press, pp. 163–190.

(1997), 'A Single-Blind Controlled Competition Among Tests of Nonlinearity and Chaos', *Journal of Econometrics*, 82, 157–92.

Bera, A.K. and Higgins, M.L. (1993), 'On ARCH Models: Properties, Estimation and Testing', *Journal of Economic Surveys*, 7, 305–66.

Beran, J.A. (1992), 'Statistical Methods for Data with Long-Range Dependence', *Statistical Science*, 7, 404–27.

Bernanke, B. (1986), 'Alternative Explanations of the Money-Income Correlation', *Carnegie-Rochester Conference Series on Public Policy*, 25, 49–100.

Berndt, E.R. (1991), *The Practice of Econometrics: Classic and Contemporary*, Reading, MA: Addison-Wesley.

Berndt, E.R., Hall, B.H., Hall, R.E. and Hausman, J.A. (1974), 'Estimation and Inference in Nonlinear Structural Models', *Annals of Economic and Social Measurement*, 4, 653–65.

Beveridge, S. and Nelson, C.R. (1981), 'A New Approach to Decomposition of Economic Time Series into Permanent and Transitory Components with Particular Attention to Measurement of the "Business Cycle"', *Journal of Monetary Economics*, 7, 151–74.

Bhargava, A. (1986), 'On the Theory of Testing for Unit Roots in Observed Time Series', *Review of Economic Studies*, 53, 369–84.

Blanchard, O.J. (1989), 'A Traditional Interpretation of Macroeconomic Fluctuations', *American Economic Review*, 79, 1146–64.

Blanchard, O.J. and Quah, D. (1989), 'Dynamic Effects of Aggregate Demand and Aggregate Supply Disturbances', *American Economic Review*, 79, 655–73.

Blanchard, O.J. and Watson, M.W. (1982), 'Bubbles, Rational Expectations, and Financial Markets', in P. Wachtel (ed.), *Crises in the Economic and Financial Structure*, Lexington, MA: Lexington Books, pp. 295–315.

Bollerslev, T. (1986), 'Generalised Autoregressive Conditional Heteroskedasticity', *Journal of Econometrics*, 31, 307–27.
(1987), 'A Conditionally Heteroskedastic Time Series Model for Speculative Prices and Rates of Return', *Review of Economics and Statistics*, 69, 542–6.
(1988), 'On the Correlation Structure for the Generalised Autoregressive Conditional Heteroskedastic Process', *Journal of Time Series Analysis*, 9, 121–32.
Bollerslev, T., Chou, R.Y. and Kroner, K.F. (1992), 'ARCH Modelling in Finance: A Review of the Theory and Empirical Evidence', *Journal of Econometrics*, 52, 5–59.
Bollerslev, T., Engle, R.F. and Nelson, D.B. (1994), 'ARCH Models', in R.F. Engle and D.L. McFadden (eds.), *Handbook of Econometrics, Volume IV*, New York: North-Holland, pp. 2959–3038.
Bollerslev, T. and Wooldridge, J.M. (1992), 'Quasi Maximum Likelihood Estimation and Inference in Dynamic Models with Time Varying Covariances', *Econometric Reviews*, 11, 143–72.
Bougerol, P. and Picard, N. (1992), 'Stationarity of GARCH Processes and of Some Nonnegative Time Series', *Journal of Econometrics*, 52, 115–28.
Box, G.E.P. and Cox, D.R. (1964), 'An Analysis of Transformations', *Journal of the Royal Statistical Society, Series B*, 26, 211–43.
Box, G.E.P and Jenkins, G.M. (1976), *Time Series Analysis: Forecasting and Control*, Revised Edition, San Francisco: Holden Day.
Box, G.E.P and Pierce, D.A. (1970), 'Distribution of Residual Autocorrelations in Autoregressive Moving Average Time Series Models', *Journal of the American Statistical Association*, 65, 1509–26.
Brock, W.A. (1986), 'Distinguishing Random and Deterministic Systems: Abridged Version', *Journal of Economic Theory*, 40, 168–95.
(1988), 'Nonlinearity and Complex Dynamics in Economics and Finance', in P. Anderson, K. Arrow and D. Pines (eds.), *The Economy as an Evolving Complex System*, Reading, MA: SFI Studies in the Sciences of Complexity, pp. 77–97.
Brock, W.A. and Dechert, W.D. (1991), 'Non-Linear Dynamical Systems: Instability and Chaos in Economics', in W. Hildenbrand and H. Sonnenschein (eds.), *Handbook of Mathematical Economics*, Amsterdam: North-Holland, pp. 2209–35.
Brock, W.A., Hsieh, D. and LeBaron, B. (1991), *A Test for Nonlinear Dynamics, Chaos and Instability*, Cambridge, Mass.: MIT Press.
Brock, W.A., Lakonishok, J. and LeBaron, B. (1992), 'Simple Technical Trading Rules and the Stochastic Properties of Stock Returns', *Journal of Finance*, 47, 1731–64.
Brockwell, P.J. and Davis, R.A. (1991), *Time Series: Theory and Methods*, Second Edition, New York: Springer-Verlag.
Brown, R.L., Durbin, J. and Evans, J.M. (1975), 'Techniques for Testing the Constancy of Regression Relationships Over Time', *Journal of the Royal Statistical Society, Series B*, 39, 107–13.

Cai, J. (1994), 'A Markov Model of Switching-Regime ARCH', *Journal of Business and Economic Statistics*, 12, 309–16.

Campbell, J.Y. (1991), 'A Variance Decomposition for Stock Returns', *Economic Journal*, 101, 157–79.

Campbell, J.Y., Lo, A.W. and MacKinlay, A.C. (1997), *The Econometrics of Financial Markets*, Princeton, NJ: Princeton University Press.

Campbell, J.Y. and Mankiw, N.G. (1987), 'Permanent and Transitory Components in Macroeconomic Fluctuations', *American Economic Review, Papers and Proceedings*, 77, 111–17.

Campbell, J.Y. and Perron, P. (1991), 'Pitfalls and Opportunities: What Macroeconomists Should Know about Unit Roots', *NBER Macroeconomics Annual*, Cambridge, Mass.: MIT Press, pp. 141–201.

Campbell, J.Y. and Shiller, R.J. (1987), 'Cointegration and Tests of Present Value Models', *Journal of Political Economy*, 95, 1062–88.

(1988a), 'Interpreting Cointegrated Models', *Journal of Economic Dynamics and Control*, 12, 503–22.

(1988b), 'Stock Prices, Earnings, and Expected Dividends', *Journal of Finance*, 43, 661–76.

(1988c), 'The Dividend-Price Ratio and Expectations of Future Dividends and Discount Factors', *Review of Financial Studies*, 1, 195–228.

Campos, J., Ericsson, N.R. and Hendry, D.F. (1996), 'Cointegration Tests in the Presence of Structural Breaks', *Journal of Econometrics*, 70, 187–220.

Caner, M. (1998), 'Tests for Cointegration with Infinite Variance Errors', *Journal of Econometrics*, 86, 155–75.

Chan, L.K.C. and Lakonishok, J. (1992), 'Robust Measurement of Beta Risk', *Journal of Financial and Quantitative Analysis*, 27, 265–82.

Choi, I. and Chung, B.S. (1995), 'Sampling Frequency and the Power of Tests for a Unit Root: A Simulation Study', *Economics Letters*, 49, 131–6.

Chow, G.C. (1960), 'Tests of Equality Between Sets of Coefficients in Two Linear Regressions', *Econometrica*, 28, 591–605.

Chu, C.-S.J., Hornik, K. and Kuan, C.-M. (1995), 'The Moving-Estimates Test for Parameter Stability', *Econometric Theory*, 11, 699–720.

Christiano, L.J. (1992), 'Searching for a Break in GNP', *Journal of Business and Economic Statistics*, 10, 237–50.

Cioczek-Georges, R. and Taqqu, M.S. (1995), 'Form of the Conditional Variance for Symmetric Stable Random Variables', *Statistica Sinica*, 5, 351–61.

Clark, P.K. (1973), 'A Subordinated Stochastic Process Model with Finite Variances for Speculative Prices', *Econometrica*, 41, 135–55.

Cochrane, J.H. (1988), 'How Big is the Random Walk in GNP?', *Journal of Political Economy*, 96, 893–920.

(1991), 'A Critique of the Application of Unit Root Tests', *Journal of Economic Dynamics and Control*, 15, 275–84.

Cooley, T.F. and LeRoy, S.F. (1985), 'Atheoretical Macroeconometrics: A Critique', *Journal of Monetary Economics*, 16, 283–308.

Cootner, P.A. (ed.) (1964), *The Random Character of Stock Market Prices*, Cambridge, Mass.: MIT Press.

Coutts, J.A., Mills, T.C. and Roberts, J. (1994), 'Misspecification of the Market Model: The Implications for Event Studies', *Applied Economics Letters*, 2, 143–5.

Coutts, J.A., Roberts, J. and Mills, T.C. (1997), 'Parameter Stability in the Market Model: Tests and Time Varying Parameter Estimation with UK Data', *The Statistician*, 46, 57–70.

Cowles, A. (1933), 'Can Stock Market Forecasters Forecast?', *Econometrica*, 1, 309–24.

(1944), 'Stock Market Forecasting', *Econometrica*, 12, 206–14.

(1960), 'A Revision of Previous Conclusions Regarding Stock Price Behaviour', *Econometrica*, 28, 909–15.

Cowles, A. and Jones, H.E. (1937), 'Some A Posteriori Probabilities in Stock Market Action', *Econometrica*, 5, 280–94.

Cramer, H. (1961), 'On Some Classes of Non-Stationary Processes', *Proceedings of the 4th Berkeley Symposium on Mathematical Statistics and Probability*, University of California Press, pp. 57–78.

Cuthbertson, K. (1996), *Quantitative Financial Economics: Stocks, Bonds, and Foreign Exchange*, New York: Wiley.

Dacarogna, M.M., Müller, U.A., Nagler, R.J., Olsen, R.B. and Pictet, O.V. (1993), 'A Geographical Model for the Daily and Weekly Seasonal Volatility in the Foreign Exchange Market', *Journal of International Money and Finance*, 12, 413–38.

Daniélsson, J. and de Vries, C.G. (1997), 'Tail Index and Quantile Estimation with Very High Frequency Data', *Journal of Empirical Finance*, 4, 241–57.

Dechert, W.D. (1996), 'Testing Time Series for Nonlinearities; The BDS Approach', in W.A. Barnett, A.P. Kirman and M. Salmon (eds.), *Nonlinear Dynamics and Economics*, Cambridge University Press, pp. 191–200.

De Gooijer, J.G. (1989), 'Testing Non-Linearities in World Stock Market Prices', *Economics Letters*, 31, 31–5.

DeJong, D.N., Nankervis, J.C., Savin, N.E. and Whiteman, C.H. (1992a), 'The Power Problems of Unit Root Tests in Time Series with Autoregressive Errors', *Journal of Econometrics*, 53, 323–43.

(1992b), 'Integration Versus Trend Stationarity in Time Series', *Econometrica*, 60, 423–33.

DeJong, D.N. and Whiteman, C.H. (1991a), 'The Temporal Stability of Dividends and Stock Prices: Evidence from the Likelihood Function', *American Economic Review*, 81, 600–17.

(1991b), 'Trends and Random Walks in Macroeconomic Time Series: A Reconsideration Based on the Likelihood Principle', *Journal of Monetary Economics*, 28, 221–54.

Dekkers, A.L.M. and de Haan, L. (1989), 'On the Estimation of the Extreme-Value Index and Large Quantile Estimation', *Annals of Statistics*, 17, 1795–832.

Demos, A. and Sentana, E. (1998), 'Testing for GARCH Effects: A One-Sided Approach', *Journal of Econometrics*, 86, 97–127.

Diba, B.T. (1990), 'Bubbles and Stock-Price Volatility', in G.P. Dwyer and R.W. Hafer (eds.), *The Stock Market: Bubbles, Volatility, and Chaos*, Boston, Mass.: Kluwer Academic, pp. 9–26.

Diba, B.T. and Grossman, H.I. (1987), 'On the Inception of Rational Bubbles', *Quarterly Journal of Economics*, 103, 697–700.

(1988), 'Explosive Rational Bubbles in Stock Prices?', *American Economic Review*, 81, 600–17.

Dickey, D.A. and Fuller, W.A. (1979), 'Distribution of the Estimators for Autoregressive Time Series with a Unit Root', *Journal of the American Statistical Association*, 74, 427–31.

(1981), 'Likelihood Ratio Statistics for Autoregressive Time Series with a Unit Root', *Econometrica*, 49, 1057–72.

Dickey, D.A. and Pantula, S. (1987), 'Determining the Order of Differencing in Autoregressive Processes', *Journal of Business and Economic Statistics*, 5, 455–61.

Diebold, F.X. and Nerlove, M. (1990), 'Unit Roots in Economic Time Series: A Selective Survey', in G.F. Rhodes and T.B. Fomby (eds.), *Advances in Econometrics, Volume VIII*, Greenwich, CT: JAI Press, pp. 3–69.

Diebold, F.X. and Rudebusch, G.D. (1991), 'On the Power of Dickey-Fuller Tests Against Fractional Alternatives', *Economics Letters*, 35, 155–60.

Ding, Z. and Granger, C.W.J. (1996), 'Modeling Persistence of Speculative Returns: A New Approach', *Journal of Econometrics*, 73, 185–215.

Ding, Z., Granger, C.W.J. and Engle, R.F. (1993), 'A Long Memory Property of Stock Returns and a New Model', *Journal of Empirical Finance*, 1, 83–106.

Doan, T.A., Litterman, R.B. and Sims, C.A. (1984), 'Forecasting and Conditional Projection Using Realistic Prior Distributions', *Econometric Reviews*, 3, 1–100.

Dolado, J.J., Jenkinson, T. and Sosvilla-Rivero, S. (1990), 'Cointegration and Unit Roots', *Journal of Economic Surveys*, 4, 249–73.

Domowitz, I. and Hakkio, C.S. (1985), 'Conditional Variance and the Risk Premium in the Foreign Exchange Market', *Journal of International Economics*, 19, 47–66.

Doornik, J.A. and Hendry, D.F. (1996), *GiveWin: An Interface to Empirical Modelling*, London: International Thomson Business Press.

(1997), *Modelling Dynamic Systems using PcFiml 9.0*, London: International Thomson Business Press.

Drost, F.C. and Nijman, T.E. (1993), 'Temporal Aggregation of GARCH Processes', *Econometrica*, 61, 909–27.

Drost, F.C. and Werker, B.J.M. (1996), 'Closing the GARCH Gap: Continuous Time GARCH Modeling', *Journal of Econometrics*, 74, 31–57.

Dufour, J.-M. (1982), 'Recursive Stability Analysis of Linear Regression Relationships: An Exploratory Analysis', *Journal of Econometrics*, 19, 31–75.

EViews (1995), *EViews User Guide Version 2.0*, Irvine, California: Quantitative Micro Software.

Edgerton, D. and Wells, C. (1994), 'Critical Values for the CUSUMSQ Statistic in Medium and Large Sized Samples', *Oxford Bulletin of Economics and Statistics*, 56, 355–65.

Efron, B. and Tibshirani, R.J. (1993), *An Introduction to the Bootstrap*, London: Chapman and Hall.

Eitrhem, Ø., and Teräsvirta, T. (1996), 'Testing the Adequacy of Smooth Transition Autoregressive Models', *Journal of Econometrics*, 74, 59–75.

Elliott, G., Rothenberg, T.J. and Stock, J.H. (1996), 'Efficient Tests for an Autoregressive Unit Root', *Econometrica*, 64, 813–36.

Engle, C.R. and Hamilton, J.D. (1990), 'Long Swings in the Dollar: Are They in the Data and Do Markets Know It?', *American Economic Review*, 80, 689–713.

Engle, R.F. (1982), 'Autoregressive Conditional Heteroskedasticity with Estimates of the Variance of U.K. Inflation', *Econometrica*, 50, 987–1008.

(1990), 'Discussion: Stock Market Volatility and the Crash of 1987', *Review of Financial Studies*, 3, 103–6.

Engle, R.F. and Bollerslev, T. (1986), 'Modelling the Persistence of Conditional Variances', *Econometric Reviews*, 5, 1–50.

Engle, R.F. and Gonzalez-Rivera, G. (1991), 'Semiparametric ARCH Models', *Journal of Business and Economic Statistics*, 9, 345–59.

Engle, R.F. and Granger, C.W.J. (1987), 'Cointegration and Error Correction: Representation, Estimation and Testing', *Econometrica*, 55, 251–76.

Engle, R.F. and Hendry, D.F. (1993), 'Testing Super Exogeneity and Invariance in Regression Models', *Journal of Econometrics*, 56, 119–39.

Engle, R.F., Hendry, D.F. and Richard, J.-F. (1983), 'Exogeneity', *Econometrica*, 51, 277–304.

Engle, R.F., Hendry, D.F. and Trumble, D. (1985), 'Small Sample Properties of ARCH Estimators and Tests', *Canadian Journal of Economics*, 43, 66–93.

Engle, R.F. and Issler, J.V. (1995), 'Estimating Common Sectoral Cycles', *Journal of Monetary Economics*, 35, 83–113.

Engle, R.F. and Kozicki, S. (1993), 'Testing for Common Features', *Journal of Business and Economic Statistics*, 11, 369–80.

Engle, R.F., Lilien, D.M. and Robbins, R.P. (1987), 'Estimating Time Varying Risk Premia in the Term Structure: the ARCH-M Model', *Econometrica*, 55, 391–408.

Engle, R.F. and Russell, J.R. (1997), 'Forecasting the Frequency of Changes in Quoted Foreign Exchange Prices with the Autoregressive Conditional Duration Model', *Journal of Empirical Finance*, 4, 187–212.

Fama, E.F. (1965), 'The Behaviour of Stock-Market Prices', *Journal of Business*, 38, 34–105.

(1975), 'Short Term Interest Rates as Predictors of Inflation', *American Economic Review*, 65, 269–82.

Fama, E.F. and MacBeth, J.D. (1973), 'Risk, Return, and Equilibrium: Empirical Tests', *Journal of Political Economy*, 81, 607–36.

Feller, W. (1966), *An Introduction to Probability Theory and its Applications, Volume II*, New York: Wiley.

French, K.R., Schwert, G.W. and Stambaugh, R.F. (1987), 'Expected Stock Returns and Volatility', *Journal of Financial Economics*, 19, 3–29.

Fuller, W.A. (1976), *Introduction to Statistical Time Series*, New York: Wiley.

(1996), *Introduction to Statistical Time Series*, Second Edition, New York: Wiley.

Gallant, A.R. and White, H. (1988), *A Unified Theory of Estimation and Inference for Nonlinear Dynamics*, Oxford: Blackwell.

Geweke, J. (1978), 'Testing the Exogeneity Specification in the Complete Dynamic Simultaneous Equations Model', *Journal of Econometrics*, 7, 163–85.

(1984), 'Inference and Causality in Economic Time Series Models', in Z. Griliches and M.D. Intriligator (eds.), *Handbook of Econometrics, Volume II*, Amsterdam: North-Holland, pp. 1101–44.

Geweke, J. and Porter-Hudak, S. (1983), 'The Estimation and Application of Long Memory Time Series Models', *Journal of Time Series Analysis*, 4, 221–38.

Ghose, D. and Kroner, K.F. (1995), 'The Relationship Between GARCH and Symmetric Stable Processes: Finding the Source of Fat Tails in Financial Data', *Journal of Empirical Finance*, 2, 225–51.

Gibbons, M.R. (1982), 'Multivariate Tests of Financial Models', *Journal of Financial Economics*, 10, 3–27.

Gibbons, M.R., Ross, S.A. and Shanken, J. (1989), 'A Test of the Efficiency of a Given Portfolio', *Econometrica*, 57, 1121–52.

Glosten, L.R., Jagannathan, R. and Runkle, D. (1993), 'Relationship Between the Expected Value and the Volatility of the Nominal Excess Return on Stocks', *Journal of Finance*, 48, 1779–801.

Godfrey, L.G. (1979), 'Testing the Adequacy of a Time Series Model', *Biometrika*, 66, 67–72.

(1988), *Misspecification Tests in Econometrics*, Cambridge University Press.

Gonzalo, J. and Granger, C.W.J. (1995), 'Estimation of Common Long-Memory Components in Cointegrated Systems', *Journal of Business and Economic Statistics*, 13, 27–35.

Goodhart, C.A.E. and O'Hara, M. (1997), 'High Frequency Data in Financial Markets: Issues and Applications', *Journal of Empirical Finance*, 4, 73–114.

Granger, C.W.J. (1966), 'The Typical Spectral Shape of an Economic Variable', *Econometrica*, 34, 150–61.

(1969), 'Investigating Causal Relations by Econometric Models and Cross-Spectral Methods', *Econometrica*, 37, 424–38.

(1998), 'Extracting Information from Mega-Panels and High-Frequency Data', UCSD Discussion Paper 98–01.

Granger, C.W.J. and Andersen, A.P. (1978), *An Introduction to Bilinear Time Series Models*, Gottingen: Vandenhoeck and Ruprecht.

Granger, C.W.J. and Ding, Z. (1995a), 'Stylized Facts on the Temporal and Distributional Properties of Daily Data from Speculative Markets', Department of Economics, University of California, San Diego, mimeo.

(1995b), 'Some Properties of Absolute Returns: An Alternative Measure of Risk', *Annales d'Economie et de Statistique*, 40, 67–91.

(1996), 'Varieties of Long Memory Models', *Journal of Econometrics*, 73, 61–78.

Granger, C.W.J. and Hallman, J.J. (1991), 'Long Memory Series with Attractors', *Oxford Bulletin of Economics and Statistics*, 53, 11–26.

Granger, C.W.J., Inoue, T. and Morin, N. (1997), 'Nonlinear Stochastic Trends', *Journal of Econometrics*, 81, 65–92.

Granger, C.W.J. and Joyeux, R. (1980), 'An Introduction to Long Memory Time Series Models and Fractional Differencing', *Journal of Time Series Analysis*, 1, 15–29.

Granger, C.W.J. and Lin, J.-L. (1995), 'Causality in the Long-Run', *Econometric Theory*, 11, 530–6.

Granger, C.W.J. and Morgenstern, O. (1970), *Predictability of Stock Market Prices*, Heath: Lexington.

Granger, C.W.J. and Morris, M.J. (1976), 'Time Series Modelling and Interpretation', *Journal of the Royal Statistical Society, Series A*, 139, 246–57.

Granger, C.W.J. and Newbold, P. (1974), 'Spurious Regressions in Econometrics', *Journal of Econometrics*, 2, 111–20.

(1986), *Forecasting Economic Time Series*, Second Edition, New York: Academic Press.

Granger, C.W.J. and Orr, D. (1972), '"Infinite Variance" and Research Strategy in Time Series Analysis', *Journal of the American Statistical Association*, 67, 275–85.

Granger, C.W.J. and Swanson, N. (1996), 'Future Developments in the Study of Cointegrated Variables', *Oxford Bulletin of Economics and Statistics*, 58, 537–553.

(1997), 'An Introduction to Stochastic Unit Root Processes', *Journal of Econometrics*, 80, 35–62.

Granger, C.W.J. and Teräsvirta, T. (1993), *Modeling Nonlinear Economic Relationships*, Oxford: Oxford University Press.

Gregory, A.W. and Hansen, B.E. (1996), 'Residual-Based Tests for Cointegration in Models with Regime Shifts', *Journal of Econometrics*, 70, 99–126.

Gregory, A.W., Nason, J.M. and Watt, D.G. (1996), 'Testing for Structural Breaks in Cointegrating Relationships', *Journal of Econometrics*, 71, 321–41.

Groenendijk, P.A., Lucas, A. and de Vries, C.G. (1995), 'A Note on the Relationship Between GARCH and Symmetric Stable Processes', *Journal of Empirical Finance*, 2, 253–64.

Guégan, D. (1987), 'Different Representations for Bilinear Models', *Journal of Time Series Analysis*, 8, 389–408.

Haan, L. de, Jansen, D.W., Koedijk, K. and de Vries, C.G. (1994), 'Safety First Portfolio Selection, Extreme Value Theory and Long Run Asset Risks', in J. Galambos et al. (eds.), *Extreme Value Theory and Applications*, Boston, MA: Kluwer Academic, pp. 471–87.

Haan, L. de and Resnick, S.I. (1980), 'A Simple Asymptotic Estimate for the Index of a Stable Distribution', *Journal of the Royal Statistical Society, Series B*, 42, 83–7.

Haan, L. de, Resnick, S.I., Rootzén, H. and de Vries, C.G. (1989), 'Extremal Behaviour of Solutions to a Stochastic Difference Equation with Applications to ARCH Processes', *Stochastic Processes and Their Applications*, 32, 213–24.

Hæfke, C. and Helmenstein, C. (1996), 'Forecasting Austrian IPOs: An Application of Linear and Neural Network Error-Correction Models', *Journal of Forecasting*, 15, 237–52.

Haggan, V., Heravi, S.M. and Priestley, M.B. (1984), 'A Study of the Application of State-Dependent Models in Non-Linear Time Series Analysis', *Journal of Time Series Analysis*, 5, 69–102.

Haggan, V. and Ozaki, T. (1981), 'Modelling Non-linear Vibrations Using an Amplitude Dependent Autoregressive Time Series Model', *Biometrika*, 68, 189–96.

Hall, A. (1989), 'Testing for a Unit Root in the Presence of Moving Average Errors', *Biometrika*, 76, 49–56.

Hall, P. (1982), 'On Some Simple Estimates of an Exponent of Regular Variation', *Journal of the Royal Statistical Society, Series B*, 44, 37–42.

Hall, P. and Welsh, A.H. (1985), 'Adaptive Estimates of Parameters of Regular Variation', *Annals of Statistics*, 13, 331–41.

Hamilton, J.D. (1986), 'On Testing for Self-Fulfilling Speculative Price Bubbles', *International Economic Review*, 27, 545–52.

(1989), 'A New Approach to the Economic Analysis of Nonstationary Time Series and the Business Cycle', *Econometrica*, 57, 357–84.

(1990), 'Analysis of Time Series Subject to Changes in Regime', *Journal of Econometrics*, 45, 39–70.

(1994), *Time Series Analysis*, Princeton, NJ: Princeton University Press.

Hamilton, J.D. and Susmel, R. (1994), 'Autoregressive Conditional Heteroskedasticity and Changes in Regime', *Journal of Econometrics*, 64, 307–33.

Hamilton, J.D. and Whiteman, C.H. (1985), 'The Observable Implications of Self-Fulfilling Expectations', *Journal of Monetary Economics*, 16, 353–73.

Hansen, B.E. (1992), 'Testing for Parameter Instability in Linear Models', *Journal of Policy Modelling*, 14, 517–33.

Hansen, L.P. (1982), 'Large Sample Properties of Generalized Method of Moments Estimators', *Econometrica*, 50, 1029–54.

Hansen, L.P. and Hodrick, R.J. (1980), 'Forward Exchange Rates as Optimal Predictors of Future Spot Rates', *Journal of Political Economy*, 88, 829–53.

Harvey, A.C. (1989), *Forecasting Structural Time Series Models and the Kalman Filter*, Cambridge University Press.

Harvey, A.C., Ruiz, E. and Sentana, E. (1992), 'Unobserved Component Models with ARCH Disturbances', *Journal of Econometrics*, 52, 129–57.

Harvey, A.C. and Shephard, N. (1992), 'Structural Time Series Models', in G.S. Maddala, C.R. Rao and H.D. Vinod (eds.), *Handbook of Statistics, Volume XI: Econometrics*, Amsterdam: North-Holland.

Hassler, U. and Wolters, J. (1994), 'On the Power of Unit Root Tests Against Fractionally Integrated Alternatives', *Economics Letters*, 45, 1–5.

Haug, A.A. (1996), 'Tests for Cointegration: A Monte Carlo Comparison', *Journal of Econometrics*, 71, 89–115.

Hendry, D.F. (1995), *Dynamic Econometrics*, Oxford: Oxford University Press.

Hendry, D.F. and Doornik, J.A. (1996), *Empirical Econometric Modelling Using PcGive 9.0 for Windows*, London: International Thomson Business Press.

Hendry, D.F., Pagan, A.R. and Sargan, J.D. (1984), 'Dynamic Specification', in Z. Griliches and M.D. Intriligator (eds.), *Handbook of Econometrics, Volume II*, Amsterdam: North-Holland, pp. 1023–100.

Hentschel, L. (1995), 'All in the Family: Nesting Symmetric and Asymmetric GARCH Models', *Journal of Financial Economics*, 39, 71–104.

Hiemstra, C. and Jones, J.D. (1997), 'Another Look at Long Memory in Common Stock Returns', *Journal of Empirical Finance*, 4, 373–401.

Higgins, M.L. and Bera, A.K. (1988), 'A Joint Test for ARCH and Bilinearity in the Regression Model', *Econometric Reviews*, 7, 171–81.

(1992), 'A Class of Nonlinear ARCH Models', *International Economic Review*, 33, 137–58.

Hill, B.M. (1975), 'A Simple General Approach to Inference About the Tail of a Distribution', *Annals of Statistics*, 3, 1163–74.

Ho, M.S. and Sørenson, B.E. (1996), 'Finding Cointegration Rank in High Dimensional Systems Using the Johansen Test: An Illustration Using Data Based Monte Carlo Simulations', *Review of Economics and Statistics*, 78, 726–32.

Hoaglin, D.C. (1985), 'Summarizing Shape Numerically: The *g*-and-*h* Distributions', in D.C. Hoaglin, F. Mosteller and J.W. Tukey (eds.), *Exploring Data Tables, Trends and Shapes*, New York: Wiley, pp. 461–513.

Hols, M.C.A.B. and de Vries, C.G. (1991), 'The Limiting Distribution of Extremal Exchange Rate Returns', *Journal of Applied Econometrics*, 6, 287–302.

Hong, Y. (1997), 'One-Sided Testing for Conditional Heteroskedasticity in Time Series Models', *Journal of Time Series Analysis*, 18, 253–77.

Hosking, J.R.M. (1981), 'Fractional Differencing', *Biometrika*, 68, 165–76.

(1984), 'Modelling Persistence in Hydrological Time Series Using Fractional Differencing', *Water Resources Research*, 20, 1898–908.

Hsiao, C. (1997), 'Cointegration and Dynamic Simultaneous Equation Model', *Econometrica*, 65, 647–70.

Hsieh, D.A. (1989a), 'Modelling Heteroskedasticity in Daily Foreign Exchange Rates', *Journal of Business and Economic Statistics*, 7, 307–17.

(1989b), 'Testing for Nonlinear Dependence in Daily Foreign Exchange Rates', *Journal of Business*, 62, 339–68.

(1991), 'Chaos and Nonlinear Dynamics: Application to Financial Markets', *Journal of Finance*, 46, 1839–77.

Hurst, H. (1951), 'Long Term Storage Capacity of Reservoirs', *Transactions of the American Society of Civil Engineers*, 116, 770–99.

Hylleberg, S. and Mizon, G.E. (1989), 'A Note on the Distribution of the Least Squares Estimator of a Random Walk with Drift', *Economic Letters*, 29, 225–30.

Jacquier, E., Polson, N.G. and Rossi, P.E. (1994), 'Bayesian Analysis of Stochastic Volatility Models (with Discussion)', *Journal of Business and Economic Statistics*, 12, 371–417.

Jansen, D.W. and de Vries, C.G. (1991), 'On the Frequency of Large Stock Returns: Putting Booms and Busts into Perspective', *Review of Economics and Statistics*, 73, 18–24.

Jarque, C.M. and Bera, A.K. (1980), 'Efficient Tests for Normality, Homoskedasticity and Serial Dependence of Regression Residuals', *Economics Letters*, 6, 255–9.

Johansen, S. (1995), *Likelihood-Based Inference in Cointegrated Vector Autoregressive Models*, Oxford: Oxford University Press.

Johansen, S. and Juselius, K. (1994), 'Identification of the Long-Run and Short-Run Structure: An Application to the ISLM Model', *Journal of Econometrics*, 63, 7–36.

Johnston, J. and DiNardo, J. (1997), *Econometric Methods*, 4th Edition, New York: McGraw-Hill.

Jong, F. de and Nijman, T. (1997), 'High Frequency Analysis of Lead-Lag Relationships Between Financial Markets', *Journal of Empirical Finance*, 4, 259–77.

Jorion, P. (1988), 'On Jump Processes in the Foreign Exchange and Stock Markets', *Review of Financial Studies*, 1, 427–45.

Judge, G.G., Griffiths, W.E., Carter Hill, R., Lütkepohl, H. and Lee, T.C. (1985), *The Theory and Practice of Econometrics*, Second Edition, New York: Wiley.

Keenan, D.M. (1985), 'A Tukey Nonadditivity-Type Test for Time Series Nonlinearity', *Biometrika*, 72, 39–44.

Kendall, M.J. (1953), 'The Analysis of Economic Time Series, Part I: Prices', *Journal of the Royal Statistical Society, Series A*, 96, 11–25.

Kim, K. and Schmidt, P. (1990), 'Some Evidence on the Accuracy of Phillips-Perron Tests Using Alternative Estimates of Nuisance Parameters', *Economics Letters*, 34, 345–50.

Kleidon, A.W. (1986a), 'Variance Bounds Tests and Stock Price Valuation Models', *Journal of Political Economy*, 94, 953–1001.

(1986b), 'Bias in Small Sample Tests of Stock Price Rationality', *Journal of Business*, 59, 237–61.

Koedijk, K.G. and Kool, C.J.M. (1992), 'Tail Estimates of East European Exchange Rates', *Journal of Business and Economic Statistics*, 10, 83–96.

Koedijk, K.G., Schafgans, M.M.A. and de Vries, C.G. (1990), 'The Tail Index of Exchange Rate Returns', *Journal of International Economics*, 29, 93–108.

Koedijk, K.G., Stork, P.A. and de Vries, C.G. (1992), 'Differences Between Foreign Exchange Rate Regimes: The View From the Tails', *Journal of International Money and Finance*, 11, 462–73.

Koenker, R. (1982), 'Robust Methods in Econometrics', *Econometric Reviews*, 1, 213–55.

Kokoszka, P.S. and Taqqu, M.S. (1994), 'Infinite Variance Stable ARMA Processes', *Journal of Time Series Analysis*, 15, 203–20.

(1996), 'Infinite Variance Stable Moving Averages with Long Memory', *Journal of Econometrics*, 73, 79–99.

Kon, S. (1984), 'Models of Stock Returns – a Comparison', *Journal of Finance*, 39, 147–65.

Koop, G. (1992), '"Objective" Bayesian Unit Root Tests', *Journal of Applied Econometrics*, 7, 65–82.

Koop, G., Pesaran, M.H. and Potter, S.M. (1996), 'Impulse Response Analysis in Nonlinear Multivariate Models', *Journal of Econometrics*, 74, 119–47.

Koopman, S.J., Harvey, A.C., Doornik, J.A. and Shephard, N. (1995), *Stamp 5.0: Structural Time Series Analyser, Modeller and Predictor*, London: Chapman and Hall.

Krämer, W. and Ploberger, W. (1990), 'The Local Power of CUSUM and CUSUM of Squares Tests', *Econometric Theory*, 6, 335–47.

Kuan, C.-M. and White, H. (1994), 'Artificial Neural Networks: An Econometric Perspective (with Discussion)', *Econometric Reviews*, 13, 1–143.

Kwiatkowski, D., Phillips, P.C.B., Schmidt, P. and Shin, Y. (1992), 'Testing the Null Hypothesis of Stationarity Against the Alternative of a Unit Root', *Journal of Econometrics*, 54, 159–78.

Lam, P.S. (1990), 'The Hamilton Model with a General Autoregressive Component: Estimation and Comparison with Other Models of Economic Time Series', *Journal of Monetary Economics*, 20, 409–32.

Lee, D. and Schmidt, P. (1996), 'On the Power of the KPSS Test of Stationarity Against Fractionally Integrated Alternatives', *Journal of Econometrics*, 73, 285–302.

Lee, J.H.H. and King, M.L. (1993), 'A Locally Most Mean Powerful Based Score Test for ARCH and GARCH Regression Disturbances', *Journal of Business and Economic Statistics*, 11, 17–27.

Lee, T.-H., White, H. and Granger, C.W.J. (1993), 'Testing for Neglected Nonlinearity in Time Series Models: A Comparison of Neural Network Methods and Alternative Tests', *Journal of Econometrics*, 56, 269–90.

LeRoy, S.F. (1982), 'Expectations Models of Asset Prices: A Survey of the Theory', *Journal of Finance*, 37, 185–217.

(1989) 'Efficient Capital Markets and Martingales', *Journal of Economic Literature*, 27, 1583–621.

Leybourne, S.J. and McCabe, B.P.M. (1994), 'A Consistent Test for a Unit Root', *Journal of Business and Economic Statistics*, 12, 157–66.

(1996) 'Modified Stationarity Tests with Data Dependent Model Selection Rules', mimeo, University of Nottingham.

Leybourne, S.J., McCabe, B.P.M. and Mills, T.C. (1996), 'Randomized Unit Root Processes for Modelling and Forecasting Financial Time Series: Theory and Applications', *Journal of Forecasting*, 15, 253–70.

Leybourne, S.J., McCabe, B.P.M. and Tremayne, A.R. (1996), 'Can Economic Time Series be Differenced to Stationarity?', *Journal of Business and Economic Statistics*, 14, 435–46.

Leybourne, S.J., Mills, T.C. and Newbold, P. (1998), 'Spurious Rejections by Dickey-Fuller Tests in the Presence of a Break Under the Null', *Journal of Econometrics*, 87, 191–203.

Leybourne, S.J., Newbold, P. and Vougas, D. (1998), 'Unit Roots and Smooth Transitions', *Journal of Time Series Analysis*, 19, 83–97.

Linton, O. (1993), 'Adaptive Estimation of ARCH Models', *Econometric Theory*, 9, 539–69.

Ljung, G.M. and Box, G.E.P. (1978), 'On a Measure of Lack of Fit in Time Series Models', *Biometrika*, 65, 297–303.

Lo, A.W. (1991), 'Long-Term Memory in Stock Market Prices', *Econometrica*, 59, 1279–313.

Lo, A.W. and MacKinlay, A.C. (1988), 'Stock Prices do not Follow Random Walks: Evidence from a Simple Specification Test', *Review of Financial Studies*, 1, 41–66.

(1989), 'The Size and Power of the Variance Ratio Test in Finite Samples: A Monte Carlo Investigation', *Journal of Econometrics*, 40, 203–38.

Loretan, M. and Phillips, P.C.B. (1994), 'Testing the Covariance Stationarity of Heavy-Tailed Time Series. An Overview of the Theory with Applications to Several Financial Datasets', *Journal of Empirical Finance*, 1, 211–48.

Lütkepohl, H. (1985), 'Comparison of Criteria for Estimating the Order of a Vector Autoregressive Process', *Journal of Time Series Analysis*, 6, 35–52.

(1991), *Introduction to Multiple Time Series Analysis*, Berlin: Springer-Verlag.

MacKinlay, A.C. (1987), 'On Multivariate Tests of the CAPM', *Journal of Financial Economics*, 18, 431–71.

MacKinnon, J.G. (1991), 'Critical Values for Cointegration Tests', in R.F. Engle and C.W.J. Granger (eds.), *Long-Run Economic Relationships*, Oxford: Oxford University Press, pp. 267–76.

(1996), 'Numerical Distribution Functions for Unit Root and Cointegration Tests', *Journal of Applied Econometrics*, 11, 601–18.

McCabe, B.P.M. and Tremayne, A.R. (1995), 'Testing a Time Series for Difference Stationarity', *Annals of Statistics*, 23, 1015–28.

McCulloch, J.H. (1996), 'Financial Applications of Stable Distributions', in G.S. Maddala and C.R. Rao (eds.), *Handbook of Statistics, Volume 14: Statistical Methods in Finance*, Amsterdam: Elsevier Science, pp. 393–425.

(1997), 'Measuring Tail Thickness to Estimate the Stable Index α: A Critique', *Journal of Business and Economic Statistics*, 15, 74–81.

McDonald, J.B. (1996), 'Probability Distributions for Financial Models', in G.S. Maddala and C.R. Rao (eds.), *Handbook of Statistics, Volume 14: Statistical Methods in Finance*, Amsterdam: Elsevier Science, pp. 427–61.

McDonald, J.B. and Newey, W.K. (1988), 'Partially Adaptive Estimation of Regression Models via the Generalized *t* Distribution', *Econometric Reviews*, 4, 428–57.

McKenzie, E. (1988), 'A Note on Using the Integrated Form of ARIMA Forecasts', *International Journal of Forecasting*, 4, 117–24.

McLeod, A.J. and Li, W.K. (1983), 'Diagnostic Checking ARMA Time Series Models Using Squared-Residual Correlations', *Journal of Time Series Analysis*, 4, 269–73.

Mandelbrot, B.B. (1963a), 'New Methods in Statistical Economics', *Journal of Political Economy*, 71, 421–40.

(1963b), 'The Variation of Certain Speculative Prices', *Journal of Business*, 36, 394–419.

(1966), 'Forecasts of Future Prices, Unbiased Markets and "Martingale" Models', *Journal of Business*, 39, 242–55.

(1969), 'Long-Run Linearity, Locally Gaussian Process, *H*-Spectra, and Infinite Variances', *International Economic Review*, 10, 82–111.

(1972), 'Statistical Methodology for Nonperiodic Cycles: From the Covariance to *R*/*S* Analysis', *Annals of Economic and Social Measurement*, 1/3, 259–90.

(1989), 'Louis Bachelier', in J. Eatwell, M. Milgate and P. Newman (eds.), *The New Palgrave: Finance*, London: Macmillan, 86–8.

Mandelbrot, B.B. and Wallis, J.R. (1969), 'Some Long-Run Properties of Geophysical Records', *Water Resources Research*, 5, pp. 321–40.

Mantegna, R.N. and Stanley, H.E. (1994), 'Stochastic Process with Ultraslow Convergence to a Gaussian: The Truncated Lévy Flight', *Physical Review Letters*, 73, 2946–9.

(1995), 'Scaling Behaviour in the Dynamics of an Economic Index', *Nature*, 376, 46–9.

Maravall, A. (1983), 'An Application of Nonlinear Time Series Forecasting', *Journal of Business and Economic Statistics*, 3, 350–5.

Markellos, R.N. (1997), 'Nonlinear Equilibrium Dynamics', Loughborough Economic Research Paper 97/6.

Marsh, T.A. and Merton, R.C. (1987), 'Dividend Behaviour for the Aggregate Stock Market', *Journal of Business*, 60, 1–40.

Meese, R.A. (1986), 'Testing for Bubbles in Exchange Markets: A Case of Sparkling Rates?', *Journal of Political Economy*, 94, 345–73.

Meese, R.A. and Singleton, K.J. (1982), 'On Unit Roots and the Empirical Modelling of Exchange Rates', *Journal of Finance*, 37, 1029–35.

Merton, R.C. (1973), 'An Intertemporal Capital Asset Pricing Model', *Econometrica*, 41, 867–87.

(1980), 'On Estimating the Expected Return on the Market: An Exploratory Investigation', *Journal of Financial Economics*, 8, 323–61.

Milhøj, A. (1985), 'The Moment Structure of ARCH Processes', *Scandinavian Journal of Statistics*, 12, 281–92.

Mills, T.C. (1990), *Time Series Techniques for Economists*, Cambridge University Press.

(1991a), 'Equity Prices, Dividends and Gilt Yields in the UK: Cointegration, Error Correction and "Confidence"', *Scottish Journal of Political Economy*, 38, 242–55.

(1991b), 'The Term Structure of UK Interest Rates: Tests of the Expectations Hypothesis', *Applied Economics*, 23, 599–606.

(1993), 'Testing the Present Value Model of Equity Prices for the UK Stock Market', *Journal of Business Finance and Accounting*, 20, 803–13.

(1995), 'Modelling Skewness and Kurtosis in the London Stock Exchange FT-SE Index Return Distributions', *The Statistician*, 44, 323–32.

(1996a), 'Non-Linear Forecasting of Financial Time Series: An Overview and Some New Models', *Journal of Forecasting*, 15, 127–35.

(1996b), 'The Econometrics of the "Market Model": Cointegration, Error Correction and Exogeneity', *International Journal of Finance and Economics*, 1, 275–86.

(1997a), 'Stylized Facts on the Temporal and Distributional Properties of Daily *FT-SE* Returns', *Applied Financial Economics*, 7, 599–604.

(1997b), 'Technical Analysis and the London Stock Exchange: Testing Trading Rules Using the FT30', *International Journal of Finance and Economics*, 2, 319–31.

(1998), 'Recent Developments in Modelling Nonstationary Vector Auto-Regressions', *Journal of Economic Surveys*, 12, 279–312.

Mills, T.C. and Coutts, J.A. (1995), 'Anomalies and Calendar Affects in the New FT-SE Indices', *European Journal of Finance*, 1, 79–93.

(1996), 'Misspecification and Robust Estimation of the Market Model: Estimating Betas for the FT-SE Industry Baskets', *European Journal of Finance*, 2, 319–31.

Mills, T.C. and Stephenson, M.J. (1985), 'An Empirical Analysis of the U.K. Treasury Bill Market', *Applied Economics*, 17, 689–703.

Mittnik, S. and Rachev, S.T. (1993a), 'Modeling Asset Returns with Alternative Stable Distributions', *Econometric Reviews*, 12, 261–330.

(1993b), 'Reply to Comments on "Modeling Asset Returns with Alternative Stable Distributions" and Some Extensions', *Econometric Reviews*, 12, 347–89.

Montañés, A. and Reyes, M. (1998), 'Effect of a Shift in the Trend Function on Dickey-Fuller Unit Root Tests', *Econometric Theory*, 14, 355–63.

Müller, U.A., Dacarogna, M.M., Davé, R.D., Olsen, R.B., Pictet, O.V. and von Weizsäcker, J.E. (1997), 'Volatilities of Different Time Resolutions – Analyzing the Dynamics of Market Components', *Journal of Empirical Finance*, 4, 213–39.

Muth, J.F. (1960), 'Optimal Properties of Exponentially Weighted Forecasts', *Journal of the American Statistical Association*, 55, 299–305.

Nelson, C.R. and Plosser, C.I. (1982), 'Trends and Random Walks in Macroeconomic Time Series', *Journal of Monetary Economics*, 10, 139–62.

Nelson, C.R. and Schwert, G.W. (1977), 'Short-Term Interest Rates as Predictors of Inflation: On Testing the Hypothesis that the Real Rate of Interest is Constant', *American Economic Review*, 67, 478–86.

Nelson, D.B. (1990a), 'Stationarity and Persistence in the GARCH(1,1) Model', *Econometric Theory*, 6, 318–34.

(1990b), 'ARCH Models as Diffusion Approximations', *Journal of Econometrics*, 45, 7–38.

(1991), 'Conditional Heteroskedasticity in Asset Returns', *Econometrica*, 59, 347–70.

Nelson, D.B. and Cao, C.Q. (1992), 'Inequality Constraints in Univariate GARCH Models', *Journal of Business and Economic Statistics*, 10, 229–35.

Nelson, D.B. and Foster, D.P. (1994), 'Asymptotic Filtering for Univariate GARCH Models', *Econometrica*, 62, 1–41.

Newbold, P. and Agiakloglou, C. (1993), 'Bias in the Sample Autocorrelations of Fractional White Noise', *Biometrika*, 80, 698–702.

Newey, W.K. and West, K.D. (1987), 'A Simple Positive Semidefinite, Heteroskedasticity and Autocorrelation Consistent Covariance Matrix', *Econometrica*, 55, 703–8.

Nickell, S. (1985), 'Error Correction, Partial Adjustment and all That: An Expository Note', *Oxford Bulletin of Economics and Statistics*, 47, 119–29.

Nychka, D.W., Stephen, E., Gallant, A.R. and McCaffrey, D.F. (1992), 'Finding Chaos in Noisy Systems', *Journal of the Royal Statistical Society, Series B*, 54, 399–426.

Osborne, M.M. (1959), 'Brownian Motion in the Stock Market', *Operations Research*, 7, 145–73.

Ouliaris, S. and Phillips, P.C.B. (1995), *COINT 2.0a: GAUSS Procedures for Cointegrated Regressions*.

Pagan, A.R. (1996), 'The Econometrics of Financial Markets', *Journal of Empirical Finance*, 3, 15–102.

Pagan, A.R. and Schwert, G.W. (1990a), 'Alternative Models for Conditional Stock Volatility', *Journal of Econometrics*, 45, 267–90.

(1990b), 'Testing for Covariance Stationarity in Stock Market Data', *Economics Letters*, 33, 165–70.

Palm, F. (1996), 'GARCH Models of Volatility', in G.S. Maddala and C.R. Rao (eds.), *Handbook of Statistics, Volume 14: Statistical Methods in Finance*, Amsterdam: Elsevier Science, pp. 209–40.

Pantula, S.G. and Hall, A. (1991), 'Testing for Unit Roots in Autoregressive Moving Average Models: An Instrumental Variable Approach', *Journal of Econometrics*, 48, 325–53.

Park, J.Y. (1990), 'Testing for Unit Roots and Cointegration by Variable Addition', in G.F. Rhodes and T.B. Fomby (eds.), *Advances in Econometrics, Volume VIII*, Greenwich, CT: JAI Press, pp. 107–33.

Park, J.Y. and Phillips, P.C.B. (1988), 'Statistical Inference in Regressions with Cointegrated Processes: Part I', *Econometric Theory*, 4, 468–97.

Pearson, K. and Rayleigh, Lord (1905), 'The Problem of the Random Walk', *Nature*, 72, 294, 318, 342.

Peel, D. and Davidson, J. (1998), 'A Non-Linear Error Correction Mechanism Based on the Bilinear Model', *Economics Letters*, 58, 165–70.

Perron, P. (1988), 'Trends and Random Walks in Macroeconomic Time Series: Further Evidence from a New Approach', *Journal of Economic Dynamics and Control*, 12, 297–332.

(1989), 'The Great Crash, the Oil Price Shock, and the Unit Root Hypothesis', *Econometrica*, 57, 1361–401.

(1990), 'Testing for a Unit Root in a Time Series with a Changing Mean', *Journal of Business and Economic Statistics*, 8, 153–62.

(1991), 'Test Consistency with Varying Sampling Frequency', *Econometric Theory*, 7, 341–68.

(1997), 'Further Evidence on Breaking Trend Functions in Macroeconomic Variables', *Journal of Econometrics*, 80, 355–85.

Perron, P. and Ng, S. (1996), 'Useful Modifications to Some Unit Root Tests with Dependent Errors and their Local Asymptotic Properties', *Review of Economic Studies*, 63, 435–63.

Pesaran, M.H. and Pesaran, B. (1997), *Working with Microfit 4.0: Interactive Econometric Analysis*, Oxford: Oxford University Press.

Pesaran, M.H. and Shin, Y. (1996), 'Long Run Structural Modelling', *Econometrica*, forthcoming.

(1997), 'Generalized Impulse Response Analysis in Linear Multivariate Models', *Economics Letters*, 58, 17–29.

Pesaran, M.H., Shin, Y. and Smith, R.J. (1996), 'Testing for the Existence of a Long-Run Relationship', DAE Working Paper No. 9622, Department of Applied Economics, University of Cambridge.

Phillips, P.C.B. (1986), 'Understanding Spurious Regressions in Econometrics', *Journal of Econometrics*, 33, 311–40.

(1987a), 'Time Series Regression with a Unit Root', *Econometrica*, 55, 227–301.

(1987b), 'Towards a Unified Asymptotic Theory for Autoregression', *Biometrika*, 74, 535–47.

(1987c), 'Asymptotic Expansions in Nonstationary Vector Autoregressions', *Econometric Theory*, 3, 45–68.

(1990), 'Time Series Regression with a Unit Root and Infinite-Variance Errors', *Econometric Theory*, 6, 44–62.

(1991), 'Optimal Inference in Co-Integrated Systems', *Econometrica*, 59, 282–306.

(1995), 'Fully Modified Least Squares and Vector Autoregression', *Econometrica*, 63, 1023–78.

(1998), 'Impulse Response and Forecast Error Asymptotics in Nonstationary VARs', *Journal of Econometrics*, 83, 21–56.

Phillips, P.C.B. and Durlauf, S.N. (1986), 'Multiple Time Series Regression with Integrated Processes', *Review of Economic Studies*, 53, 99–125.

Phillips, P.C.B. and Hansen, B.E. (1990), 'Statistical Inference in Instrumental Variables Regression with *I*(1) Processes', *Review of Economic Studies*, 57, 407–36.

Phillips, P.C.B. and Loretan, M. (1991), 'Estimating Long-Run Economic Equilibria', *Review of Economic Studies*, 58, 407–36.

Phillips, P.C.B., McFarland, J.W. and McMahon, P.C. (1996), 'Robust Tests of Forward Exchange Market Efficiency with Empirical Evidence from the 1920s', *Journal of Applied Econometrics*, 11, 1–22.

Phillips, P.C.B. and Ouliaris, S. (1988), 'Testing for Cointegration Using Principal Components Methods', *Journal of Economic Dynamics and Control*, 12, 205–30.

(1990), 'Asymptotic Properties of Residual Based Tests for Cointegration', *Econometrica*, 58, 165–94.

Phillips, P.C.B. and Perron, P. (1988), 'Testing for Unit Roots in Time Series Regression', *Biometrika*, 75, 335–46.

Pierce, D.A. (1979), 'Signal Extraction Error in Nonstationary Time Series', *Annals of Statistics*, 7, 1303–20.

Pierse, R.G. and Snell, A.J. (1995), 'Temporal Aggregation and the Power of Tests for a Unit Root', *Journal of Econometrics*, 65, 333–45.

Ploberger, W., Krämer, W. and Kontrus, K. (1989), 'A New Test for Structural Stability in the Linear Regression Model', *Journal of Econometrics*, 40, 307–18.

Plosser, C.I. and Schwert, G.W. (1978), 'Money, Income, and Sunspots: Measuring Economic Relationships and the Effects of Differencing', *Journal of Monetary Economics*, 4, 637–60.

Poskitt, D.S. and Tremayne, A.R. (1987), 'Determining a Portfolio of Linear Time Series Models', *Biometrika*, 74, 125–37.

Poterba, J.M. and Summers, L.H. (1988), 'Mean Reversion in Stock Prices: Evidence and Implications', *Journal of Financial Economics*, 22, 27–59.

Priestley, M.B. (1980), 'State-Dependent Models: A General Approach to Nonlinear Time Series Analysis', *Journal of Time Series Analysis*, 1, 47–71.

(1988), *Non-Linear and Non-Stationary Time Series Analysis*, London: Academic Press.

Qi, M. (1996), 'Financial Applications of Artificial Neural Networks', in G.S. Maddala and C.R. Rao (eds.), *Handbook of Statistics, Volume 14: Statistical Methods in Finance*, Amsterdam: Elsevier Science, pp. 529–52.

Quintos, C.E. (1997), 'Stability Tests in Error Correction Models', *Journal of Econometrics*, 82, 289–315.

Quintos, C.E. and Phillips, P.C.B. (1993), 'Parameter Constancy in Cointegrating Regressions', *Empirical Economics*, 18, 675–706.

Ramsey, J.B. (1969), 'Tests for Specification Errors in Classical Linear Least Squares Regression Analysis', *Journal of the Royal Statistical Society, Series B*, 31, 350–71.

Rappoport, P. and Reichlin, L. (1989), 'Segmented Trends and Non-Stationary Time Series', *Economic Journal*, 99 (Supplement), 168–77.

Reichlin, L. (1989), 'Structural Change and Unit Root Econometrics', *Economics Letters*, 31, 231–3.

Reimers, H.-E. (1992), 'Comparisons of Tests for Multivariate Cointegration', *Statistical Papers*, 33, 335–59.

Reinsel, G.C. and Ahn, S.K. (1992), 'Vector Autoregressive Models with Unit Roots and Reduced Rank Structure: Estimation, Likelihood Ratio Test, and Forecasting', *Journal of Time Series Analysis*, 13, 353–75.

Richardson, M. and Stock, J.H. (1989), 'Drawing Inferences from Statistics Based on Multi-Year Asset Returns', *Journal of Financial Economics*, 25, 323–48.

Roberts, H.V. (1959), 'Stock-Market "Patterns" and Financial Analysis: Methodological Suggestions', *Journal of Finance*, 14, 1–10.

Robinson, P. (1977), 'The Estimation of a Non-Linear Moving Average Model', *Stochastic Processes and Their Applications*, 5, 81–90.

(1994), 'Time Series with Strong Dependence', in C.A. Sims (ed.), *Advances in Econometrics: Sixth World Congress, Vol. I*, Cambridge University Press, pp. 47–95.

Rocke, D.M. (1982), 'Inference for Response-Limited Time Series Models', *Communications in Statistics: Theory and Methods*, 11, 2587–96.

Runde, R. (1997), 'The Asymptotic Null Distribution of the Box-Pierce *Q*-Statistic for Random Variables with Infinite Variance. An Application to German Stock Returns', *Journal of Econometrics*, 78, 205–16.

Ruppert, D. and Carroll, R.J. (1980), 'Trimmed Least Squares Estimation in the Linear Model', *Journal of the American Statistical Association*, 75, 828–38.

Rydén, T., Teräsvirta, T. and Åsbrink, S. (1998), 'Stylized Facts of Daily Return Series and the Hidden Markov Model', *Journal of Applied Econometrics*, 13, 217–44.

Said, S.E. and Dickey, D.A. (1984), 'Testing for Unit Roots in Autoregressive Moving-Average Models with Unknown Order', *Biometrika*, 71, 599–607.

(1985), 'Hypothesis Testing in ARIMA(p,1,q) Models', *Journal of the American Statistical Association*, 80, 369–74.

Saikkonen, P. (1991), 'Asymptotically Efficient Estimation of Cointegrating Regressions', *Econometric Theory*, 7, 1–21.

Saikkonen, P. and Lütkepohl, H. (1996), 'Infinite-Order Cointegrated Vector Autoregressive Processes: Estimation and Inference', *Econometric Theory*, 12, 814–44.

Saikkonen, P. and Luukkonen, R. (1993), 'Testing for a Moving Average Unit Root in Autoregressive Integrated Moving Average Models', *Journal of the American Statistical Association*, 88, 596–601.

Samarov, A. and Taqqu, M.S. (1988), 'On the Efficiency of the Sample Mean in Long Memory Noise', *Journal of Time Series Analysis*, 9, 191–200.

Samorodnitsky, G. and Taqqu, M.S. (1994), *Stable Non-Gaussian Random Processes*, New York: Chapman and Hall.

Samuelson, P.A. (1965), 'Proof that Properly Anticipated Prices Fluctuate Randomly', *Industrial Management Review*, 6, 41–9.

(1973), 'Proof that Properly Discounted Present Values of Assets Vibrate Randomly', *Bell Journal of Economics and Management Science*, 4, 369–74.

Sargan, J.D. and Bhargava, A.S. (1983), 'Testing Residuals from Least Squares Regression for being Generated by the Gaussian Random Walk', *Econometrica*, 51, 153–74.

Schmidt, P. (1990), 'Dickey-Fuller Tests with Drift', in G.F. Rhodes and T.B. Fomby (eds.), *Advances in Econometrics, Volume 8*, Greenwich, CT: JAI Press, pp. 161–200.

Schwarz, G. (1978), 'Estimating the Dimension of a Model', *Annals of Statistics*, 6, 461–4.

Schwert, G.W. (1987), 'Effects of Model Specification on Tests for Unit Roots in Macroeconomic Data', *Journal of Monetary Economics*, 20, 73–105.

(1989), 'Why does Stock Market Volatility Change Over Time?', *Journal of Finance*, 44, 1115–53.

Sentana, E. (1995), 'Quadratic ARCH Models', *Review of Economic Studies*, 62, 639–61.

Shazam (1993), *SHAZAM User's Reference Manual Version 7.0*, New York: McGraw-Hill.

Shephard, N. (1996), 'Statistical Aspects of ARCH and Stochastic Volatility', in D.R. Cox, D.V. Hinkley and O.E. Barndorff-Nielsen (eds.), *Time Series Models. In Econometrics, Finance and Other Fields*, London: Chapman and Hall, pp. 1–67.

Shiller, R.J. (1979), 'The Volatility of Long Term Interest Rates and Expectations Models of the Term Structure', *Journal of Political Economy*, 87, 1190–209.

(1981a), 'Do Stock Prices Move Too Much to be Justified by Subsequent Changes in Dividends?', *American Economic Review*, 71, 421–36.

(1981b), 'The Use of Volatility Measures in Assessing Market Efficiency', *Journal of Finance*, 36, 291–304.

Shiller, R.J. and Perron, P. (1985), 'Testing the Random Walk Hypothesis: Power Versus Frequency of Observation', *Economics Letters*, 18, 381–6.

Shlesinger, M.F. (1995), 'Comment on "Stochastic Process with Ultraslow Convergence to a Gaussian: The Truncated Lévy Flight"', *Physical Review Letters*, 74, 49–59.

Siklos, P.L. and Granger, C.W.J. (1997), 'Regime Sensitive Cointegration with an Application to Interest Rate Parity', *Macroeconomic Dynamics*, 1, 485–512.

Silverman, B.W. (1986), *Density Estimation for Statistics and Data Analysis*, London: Chapman and Hall.

Sims, C.A. (1980), 'Macroeconomics and Reality', *Econometrica*, 48, 1–48.

(1981), 'An Autoregressive Index Model for the US 1948–1975', in J. Kmenta and J.B. Ramsey (eds.), *Large-Scale Macroeconometric Models*, Amsterdam: North-Holland, pp. 283–327.

(1988), 'Bayesian Skepticism of Unit Root Econometrics', *Journal of Economic Dynamics and Control*, 12, 463–75.

Sims, C.A., Stock, J.H. and Watson, M.W. (1990), 'Inference in Linear Time Series with Some Unit Roots', *Econometrica*, 58, 113–44.

Sims, C.A. and Uhlig, H. (1991), 'Understanding Unit Rooters: A Helicopter Tour', *Econometrica*, 59, 1591–9.

Sowell, F.B. (1990), 'The Fractional Unit Root Distribution', *Econometrica*, 58, 498–505.

(1992a), 'Maximum Likelihood Estimation of Stationary Univariate Fractionally Integrated Time Series Models', *Journal of Econometrics*, 53, 165–88.

(1992b), 'Modelling Long-Run Behaviour with the Fractional ARIMA Model', *Journal of Monetary Economics*, 29, 277–302.

Spanos, A. (1986), *Statistical Foundations of Econometric Modelling*, Cambridge University Press.

Stock, J.H. (1987), 'Asymptotic Properties of Least Squares Estimators of Cointegrating Vectors', *Econometrica*, 55, 1035–56.

(1991), 'Confidence Intervals for the Largest Autoregressive Root in US Macroeconomic Time Series', *Journal of Monetary Economics*, 28, 435–69.

(1994), 'Unit Roots, Structural Breaks and Trends', in R.F. Engle and D.L. McFadden (eds.), *Handbook of Econometrics, Volume IV*, New York: North-Holland, pp. 2739–841.

(1996), 'VAR, Error Correction and Pretest Forecasts at Long Horizons', *Oxford Bulletin of Economics and Statistics*, 58, 685–701.

(1997), 'Cointegration, Long-Run Movements, and Long-Horizon Forecasting', in D.M. Kreps and K.F. Wallis (eds.), *Advances in Economics and Econometrics: Theory and Applications, Volume III*, Cambridge University Press, pp. 34–60.

Stock, J.H. and Watson, M.W. (1988), 'Testing for Common Trends', *Journal of the American Statistical Association*, 83, 1097–107.

(1993), 'A Simple Estimator of Cointegrating Vectors in Higher Order Integrated Systems', *Econometrica*, 61, 783–820.

Subba Rao, T. (1981), 'On the Theory of Bilinear Models', *Journal of the Royal Statistical Society, Series B*, 43, 244–55.

Subba Rao, T. and Gabr, M.M. (1984), *An Introduction to Bispectral Analysis and Bilinear Time Series Models*, Berlin: Springer-Verlag.

Swanson, N.R. and Granger, C.W.J. (1997), 'Impulse Response Functions Based on a Causal Approach to Residual Orthogonalization in Vector Autoregressions', *Journal of the American Statistical Association*, 92, 357–67.

Tanaka, K. (1990), 'Testing for a Moving Average Unit Root', *Econometric Theory*, 6, 433–44.

Tauchen, G.E. and Pitts, M. (1983), 'The Price Variability-Volume Relationship on Speculative Markets', *Econometrica*, 51, 485–505.

Taylor, S.J. (1986), *Modelling Financial Time Series*, New York: Wiley.

(1994), 'Modelling Stochastic Volatility: A Review and Comparative Study', *Mathematical Finance*, 4, 183–204.

Teräsvirta, T. (1994), 'Specification, Estimation, and Evaluation of Smooth Transition Autoregressive Models', *Journal of the American Statistical Association*, 89, 208–18.

Teräsvirta, T., Lin, C.-F. and Granger, C.W.J. (1993), 'Power of the Neural Network Test', *Journal of Time Series Analysis*, 14, 209–20.

Teräsvirta, T., Tjostheim, D. and Granger, C.W.J. (1994), 'Aspects of Modelling Nonlinear Time Series', in R.F. Engle and D.L. McFadden (eds.), *Handbook of Econometrics, Volume IV*, New York: North-Holland, pp. 2919–57.

Thaler, R. (1987a), 'The January Effect', *Journal of Economic Perspectives*, 1(1), 197–201.

(1987b), 'Seasonal Movements in Security Prices II: Weekend, Holiday, Turn of the Month, and Intraday Effects', *Journal of Economic Perspectives*, 1(2), 169–77.

Toda, H.Y. (1994), 'Finite Sample Properties of Likelihood Ratio Tests for Cointegrating Ranks when Linear Trends are Present', *Review of Economics and Statistics*, 76, 66–79.

(1995), 'Finite Sample Performance of Likelihood Ratio Tests for Cointegrating Ranks in Vector Autoregressions', *Econometric Theory*, 11, 1015–32.

Toda, H.Y. and Phillips, P.C.B. (1993), 'Vector Autoregression and Causality', *Econometrica*, 61, 1367–93.

(1994), 'Vector Autoregression and Causality: A Theoretical Overview and Simulation Study', *Econometric Reviews*, 13, 259–85.

Toda, H.Y. and Yamamoto, T. (1995), 'Statistical Inference in Vector Autoregressions with Possibly Integrated Processes', *Journal of Econometrics*, 66, 225–50.

Tomczyck, S. and Chatterjee, S. (1984), 'Estimating the Market Model Robustly', *Journal of Business Finance and Accounting*, 11, 563–73.

Tong, H. and Lim, K.S. (1980), 'Threshold Autoregression, Limit Cycles, and Cyclical Data', *Journal of the Royal Statistical Society, Series B*, 42, 245–92.

Tsay, R.S. (1986), 'Nonlinearity Tests for Time Series', *Biometrika*, 73, 461–6.

Tukey, J.W. (1977), *Exploratory Data Analysis*, Reading, Mass.: Addison-Wesley.

Vahid, F. and Engle, R.F. (1993), 'Common Trends and Common Cycles', *Journal of Applied Econometrics*, 8, 341–60.

(1997), 'Codependent Cycles', *Journal of Econometrics*, 80, 199–221.

Vogelsang, T. (1997), 'Wald-Type Tests for Detecting Breaks in the Trend Function of a Dynamic Time Series', *Econometric Theory*, 13, 818–49.

Wecker, W. (1981), 'Asymmetric Time Series', *Journal of the American Statistical Association*, 76, 16–21.

Wegman, E.J. (1995), 'Huge Data Sets and the Frontiers of Computational Feasibility', *Journal of Computer and Graphical Statistics*, 4, 281–95.

Weiss, A.A. (1984), 'ARMA Models with ARCH Errors', *Journal of Time Series Analysis*, 5, 129–43.

(1986a), 'Asymptotic Theory for ARCH Models: Estimation and Testing', *Econometric Theory*, 2, 107–31.

(1986b), 'ARCH and Bilinear Time Series Models: Comparison and Combination', *Journal of Business and Economic Statistics*, 4, 59–70.

West, K.D. (1987), 'A Specification Test for Speculative Bubbles', *Quarterly Journal of Economics*, 102, 553–80.

(1988), 'Asymptotic Normality, When Regressors have a Unit Root', *Econometrica*, 56, 1397–418.

White, H. (1980), ' A Heteroskedasticity Consistent Covariance Matrix Estimator and a Direct Test for Heteroskedasticity', *Econometrica*, 48, 817–38.

(1984), *Asymptotic Theory for Econometricians*, New York: Academic Press.

(1989), 'Some Asymptotic Results for Learning in Single Hidden-Layer Feedforward Network Models', *Journal of the American Statistical Association*, 84, 1003–13.

White, H. and Domowitz, I. (1984), 'Nonlinear Regression with Dependent Observations', *Econometrica*, 52, 643–61.

Wickens, M. (1996), 'Interpreting Cointegrating Vectors and Common Stochastic Trends', *Journal of Econometrics*, 74, 255–71.

Wilmott, P., Howison, S. and DeWynne, J. (1995), *The Mathematics of Financial Derivatives,* Cambridge University Press.

Wold, H. (1938), *A Study in the Analysis of Stationary Time Series*, Stockholm: Almqvist and Wiksell.

Working, H. (1934), 'A Random-Difference Series for Use in the Analysis of Time Series', *Journal of the American Statistical Association*, 29, 11–24.

(1960), 'Note on the Correlation of First Differences of Averages in a Random Chain', *Econometrica*, 28, 916–18.

Yadav, P.K., Pope, P.F. and Paudyal, K. (1994), 'Threshold Autoregressive Modelling in Finance: The Price Differences of Equivalent Assets', *Mathematical Finance*, 4, 205–21.

Yamada, H. and Toda, H.Y. (1997), 'A Note on Hypothesis Testing Based on the Fully Modified Vector Autoregression', *Economics Letters*, 56, 27–39.

(1998), 'Inference in Possibly Integrated Vector Autoregressive Models: Some Finite Sample Evidence', *Journal of Econometrics*, 86, 55–95.

Yap, S.F. and Reinsel, G.C. (1995), 'Results on Estimation and Testing for a Unit Root in the Nonstationary Autoregressive Moving-Average Model', *Journal of Time Series Analysis*, 16, 339–53.

Zakoian, J.M. (1994), 'Threshold Heteroskedastic Models', *Journal of Economic Dynamics and Control*, 18, 931–55.

Zivot, E. and Andrews, D.W.K. (1992), 'Further Evidence on the Great Crash, the Oil Price Shock, and the Unit Root Hypothesis', *Journal of Business and Economic Statistics*, 10, 251–70.

Index